A History of Education in Kentucky

Topics in Kentucky History

James C. Klotter, SERIES EDITOR

Books in the Series

A History of Education in Kentucky

William E. Ellis

THE UNIVERSITY PRESS OF KENTUCKY

Scholarly publisher for the Commonwealth,
serving Bellarmine University, Berea College, Centre
College of Kentucky, Eastern Kentucky University,
The Filson Historical Society, Georgetown College,
Kentucky Historical Society, Kentucky State University,
Morehead State University, Murray State University,
Northern Kentucky University, Transylvania University,
University of Kentucky, University of Louisville,
and Western Kentucky University.
All rights reserved.

Editorial and Sales Offices: The University Press of Kentucky
663 South Limestone Street, Lexington, Kentucky 40508-4008
www.kentuckypress.com

15 14 13 12 11   5 4 3 2 1

Library of Congress Cataloging-in-Publication Data

Ellis, William E. (William Elliott), 1940–
A history of education in Kentucky / William E. Ellis.
    p.   cm.— (Topics in Kentucky history)
Includes bibliographical references and index.
ISBN 978-0-8131-2977-8 (hardcover : alk. paper) —
ISBN 978-0-8131-2984-6 (ebook)
1. Education—Kentucky—History. I. Title.
LA292.E44 2011
370.9769—dc22
                                        2010044903

This book is printed on acid-free recycled paper meeting
the requirements of the American National Standard
for Permanence in Paper for Printed Library Materials.

∞ ⊛

Manufactured in the United States of America.

Member of the Association of
American University Presses

To THOMAS D. CLARK,
whose keen vision, wise counsel, and clear voice
are missed by all Kentuckians

Contents

Illustrations follow page 264

Preface

THE IDEA FOR THIS BOOK originated in a conversation between Thomas D. Clark, just a few weeks before he died, and Stephen M. Wrinn, director of the University Press of Kentucky. In their conversation about what books needed to be written about the history of the Commonwealth of Kentucky, Tom mentioned that something should be done about education. My name came up in the conversation, and Tom said I was the one to attempt to do so. Steve Wrinn and I have chuckled about this challenge several times. Actually, I had thought of writing a history of higher education in Kentucky, but now I changed my approach to include K–12, public and private. Humbled by Tom's confidence in my work, I accepted this daunting challenge.

I come to this task as a product of the private and public schools of Kentucky. My educational opportunities set me on a life course that I have found satisfying. Yet, in the following pages, I point out not only the many good things about education in Kentucky but also where the state has failed its young people. Unfortunately, although Kentucky has taken many steps forward in education, it has also often taken steps backward. The subtitle for this book could well be "The Struggle for Equity and Equality."

The book is divided into four periods often used by historians: 1775 to the beginning of the Civil War, the Civil War to 1900, 1900 to 1941, and World War II to the mid-1980s. Where K–12 and higher education intersect, as they often do, these connections are developed and explained. The epilogue examines the reforms brought about through the Kentucky Education Reform Act and the changes that occurred in higher education from the Patton years to the near present.

The history of education in Kentucky cannot be understood without a grounding in political, social, economic, and ethnic history. Moreover, what happens in Kentucky is always part of a larger world, including the southern and midwestern regions of the United States. For these reasons the context of the times is explicit throughout the book.

Though this book is longer than I intended, some readers will be disappointed that their favorite school or teacher has been omitted. I have been forced to find a representative sample of schools, administrators, teachers, and students in each time period.

The book is primarily a synthesis based on the wealth of writings about Kentucky. First, the "Kentucky canon" of fine histories by Thomas D. Clark, Lowell Harrison, James C. Klotter, Marion B. Lucas, John A. Hardin, James Ramage, George C. Wright, Frank L. McVey, and a few others is indispensable for the study of Kentucky history. Second, numerous entries in the *Kentucky Encyclopedia*, the *Encyclopedia of Louisville*, and the *Encyclopedia of Northern Kentucky* have benefited my study. Third, I have found many articles in the *Register of the Kentucky Historical Society* and the *Filson Club History Quarterly* to be useful. Fourth, the works of Jurgen Herbst, John R. Thelin, Lawrence A. Cremin, Henry J. Perkinson, William J. Reese, and others, with their regional and national perspectives on education, added immeasurably to this study. Fifth, I have made use of specialized studies, theses and dissertations, government documents and studies, and journal articles. Many fine theses and dissertations have been produced by the University of Kentucky and other universities over the years. I have perused more than ninety such writings in preparation for this work. In the first half of the twentieth century, outstanding theses and dissertations on early Kentucky education came out of George Peabody College and the University of Chicago, and several of those from George Peabody College were released in printed form. The reports of the state superintendents of public instruction and others were also most useful. C. W. Hackensmith, Barksdale Hamlett, Moses Edward Ligon, Alvin Fayette Lewis, H. W. Peters, and others published important studies of Kentucky education. As the following pages reveal, Kentucky education has been much studied by private and public entities, particularly state commissions, over the years. Unfortunately, most of these studies have been ignored by private citizens, governors, and the General Assembly. Sixth, I have consulted original sources including government documents and newspaper articles and editorials and have supplemented these sources with additional research, including the study of oral histories.

Ever since the days of John Dewey, America's most famous educationist, a person studying to become a teacher has always been asked to develop a philosophy of education. My own philosophy is a product of my upbringing on the outskirts of Shelbyville, Kentucky, where I attended the public schools; my student life at Georgetown College, Eastern Kentucky University (EKU), and the University of Kentucky; and my four years of public school teaching and coaching, three years of teaching at Lees Junior College, and twenty-nine years of teaching at EKU. Most of my experiences in education have been positive. I have been privileged to study under some of the most dedicated, best-trained, and hard-working teachers in America and to teach alongside others from that select group. However, I have also had teachers and colleagues who were ill-trained and inept, persons who were in the teaching trade for the single reason that they could do hardly anything else.

Overall, my philosophy of education, and of life as well, is old-fashioned progressivism. I believe in "progress," but only if we fight the constant, uphill battle against forces that try to pull us down. Nevertheless, as an ironist, in the sense in which theologian Reinhold Niebuhr used the term, I am fully aware that we always fall far short of our goals. The vast majority of our children, but not all, can benefit from a well-grounded education; and most teachers, but not all, make a good effort. Cynics will say that for all the effort and money put into education in Kentucky, particularly at the preschool–12 level, we still fall woefully short of national norms. My baseline reply is always this: until we reach at least the average of statistical analyses, we can't let up in pushing harder.

I wish to thank the following persons, who by reading and critiquing one or more chapters have greatly enhanced this book. They include Lowell Harrison for chapters 1 and 2; James C. Klotter for chapter 3; James Ramage for chapter 4; Nancy Forderhase, John Kleber, and John A. Hardin for chapter 5; Terry Birdwhistell and Duane Bolin for chapter 6; Elizabeth Fraas, John Kleber, Nelson Dawson, David Hawpe, and Richard Day for chapter 7; Richard Wilson, Gary Cox, and David Hawpe for chapter 8; and Paul Blanchard, Elizabeth Fraas, Linda Blackford, and Lindsey Apple for the epilogue. I also thank the anonymous readers of this book. I am grateful as well to the librarians and archivists at Eastern Kentucky University, Western Kentucky University, the University of Kentucky, and the University of Louisville for their help in research over the past several years. I, of course, take full responsibility for mistakes and omissions.

Kentucky counties and county seats (map by Dick Gilbreath).

Burlington

BOONE Independence Alexandria

KENTON CAMPBELL

GALLATIN

Warsaw PENDLETON BRACKEN

Carrollton GRANT Brooksville Maysville

TRIMBLE CARROLL Williamstown Falmouth MASON

OWEN ROBERTSON

Bedford New Mount LEWIS Vanceburg GREENUP Greenup

La Castle Owenton Olivet Catlettsburg

Grange HENRY HARRISON CARTER

OLDHAM Cynthiana NICHOLAS Flemingsburg Grayson BOYD

SCOTT FLEMING

Shelbyville FRANKLIN George- Carlisle ROWAN

Frankfort town BOURBON Owingsville Morehead ELLIOTT Louisa

lle SHELBY Paris Mt. Sterling BATH Sandy Hook LAWRENCE

WOOD- FAYETTE

SPENCER FORD Lexington CLARK MONT- Frenchburg MORGAN

le Lawrenceburg Versailles Winchester GOMERY MENIFEE West Liberty JOHNSON

Taylorsville ANDERSON Nicholas- Stanton Paintsville Inez

ville POWELL Salyersville MARTIN

NELSON MERCER JESSAMINE Irvine WOLFE MAGOFFIN

WASHINGTON Harrods- MADISON Campton Prestonsburg

Spring- burg GARRARD Richmond Beattyville Jackson PIKE

field Danville Lancaster ESTILL LEE BREATHITT FLOYD Pikeville

enville Lebanon BOYLE

MARION Stanford JACKSON Booneville KNOTT

Campbellsville LINCOLN ROCK- McKee OWSLEY PERRY Hindman

EN TAYLOR CASEY Liberty CASTLE Mt. Vernon Hazard LETCHER

nsburg Manchester Hyden Whitesburg

ADAIR PULASKI London CLAY LESLIE

Columbia RUSSELL Somerset LAUREL

dmonton

ALFE Jamestown Barbourville Harlan

UMBERLAND WAYNE KNOX Pineville HARLAN

Burkesville CLINTON Monticello Whitley Williamsburg

Albany City BELL

ile McCREARY WHITLEY

Part 1

1775 TO THE BEGINNING OF THE CIVIL WAR

Chapter 1

Tragedies, Blunders, and Promises

Creating a Public School System

Settlers brought great hopes with them across the Appalachian Mountains and down the Ohio River into the "Kentucke" country. While efforts were made to develop schools, children, if they had literate parents, received a modicum of education at home. First settled by European Americans from the American colonies during the tumultuous 1770s, when the fate of independence was still in doubt, Harrodsburg and Boonesborough were the first new "western" settlements. Those who championed education faced daunting odds. The institution of slavery and an incongruous, undemocratic land-distribution system combined to further complicate their pursuit.[1]

Much has been written about the early exploration, settlement, and conquest of Kentucky. A 1996 book by Stephen Aron takes a different tack from that of most previous histories. Kentucky represented the "New West" in the trans-Appalachian region, according to Aron in *How the West Was Lost: The Transformation of Kentucky from Daniel Boone to Henry Clay.* The author advises his readers to suspend "the sense of inevitability that inspired histories of how the West was won," as seen, for example, in the accounts written by Frederick Jackson Turner and his followers. Kentucky, Aron maintains, had a brief moment to develop into a society different from the more settled East. Could white settlers and Native Americans coexist in some sort of hunting-gathering–small holding agricultural utopia? An amalgam of settlers, the poor, as well as the middle and upper classes with their chattel property, went to Kentucky. Very soon litigation relieved original freeholders such as Daniel Boone of their land. (Kentucky was a paradise for young lawyers like Henry Clay.) Early opposition to slavery by many evangelicals, particularly during the initial stages of the Great Revival, 1800–1801, was soon quelled by those who wanted stability in their otherworldliness. When religion became subservient to the status quo, the landed class, who controlled the government and the writing of Kentucky's constitutions, oversaw the commonwealth's future. Although the majority of white Kentuckians did not own slaves, those who did dominated the mores, politics, and economy of the state. Henry Clay's "American System" of internal improvements and its accumulated debts nearly bankrupted the state while stealing valuable resources from the commonwealth's children. If there was never enough money to build locks and dams, roads, canals, and railroads, then education would perpetually suffer.[2]

From the earliest days of settlement in "Kentucke," there were children to be educated. Elementary, or grammar, school education began early. Jane Coomes, who came from Maryland with her husband William, started a dame school at Fort Harrod in 1775 or 1776. The dame school originated in Reformation England and, transferred to America by the Puritans, eventually evolved into the American elementary school. In this most primitive of schools, Coomes charged families a few pennies a week to teach their children the rudiments of knowledge in her home. She used a horn book, or alphabet board, to instruct students in this prototypical English subscription school. The horn book probably included letters of the alphabet illustrated with rhymed couplets from the *New England Primer* of about 1690. From "A" for "In Adam's fall/we sinned all" through "I" for "The idle Fool/is whipt at school" to the end, students received a strong dose of religious and moral lessons.[3]

Other early schoolmasters included Joseph Doniphan in the summer of 1779 at Fort Boonesborough, where he taught the young children of Daniel Boone, Richard Calloway, and others. Doniphan used printed spelling and geography books as well as an arithmetic manuscript brought to the fort from Virginia. As always, the Bible was a primary source for reading. John May at McAfee's Station and Elijah Craig at McClellan's Station also formed early central Kentucky elementary schools. "This was an era when most of the schoolteachers were chiefly men," concluded Thomas D. Clark.[4]

Just a few years after settlements were established at Harrodsburg and Boonesborough, the 1780 Virginia General Assembly chartered a "public school or Seminary of Learning," granting it eight thousand acres, confiscated from loyalists, as an endowment. The original charter, entitled "An Act to vest Escheated Lands in the County of Kentucke in Trustees for a Public School," was aimed at educating the populace. As John D. Wright Jr. has pointed out in *Transylvania: Tutor to the West*, the almost startling point is that the school was intended to be "public." Progress, however, was slow. In 1783 more land was added and the trustee board was expanded from 13 to 23 for the officially named Transylvania Seminary. While still fending off Indian attacks and adjusting to the rigors of frontier life, the trustees eventually authorized a grammar school.[5]

Long before white settlement of Kentucky and the founding of Tran-sylvania Seminary, the academy had become an established institution. Although some say its origins were in the dissenting religions of the earliest settlement of the eastern seaboard, the traditions that formed these schools go back to Europe. Coming out of the Latin grammar school, with its emphasis on Greek and Latin instruction, the academy in America quickly came to focus on English-language education. Until true public schools were founded, academies filled an enormous educational gap in the developing western democracy. Organized by individuals; groups, religious and secular; and towns, the academy, or seminary, so named often if a school for girls, dominated early childhood education until the time of the Civil War.[6]

In 1785 the first classes of Transylvania Seminary, taught by Rev. James Mitchell, were held near Danville in a cabin owned by Rev. David Rice, one of the founders of Presbyterianism on the frontier. Tuition could be paid in Spanish gold, the preferred currency of the frontier, or in produce or other commodities. A year later the school moved to Lexington and a year after that met in the home of Rev. James Moore, a Lexington Episcopalian rector. In 1799 the school combined with Kentucky Academy, a competing Pres-byterian school, to form Transylvania University, which began then to offer college-level courses. The eastern seaboard conflict between sectarianism and the newer thoughts of Enlightenment secularism that had been developing for more than a century was transmitted to the Kentucky frontier and played out in the forming of Transylvania.[7]

Other schools were being started as well. Rev. David Barrow, to supple-ment his income, organized and taught a subscription school on Lulbegrud Creek in Montgomery County beginning in January 1801. The school rules he published mirrored many others of the time. The first rule was "The Teachers and Scholars [are] to appear at the school House each morning if possible by an half Hour by Sun; with Hands and Face cleanly washed, and Hair neatly combed." "Each one is to mind his or her business during Book Time," the rules continued, "and there is to be no Fleering, Laugh-ing, Hunching, whispering, or making Mouths to provoke others during the Hours of Exercise." There were seventeen other irrevocable dicta among Barrow's rules of order, but no record remains of his success as a pioneering teacher on the Kentucky frontier.[8]

Schools soon dotted the Kentucky landscape. Robert B. McAfee, who went on to serve in the War of 1812 and as lieutenant governor of Kentucky from 1820 to 1824, attended a school built on family property in Mercer County for his earliest education. He recalled that "an old English gentleman who used his rod pretty freely" briefly taught there. Another year McAfee "went to school to an Irishman by the name of John Forsythe." Once,

McAfee and his classmates, in a high-spirited assertion of independence, barricaded the doors of the school to force Forsythe to give them a holiday on Christmas Day. As a reward for their audacity, McAfee's father treated the boys to all the beer they could drink, which was produced at the family brewery. Like all schoolboys, McAfee was smitten by a pretty schoolgirl. "I do not know that [the feeling] was reciprocated," he said, "as I never told her except by my looks and constant effort to make myself agreeable to her." As for many children of the late eighteenth and early nineteenth centuries, much of McAfee's education took place at home. Both parents encouraged his reading and writing. From an early age he was required by his mother to read aloud a chapter from the Bible every Sunday.[9]

Susannah Johnson attended one of the earliest schools in western Kentucky, at Eddy Grove (now Princeton) in Caldwell County. Her first teacher was a "Brother Elijah," who held forth in "an old corn crib," improved by having a larger door cut out and the addition of a fireplace. For three months of schooling, each student paid him "a silver dollar on the last day of school." The students sat on split-log seats across from larger log slabs that served as their desks. "Every scholar studied at the very top of his voice, each one seeming intent to excel his neighbor," said Johnson. "And the result was, a noise 'as of many waters' that might at times be heard at the distance of half a mile." The second teacher at Eddy Grove was an itinerant Irishman by the name of Hugh McClellan, who was "rough and passionate." "If a large boy showed the least impertinence, he would knock him down with his fist in an instant. Yet he was very kind when not enraged, especially to the little girls. . . . Like all the Irish teachers—and most of those in the early days were Irish—he pretended to be very learned; and would frequently astonish us by the fluency with which he quoted Latin, Greek, and Hebrew." She attended only twelve months of school in all, while also learning at home, but Johnson believed she got a good education. About 1809, in a new "neat and spacious school-house," she received the last of her formal schooling. "Here I completed my education by learning to write. For a girl to study arithmetic, grammar, or geography, was a thing we never thought of. The two latter studies were scarcely known even among the boys." This comparatively well-educated frontier Kentucky woman later married a Methodist circuit rider and chronicled their lives in a well-written book edited by one of her sons.[10]

Finding a competent teacher proved a daunting task, because there were no teacher-training programs, nor certification, nor standards of compensation in the late eighteenth and early nineteenth centuries. School organizers had to take whomever they could find. Sometimes itinerant teachers from New England wandered their way. Many teachers were ministers, lawyers, surveyors, or other professionals looking to supplement their incomes. Private academies usually offered such esoteric subjects as Latin and Greek if taught by a trained minister. Those teachers who led proprietary efforts were no better and often worse than those hired for the task.[11]

The experiences of John McKinney, recounted by Lewis Collins, illustrate the rigors of frontier teaching. In 1780 McKinney arrived in Lexington and soon began a school. Three years later, while working at his desk alone, he was startled by a noise at the door of his school. A wildcat entered the room, "her tail curled over her back, her bristles erect, and her eyes glancing rapidly through the room, as if in search of a mouse." Although McKinney dared to face down the beast, "puss was not to be bullied. Her eyes flashed fire, her tail waved angrily, and she began to gnash her teeth, evidently bent upon serious hostility." When the distraught teacher tried to flee, "she fastened upon his side with her teeth, and began to rend and tear with her claws like fury. McKinney's clothes were in an instant torn from his side, and his flesh dreadfully mangled by the enraged animal." Bleeding profusely, McKinney managed to pin the animal against his desk. "The cat now began to utter the most wild and discordant cries," Collins continued, "and McKinney, at the same time, lifting up his voice in concert, the two together sent forth notes so doleful as to alarm the whole town." Rushing to the scene, townspeople found a dead wildcat and a teacher nearly so. "Wildcat" McKinney survived, later moved to Bourbon County, and in recounting the tale said he "would rather fight two Indians than one wild cat."[12]

Life in pioneer Kentucky was indeed perilous, as much for the teacher as for anyone else. John Filson, who briefly taught school in Lexington and wrote a famous promotional account of Kentucky, *The Discovery, Settlement, and Present State of Kentucke*, in 1784, later disappeared, presumably killed by Indians. Moreover, six trustees of Transylvania University in its early days died at the hands of Indian warriors.[13]

Organizing a rational educational program for the fledging commonwealth proved difficult. The first two Kentucky constitutions were of no help in developing a system, as neither specifically provided for, nor even mentioned, education. The first one was written in 1792, before Kentucky's entry into the Union. Influenced by the constitutions of the nation and of several other states, it created a tripartite government and a bicameral legislature and contained a bill of rights. Like the U.S. Constitution, it established a house of representatives elected by popular vote and a senate and a governor elected by electors.

Seven years later, the constitution of 1799 made Kentucky a bit more democratic by abolishing the electoral college in favor of direct election of the governor and the senators. More power was given to county governments, what Robert Ireland has called the "little kingdoms" of the Commonwealth of Kentucky. With its principal powers over taxation, the county in many ways became a retrogressive influence in Kentucky. Unfortunately, the 1799 constitution also took the franchise away from freed slaves. Even more ominous, both constitutions firmly entrenched the institution of slavery, tying Kentucky's present and future to the South rather than the more progressive territories and states north of the Ohio River. Again, the new constitution made no provision for education.[14]

One key to the success of public education is permanent funding. In the old Northwest Territory, public education was funded from the beginning by the Land Ordinance of 1785. In each township, one section, or one square mile, was set aside for the maintenance of public education. The 1787 Northwest Ordinance decreed that seventy-two sections in each state were to be used for developing an institution of higher education. Perhaps even more important, slavery was strictly prohibited; this provision was suggested by slave-owner Thomas Jefferson. In Kentucky there were no such provisions. Kentucky and its southern counterparts were forced to fall back on the Virginia style of education. And the Ohio River became the boundary between slave and free territory.[15]

From the beginning of settlement, an inherent conflict developed between localism and the needs of the state. The slave-owning society and its elites did not believe in a democratic public school system. Consequently, Kentucky followed not the New England pattern but a Virginia one: establishing academies "to give an elementary education to a more or less select group of students to serve the professions, unsupported by taxes." The prevailing belief of the elites was that the commonwealth needed trained ministers, businessmen, lawyers, and other public servants and not an educated general population. The prevailing slavocracy set the tone for Kentucky society and dominated the state government until the end of the Civil War. Sadly, as Kentucky's population more than doubled from 1790 to 1800, educational efforts fell far short of what was necessary to develop an informed public.[16]

In December 1794, the Kentucky General Assembly chartered Kentucky Academy at Pisgah in Woodford County, in opposition to the seminary founded by Transylvania. Though Kentucky Academy was denominationally a Presbyterian school with a state charter, its trustees promised to maintain religious freedom. Subsequent individual legislative acts from 1798 to 1850 created numerous land grant academies, each initially given a grant of six thousand acres for its maintenance. In 1808 a legislative session provided that each county could apply for a grant to charter an academy. By 1860 nearly 450,000 acres of public land had been set aside for the academy system. Only a few of the counties had land grants within their own county; the vast proportion were granted south of the Green and Cumberland rivers. Originally, the trustees were named in each individual charter. In order to gain any funds at all, the trustees had to pay to have the land located, surveyed, and registered. In most cases, only enough money was received to pay for a small plot of land and build a modest school. All of the academies, sometimes called seminaries or institutes, especially if the school was limited to female enrollment, charged tuition, ranging anywhere from ten to twenty dollars a year. Often produce was accepted in lieu of money. Some academies existed only on paper for a brief time before fading away, because of inactivity on the part of their trustees and lack of local interest in education. Privately funded academies also lingered on the brink. For example, Bethel Academy, founded as only the second chartered Methodist educational institution in America, opened in 1794 near Wilmore. After floundering there, it moved to Nicholasville in 1805, where it never became an important institution.[17]

The legislature tinkered from time to time with the funding of the academies. Several received permission from the legislature to raise funds, usually limited to a few hundred dollars a year, through a lottery. Special legislation allowed some counties to levy taxes to at least partially support an academy. Escheated lands, which reverted to the state when there was no legal heir, sometimes were made available to aid an academy or seminary. For example, in 1837 the escheated property of a Madison County man was donated, as always by special legislative act, for the benefit of the Madison Seminary, an all-male school founded in 1816.[18]

Private academies, mostly founded by religious organizations, partially filled the void created by the lack of support for public education. Jefferson Seminary in Louisville was one of the earliest academies not funded by a church group. Founded in 1798 on a land grant in Christian County and using a lottery, the school, for males only, did not open until 1813. Principal Mann Butler intended the school, "from the beginning elitist in character," to exude his Unitarian ethos. The school had difficulty with finances as well as a declining enrollment. One critic charged that for the cost of Jefferson Seminary, every child in the county could receive a basic common school education. As David Post has pointed out, the school was caught between the "populism" of Louisville tradesmen and the elitism of the well-to-do. The hybrid school became "free" only briefly. A "Female Department" was developed, adding to the movement toward a common school system in Louisville. Jefferson Seminary operated for only twelve years.[19]

In 1828 the General Assembly granted a charter authorizing "free schools" for the city of Louisville. The next year the city council passed an ordinance with the ambition of establishing public schools in each ward of the city, levied a property tax, and appointed Mann Butler as head of the first new school. The school was free only to the indigent; until 1851 others paid small fees. From October to April the school met from eight to twelve in the morning and then from two in the afternoon until six, five days a week, with one week off for Christmas. Teachers soon began using the monitorial, or Lancastrian, system of teaching, in which senior students acted as monitors and aides in the instruction of younger pupils. By 1837, 716 students were enrolled. Also by that date, Louisville had a city superintendent of schools. In 1851 two institutions, the Male High School and the Female High School, opened. More schools had been founded by then, and 4,303 students were enrolled citywide. Louisville had the best school system in the state by the beginning of the Civil War.[20]

Some academies were organized to educate young ladies in the finishing-school tradition. For example, in 1798 a French émigré couple, who had escaped the ravages of the French Revolution, founded Mentelle's for Young Ladies, a female academy in Lexington. At the age of fourteen, Mary Todd, who later married Abraham Lincoln, went there to be educated. Madame Victorie Charlotte LeClerc Mentelle and her husband Augustus Waldemar Mentelle lent a Continental air to Lexington with their school on Richmond Road across from Henry Clay's Ashland estate. The school, which lasted until the middle of the nineteenth century, taught etiquette, literature, dancing, and, of course, French, which was a particular love of the future first lady throughout her life.[21]

One of the most interesting early educational experiments in Kentucky involved an Austrian schoolmaster, Joseph Neff, who was a disciple of the Swiss innovator Johann Heinrich Pestalozzi. With exercises in language and in studying nature firsthand, the Pestalozzian method became known as "the Art of Sense Impressionism." Neff studied with the master in Switzerland and then migrated to the United States at the request of William Maclure, initially settling in Pennsylvania. Pestalozzi's ideas about elementary and vocational education were far ahead of the time, particularly for an educational backwater like Kentucky. Neff established a boys' school outside Philadelphia in 1809 that received national publicity. Apparently with the usual complement of books and other educational aids, Neff used mental exercises and games to challenge his students. Dr. Joseph Buchanan, a liberal-minded physician from Lexington who dabbled in inventions, including the steam engine, and whom Niels Henry Sonne called "unquestionably Kentucky's greatest intellectual of the period," visited Neff's school in 1812.[22]

In 1813 Buchanan advertised the opening of a Pestalozzian school in Lexington, which would cater primarily to boys six to ten years of age. Buchanan expected the students to complete their education there "or until they have arrived at the age of manhood." He said he would exclude all religious instruction of any form. As a sign of the times, academies in Versailles and

Paris also offered no religious studies. However, within two years the school failed, owing in part to the strong censure of local Presbyterian clergy. Rev. John P. Campbell denounced the effort and compared Buchanan to the "atheist Hobbes, and the vermine [*sic*] of the ancient Epicurean style."[23]

But the Pestalozzian experiment was not yet over in Kentucky. Louisville physician William C. Galt, whose two sons had studied with Neff in Pennsylvania, lured the Austrian American to Louisville. Opening in 1815, the Louisville school had a disappointing enrollment, and Neff's wife Eloise did not feel comfortable in what she called the "backwoods" after living in cosmopolitan Philadelphia. Neff also got caught up in another idea, founding a "farming school" supported by Shelby County farmer Thomas Buckner. Neff theorized that young boys would flock to him to learn modern agricultural methods and believed he was the person to teach them. After Neff purchased a farm from Buckner, the grand idea went nowhere fast; Neff ended up cultivating the farm to eke out a living for his family. He finally escaped to Robert Owen's utopian experiment in New Harmony, Indiana, where his theories about education found a willing audience. His students there also took instruction in an industrial school that was much like a trade school. Considered one of the true pioneers in early-nineteenth-century education, unfortunately, Neff found no success in Kentucky.[24]

Other, more practical schools were being founded. Two of the most famous private academies, Science Hill Female Academy and the Choctaw Academy, illustrated both the success and the failure of such enterprises. Both began with promise, but only one lasted into the twentieth century.

Science Hill Female Academy in Shelbyville, founded by Methodists Rev. John and Julia Ann Tevis, opened in March 1825. Julia Tevis served as principal of the school until 1879. With no endowment or state aid, supported only by tuition and payments for board, the school nevertheless flourished. Basic tuition for a five-month term cost $10, with music instruction an additional $16 and French another $12. Board was $40 a term. The day and boarding students, ages six though twenty-one, received more than a "finishing" school education. Fighting the prejudices of the time against female education, Tevis made sure her students received a well-rounded education, including studies of history and astronomy. She used recitation as a teaching method throughout her career. The school's enrollment, drawn from most of the states but primarily from the South, grew to as many as 250 students in the 1850s. Julia Tevis spoke courageously on the brink of Civil War, asserting, "The Negroes must be freed." The school changed hands in 1879 and began to send more young women to college. Stressed by the economic hardships of the Great Depression, Science Hill School closed in 1939.[25]

The Choctaw Academy was not so fortunate. Founded by the Baptist

Mission Society of Kentucky in 1818 at Great Crossing in Scott County, the school closed for lack of funds in 1821. U.S. senator Richard Mentor Johnson, a hero of the Battle of the Thames and the alleged slayer of Tecumseh, reopened the school in 1825 at the request of the Choctaw Nation. This development created some controversy because Johnson's brother-in-law, William Ward, was the agent at the time for the Choctaw in Mississippi. There was some sentiment that Johnson was interested more in money than in the intellectual benefit of Choctaw youth. Nevertheless, from an original class of 25, enrollment grew to as many as 188 in 1835, including students from several other tribes. After ratification of the Treaty of Dancing Rabbit in 1830 and subsequent removal of the Choctaw to Oklahoma, the school declined, and it finally closed in 1842.[26]

Another group of settlers in the central part of the state, the Shakers of Pleasant Hill, had about the same attitudes toward education as "those of their rural Kentucky neighbors," according to Thomas D. Clark and F. Gerald Ham. In other words, only a modicum of education was needed for full citizenship. From November to February, classes were held for elementary students, girls taught by the Sisters and boys by the Brethren. Arithmetic, geography, reading, writing, and religion, of course, as well as some work instruction completed their education. Although Shakers believed in keeping a certain distance from the "world," which meant outsiders, their students were given some exposure to "worldly textbooks." Shaker education did not proceed past a basic elementary level.[27]

The private academies offered a passable education for the children of the elite landholders, most of whom owned slaves. At the other end of the spectrum were schools of a different type, probably brought over the mountains from Virginia. Called "blab schools" because of the cacophony of voices repeating a lesson, they offered a partial education that was the most a child of the white nonelite, nonlandowning class could expect. In such schools, which often lacked books, blackboards, and chalk, students repeated their assignments aloud in a singsong fashion, over and over, until the lesson sank in. Old-timers explained to Ellis Hartford, author of *The Little White School House*, "This was the only way the schoolmaster knew that the pupils were busy." "It generally turned into a contest to see which one could drown out the others," said one observer. "An energetic girl with a high pitched and strident voice could raise havoc and her competitors usually retired from the field." "A roar ensued not unlike that of a park artillery," recalled another observer. "The air seemed filled with splinters of words and syllables. After the first burst of enthusiasm ceased, sundry diligent [students] kept up a running fire, which continued till we left." One of the most famous characters in Kentucky fiction, young Chad in *The Little Shepherd of Kingdom Come*, studied at such a school. This antiquated teaching method continued in the more isolated areas of the state, particularly in the mountains, until the 1870s. Harriette Simpson Arnow, author of *The Dollmaker* and other books, tried the blab-school technique while teaching in a one-room school in Pulaski County many years later. She and her students found the method useful until "a child got started wrong on a multiplication; I then had to let him run on in his ignorance, or risk stopping all with curiosity while I got him back on the right track."[28]

The early "schoolhouses" themselves varied widely. Some classes were held in private homes or local churches. Where frontier conditions still existed in poorer communities, a simple log cabin with a dirt or split-log floor was about the best one could expect. Children sat on split-log benches, warmed themselves at a fireplace, drank from a common dipper and bucket, and ate the meager meals they brought from home. Winter was the best time for school, because many children had to work during the growing season. Most working-class and farm people worked "from can 'til can't," from daylight to dark. Both before and after school, most children had "chores" to do. The school had to be within walking distance, usually less than three miles, of a child's home. Over hill and dale and often through a muddy creek or two, poorer Kentucky children trudged to school. In contrast, the best private academies resided in brick or stone buildings with better amenities, perhaps even an outhouse of similar design and construction. The children who attended those schools were better dressed, went to school for a longer term, probably did not work in the fields, had better instructional materials, and warmed themselves by a brick fireplace.[29]

Having sufficient textbooks remained a problem for most schools during the antebellum period. The few books and manuscripts that had been brought over the mountains in the early pioneer days were supplemented by texts printed for sale in newspaper offices or bookshops. A Lexington paper advertised such textbooks as *Geography and Children,* the *Webster Speller,* the *Harrison Grammar,* and *The New England Primer* for sale in 1809. Book publishers and binderies in Frankfort, Lexington, and Louisville soon appeared and made Humphrey Marshall's *History of Kentucky* and other textbooks available. *An Easy Introduction to the Study of Arithmetick,* by President Martin Ruter of Augusta College (in Augusta, Kentucky) could be purchased for eighteen and three-quarters cents. Until 1851, parents had the sole right to choose textbooks for their children, "providing the same are not immoral," according to an 1844 law.[30]

One of the most important figures in nineteenth-century American education, William Holmes McGuffey, had at least a temporary Kentucky connection, having taught school in Paris during college breaks while he attended Miami University in Ohio. In 1823 he held classes for seven students in the dining room of a local minister. After becoming professor of languages at Miami University, McGuffey embarked on a long career as a textbook author, beginning with his "eclectic" readers, which became the standard of the day. McGuffey's books had a distinctive "western" rural flavor, in contrast to older books written by northeasterners. Beginning with first- and second-grade books published in 1836, each lesson in his readers "contained a moral that was supposed to impress the pupil and give him a set of precepts which would develop his character." McGuffey's readers were read widely in Kentucky because they fit the Protestant ethos that pervaded the state; they continued to be used well into the twentieth century in some schools.[31]

The academy system failed for several reasons. First, there were too few academies created, and they were not always situated in the right places. By 1850 a total of eighty-eight county academies had been chartered, but many lasted only a short time. They were not adequately funded, nor was there central oversight of their operations. In many ways they were considered secondary schools with lower grades appended. The trusteeships were self-perpetuating bodies that usually included men who knew little if anything about education. Some trustees used their positions for personal gain. The land grant academy system utterly failed to create the funding necessary for an adequate elementary and secondary public school system statewide. The most positive outcome of the land grant system is that several of the more successful academies evolved into colleges. For example, Rittenhouse Academy became the core for the establishment of Georgetown College, and Bethel Female Institute in Hopkinsville, founded in 1854, evolved into Bethel Female College in 1890.[32]

While Baptists, Presbyterians, Methodists, and other Protestants were organizing private academies and seminaries, Catholics formed their own schools, first centering in Marion, Nelson, and Washington counties and later scattering along the Ohio River counties. St. Thomas of Aquin College, founded by Dominican priests near Springfield in 1809, was the first organized Catholic school in Kentucky. It was a preparatory school for boys rather than a college in the twentieth-century sense. Jefferson Davis attended it for two years, continued his education nearer his Mississippi home, and then enrolled in Transylvania University. "Sectarianism did not characterize St. Thomas," and Protestants who attended there were not proselytized to by the teachers. As one of the youngest students there, Davis was doted on by the priests. When the eight-year-old told Father Wilson he wanted to convert to Catholicism, Davis reported, the old priest "received me kindly, handed me a biscuit and a bit of cheese, and told me that for the present I had better take some Catholic food." The young Mississippian received a good classical grounding at the Kentucky school, which he appreciated throughout his life. After two nearby Catholic colleges, St. Joseph's and St. Mary's, were founded, St. Thomas's closed in 1828.[33]

One of the founding members of the Sisters of Loretto, Mary Rhodes, began teaching children in an abandoned log cabin near Bardstown in 1811. In the nineteenth century, the Sisters of Loretto founded more than forty schools among the Catholic communities clustered along the Ohio River from Owensboro to Louisville to Maysville. Loretto Academy, founded in 1812, lasted more than a century in Marion County. In 1814 the Sisters of Charity of Nazareth organized a girls' school on a farm in Nelson County. The Jesuits, not to be outdone, founded several schools of short duration before the Civil War.[34]

Like Kentucky's constitutions, the earliest governors and state legislators took little notice of education. After all, there was a frontier to civilize and a Native American population to subdue and supplant. From the base in central Kentucky, white settlements spread in all directions. As the better land was swallowed up by slave-owners and speculators, poorer settlers filled up unclaimed land in the Appalachian Mountains. The population of the commonwealth grew rapidly. From 73,077 souls in 1790 the population ballooned to 1,155,684 by 1860; 20 percent of that number were slaves or free blacks. Lexington; Louisville; and Newport and Covington, on the south bank of the Ohio River, across from Cincinnati, grew rapidly. Louisville's location at the Falls of the Ohio soon made it a commercial center. Though lacking the large slave populations of the Deep South, Kentucky slave-owners wielded a strong hand in the state. According to the 1850 census, for example, 28 percent of white families in the commonwealth owned slaves. Emancipation was discussed from time to time, but after 1830 slavery became the "solvent" that melded all classes of whites into a pliant slavocracy. "Kentucky's slave society managed to live with itself under an invented myth of republicanism," while maintaining "near oligarchical rule," said historian Frank Mathias. In *Evil Necessity: Slavery and Political Culture in Antebellum Kentucky,* Harold D. Tallant makes a strong case supporting Jefferson's famous dictum "We have the wolf by the ears, and we can neither hold him, nor safely let him go."[35]

In the early nineteenth century, Kentucky always seemed to be just behind the curve in educational progress. Kentuckians were also bound up in the nation's triumphs and woes. The War of 1812 devastated Kentucky; 64 percent of the Americans killed in the war were Kentuckians. "The Hunters of Kentucky" proved to be invaluable warriors in battles ranging as distant as Canada and New Orleans. Political careers were made as a result of the war; for example, George Madison, who survived the infamous slaughter of prisoners after the Battle of the Raisin, won the governorship without opposition in 1816.[36]

Kentucky's governors eventually took notice of the educational woes of the commonwealth, beginning with Gabriel Slaughter, who as lieutenant governor succeeded Governor George Madison upon his death in 1816. During his time in office (1816–1820), Slaughter, a Democratic-Republican, soon gained additional political enemies. His views on education, penal reform, improved transportation, and the creation of a state library were enlightened but, regrettably, ahead of the times. "Every child born in the state," he said in an address to the legislature in 1816, "should be considered a child of the republic, and educated at public expense, when the parents are unable to do it." The next year he proposed a public system of district schools that would be free to the poor. Slaughter's prickly relationship with legislators worked against the obvious needs of Kentucky's poorer youth, and what made matters worse was that the state was mired in an economic depression owing to the Panic of 1819. The General Assembly paid no attention to his pleas for creation of a public school system and refused to approve his plan for creation of a school fund. Instead it approved lotteries to support individual schools, the usual legislative expedient, over the governor's vetoes.[37]

Governor John Adair (1820–1824), a Jeffersonian Republican, had a progressive agenda like Slaughter's, but he spent most of his time trying to push debtor relief. With creation of the Bank of the Commonwealth, which loaned money and printed currency, conditions only worsened. However, the legislature did create the Literary Fund on December 18, 1821, to be made up of profits "from the operations of the Bank of the Commonwealth . . . for the establishment and support of a system of general education, to be distributed in just proportions to all the counties of the state." This act also authorized a six-man committee headed by Lieutenant Governor William T. Barry to study a plan to develop a system of "Common Schools."[38]

The Barry Report, submitted to the House of Representatives a year later, won wide support, including accompanying letters from such luminaries as former presidents John Adams, Thomas Jefferson, and James Madison. The latter applauded the effort of Kentucky. "Knowledge will ever govern ignorance, and a people who mean to be their own governors must arm themselves with the power which knowledge gives," Madison said. While Adams lauded the public schools of Massachusetts, Jefferson criticized Virginia and its public expenditures for education. "If a single boy has received the elements of common [school] education," the third president grumbled, "it must be in some part of the country not known to me." All three letters reveal an implicit fear that the Republic might be losing the educated citizenry needed to maintain freedom. The evident sense of the social contract was strong and was a continuing sign of the ideas of the revolution generation.[39]

Written by Amos Kendall, editor of the *Frankfort Argus,* the Barry Report declared the Literary Fund to be insufficient for its task. Instead, it proposed an optional county school tax, a school census, and the creation of a system of "Common Free Schools." One-half of the profits of the Bank of the Commonwealth, about $60,000, would be placed in the Literary Fund, available only to those counties that passed their own tax. Referring to studies of the New England and the mid-Atlantic states, the report maintained that common schools were possible and could be adequately funded. If a system was to win broad acceptability, the report asserted, it must include all students, not just the poor or indigent. For the children of poor families to be made separate from the rest of the community "is a degradation too humiliating for the pride of freedmen."[40]

The Barry Report also enumerated the failures of the land grant academy system, which appeared to work only in towns or areas where families could afford to send their children to boarding schools in the towns. Maintaining that "common schools" were the answer, the report tried to convince "the rich" that they would save money with such a system. "In the pecuniary view, therefore," the report said, "the rich will be benefited by the introduction of a system of schools, and its advantages to the poor, and to the state at large, are wholly incalculable." More important, "a well-educated people will never be the slaves of tyrants or the tools of demagogues." Money would be appropriated out of state coffers and obtained through local county taxation. Unfortunately, the General Assembly completely ignored the report. Tom Clark called this "a great Kentucky tragedy" and "one of the most egregious blunders in American educational history." Adding insult to injury, the state continually borrowed from the Literary Fund for internal improvements, proving again the supremacy of Henry Clay's Whiggish American System over the hearts and minds of Kentuckians, who believed, along with their venerable senator, in excessive investment in internal improvements.[41]

The economic doldrums of Kentucky worsened during the governorship of Joseph Desha (1824–1828). The key issue of the day was relief for debtors. Desha's election was a referendum for debt relief, and his forces won enough seats in the legislature to vote out the "Old Court," the state's highest court, and create an amenable "New Court" that would grant debt relief without question. Incongruously, Kentucky had two high courts in session at the same time. A year later the Old Court forces retook the House of Representatives, and by 1826 it abolished the New Court. Controversy dogged Desha's term. He was roundly condemned for pardoning his son Isaac, who had been sentenced by two local juries to hang for the murder of a Mississippi man.

Desha took little notice of education except to support the forces seeking the ouster of Horace Holley, a New England Unitarian who had assumed the presidency of Transylvania University in 1818. Orthodox Christians in the state had mounted an attack on the liberal Holley. Desha, capitalizing on their position and that of other enemies of education, saw to it that Holley's salary was reduced by $1,000. In 1826 Holley resigned after Governor Desha attacked him in his annual message to the legislature.[42]

Governor Thomas Metcalfe (1828–1832), a National Republican and a devotee of Henry Clay, demonstrated a serious concern for the educational well-being of the state. In a message to the legislature in 1828, the governor scolded the state: "Kentucky is in the rear of a majority of her sister states . . . Is this not a reproach? Does it not rebuke us for our unprofitable and wasteful party strifes and struggles?" All the General Assembly did was to call for a new study to be made by President Alva Woods and Professor Benjamin O. Peers of Transylvania University, an 1821 graduate of that school. Their report of 1830 reiterated the call for a state-supported public school system, free to all; the creation of a state board of education; and a compilation of data based on the federal census. The results of the latter showed that there were nearly thirty-two thousand students in more than eleven hundred schools but "nearly four times as many children out of school as in school." The counties spent a total of $277,706 on education, and annual tuition per pupil varied from $12.91 in Logan County to $6.74 in Pulaski County. The legislature again ignored a well-intentioned report, but at least the call for change had been well founded and well publicized.[43]

If public education in Kentucky in the first third of the nineteenth century, particularly in the more rural counties, lagged behind education in the rest of the nation, there were some signs of progressivism with the chartering of state-supported schools for the deaf and the blind.

Kentucky organized the first state-supported school for the deaf in the nation and the first deaf school west of the Appalachian Mountains. State senator Elias Barbee, whose daughter Lucy was deaf, helped write the bill that became law on December 7, 1822. The Kentucky Asylum for the Tuition of the Deaf and Dumb, its first official name, opened on April 10, 1823, with three students. After renting property for two years, the Kentucky School for the Deaf moved to its present location on South Second Street in Danville. Because deaf education was still in its infancy, KSD had difficulty finding trained teachers. Finally a Centre College student, John Adamson Jacobs, received training with Thomas Gallaudet and Laurent Clerc, two of America's earliest leaders in deaf education, and joined the Danville campus.[44]

Henry Clay helped the deaf school obtain two federal land grants that were eventually sold to finance construction costs. Until other nearby states developed their own deaf schools, several sent their students to Danville. The board of trustees of Centre College operated the school until 1870. Jacobs, some of whose methods became controversial, became one of the nation's leaders in developing deaf education. The Civil War placed great stress on the Danville school, as on most institutions, and its enrollment suffered.[45]

Kentucky also became one of the leading western states in providing education for the blind. Bryce McLellan Patten, president of the Louisville Collegiate Institute, invited his brother Otis to teach a few blind students in afternoon classes, beginning in the summer of 1839. Two years later Patten tried to get the General Assembly to fund a blind school. In early 1842, the Patten brothers and several citizens of Louisville invited Samuel Gridley Howe, founder and director of the Perkins School for the Blind in Massachusetts, and four of his students to demonstrate methods of educating the blind. In 1842 the General Assembly passed legislation creating the Kentucky School for the Blind, the sixth such school in the nation, and the school opened on May 9, 1842, with five students directed by the Patten brothers. The city of Louisville also appropriated money to help found the school. After moving around several times in Louisville, KSB moved to its permanent site on Frankfort Avenue in 1855.[46]

Perhaps even more amazing than the creation of deaf and blind schools in Kentucky during the antebellum period is that some black children received an education. While slavery represented an important institution in Kentucky, the state never prohibited by law the education of slaves or free blacks. Most masters did not want their slaves to be literate, though, fearing it would aid them in running away to nearby free territory across the Ohio River. For example, advertisements for runaways sometimes contained such notices as "a pretty good scholar."[47]

The earliest effort at Negro education may have been a "Sunday School" in Lexington in 1798. "Those who wish their servants taught," said a notice in the *Kentucky Gazette*, "will please to send a line, as none will be received without." No doubt, some owners believed that moral and biblical instruction, either delivered orally or by teaching slaves to read and write, would promote "morality, good health, and faithful service," resulting in contented, nonrebellious slaves. Sympathetic antislavery whites also established schools, which usually lasted only a short time, for example, in Louisville in 1827, 1833, and 1834, and in Lexington in 1839 and 1840. In 1841 the Fifth Street Baptist Church in Louisville, a black institution, opened the Adams's School, named for Rev. Henry Adams. William H. Gibson Sr., a free black from Baltimore, opened a school for the children of black Methodists in Louisville in 1847 that flourished until the beginning of the Civil War. He also formed grammar schools in Lexington, Bowling Green, Richmond, and Frankfort before the war. Having fled the state during the war, Gibson returned in 1866 to again become a leader in the black community. In the mid-1850s abolitionist John G. Fee and antislavery advocate Cassius Marcellus Clay cooperated in proposing an integrated, coeducational colony in Berea. Because of their conflicts with each other, along with the opposition of Madison County slaveholders and those in surrounding counties, Berea College was only a short-lived primary school before the beginning of the Civil War. Against all these odds, a surprising number of African Americans in Kentucky learned to minimally read and write. Marion B. Lucas has concluded from census data and other studies that by 1860 perhaps slightly more than half of the freedman over age nineteen were literate, although the percentage of literate slaves was far lower. One study indicated that as many as 10 percent of slaves across the South may have been literate.[48]

All was not lost with the failure of the Woods-Peers suggestions to immediately win over the legislature. Although Governor Slaughter put internal transportation concerns first, he did not forget about the needs of education. The 1830 legislature authorized county courts to establish school districts and levy taxes, but because the system was voluntary, it met with little initial success. Peers continued to publicize the need for "universal education," although he meant education only for boys through the fourth grade. He was like many leaders of that era in that his conservatism predominated over his more liberal side. For example, he feared that without educated voters, democratic excesses in America might overcome the republic. Biographer Doris Lynn Koch Moore has called Peers "a social conservative" but also "a pedagogical liberal." Moreover, Peers argued that government officials could do only so much if the people of the state did not support a public school system. In his book *American Education: Our Strictures on the Nature, Necessity, and Practicability of a System of National Education, Suited to the United States,* Peers made one last attempt to influence Kentucky and national educational policy. He argued, as an Episcopal theologian, that all public education should be grounded in religious values actively presented in the classroom.[49]

Momentum began to build for change. As early as April 1828, educators began meeting periodically, led by Transylvania University faculty. The idea of professionalizing teaching took root slowly. A survey in 1832 revealed that the private and public academies were educating only about one-quarter of the children of the state between ages five and fifteen. Most schools were clustered in towns and cities. Russell County, for example, had only one school. Parents who could afford to send their children to boarding schools did so. The majority of Kentuckians were illiterate. It took organization to move Kentucky forward. The Kentucky Association of Professional Teachers, formed in 1833 and led by Professor Peers, and the Kentucky Common

School Society, formed in 1834 with Governor John Breathitt as its first president, began to cooperate in publicizing the educational needs of the commonwealth. The Kentucky Education Association, planned by a group of educators in Louisville, met for the first time in that city in late December 1857. However, the Civil War intervened before the organization could do much to promote education in the commonwealth.[50]

Many of Kentucky's leaders understood that neither the Literary Fund of 1821 nor the 1830 act had much impact on the state. Governor James Clark (1836–1839), in his first message on December 6, 1836, asked the General Assembly to consider establishing a common school system. The legislature took little notice. However, in the middle of 1836, the U.S. Treasury, at the behest of the tight-fisted administration of President Andrew Jackson, began distributing excess federal funds, and Kentucky received $1,433,757. After agreeing to set aside $1 million of this fund to support education, the legislature finally listened to Governor Clark's pleas and in February 1838 adopted a statute creating a common school system. The short-sighted General Assembly soon reduced the school fund by $150,000, shifting that amount over to the internal improvements so popular with a society still in the making.[51]

The 1838 law had important features that could bring about potentially epic changes for the youth of Kentucky. Most crucial was the School Fund. A superintendent of public instruction, appointed by the governor for a two-year term, would be part of a state board of education, and the secretary of state and the attorney general would be its other members. County courts were to divide the counties into districts and "to take the sense of the legal voters" on the questions of forming a school system and levying taxes to support it. Each county could levy taxes equal to the amount from the School Fund received from the state. The State Board would appoint five commissioners in each county, in effect a county board, to oversee the schools. Five trustees in each district would "have full charge" of the schools and would select teachers. They also had the power to levy a poll tax on every white male over age twenty-one. Generally, students attended only through the third grade, if at all, in this most rudimentary of the public common schools. If a child knew enough of the "three R's to read the Bible, write a simple letter, and cipher through the rule of three," his or her education was considered complete. The act of 1838 did not apply to independent school districts in Louisville, Lexington, and Maysville, where schools were already funded on a local tax and tuition basis.[52]

Like previous education laws in the commonwealth, this one failed to work because it was simply unenforceable. First and foremost, the majority of Kentuckians did not see a real need for common schools. Isolation, localism, and a plain lack of interest defeated the reformist impulse. The state superintendent was little more than an office clerk, a record keeper without power to enforce the new law. Moreover, the all-powerful county courts did not want to give up any control over their "little kingdoms" to other bodies. By law, the School Fund was to be invested, and the interest used to support schools. The interest that accrued would have been too small to do much good on a large scale. But the worst was yet to come.[53]

In 1840 "the fallacy" of the School Fund became apparent when Kentucky got caught up in another economic downturn. In the fall of that year, Robert Perkins Letcher (1840–1844), known as "Black Bob" to some, whom historian Lowell Harrison called "one of the most entertaining Whig governors" because of his colorful speeches and fiddle-playing ability, assumed the governorship. A fiscal conservative, Letcher proceeded to cut expenditures to balance the overextended state budget. As chairman of the Commissioners of the Sinking Fund, the governor announced that there "was not enough money available to pay the interest on the bonds in the School Fund." With interest due on bonds sold for internal improvements, the commissioners decided to take any income from the school bonds. For the next three years, the commissioners continued this thievery, paying little back into the School Fund. No money went to local schools from the state coffers.[54]

The 1840 census revealed the dilemma of Kentucky education, especially compared with education in Ohio, one of the states founded on the basis of the Land Ordinance of 1785 and the Northwest Ordinance. While both states had about the same number of students attending academies, Ohio's total population was 1,519,500 and Kentucky's was 779,828. In the "common school" Kentucky's northern neighbor listed 218,609 students to the commonwealth's 24,614. Whereas in Tennessee 22.2 percent of students were being "educated at public expense," only 1.4 percent were so blessed in Kentucky. On both the state's northern and southern borders, public school education was improving while Kentucky's schools languished.[55]

Moreover, out-and-out political flimflam was also afoot. By January 1844, the interest owed to the School Fund from the Sinking Fund, a "rainy day" fund used to pay accumulated state debts, was more than $400,000, which made the School Fund now total precisely $1,258,368.66. With continued stress on building roads and improving the rivers, coupled with poor credit ratings in eastern banking circles, Governor William Owsley (1844–1848), looked for a way to "stop the snowballing of interest due on the School Fund." In what Tom Clark called "one of Kentucky's public scandals" and what University of Kentucky president Frank L. McVey termed "chicanery," the General Assembly on February 10, 1845, passed the "act to increase the resources of the Sinking fund, and to provide for the burning of certain State bonds." This cowardly statute ordered all bonds held by the Board of Education to be turned over to the governor so that he could burn them in the presence of the state auditor and the state treasurer. In political doublespeak, Governor Owsley justified his act by saying, "It was not imperative to borrow money at six per cent to pay the state a debt it owned itself." Ironically, the act also ordered duplicate lists to be made, "presumably on the ground that the state might someday do something about the bonds." Kentucky had again missed a golden opportunity, the third such misstep since its founding, to break free from its dismal education past.[56]

The school law of 1838 established numerous standards, both positive and negative, that guided public school education in the commonwealth for more than a century. The creation of the State Board of Education and county boards set precedents that continue to the present. Each county was to be divided into convenient districts, ranging from no fewer than thirty students to as many as one hundred, in effect a single school in each district. Lawmakers hoped that such small districts would encourage parent involvement and local pride. The number of district trustees, originally five, was reduced to three in 1842. As the trustee system entrenched itself into the county systems, it became one of the leading causes for the inefficiency of education. Many times a teacher was forced to pay a kickback from her or his already meager salary to inept, corrupt, and often quite ignorant trustees. Tom Clark summed it up best when he called the local district trustee system the "black beast of Kentucky educational history from 1838 to 1920." County commissioners were not much better; their numbers were reduced from five to three and finally to one by 1856. Characteristic of the times, some counties refused to levy local school taxes until the late nineteenth century. "Teachers were paid starveling salaries ranging from twelve to thirty-five dollars for three-month terms," exclaimed Clark, "a sum insufficient to sustain a person without a secondary source of employment."[57]

Section 41 of the 1838 law provided for independent school districts, separate from the schools of the county. Louisville, Lexington, and Maysville were permitted to operate separate districts "so long as they continue to maintain public schools by taxation." This development had been progressing for some time, dating back to the formation of the public academies. Subsequent laws in 1845 and 1859 enlarged the independent-district system so that it applied to more towns and even to parts of some counties. The 1838 law primarily was intended to protect the surplus fund and its income; it neither proposed nor defined what a common school should do. Most schools met for three months at most, although some extended a bit longer by subscription. Completion of the fourth grade was considered to be terminal in the common schools of the time. At that level a student was assumed to have rudimentary knowledge, enough of the "three R's" to "read a newspaper and the Bible, write a simple sentence of social correspondence or business, and 'cipher through the rule of three' (add and subtract)."[58]

Teaching was not much advanced by the new law. Trustees certified and employed teachers based on annual examinations. It helped to have family or political connections. Examinations of prospective teachers were sometimes spurious and the applicants suggestible. When asked whether he taught that the world was flat or round, one applicant reportedly said, in effect, "that while he was a little uncertain on the subject, he would teach whichever one the trustees wanted." This situation did not improve until the state took over teacher examinations and the issuance of certificates, beginning in the 1870s. In 1827, the trustees of Transylvania University proposed to teach pedagogy along with liberal arts courses, but the plan never materialized because of a lack of state support. Professor Peers of Transylvania established the Eclectic Institute for boys in Lexington in 1832 and used progressive teaching methods. He encouraged the use of the Pestalozzian method of active learning and the "Rensselaerean method of science instruction, which stressed laboratory work and student demonstration of experiments."[59]

The creation of the office of state superintendent had a long-lasting influence. In February 1838, Governor Clark appointed Rev. Joseph J. Bullock as the first superintendent. He served only one year of a two-year term. Before the professionalization of education, Protestant ministers often held such posts in America. The first of seven ministers to hold the post in succession, Bullock had been one of the progressives advocating the common school cause. Bullock spent much of his year traveling the state, finding that Kentuckians "do not value education as it deserves." He made a special effort to study the problem of literacy, but most county commissioners ignored his request for information. Even so, he "declared that one-third of the white population was entirely uneducated." Bullock found it difficult to keep up the pace the job warranted. In his report to the General Assembly, he argued that future superintendents needed a larger salary to keep them focused on the school work and not in need of other employment to supplement their income.[60]

State superintendents from 1839 through 1847 faced many of the same problems as Bullock. Protestant ministers of the Gospel all, their reports complained about the inadequacy of the School Fund, the need for normal schools, the reduction of the superintendent's annual salary from $1,000 to $750, and lack of interest by parents and the general public. Because too few native Kentuckians were being trained, the Right Reverend Benjamin Bosworth Smith, an Episcopalian prelate, found "a regular invasion of the State by pedagogues from the older states," particularly "teachers from the Old Dominion and the Yankee School Marms." Another superintendent complained about "transient teachers," who only taught for a short time until they found better employment in another trade or profession.[61]

Governor Owsley shamelessly burned school bonds and repudiated the trust of his office, but he did one thing that abruptly changed common school education when he appointed Presbyterian minister Robert J. Breckinridge state superintendent in 1847. A somewhat intolerant man, particularly toward Catholicism but also toward anyone else who disagreed with him, Breckinridge returned to Kentucky for his appointment after serving as president of Jefferson College in Pennsylvania. Although he held slaves, he bitterly opposed the slave system, even running unsuccessfully as an emancipation candidate for the 1849 Constitutional Convention. It took all of Breckinridge's considerable talents as a publicist and a persuader to overcome what the *Frankfort Commonwealth* declared in 1847: "The Common School System of Kentucky is a mockery."[62]

Considered as one of the early leaders of "the Awakening" of the national public school movement, Breckinridge's first term as an appointed state superintendent, 1847–1850, coincided with a finally successful attempt to write a new constitution. He hit the ground running. Like his predecessors, he traveled the state pushing the cause of education, collecting data while cajoling and pestering politicians and other civic leaders. Most important, he was determined to keep the legislature's hands off the School Fund. He immediately set about organizing new districts and compiling statistics. Studying all school laws, he cooperated with like-minded citizens. Breckinridge worked on simplifying the system used for distributing the School Fund while trying to increase resources.[63]

The indefatigable superintendent's surveys indicated that not enough children were attending school and that state funds were not being distributed equitably. Since the beginning of state support, such as it was, money had been distributed by total child count in a county rather than by those actually attending school there. As a result, local officials exaggerated their census in order to get as much money as possible while dragging their feet in organizing new schools. Breckinridge tried to change this inequity.[64]

Breckinridge's efforts were soon rewarded. School legislation of February 29, 1848, directed the governor to issue new school bonds for $308,268.42, to replace the funds lost in 1845. Moreover, the state was now allowed to levy a property tax of two cents per $100 of value. The tax, to benefit schools, was to be approved by vote of the citizens of the commonwealth. The number of children in school increased rapidly in the first four years of Breckinridge's tenure. From 1847 to 1850 the number of children in school increased from 20,775 to 178,559. The number of counties reporting educational progress increased from twenty-seven to ninety-eight, with only two counties not responding. Even more amazingly, the number of schools increased from 170 to 3,704. Just as important, money began flowing to the schools as average attendance improved.[65]

Nonetheless, Breckinridge and other state leaders understood that the 1799 constitution hamstrung needed change. They supported the idea of a new document that would specifically safeguard education. Critics of the 1799 constitution had tried several times over the years to call for a new charter. Finally, in January 1847, a vote for a convention cleared the legislature and voters approved the measure overwhelmingly on two separate required ballots. Education, slavery, and fiscal policy were key issues to be discussed at the meeting held in 1849. The constitution of 1850 was the result of growing dissatisfaction with government mischief, the raiding of the School Fund by Governor Owsley and the General Assembly being only one example. Furthermore, private legislation took up an inordinate amount of the legislature's time.[66]

The convention began on October 1, 1849; delegates were chosen by ballot, and Democrats held a slight majority. Henry Clay and John J. Crittenden did not seek seats, and Superintendent Breckinridge lost his election bid. The new constitution included important new measures. Elections were to be held every two years rather than every year, and nearly all county officials as well as judges were to be elected by popular vote. The balloting, voting by voice, would now be limited to one day. While no major change was made in the governorship, the judiciary was now to be elected for fixed terms, and financial controls were placed on the legislature. With an obligation of $4.5 million on the books, the state was deeply in debt and found it increasingly difficult to borrow money in the East. Now, by law, the Sinking Fund could no longer be expanded outrageously; there was a provision for oversight by the people. The General Assembly could not contract for more than $500,000 unless it imposed a tax increase to pay the interest each year, after first gaining the electorate's approval. Legislative sessions were limited to sixty days biennially, unless two-thirds of the General Assembly's members voted otherwise.[67]

Although increased popular controls were imposed on government power, protecting the "peculiar institution" was the first order of the day. Ominously, slavery was given even more protection than in the previous constitutions. The new constitution stated: the "right of the owner of a slave to have such slave and its increase is the same and as inviolable as the right of any property whatsoever."[68]

Despite the momentum that had built for making education prominent in the document, the idea of a common school system still faced considerable opposition, and education was placed "last on the agenda." The statement on education followed the language of a document adopted earlier in New Hampshire. Ben "Kitchenknife" Hardin, a Catholic representative from Nelson County, as well as many Protestants, stoutly opposed including public schools in the constitution. Thomas D. Clark said Hardin's statement against public funding of public schools "almost stands alone as an American anti-intellectual classic." The irascible Hardin railed against the common schools as being "generally under the management of a miserable set of humbug teachers at best." Claiming that private schools were best, he declared it took him years to overcome the terrible impact of attending a blab school. "I would not send a child to a free school," he said, "and would rather pay for his education myself." Former governor Charles A. Wickliffe, a cousin of Hardin, voiced his opposition as well. Like Hardin and Wickliffe, many Kentuckians expressed the belief that since all taxation to support schools was a tax on land, any farmer, of high or low income, would be opposed to the idea.[69]

Ira Root, a Louisville lawyer and delegate, expressed his exasperation with Hardin in sarcastic oratory. "Would to God that the powerful talents of the gentleman from Nelson—for his talents must be felt wherever he shall take part—could have been exerted, at this late hour of his life, upon one of the greatest and most ennobling theatres, that would crown every other act of his honorable career." Root went on to explain that only with public schools financed by the citizenry could Kentucky reach its true potential. Further, he reminded the delegates that most of the "wealthy" sent their children to private schools. Larkin J. Proctor of Warsaw told his colleagues that the majority of Kentuckians of school age, two hundred thousand, had no schooling at all nor an opportunity to attend school at public expense. Another delegate, John D. Taylor, also struck at Hardin's agrarian pessimism: "Great God, can it be possible that we shall be non-combatants in the great battle for life—for knowledge is life." In the popular style of mid-nineteenth-century florid oratory, he declared that "under the new organization, schools are to spring up in every neighborhood, to be as free as the gush of waters from the mountain rock. . . . They will arise like fireflies at summer sunset, giving life and hope to each other—light to the young, hope to the middle aged, and consolation to the old."[70]

In the end, the delegates approved what Tom Clark called "a vague educational clause," one creating a common school system and a School Fund protected from "legislative raids." Most of the opposition to ratification of the new constitution came from Whigs who believed the document to be evidence of Democratic Party reformism, but it was adopted by a vote of more than three to one. Perhaps education had fared better this time; at least a public, or common, school system was part of the 1850 constitution.

Article XI appeared to protect "the capital of the fund called and known as the 'Common School Fund'" by declaring in strong language that the money must be "held inviolable for the purpose of sustaining a system of common schools." Like all other state officials, the state superintendent was made an elected office. This article also authorized the General Assembly to distribute the fund's income to the counties.[71]

Governor John Jordan Crittenden (1848–1850) strongly supported Breckinridge and the improvement of education in the state. Early on he backed up the General Assembly of 1848–1849 by reissuing new bonds to the State Board of Education for all interest in arrears to the School Fund and thoroughly supported the property tax of two cents per $100 of value to support schools. The voters overwhelmingly voted to approve the new tax, a first for the state of Kentucky. Historian Victor Howard found that "during Crittenden's administration the common school system was given a sound financial foundation." When Crittenden resigned in July 1850 to accept the attorney general post in the cabinet of President Millard Fillmore, the governorship passed to Lieutenant Governor John Larue Helm. By this time, an estimated 90 percent of Kentucky children were in school, although that figure was probably considerably inflated.[72]

Helm and Breckinridge immediately clashed. Helm, who had never been a supporter of a common school system, attempted to scuttle it by reigniting the old battle for control of the School Fund. The new governor "took the position that the School Fund was a debt the state owed to itself and, therefore, the state could refuse to pay the interest in the fund without dishonor." When the state legislature overrode his veto and directed the commissioners of the Sinking Fund to pay the interest due to the School Fund, Helm refused to obey the law. Fortunately, this impasse was circumvented when Helm, called by one historian "public education's strongest opponent" of all pre–Civil War governors, resigned. He was replaced by a pro-education governor, Lazarus Whitehead Powell, the first Democrat governor elected since 1832 and the first elected under the 1850 constitution.[73]

Powell ordered the state treasury to pay the State Board of Education $67,013 in back interest on the school bonds, the money due it from the Sinking Fund. He later signed a bill putting before the voters in 1855 a measure to benefit education by increasing the ad valorem tax on property from two to five cents per $100 of property. The voters of the commonwealth approved it by more than three to one. Powell saw the advantages of having an educated populace. "The surest guaranty we can have for the continuance and perpetuity of our free institutions," he explained, "is the education of our children." Breckinridge appeared to be victorious. "Too much praise cannot be given Superintendent Robert J. Breckinridge in winning this contest for the establishment of a common school system for the people of the state," said Moses Edward Ligon, the author of an early history of Kentucky public school education.[74]

When things quieted a bit, Breckinridge wrote a report (an activity at which he excelled) in flowery self-promotion, to the Senate. Breckinridge saw only in shades of black and white. He took no prisoners, displaying an attitude that bordered on immodesty and arrogance. "For myself I expect nothing and I fear nothing," he said. "I have done my duty, and whatever personal verdict the government or the people may pass, will be received by me with perfect tranquility." All things considered, Breckinridge was probably the only person in the commonwealth who could have pulled off so much change so quickly. The defeat of Helm's veto once and for all, as well as the constitution of 1850, established the School Fund as a permanent part of state institutional funding and made the state responsible for the common schools. The old academy system of English origin and Virginian derivation had never worked well in the Kentucky context and never educated enough children to justify its existence and the unworkable state land grant system.[75]

Breckinridge remained in his formerly appointive post without interruption when he was elected the first state superintendent of public instruction in the general election of 1851. He ran as a Whig, winning over five other candidates. Section 2 of Article XI of the 1850 constitution made the office permanent, to be elected every four years. He continued to take his charge with typical Calvinist assurance. "The Superintendent of Public Instruction is not the clerk of the board of education," he averred, "but is the head of one of the most difficult and important enterprises ever untaken by the State." Breckinridge had served two years of his term when he resigned in 1853 to found the Danville Theological Seminary.[76]

The constitution of 1850 offered a somewhat firmer foundation than ever before on which to make educational progress. In 1851 the General Assembly defined the common school as "one in which a competent teacher was employed for three months in the year, and which received all white children between the ages of six and eighteen, who resided in the district." A law in 1852 provided for teacher certification, such as it was. "The county commissioners were the key men in the success of the whole system," one observer said. The commissioners, their number reduced to one in 1856, often either ran the county's schools as a personal fiefdom or demonstrated a "lack of interest." The commissioner had responsibility for examining and supervising teachers, establishing districts, receiving state money, and making reports to the state board. Management of the districts resided in the trustees, who could range from the illiterate to the semicriminal to the diligent. Trustees continued to supervise the buildings, hire and fire teachers, take a census of children, and make annual reports to the commissioners.[77]

After being elected state superintendent and seeing the realization of decades of efforts to create a true common school system, Breckinridge remained just as combative during his remaining tenure as during his first years. And he lost some battles during his second term. In 1851 the legislature passed a law giving the state board the power to recommend textbooks for a course of study but leaving the final say up the local school trustees. It was a long-sought "reform," going back at least to 1840 and Superintendent H. H. Kavanaugh, but some thought it attacked the sanctity of parental rights. Moreover, parents now had to pay for the suggested books rather than depending on what they had in their homes.[78]

Another school law of 1851 recreated a state school board of the same consistency as before; it included the attorney general and the secretary of state, in effect ex officio members, along with the state superintendent. Some critics claimed that the first two normally had little or no knowledge of education. Nor would they have sufficient time to devote to choosing textbooks, developing courses of instruction, and other tasks if they were doing their own jobs in state government well. The prevailing feeling of legislators was that since these were elected officials, they could provide proficient oversight over public school education in the commonwealth.[79]

In 1852 parents and guardians also lost control of curriculum. The state board was authorized to provide "a plain education," to include English, grammar, arithmetic, and geography. In reaction, the Friends of Education in Kentucky, spearheaded by Breckinridge, declared the curriculum inadequate. The Friends resolved "that a course of good common school instruction should contemplate a thorough knowledge of spelling, reading, writing, geography, with maps, arithmetic, the history of the United States, English grammar, in its elementary principles, including composition, and the elements of general history." This report also encouraged the use of the Bible in the classroom as long as it did not stir up religious difficulties.[80]

Another improvement statewide came with the mandate for a three-month school term for the common schools that would be free to all students. But Breckinridge wanted the school term to be longer and still free to students; he opposed charging tuition for schools that lasted longer than the required three months. He railed against what he considered to be "imported" ideas from other states, one of the most objectionable being the new process of choosing textbooks and organizing the curriculum. This development "puts parents and guardians aside as unworthy to be trusted with the culture of the minds and hearts of their own children and wards."

Breckinridge also feared that the "indigent" would still be discouraged from attending school, as they had been at the academies. Moreover, he believed that the School Fund distribution to the counties should be based on the number of children actually attending school rather than the total number of children. Ultimately, the Friends of Education in Kentucky, dominated by Breckinridge, became his rearguard action against education policies that he opposed.[81]

In Breckinridge's "Farewell Report," submitted in late 1853, he pointed with pride to his accomplishments as state superintendent and the great strides that had been made in education during his tenure. He repeated his major complaints against what had been created. The new school laws regarding the status of the state superintendent he characterized as "improper and injurious." With complaints from inadequate compensation and staffing to a less-than-proper status for the post, this haughty Presbyterian minister found the position wanting. Breckinridge counted himself among the angels. In his most flowery mid-nineteenth-century prose, he exclaimed: "It may be that men will not always bear to hear it, and it may be, too, that it is not the part of carnal wisdom to utter it. But wise and thoughtful men all know it, and they who have long toiled in the sacred cause [education] may not ever be silent and forbear to proclaim it, where none will hear."[82]

It was past time for Breckinridge to move on. For all his bombast, though, he had done what no one else could have done in the late 1840s and early 1850s: he bridged the gap between the old system of education in Kentucky and the new. And he set a precedent for a strong state superintendency. He wisely saw that Kentucky had a long way to go to develop an adequate common school system. Called the Kentucky "Horace Mann" by the *Louisville Morning Courier* at the end of his tenure and "the father of the public school system in Kentucky" by James C. Klotter, Breckinridge would hardly take no for an answer, and that trait proved to be invaluable during his time as state superintendent. He was one of the important "Crusaders for the Common School" in the South, along with Calvin Wiley in North Carolina and Charles Fenton Mercer in Virginia. Lowell H. Harrison claimed that by the end of Breckinridge's term in 1853, "only North Carolina among the slave states could match Kentucky's educational progress." However, in contrast to Breckinridge's Kentucky, Mann's Massachusetts moved to a six-month school term during Mann's twelve years as director of the state school board and had founded three state-supported normal schools by 1840. On the positive side, education officials now claimed, quite obviously exaggerating, that 90 percent of Kentucky white youths attended school of some sort. Educational opportunities in the mountains of Kentucky were indeed challenging. The 1850 census in Appalachia indicated that Perry and Owsley counties had no public schools at all. In other counties enrolled students ranged from 80 in Breathitt to 298 in Letcher to 1,197 in Whitley.[83]

By the time Breckinridge left his post, the country had moved closer to a showdown over the slavery issue. The Compromise of 1850, the last brokered by Kentucky's "Great Compromiser," Henry Clay, with old warhorses Daniel Webster and John C. Calhoun also playing key roles, first appeared to be a workable solution to the slavery problem. The agreement included provisions that allowed California to enter the union as a free state and ended the slave trade but not slavery in Washington, D.C. The fugitive slave issue was of paramount concern to Kentucky slave-owners, with freedom beckoning to slaves across the Ohio River. Clay's compromise strengthened the penalties for helping fugitive slaves. Ironically, in 1850 there were only 96 fugitives out of the nearly 211,000 slaves in the commonwealth. Ten years later, on the eve of the Civil War, there were only 119 fugitives out of about 225,000 bonds-men. This issue was obviously more important as an emotional issue than as a practical one. The "cold war" that existed between North and South, with its brief periods of violence, could not last much longer.[84]

For the remainder of the 1850s, common school education in Kentucky appeared to improve. After the bombastic Breckinridge, the administration of another minister, Rev. John Daniel Matthews (1853–1859) proved to be less exciting, one of the episodic steps backward. Like his predecessors, Matthews deplored the lack of training of teachers and, like them, proposed that Kentucky join the national movement of developing "normal" schools for teacher training. The normal school, a movement that began in France with the *école normale* and spread to England and then to the United States, usually consisted of a short course in the rudiments of teaching. Most Kentucky common school teachers had no training; their preparation amounted to cramming to pass an examination mandated by the school law of 1852. For a fee of fifty cents, prospective teachers took a test in "plain English Education," administered by examiners appointed by the county school commissioner. If the teacher passed the exam, a certificate was issued for one or more years.[85]

In the mid-1850s, Kentucky had another opportunity to make a modest step forward in common school education. The cause, however, got caught up in a combination of growing nativism, the closing of the ranks of white Kentuckians to extinguish criticism of the institution of slavery, and continued religious turmoil in the commonwealth. Transylvania University, after thrashing about trying to find a sure denominational direction (it had been, over the years, Baptist, Episcopal, and then Presbyterian), lost Methodist support in 1850. The school's trustees looked for a way for the state of Kentucky to take over the floundering institution. Matthews lobbied the legislature with the same argument used by previous superintendents, that outsiders were filling the state's teaching positions because not enough native Kentuckians had training. Also, owing to the growing defensiveness of slaveholders, he painted "Yankee" teachers as subversives and a threat to local mores. This charge illustrated the times. Charles Slaughter Morehead, who joined the American, or "Know-Nothing," Party after the death of the Whig Party in the early 1850s, won the governorship in 1855 and served until 1859. A "rowdy element" within the nativist movement in Louisville touched off "Bloody Monday" not long after his election. Morehead fully supported the normal school measure. An act of the General Assembly on March 10, 1856, passed by a narrow margin, made Transylvania the state's first state school of higher education and its first normal school. A dual board of former trustees and some state officials was designated, and the legislature promised annual support of $12,000. In effect, Transylvania became a state institution as well as the nation's ninth state-funded teachers' college.[86]

Superintendent Matthews reported a booming start for the Transylvania normal school in September 1856: eighty men were beginning six months of instruction "in the beautiful and refined city of Lexington," using "the large and commodious college building and dormitory." Although Morehead continued his support, Kentucky's legislators soon cooled to what they considered to be an overly expensive institution. Many claimed that the state had no constitutional right to form a public university or college. Moreover, to them there always seemed to be a better, more profitable way to spend the state's money. So the General Assembly, this time overwhelmingly, killed the normal school at Transylvania in 1858, an act that Superintendent Matthews rightly termed "a retrograde movement." Kentucky had lost another chance to join a growing national trend in public school education.[87]

Perhaps the highlight of the 1850s in education, as well as of the administration of Matthews, was the successful increase in the state school tax in mid-decade, raising the levy from two cents to five cents per $100 evaluation. Voters of the state approved the measure by a vote of more than two to one. However, Superintendent Robert Richardson reported in 1860 that a majority of counties did not impose a local tax but relied entirely on state school funds for support of their schools. Those counties rarely had more than a three-month school term. It was difficult to get over the stigma attached to poverty. "It shall be the duty of the trustees to invite and encourage all of the indigent children of the district to attend the school," the new law read. An earlier historian of Kentucky education, C. W. Hackensmith, found that "in the more favored sections of the state where private schools flourished, it was not uncommon to hear the public school referred to as the school for the poor people."[88]

Nevertheless, many new schools were being founded. As a matter of fact, on the eve of the Civil War, Superintendent Richardson called for the "consolidation of schools," owing to the unnecessary "multiplication of districts." The classic one-room school, which dotted the landscape from early American history well into the twentieth century, served as the center of community life for thousands of Kentuckians. As the community grew, the school might be expanded into two rooms or more, and establishment of a high school could be considered. In small communities and the more isolated rural areas, high schools might not be added until after the turn of the twentieth century.[89]

The academy and the seminary filled an important void as Kentucky struggled to found and sustain a public school system. From 1792 to 1850, Kentuckians founded approximately 85 academies and 58 seminaries, according to a 1926 master's thesis at the University of Chicago. With a charter from the General Assembly, these quasi-public institutions used various means of funding, including state land grants, donations, subscriptions, tuition, and lotteries. As corporate entities, their success depended on good leadership. The success of the academies and seminaries retarded the growth of purely public institutions, but particularly for girls, these schools offered a creditable education for the time. Teenager Bettie Woodford of Clark County could report to her aunt with a considerable sense of pride in February 1858, "I am studying History, Colburn's Arithmetic, Ray's Arithmetic, Michel's Large Geography, and grammar and spelling."[90]

Only a few schools went against the grain of antebellum social and educational mores. Columbia Male and Female High School in Adair County, founded by Presbyterians, operated in the 1850s as a "mixed school," a quite forward thought for conservative Kentucky. The 1858 Triennial Catalogue of the school declared, "Providence has not so ordered the affairs of the human race that one family or one community should raise females and another males. . . . The mutual influence of the sexes upon each other is necessary to the highest development and happiness of the family, and society at large." In its third year of operation, the school boasted a student body of nearly three hundred in the primary, preparatory, and collegiate departments. Strict rules of attendance, religious instruction, and Friday afternoon "Public Exercises" to demonstrate that "all" students learned skills, indicated the seriousness of this endeavor at groundbreaking education. The trend, though, was to separate the sexes in private schools, such as Daughters College in Harrodsburg, founded by John Augustus Williams in 1856, after the purchase of Greenville Springs Institute.[91]

How effective were public- and private-school elementary and secondary education in antebellum Kentucky? The education varied from child to child, based on local circumstances, the interest of the parents, and the intelligence and inquisitiveness of the child. Abraham Lincoln had enough of the latter to catapult himself into the White House at the most critical time in American history. Young Abe Lincoln, having already been taught his letters, went to a school near his Knob Creek home at the age of six. He attended school only for a few short months after moving with his family to Indiana and then Illinois. Most poor children in his circumstances would have been worn down and lucky to have a smattering of the "three R's" as they entered adulthood. The academies and seminaries did a bit better than the public schools. Even the wellborn had their problems. In early January 1852, from Bowling Green, Elizabeth Cox Underwood wrote to her husband, U.S. senator Joseph R. Underwood, in the nation's capital, reporting on the education of her children. Her letter encapsulated the fears, hopes, and realities of many Kentucky parents. "The schools for boys in this Town are of no account," she said. "They are not conducted in a proper manner. Teaching ought to be a labor of love; but it is seldom we meet with such. And indeed, I pity the poor schoolmaster, with three or four dozen turbulent boys, and hardly wonder how they can do better." She was not hopeful.

> Our John has no natural love of learning from books, so it is an uphill work with both teacher and pupil. . . . Sometimes I think I will take him from school and instruct him myself, but fear my patience would give out. If he showed the assiduity and thirst for knowledge of little Robert, I would love to teach him. The labor then would not be so arduous, as it would be mutual. But I have some hopes that John will spend his time more profitably this year, as he is rid of some very objectionable playmates.

John Cox Underwood did indeed turn out well. Although his father was an emancipationist and a unionist, John joined the Confederate Army in 1862 after graduating from Rensselaer Polytechnical Institute in Troy, New York. When the Civil War ended, he returned to Bowling Green and pursued a career in engineering and architecture. He served as mayor of Bowling Green, then lieutenant governor of Kentucky (1875–1879), but lost a bid for the governorship as a Democrat in 1879. In his later years he edited a newspaper in Cincinnati.[92]

As part of an "Educational Awakening" nationally in the period from 1820 to 1860, Kentucky made significant strides, considering its impediments. In 1860 Kentucky lagged behind its northern cohorts. With a population double that of Kentucky, Ohio had 10,501 teachers compared to 2,617 in the commonwealth. On the other hand, Kentucky had 431 more teachers than Tennessee, which had a similar population. Organized efforts to create a public school system were only partially successful. Before Presbyterian minister Robert Jefferson Breckinridge became state superintendent in 1847, for every step forward there always seemed to be one backward. Momentum for change, coupled with a new constitution in 1850, finally created a common school system. By 1853 Kentucky ranked second only to North Carolina among the slave states in providing for public education. But was that enough? And what challenges would the impending Civil War place on education?[93]

Chapter 2

The Early History of Higher Education

W AR AND RUMORS OF war, funding difficulties, reticent and sometimes rebellious students, underpaid and overworked faculty, sectarian strife, helpful as well as meddling alumni and supporters, and feckless and sometimes downright hostile legislators and governors are all problems we are familiar with today in higher education. Yet the same could be said for the earliest days of higher education in Kentucky.

One of the most provocative books about the early history of the commonwealth probed the history of ideas in the frontier environment in the early Republic. Niels Henry Sonne, in *Liberal Kentucky, 1780–1828,* published in 1939, described the late-eighteenth- to early-nineteenth-century battle between "infidel" liberals, or sons of the Enlightenment, and the proponents of orthodoxy, in this case overzealous conservative Presbyterians. Sonne examined the conflict played out in Kentucky during its earliest days as a state over the struggle for control of Transylvania University. There is no doubt that his heroes were the liberals Horace Holley, president of the university, and alumnus Joseph Buchanan.[1]

The designation *college* or *university* in the early nineteenth century did not mean that an institution with either title offered what would be considered today college-level coursework. Moreover, there were no state, regional, or national accreditation agencies. "Many Kentucky towns still have a College Street," Lowell Harrison explained, "named for some long-ago educational institution. Most of those schools were actually no more than academies [elementary and high schools at best], and most had short lives."[2]

Shortly after white settlement began, and a dozen years before Kentucky became a state, there was a positive attempt to bring public education to the frontier. Chartered in 1780 while Kentucky was a county in far western Virginia, Transylvania University's forerunner was the first such school founded west of the Allegheny Mountains. The Virginia General Assembly chartered a "public school or Seminary of Learning" and granted it eight thousand acres of "escheated" land, confiscated from three loyalists who had large Kentucky land grants. Three years later Caleb Wallace, representing Woodford County in the Virginia legislature, introduced legislation to recharter the school and amend the original charter by increasing to twenty-five the number of trustees of a self-perpetuating board and adding twelve thousand acres to the endowment.[3]

As John D. Wright Jr. pointed out in *Transylvania: Tutor to the West*, it is surprising that the school was intended to be "public" from the beginning and that it functioned at all on the frontier during the early settlement of Kentucky. Among the early trustees was Wallace, a Presbyterian minister now practicing law; Revolutionary War veteran and future governor Isaac Shelby; and Christopher Greenup, one of the commonwealth's first representatives to Congress, who was elected governor in 1804. Even the infamous General James Wilkinson served on the board for two years, while secretively hatching plans to separate Kentucky and the new west from the United States.[4]

Transylvania's trustees faced a daunting task. The quasi-public school never received the one-sixth of surveyors fees collected within the county of Kentucky for its maintenance, as promised by the Virginia General Assembly. The trustees took a leap of faith and opened a school anyway. Because there was no national currency at the time, tuition was set in Spanish coin, four pistoles a year. The first classes at the academy level of Transylvania Seminary were held in the home of Rev. David Rice, one of the founders of Presbyterianism in Kentucky, near Danville in 1785. With all its failings, "it was a beginning," said Wright in his magisterial history of the school. Rev. James Mitchell, another Presbyterian minister, received an annual salary of thirty pounds as the school's first teacher. During these early days of Transylvania, as it searched for its identity, such observers as the pseudonymous "Catholicus" maintained that orthodoxy was the best protection against Jefferson's idea of religious neutrality. Probably a trustee of the school, Catholicus feared "that the students may embrace that which is erroneous." When Mitchell returned to a ministry in Virginia, the school languished for a few months before moving to Lexington in 1789.[5]

Before Louisville became a larger city owing to its position on the Ohio River and the expansion of trade by development of the steamboat, Lexington shone as the business and the cultural center of the state. Presbyterians intended to keep control of the school and its curriculum, but newspaper columns in John Bradford's *Kentucky Gazette* criticized their leadership, arguing for "the newly established American principle of the separation of church and state." Transylvania Seminary, a grammar school at the time, began operations in Lexington with Rev. James Moore, an Episcopalian rector, as schoolmaster in 1791. Classes met in his home.[6]

In 1793 a group of Lexingtonians purchased a lot in what is now Gratz Park and built a brick structure. They offered both to Transylvania if the school would remain in Lexington. Meanwhile, newer trustees such as editor Bradford expressed discontent with "the strongly-orthodox Presbyterian influence on the Board."[7]

In a February 1794 board meeting, some liberal members of the board of trustees pushed through the election of Harry Toulmin, a personal friend of Thomas Jefferson, as the new president of Transylvania. Toulmin, the son of a dissenting English minister, was himself a Unitarian minister with "republican sentiments." In protest, Moore and most of the Presbyterian trustees resigned and formed Kentucky Academy at Pisgah Presbyterian Church, eight miles from Lexington. Americans as well known as President George Washington and the soon-to-be infamous Aaron Burr pledged funds for the new school. The "peripatetic James Moore" became director of the new academy.[8]

"The whole affair, in retrospect," asserted John Wright, had "all the appearances of an academic charade," a ploy by the Presbyterian power structure to regain control over Transylvania. Being the center of the dispute, Toulmin reluctantly resigned in 1796. However, being a Jeffersonian, he was soon named secretary of state by Governor James Garrard (1796–1804), and in 1804 President Thomas Jefferson appointed him to a federal judgeship. Meanwhile, the two schools began talking about unification; the first meeting was at Lexington's McGowan's Tavern on September 14, 1796. By the fall of 1798, details had been worked out. The Kentucky legislature approved the reconstituted Transylvania, and the "new institution became legally alive on January 1, 1799."[9]

Now using the title of Transylvania University for the first time, the trustees at their first united meeting appointed two professors of medicine and a professor of law and politics. Transylvania made little headway in either medical or legal education until 1818. Since there was no adequate secondary education locally, Transylvania established a preparatory department, where students received a heavy dose of Greek, Latin, English, and arithmetic in preparation for university studies. Students in the liberal arts department received a typical early-nineteenth-century college education, with a heavy emphasis on the classics. A two-year college in the beginning, Transylvania stressed mathematics and English composition in the first year and natural philosophy (science), astronomy, moral philosophy, history, rhetoric, and belles lettres in the second year. Later, when four-year studies became common, Transylvania and other early Kentucky colleges followed a basic eastern-college curriculum with sometimes considerable variations, which included instruction in Latin, Greek, Hebrew, rhetoric, and logic in the first year; Greek, Hebrew, logic, and natural philosophy in the second year; natural philosophy, metaphysics (philosophy of being), and ethics in the third year; and mathematics and a review of Greek, Latin, logic, and natural philosophy in the fourth year.[10]

If "the ultimate product of an American college education in this era was the Christian gentleman," as asserted by Wright, what better person would there be to oversee the consolidated Transylvania than James Moore. Wright found that Moore, "as a man of traditional views and moderate manners, relatively uncontroversial," was "generally acceptable to both sides of the previously-opposing camps." Described as "tall, gaunt, and somewhat neglectful of dress," Moore urged his students to be diligent in their studies, disciplined, and mannerly. "Be kind, affectionate, and forgiving towards one another," he told his charges.[11]

Transylvania grew slowly as conditions on the frontier eased in the first decade of the nineteenth century. Medical and law students "most likely" met in the homes of their professors. In 1799 the school had collected enough library books to place them in a building separate from the seminary building. A new professor and another building gave the campus north of Main Street a growing sense of what a western university should be. Adding a boarding house and publicizing the school more widely established its viability. In April 1802, Robert Barr received the first A.B. degree conferred by the school.[12]

When the school did not seem to be progressing rapidly enough, thirty-nine leading citizens in Lexington signed a petition in 1802, urging the trustees to bring the president of William and Mary to Transylvania, even offering to guarantee the unheard-of annual salary of $1,000. Although Moore appeared willing to resign and the president of the Virginia school was also agreeable, nothing came of the effort. Then in the fall of 1804 Moore resigned. The Presbyterian-dominated board of trustees appointed Rev. James Blythe, "a staunch Presbyterian," as acting president. Blythe continued in that role, after the trustees apparently, in the short run, gave up the idea of finding another perhaps more qualified person.[13]

Blythe's tenure at Transylvania coincided with further religious turmoil in Kentucky. The Great Revival, a religious upheaval that attacked Calvinism with ideas of free grace, strained the bounds of predestination even among Presbyterians in the first decade of the nineteenth century. To combat this new heresy, Blythe brought in, as professor of moral philosophy, Robert Hamilton Bishop, who had published a defense of Calvinism against apostate Presbyterian Barton W. Stone. Stone, along with Alexander Campbell, led in the development of the Cane Ridge revivals in Bourbon County and in the founding of the Disciples of Christ and various other "Christian" churches.[14]

In addition to the roiling religious atmosphere, lack of funds and dwindling enrollment confounded the trustees and President Blythe. However, small investments continued to be made in books for the library and scientific apparatus. Selling off and renting some of the school's land brought in money to begin building a modest endowment. There were few graduates in the early days, but one in particular, Louisvillian Joseph Buchanan in 1809, is of special significance. Buchanan became one of the leading liberals in opposing the Presbyterian hierarchy and was, according to Sonne in *Liberal Kentucky*, "unquestionably Kentucky's greatest intellectual of the period." Keeping faculty proved to be no small problem. The appointment of Henry Clay as professor of law in 1805 began his long association with Transylvania. Although Clay taught for only two years, he served occasionally as a valuable trustee and "loyal friend and counselor to the institution until his death in 1852."[15]

The Transylvania family, along with the rest of Kentucky, divided over the War of 1812. While Congressman Henry Clay was one of the leading "War Hawks" pushing for expansion and war with Great Britain, President Blythe and other conservative Presbyterians opposed the war and the demise of the Federalist Party and abhorred the rise of Jeffersonianism. Some of the trustees had never been supporters of Blythe, but he served a total of fourteen years as president, ironically never having been given permanent status. A presidential search in 1812 fell through because of the war. Three years later the trustees barely tabled a resolution to not reappoint Blythe. Instead they elected another Presbyterian divine from New York, who promptly refused the post. When students became involved and passed a no-confidence vote against the beleaguered acting president, the board of trustees chastised them. Transylvania continued to drift rather aimlessly in this comedy of errors as enrollment declined.[16]

Then in 1816 issues came to a head and the trustees issued a call to Rev. Horace Holley, a leading Boston Unitarian minister, who had migrated spiritually and intellectually from his Congregationalist roots. However, when the Presbyterian conservatives on the board found out that Holley was too liberal for their tastes, they rescinded the offer. Two other gentlemen elected to the post declined the offer. Dr. Joseph Buchanan began writing articles for Kentucky newspapers under pseudonyms urging immediate change at Transylvania. Meanwhile, the General Assembly got involved: legislators Francis Johnson, John Crittenden, and Joseph C. Breckinridge asked for an investigation of the goings-on in Lexington. Their findings criticized Presbyterian sectarianism as well as some "unpatriotic" (anti-Jeffersonian-Republican) statements made in classes. Again, Holley's name came up. This time he knew full well the problems as well as the promises of the post in Lexington. When he was first nominated again, on October 25, 1817, six trustees voted for him while five turned in blank ballots. On a final consideration the next month, the trustees elected Holley as president, though only eleven of the seventeen men present voted for him.[17]

On February 3, 1818, the General Assembly, controlled by the Democratic-Republicans and with a pro-education governor, Gabriel Slaughter (1816–1820), overwhelmingly abolished the old board, voting 102-19 for an "Act Further to Regulate the Transylvania University." The legislature appointed a new board of thirteen men to serve for two years, one of whom, Henry Clay, probably had the most to do with enticing New Englander Holley to Kentucky. Though a religious liberal, the new president was not overly liberal politically, as a Federalist and a good friend of John Adams. After Holley made an initial visit to Lexington and Frankfort and was shown around by Clay, the trustees raised his salary offer to $3,000, making him one of the highest-paid academicians in the nation.[18]

When Holley and his wife moved to Lexington in late November 1818, the *Lexington Reporter* hailed him as an "accomplished scholar and gentleman of talents." At his inauguration on December 19, held at the Episcopal Church, he gave a brilliant address covering most areas of education. Even a Presbyterian foe commented on the new president's "remarkable presence," distinguished by his "mellifluent voice, great vivacity, fascinating manners, splendid conversational powers, and brilliant oratory."[19]

"There was no doubt as to Holley's goal for Transylvania," according to Wright. "It was nothing else than to create in the West an outstanding state university." Since Transylvania's charter created, nominally, "a public non-denominational" university, he felt it was a perfect location for his ambitious plans. "And falling into the cliché of the time and place," Wright continued, "Holley suggested that Kentucky was the Attica and Lexington the Athens of the West."[20]

Holley set about his task energetically, particularly looking for faculty to match his vision by keeping up with his contacts in the East. In the Academic Department, where he served as professor of mental and moral philosophy, Holley lent an air of immediate erudition; Bishop moved over to teach natural philosophy. Bishop and former acting president James Blythe disparaged Holley's leadership at every turn. Enrollment improved immediately, soon challenging the leading Eastern schools. For example, in 1821 Transylvania had 282 students while Yale had 319, Harvard 286, and Princeton 150. Except for the vast improvements being made in the Medical Department, probably the most dynamic development came with the advent of Constantine S. Rafinesque on the Lexington campus.[21]

Perhaps more multitalented than anyone else who has ever taught in the commonwealth, the peripatetic Rafinesque, born in Constantinople, the son of a French father and a German mother, came to Transylvania by a circuitous route. An acquaintance of the great naturalist John James Audubon, Rafinesque was known for his genius in finding and classifying plants and animals. He made his way down the Ohio River identifying fish and on to Lexington in 1819, where a former employer, the influential merchant John D. Clifford, secured his professorship of botany and natural science at Transylvania.[22]

Rafinesque initially viewed Lexington and Kentucky quite favorably. "The surname of *Athens of the West* has already been given to this town," he said, "and methinks on very plausible and reasonable grounds. . . . Let Pittsburgh become the Manchester of the Western States, Cincinnati their Liverpool, and Louisville their Bristol; but Lexington must be their Edinburgh." Rafinesque, "the most extraordinary figure on the campus," was unkempt and absentminded but lectured brilliantly and inspired students. Though looked upon with some reverence for his hard work, he never received a salary greater than bare subsistence, being "pitilessly exploited by the school authorities," according to his latest biographer. However, he could charge for courses, and he attracted crowded lectures. One of his botany courses drew 108 paying students, so he was not indigent. General George W. Jones, who graduated in 1825, said his lectures were delivered "in a most entertaining manner to the great delight of his audiences."[23]

Rafinesque was not just a different "personality"; he exuded a Continental flair of "high culture" that appealed to student and citizen alike of "the Athens of the West." Never one-dimensional, he wrote poetry; works on geology, astronomy, and meteorology; and pieces about Native American archaeology, history, and language. When his patron Clifford died suddenly in 1820, Rafinesque lost "the major stabilizing force" in his life and his financial security. Increasingly he came into conflict with Holley and the rest of the faculty, "and for the remaining eighteen years of his life he met with repeated failings and disappointment—the underlying cause of bizarre and even psychotic behavior that manifested from time to time." Perhaps Holley felt upstaged by his eccentric and popular professor; Rafinesque's style rubbed him the wrong way, as did the professor's frequent absences from the school. When Rafinesque left Lexington for the last time in 1826, looking for greener pastures in the East, he had given up hope of making great strides in his scientific quests in the West. However, he was not done with Transylvania University. Rafinesque said he cursed Holley and Transylvania upon his exit from the city. In 1924 what may or may not be his remains were reinterred in a crypt in the basement of Old Morrison. Today, on a day close to Halloween, "Rafinesque Day" is set aside for student frivolity and the reenactment of folkloric fears, mostly tongue-in-cheek, that the "spirit" of this unique individual still prowls the campus.[24]

Initially, things went well with Holley's career at Transylvania, which could now legitimately be called a university. Even as early as 1799, Vice President Thomas Jefferson advised young Virginians to attend Transylvania because of the republican leanings of some professors. He was even more impressed by the early Holley years, declaring that if Virginians did not step up their efforts in founding what became the University of Virginia, "We must send our children for education to Kentucky or Cambridge [Harvard]."[25]

Holley's coming to Lexington in 1818 led to more sectarian conflict, not less, and to the founding of other colleges. Embittered Presbyterians, having lost control of Transylvania, looked for another outlet, "a new, purified Presbyterian institution." They petitioned the General Assembly and on January 21, 1819, received a charter for Centre College, named for its central location in the state in Danville. With a self-perpetuating board of thirteen that included Isaac Shelby as well as Ephraim McDowell, the pioneer physician who performed the world's first ovariotomy, Centre initially operated as a quasi-public school like Transylvania.[26]

When the state failed to provide adequate funds, Presbyterians took firm control of Centre College in 1824. However, the legislature specifically required "liberal, free, and enlightened principles, and [that] no student shall be excluded in consequence of his religious opinions" at the Danville school. The legislature further insisted that "no religious doctrine peculiar to any one sect of Christians shall be inculcated by any professor in said college," a dictum the Presbyterian school must have found unwanted and challenging at times. When Rev. John Clarke Young became president in 1830, Centre had a young leader who went on to lead the school for the next twenty-seven years. One prominent Presbyterian said Young was the "dominant, controlling, moulding spirit" of Centre College. During Young's tenure, enrollment grew from less than 30 to 225, the endowment added $100,000, and new faculty challenged students to ever-higher standards. By 1838, Centre students received, in addition to a classical course of study, a heavy dose of Bible instruction, including "daily chapel, church attendance and a Bible lesson on Sunday." At the same time, the Deinologian Literary Society debated current issues such as "Should women receive the same amount of education as men?" and "Are Republican Governments more favorable to the cause of learning than monarchial governments?"[27]

Religious schism among Protestants and the lingering effects of the Great Revival in Kentucky continued to reverberate. At the other end of the Presbyterian spectrum from the dominant beliefs in Danville, the evangelically minded in far western Kentucky came out of the Great Revival with their own, quite different worldview. Rejecting election, or predestination, these radicals tried to remain within the Kentucky synod but were denied permission to ordain and license ministers under the synod's authority. They split off and formed the Cumberland Presbyterian Church, or Cumberland Presbytery, a small denomination but one adamantly opposed to their high-church brethren in central Kentucky. As a result they established their own school of higher education, Cumberland College, in 1826 near Princeton in Caldwell County, primarily to educate ministers in a liberal arts atmosphere. Students spent part of the day working on the campus to pay for their upkeep. By 1842 the college had graduated fifty-two ministers, but it left Princeton because of financial difficulties and merged with what became Cumberland University in Lebanon, Tennessee.[28]

Methodists formed their first institution of higher learning west of the Appalachian Mountains in 1822, when they received a charter for Augusta College, built on the six-thousand-acre endowment of Bracken Academy in Augusta, Kentucky. Ohio and Kentucky Methodist conferences jointly supported the school. Classes opened there in 1825 after a three-story building was constructed. Rev. Martin Ruter led Augusta during its best days. In the 1830s enrollment neared two hundred students "from both free and slave states." Joseph S. Tomlinson, the uncle of Stephen Collins Foster, taught there and was visited by his famous nephew on at least one occasion. Henry Bascom, later to become president of Transylvania, briefly taught there. Some of Augusta College's most prominent alumni included John G. Fee, cofounder of Berea College, and Randolph S. Foster, future president of Northwestern University. The slavery issue split Methodists, and when the Ohio conference pulled out, Augusta College died in 1849.[29]

Baptists also wanted to protect their denomination from the inroads of liberalism at Transylvania, the same threat that Presbyterians feared, by founding a school of higher learning. Issachar Pawling, a prominent Mercer County farmer and layman, offered his estate as an investment to train Baptist ministers. Meanwhile, Silas Noel, a Frankfort lawyer and minister, led in the chartering of the Kentucky Baptist Education Society (KBES). The society first considered forming a college as part of Transylvania just as Holley was about to leave, but it decided instead to take advantage of an earlier Baptist institutional development. Absorbing the assets of Rittenhouse Academy in 1829, the KBES founded Georgetown College, which became the first Baptist college west of the Allegheny Mountains. Philadelphia Baptist educator William Staughton, elected as Georgetown's first president, died en route to the campus, but his place was soon taken by Rev. Benjamin Farnsworth.[30]

Episcopalians also joined the race to form colleges. Growing out of Shelbyville Academy, one of the earliest formed by legislation, Shelby College was chartered in 1836. In 1841, the Protestant Episcopal Church of Kentucky assumed leadership of the school, on what is still called College Street in Shelbyville. Replete with a preparatory department (most colleges of the day had one, because of inadequate public education), the school offered liberal arts courses as well as instruction in the military arts leading to a degree. Never very large, it closed after the Civil War, owing to a dispute over using a lottery for its upkeep.[31]

Kentucky's Catholics, a distinct minority in the heavily Protestant state, also went about organizing their own schools of higher learning. Though on the periphery of the Great Revival and the schisms racking Protestantism, Catholics had much in common with other religionists, living in an expanding stressful society. They were under the leadership of Bishop Benedict Joseph Flaget of Bardstown, the first inland diocese in the United States. Education at all levels was always of primary concern to Kentucky Catholics in the early nineteenth century. With the founding of St. Joseph's College in Bardstown in 1819 and St. Mary's College in Marion County in 1821, Catholics offered their youth and others as well an opportunity for structured higher education. After attending St. Joseph's in Bardstown, Theodore O'Hara, author of the poem "The Bivouac of the Dead," taught there briefly before moving on to read law in Frankfort. Another famous Kentuckian, Cassius M. Clay, attended St. Joseph's before attending Transylvania. St. Mary's College was led by Father William Byrne for a time, and then Jesuits took over leadership of that institution until 1846, when they moved on to found what later became Fordham University in New York City. While St. Joseph's closed because of wartime conditions in 1862, St. Mary's survived as a seminary until 1975.[32]

In antebellum Kentucky, as elsewhere, as many as one-third of the students in Catholic schools might be Protestants. The Catholic hierarchy was a bit leery of such numbers, wanting to keep control over what they viewed as their own realm in a Protestant-dominated culture. While it might be relatively easy to obtain a charter from the Protestant-dominated state legislature to found a Catholic school, there was friction occasionally. For example, "in 1850, eighteen Protestant students withdrew from St. Joseph's, Bardstown, after unsuccessfully protesting the requirement that they attend religious services," according to renowned Catholic historian Philip Gleason. Most Catholic "colleges," like most other colleges, accepted young students and operated as elementary and secondary schools as well as offering college-level courses, taking students where they found them. Moreover, most Catholic colleges also served as seminaries, training priests for the work in the West.[33]

The highlight of early higher education in Kentucky was Holley's leadership at Transylvania, which produced great changes in the Lexington school. The rejuvenation of the medical education meant much for the state and region. With Dr. Benjamin Dudley, "the very mainstay of the Medical Department for many years," remaining, the unit improved immeasurably when Dr. Charles Caldwell was lured away from the University of Pennsylvania in 1819. Dr. Samuel Brown, noted for experimentation with smallpox vaccines, taught at the school during the Holley administration. Enrollment in the department grew from only 37 when Holley arrived to 138 two years later, and the number continued to increase. In 1821 Caldwell made a successful trip to Europe, purchasing medical books and apparatus. Transylvania also began to professionalize medicine by requiring not only two years of classroom work but a thesis and successful examinations before a candidate received a degree. As in other medical schools of the day, students were responsible for acquiring their own human "subjects" for dissection, and sometimes this was done by illegal means from fresh graves. One time, said a graduate, "We were pursued when making our way to our horses hitched outside an orchard fence, and one ball of several fired lodged in the subject, on my back."[34]

The Law Department at Transylvania also flourished during the Holley years. When William T. Barry's duties as lieutenant governor kept him from teaching, Holley, who had considered becoming a lawyer before settling on the ministry, taught for him. Jesse Bledsoe, a Virginian by birth like Barry, also taught law courses. While Barry remained in the profession, becoming postmaster general under President Andrew Jackson, Bledsoe eventually became a Disciples of Christ minister. In the Holley years, the law course increased to more than forty students a year.[35]

From the time Holley arrived in Lexington, his enemies kept up an unrelenting assault. One late-nineteenth-century chronicler of higher education in Kentucky euphemistically stated it best: he said this began as soon as Holley's religious opinions "began to be noised about." Taking notes when he delivered sermons in college chapel services or gave public addresses, his foes attacked his theology. Holley usually preached about morality, his primary concern, and, being a son of the Age of Reason, he had to invent a way to interpret the miracles of the Bible. While he was "a firm believer in the immortality of the soul," it was as a skeptic about the Trinity and the divinity of Christ that he received the greatest criticism. When he stopped preaching, critics said he had literally run out of things to say, which they disagreed with anyway. Moreover, conservatives attacked Holley's obvious pleasure in dancing and attending horse racing. And, according to Wright, "they condemned the worldly social gatherings in his home where improper conversation was heard (spies apparently had infiltrated these parties), undraped female statuary displayed and carefree songs sung."[36]

There appeared to be a genuine attempt by state government to contribute to the success of Transylvania during the early Holley years. The General Assembly made several appropriations, including $5,000 at one time to pay for medical books and apparatus. Some of the profits of two chartered state banks went to Transylvania for a short time. The legislature also approved a lottery, not to exceed $25,000, for the benefit of the Medical Department. One year, 2 percent of auctioneers' sales in Fayette County went to purchase medical books. The city of Lexington, as well as private citizens of the community, also made donations from time to time. Unfortunately, there was only enough money for immediate investments and to pay current bills and never sufficient funds to add substantially to the endowment. In Governor John Adair (1820–1824), Transylvania had a friend. In 1822 he claimed in his annual message to the legislature: "The State University continues to flourish. Its growth is unrivaled; and the benefits it dispenses are diffused beyond the limits of our own state." This was indeed an excellent summary of the state of Transylvania after three years of Holley's leadership.[37]

Unfortunately, Holley and Transylvania got caught up in that maelstrom known as Kentucky politics. The "monetary honeymoon" and cooperation of the governor and the state legislature "ended with the rise of the Relief controversy, the Old and New Court struggle, and the ascension of Joseph Desha to the governor's office." Holley and his school became a convenient whipping boy for Governor Desha (1824–1828), who attacked the school and its president as elitist. When the attacks reached a climax, state funds were cut off.[38]

Holley had his supporters. All did not seem lost, even as late as 1826. Henry Clay, for example, persuaded Colonel James Morrison to leave much of his estate to the school, money that funded a new building, known today as Old Morrison. Lexington's elite appeared to support the beleaguered president, as did most of Transylvania's students, faculty, and the board of trustees. Although Holley was occasionally attacked as being a "Yankee," he was actually quite soft on the slavery issue, following the ideas of his patron Henry Clay. Dr. Charles Caldwell believed that Holley might have weathered the storm if he had been a bit less outgoing, but it was not in the New Englander's nature to be so. Others thought he did not defend himself enough, "hoping always to kill false accusations with silence."[39]

What are we to make of Transylvania under Holley's guidance? Wright's opinion is evident as he concludes the Holley episode in a chapter entitled

"The Making of a Martyr." In *The Frontier Mind*, Arthur K. Moore characterizes the departure of Holley as "the Rejection of Athens." Another writer found that "Dr. Holley had committed the unpardonable sin. He had been too successful." Lowell Harrison declared that "Holley's resignation in 1827 ended the university's most glorious period of achievement." Sonne, of course, also finds that Holley fought the good fight for liberalism. In the end, however, according to Sonne, "the ideal of a great central state university, open to all religious denominations, and conducted on liberal principles, had been effectively quashed." Thomas D. Clark asserted that Holley's tenure "formed the golden years of promise of real intellectual maturity for both Lexington and the Ohio Valley." All of these authors concluded that Kentucky had lost a once-in-a-lifetime opportunity to lead not only the West but also the nation in development of public higher education. A combination of religious conservatism and parochialism, political timidity, self-serving politicians, and class conflict extinguished another noble experiment in Kentucky education. "It would indeed be a bold man who would expose his reputation and talents to an onslaught such as suffered by Holley," said one historian of higher education in the Ohio valley, C. W. Hackensmith. "It would be a rash board of trustees which would invite such opposition to their institution." The battle for control of Transylvania had national significance. George M. Marsden in *The Soul of the American University*, a magisterial study of the evolution of higher education from Protestant control to that of "Established Nonbelief," positions the story of Holley squarely in the middle of the early battle, one in which Protestantism and secularism contended for domination of American higher education.[40]

Holley ably defended himself to the last against his conservative foes. In his final report to the Board of Regents, the president compared his tenure with the entire previous history of the school. Under his watch 644 degrees had been awarded, compared with 22 in the previous nineteen years. "'We are satisfied with the contrast,' said Holley. 'Are they?'" Holley left Lexington on March 27, 1827. Unfortunately, he never again led a university like Transylvania. After departing New Orleans to escape the summer heat, he died of yellow fever on July 31, 1827, while at sea en route to New York.[41]

Yet another early Kentucky school resulted in schism growing out of the Great Revival, this time between Georgetown College and three professors who were members of the Disciples of Christ faith. They resigned in 1836 and, under the leadership of Thornton F. Johnson, a West Point graduate, founded Bacon College, receiving a state charter in 1837. Named in honor of Sir Francis Bacon, the school soon moved from Georgetown to Harrodsburg, where Mercer County residents had pledged $50,000, of which only

$18,000 materialized. Although Bacon enrolled as many as 180 students in 1847, the school constantly faced financial restraints.[42]

With Louisville becoming the largest city in Kentucky, pressure built to found an institution of higher learning to supply its needs. Its location on the Ohio River, now more navigable because of the advent of the steamboat and construction of the Louisville and Portland Canal, could be a bigger draw to students and faculty. As early as 1833, the city created the Louisville Medical Institute, although it did not function. Meanwhile, the Transylvania Medical Department flourished while its Academic Department declined disastrously. But Dr. Caldwell became disenchanted with Lexington and new Transylvania president Thomas Coit. Even cadavers seemed in short supply in the smaller city of Lexington. Medical professors Dudley and Caldwell fell out over a discussion of possibly moving to Louisville, where the latter thought medical education would have advantages over the situation in Lexington. An "emotional outburst which matched the virulent sectarian controversies of the previous decade" apparently tore the heart out of one of the finest medical schools in America. The Louisville City Council, led by James Guthrie, stepped in and reinvigorated the efforts to found the Louisville Medical Institute (LMI) as well as the Louisville Collegiate Institute, which was to be an undergraduate college, in 1837. Louisville and Lexington newspapers and governments joined in the fray and made charges and countercharges as they vied for this valuable resource.[43]

There is little doubt that Caldwell and Louisville officials were acting in concert. Because Louisville was a larger city with the possibility of drawing more students, as Transylvania's fortunes declined, the offer became too good to resist. The city council pledged money and land, and Caldwell gave a public address in Louisville advocating immediately founding a medical school there. Louisville Medical Institute became a reality when Dr. Caldwell pulled out of Transylvania in 1837, after nearly two decades there, with three of his colleagues. With $50,000 in pledges in hand, LMI opened in the fall of 1837 with one hundred students. The trustees chose Judge John Rowan, who had survived an 1801 duel in which he killed a drinking companion, as the first president of LMI. After first holding classes in the city workhouse, the school found a permanent home at Eighth and Chestnut, thus adding to LMI's reputation as one of the best medical schools in America. "The Louisville Medical Institute was a ringing success," reported the historians of the University of Louisville. "Between 1838 and 1861, the school produced nearly 1,500 medical doctors." In 1846 a new charter from the General Assembly combined Louisville Medical Institute and Louisville Collegiate Institute into the University of Louisville, which also added a law school. However, LCI, the academic department of the school, "remained dormant until the twentieth century." As at Transylvania, students at LMI attended two years of classes before having to pass extensive examinations for licensure.[44]

Because of all the forming of colleges and universities, it was said that by 1847 Kentucky "had more colleges than any other state in the Union." It should be recalled, though, that the appellation *college* was used loosely at the time. John R. Thelin in *A History of American Higher Education* described this era as part of the "college-building boom" from 1820 to 1860, when "higher education would become America's 'cottage industry.'" Some have argued that the decision in the Dartmouth College Case made it difficult for public universities to organize before the Civil War. Transylvania, of course, vacillated between public and private in this period. Nearly all Kentucky colleges had a denominational affiliation. One was even ecumenically Protestant. Chartered in 1844, Masonic University at LaGrange in Oldham County struggled for a few decades under the control the Grand Lodge of Kentucky. Primarily intended to be a haven for orphans and the sons of indigent Masons, the school never was well funded and, lacking the resources to become a true university, closed for good in 1881.[45]

Before the Civil War, several schools formed that were aimed at educating young women in a higher-education environment. In 1846 Methodists opened Russellville Academy, a coeducational institution in southern Kentucky. Renamed Russellville Collegiate Institute in 1860, the school suffered through the Civil War, being reorganized and rechartered in 1867 as Logan Female College. It never had a substantial student body or adequate financial backing, but it endured until disbanded by the Louisville Conference of Methodists in 1931. Western Kentucky Baptists secured a charter for a high school for young women in Hopkinsville in 1854. Two years after the school opened, it was rechartered as Bethel Female Institute; it offered a rudimentary college education. Beginning with a three-story Greek Revival building as its base, BFI struggled for more than one hundred years in one form or another, to educate first women and then both sexes, but always as a stoutly Baptist institution. Millersburg Female College, a female college formed in 1860, just before the outbreak of war, had begun as a coeducational school in 1856. It struggled on as a junior college until finally succumbing to the rigors of increasing competition for students in the early twentieth century.[46]

The sectarianism that encouraged the development of higher education in Kentucky also led to the founding of several schools of theology. The Episcopalians were first, receiving a charter for the Theological Seminary of the Protestant Episcopal Church in Kentucky in Lexington from the General Assembly on February 24, 1834. Benjamin Bosworth Smith, the first bishop of the Kentucky diocese as well as superintendent of public instruction from 1840 to 1842, initially led the seminary. In 1836 he became embroiled in a controversy, the intensity of which was hinted at by a report that said, "It is not necessary to indicate the charges made against the bishop, or the progress of the angry discussion behind closed doors." Smith was acquitted and soon moved the school to Shelbyville as part of the Episcopalian Shelby College, where it remained until that college closed in 1870. A student could earn seventy-five cents a day working in the campus garden, toward the annual expenses of seventy-five dollars. One professor continued teaching classes until 1895. In 1951 Lexington bishop William R. Moody revived the school after discovering that the charter had never been revoked.[47]

Not long after the Episcopalians formed their seminary, Baptists founded the Western Baptist Education Society in Cincinnati in 1834. Although the Kentucky legislature chartered the Western Baptist Theological Institute six years later, the school did not open until 1845 in Covington. Enrollment increased briefly to more than fifty students, but the slavery issue soon divided Northern and Southern Baptists. President Robert Everett Pattison and two of the school's three other professors were forced to resign. Legal battles between antislavery and proslavery Baptists led to a Solomon-like decision by the arbitrator, U.S. Supreme Court justice John McLean, who suggested dividing the property between the two sides. The Kentuckians moved their assets to Georgetown College, where WBTI "nominally existed until 1879."[48]

Not to be outdone, Presbyterians organized Danville Theological Seminary in October 1853, with twenty-three students, four professors, and recent superintendent of public instruction Rev. Robert J. Breckinridge as its first president. A result of the Old School–New School split among Presbyterians, DTS became a "bastion of Old School thought." Enrollment increased to as many as fifty students until the Civil War nearly brought education to a standstill. Presbyterians, like all denominationalists in Kentucky, split over the issue of slavery and the impending crisis leading to the Civil War.[49]

In addition to education for the professions and education to protect the souls of Kentuckians, there was also instruction in the military arts, mostly modeled after West Point and Virginia Military Academy and their training in engineering and applied science. Kentucky Military Institute and Western Military Institute began operation in the mid-1840s, during the era encompassing the Mexican War and a growing militancy in America. Both operated prep schools, with better preparation than the usual high school instruction but somewhat below that of a classical college education of the age.[50]

Beginning in 1845, Robert Thomas Pitcairn Allen, a graduate of West Point, founded Kentucky Military Institute six miles from Frankfort on the Lawrenceburg Road, maintaining that "an advantage possessed by this Institute, of the great importance, is the distance of its location from the tempting and corrupting influences of the city." Beginning students studied Virgil, Latin, English grammar, and American history in a school somewhat below college level. According to historian Nicky Hughes, "graduating seniors had completed a semester each in architecture, political economy, physiology, international and constitutional law, history and statistics of the United States, and the lives of the founding fathers." KMI students went off to fight for both North and South during the Civil War, a war that severely weakened the school.[51]

In 1847 Thornton F. Johnson, who had earlier left Georgetown College to organize Bacon College, founded Western Military Institute in Georgetown, beginning with students at age thirteen. The curriculum included engineering, mathematics, and military science and led to A.B. and M.A. degrees. Searching for a home, the school moved from Georgetown to Blue Lick Springs in Nicholas County, thence to Drennon Springs in Henry County, and finally to Nashville, Tennessee. James G. Blaine, a future Maine Republican senator narrowly defeated by Grover Cleveland in the 1884 presidential election, taught Greek, Latin, and algebra from 1848 to 1851. WMI officials noted some difficulty with their students, indicating that "rowdiness" and malingering led the offenses. At the Blue Lick Springs site, a fight broke out between the owners of a building used by the school and students and faculty when WMI prepared to move, and Blaine even participated in the fisticuffs. After a terrible outbreak of cholera at Drennon Springs in 1854, WMI moved to Nashville, eventually becoming part of the University of Nashville. On January 17, 1861, its students received their last orders, and "faculty and students marched away to defend the Southland they loved," according to one account.[52]

Who were the young men who attended KMI and WMI? The two schools served a vital function in the late antebellum South, preparing young men from an often poor economic background for "the developing southern middle class." A study by Jennifer R. Green found that when war broke out in 1861, "more than 11,000" young men who had attended either state or private military schools in the South not only were prepared to fight for the Confederacy but "also participated in the modernization of the Old South." She studied nearly one-tenth of that number, including some Kentuckians, through their biographies and correspondence. These men entered the "white-collar" middle class before the war and remained there as leaders in the postbellum South. Most of them moved into nonagricultural professional occupations, including medicine, law, and education. Americus Cartwright, while a student at KMI in 1858, pursued the nonclassical course, while considering entering the law profession. He clearly understood what was at stake. "The next two years will tell a great deal for me," he said in a letter. "If I don't seize and improve each moment which presents itself to me for improvements I will regret as long as I live and therefore I will make a good use of my time and try to make a man of myself." Many of the men of Cartwright's generation made lifelong friends and contacts in their professional life outside the planter aristocracy. Large state military schools like Virginia Military Institute in the South even developed well-defined alumni networks. Before the war, Green contended, these men proved that not all elites aspired to become planters. For example, another Kentuckian, Hervey McDowell, attended WMI before graduating from KMI, for his early education, and then became a physician.[53]

The history of Kentucky's liberal arts colleges entered a new phase after Horace Holley left the state in 1827. Turmoil and schism diminished only slightly in the era that historians call the Middle Period, as slavery became a divisive issue. Moreover, new courses of study and the role of the liberal arts became controversial.

Post-Holley Transylvania idled along as it continued to search for its role. Primarily because of the influence of Henry Clay, Alva Woods, acting president of Brown University and a New Englander like Holley, went to the Lexington school in 1828. The Medical Department drove enrollments at Transylvania as long as Caldwell taught there. However, it soldiered on even after he left, continuing to graduate physicians for Kentucky and the slave-holding areas to the south and the west. Woods, a Baptist, tried to resurrect the Academic Department by making education less elitist; he instituted a course of study that placed less emphasis on classical languages in the new Department of English Literature. Things improved in the short run as even the Law Department revived. With its completion in 1833, the neoclassical Morrison Hall, designed by renowned architect Gideon Shryock, replaced the main college building, which had burned down in 1829. Woods and the trustees became disenchanted with each other, and he moved on to become president of the new University of Alabama in 1831.[54]

This time the Transylvania trustees elected Benjamin O. Peers, a professor of moral philosophy who was already serving as acting president. A devotee of Pestalozzian education who had formed the Eclectic Institute for teaching younger children, Peers was the most innovative educational thinker in Lexington. Following the lead of President Francis Wayland of Brown University, Peers supported dropping the old "cut-and-dried recitation method in classes." Recitation included studying a long passage in a book and being able to demonstrate knowledge before the class. Natural science should play a bigger role in the newer higher education, Peers averred. But he soon came a cropper. When Peers complained about trustees' appointing new faculty without his input, it was not long before he resigned. Meanwhile, the law and medical departments continued to expand; they operated as separate entities from the university in the thirties and forties. Even after the split in the Medical Department in 1837, it did not decline immediately. Moreover, the addition of Judge George Robertson to the Law Department added to its prestige and strength.[55]

Still, something was missing at Transylvania. It might have been that Lexington was no longer Kentucky's premier business hub, or that times were changing. The trustees finally gave up on the idea of nondenomination-alism and in September 1841 offered control of Transylvania University to the Methodist Episcopal Church of Kentucky, the obvious reason being the decline of the Academic Department, now called Morrison College, to only eight paying students. Acting President Rev. Robert Davidson opposed the move, but Kentucky Methodists generally approved. The slavery issue had already doomed joint Kentucky and Ohio Methodist cooperation at Augusta College. Kentucky Methodists pulled out in 1842 as Henry B. Bascom, a professor at Augusta, accepted the presidency of Transylvania. Known for his "great oratorical and administrative ability," Bascom led the revival of the school, particularly Morrison College. Denominational affiliation initially seemed to work for Transylvania, as did Bascom's leadership. Methodist parents sent their children to the school, just as Baptists did for George-town, Presbyterians for Centre, and Catholics for their colleges. Enrollment increased at Transylvania, and new faculty joined the school in the early Bascom years.[56]

After three Disciples of Christ members, led by Thornton F. Johnson, rebelled in 1836 and founded Bacon College, Georgetown College kept true to its Baptist roots. However difficult it may be to believe today, in the early to middle nineteenth century, Baptists and Disciples of Christ adherents fought tooth and nail over such issues as baptism, Communion, and the role of the ministry. Moreover, Particular, Regular, and independent Bap-tists often warred with each other. When Johnson opened Bacon College nearby with six professors and one hundred students, Georgetown president B. F. Farnsworth was left with only one teacher besides himself and twenty students. Georgetown barely existed when Rockwood Giddings became the school's fourth president in 1838. As Bacon College moved to Harrodsburg, Georgetown College began to recover quickly; Giddings canvassed the state for Baptist money while preaching unity. Exactly one year after accepting the presidency, Giddings collapsed from overwork and died within a few days. The Campbellite threat of the Disciples of Christ to Georgetown subsided through Giddings's efforts to solidify Baptist support.[57]

During the brief administration of President Howard Malcolm of Philadelphia, Georgetown organized literary societies and developed a classical-style curriculum, with some room for Francis Wayland's modern idea of electives. With the opening of Pawling Hall, a men's dormitory for ministerial students, in 1845, President Malcolm reported the beginning of a new day for the college. Under his direction the college grew in students and faculty. Unfortunately, his antislavery views clashed with what was happening in the South. In 1845 Baptists in the slave states split away from their Northern brethren, organizing the Southern Baptist Convention. Malcolm not only voted for an emancipationist candidate in the election leading to the constitutional convention of 1849, he also distributed antislavery pamphlets on campus. With his life threatened anonymously and gaining the disdain of the proslavery board of trustees, Malcolm resigned. He later became president of Bucknell University.[58]

Throughout the antebellum period, the primary goal of higher education continued to be the education of a "Christian gentleman" and, in the case of women's colleges, educating a proper Victorian Christian helpmeet. The administrators of Kentucky colleges believed in a strong dose of in loco parentis for their charges, following the examples of such schools as Harvard and William and Mary. A classical education, with all its virtues of good thoughts and deeds, was aimed at creating a scholarly gentleman or lady. During his reign, Holley taught classes in gentlemanly manners as well as in the proper reading of novels. As free-thinking as he was, the Transylvania president still gave students a strong dose of religion along with his belief in the bounties of reason. Literary societies served a vital role in Kentucky colleges. For example, the Chamberlain Philosophical and Literary Society at Centre College not only held cerebral events but also sponsored an annual celebration of Washington's birthday and the Commencement Ball. At Georgetown College, the Tau Theta Kappa and Ciceronian literary societies competed against each other for students. They held secret meetings and open competitions where they debated the issues of the day and developed some of the trappings of social fraternities. Jefferson Davis joined the Union-Philosophical Society at Transylvania, participating in debates as well as social events. Discipline was the key. College administrators, believing idle hands were the devil's workshop, tried to fill students' days with endless routine. At early Transylvania, for example, student study hours were to begin at sunrise and continue throughout the day, with interruptions only for attending classes and mealtimes. Centre College prohibited attendance at "theatre, ball, dancing-party, or horse-race, during term-time" and at all times "profane swearing, intemperance, obscenity, licentiousness, impiety, playing at cards or at any game of wager." Of course, students always found diversions, sometimes not altogether wholesome ones.[59]

The foregoing description of student behavior and college administrations' proscriptions in the early days of college education in Kentucky places the state's colleges within a southern context. In *Halls of Honor: College Men in the Old South*, Robert F. Pace details the social and intellectual history of an elite group, the sons of privilege who had some difficulty passing over into full manhood and participation in the antebellum world. More homogeneous than their counterparts in the free states, these young men adhered to a code of honor that was imposed on them. "Southern honor consisted of a set of rules that advanced the *appearance* of duty, pride, power, and self-esteem," Pace asserted, "and conformity to these rules was required if an individual were to be considered an honorable member of society." The author emphasized that "appearance superseded content." "This ethic . . . did not say that one actually had to *be* dutiful, respectful, or honest," the author maintained; "one simply had to *appear* to be a man of duty, respect, and honesty." For the most part, students felt an "us versus them" relationship with the faculty and administration, so that even cheating was seen as a way of saving face in a competitive world not of their making. A reviewer correctly chastised Pace for developing too simplistic a view of southern young men and overstating the case for honor as the engine that drove everything. Nevertheless, a tragicomic duel between two members of Transylvania's medical faculty illustrated the "southernness" of Kentucky's culture. In a confusing affair of honor in 1817, apparently over a postmortem examination, Professor Benjamin Dudley wounded Professor William Richardson in the groin, severing an artery. Then Dudley went to Richardson's side, after receiving his permission, and staunched the flow of blood, thus saving his opponent's life. Is it any wonder that Transylvania students such as Jeff Davis and Cassius Clay followed code duello throughout their lives?[60]

Early higher education in Kentucky was mostly for the well-to-do. Sons of planters, merchants, and professionals stood a better chance at getting into college and finishing their education that those from the lower classes. It boiled down to money and class. During Jefferson Davis's days at Transylvania, 1821–1824, tuition was $35 a year, plus $105 annually for room and board and fuel, light, and laundry. Slaves sometimes accompanied their masters to college. Transylvania student Cassius Marcellus Clay, who later became an antislavery advocate, brought his manservant. "This arrangement proved successful" until one evening when the slave accidentally ignited with a "tallow candle" the steps on which he was shining Clay's shoes. As today, students tried to keep up with or surpass their peers in appearance. Future Iowa senator George W. Jones, a lifelong friend of Jefferson Davis, recalled: "I was fastidious in the manner of dress—'full dress' consisting of canton crepe trousers, buff-colored buckskin boots, dark blue or black swallow tail coat with brass buttons which were sometimes flat and sometimes bullet-shaped, white waist-coat, shirt ruffled at the bosom and sleeves, very stiff and high-standing collars, and the white or black broad silk cloth; I used to beg my laundress, Tiny, to starch my collars so stiff that they would draw blood from my ears." A few years later at Augusta College, Virginian Robert Whitehead reported that the president of the school tried to mute class-based dress, favoring instead "a cheap uniform." He said the trustees passed rules "enacting that, No student shall wear broad cloths and prohibiting them also from wearing ruffle shirts; they are permitted to wear jeans, casinetts or satinetts for there are some right extravagant students which [President] Doct Ruter considers as a disrepute to the College."[61]

In the absence of the modern view of adolescence, antebellum administrators warned parents about sending too much money to young males, who might spend it on a city's too-evident diversions. Rule 33 at early Transylvania prohibited "possessing or exhibiting licentious pictures and lascivious and immoral books, and lying, swearing, playing unlawful games, and practicing other gross immoralities," the latter presumably covering any remaining sinful possibilities. In the 1840s discipline was meted out to Georgetown students for infractions that "ranged from card playing, carrying a deadly weapon, locking the chapel doors before prayers, stealing chickens, and prolonged absence from class—someone reported students attending the circus or the races in Lexington instead of going to school." Duels were prohibited, as were "any frolics of a noisy nature." One student's public drunkenness at the Baptist school drew probation rather than expulsion when he successfully argued that his physician had prescribed strong drink for an ailment. The appearance of Whig presidential candidate William Henry Harrison in 1840 must have elevated the students' and faculty's horizons, possibly offsetting a bear fight against dogs on the Georgetown campus that same year. President Malcolm admonished students to toe the line as Christian gentlemen but reported, "It has been my painful duty to request several parents to withdraw their sons, on account of idleness or extravagant expenditures."[62]

Students were not always happy and looked for diversions. One student at Augusta College felt isolated and lonely at this outpost of Methodism on the Ohio River. In 1830, Robert Whitehead wrote home: "This place here is but a small one right on the banks of the river. Nothing here to cheer one's spirits. It is one of the most lonesome places I ever was at." Pranks and mischief were normal among high-spirited youngsters. There were limits, however, as in the case of two "prominent" students who were expelled from Georgetown College in 1841 after they marched to the homes of two faculty members from New England shouting, "Down with the Yankees." Nevertheless, without organized sports or recreation, students still found time for ice skating, competitions involving running and walking, and other impromptu outings. At Transylvania students sometimes played a rudimentary form of football, more like soccer, a "rough and tumble sport" that resulted in "many bruised shins." Jefferson Davis "stood aloof from this game," according to the testimonies of his classmates. T. T. Crittenden, a future governor of Missouri and a member of the class of 1855 at Centre, later praised Danville for its excellent blending of town, gown, and student. "There is an indefinable something in the air, soil, and society of this place which makes it the natural location of colleges," he said.[63]

Like Davis, who went on to West Point for the completion of his higher education, other young Kentuckians from prominent families also left the state for educational opportunities. The Breckinridges of Kentucky were prime examples. Joseph Cabell Breckinridge, known by his middle name, attended Princeton in the first decade of the nineteenth century. Robert J. Breckinridge studied at Princeton and Union College in Schenectady, New York. John C. Breckinridge, who later became vice president of the nation in the James Buchanan administration and a Confederate general and secretary of war, attended Princeton to study law after graduating from Centre College.[64]

Even with all the problems of the 1840s, the Mexican War, and increasing turmoil over the slavery issue, new colleges still formed in Kentucky. Several colleges were chartered on the verge of war that survived into the next century in one form or another. McLean College in Hopkinsville began classes in the fall of 1849. Kentucky Catholics did not rest. In 1851 the Trappist monks of Gethsemani founded what became Gethsemani College officially by act of the legislature in 1868. Millersburg Female College became a reality in 1860 after the demise of Millersburg Male and Female Collegiate Institute. Methodists organized what became Warren College in 1859 in Bowling Green and also Logan Female Institute a year later in Russellville.[65]

There is even an example of a Kentucky school, Eminence College, that was tied directly to the fortunes of one man, Rev. W. S. Giltner, a leader of the Christian Church. In 1855 the citizens of the Henry County community formed a company to raise funds to build a high school. That school folded three years later and sold its assets to a company headed by Giltner, who finally got a state charter for a coeducational institution in 1861 that offered a basic college course. Like other Kentucky colleges, it muddled through the Civil War. Although brighter days appeared with the addition of a commercial department in 1880 and a normal school in 1885, the school floundered after Giltner retired in 1893, and it closed two years later.[66]

Because the General Assembly failed to sustain Transylvania as a normal training school in the late 1850s, Transylvania became little more than a high school with the closing of the Medical Department in 1859. Transylvania University's star fell, but its record as "Tutor to the West" is commendable, as judged by higher education historian John R. Thelin. Many early national leaders received training there, including "50 United States senators, 101 members of Congress, 36 governors, and 34 ambassadors." Alumni and former students included Jefferson Davis, Cassius Clay, and Stephen Austin. Unlike other southern slave states, such as Virginia, North Carolina, Alabama, and Mississippi, the Commonwealth of Kentucky had no viable state-funded university when the Civil War began.[67]

However, what Lowell Harrison has called the "remote origins" of what eventually became the University of Kentucky can be traced to the antebellum years, the nadir of Transylvania, and the rebirth of another school. After the closing of Bacon College in 1850, John Bryan Bowman, an 1842 alumnus, raised $180,000 to help create what he hoped would be a major university in the West. He petitioned the state in 1858 to create a new school, Kentucky University, to be "a first class university." The Christian Church of Kentucky was to have control of two-thirds of the seats on the governing board. KU operated in Harrodsburg until 1864, when a fire destroyed its only building. After considering offers from Louisville and Covington, the school moved to Lexington in 1865 and merged with Transylvania.[68]

The plethora of colleges in Kentucky, or at least the plethora of attempts to form them, illustrated the growing sense of the possible in America. As noted, some of the attempts appeared foolhardy, while others were driven by competition and downright animosity between religious denominations and sects. Schism seemed the theme of the history of higher education in Kentucky before the Civil War. Out of the sectarian strife at Transylvania came Centre and Georgetown. Out of controversy at Georgetown came Bacon, and the list goes on. In 1850 opponents of the medical department at the University of Louisville, which had withdrawn from Transylvania in 1837, seceded and established a second medical school in Louisville. According to Frank L. McVey, the labyrinthine antebellum history of Transylvania made it the progenitor, the "mother of these institutions," which included Kentucky University, Central University, the University of Louisville, and the University of Kentucky, as is explained in detail in later chapters. There had been much progress in higher education in Kentucky in the antebellum period, with more than fourteen hundred students reported in the 1860 census. However, there were nearly as many "rag collectors" (70) identified in the census as "professors" (75).[69]

In the late 1850s, the slavery issue overrode all others. Although Kentucky was a border slave state, proslavery advocates dominated the state, pressuring all institutions into conformity. The slavery issue resulted in President Bascom's departure from Transylvania after Northern Methodists withdrew their support, as well as the demise of Augusta College in the mid-1840s. Baptists also divided, with the result that President Malcolm fled Georgetown College and President Robert Everett Pattison resigned his position at Western Baptist Theological Institute. Moreover, when proslavery advocates forced John G. Fee to seek refuge, higher education at Berea College remained a dream until after the Civil War.[70]

After the presidential election of 1860, all attempts at compromise went for naught. Secession began to command the attention of Kentuckians, particularly with the firing on Fort Sumter. The most prominent families in the state, the Breckinridges, the Crittendens, the Clays, and others, divided, father against son, brother against brother. Students, faculty, and administrators at Kentucky's colleges chose sides as well.[71]

What happened at Georgetown College illustrated the turmoil and passions of the day. Not long after the election of Abraham Lincoln, the Tau Theta Kappa Literary Society for the tenth time in twenty years debated whether "a Southern Confederacy should be formed in the event of aggression upon our constitutional rights." After the crisis at Fort Sumter, tempers flared when pro-South students gathered on one side of the campus and unfurled a makeshift Confederate flag. When they tried to mount the stars and bars on Recitation Hall, pro-Union students protested. The faculty intervened and allowed a debate and then a student vote on the question of secession, which turned out in favor of the southern cause, and the "flag was hoisted on the northeast corner of the Hall." When Union sympathizer Stephen Gano, a Georgetown resident and president of the trustees, heard the furor, he rushed to the campus, climbed to the roof with his personal slave, and cut down the southern flag. Miraculously, only minor fisticuffs disrupted the peace. However, President Duncan Campbell, "on account of the increasing excitement among the students caused by the agitated condition of the country," closed down the college in late April. The majority of Georgetown College students separated and marched off to war, a pattern repeated at all Kentucky colleges.[72]

Part 2

THE CIVIL WAR TO 1900

Chapter 3

Elementary and Secondary Education

Fʀᴏᴍ 1860 ᴀɴᴅ ᴛʜᴇ election to the presidency of native son Abraham Lincoln, to 1900 and the turmoil surrounding the assassination of William Goebel, Kentuckians faced increasing challenges. The Commonwealth of Kentucky, based on its population, its economy, and its location, declined from being one of the major states in the Union to being one of the poorest, bypassed by many of the important changes of the latter nineteenth century. White and black Kentuckians struggled with the social, political, and economic issues that accompanied the end of slavery. Many people sought to improve education at all levels in the state. But questions had to be answered. Could Kentuckians agree on what needed to be done? Was there enough public will to build on the surprising educational advances made before the Civil War? Could the commonwealth's often self-seeking and sometimes corrupt political structure follow through on needed reform? Would Kentuckians be willing to pay for an adequate public school education for all the children in the state? Moreover, beneath a thin veneer of civility after the Civil War, a culture of violence seemed to vitiate signs of progress in the state. From the bushwhackers of postwar days, to lynching of blacks, to mountain feuds, Kentucky developed a reputation as one of the more violent places in America. The aptly named history of this era by Hambleton Tapp and James C. Klotter, *Kentucky: Decades of Discord, 1865–1900*, chronicles this period when Kentuckians somewhat blindly reacted to modernity and the changing forces of the late nineteenth century.

Raw statistics tell something about the condition of Kentucky education just before the Civil War. The 1860 census reported 4,507 public schools in the commonwealth with 4,646 teachers and a total income from all sources of nearly $500,000. Clearly, the typical public school on the eve of the Civil War was a one-room structure with one teacher. A perusal of other states at the time indicates much the same pattern. For example, among the original states, even Massachusetts had only 5,308 teachers for 4,134 public schools. The census for Kentucky also enumerated 223 private academies and "other schools," with 639 teachers and an income of nearly $450,000. Another indicator of educational opportunities was the presence of libraries and the numbers of volumes held. The Eighth Census for Kentucky listed 95 public libraries with a grand total of 106,175 volumes. With schools, Sunday schools, colleges, and churches added in, more than 148,000 books were available for the readers in Kentucky. However, Massachusetts libraries held nearly 2 million volumes, Indiana had more than 467,000 books, and even Tennessee outnumbered Kentucky with 245,000 books.[1]

During the election of 1860 and afterward, the compromises of the past failed. Republican Abraham Lincoln's stated ambition to hem in the expansion of the peculiar institution into the new western territories did not set well with Kentucky voters, who rewarded him with less than 1 percent of the votes cast. Kentucky's slavocracy dominated, splitting the state's vote between John Bell, the candidate for the Constitutional Union Party, and John C. Breckinridge, a native son and a southern Democrat. After the election, new attempts at compromise, led by such stalwarts as Kentucky senator John J. Crittenden, also failed, as did the Peace Commission held in the nation's capital just before Lincoln's inauguration.[2]

With the firing on Fort Sumter, all institutions in Kentucky faced the terrible consequences of war. At first, Governor Beriah Magoffin (1859–1862) tried to steer a neutral course, believing, perhaps quixotically, that Kentucky and Kentuckians could remain above the fray. Could Kentucky be the mediating point where a bloody war was ended in its early months? Many Union-leaning Kentucky slave-owners, hoping they could keep their slaves, followed this path. Both Confederate and Union governments and armies understood the importance of borderland Kentucky, with its long Ohio River shoreline and plentiful population and farm products. In September 1861, Abraham Lincoln said it best: "I think to lose Kentucky is nearly the same as to lose the whole game. Kentucky gone, we cannot hold Missouri, nor, as I think, Maryland. These all against us, and the job on our hands is too large for us. We would as well consent to separation at once, including the surrender of the capital."[3]

The war in Kentucky ebbed and flowed, with Confederate forces first controlling a line across the southern part of the state and then Union forces dominating the state after the Battle of Perryville in the fall of 1862. Thereafter, only occasional raids by General John Hunt Morgan and his ilk threatened federal control. While Louisville generally prospered as a Union stronghold and shipping point, the rest of the state suffered from marauding bands of regular and irregular soldiers. Even though Kentucky never officially seceded from the United States, secessionists formed a government, which had little impact on the fate of the commonwealth. Kentuckians did not join Confederate general Braxton Bragg's "army of liberation" in sufficient numbers to offset his losses in his 1862 campaign in the state. The war in Kentucky then degenerated into guerrilla atrocities having little strategic impact on the war. James Beauchamp "Champ" Clark, an Anderson County native and later speaker of the U.S. House of Representatives, recalled that "the land swarmed with cutthroats, robbers, thieves, firebugs, and malefactors of every degree and kind, who preyed upon the old, the infirm, the helpless, and committed thousands of brutal and heinous crimes—in the name of the Union or the southern Confederacy."[4]

The Civil War placed Kentucky's slave population in a difficult situation. Should they flee across the Ohio River or remain in place waiting for the outcome of war? Joining the Union Army offered men and their dependents a chance for freedom. Those African American soldiers who could read and write advanced quickly in the ranks. Many black men walked off into the night, uncertain of the future but, as one man recalled about his four uncles, with "'the light of adventure shining' on their faces." In 1863 the creation of Camp Nelson, located south of Nicholasville in Jessamine County, became the sanctuary for thousands of slaves, technically "impounded" to work on Union-controlled railroads. Camp Nelson became the primary recruiting center for slaves into Union Army service in March 1864. Abolitionist and Berea cofounder John G. Fee went to the camp in July 1864 and immediately formed schools. Fee's Ariel Academy and Camp Nelson School for Colored Soldiers offered many slaves their first taste of education in a seven-room schoolhouse. Though never intended to be a refuge for all slaves—it was only officially a recruiting center—Camp Nelson saw hundreds of men, women, and children pour into the camp for protection, food, and labor. Unfortunately, the history of Camp Nelson was replete with missteps, maladministration, and callousness. For example, four hundred women and children were ordered off the base in November 1864, and more than one hundred of them died before the order was reversed.[5]

"Like the Revolution, the Civil War disrupted and destroyed, in education as in other domains," claimed education historian Lawrence A. Cremin. Historian E. Merton Coulter took a more cynical slant: "Education, never a very great concern of the Kentuckians, was dealt a severe blow by the war." Teachers went off to war, as survival became uppermost in people's minds. Churches and schools usually closed before advancing armies. However, it was impossible to anticipate all dangers. For example, in Wayne County, life could be dangerous for school-age children. Near an old schoolhouse one day, "two guerillas shot a runaway mule near some children who were play-ing marbles. This scattered the youngsters and 'abruptly ended the school.'" Presbyterian minister and Confederate officer Edward O. "Ned" Guerrant expressed surprise when he saw schoolchildren in a Kentucky mountain town in April 1863. "While grazing my horse, the children came laughing from school—! From School—!" he exclaimed in his diary. "So strange to see a schoolhouse, and school children."[6]

Superintendent of Public Instruction Robert Richardson (1859–1863), a Unionist and a lawyer, reported in 1861 that school attendance had fallen from 165,000 to about 90,000 in one year. At the same time the state School Fund diminished from $340,000 to $200,000. Some children were "home-schooled" by their parents. For example, Caroline Carter of Clark County taught the children of several families in her home. She had eight in at-tendance in June 1861 and the possibility of more to come. However, many children, particularly the poor, received no instruction at all during the most important years of their education. Richardson tried to hold together a sys-tem increasingly beset by war and fought his own battle against a declining School Fund and falling enrollment. During these stressful times, he urged that schools be consolidated, "to prevent the multiplication of districts." Moreover, he returned to the previous pleas of other state superintendents for normal schools and teacher training. Only in a few towns and cities did he find adequate financial support for schools. Rural districts simply would not vote to tax themselves for education, preferring instead to depend entirely on the state School Fund. Rural districts had only three-month schools, if that much. For the remainder of the Civil War era, Kentucky again had a min-ister as state superintendent, in this case Rev. Daniel Stevenson (1863–1867), a Methodist educated at Transylvania. While trying to hold the educational system together, Stevenson revised the common school laws, promoting the office of superintendent as a full-time position. There were continued efforts to educate the youth of the state. Catholics kept up their zeal with the found-ing of the Panther Creek School in Daviess County in 1862. St. Francis de Sales Academy in Maysville, a girls' school, also founded during the war, operated into the twentieth century.[7]

Kentucky's divided mind over the fate of slavery and of the Union led to the breakup of families and friendships as kith and kin joined the contend-ing camps. Estimates vary from source to source, but apparently more than twice as many men joined the Union forces as those of the Confederacy, approximately 100,000 to about 40,000. Lowell Harrison estimates that as many as one-third of these men died of wounds or disease. A census toward the end of the war listed 21,000 fewer white males over age twenty-one than in 1861. Guerrillas on both sides scourged the countryside. Presbyterian Rev.

Robert J. Breckinridge, a staunch unionist and a former state superintendent (1847–1853), whose sons fought on both sides, proposed a cure for guerrillas: "Treat them all alike, and if there are any among them who are not rebels at heart, God will take care of them and save them at least." Wartime grudges led to postwar feuds and ill will. One western Kentucky Union veteran doubted he could live with his Confederate neighbors. "One or the other of us will have to leave the country forever," he said. In Lexington, Union supporter Frances Dallam Peters observed the heartache and turmoil in a divided town. The "secesh" tended to gravitate around General John Hunt Morgan's home whenever word of the war gave them hope of victory. Once, when the general's cavalry passed through town, Peters reported that a brave lady exclaimed, "I say Hurra for Lincoln." Though shouted down by the Confederate troops, she stood her ground.[8]

Most historians view the Civil War as an unmitigated disaster for Kentucky, the beginning of its descent into the bottom rung of states. "Kentucky emerged from the Civil War in virtual ruin," declared Melba Porter Hay. Michael C. C. Adams said: "Kentucky was in the top ten states by per capita income in 1860. It has been in the bottom ten since 1865." Although Union-controlled Louisville thrived during the war, most of the remainder of the state was hard pressed. Lowell Harrison takes a more moderate tack, finding that many farmers prospered because of high prices, especially if they could avoid Confederate currency and foragers. Moreover, Thomas D. Clark found that much of the decreases in values of property "resulted from neglect rather than from destruction." Whatever the causes or results, Kentucky has never again been a leading state in any chosen category.[9]

The end of the Civil War in April 1865 officially decided the fate of slavery and the idea that states' rights superseded those of the nation and the federal government. Wartime animosities took several generations to heal. The war only seemed to exacerbate peacetime violence. "Across the commonwealth, vigilantes, the Ku Klux Klan, and individual groups killed and lynched blacks with seeming impunity," concluded historian Klotter. "Skaggs Men," a 120-man "gang of villains," according to Ross A. Webb, terrorized Marion, Boyle, and adjoining counties. Governor Thomas Elliott Bramblette (1863–1867) warned the legislature of the increasing lawlessness as postwar tempers cooled only slightly. Moreover, Kentuckians had to be pulled kicking and screaming into the new era. As a sign of the state's obstinacy, its representatives in Congress voted against submission of the Thirteenth Amendment in 1865. Kentucky did not add its vote to the ratification of the Thirteenth, Fourteenth, or Fifteenth Amendments. It was as if the war had never happened.[10]

Kentucky, owing to its native conservatism, fear of black freedom, and lack of education, drifted toward the South, ideologically, after the conclusion of the Civil War. "In fact," explained Hay, paraphrasing E. Merton Coulter, "it has been said that Kentucky seceded from the Union *after* the Civil War." "It is strange indeed that the vanquished ruled the victors," explained historian Hambleton Tapp. Although it "appears bizarre," or certainly ironic, because of Kentucky's greater number of Union than Confederate servicemen, the commonwealth's political system, including local officials, the governorship, and the General Assembly, quickly came under the control of ex-Confederates. Their southern-leaning Democratic Party became almost unbeatable except in the mountains and other isolated parts of the state. With control of the legislature and the governorship, Democrats, unless disrupted by factionalism, set the agenda for the commonwealth. When challenged, they evoked "the Lost Cause" and "the bloody shirt" to whip their constituents into shape. If that failed, the specter of the Klan struck fear into their opponents. Ironically, Louisville, which had a decidedly Union flair during the war, quickly became a haven for ex-Confederates, who soon established themselves as the ruling elite. They controlled the city's newspapers, schools, courts, businesses, and churches. Basil Duke, the right-hand man of John Hunt Morgan, moved to Louisville and edited the *Southern Magazine*. Confederate war veterans held numerous meetings in the river city in the late nineteenth century. Is it any wonder that not only blacks but some whites concluded that life would never improve and left the state?[11]

Having thrown in its lot with that of its southern neighbors, Kentucky faced an uphill battle, one that was, unfortunately, self-willed. "The bald fact is that the South was in no position to come to terms with its public education, nor, for that matter, was it in the mood," declared education historian Adolph E. Meyer. In the latter nineteenth century, Kentucky faced many problems, including economic and political ones, as well as an intellectual dearth of new ideas. "The world of many Kentuckians was one of limited learning, narrow geographical boundaries, and restricted mental horizons," Harrison and Klotter concluded. "Places of finite options and confined imaginations would long survive." Picking up the pieces after the war proved difficult, particularly for education of the youth of the state. For example, the 1870 census indicated that one-quarter of Kentuckians over age ten were illiterate. Leadership in Frankfort, either from the governor's or the state superintendent's office, varied from the Civil War to the end of the century, but most officeholders were competent. One sign of weakness continued to be the basic political nature of the state superintendent's post. Candidates thought first of getting elected and only then about what they would do once in the office of state superintendent. Moreover, from 1859 to 1891, as C. W. Hackensmith pointed out, "not a man was elected to this high office who was directly connected with the public school system." Most of them needed a quick study just to find out the basics of the system. Perhaps even more important, what Clark called "the black beast of Kentucky educational history," the district trustee, in one form or another continued well into the twentieth century as the overlord of the local school. And the county commissioner, changed to county superintendent in 1884, needed no education credentials until an 1893 law required a teaching certificate as a minimum.[12]

Superintendent Stevenson's term extended into the immediate postwar era, often called Reconstruction in the South, and into the remaining years of Governor Bramblette's tenure. Of immediate concern was the end of slavery. While Bramblette railed against the entry of the Freedmen's Bureau into Kentucky because of "atrocities committed" against blacks, he pushed the General Assembly to pass some needed measures. A series of seven acts granted ex-slaves minimal civil rights and authorized the development of a school system for Kentucky blacks. But Bramblette, like most unionist Kentuckians and certainly most Confederate veterans, stoutly opposed the Fourteenth and Fifteenth amendments.[13]

Kentucky's postwar school laws proved to be both progressive and puzzling. While a new school law of 1869 provided that a district could, by majority vote, impose a local tax of five cents on each $100 of taxable property value for the upkeep of the school and the teacher, at the state level a dog tax of one dollar per animal, with two exemptions per household, was seen as landmark legislation by some. However, Stevenson worked to get the legislature to codify black education, creating an entirely separate system. He supported a February 16, 1866, act providing that "all taxes derived from the property of negroes and mulattoes" would be "used to provide for taking care of their paupers and the education of their children." Black schools would be under the jurisdiction of white trustees. Now both black and white teachers would be issued state certificates based on a two-tier system. The first-class certificate would be "renewable, good for two years, granted to persons well qualified to teach"; the second-class one would be good for one year only and "not renewable unless [the] teacher shows improvement to persons 'passably qualified' to teach." School finances appeared safe. Fortunately, since Kentucky never officially seceded from the Union, neither its money nor its bonds became worthless like those of the Confederate States of America. The old School Fund, with its assets in state bonds and bank stock, survived the Civil War intact. However, as pointed out by University of Kentucky president Frank L. McVey, "outside the shares of the Bank of Kentucky stock there was in reality no common school fund," because each year the interest paid on the bonds to support schools had to come from tax revenues.[14]

State politics of the era had an important impact on the education of both whites and blacks. Within the Democratic Party, two factions vied for dominance. The "Bourbons" wanted a return to the old antebellum days of privilege and dominance, without even granting a rudimentary education for blacks. They opposed new economic development, preferring instead to depend on the old agrarianism. Like the French Bourbons, this group "seemed to worship at the shrine of the dead past." The "New Departure" faction, led by editors Henry Watterson of the *Louisville Courier-Journal* and W. C. P. Breckinridge of the *Lexington Observer and Reporter*, advocated following the "New South" ideal of accepting defeat and the end of slavery. They pushed for industrialization of the region and improved transportation, and they decried the role of the Klan and its many imitators. But Watterson was not a social liberal by any means, and the New Departure's view of African Americans differed little from that of the Bourbons. Historian George C. Wright claims that Watterson's views of race were "not out of genuine concern for [freedmen] but out of fear that the federal government would intervene in Kentucky." Publicly and privately, Watterson apparently used the word *nigger* with abandon and without regret. Until the mid-1890s, the commonwealth's Bourbons and New Departure Democrats continued their battles over party leadership.[15]

In the immediate postwar period, that of Reconstruction, the administrations of Governor John W. Stevenson and Superintendent Zachary F. Smith (1867–1871), both Democrats, of course, brought education back into focus as having importance. Stevenson, elected second on the ticket, succeeded Governor John L. Helm five days after the latter died. In 1868 he won a special election to serve out the remaining three years of the term. While lawlessness still pervaded the commonwealth and Stevenson opposed federal efforts on behalf of blacks, some progress occurred in education. He supported a successful referendum to levy an additional local tax for schools.[16]

Smith, a farmer and businessman who had attended Bacon College, declared the common schools to be "in a state of decay." Claiming that the entire system needed "remodeling," he proposed six recommendations, including improving the county commissioners, creating "a corps of professionally trained teachers," adopting a "uniformity" of textbooks, and consolidating districts. In 1869 Smith's records revealed that there were nearly 4,500 school districts, usually with a single school in each, scattered across the state, sharing $242,989.61 from the School Fund, which amounted to $54.63 per district. Smith also criticized the system for allowing commissioners to "baffle and delay payment of teachers' wages for months longer than is necessary, and finally worry him [or her] into taking it out in a bill of merchandise" at a discount. The state superintendent claimed that people were leaving the state because of the poor state of education. He displayed unusual energy for his task. Just after taking office, he and Governor Stevenson took on a balky state legislature, campaigning for a substantial increase in state taxation for schools. By referendum in 1869, the voters passed a property tax increase from five cents to twenty cents per $100 of evaluation. "This date stands as a red letter day in Kentucky's educational progress," extolled Thomas D. Clark. By 1871 the amount available to disburse to the public schools increased by $185,000 to $968,000. This state school tax on property, interest from the state School Fund, taxes on several banks' stocks, and the taxes collected on dogs and even billiard tables, all increased substantially during Smith's term. Other highlights of his tenure included extending the school term in most districts from the old standard of three months to five and increasing white pupil attendance by 29,000 students to 405,000, from 1869 to 1871.[17]

After the decline of the common schools during the Civil War, public education again appeared on the rise. While Stevenson's and Smith's administrations took some steps forward for white students, the education picture for black students continued to be difficult. Life for most blacks in postwar Kentucky was hard. An 1866 law that allowed ex-slave couples to purchase for fifty cents a certificate legitimating their marriages and children also prohibited interracial marriage. The Freedmen's Bureau's Educational Division eventually established 219 schools in Kentucky, enrolling more than ten thousand students by 1870. However, only a small amount of state money went into African American education, because blacks owned little property to be taxed by the 1866 and 1867 laws. In a few places hostile whites broke up school sessions or, as in the case of Crab Orchard, a mob torched the black school. From their beginnings, black schools were underfunded. "Though constantly short of money," Marion B. Lucas declared in *A History of Blacks in Kentucky: From Slavery to Segregation, 1760–1891,* "the bureau made its greatest contribution to black education in Kentucky through a financial assistance program." Working through black churches, the bureau passed out "admission" tickets to schools, providing a free education "for indigent black pupils." Black teachers outnumbered white ones in Kentucky's schools sponsored by the bureau. After the Freedmen's Bureau was dissolved in February 1874, the state legislature created a school system for blacks. State and county officials insisted that black paupers be provided for first from the "capitation tax" on African Americans, leaving little money for their schoolchildren. Although the number of black school districts nearly doubled and more students attended school from 1875 to 1881, the amount of money made available per capita increased only slightly, from fifty to fifty-eight cents.

Change came slowly for black education in Kentucky because many whites, either through "indifference" or open "hostility," deprecated the need for an educated black population.[18]

Postwar lawlessness in Kentucky tore the heart out of civility. "It is remarkable the Freedmen's Bureau schools did as well as they did, for almost every effort was met with resistance," claimed Harrison and Klotter. Blacks were driven across the Ohio River from Gallatin County, and beatings of ex-slaves elsewhere went unpunished. Dozens of blacks were killed and more than one hundred lynched between 1867 and 1871. Self-styled "Regulators" dominated several central Kentucky counties, dispensing their own brand of justice. Moreover, the Ku Klux Klan in Kentucky was just as violent, destructive, and insidious as its brotherhood in the Deep South. But many blacks ably defended themselves. When threatened by the Klan, Elijah P. Marrs, a Henry County teacher, organized the Loyal League for the Protection of Negroes. He later recalled: "I slept with a pistol under my head, an Enfield rifle at my side, and a corn knife at the door, but I never had occasion to use them." In such an atmosphere, it is a wonder that black education advanced at all.[19]

One American Missionary Association teacher went to Louisville unrealistically expecting to find "a kind of noble savage, with boundless energy for learning." Instead, "hundreds of filthy, squalid, untaught children" confronted Sarah Stanley. She blamed their unresponsiveness on the "brutalizing influence of slavery." Although she found the work "laborious and exhausting," she kept up a brave front. "There is no alternative," she claimed; "the work must be done and there are none to do it." After organizing her students into "primary, secondary, and intermediate grades," she began to see improvement in her charges. Even some ex-Confederates who visited the school, she reported, were "surprised at the order, decorum, and general proficiency of the pupils."[20]

After the Civil War, African Americans of the Appalachian region, never in as large numbers there as in other regions of the Commonwealth of Kentucky, migrated out into other parts of the state. Economic conditions in the more remote areas had deteriorated. A case study of one such area, Beech Creek in Clay County, offers lessons in what happened and why it occurred. Coming out of slavery, most blacks had to struggle to find niches in the local economy, owing to a lack of property. With the decline of the Clay County salt industry, many worked for white families or were tenants on subsistence farms. When opportunities for work developed in timber and coal outside the county, the poorest whites left, but the poorest blacks did not. Other blacks did leave, though. Whereas in 1840 blacks made up 15 percent of the Clay County population, by 1890 they accounted for only 3 percent. The same study found that those blacks and whites who had some education prospered at the expense of those who did not. "Landless whites and blacks, with few resources in land, had little access to the educational and occupational opportunities of the commercial marketplace," the authors declared. "They either left the county or remained as its poor." Educational opportunities came slowly in Clay County. Still, and somewhat amazingly, by 1880 one-third of black heads of household could read and one-half of whites could read. Among both blacks and whites, lower percentages of women than of men demonstrated literacy. At the turn of the twentieth century, about half of the black males could read and write.[21]

As soon as the Civil War ended, John G. Fee returned to Berea. In January 1866, the Berea Literary Institute opened, divided into a primary school and the Academic Department, which offered secondary education. A few weeks later, in early March, the first black students entered, and Principal J. A. R. Rogers proclaimed that "from this hour the school was open to all." Fee's dream of an interracial enclave now seemed possible with the abolition of slavery. However, some white students left the school because of integration as the first black students began to arrive. Angus Augustus Burleigh, an eighteen-year-old veteran, received direct encouragement from Fee to attend school in Berea as a grammar school student. After attending the institute, Burleigh graduated from Berea College in 1875, becoming its first black graduate. Shannon Wilson, in *Berea College: An Illustrated History*, estimated that by 1870 "some forty to fifty African American families" had moved into the Berea community, "their lots and parcels interspersed with those of whites," making Fee's experiment in a biracial society appear possible. Fee was already trying to raise money for buildings in Berea as well as trying to keep the older Camp Nelson school open. Into the 1880s, enrollment at the Berea Literary Institute remained about half white and half black. As an example of Berea's boldness, interracial dating was permitted between 1872 and 1892. As in most schools of its type, teacher preparation became one of the main thrusts of the institute. Through the presidency of William Goodell Frost (1892–1920), Berea Literary Institute kept its commitment to four divisions: college, normal, academic (secondary), and elementary. Berea College, the upper division of Fee's dream, after the disappointments of pre–Civil War years, began to develop as well. As Berea College neared the conclusion of the nineteenth century, it was hard put to keep a racial balance among its students.[22]

After starting from near zero, black education made some progress, particularly in the Ohio River towns and counties, such as Paducah, Gallatin County, Covington, Daviess County, and Louisville, where the Freedmen's Bureau had a strong presence. Black churches, with the financial assistance of such groups as the American Missionary Association, became the center of efforts to found schools. In 1883 organized education for African American youth began at Bowling Green with the founding of State Street School. The school grew so much that a third floor was added to the building in 1890. The 1870 city charter of Louisville provided for black education, and the city began establishing schools, one at the Center Street African Methodist Church, with Sallie Adams as principal, and one at the Fifth Street African Baptist Church, with Suzie Adams as principal. In 1873 the first school building for blacks, Central Colored School, opened at Sixth and Kentucky streets. Other schools soon organized in "neighborhoods of growing black concentration" in Louisville, which included those in Smoketown and California. There were heroes among these educators. For example, Bell Mitchell Jackson taught briefly at Camp Nelson, attended Berea College, and then taught in Lexington's black schools for more than three decades.[23]

Private schools, seminaries, and academies for whites briefly flourished after the Civil War, partially filling the void left by the commonwealth's lack of public schooling. Founding of these private schools continued, and fifteen thousand students attended such institutions in 1870. For example, in September 1869 Principal John O'Flaherty, in a "School Prospectus," invited interested parties to meet at the "Old School House" in Auburn, Logan County, where primary, intermediate, and senior departments were set up and the costs ranged from ten to eighteen dollars per session. Only a few such schools survived into the twentieth century. Transylvania Female Institute, now known as Sayre School, was an exception; it has remained in continuous operation since its founding in 1854. Boys were admitted to the primary school in 1876, and Sayre has gone through several permutations down to the present day. Powell Academy in Catlettsburg served a clientele in northeastern Kentucky, promising a "thorough practical education to both male and female pupils at the lowest possible rates." It offered primary to college preparatory courses and listed four faculty and more than one hundred students in attendance in its 1868–1869 catalog. Another school founded just before the Civil War, Laurel Seminary, lingered into the early twentieth century, following the old nineteenth-century pattern of offering a wide range of courses in the seminary or academy tradition. Eventually it melded into the common school system of London. Eminent pre–Civil War institutions like Science Hill Female Academy in Shelbyville and Madison Female Institute (1858–1919) in Richmond flourished at least briefly as "southern finishing schools" until overcome by changing times in the early twentieth century. A succession of such schools in Danville included Danville Female Academy, Henderson Female Institute, and the Caldwell Institute, which also offered a college curriculum.[24]

What were the common schools of the commonwealth like in the second half of the nineteenth century for the pupils and teachers? What was taught, and how was it taught? Thomas D. Clark, in the *Kentucky Encyclopedia*, summed up the common school education, in his inimitable fashion, "as being of shabby, backwoods, log-cabin quality."[25]

In the Common School Report of 1871, Superintendent H. A. M. Henderson (1871–1879) eloquently and harshly described the physical environment of the typical district county or village school as "exceedingly rude and unsuitable."

They are too frequently located on some barren and treeless hillside, where the hot suns of summer pelt down upon them; and the cold winds of winter have unbroken sweep; or on a narrow strip of land at the junction of highways, where the dust is sure to blow into the house from one or the other road; or by streets and railroads, in the neighborhood of factories, or the busiest portions of villages, where study will be interrupted and the persons and morals of the children endangered. Broken windows, swinging weather-boards, leaky roofs, are noticeable from without. Inside are filthy floors, smoked ceilings, and walls defaced with obscene images. The furniture is of the most primitive kind, and constructed with little or no reference to the comfort of those who are to use it. Appliances promotive of order and cleanliness are neglected. Hats and clothing are thrown on the floor or tossed over the benches. If there is a privy, it is a den of loathsomeness. Altogether, the common school seems to be a place which has few attractions, but much that is offensive and repulsive.[26]

Governor Preston Leslie (1871–1875) made similarly condemning statements three years later, lamenting that the buildings "seem to have been built simply for a pen for prisoners." Superintendent Henderson included "a law providing for the building of good school-houses upon a uniform plan" among "The Great Desiderata," his wish list of necessities for improving Kentucky education. He assumed that increasing local participation would enhance local pride and lead to better schools, with the county commissioners and district trustees being held responsible. Another critic found that "the poor schoolhouses were the outward expression of the attitude of the people." Although taxes could be levied to build schools, most county district buildings continued to be built directly from local sources and maintained by the parents and concerned citizens, without concern for a common type. School buildings slowly improved, particularly after passage of a law in 1894 that placed the onus directly on the school trustees to provide for an adequate structure. Between 1881 and 1901, the number of log school buildings decreased from 3,360 to 1,238, while the number of brick and frame structures increased. There was notable construction in some places. The new Second Street School in Frankfort, the city's first high school, completed in 1868 at a cost of $30,000, contained a library and a science laboratory. However, the one-room school, as well as the common water pail and dipper, continued to predominate in most regions of Kentucky, outside of the towns and cities, well into the twentieth century. One late-nineteenth-century school superintendent exclaimed: "The difficulty I meet in the work of improving our [school] houses, is to get the people to understand that a Woodford County child is worth as much as a race-horse, and is entitled to as good a house in which to study."[27]

Most sources assume that rural schools, particularly in the South, were inferior in every way to those of the towns, the independent districts. A contemporary "Yankee" educationist condemned the rural schools in the South as "unspeakably bad." Most Kentucky counties did not impose a special tax for their schools, continuing to rely entirely on state funds. In some counties, especially in the mountains, schools were few and far between. None of the mountain counties had public county high schools. Superintendent Smith pushed the legislature to pass a law on January 23, 1869, allowing Louisville to elect a city education commissioner, and other towns soon followed. Studying what passed as high school curriculum, prospective elementary teachers made their way haltingly into the profession. However, it would take teachers' institutes and normal school education to more fully develop a cadre of teachers capable of improving Kentucky's abominable system. Already states north of the Ohio River were rushing to improve their school systems. Kentucky, as usual, was playing catch-up while now comparing itself with its sister "southern" states. By 1875 most states outside the South had fully functioning public normal schools, offering a two-year study in the arts of teaching. In the more progressive areas, schools were becoming "graded" and teachers were being taught to teach. Early normal school education was no more than a basic high school course with emphasis on preparing a student to teach in the elementary or grammar school grades. Outside the South, the public high school evolved rapidly as the old academy system declined. "As an upward extension of the educational ladder," said one educationist, "the high school could not proceed until elementary school development was well advanced." Kentucky and its southern counterparts faced an uphill battle.[28]

Many institutions, like Pleasant Grove Grade School in south-central Jefferson County, slowly evolved into a "graded" form from their antebellum days as one-room schools. The experiences of Pleasant Grove's teachers and pupils alike were replicated in other Kentucky rural schools in the second half of the nineteenth century. Although one former student of the school glow-ingly declared, "The teachers in those schools did all in their power to give pupils the fundamentals on which to build an education," another recalled, "The school building was old when I was there—with hand-made desks—and, oh, those seats! Backs straight, and 3 to a seat, huge wooden shutters, closed after school, when anyone was kept for punishment." In the middle to late nineteenth century, students learned through the drill method and progressed through McGuffey's Readers in an ungraded class "mixed up like boarding house hash," said one informant. Because Pleasant Grove School was the center of the community, "most children knew that if the teacher had to punish them at school the parents would do likewise for that same offense when they arrived home." Sometimes students as old as eighteen would be in attendance. Recitations, "pie suppers," and other events filled the school with delighted parents, relatives, and children throughout the year. Eventually Pleasant Grove became graded, offering grades one through eight, with an annual graduation ceremony for those who completed the eighth grade. A picnic at Fontaine Ferry Park often concluded the school year for everyone. A new two-room building eventually graced the school grounds, but it was not enough to save Pleasant Grove from "progress." On June 7, 1949, the Jefferson County School Board closed the school, consolidating Sub-district No. 9 into the larger system.[29]

Who were the teachers in the second half of the nineteenth century? Young men often began professional careers by teaching for a few years un-til they could save enough money for more training or to start a business. Young women sometimes taught for a few years before they married. Mar-ried women were generally not hired as teachers. Men and women had few options in teaching other than staying in the classroom with no opportunity for promotion, unless they lived in a larger town or a city like Louisville. Moreover, teacher pay was so low that it discouraged prospective teachers from increasing their learning beyond the rudimentary knowledge needed to "keep" school. Of course, there were always the dedicated teachers who saw their job as a calling worthy of the sacrifice, and they made a difference in the lives of thousands of Kentucky youth. Teachers were often tested by their students. "In many cases," said Thomas D. Clark, "a teacher was considered to be a good one if he could whip every boy in school." Female teachers had to rely more on guile, one supposes. Discipline was crucial to learning, and teachers' institutes of the time often spent much time on it. Standing in the corner or wearing a dunce cap were older forms of punishment for minor of-fenses. For such pranks as stuffing paper down the chimney or the stovepipe to smoke up the schoolroom or throwing a .22 caliber rifle shell into the stove to cause havoc, the teacher would have to resort to sterner punishment. Although an 1877 State Department of Education dictum ruled that "in no case shall resort be had to cruel and unusual punishment as a mode of discipline," most schools permitted the spanking of miscreants. "Spare the rod and spoil the child" was an aphorism that fit the times. Teachers often took matters into their own hands. After Villah Bratt at the Arnold School in Newport failed to persuade a large boy to bathe, the ninety-pound teacher "scrubbed him thoroughly" one day. "She expected a 'peppering time' the next day," but the boy's parents instead "sent her a bar of soap."[30]

The local school trustee in the county rural areas chose the teacher for his district. Because the trustee was elected by his constituents in the district, he was susceptible to all the foibles of any politician, and the teacher was caught in the middle of this inefficient and often corrupt system. If a teacher was not a local person, he or she had to stay with a family, "boarding out," as it was known, paying for room and board out of an already meager salary. Only a few districts provided free room and board to a teacher. Salaries varied, ranging in 1883–1884 from $9.33 to $28.00 a month for a three- to six-month school. Teachers normally were not paid anything until half the term was completed. Most rural schools began their sessions later than urban ones. The salary depended on whether a teacher taught the minimum or the maximum number of students in the district. Only in Louisville, where its citizens passed a tax to supplement state funds, did salaries (from $350 to $700 per term) rise above the average wages of a farmhand or a day laborer. Moreover, teachers often did not receive their salaries on time, owing to inefficient state administration and inept county commissioners and district trustees. Many teachers were not paid until the school term was completed. Slow payments encouraged a "racket," in which a teacher could get money, at a discount, from a bank, from individuals, or even from the superintendent. Superintendent Smith railed against this system and the "shaver," who "at a savage discount," made money off the teacher. In 1886 a state law finally prohibited superintendents from trading in this nefarious way. For all these troubles, teachers were expected to arrive before the students did and prepare for the school day, including building a fire in a fireplace or a potbellied stove if the weather required it. It is no wonder that teacher quality continued to be low in many counties. One county superintendent lamented, "The trouble is that schools are sometimes 'let out' to the lowest bidder, thereby securing a low grade teacher."[31]

In the typical Kentucky classroom, only rudimentary equipment aided the teacher in her or his efforts. Chalk, erasers, a coal bucket, a water bucket, and a mop might be all a teacher received at the beginning of the school term. Teachers in the country schools might have more than forty students in class, in a school term that might last three to four to five months, depending on local support. The school day usually lasted from eight o'clock in the morning until four in the afternoon. Recitations took up most of the day, with time out for recess and lunch. After 1888 schools were to provide six hours of actual classroom work. Most students, unless they lived near the school, brought their lunches, which usually consisted of leftovers from supper or breakfast. Sometimes an enterprising teacher might put a pot of beans or stew on the stove for a noonday meal made up of vegetables that students had brought from their homes and farms. Recess was a time for games. If weather permitted, students poured into the fields, waded streams, and invented "play like" imaginary games and adventures. Ante-over, hide-and-seek, London Bridge, and other folk games of ancient origin did not exhaust the students' inventiveness. One of Winslow Homer's most famous works, "Snap the Whip," is a poignant painting of grade-school boys whirling around, the ones on the end falling as they run faster and faster. This 1872 idealized view of country life, with a little red schoolhouse in the background, belies the difficulties of life at the time. It should be remembered that most children of this era and their parents faced lives of unending drudgery on farms.[32]

How did one become a teacher in the second half of the nineteenth century? Hackensmith, in *Out of Time and Tide*, stated the method succinctly: "The teachers secured their training wherever and whenever they could and were certified to teach on the basis of examination." Like other states, Kentucky, though at a glacial pace, began to professionalize teaching in the second half of the nineteenth century. First Massachusetts and then New York founded public normal schools before the Civil War. Not until landmark legislation was passed in 1906 did Kentucky follow suit, but many educators and public-spirited citizens saw the need for such education much earlier. In 1871 the city of Louisville formed its own normal school, leading to an internship-type program for its schools. Until 1911 Louisville Normal School offered a one-year program preparing female teachers for grades one through eight. In 1897 the Louisville Colored Normal School opened, located at Central Colored High School, to train primary school teachers. Other private Kentucky colleges also offered some teacher education. Private normal schools, following the entrepreneurial spirit of the time, proliferated after the Civil War. Between 1868 and 1905, thirty-four normal schools, some of which lasted only a short while, received charters from the General Assembly. Some Kentucky teachers also attended the Lebanon National Normal School in Ohio. The Glasgow Normal School and Business College, founded in 1876 by A. W. Mell, was modeled after the school in Ohio and could offer a twenty-week term, including tuition, board, and supplies, for sixty-five dollars. Each of its graduates received a first-class teacher's certificate. When the school outgrew its facilities, Mell and his partner, J. Tom Williams, moved it to Bowling Green, adopting the name Southern Normal School and Business College in 1884. After several trying years and ownerships, Henry Hardin Cherry, a "promotional genius," became sole owner of the school, and by 1899 it had nearly seven hundred students, most of them taking a high school course leading to a teaching career. Cherry set a high standard for himself, his faculty, and his students. His "Declaration of Principles and Policies" for Southern Normal included this maxim: "To be a live school and to impart to its students a burning zeal to do and be something."[33]

State superintendents from before the Civil War continually urged the state legislature to pass enabling legislation for public normal school education. Perhaps the ill-fated two-year normal school experiment at Transylvania in the mid-1850s soured legislators from again joining this growing national trend. Prospective teachers picked up education where they could. Many who gravitated toward teaching at the common graded school level had, at most, an eighth-grade education. As the high school developed in Kentucky towns, teachers might even have some college training. However, until the late nineteenth century, many teachers with only an elementary school education studied on their own to pass the certification examinations. After 1870 they attended the mandated five- to six-day teachers' institutes, each of which cost the teacher two dollars. The institute usually covered all school subjects, management of the school and students, and school laws, and it crammed all this into a period of five or six days. Private normal schools only filled part of the void. In the summers of 1878 and 1879, at the urging of Superintendent Henderson, the state operated ten-week normal sessions, allowing free tuition for three students per county. However, nothing was done to make this an annual event. In 1880 the Agricultural and Mechanical College in Lexington added a new Normal Department. The first sustained attempt to regularize public normal school education came with the founding of Kentucky State Normal School for Colored Persons in Frankfort in 1886.[34]

In the period from 1868 through 1905, at least thirty-four schools, academies, and institutes in Kentucky offered normal school education of one sort or another. Some were little more than fly-by-night efforts of a teacher or two to make some extra money. Most of these "schools" lasted for only a short time. It is difficult to call them more than feeble attempts to "teach teachers to teach." Some became important and evolved into such schools as Murray, Morehead, and Western state normal schools. Most were inexpensive coeducational schools offering a high school education, and they served a vital function for the time. The established private colleges, including Georgetown College and Berea College, offered teaching courses of varying degrees of efficiency. National Normal University in Lebanon, Ohio, had an influence on the development of normal school education in Kentucky. It not only offered a template for how such a school should be conducted but also educated some Kentucky teachers and educational leaders.[35]

An 1852 school law provided for state-funded county examiners to examine prospective teachers for a fifty-cent fee, the cost raised to one dollar in 1870. Teachers were to be able to teach the "elements of a plain English education." In 1874 the state superintendent's office began to recommend printed questions for written examinations. If a prospective teacher graduated from a normal school or passed the examination, he or she received a certificate. The certification process evolved from one classification in 1852 to three in 1870. The first class "signified thorough and accurate knowledge of the branches taught" and was good for two years. The second class, good for one year, indicated "imperfect knowledge," and the third class, also good for one year, signified "indifferent knowledge." The system returned to two classifications in 1871, but then in 1884 three certificates were again instituted, with emphasis on encouraging teachers to acquire the first-class certificate. Four years later another law changed the system so that a second-class certificate could be renewed only once, for a second year, and the third-class certificate could not be renewed. At first certificates were good only for one county, but in 1893–1894 provision was made for a state diploma, good for life and permitting the holder to teach in all the state's schools. To qualify, a teacher had to be at least twenty-four years of age, "of good moral character, and make an average grade of ninety in several subjects, including English Literature, algebra, physics, and elementary Latin."[36]

In the state system emerging from the Civil War, there was evidence of corruption as well as inefficiency, incompetence, and bad faith. Some district trustees took a kickback on a teacher's salary for appointing that person. In the absence of state laws against nepotism, it was not unusual for a trustee to appoint a relative to a school. As the state examinations became more and more important in obtaining a teaching certificate, some trustees gave the questions to their favorites in advance of the examination. Also, individuals known as "question peddlers" stole the questions and sold them to prospective teachers unwilling to play by the rules. As time went on, the county superintendent might become the largest employer in the county and the source of political largesse. The administration of the local school did not improve much from 1860 to 1900. State Superintendent Harry V. McChesney (1899–1903), railed against the trustee system, which he evaluated as unworkable at best and corrupt at worst. The politicization of the county school system produced abuses that carried long into the twentieth century. All of these problems, coupled with low expectations, led to poor performance by teachers and the short-changing of students.[37]

Before the turn of the twentieth century, the majority of common school system teachers were men (in 1907 the percentage was 58). During a Campbell County teachers' institute held in September 1878, Sallie S. Armstrong read an essay pleading for more "lady" teachers in a profession dominated by men. "Many gentlemen teach for a year to two in order to obtain the money to attend lectures, that they may follow some other profession," she claimed. "There are some of us who do not teach simply to procure money to buy our wedding finery or dress in the latest style." She argued that men usually got teaching jobs because of discrimination. "Yet when we teach," Armstrong said, "we must do it for about half the money that they obtain. Not because we are less worthy, but because we are women." In Victorian cadence and metaphor, she asked for equality and justice: "Do not cast aside woman's government as something worthless, for there are too many precious mothers in this land. Perhaps we might not always be successful in governing, if the only avenue to a human heart was a stormy path, but often the sunshine and pleasant April rain accomplish marvels which the blustering March wind fails to produce."[38]

The curriculum of the public schools included a good dose of the "three R's" at all levels. Legislative acts of the General Assembly dictated the minimal course to be taught, beginning with an 1852 law. In the elementary grades, the "three R's," geography, and American history were emphasized in most schools. In the secondary school, courses included the "three R's" plus "spelling, grammar, composition, geography, American history, and 'laws of health.'" In 1888 the elements of civil government were added, and physiology and hygiene replaced the "laws of health." A study of Kentucky history was added in 1893. Teachers learned from "prescribed aids" suggested by superintendents or other educators. The duller, less prepared teachers had a hard time keeping one jump ahead of their sharper students. "In most cases, teachers knew no more of the subjects which they taught than was contained in their handbooks," Tom Clark claimed. "It was once a favorite pastime for bright students to catch their teachers working arithmetic problems from their handbooks." Although there were exceptions, Ligon declared, "generally speaking, the county superintendent was a failure in his supervision of instruction."[39]

Textbooks were always a great concern because of their cost. Books were the total responsibility of the parents until an 1852 law authorized the state board to recommend texts to be purchased by parents. Some students did not go to school because their parents were unable or unwilling to pay for textbooks. The most popular texts of the day included William Holmes McGuffey's readers, Noah Webster's spellers, and Joseph Ray's arithmetic books. Books were at the center of the curriculum and the focus of all study. Although the blab school received censure by law in 1870, recitation continued to be the main method of study. In the one-room school, older students often helped educate the younger ones, following the Lancastrian monitorial system in its most basic format. Superintendent Smith asked for "uniformity" of texts. "The great variety and frequent changes of those now in use have become a costly and serious evil, under our unprotected system," he claimed. His successor, H. A. M. Henderson, pushed for a list of texts that local schools could choose from. The Bible was no longer the center of education, but moral and ethical lessons from the Bible were an intrinsic, even subliminal, part of the textbooks of the day. Unfortunately, textbook selection became embroiled in Kentucky politics as book companies such as the John P. Morton Company of Louisville vied to have their publications given foremost attention. The American Book Company, formed by a consolidation of several smaller publishers, became a virtual monopoly in the late nineteenth century, adding constant pressure on education.[40]

Who were the students who attended Kentucky's public schools? They ranged in age from six or younger to eighteen or more. It was not unusual in a one-room school to have a few students who were older than the teacher. School attendance was poor. In 1882 only 33 percent of the commonwealth's youth were in school. The passage of a compulsory attendance law in 1896, the first in the South, without Governor William O. Bradley's signature, required children between ages seven and fourteen to attend a minimum of eight weeks a year. But the law was not enforced. Kentucky's mostly agricultural economy depended on the labor of farm families, children included. Although rural schools were scheduled to coincide with the slow season of agriculture, the late-fall and winter months, many farm children still did not attend school. The school year officially began July 1, but most schools did not begin their session until August or September, or even later in the county districts. School terms in rural areas lasted only two-thirds as long as those in towns, and a study revealed "that students in rural schools tested about two and a half years behind those in urban districts."[41]

Public school education in Kentucky made advances as well as the occasional missteps in the late nineteenth century. H. A. M. Henderson, judged by many, including Thomas D. Clark, as "perhaps the most distinguished superintendent of public instruction before 1907," led the commonwealth's common schools during a period of significant change. Henderson was a Yale graduate, a Confederate veteran, and a Methodist minister, and he served two terms as state superintendent, from 1871 through 1879, during the governorships of Preston Hopkins Leslie (1871–1875) and James B. Mc-Creary (1875–1879). Both of these Democrats supported educational advance, which, in the context of Kentucky's political, cultural, and economic milieu, "of necessity followed a zigzag course," according to Clark. Though abrasive at times and occasionally displaying an arrogant intellectualism, the politically ambitious Henderson had the right idea about education in Kentucky. Unless radical changes were made, Kentucky would continue to languish educationally.[42]

Henderson energetically approached his job with "a desire to build a system of public education." Apparently, he had made a study of the system before he took office. Governor Leslie, a Civil War Union supporter and an antisecessionist, adopted New Departure themes in order to defeat his Republican opponent, John Marshall Harlan, in the 1871 gubernatorial election. Leslie supported increased appropriations for education. The big issue during the first General Assembly meeting during Leslie's tenure was the bill to authorize the building of the Southern Railroad through Kentucky, but he did get the legislature to pass a law legalizing African American testimony in the courts, his only sign of progressivism. The only major education legislation officially sanctioned a "uniform system of common schools for the Colored Children," officially separating the already segregated state public schools.[43]

Governor McCreary, a Confederate veteran, also defeated Union veteran Harlan, in the 1875 gubernatorial race. McCreary was not an effective chief executive. Most of the legislature's time was spent passing more than a thousand insignificant private bills. McCreary pushed gently on the issue of state normal schools, which did not pass, and oversaw a decrease in the state property tax. As far as education was concerned, a new law establishing a state board of health included providing "health books for schools." Neither Leslie nor McCreary had much impact on the problems of violence in the state, one of which was the developing feuds in eastern Kentucky, as the term "Bloody Breathitt" (a reference to Breathitt County) became nationally known.[44]

In this atmosphere, Henderson accomplished much. He played politics well, winning election in 1871 and reelection in 1875 in the hurly-burly world of Kentucky politics. His successes included encouraging development of the "graded" school, getting the General Assembly to approve local direct taxation of up to twenty-five cents per $100 in property evaluation, mandating teachers' institutes, updating teacher certification, changing to the single-trustee system, and setting standards for the high school curriculum. He called attention to the poor physical condition of many schools. Many systems, particularly in urban areas, moved from the three-month to a five-month school term. He was not able to persuade the legislature to approve his suggestion to establish three permanent public normal schools, after the two summers of normal school experimentation, or to pass a compulsory school attendance law. Nor was he able to advance the qualifications or efficiency of the county superintendents. Moreover, the legislature, under duress from local interests, repealed the one-trustee law in 1878, returning to the three-trustee system.[45]

Superintendent Henderson encouraged the organization of black and white teachers. In its early days dominated by the state superintendent and the state board, what eventually became the Kentucky Education Association began its efforts in 1857 as the Kentucky Association of Teachers, in support of public school education in the commonwealth. After the Civil War, Smith and Henderson both served as ex officio presidents of the association until 1878, at which time began an ongoing struggle for control of KEA that continued well into the twentieth century. Should it be directly controlled by the State Board of Education, by administrators, or by teachers? At the 1884 KAT convention, a new constitution highlighted the need for educational reform, and new president R. D. Allen said the association had not exerted any "discoverable influence on the well-being of public education." At that meeting resolutions passed urging the legislature to raise taxes for education and higher teacher salaries and develop normal schools and asking that Congress assign funds from the federal surplus to education. Association meetings for the remainder of the nineteenth century took on the trappings of the growing trend toward professionalization of teaching in the United States with better organization and the formation of committees.[46]

Henderson's shortsightedness on the issue of race perfectly fit the mood of white dominance. He displayed all the impedimenta of Kentucky whites, particularly those who had fought for or supported the "Lost Cause." "The most perplexing question connected with our school interest is that which relates to the education of the children of the colored people," he said.

> In every social aspect of the case they constitute a non-conformable element. Different in history and color, there seems to be no natural affinity between them and the white race. . . . Whatever view we may entertain of the proprietary of the amendment to the Federal Constitution conferring this dignity upon them, it confronts us as a fact, and necessitates that we should deal with it as a practical problem, pressing upon us for its proper solution. If education be the basic of civil order, then to elevate the ignorant Africans, who are invested with the tremendous power of suffrage, becomes at once a necessary duty.

Henderson assumed that the races must never mix in the public schools. Furthermore, he believed that blacks should pay for their own education though property taxes, a capitation, or poll tax on all males over the age of twenty-one, and from the collection of fines on black residents.[47]

Black education presented a challenge, the solution to which seemed to be only to create a dual system of education by law in 1866, with African Americans paying their own way. However, the Colored School Fund never generated enough money for even Henderson's modest ambitions. The fund accumulated little money after funding aid to the poor, as mandated by the General Assembly. Meanwhile, whites began to recognize the need for a system of black education, either because of a sense of "moral obligation" or "linking civil order to education." At the national level pending civil rights legislation "raised the specter of race-mixing, and the creation of black schools would ensure racial separation." When Congress proposed appropriating money to improve black schools in the South, Henderson, arguing that Kentucky might miss its share, "could not resist the bait." Therefore, at his urging, in February 1874 the Kentucky General Assembly created "a separately maintained, segregated, unequal system of black public schools." The act, at Henderson's insistence, included his idea that African Americans would pay for their own education. The state superintendent would distribute the fund. Three appointed black trustees in each district would report directly to the white county commissioner. Black schools could be no closer than one mile to a white school in a rural area or no closer than six hundred feet in an urban area. Districts of no more than 120 black students, between the ages of six and sixteen, would be arranged by the county commissioner. In the first year of operation, ninety-three counties formed 452 black school districts.[48]

The new law did not work well for black children. During this period Kentucky never received federal funding for their education. State funds per black student averaged forty-nine cents per annum between 1876 and 1882, about one-third the amount spent on white students. Classes averaged about fifty students per teacher, and many black district schools failed to be in session for even three months. A Madison County black student, Henry Allen Laine, later recalled his school as an "old slave cabin" heated by a fireplace. His only textbook in 1879 was a well-worn *Webster's Speller*. While most white Kentuckians displayed only a passing interest in black education, if that, President E. H. Fairchild of Berea College, John Marshall Harlan, and a few others wholeheartedly supported their cause. Fairchild pushed others for action. Black leaders had met periodically since the Civil War to try to improve their lot generally. In November 1875, a convention of blacks in Lexington called for legislation to "provide equal education advantages to every child in the State," decrying the disparity between expenditures for black and white education. Resolutions at this and later meetings asked for equal funding. Superintendent Henderson, to his credit, at a black educators meeting in 1877, urged creation of the Colored Teachers' State Association, reorganized as the Kentucky Negro Education Association in 1913. The CTSA was the first African American teacher group organized in the South.[49]

Two federal court cases eventually dealt with this problem. Two black leaders from Louisville, Horace Morris and John H. Jackson, the first president of the CTSA, pressed for relief from the legislature. When that failed, they filed a lawsuit. A simultaneous Ohio case established legal precedent: the decision in *U.S. v. Buntin*, handed down in February 1882, addressed that state's equalization problem. In April 1882 the commonwealth's separate funding plan was found unconstitutional in the case of *Kentucky v. Jesse Ellis*. Faced with integration, closing down the state's schools, or equalizing funding, the legislature took the latter course. The General Assembly on April 24, 1882, passed a law, to be voted on by the people, combining the school funds, establishing the same tax rate for blacks and whites, raising the tax rate from twenty cents to twenty-two cents, and abolishing the black poll tax. Most black voters supported the moves. In an August 1882 referendum, the voters of the state adopted the plan by a nearly seventeen-thousand-vote margin. This law, however, applied to state funding and not that of local system. Only Louisville and Paducah appeared to equally fund black and white education with local taxes. Sensing a lack of concern about equalization, blacks in Owensboro tried to enroll some students in a white school. When the students were turned away, they filed a lawsuit. In April 1883, in *Claybrook v. Owensboro,* a federal court ruled discrimination based on the Fourteenth Amendment. Although black and white schools remained separate, "on the surface at least," as far as funding was concerned, they were to be equal. That same year a new state law increased per capita funding for both races. Funds spent on black education doubled, as did per capita spending, between 1882 and the end of the decade. The school age was extended to twenty. Unfortunately, most white Kentuckians, even the best educated, would probably have agreed with a South Carolina Presbyterian minister who claimed that an educated African American "is just as much Negro as before, just the same raw hide volume with the incongruous addition of a gilt edge; he is only a little more aggressively offensive than his less ornate brother."[50]

Bitten by the political bug and cocksure of his abilities and agenda, Henderson sought a third consecutive term in 1879. This time he appeared a bit too zealous even for many Democrats. At the state convention, he ran against Joseph Desha Pickett, a professor who had been president of the Agricultural and Mechanical College and chaplain of the storied Confederate Orphan Brigade. Why all this hullabaloo about the office of state superintendent? With a state budget of more than $1 million, the office was now "regarded by many at that time as the most important in state government." Apparently, Democratic leaders and others were tired of Henderson's seeming arrogance and his ambition, and they swung their votes for Pickett, who won the nomination and ran on the ticket with Luke P. Blackburn. During the general election, rising Republican star William O. Bradley scolded the Democrats for their lack of leadership. "If we would preserve this government for posterity, if we would consecrate this land to Freedom, we must encourage a liberal system of common schools," he said, adding, "The Democratic Party has forgotten the minds of our children." He deplored how far behind the commonwealth had fallen in educating its youth. Notwithstanding Bradley's rhetorical barbs, the Democrats swept the general election as usual, with Blackburn and Pickett winning, and again dominated the legislature. If educational or other reforms were to come at this time, they would have to be generated within the all-powerful Democratic Party.[51]

Like his predecessor, Pickett served two terms as state superintendent, in the administrations of governors Luke P. Blackburn (1879–1883) and J. Proctor Knott (1883–1887). Blackburn, a physician, had served the Confederate cause as an agent, planning and carrying out such schemes as infecting Northern cities with yellow fever. After escaping federal indictment, he returned to the United States and helped fight yellow fever outbreaks in the South. Without much political experience, he easily won the governorship over a weak Republican candidate. Rightly known as "the father" of badly needed prison reform, "lenient Luke" opened the gates of the Frankfort prison for many minor offenders and encouraged construction of a prison at Eddyville. Under his leadership the General Assembly did some good for education by increasing property taxes, reorganizing the Agricultural and Mechanical College, and developing the Board of Health.[52]

With two years' service as president of the Agricultural and Mechanical College of Kentucky University, Pickett had some educational experience, unlike most of his predecessors. His 1881 report to the legislature encouraged textbook reform. Three years later the General Assembly passed a law empowering the state board to recommend a "suitable list of books" for the schools, to be finally approved by the district trustees. In 1888 the legislature gave this authority for final approval to the county board of education. Although both Blackburn and Pickett tried to interest the legislature and the people in adopting local taxation to supplement the state school funds, hard economic times, the aftershock of the Panic of 1873, and agrarian Kentucky's natural conservatism kept this idea from gaining much support. On May 12, 1881, white and black schools at the county level were consolidated into a single system, though still in separate schools.[53]

A sampling of "The Voice of the Commissioners," written comments addressed to Pickett in 1881, illustrated the problems faced by the common school system in Kentucky. While the Bourbon, Boone, and Campbell

County commissioners could point with pride to improved schools, resulting from local taxation in some of the districts under their control, others lamented the lack of foresight in their counties. "The teachers do not get enough pay, and few districts will pay more than free [state] money," said the Butler County commissioner. "There are not enough professional teachers in this county." The commissioners from Jefferson, Johnson, Lewis, McCracken, and Perry counties all complained about inadequate school buildings. The Rockcastle County commissioner found that "many of the log cabins called district schools are places of punishment rather than learning." The Carter County commissioner summed up the problem for many rural districts without local taxation. "Teachers are in great measure made up from failures from other occupations," he cried. "No capable man will prepare himself for a profession that gives employment for only five months of the year at 'starvation prices.'" Knott, Pickett, and others interested in improving educational opportunities in Kentucky faced an uphill battle. Progress would come only with increased funding at the local district level, professionalizing teaching, and, more generally, greater public support.[54]

Governor Knott was more of a professional politician than his predecessor, having served in the U.S. House of Representatives for several terms. He had also unsuccessfully sought the Democratic nomination for governor in 1871 before winning in 1883. Though a fiscal conservative, Knott, according to historian Robert Ireland, turned out to be "one of the most effective governors of the postwar nineteenth century." First, he completed some of Blackburn's penal reforms. The General Assembly complied with his request for tax reform by creating the State Board of Equalization to "equalize tax assessments," reconciling the disparity between market value and assessed value.[55]

When the state legislature failed to pass much-needed education reform in the early 1880s, some private citizens, as well as Governor Knott and Superintendent Pickett, began to look for a better outcome. William Morgan Beckner, a Winchester newspaper editor and lawyer who also served as Clark County judge, became one of the leading and most successful advocates for education reform. Beckner began to coalesce with others on what they called the "school question." Like many other white Kentuckians, he did not go against the racial mores of the day, but he did advocate equal funding for black schools. In a speech titled "A Problem to Be Solved," delivered at the 1882 meeting of the Kentucky Association of Teachers, he "decried" the illiteracy problem of the state. He even pushed the idea of federal aid for education, particularly for such a poor state as Kentucky. Praising "the shrewd, energetic Yankee" states for their educational efforts, in contrast to those of the South, Beckner urged his audience, in strong religious overtones, to "arouse the people until they compelled their representatives to do their duty." Henry Watterson, though he did not approve of federal aid for schools, supported Beckner's call for action, as did the *Louisville Commercial,* a Republican organ.[56]

Beckner led in the organization of an "Educational Convention" held in Frankfort on April 5–6, 1883, that included whites and blacks, Republicans and Democrats. The meeting called for federal action and asked that the Southern Exposition in Louisville set aside two days for a "consideration of the question of common-school education" in the South. Momentum built in the state, with several newspapers taking up the fight. Henry Watterson, in the *Courier-Journal,* praised the effort with his usual pithiness, theorizing that "Public Education doesn't make angels of us, but it does kill off illiteracy." At the Southern Exposition in September 1883, a summit of common school advocates from nearly two dozen states met, and Beckner was elected chairman. At his suggestion the delegates approved a resolution for federal distribution of money based on illiteracy. True to his southern heritage, Beckner skirted the race issue, asking that the money be distributed "under state laws and by state distribution," not by federal agents or agencies.[57]

The Southern Exposition of 1883–1887 highlighted Louisville as a modern commercial center. With technology as its main theme, the exposition housed many exhibits in a two-story wooden building that covered thirteen acres. At the time it was the first such event to be illuminated by Thomas Edison's incandescent light system. The exposition was so successful that it lasted beyond the one year planned.[58]

Beckner soon returned to his first concern, getting legislation through the Kentucky General Assembly. Governor Knott followed recommendations made by a surprisingly successful nonpartisan group that included Beckner, former Union general Don Carlos Buell, W. C. P. Breckinridge, Pickett, and Louisvillian John Mason Brown. They had met in Louisville on April 29, 1883, "to devise a plan for a complete educational organization throughout the state." Its recommendations comprised a general reshaping of the common schools in Kentucky. Knott approved their work and forwarded the recommendations to the legislature.[59]

The Common School Law of 1884 included some but not all of Beckner's and the committee's suggestions. As previously mentioned, the 1884 law specified courses for the curriculum and included health and civil government. It spelled out the requirements for a "uniform system of schools," including length of the school year and the duties of the county and state boards of education and trustees. One of its stipulations was close to Beckner's heart: forbidding sectarianism in the public schools. The law disestablished the county commissioner system, renaming the official superintendent, who would be elected for a two-year term by popular vote in each county. In 1886 the term was changed to four years. The law of 1884 dictated that the State Board of Education would be made up of the state superintendent, the attorney general, the secretary of state, and two members elected by them. The state board was given control over curriculum, courses of study, the new health education initiative, and almost everything else having to do with the common schools. The law required annual county teacher institutes and added a provision to improve school buildings. Books for indigent children were to be paid for by the state board. Beckner called the law "a step forward," but like most other critics of Kentucky's common schools, he found the legislature wanting because of "ignorance and timidity on the one side, and . . . secret hostility to free schools on the other." Most prominently, there was no strong movement to push for local taxation. The state school fund was not enough by itself to improve schools. Only those schools supplemented by local taxes stood a chance to improve significantly in the late nineteenth century.[60]

In Louisville, public school education more closely resembled that north of the Ohio River, because of the infusion of local taxes. With one-tenth of the state's population, the River City spent $250,000 on education annually at the end of the nineteenth century, or "almost a third of the whole cost of education in the state." Therefore, Louisville led the state in academic advances and innovations. Albert Victor du Pont, of the fabulously wealthy and powerful New Jersey family, moved to Louisville in 1854 and made his own fortune in railroads, coal, iron, and steel companies. He helped found a new type of school for Kentucky: vocational education came to the commonwealth in 1892 with the founding of du Pont Manual Training High School, later renamed du Pont Manual High School. The school opened with 121 students and new equipment, comparable with the best in the nation. Before the turn of the century, other educators began talking about adding similar studies, practical courses for the industrial age.[61]

Louisville Female High School, whose name was changed to Louisville Girls' High School in 1912, and Male High School, both founded in 1856, remained committed to classical education in the nineteenth century. Girls' High moved into a new building with four stories and a basement in 1873 and remained there until 1899. Both schools had admission-by-examination policies. Male High, which also moved to a new site in 1899, exposed its students to a traditional nineteenth-century classical education. In 1895 the school's three-hundred-plus students were offered classes in Latin, Greek, German, English, algebra, chemistry, geometry, and political economy. These two schools ranked with the finest in the South and, probably, in the nation.[62]

Louisville also led Kentucky in primary school education. One of the true innovators in late-nineteenth-century Kentucky, Patty Smith Hill, who became interested in primary school education, graduated from the first kindergarten training school in Louisville in 1887. That same year "a group of prominent Louisvillians established the Free Kindergarten Association." By the middle of the 1890s, Hill directed the association's ten kindergartens. She "experimented with the idea that children should be placed in settings that stimulated creative thought and openness" and "used music, poetry, stories, and plays to instruct children." "The world moves forward on the feet of little children," she once said. Hill's ideas even drew the attention of progressive educator John Dewey, who traveled to Louisville to study her efforts. By 1900 kindergarten programs were offered in several Louisville primary schools. That same year Hill spoke to the Louisville Education Association on the subject "Education through Play." She went on to lecture at Columbia University's Teachers College and eventually became a renowned faculty member there.[63]

The Catholic schools of Louisville also led in offering new educational opportunities. Bishop Martin John Spalding presided over the creation of twenty parochial schools, a testimony to Catholic desire for education, before he left Louisville for Baltimore in 1864. The Xaverian Brothers founded St. Aloysius Select School in 1863. A year later it moved and combined with another school under the new name "St. Xavier Institute." It had students from age six through age eighteen in attendance, "largely the children or grandchildren of Irish and German immigrants." In 1890 the school received a new charter, granting it the power to offer college courses as St. Xavier College. In the latter part of the nineteenth century, new parishes were formed along with new schools.[64]

In eastern Jefferson County, along LaGrange Road, Anchorage offered several early educational opportunities. Boarding schools such as Bellewood Female Academy, Pine Hill, and Forest Military Academy taught elementary through high school students but began declining in the latter nineteenth century. Public school education evolved more slowly, as the Anchorage public school, known as "Sleepy Hollow," filled the need for poorer students. Not until 1911 did the town develop enough of a tax base to build the Anchorage Graded and High School.[65]

Louisville played an important role in the development of sports in Kentucky schools. On November 18, 1893, Male and Manual high schools played the first of many football games. Early football games closely resembled the English game of rugby and sometimes amounted to out-and-out brawls. In 1877 the city of Maysville prohibited the playing of football because of the game's violence. Baseball caught on after the Civil War, because many troops had first seen and played the game during lulls in training, maneuvers, and battles. In 1867 professional baseball came to Louisville, and younger men caught on to the game's allure as well; the game quickly became the "National Pastime." "Pickup" games of "sandlot" baseball and football were played in towns and at rural crossroads. By the late nineteenth century, many city or town high schools had organized baseball and football teams. In rural areas young people might have to be content with footraces and other less-organized sports and folk games. The organization of sports into teams and leagues began in the late nineteenth century, a sign of the times, in which many things American became regularized. Basketball did not become a noted sport until the beginning of the twentieth century.[66]

In the latter part of the nineteenth century, the American high school came of age. By the 1880s, the academy was being eclipsed by the public high school as the dominant form of secondary education. When America was primarily an agrarian nation, there appeared to be little need for secondary school education, since most young people went into the workforce as farm laborers. As the nation became more urbanized, particularly after the Civil War, the need for a better-trained workforce encouraged the development of the high school. The high school became an extension of the public elementary school as it developed in a graded form. For some time there was no clear dividing line between the upper level of an academy education and what constituted a college curriculum, but by the latter nineteenth century, curricula were changing. The Committee of Ten, established by the National Education Association in 1892, was given the task of "standardizing the high school curriculum." Its recommendations included making eight years of elementary school and four years of secondary school education the standard for America. Four separate curricula were suggested, including classical, Latin-scientific, modern language, and English, which all came with modifications. The English language high school became the alternative to the Latin school or the academy. "Where a local high school developed as a continuation of the primary or grammar or intermediate school," explained education historian Lawrence Cremin, "it constituted an additional rung on what was increasingly perceived as an American educational ladder."[67]

The public high school in Kentucky followed the national trend growing out of the development of the graded school in urban areas. With school attendance beginning about age six, most children attending schools in the commonwealth's urban areas finished the eighth grade at about age fourteen. With at least four years left of legal school age, it seemed natural for education leaders to expand schools for four more years. Depending on their resources, towns and cities began adding one grade at a time up to the total of four for high school. For example, in 1875 the board of education in Paris added one year of study beyond the eighth grade, to include the study of "Latin, algebra, general history, natural philosophy, and physiology." Covington had begun the process, like Louisville, before the Civil War. Most towns and cities followed the trend set by Paris. Henderson, Owensboro, Cynthiana, Carrollton, Shelbyville, Paducah, Newport, Catlettsburg, Danville, and Frankfort all reported high schools by the mid-1870s. For example, Henderson issued $50,000 in bonds to build a new school that opened in September 1870. In 1898 Ashland completed a new building with a soaring bell tower. Second-class-city Lexington kept pace with educational progress by raising the local tax from ten to fifteen cents after receiving a new charter in 1882. Four years later the city received permission from the state to issue up to $30,000 in educational bonds. Although Lexington continued to expand its public school offerings (it built its "first large consolidated elementary school" at Picadome in 1888 and offered its first kindergarten classes at the Dudley School in 1892), this major central Kentucky city did not open its first public high school until 1905. State superintendents continually urged the development of public county high schools, but by 1900 there were none in Kentucky.[68]

The Kentucky political atmosphere in the 1880s finally prepared the way for the writing of a new constitution. Democrats were able to keep a near stranglehold on Frankfort, electing as governor Simon Bolivar Buckner (1887–1891), a West Point graduate and a Confederate veteran, along with Ed Porter Thompson, another ex-Confederate, who served two terms as superintendent of public instruction (1887–1895). Buckner's opponent, Republican attorney William O. Bradley, ran a strong race, losing more narrowly than previous Republican candidates. Agrarian reform was in the air, and third-party candidates drew votes away from the Democrats. The Farmers' Alliance and populism, promising reform to alleviate pressures on the poorer farmers, swept across the state. Although Buckner had some successes as governor, he is best known for becoming involved in a tragic-comical conflict with the governor of West Virginia over the Hatfield-McCoy feud and the unfolding of a major scandal during his administration, the absconding of Kentucky state treasurer James W. "Honest Dick" Tate. The latter was in his twentieth year as treasurer when on March 14, 1888, he left the state and was never seen again. An investigation soon revealed that he had embezzled upwards of $250,000 from state coffers.[69]

Meanwhile, pressures had been building to write a new constitution for the commonwealth, and the "Honest Dick" debacle tipped the commonwealth's voters in favor of such a step because it could include a provision limiting elected officials to a single four-year term. William Morgan

Beckner played a key role. Elected as a delegate from Clark County to the meeting, scheduled to begin in September 1890, Beckner "arrived at the constitution convention well known as one of Kentucky's most vocal and articulate advocates for public education." During the 226-day session of the convention, he kept up the pressure to improve the stature of education over that of the 1850 constitution. The 1850 constitution had addressed education for the first time, with a feeble attempt at solidifying education's role in the commonwealth and the body politic, but Beckner asked for much more.[70]

Beckner offered the following "portentous addition" to the proposed constitution:

> The General Assembly shall have power, and it shall be its duty, to provide by appropriate legislation for an adequate and efficient system of popular education; and to this end, may fix the terms and conditions on which the common school fund of the State, now existing or hereafter to be raised, shall be distributed. In distributing the common school fund, no distinction shall be made on account of race or color, but schools for white and colored children shall be kept separate. No tax now levied for educational purposes shall ever be repealed or diminished.[71]

Beckner also took a stand for religious rights, proposing a stipulation for the new bill of rights that there should be no coercion on any parent to "send his child or children to any school to which he may be conscientiously opposed." Many issues arose at the convention, including the hot issue of the role of Catholic parochial schools in America. To keep Kentucky from adopting draconian laws restricting Catholic schools, such as in Illinois or Oregon, the convention eventually adopted the ideas of Beckner, who kept up the pressure for creating an "efficient" school system.[72]

On March 11 the delegates to the convention approved Sections 183–89 on education, devised by Beckner and his supporters. Beckner's biographer concluded: "William Morgan Beckner left the convention with his reputation as Kentucky's most visible and vocal advocate for the cause of popular education soundly reinforced."[73]

Tom Clark perhaps best summed up the educational outcomes of the convention. He said, "Where there was a superfluity of orating, debating, and legalistic pawing of the constitutional air, the delegates finally adopted an educational article." Unfortunately, the delegates missed an opportunity to write a long-lasting charter like the U.S. Constitution. In Clark's view, "Kentucky's fourth constitution is not so much a fundamental rule of government as a piece of omnibus legislation." The people of the commonwealth overwhelmingly approved the new constitution, 213,432 to 74,017, with full Republican support and most Democrats in favor.[74]

The sections on education in the new constitution gave the legislature the responsibility to "provide for an efficient system of common schools throughout the state" (section 183). Section 184 defined the Common School Fund and mandated that the fund could not be used for other purposes. All questions of taxation would be "submitted to the legal voters." Section 185 required the General Assembly to pay the interest on the School Fund and control the fund's holding in the Bank of Kentucky. Section 186 described the distribution of the schools fund, giving the General Assembly the power "to prescribe the manner of the distribution of the public school fund." Section 187 gave equal distribution to white and black schools but stated that "separate schools for white and colored children shall be maintained." Section 188 provided for the distribution of federal funds among the schools of the commonwealth. Section 189 concluded the education portion of the 1891 constitution by declaring that "school money" would not be allotted for any "church, sectarian, or denominational school."[75]

Other parts of the 1891 constitution dealing with education included number 5 in the Bill of Rights, the "Right of Religious Freedom." Dear to the heart of William Morgan Beckner, that item decreed that no "man be compelled to send his child to any school to which he may be conscientiously opposed." In Section 91, the state superintendent of public instruction was listed as a constitutional state officer who must be at least thirty years old and who was limited to a four-year term. Election of the superintendent would coincide with the election of the governor. Other sections dealt with taxation.[76]

Superintendent Thompson's eight years in office wrapped around the writing of the new constitution. He was reelected in 1891, at the time of the positive vote for ratification and the election of another Democrat, John Young Brown (1891–1895), as governor. Thompson supported enlightened changes in the educational system of the commonwealth. He opposed the trustee system, pushed for local taxation, and favored central county high schools and compulsory attendance. The greatest improvements appeared to be in the office of the trustee: a law even required that he "must be a man of good moral character, and when not impracticable able to read and write." In 1893 the minimum age of a trustee was set at twenty-one years. However, election in a democratic fashion led to abuses of the system. With the addition of the state diploma in 1893, aimed at improving teacher qualifications, public school education in Kentucky in the mid-nineties appeared to be on the upswing.[77]

Race relations in Kentucky followed a jagged path toward the beginning of the twentieth century. The commonwealth did not adopt the "Mississippi Plan," which included radical measures meant to completely disfranchise black voters through poll taxes, residency requirements, the grandfather clause, and literacy tests. While some Republican leaders in the state continued to support progress for blacks, most Democrats, even of the New Departure variety, thought of African Americans as an impediment to progress. Kentucky, in its conscious effort to become more southern after the Civil War, followed the trend of racial separation by Jim Crow laws. Already the segregation of schools had been codified in the constitution of 1891. The next year the legislature passed the Separate Coach Law, requiring separate railroad coaches for blacks and whites. Other southern states also wrestled with separate-accommodation laws. In 1896 the Supreme Court established precedent when it found in favor of the state of Louisiana in a test case, *Plessy v. Ferguson,* the "separate but equal" dictum that haunted America well into the twentieth century. The sole dissenter in that case, as in the earlier *Civil Rights Cases,* Kentucky native John Marshall Harlan, wrote, "In my opinion the judgment this day rendered will, in time, prove to be quite as pernicious as the decision made by this tribunal in the Dred Scott Case." Although initially struck down by a U.S. district court, the Supreme Court ruled Kentucky's separate-coach law valid in 1900. In *Chesapeake and Ohio Railway Company v. Kentucky,* Harlan again cast the lone dissenting vote. At an ever-expanding rate, the commonwealth joined the rush to implement Jim Crow laws. Towns and cities enacted laws not allowing blacks equal access to public accommodations, parks, housing, and libraries. At the state level, even schools for the blind and deaf were segregated. Moreover, the lynching of African Americans never stopped. "From 1880 to 1940 more than two hundred Kentucky blacks died at the hands of lynch mobs," wrote George C. Wright.[78]

Under these conditions, African Americans in Kentucky made remarkable progress in educating their youth. The education of teachers continued to trouble black educationists as well as whites. After a campaign by the Colored Teachers State Association, the Kentucky General Assembly chartered a normal school in Frankfort, appropriating $7,000 to erect two buildings and $3,000 for teachers' salaries, and the City of Frankfort donated forty acres on a hill on the east side of town on Georgetown Pike. The State Normal School for Colored Persons opened on October 11, 1887, with John Jackson, a graduate of Berea College, as president. Two departments, literary and industrial, trained teachers for elementary schools. In 1890, after federal legislation provided for establishing African American land grant colleges, State Normal developed departments in agriculture and mechanics. The school's name was changed in 1902 to Kentucky State Normal and Industrial Institute for Colored Persons. Location in the state capital kept the school under the direct supervision of the sitting governor, who appointed all the members of the board of trustees. The school did not offer college-level courses until well into the twentieth century. Participation in politics by State Normal personnel could be problematical. For example, when Professor C. C. Monroe spoke out against the Separate Coach Law, he lost his teaching position.[79]

The education of blacks at all levels in the latter nineteenth century led to debates not only over the types of education they should be receiving but also their role in the postwar era. Should blacks accommodate themselves to the mores of the day and accept a second-class status? Or should they more aggressively face the era of segregation? Both views had supporters, black and white, and prominent spokesmen, particularly Booker T. Washington and W. E. B. Du Bois. Washington, the president of Tuskegee Institute in Alabama, argued that African Americans "should first establish an economic base for their advancement." They should first focus "upon the everyday practical things of life, upon something that is needed to be done, and something which they will be permitted to do in the community in which they reside." Vocational education would be the key to black advancement. In a famous speech in Atlanta in 1895, he omitted any mention of politics and apparently endorsed segregation. In contrast, Du Bois, a Harvard-trained professor at Atlanta University, said this was only part of the answer and that a "talented tenth" of black leaders should be educated for leadership roles at the college level. Moreover, he insisted that both political and economic progress could be achieved.[80]

George Wright has found that in Louisville, the largest city in Kentucky and its most dominant economic engine, blacks made few gains in employment between 1870 and 1915. "By 1915 blacks remained underrepresented in the skilled trades and overrepresented as common laborers and domestics." This coincided with "worsening race relations." William J. Simmons gravitated toward Washington's viewpoint. In 1890 Simmons resigned from State University and became president of Eckstein Norton Institute in Bullitt County, named for the president of the L&N Railroad. Backed by several wealthy white Louisvillians, his school offered manual training, including carpentry, farming, cooking, and dressmaking. Charles Parrish Jr. took over at Simmons's death in late 1890. Eckstein Norton Institute's motto, "Education of the hands, head, heart, and mind," fit the ideals of both its white benefactors and its black founders. Central High School, Louisville's only black secondary school, founded in 1874, followed that view as well. Wright concluded: "So despite the proliferation of industrial schools and the emphasis on learning a trade at Central High, blacks often acquired skills that were essentially outdated or, because of racism, were of little use to them." At least in the short run, Washington's view seemed to have more supporters than that of Du Bois. Washington's belief system embodied the idea of "the self-made man." Most people of that era, black and white, believed in that concept, whether fact or myth. "I have learned that success is to be measured not so much by the position that one has reached in life as by the obstacles which he has overcome while trying to succeed," the Tuskegee president said. Was Washington an accommodationist or a realist? The debate still rages over who was right, or at least more correct: Washington or Du Bois.[81]

After implementation of the 1891 constitution, education in Kentucky made little progress in the nineties. The General Assembly updated all school laws, including those for first- through fourth-class cities. Louisville was the only first-class city in the state, and Newport, Covington, and Lexington were second-class cities. A new law in 1891 completed the evolution of city and town boards of education, giving them oversight of all school functions in their districts except that of raising taxes by the city council. State and national politics became embroiled in the silver issue, with Henry Watterson supporting the gold Democrats. Farmers, small businessmen, and laborers were pressed to the wall by the Panic of 1893. This was not a time when voters would think much about raising taxes for any purpose, much less improving education in the hinterlands of Kentucky. "Bonded in a weak philosophical way by a devotion to low tariffs, a limited role for government, and opposition to Republicans," maintained Harrison and Klotter, "Democrats had never had a fully united party." Republicans were more compatible, but they could not muster enough strength to win control of the governor's mansion or the legislature. Populists in the early nineties drew support from both parties, mostly in the western part of the state, but not enough to control the state by themselves. Meanwhile, the legislature, reacting to the new constitution, remained in session to replace old laws and became known as the "Long Parliament." The silver issue continued to agitate the body politic nationally. "Sound money" advocates, those who supported keeping the gold standard, became the enemies of the free silverites. Democrats split over the gold issue in 1895, nominating P. Wat Hardin for governor. Although the party adopted a platform in support of sound money, Hardin, trying to get support from hard-pressed farmers, came out for free silver. William O. Bradley, the Republican candidate, won the 1895 gubernatorial race over Hardin, 172,436 to 163,524, and the Populist candidate, former Democrat Thomas S. Pettit, garnered 16,911 votes. The next year in the presidential election, Republican

William McKinley defeated William Jennings Bryan by 281 votes in Kentucky. For the foreseeable future, Kentucky politics would be competitive and often attended by violence.[82]

William Jefferson Davidson, the superintendent of Pulaski County schools, won the state post in 1895, the first Republican elected to that office. Like most other superintendents in their reports to the General Assembly, he pointed out the abuses that occurred in the district trustee system. "Many men, without special fitness, moral or educational, or without personal interest in the conduct of the school," he argued, "seek positions on these boards either for mercenary purposes or to reward some friend or to turn the school over to some relative." Because the trustees were elected each year, the districts were in constant political turmoil. Davidson, like his Democratic predecessors, maintained that schools would never be able to provide seven months of instruction unless the people of the district voted to tax themselves. And he stressed the need for public normal schools.[83]

Governor Bradley recommended "striking" reforms for education in Kentucky. He wanted to abolish the trustee system, making the "county system" supreme, and even proposed "fairer support for black education" among other progressive measures. Although a weak compulsory attendance law passed the legislature in 1891, with Republicans controlling the House and the Democrats the Senate, little else was done for education by the state's lawmakers during the tenure of "Billy O.B." Students between ages seven and fourteen were to attend school for at least eight consecutive weeks in either a public or a private school. The law was easily evaded, however, and was not enforced in most places. It seemed there were more important things on the agenda of the state and the nation, continued political wrangling over a multitude of issues or fighting a successful war against Spain.[84]

An 1895 report on rural education by the National Education Association fit Kentucky precisely when it "concluded that most normal school graduates—the teachers most sought after and best informed on progressive pedagogy—flocked to the cities, where hierarchy and order were the pillars of the system." Moreover, in the 1890s most poorly prepared rural teachers still relied on memorization and recitation, a modern rendition of the old blab school mentality.[85]

Richard B. Drake, in *A History of Appalachia*, is only partially correct when he declares: "On the pre-collegiate level, each state with Appalachian areas developed an increasingly satisfactory system of primary and secondary students which by 1900 provided a quite respectable education for students in the towns and cities of the region." It would have been difficult to persuade residents of many towns that that assertion was true. More important, the great majority of students lived in the more isolated areas of the region and received much less opportunity for a "respectable education."[86]

In the Appalachian area, a movement began in the last part of the nineteenth century to bring education to a vastly underserved region. Religious and secular organizations, with much the same missionary zeal, found many places with few if any educational opportunities. John Jay Dickey, a Methodist minister, witnessed the worst aspects of mountain behavior and determined to have an impact on the drinking, moonshining, and violence that he saw in several counties. He observed the terrible feuds wracking the region in the late nineteenth century, including the infamous ones such as in Breathitt County. Noting the poor educational opportunities in Jackson, he established a school there in the early 1880s. He had to battle indifferent teachers, immorality, and corruption. In 1887 the school became Jackson Academy, a preparatory arm of Presbyterian-controlled Central University, and the name changed again in 1897 to S. P. Lees Collegiate Institute. Dickey later went to London in 1895 to begin the battle all over again.[87]

At the end of the nineteenth century, a movement known as "settlement schools," akin to the "settlement houses" effort in America's cities, began in Appalachia. Between 1899 and 1901, May Stone and Katherine Pettit, both well-educated central Kentuckians, held summer schools in Hazard and Hindman. Encouraged by their success, they founded Hindman Settlement School, "the first rural social settlement school in the United States," in 1902 in Knott County. In 1913 Pettit along with Ethel de Long Zande founded Pine Mountain Settlement School in Harlan County. Though secular in nature, both founders and their schools exuded a religiosity in fund-raising and teaching. These schools provided much-needed social services as well as education in a residential setting. Other similar schools founded in the first third of the twentieth century included Henderson Settlement School in Bell County and Lotts Creek Community School in Knott County.[88]

Two other mountain schools, Hazel Green Academy and Oneida Baptist Institute, represented another type of school, operated directly by a religious organization. The first town incorporated in Wolfe County, Hazel Green, became the site of a residential school in the 1880s. The idea originated with Lou Mize, the wife of state senator William Oldham Mize, who obtained a charter from the legislature. The National Christian Board of Missions of the Disciples of Christ Church assumed control in 1900. Oneida Baptist Institute, on the Kentucky River in Clay County, opened in 1900. Baptist minister James Anderson Burns, "Burns of the Mountains," believed that the enlightenment of education in a religious setting would cure the area of its violence, made nationally famous in the Baker-Howard feud. Other religion-oriented schools, as well as coal-camp schools, were founded in the early twentieth century to fill the needs not served by public school education in the eastern mountains of the commonwealth.[89]

Kentuckians slowly began to embrace the major national curriculum changes of the late nineteenth century. One area, vocational education, seemed to be encouraging. By the mid-1890s, several schools, for example those in Frankfort and Bellevue, were attempting to follow the example of Manual High School. At the same time, the annual meetings of the Kentucky Education Association discussed ways of improving high school education. The 1895 KEA meeting appointed a "Committee of Ten," made up of prominent educators and chaired by Superintendent John Grant Crabbe of Ashland, to consider in detail what the high schools should be teaching. Kentucky's committee adopted the National Education Association's recommendations, which emphasized "traditional" curricula, including classical, scientific, and Latin-English courses. To be accredited, Kentucky high schools had to follow these guidelines. Ruric Nevel Roark, dean of the Department of Pedagogy at State College in Lexington, suggested in a paper presented to the 1896 KEA meeting "that there must be manual training in the public school, or as it is better named, 'manumental training.'" He did not mean manual training in a modern sense, but "that there should be a training of eye and hand and mind all together." Most Kentucky educators tepidly entered this brave new world of curriculum change. Nevertheless, they at least began a dialogue about vocational and manual training; it continued into the new century.[90]

As Kentucky rushed toward the twentieth century, several key factors depressed the state into further ignominy, centering on the gubernatorial election of 1899. William Goebel, "the most controversial man in Kentucky," rose to a position of leadership in the Democratic Party. A new leader, outside the old Confederate circle, he aroused the best and the worst in political circles, preaching help for laborers and controls over corporations like the L&N. In 1895 Goebel killed a rival in downtown Covington, the base of his power. After the votes were counted in the governor's race, and undoubtedly manipulated by both parties, Republican William S. Taylor apparently won by 2,383 votes and was sworn in. Hundreds of armed men descended on Frankfort. The Democrat-controlled General Assembly challenged the results. On January 30, 1900, Goebel was shot down in front of the capitol. Both sides brought in more armed men as the state appeared on the brink of civil war. Then the legislature, after throwing out thousands of votes for Taylor, declared Goebel the winner. Eventually, the Kentucky Court of Appeals ended the squabble and was backed up by the refusal of the U.S. Supreme Court to intervene. Taylor fled to Indiana, and although several men went to jail, no one was ever sure who really killed William Goebel. The temper of the times was well illustrated when a young girl sent a dollar to the Goebel Memorial Committee with the bellicose admonition, "Won't you please kill the man that killed Mr. Goebel?"[91]

Kentucky was already known as a state with a high murder rate, innumerable mountain feuds, poverty, low education expectations, illiteracy, and a general backwardness, so the occurrence of another violent incident only a few months after the Goebel assassination illustrated that even the "best" of Kentucky's citizens were only a hair-trigger away from mayhem. This incident took place in Richmond. French Tipton, a staunch Republican, and Clarence Woods, an avid Democrat, would have appeared the last persons in the world to engage in violence. Both were progressive and well educated, graduates of Central University, a southern Presbyterian school in Richmond. They had been verbally feuding for years, beginning with the free silver issue, and they ended up arguing the merits of municipal control of the local water company in the pages of two contending Richmond newspapers. "In a fatal encounter" one evening on Richmond's Main Street, Tipton apparently came from behind and struck Woods on the side of the head. The latter fell to his knees and then rose with pistol in hand, firing a shot into Tipton's abdomen. On his deathbed Tipton exonerated Woods from any blame. Woods soon resumed his career as newspaper editor and later served as mayor of Richmond.[92]

The Goebel assassination, the killing of French Tipton, the mountain feuds, and the lynching and suppression of blacks all seemed to be symptomatic of a general malaise in the commonwealth. Something was amiss. Was it a lack of religion, education, or civility, or a combination of all of these? Citizens of the time and historians of the era all point to the decline of Kentucky from its pre–Civil War eminence as one of the leading states of the Union.

What was the state of education in the Commonwealth of Kentucky at the turn of the twentieth century? Whereas 37.4 percent of eligible students attended school in 1860, only 36.3 percent attended in 1900, indicating a nearly total disregard of the compulsory attendance law of 1896. Teachers received paltry compensation on average, $34.10 per month for white teachers and $29.95 for black teachers. Tapp and Klotter concluded that although the commonwealth "ranked high among southern states," education, even with some reforms, "through the 1890s seemed a drab, perfunctory affair indeed." However, there were some dramatic changes in the 1890s. African American illiteracy dropped from 55.9 percent to 40.1 percent. Native white Kentuckian illiteracy fell from 12.6 percent to 8 percent. For all Kentuckians over the age of ten, illiteracy dropped from 29.9 percent in 1880 to 21.6 percent in 1890 to 16.5 percent in 1900. Ligon called the period from 1860 to 1900 one of "marking time." Even with state tax increases for the School Fund, in forty years expenditure per student increased only from $1.00 to $2.45 per capita.[93]

One bright spot was that of Kentucky's 714 black high school students in 1900, 93 graduated that year, a number that led the South. By 1907 a higher percentage of blacks than of whites attended high schools. However, there was little progress in racial reconciliation, and Kentucky remained very much a southern state in attitude and action. The commonwealth's leading editor and opinion-maker, Henry Watterson, had the same beliefs as most white Kentuckians, educated or illiterate, consciously or unconsciously, on the matter of race. The old ex-Confederate fully accepted black citizenship as long as it was subordinate to the will of his own race. His most recent biographer explained it this way: "He argued that the best way to approach domestic race relations was with the 'supervision and benevolent assistance of white men.'"[94]

Furthermore, Tapp and Klotter found that "economically, Kentucky entered the twentieth century in the same relative condition that had existed in 1865." Although there had been a rise in farm tenancy, Kentucky probably had the best, most diversified farm economy in the South. Again, comparisons with the South now proved crucial.[95]

In summation, if a student, black or white, lived in a town or city, her or his chance of getting a decent public school education was good. Louisville, with one-tenth of the school population, spent about one-third of the total money spent for education in the entire state. But rural students, unless their parents could afford to send them to live in a town or at a residential school, typically received a rudimentary education at best. That was not enough to benefit from the increasing economic opportunities of the twentieth century.[96]

The early life of Louisa native Frederick Moore Vinson, thirteenth chief justice of the U.S. Supreme Court, illustrated that opportunities for a creditable education existed in Kentucky for those who took advantage of what was available. His education straddled the end of the nineteenth century and the beginning of the twentieth. Vinson liked to say that he was born in the Lawrence County jail (his father was a jailer there). His education included the "free run" of the jail and the courthouse. In his county-seat town, he was allowed to "romp in and out of the judge's chambers and sit lazily in the open courthouse windows on hot summer days listening to lawyers matching forensic eloquence." From an early age he determined to become a lawyer and got an education in the real world. At the tender age of four, he surreptitiously took his father's hatchet to a prisoner who he had decided "had done nothing to merit durance vile." The prisoner immediately returned the hatchet to Fred's father. Though a somewhat indifferent student at times,

Vinson displayed a love of reading, devouring everything in the local library. He played baseball whenever possible. The railroad station and the river wharves on the Big Sandy also contributed to his education. His mother "always encouraged her son's interest in school and reading, silently enduring his passion for baseball." After attending elementary school in Louisa, where "his teachers continued to be impressed with his brilliance and unusual intellectual promise," he went to high school in Catlettsburg, including the local normal school. He continued his love of reading and baseball, even considering a career in the nation's pastime. However, an education at Centre College, graduating from the law school in 1911, catapulted him into the profession of law. He served in Congress as a Democratic member in the House of Representatives and became a strong supporter of Roosevelt's New Deal. Truman appointed him secretary of the treasury and later to the Supreme Court in 1946, where he served until his death in 1953. Vinson's early education may have represented the best of the practical, observing and participating in his environment, as well as formal schooling. No doubt the love of reading was his forte.[97]

There were signs of educational progress since the Civil War. County superintendents were now elected for four-year terms with some qualifications added; the trustee system had been modified so that there was only one trustee per district; and teacher certification was now established at the state level, with an examination controlled by a board of examiners. Although most teachers continued to be paid based on the number of students in their care, they were a little better trained than in 1860. There was hope for better things in the new century because a groundswell of opinion was urging improved teacher education via annual institutes and public normal schools.

Chapter 4

Higher Education in an Age of Flux

On August 7, 1869, Professor Joseph Winlock, director of the Harvard College Observatory, trained what was said to be the third-best telescope on a college campus into the heavens. With this twenty-five-hundred-dollar device, Winlock and a cadre of Harvard professors and scientists from the U.S. Coastal Survey gazed into the heavens and took eighty-five timed photographs as a total eclipse of the sun took place. "Eight minutes before the total phase the usual phenomena of distraction among birds of the air and cattle occurred," a newspaper reported. "When the sunlight commenced to become dim, a large number of citizens rushed to the college grounds, the headquarters of the observers," the newspaper piece continued. "Six minutes before totality, a deadly ashen hue overspread the countenances of all present, and for awhile the faint-hearted were terrified. The scene during the totality was an awful one, and when the sunlight appeared again a shout of exultation went up from the great crowd on the college grounds." During the total darkness, a highly visible shower of meteors added to the spectacle.[1]

The location of these observations might surprise the reader. "The great crowd on the college grounds" was not in Cambridge, Massachusetts, the home of Harvard University, but in Shelbyville, Kentucky, and the telescope belonged to Shelby College. *Harper's Weekly* reported the story on its front page and included a photograph of the several telescopes aimed at the sky, the most impressive being the one owned by Shelby College. Eight of Bostonian J. A. Whipple's photographs revealed the phases of the eclipse of August 7.[2]

This vignette would appear to denote a strong institution with vibrant support. But the facts were otherwise. Beginning as Shelbyville Academy in 1798, the school demonstrated many characteristics of its type in nineteenth-century Kentucky. Never adequately funded, it became Shelby College in 1838, floundering along its way as an Episcopalian school with a theological school appended. Military instruction, the arts and sciences, astronomy, and other courses did not lead to growth. Several lotteries failed to sustain growth of the school. Actually, the school as a "college" had already ceased to exist by August 1869; it had reverted to town control. After one more effort to form a college in Shelbyville, St. James College, the main building on "College Street," became a graded school. In 1939 the old Shelby College building was razed, becoming the site for Northside School. (The author attended elementary school in that building from 1947 through 1952.)[3]

Kentucky higher education struggled in the era from 1860 to 1900, particularly during and just after the Civil War. Old colleges failed as newer schools, some founded as secondary schools in the mold of the old academy system, slowly moved toward offering college curricula. Masonic University, originally founded by the Grand Lodge of Kentucky in 1842 as Funk Seminary, a high school, foundered on the rocks of hard times. It ceased to exist on May 1, 1873, when the property and bequest of benefactor William Funk returned to high school status in Oldham County. But other colleges survived. Transylvania University, Centre College, and Georgetown College revived slowly after the Civil War. Schism brought on by the slavery issue and the Civil War continued to divide Kentucky churches, leading to the founding of new colleges. In the public sector, what eventually became the University of Kentucky took a circuitous path toward its founding. Normal school education in Kentucky evolved more slowly than in northern states such as Wisconsin. But over time, Kentucky colleges in the late nineteenth century began to incorporate courses of study for teachers, as elementary and secondary education became more distinct. Although little progress was made in racial integration, by the end of the century coeducation came to several colleges.[4]

Nationally, an "emerging national consensus" after the Civil War began to place greater importance and emphasis on education. Cremin found that in the latter nineteenth century "there was a drift in educational policy toward ever greater reliance on the schools and colleges as institutions of social reform and uplift." William T. Harris, "a philosophical idealist" who served as superintendent of the St. Louis School System and later became U.S. commissioner of education, worked for improvement in educational opportunities for America's youth and wrote extensively about the topic. As children finished "elementary" schools, they entered "high" schools as more and more districts extended the grades. In *The Theory of Education*, published as the nineteenth century closed, Harris championed progressivism in education. He claimed, "The sooner we can make a youth able to pursue his course of culture by himself, the sooner we may graduate him from the school." In his view, "education should excite in the most ready way the powers of the pupil for self-activity." Harris, like many others in this optimistic age, believed that the United States offered an unusually fertile ground for the rise of the "common man," but only if education fulfilled its key role in a democratic society.[5]

Just as it did for elementary and secondary education, the onset of the Civil War disrupted higher education in Kentucky. A sometime battle zone, the commonwealth's colleges suffered along with those in the Deep South when marauding armies moved across the countryside. While most colleges remained in session, it was not without difficulty.[6]

Tempers ran high on both sides. Georgetown College closed down in 1861, when its students marched off to war. After the school's doors opened again the next year, Georgetown College officials refused to grant a diploma to "a young Mr. Grant," judging him to be "a violent secessionist." That same year Confederate general John Hunt Morgan recruited several students from the college as his forces paused briefly in Georgetown on a raid through the Bluegrass. Two years later, in 1864, Georgetonian Union general Stephen Gano Burbridge, nicknamed "Butcher" by southern sympathizers in Kentucky, had three Confederate "prisoners of war chosen at random and shot in Scott County in reprisal for alleged guerilla murders." Dwindling to only 35 students in 1863, by 1870 enrollment rebounded to 145 at Georgetown.[7]

Other Kentucky colleges also struggled through the war years. The failure of the normal school idea at Transylvania appeared to sound the death knell for the idea of a university in Lexington, "the Athens of the West." The Academic Department limped through the Civil War as Transylvania High School. After the Battle of Perryville in fall 1862, the Union army took over Morrison Hall and the other Transylvania buildings as hospitals, where, as historian E. Merton Coulter explained, "the groans of the wounded and the dying filled the classic halls which had so often echoed to the logic of Holley, the fire of Bascom, or the eloquence of Clay." Medical Hall rather mysteriously burned on May 22, 1863, and wounded and ill soldiers were successfully evacuated. Medical equipment and library books were consumed. After 35 men graduated from Centre College in 1860, 28 graduated the next year, as the war set in. More Centre men joined the Confederate forces than those of the Union. In 1866 only 11 men graduated at the Danville campus. This small school was hit particularly hard by the war, which caused the deaths of twenty-six Centre College alumni and students.[8]

Although Bacon College transformed itself into Kentucky University by charter from the General Assembly at the insistence of John Bryan Bowman in 1858, it did not prosper. While 150 students matriculated in 1859, by 1863 that number was down to 62. KU operated in Harrodsburg until a fire on February 10, 1864, destroyed its only building. Bowman began considering moving the school to Louisville, Covington, or Lexington. Mercer County donors and supporters voiced strong opposition when KU's board of curators decided to relocate the institution in Lexington. With the Civil War continuing to stress higher education as well as life in general in Kentucky, discussions were taking place on how to resuscitate both Kentucky University and Transylvania. The boards of both schools began serious negotiations about merger.[9]

Even before the war ended, there were negotiations to create a new university, building on the past. The result would be a "new hybrid institution," something never envisioned before the war began. Bowman, a graduate of Bacon College and the founder of Kentucky University, believed the time was ripe to develop a new major western university, one that would surpass even the dreams of the old Holley days at Transylvania University. He wanted something that would make Kentucky an educational center, in contrast to the "scores of unendowed, half-starved, sickly, puny institutions, called colleges and universities," in the western states. In short, Bowman wanted what was then developing as "an amalgam of the emerging American university," one that was broad-based and well funded and would include all areas of study. Questions remained about how the new school would be founded. Many Kentuckians had opinions on the topic. Former governor Beriah Magoffin urged that the state "make no union of Church and state."[10]

With Transylvania University and Kentucky University nearing a merger, another part of the new "hybrid" institution came into play. Bowman again led the way. The Kentucky General Assembly found a way to take advantage of the Morrill Act, passed by Congress in June 1862, when the southern states, opposed to such federal legislation, were in revolt. The Morrill Act built on previous laws passed between 1796 and 1861 providing federal land grants to states for the support of higher education. This new law specified a gift of thirty thousand acres of public land for each member of a state's congressional delegation. Because Kentucky had no public land remaining, the state would be granted "land scrip" on western public domain. The land would then be sold in order "to fund advanced instructional programs." Only the principal from the sale of the land, "safely" invested, could be used for the "endowment, support, and maintenance of at least one college." The state then had to establish "collegiate programs in such 'useful arts' as agriculture, mechanics, mining, and military instruction—hence the 'A&M' [usually Agricultural & Mechanical] in the name of many land-grant colleges." Military training was required, because of the current hostilities, but courses in the traditional liberal arts were not excluded.[11]

As the idea of taking advantage of the Morrill Act surfaced in Kentucky to found a new partly public, partly private institution, old wounds reopened when the curators of Transylvania opened their school to hosting such a college. KU founder Bowman and Madison C. Johnson, chairman of the Transylvania board, met in Frankfort to iron out plans of merging their two schools. Transylvania's Disciples of Christ leaders worked the legislative halls to secure the merger. Bowman envisioned something larger, the continuation of his dream of a major university in the West, and he also lobbied members of the General Assembly to pass enabling legislation. Combining a state-funded college with the moribund Transylvania, along with Kentucky University, a Disciples of Christ institution, found stout opposition among Baptists, Methodists, and Presbyterians, "who accused the Disciples of Christ of having used state resources to further their own sectarian ends." The idea of state tax money going to a quasi-public institution infuriated Baptist Richard M. Dudley, who argued that the money could be better spent on the public schools of the commonwealth. Moreover, residents of Harrodsburg and Mercer County were still angry about the removal of Kentucky University to Lexington.[12]

Nevertheless, the General Assembly passed a law on February 22, 1865, enabling Kentucky to benefit from the Morrill Act. A second act six days later merged Transylvania with Kentucky University, using the name of the latter for the new amalgam of higher education in Lexington. The state laws stipulated that KU must raise $100,000 on its own in order for the acts to take effect. Regent John B. Bowman soon gathered more than $125,000 in pledges for the project. He used the funds to purchase two Lexington estates, the Woodlands and "Ashland," the Henry Clay estate, totaling 433 acres. When the A&M College opened on October 1, 1866, 190 students enrolled.[13]

"The dream of Regent Bowman for a great state university embracing all departments of learning and preparing young men to take their places in American life in all the professions seemed about to be realized," asserted a historian of Bacon College. Each of the one hundred state representative districts could send one student to KU tuition free. A&M College existed as a separate college within the framework of KU. Cornell University in New York followed a different course, as a completely secular school under the leadership of Ezra Cornell, Andrew Dixon White, and Liberty Hyde Bailey in its early years.[14]

The revived hybrid Kentucky University was an initial success, with A&M being an entirely new venture. KU opened before A&M, in the fall of 1865; classes were held for the first time in the College of Science, Literature, and the Arts, the Ministerial College (soon to be known as the College of the Bible), and the College of Law. Retaining his title of regent, but without the title of president, Bowman served as KU's chief executive. Old Morrison Hall on the former Transylvania campus echoed again to the sounds of lectures and student chatter. Many of the 297 students who had enrolled by mid-September had just returned from war service. One of them, J. H. Stover, believed that they were mostly diligent. "No college or school, in my opinion, ever had a larger percentage of studious men than the class which entered Kentucky University in 1865," he said. Within five years more than seven hundred students attended all the schools within the KU framework, public and private. Bowman wanted an affordable college education for all and tried to keep costs low.[15]

Kentucky, like many eastern states, sold its land scrip allotment too soon and for too little, but it did receive about $165,000, which brought in an annual income of nearly $10,000 from the investment of the principal. The price received by the commonwealth fell somewhere between the lowest return per acre of Rhode Island (41 cents) and that of New York ($6.73). Bowman was disappointed, particularly since he was one of the greatest supporters of the Morrill Act. In addition, students paid an annual fee of ten dollars, and KU received income from the sale of crops and the making of equipment. A&M used the Tilford home at Woodlands for classrooms and assemblies. Students drilled nearby under the watchful eye of the unsalaried Regent Bowman, who moved into Henry Clay's home. The early faculty included Dr. Robert Peter, who combined thirty years of teaching chemistry at Transylvania with another three decades at A&M. James G. White taught mathematics, and James K. Patterson, who had been principal of the high school at Transylvania during the Civil War, taught history and moral philosophy. In 1868 the school received a windfall when G. W. N. Yost donated $25,000 to build the Ashland Mechanical Building after using the campus to test the prototype for his new mowing machine.[16]

Three years after A&M opened, James Kennedy Patterson, under the benevolent eye of Regent Bowman, became its first official president. A native of Scotland, Patterson found his way to Lexington at the beginning of the Civil War to become principal of Transylvania's high school. Serving from 1869 as president of A&M through several transitions until 1910, when the University of Kentucky entered its modern period, Patterson has been described as a "dictator," a "benevolent dictator-president," a "benevolent despot," a "somewhat cantankerous educator," and the "master of his domain" by various observers and historians. Education historian John Thelin places a high value on Patterson's leadership in a particularly difficult time in higher education, believing he deserves "his rightful place in the history of American higher education." There is little doubt that Patterson knew what A&M should become. As the history of A&M and its later permutations unfolded, Patterson proved to be insightful as well as spiteful.[17]

Initially, more students attended A&M than the other colleges of KU. They worked hard, studied long hours, and drilled daily on the field, as required by "the semimilitary regimen mandated by the Morrill Act." Those who wanted or needed to work extra made ten cents an hour for on-campus labor. A "Jacksonian agrarian," according to one of his biographers, Bowman believed that by working, a student, particularly one engaged in the study of agriculture, gained a greater appreciation of the effort that went into production. Because Bowman wanted to allow as many students as possible to attend KU, he believed that student work would ensure that even the "pauper" could get an education. His devotion to the Christian Church an overriding feature of his life, Bowman made sure that Sunday was taken up with church attendance by his charges. He even vilified Thomas Jefferson for founding the University of Virginia without a strong Christian ethic.[18]

Bowman believed he could build on the past efforts before the Civil War and construct "a first class university" in the West. His vision appeared limitless, as when he wrote, "We want ample grounds and buildings and libraries, and apparatus, and museums, and endowments, and prize-funds, and professors of great heads and hearts, men of faith and energy. Indeed, we want everything which will make this institution equal to any on this continent. Why should we not have them? I think we can." Only a few students completed their studies in the early years, however; William B. Munson was the first A&M graduate, in June 1869.[19]

The disruption of the Civil War and its aftermath did not deter Kentuckians from developing new colleges. Methodists, never happy with the Disciples of Christ control over Transylvania, had tried to control the Lexington school as well as founding Augusta College (1825–1849). In 1860 the General Assembly chartered Kentucky Wesleyan College, sponsored by the Kentucky Conference of the Methodist Episcopal Church, South. After being disrupted during the Civil War, six years later the school opened in one building in Millersburg, Bourbon County. With most Kentucky Methodists loyal to the ME Church, South, Kentucky Wesleyan College perfectly fit the postwar southern tilt of Kentuckians. Building on the already existing Millersburg Male and Female Seminary, a high school, Wesleyan president Dr. Charles Taylor knew well the obstacles he faced in founding a new college.[20]

Ninety students showed up for the first session at Wesleyan, the majority signing up for the preparatory department. Students in the college sessions received a general liberal arts education, with classical studies in Latin and Greek, mathematics, and the sciences. Those studying for the ministry took Hebrew and biblical literature courses. Emphasizing the liberal arts from the beginning, the school also offered courses to prepare students for business and education. Wesleyan also developed a military program. However, in what might be the first example of successful student activism in Kentucky, the program ended after one year when ministerial student Alexander Redd led a student revolt against the "military regime." Like most such schools, Wesleyan suffered from insufficient funding, particularly since the Louisville Methodist Conference still had a strong northern influence.[21]

Changing leadership and the lingering divided nature of Kentucky Methodism dogged Wesleyan in its first decades. The controversial presidency of "wheeler dealer" Rev. Benjamin Arbogast nearly destroyed the school, breaking a tenuous alliance between the Kentucky Conference and the Louisville Conference. The new president, John Darby, carried out the necessary "damage control" and soon restored "the moral and financial credibility of the college," according to the historians of the college. Financial crises came and went; the growth of the "holiness" faction among Kentucky Methodists caused more problems on the Millersburg campus. With endowment dropping while enrollment grew steadily under president David W. Batson, more and more supporters agreed that Millersburg was not the best place for the college. Perhaps the last straw was the growing holiness presence in Millersburg. In any case, discussions began about moving the school to a more hospitable town.[22]

In 1890, after a challenge by Millersburg supporters, Kentucky Wesleyan moved to Winchester. That same year another Methodist school, of a more conservative holiness nature, formed after Rev. Henry Clay Morrison, a conservative Methodist revivalist, led a long revival in Wilmore. This was just the opportunity that the holiness faction had been looking for. Rev. John Wesley Hughes, who had long opposed the "worldliness" of traditional Methodist education, organized successful fund-raising for the creation of Kentucky Holiness College, a quasi-Methodist though officially nondenominational conservative school. In 1891 Hughes and Morrison, its first president, changed the name to Asbury College, after the famous early-nineteenth-century Methodist circuit rider. Contentiousness rocked the Asbury campus early on, when some students urged the dismissal of a professor because at one time he had been a priest. President Hughes defended the professor in chapel, but one hundred students walked out in protest. At the end of the school year, the professor resigned.[23]

Methodists also looked for other regional fields of service. Union College began in Barbourville in 1879, founded by local citizens who figured that their town also needed a college. Founded with a stock company, the school represented several religious denominations in the town, "hence its name, Union," and the Union College Corporation. With a new building the next year, the school opened in 1880 but floundered six years later. The Kentucky Conference of the Methodist Episcopal Church purchased the property in

1886, under the leadership of Rev. Daniel Stevenson. Actually, he attended the sale of Union and took it upon himself to buy it outright; then the Board of Education of the Methodist group bought it from him. Stevenson became Union's president. A graduate of Transylvania in 1847, he served as state superintendent of public instruction from 1863 to 1867, during the crucial years of the Civil War and Reconstruction. Upon the death of President Stevenson in 1897, Rev. James P. Faulkner, a Union alumnus, became the new chief executive.[24]

As denominational turmoil between northern and southern branches of Protestant churches roiled the religious waters in Kentucky, southern and northern Presbyterians vied for control of Centre College after the Civil War. During the war a majority of Kentucky Presbyterians supported the southern cause. Old warhorse Robert J. Breckinridge led the northern faction. "Southern Presbyterians," under the new designation of Presbyterian Church in the United States, came under the guidance of southern sympathizer Rev. Stuart Robinson, who had been forced to flee to Canada during the war, and lawyer Bennett Young, who had led the raid from across the Canadian border on St. Albans, Vermont. At stake was control of Centre College and the seminary in Danville as well as some key churches. After the northern faction won control of Walnut Street Presbyterian Church and Centre through litigation, the southern group formed the Alumni Association of Central University. With passage of enabling legislation by the legislature in 1873, Central University took its first halting steps toward independence.[25]

Centre College went off on its own, perhaps the most elite college in the state with its small theological seminary as an appendage. T. T. Crittenden, later governor of Missouri (1881–1885), and Adlai E. Stevenson, vice president under President Grover Cleveland (1893–1897), both in the class of 1855, praised the school as well as the town of Danville as fundamental to their successful lives. In 1865 only thirteen students entered Centre College, and the following year the number declined to eleven. President Ormond Beatty (1868–1888) led Centre during difficult times. However, the school proved to be resilient, even surviving the theft of about $60,000 of its bonds in 1873. That sum, representing about two-thirds of its endowment, encouraged renewed and successful efforts to raise more funds for the Danville school. After former governor J. Proctor Knott went to Centre in 1890, the school began a law course, and Knott, known as one of the commonwealth's best lawyers, became dean of the School of Law in 1894. In 1888 William C. Young, the son of a former president, replaced Beatty. With increased endowment and "the liberality" of Louisville supporters, Centre opened a new library in 1894, when enrollment had grown to nearly two hundred.[26]

Little seemed to change on the Danville campus after the Civil War. Most of the students came from Kentucky, but there was a smattering of out-of-state students, mostly from north of the Ohio River. Beginning in 1888, Centre hired an agent "to actively canvass for students." The majority of students as well as graduates continued to be from the Bluegrass state. Most of Centre's alumni stayed in the state, the largest percentage of graduates going into law or other professions. One study of late-nineteenth-century Centre indicates a slight shift from "a socio-economically elite segment of society" to a more broad-based one. As student population increased, "these students of lesser means needed financial aid and cheaper housing." However, the well-to-do continued to come to Centre, particularly from Danville, Boyle County, and central Kentucky.[27]

Georgetown College also survived the postwar years. Weathering the pre–Civil War controversies and the Campbellite attack, which led to the founding of Bacon College, had proved its hardiness. President Nathaniel Crawford served briefly at the school after the war. The coming of President Basil Manly, a professor at Southern Baptist Theological Seminary, in 1871, gave Georgetown a strong administrator and devoutly orthodox Baptist leadership. Upon arrival he found about 145 men on campus, "though most were freshmen and academy students," and four teachers. With only three buildings on campus, Manly immediately began an endowment and building campaign. He remained at Georgetown College until 1879, returning to SBTS when that seminary moved its campus to Louisville. Dr. Richard M. Dudley became president of Georgetown College in 1880 and served until his death in 1893. The first Georgetown College graduate to become its president, Dudley pushed for an increased endowment. During his administration, a library, a new chapel, a gymnasium, and a new dormitory for women were constructed.[28]

Central University struggled to find its niche in post–Civil War Kentucky higher education. Although an endowment drive oversubscribed its goal of $150,000, the Panic of 1873 struck Kentucky hard, so actual cash dribbled into the new school in much smaller quantities than had been promised. Initially choosing Anchorage in Oldham County as its site, Central University settled in Richmond after Singleton P. Walters and several other Madison County residents made the largest pledges to the cause. Richmond Presbyterian minister Rev. Robert L. Breck accepted the post of chancellor. He argued that the new school would appeal to "the southern-ness among a people homogeneous," referring to the overwhelming majority of southern Presbyterians in the state. In September 1874, Central opened in Richmond with a College of Philosophy, Letters, and Sciences and a preparatory school.

In its first year enrollment fluctuated, and only thirty-six students finished the second semester. The Richmond school eventually added preparatory schools in Jackson, Elizabethtown, and Middlesboro. A law school never found much favor, although a theological school in Louisville competed with its northern rival in Danville. The most successful arms of Central University operated in Louisville as schools of medicine and dentistry. Receiving support from the Louisville community, these professional schools graduated thirteen hundred physicians and dentists through 1901.[29]

Crises abounded as Central competed with Centre and other Kentucky colleges. Like all other Kentucky institutions of higher education of the time, it struggled with finances as Kentucky's economy fluctuated. Central had difficulty competing with nearby A&M College because of that school's cheaper tuition. Chancellor Breck, unable to resolve Central's financial woes, resigned in 1880. Another Presbyterian minister, former rebel chaplain Lindsay Hughes Blanton, took over as chancellor. For a while Central appeared to prosper. Main Building, later known as the University Building, a president's home along "Faculty Row," as well as a gymnasium and Memorial Hall, a dormitory paid for by Presbyterian women, added to the campus feel along Lancaster Avenue in Richmond.[30]

A few miles south of Richmond in Madison County, a campus antithetical to the southern-oriented Central University struggled to maintain its mission of Christian education for African Americans. Most white Kentuckians totally opposed the education of blacks in an integrated environment. Only the efforts and money of the American Missionary Association, an affiliate of the Congregational Church, and New England and northern midwestern philanthropists stood between continuing operations and closing the school. Although Berea College operated briefly (in name only) as an elementary-secondary school shortly before the Civil War, the first college students, four men and one woman, entered in 1869, the year Oberlin graduate Edward Henry Fairchild became president.[31]

In early February 1869, John G. Fee told a receptive New York City audience that the school was off to a good beginning. Emphasizing the Christian educational nature of Berea, Fee said the school had "near two hundred students, and near half of them white, the others colored. They are harmonious in a permanent degree." Even then, it operated primarily at the elementary and basic normal school levels. College education for blacks and whites became increasingly important. From 1873, when the first college students graduated, until 1889 and the end of Fairchild's presidency, "there were fifty-six graduates of the college, ladies', and normal courses." Berea's primary function in the late nineteenth century continued to be educating poor blacks and whites at the elementary, secondary, and normal school levels. "Between 1869 and 1892, when William G. Frost became president, the number of college students was never higher than 42," declared Berea historian Shannon H. Wilson.[32]

Berea graduates spread across Appalachia, Kentucky, and the nation as educators and ministers and in other professions. African American John Bate, who graduated in 1881, came out of slavery to found schools for blacks in Danville. Often referred to as "Kentucky's own Booker T. Washington," Bate continued his work until he was eighty-five years of age. Brothers James and Henry Bond distinguished themselves as Berea graduates, James as a minister, teacher, civil rights leader, and Berea trustee, and Henry as an educator and lawyer.[33]

Kentucky blacks also believed in self-help, taking the initiative to found a school in Louisville, a center of African American population. The General Assembly of Colored Baptists received a charter from the state legislature for a new school in Louisville in 1879, to be called the Baptist Normal and Theological Institute. H. C. Marrs led the effort and brought on board his brother Elijah P. Marrs as the first leader of the school. Whites became interested in the school. The American Baptist Home Missionary Society gave small donations to the school, as did the Walnut Street Baptist Church and the Southern Baptist Theological Seminary, both in Louisville. William J. Simmons became president in 1880. The school began offering college courses in 1882 and soon added law courses, and in 1883 it was renamed State University. The Louisville National Medical College trained African American physicians from 1888 to 1912 and merged with State University in 1907. How effective was Kentucky's only African American–controlled college? "State University, despite its limitations, was important to black Louisville," according to historian George C. Wright. "It was their own institution, something they had created."[34]

In the latter nineteenth century, Kentucky higher education continued to be segregated by race (except briefly at Berea College) and divided by religion. Although Louisville and northern Kentucky had the largest Catholic populations in Kentucky, Catholics did not found a major college or university as they did in other major urban areas. However, Catholics continued to treasure education as part of the Americanization process and their rise in American society. St. Joseph's College in Bardstown, first controlled by the Jesuits and then by the Xaverian Brothers, suspended educational work from 1862 to 1869. Both St. Joseph's College and St. Mary's College struggled financially without endowments, being funded only by tuition. Bishop William George McCloskey, realizing that one strong school would be better than two weak ones, merged St. Joseph's with St. Mary's College at Loretto in Marion County in 1890. The only male Catholic college in Kentucky in the late nineteenth century, St. Mary's stressed commercial education as well as the sciences and other liberal arts. St. Mary's College was conducted by the Fathers of the Resurrection.[35]

Two colleges in Bowling Green—one for men and the other for women—organized after the Civil War eventually became part of Western Kentucky State Normal School. Founded in 1877 from a bequest of a wealthy resident of Warren County, Ogden College began as a preparatory school. Slowly, college curriculum was added in the last two decades of the nineteenth century, leading to a B.A. degree. Financial constraints kept Ogden from growing, although it even added athletics teams eventually. It survived until 1928, when it was subsumed by Western Kentucky State Normal School. Potter College, a private nondenominational school for women, opened in 1889. Enrollment never rose above about two hundred students in the school's liberal arts and commercial classes. Potter closed in 1909, and its property became part of Western.[36]

Late-nineteenth-century public schools evolved from grammar schools into high schools by adding more years of education, and Kentucky colleges developed similarly. Most of them began as high schools and added college courses until they emerged as schools of higher education.

The history of Bethel College, with campuses in both Hopkinsville and Russellville, exemplified much that animated Kentucky higher education. Beginning as a Baptist-sponsored high school for girls in Hopkinsville, it developed slowly, being rechartered in 1890 as Bethel College. Bethel College in Russellville began as a boys' high school before the Civil War, again sponsored by western Kentucky Baptists. Later superintendent of public instruction James H. Fuqua (1903–1907) graduated from Bethel College and served as professor there on two separate occasions. In 1928, as Bethel Female College, the school in Hopkinsville became a junior college; it was again renamed Bethel College in 1951, when it admitted men for the first time, consolidating the Russellville and Hopkinsville campuses. In 1964 Bethel closed, when the Kentucky Baptist Convention diverted funds from it to help found a new school, Kentucky Southern College in Middletown.[37]

The spirit of entrepreneurship also animated Kentucky higher education, as proprietary professional schools opened in the late nineteenth century. Following a flourishing national trend, business educator Enos Spencer founded Spencerian College in Louisville in 1892. The school adopted the task of training office workers in an increasingly business-oriented age and slowly evolved into a college in the twentieth century. A trade school of another type operated briefly in Shelbyville. The Morse School of Telegraphy began there in 1884; in 1901 it joined Ross College of Lexington but still operated in Shelbyville. Open to both men and women, the school prepared both railway and commercial operators. It included military drill for male students as well as an orchestra and a debating society. As the telephone developed, the need for telegraph operators declined, and Ross College, after changing hands, "disappeared" in 1903.[38]

A plethora of other "colleges" in the second half of the nineteenth century deserve at least a brief mention. Most evolved out of a high school, seminary, or academy until they eventually used a true college curriculum. Some flourished for a brief time and then folded. Some, like Logan Female College in Russellville, Gethsemani College in Bardstown, Shelby College in Shelbyville, and Eminence College in Eminence, eventually failed to prosper and faded away. Eminence College advertised itself in 1870 as a "mixed school" (coeducational, in other words), which was quite daring for that early date. The rationale was simple: "God, who created man, and thoroughly understood the wants of his being, saw that it was not good for man to be alone, and all human experience attests the truth of Divine omniscience, that there is no period of man's existence, from the cradle to the grave, when it is good for him, either morally or intellectually, to be alone—apart from the refining presence of the opposite sex." The majority of graduates at Eminence College were women; for example, in 1870, of the thirteen graduating, eleven were women. Even the addition of business and normal courses could not save Eminence College, and it closed in 1895. Daughter's College in Harrodsburg later evolved into Beaumont College, which lasted until 1914. Established as Hocker Female College in 1869 in Lexington and later renamed Hamilton Female College in 1878, Hamilton became an appendage of Kentucky University in 1889. Hamilton served as a women's junior college, feeding its students into KU, and developed a reputation for its strict social rules. In 1903 Kentucky University took over Hamilton completely. Several colleges that developed in the twentieth century grew out of late-nineteenth-century high schools. Cumberland College evolved from the founding of Williamsburg Institute in 1889, Pikeville had its origins as Pikeville Collegiate Institute in 1889, and Sue Bennett College opened as a high school in London in 1897.[39]

Who attended these colleges? The sons and daughters of the middle classes predominated in Kentucky's schools of higher education. College enrollments grew slowly as the increasing number of students, at first male and then female, in the commonwealth's public and private secondary schools, many of which still operated as academies and seminaries in the pre–Civil War mode, graduated and moved on to college. Moreover, most colleges had their own academies, or preparatory departments, until the end of the nineteenth century. Most often, these departments had more students than the collegiate ones did. Hopkins, in his early history of the University of Kentucky, declared the academy at A&M and then State College to be entirely necessary, "since it bridged the gap between college and secondary school at a time when the curricula of the latter left much to be desired and were not uniform across the state." Most applicants to State College before 1896 had to pass an exam based on the curricula of the academy. Slowly, Kentucky colleges began admitting students without examination from "accredited" high schools. Although most colleges had not only entrance requirements but also entrance examinations, students were not turned away, if they could pay for their education and agreed to take what today we would call remedial work. Central University also planned a system of "feeder" schools. In addition to the one on the Richmond campus, S. P. Lees Collegiate Institute in Jackson (begun in 1891), Hardin Collegiate Institute in Elizabethtown (1892), and Middlesboro University School (1896) ultimately failed to push enough students toward the Central University campus. Some critics of this dual system of education claimed that the on-campus academies "tended to lower the tone on the campus." Centre College, Central's competitor for Presbyterian control of higher education in Kentucky, grew by using a recruiting agent as well as beginning to accept more students from a lower socioeconomic level.[40]

Tuition varied in Kentucky colleges from as low as $20 a year at State College and Asbury to $35 at Union, $45 at Georgetown, $50 at Centre, and $55 at Bethel. Although these sums appear small today, raising this much money proved difficult in a basically agricultural cash-strapped economy suffering major depressions brought on by the panics of 1873 and 1893. In addition, students had to pay room and board, often in private homes at rates of three to five dollars a week. Young Kentuckians, perhaps the most affluent, continued to find opportunities for higher education outside the commonwealth. The University of Virginia still drew Kentuckians, as did Washington and Lee, which had a Kentucky enrollment of 10 percent in 1871. Such schools as Johns Hopkins University in Baltimore became the leading dispensers "of higher learning to Southern scholars in the last quarter of the nineteenth century." Most college students, except perhaps those at Berea, easily identified with southern mores. "The aura of the Confederacy, of course, was everywhere," concluded one historian about Central University. Those same sentiments would have been found on most Kentucky campuses. Louisville, which had been a Union stronghold during the Civil War, became more "southern" in the late nineteenth century. Lexington, with a 39 percent black population, remained a racially divided city, with the "Lost Cause" mentality pervasive among the white population, young and old, student and nonstudent.[41]

College life continued in the late nineteenth century much as it had before the Civil War. However, it began to change in the eighties and nineties with the admission of women. Campus authorities tried to keep a tight rein on their charges, whom they expected to behave like Victorian and Kentucky gentlemen and gentlewomen. All the colleges spelled out exact rules in written forms and at meetings. At Central University Archie Woods, a member of the first class in 1874, complained to his father that he never had time for anything but study. He observed that two students soon quit school because the faculty was so strict, "you have to come right to the mark in everything." Students at Central had to attend daily morning prayer services and at least one Sunday service. Under the "benevolent" dictatorship of President Patterson, State College also had strict rules as part of its military environment. From reveille at 5:30 A.M. until taps at 10:00 P.M., college officials expected a student to be in class, on the drill field, or under other campus scrutiny. Otherwise they were to be in their rooms studying, not fraternizing in their rooms or hallways. At State College, "the steady knock of Patterson's wooden leg as he checked on his scholars would soon dispel any such thoughts of loafing, however," declared Tapp and Klotter. Actually, he had a lame left leg, not a wooden one. It was crippled from an accident at the age of four, and he used a crutch that would have a made a "steady knock" on the floors of State College buildings as he inspected his fiefdom.[42]

The strictures at all the colleges extended to card games and billiards. Central students were forbidden to visit downtown Richmond billiard parlors and to smoke or drink on campus. When Georgetown College enlarged Pawling Hall, new rules became more specific than ever: "There must be no card playing, swearing, vulgar language, boisterous laughing or talking, whistling, wrestling or any unnecessary noise in any of the rooms or halls of the building. No slops or trash must be thrown from the windows. There must be no congregating in the halls for any purpose." At State College in Lexington, students received demerits if found smoking or playing cards. Demonstrating that no separation of church and state existed at the time, State College students also were expected to attend Sunday services. As conditions changed, so did the rules and regulations. When some Central students apparently failed to pay their bills in Richmond stores, the 1883 General Assembly passed a law forbidding local merchants to extend them credit. Wesleyan officials prohibited students from even leaving Millersburg without permission; if a student withdrew from school, he had to exit the town immediately. All Kentucky colleges required regular class attendance, which according to their records must have been a problem.[43]

At coeducational Berea College, "restrictions regulated associations with the opposite sex even to the extent of walking across campus or attending the same classrooms or religious services. 'Calls of gents upon ladies' were limited to twice weekly in the ladies parlor and then only when chaperoned." Men found a way around "the two-visits per week restriction simply by courting different women." Two males "worked the system to perfection, occasionally 'flipping a cent' to decide which women they would visit." At least for a short time, interracial dating was permitted, though again under the strictest of rules. While many Kentucky college students worked to help pay for their education, every Berea student had to work each day. Such tasks must have left its students more tired than students on other campuses. Berea restrictions included the possession of firearms.[44]

Of course, rules were made to be broken, some infractions merely the frivolities of youth and others more serious. According to one historian, "college life was born in revolt." Since the Middle Ages, conflict has existed between students and faculty, much of it due to the differences in age. Many students believed that almost any action in academic life, including cheating on examinations, was perfectly legitimate, if not moral or ethical, in order to gain advantage over the faculty and to keep them from controlling their lives. The antagonisms at Central University, faculty versus students, fraternities versus nonfraternities, athletics versus literary societies, town versus gown, were found in all other Kentucky colleges as well.[45]

College codes of behavior clashed with students' wills and high spirits. At State College, for example, students put a horse on the second floor, which housed the chapel. When a committee of faculty gathered to study this misdemeanor, "some of those same students secretly hurried out, removed the wheels from the committee's carriage and returned quietly to their rooms." Central University students had their own versions of these pranks. On more than one occasion, they painted the president's carriage horse with alternating black and white stripes to make it look like a zebra. Other times they took a calf or a cow to the roof of the Main Building. Observers reported that it was much more difficult to entice the animal to walk down the steps than up. Drunkenness and gambling usually led to immediate expulsions. One observer who attended Central said, "I saw more drinking at Old Central University from 1884 to 1899 than at all the universities I have visited."[46]

Although Centre began to make adjustments to postwar intellectual change, particularly the onslaught of Darwinian science, it remained staunchly Presbyterian. Bible courses continued to be a centerpiece of the curriculum. Students were dismissed for infringements of rules such as intoxication and carrying firearms. Pranks like stealing "a hand car of the railroad" led to quick dismissal. The campus YMCA provided activities, mostly religious, that also included an opportunity to meet local girls, well-chaperoned, of course, in the male-dominated Centre environment. Ever rebellious, like their peers at other Kentucky colleges, Centre students on one occasion painted the word "SALOON" on a cloth over the door of the

YMCA reading room. The faculty had its own ways of countering youthful foolishness. Daily chapel brought all the Centre community together. "Each morning, one hundred adolescent and energetic males were expected to ignore their peers and morning thoughts and concentrate on the solemn words of the adult world," explained one historian of the school. Sometimes, the students would look for diversions like rolling marbles across the floor "with the assistance of many feet." [47]

Former slave and Union Army veteran A. A. Burleigh at Berea College proved to be particularly independent, primarily because of his age. In late 1873 he came under harsh criticism by the faculty for several offenses, including "his outspoken hostility to the rules, indifference to his studies and to church attendance, and threatening a teacher." With Fee's support of Burleigh, the situation was resolved. "Burleigh grumbled but the two sides eventually made peace." Berea students Charles Norton and William E. Barton pulled off one of those amazing episodic pranks that only college students could design: "They wrote Charles Guiteau, the assassin of President James A. Garfield, asking for his autograph." To their "chagrin," Guiteau read the letter during his trial in mid-January 1882 and "released it for publication in the *New York Herald*." Other students, friends of Norton and Barton, got involved and made effigies of the two miscreants. At first Norton and Barton went along with the prolonged joke, which included building a wooden monument to make it look as if they had been killed by a mob. When the incident became the subject of downtown Berea talk, things got out of hand. Norton and Barton discovered their funeral notices in the Berea post office. Then tempers flared when other students placed whips "in the reception room, with their names attached, and a card stating: 'a rod for a fool's back.'" After an ensuing "tug of war" over the whips, "President Fairchild called Barton and Norton to this office and told them flatly: 'This thing must be stopped.'" And it stopped. [48]

Students at Kentucky University on the old Transylvania campus lived under the same in loco parentis atmosphere that prevailed at other colleges. At KU, problems seemed rampant. As John Wright explained in his history of Transylvania, "One student in 1870 seemed intent to encompass all the sins. He was dismissed for 'carrying a concealed weapon, . . . engaging in an angry controversy with a fellow student, and . . . visiting in the company of a fellow student, a house of ill-fame near the College premises, this visit having been made in open day in the view of many of his classmates.'" That same year, James Beauchamp "Champ" Clark, who went on to become an important member of the U.S. House of Representatives from Missouri and the Speaker of the House from 1911 to 1919, got involved in what started as a friendly quarrel. After a tussle in which one young man pummeled Clark while he was being held by another student, Clark reached under his bed, where he had hidden, he said, "an old revolver, whose cylinder would not revolve except by hand manipulation, for which I had swapped a German grammar and a French grammar. I got that and fired at Webb. Thomson knocked up my pistol hand and the bullet went about an inch above Webb's head and lodged in the door-casing. That ended the fight." Unfortunately, it also ended Clark's career at KU in his senior year. However, he received compensation in 1917 when Transylvania awarded him an honorary Doctor of Laws degree.[49]

Time-honored traditions of college life could also turn violent. Pitched battles by students over some object, such as a class flag, appeared on many college campuses in the late nineteenth century. As reported by the *University Hot Times,* an underground student newspaper at Central University, during the "Great Flag Rush" of 1900, a war between students ended with a coalition of juniors and freshmen defeating seniors and sophomores. Fisticuffs probably took place, and some students were undoubtedly injured, but no public reports were made of them. Charges and countercharges ensued for hours that evening, with thoughts about study far from students' minds. Flags were torn down and burned. Powerless to stop such events, the faculty usually waited out the tumult before assuming control. Sometimes State College suspended classes on flag rush day, when hundreds of Lexingtonians would crowd the campus to see the mayhem.[50]

"The Hallowe'en riot of 1906" by State University students in Lexington got completely out of hand. After capturing a policeman patrolling the campus, the rioters moved downtown and placed on a streetcar line a "huge stone" that led to a wreck and injuries. They moved along breaking street lamps, and a violent confrontation ensued between students and Lexington policemen. After a stone thrown by a student struck a police captain in the mouth, explained James Hopkins in his history of the early years of UK, "the police charged; sticks, stones, fists, and revolvers were brought into use; and when the melee ended, four policemen lay injured and seven boys were under arrest." The next year President Patterson preempted possible holiday rowdiness by removing the patrolman from the campus and putting the young men "on their honor" to find a more wholesome amusement, and they apparently did.[51]

Conditions at the mostly private colleges in Kentucky differed little from those at State College. Students could be just as disruptive and obstreperous at either. At Kentucky University and Central University, student cheating remained a great concern of the faculty. At the turn of the century, Transylvania initiated an honor system. President Blanton's career at Central University exemplified some of the problems of a college administrator as well as a father. When his son violated campus rules, the faculty "voted that Dr. Blanton be requested to withdraw his son W. E. Blanton from the college." In another incident Blanton clashed with faculty over their voting the expulsion of a student accused of cheating. Bowing to the wishes of the young man's father, a prominent Kentuckian, Blanton vetoed the faculty action. Only the intervention of the university's Board of Curators settled a potentially explosive situation. In a compromise, the student received a brief suspension and then returned to CU. After graduation he became a respected citizen.[52]

Kentucky higher education, if a little late, followed most of the national patterns of the late nineteenth century. In a "nation of joiners," students sought their own organizations, just as the Moose, Elks, Eagles, Masons, and others gave adults a sense of belonging. Faculty feared secret societies, hence the reluctance to sanction Greek letter fraternities except under direct administrative control. Centre College probably had the first fraternity in the state, Delta Kappa, which organized in 1856 and was absorbed into Phi Delta Theta in 1879. Kappa Alpha, Sigma Chi, Sigma Alpha Epsilon, and Delta Kappa Epsilon had organized by the end of the century, but even then the YMCA on the Centre Campus continued to draw in nearly all the males on campus. At first operating sub rosa, the first fraternities became officially sanctioned at Central University in 1883, including Sigma Alpha Epsilon, Alpha Tau Omega, Sigma Nu, Delta Kappa Epsilon, and Phi Delta Theta. Kappa Alpha and Pi Kappa Alpha arrived on the campus of Kentucky University (Transylvania) in the nineties. Sigma Chi and Kappa Alpha came to State College in 1893. Georgetown did not allow fraternities until 1904. Berea College never permitted fraternities or sororities. Sororities did not appear on Kentucky college campuses until after the turn of the twentieth century. Fraternity-nonfraternity rivalries accompanied these new institutions. At Central University groups with whimsical names such as the Suicide Club, the Dynamite Club, the Ancient Order of Bloody Toughs, and the KHB Eating Club formed to combat the alleged snootiness of the literary societies and fraternities and flourished for a brief time.[53]

The early gains of A&M proved difficult to sustain. "By 1878, when the college separated by legislative fiat from Kentucky University," said historian Carl B. Cone, "it had graduated only 14 of the 2,200 who had enrolled during that period." By 1878 enrollment fell to only 68 students. There were several causes for this decline. First, A&M required student labor, the number of hours a week depending on the amount of fees paid by the student, and the labor itself may have become onerous for some. Then there was more physical work than true scientific study and applications of agriculture. "Moreover, the Spartan existence may have been more severe than some were willing to endure," Cone suggested. With total expenses at $200 a year, including the cost of a military uniform, the expenses of an education became prohibitive for some students.[54]

The hybrid of Kentucky University, a quasi–Disciples of Christ university with the Morrill Act–sponsored public Agricultural and Mechanical College as an appendage, never seemed to work well. Regent Bowman's dream of founding "a great state university" in the west, encompassing all studies and professions, ultimately failed. Controversy over control of A&M by a denominational school could not be quelled. With the Disciples of Christ controlling the College of the Bible as a part of Kentucky University, Baptists and other sectarians never let the issue rest. While the board of curators of KU refused to allow Bowman to resign in 1873, four years later they removed him both as regent and as board member. The Kentucky General Assembly got into the fray. Governor James B. McCreary (1875–1879) urged separation of A&M from KU, and the legislature concurred in the "divestiture." New governor Luke P. Blackburn (1879–1883) threw his support behind the new school. A legislative commission studied the problem and recommended the obvious, that A&M would be better off as a separate entity. Henry Watterson, editor of the *Louisville Courier-Journal* and one of the most influential men in the state, backed the creation of a completely public college/university in Kentucky. Renamed State College, the school remained on the Ashland and Woodlands properties until 1879, when it moved to South Limestone Street. Historian John D. Wright Jr. lamented about "the second failure of Kentucky within a half a century to erect a first-rate institution of higher education." However, it is difficult to see how such an institution as Kentucky University, with all the impedimenta of politics and religion, could have survived for long. Transylvania between 1780 and 1878 was never "public" in the modern sense. "Mixed-governance" of the school never worked well or for any length of time. Linda Raney Kiesel maintained that Bowman's "inordinate self-confidence, which at times bordered on hubris, may have much to do with his decision to follow a sectarian course in the face of Kentucky history and national trends." However, he "lived to regret his original decision to keep the school under sectarian governance." "He was a broken-hearted man, ill in body and in spirit," when he lost his dream.[55]

When A&M separated from Kentucky University in 1878, prospects did not look very bright, because "the school was bereft of all financial support except for its meager land-grant endowment of less than $10,000. It had virtually to start over again under the leadership of Patterson." John Thelin's belief that James Kennedy Patterson deserves "his rightful place in the history of American higher education" is echoed by historian Linda Raney Kiesel. "Patterson differed from Bowman in his approach to the issues and problems that besieged the early land-grant schools, but he was able to build on Bowman's vision of a great university. . . . While it may have been inevitable that Kentucky would have a land-grant institution, it was not inevitable that it would survive. To this end, the state owes James Kennedy Patterson."[56]

The new law incorporating State University, codifying Kentucky's first fully public college of higher education, provided for a twelve-member board presided over by the governor. The law stated unequivocally: "Agricultural and Mechanical College shall forever remain a State institution free from all ecclesiastical entanglement of control." Admission was to be based on competitive examinations, and one student from each representative district would receive free tuition. State University, called by most people State College, remained in Lexington because that city outbid Bowling Green. With $50,000 in city and county bonds, a small endowment, and a half-cent state property tax, prospects looked brighter for the new school, with "benevolent despot" President James Kennedy Patterson continuing at the helm. Most important for the new State University, it could now issue teaching certificates in its normal department. The idea of the normal school originated in France as the *école normale*, or a training school for teachers, giving then the rudiments of teaching skills.[57]

However, the private denominational schools in the state found a common cause in opposing State College. With tuition of only twenty dollars, State College easily offered a cheaper quality education than the private schools. In 1881 the presidents of Central University, Georgetown, Kentucky Wesleyan, Bethel, and Centre published *A Protest from Some Private Institutions against State Aid to Their Rival in the Field of Education.* They asked, "Do the people of the State desire to drive these institutions from the field and replace them with a costly State institution supported by special taxation?" Blanton at Central University declared, "The mass of the people everywhere are against taxation for college education." The private colleges argued that the tax benefited only a few in the state at the expense of a "poor boy" who wanted an education. This "surprise offensive" against State College eventually led to litigation. But the private-school presidents met their match in Patterson. President Patterson of State College lobbied the legislature and once delivered a two-and-one-half-hour impassioned testimony in defense of his school and the new tax before the General Assembly, ending with this peroration: "Let Kentucky rouse from her slumber, shake off her lethargy, and in the provision which she makes for the education of her sons dare to be free." Defeated in the legislature, the opposition went to court. The cases dragged on until 1890, when the Kentucky Court of Appeals finally declared taxation for support of State College to be constitutional. In the long run the citizens of the Commonwealth of Kentucky did indeed support having a public college, and the legislature and the courts bowed to their will.[58]

The admission of women added a new dimension to several Kentucky college campuses and prompted the first halting steps toward breaking the bounds of Victorianism. Although Oberlin pioneered coeducation before the Civil War, colleges in the South were slow to follow this growing trend. Some women's colleges, such as Caldwell College, Hamilton Female College in Lexington, and Potter College, remained separate, for a while, into the next century. Moreover, at some Kentucky colleges, women were already attending female restricted sections before the colleges became fully coeducational. In 1884 women at Georgetown Female Seminary received permission to attend classes with men at Georgetown College in a few courses. Even in sedate Georgetown, the times were changing. When President Dudley's daughter Myra graduated from the seminary in 1887, she chose for her parting essay the topic "Pin Thy Faith on No Man's Sleeve, Hast Thou Not Two Eyes of Thine Own?" Two years later women began receiving baccalaureate degrees like the men at Georgetown, and in 1892 the seminary fully merged with the college. In the same year, women attended Wesleyan for the first time; the following year there were 22 women in the total enrollment of 134. Other colleges were also allowing women to enroll. Transylvania admitted women in 1889. Centre did not admit women until much later. After some discussion of uniting Caldwell Institute with Centre in 1893, "the proposal was dropped when Centre's Board showed no enthusiasm." That year Caldwell conferred its first baccalaureate degrees.[59]

When the Kentucky General Assembly passed legislation authorizing the normal department at State College, it prepared the way for admission of women to the commonwealth's only "white" state college. The new law allowed each county to send one student of either sex to State College, with free tuition, for an education as a teacher. Men could live free in the dormitory, but "women appointees apparently received no boarding allowance." In the session of 1880–1881, 43 women entered as part of the class of 234. Among these young women was Sophonisba "Nisba" Breckinridge, the daughter of W. C. P. Breckinridge, a Civil War veteran, newspaperman, and Kentucky congressman. She went on to attend Wellesley College and then became the first woman to receive a law degree from the University of Chicago. Patterson's account of opening the school to women differed from those of others. The crusty president said that he favored such a move and, with the aid of the chair of the board of trustees, Judge William B. Kinkead, persuaded the board to allow women on campus. Nisba Breckinridge credits her father and "several gentlemen" in Lexington with encouraging the admission of women to the normal course, which soon opened the rest of State College to them. Terry L. Birdwhistell, in a study of women at State College (the University of

Kentucky) from the earliest admission of women, found that Patterson was a realist and understood that the admission of women would add revenue "for the struggling college. The President was no maverick, but he repeatedly showed that he would do most anything to assure the continued existence of his college."[60]

The admission of women to State College gave the school an immediate source of revenue, and female enrollment increased quite rapidly. When the forty-three women entered in 1880, they made up 18 percent of the total enrollment; the next year women made up 23 percent of total enrollment. The percentage varied from then to 1900, reaching as much as 28 percent in 1892–1893. In 1884 Leonora Hoeing received a normal school certificate, and women were already enrolled in other programs at State College. Belle Clement Gunn, who became the first woman to receive a degree from State College in 1888, also served as vice president of the female literary society Philosophia. Gunn, a Lexington native, when asked by President Patterson if she preferred to sit separate from the male graduates, replied, "I've been through four years of classes with them and I don't see why I shouldn't sit on the platform with them now." While female attendance at State College increased rapidly, a dormitory for them was not built until after the turn of the century. "The absence of a women's dormitory naturally limited their enrollment," concluded Birdwhistell. Women began to excel at the Lexington school from the start, two becoming valedictorians in the nineties.[61]

The admission of women to colleges strengthened the schools by increasing enrollments, adding to revenue, and bringing Kentuckians into a new age of higher education. In the case of Central University, it almost saved the school. In 1887 the first females, Elizabeth Barbour, the daughter of Professor L. G. Barbour, and Bessie McDowell, graduated with diplomas, not degrees, meaning that they had been in attendance for a one-year course of study. In 1893 the Board of Curators gave the chancellor the power to admit any "young lady" who resided in Richmond or Madison County and who passed an entrance examination. Barbour graduated the next year, as did another woman, S. Russell Letcher, who graduated magna cum laude. Letcher was described in the *Atlantis*, the student publication, with proper Victorian verbiage by an obviously male writer as follows: "Her dignified and graceful figure, dark hair and brown eyes, fair complexion and irresistible beauty command universal admiration." Women became a more common sight on campus and in Central's organizations. Near the turn of the century, Kit Chenault graduated magna cum laude with a bachelor of letters degree. Paradoxically, a graduation picture shows her and the men graduates seated and wearing hats and holding canes symbolic of their accomplishments, as southern "gentlemen." Women not only entered the halls of Central as students; Elizabeth Fauquier held the chair of elocution and oratory in 1897–1898.[62]

Student "extracurricular" activities of the late-nineteenth-century Kentucky college campus ranged from the serious to the frivolous. Literary societies, debating clubs, and oratory contests contributed identity and a spirit of competitiveness to most campuses. Every campus had student publications, sometimes even underground, unsupervised by the faculty. Literary societies, some dating from before the Civil War, predominated until the beginning of the twentieth century as the focus of campus activities. As late as 1897, Centre College's Deinologian Society had a library containing five thousand volumes, more than the college library had. Literary societies usually took names of Greek or Roman origin, such as Periclean, Cecropian, Philalethean, and Epiphyllidian. Rivalries ensued between such groups as the Union and Patterson societies at State College. Competition took on the aura of an athletic event. At Central University the literary societies dressed in contrasting uniforms, each wearing either a red or white sash. In an 1898 clash, they debated the topic "Resolved: That the flying machine would be beneficial to mankind." The affirmative side won. Founded in 1887, the Intercollegiate Oratorical Association held annual contests with sometimes controversial outcomes. Competitions were held between literary societies on every campus, and the new Opera House on Broadway in Lexington became the scene of contests between the colleges. Scouting of opponents before a contest took place. Squabbles over rules and even the number of and composition of judges led to ill feelings. The editor of the *Central News* cried sour grapes when the venerable President Patterson complained about the judging of an oratorical contest that Central won. Another time, "about forty State College students" and others from Kentucky University attended an event in Georgetown that would choose that college's representative in the upcoming intercollegiate contest in Lexington. The Lexington students were vocal enough that the judges delayed their decision until the next day so that the rivals, local and outsiders alike, would not be able to raise a ruckus. State College considered suspending both intercollegiate oratorical and athletic contests in the mid-nineties because of what it considered overemphasis on such activities and the distraction for students. Alas, some students were even caught gambling on the results of such contests.[63]

A thought-provoking book by Kolan Thomas Morelock, *Taking the Town: Collegiate and Community Culture in the Bluegrass, 1880–1917*, explores the synergic interaction of the collegiate community with a central Kentucky town, Lexington. In the era before the impact of modern and widely attended entertainment and athletic contests, high culture was acceptable to most people in central Kentucky. Student life could be disruptive, because of the students' penchant for pranks as well as the minor violence of flag rushes, and at the same time could set the pace for cultural leadership. Student cultural activities, including literary and oratorical contests, were town and not just college events, and this contact extended into the surrounding central Kentucky community. For example, after Henry Duncan Jr., of Kentucky University, gave an oration titled "The New South," the *Lexington Leader* announced that "hats whirled in the air, the band played gaily, cheers resounded from pit to dome, . . . the ladies even shed tears from excess of joy, . . . and constituents of Kentucky University and the Lexington people in general yelled themselves hoarse, stamped until the air was thick with dust, and clapped their hands red." This was not just journalistic hyperbole, because Morelock found that "this same remarkable public spectacle would be repeated and embellished over the next decade and would become a regular, almost yearly feature at the [Lexington] opera house through 1903." Moreover, the winner of the oratorical contest "would be hoisted on the shoulders of his fellow literary society members" and carried through downtown Lexington "in an exuberant victory parade."[64]

Following a national trend, Kentucky college students began taking an increasingly avid interest in athletics. Athletic competition began with what we call intramurals today, but intercollegiate sports soon became an important part of life on several Kentucky college campuses, so quickly in fact that college officials, particularly faculty, argued against "overemphasis" in the 1890s. As one historian of Centre College declared, "Centre College was a man's world. Full of high spirits and virility, the male undergraduates found great rewards from the battlefields of college sports." Football and, to a lesser extent, baseball became the centerpieces of the new rivalries between Central University, State College, Georgetown, Wesleyan, and Centre. These colleges participated in what one education historian has called "the Rise of Football" in the late nineteenth century.[65]

Although undoubtedly unstructured "sandlot" games existed earlier, on April 9, 1880, Kentucky University (which later returned to the name Transylvania) met Centre College in the first organized football game in the state. With fifteen players on a side, if a player left the field of combat with an injury or to rest, he could not be replaced. Perhaps played in a cow pasture that later became Stoll Field, the game was won by KU, 13¾ points to 0, before a crowd estimated at five hundred, who paid fifty cents' admission each. The first match between American colleges took place at Rutgers in 1869, but this one in 1880 may have been the first intercollegiate match in the South. Before long Centre was playing State College in sometimes not-so-friendly matches. By 1900 Centre was paying its coach "a salary not to exceed $700."[66]

Late-nineteenth-century football was a violent sport. Players wore only light padding and no helmet, although some protected their noses with rubber pads. With two forty-five-minute periods, no forward pass, three downs to make five yards, and goals 330 feet apart, the game resembled rugby, its progenitor, more than modern football. Five points were granted for a touchdown and two for a "kick for goal." The game was a rough contest of pushing and shoving. Unfortunately, the "flying wedge," for which several teammates locked arms and hurled themselves at their opponents as interference for their ball carrier, became a standard tactic until outlawed because of its danger to life and limb. Meanwhile, Walter Camp and others began to modernize and "Americanize" the game. As the sport became popular, some towns outlawed the game for a short while, as Maysville did in 1877. There was conflict over the eligibility of players, sometimes with "ringers" playing for several teams and for pay. And college officials began to realize that winning meant as much to alumni as it did to students.[67]

In 1881 Kentucky University and Centre split two games, but there is little record of games after that until the next decade. Berea College and Kentucky Wesleyan also began fielding football teams, but they apparently played only local teams. Beginning in the fall of 1891, Central University fielded a team after receiving a blood-inscribed sheepskin from Centre challenging them to a game. The Centre faithful shouted, "Rackyte Cax, Cowax Cowax; Rackyte Cax, Cowax Cowax; Hooray, Hooray; Centre; Centre; Rah! Rah! Rah!" Most of the Central team played in the first game of football they had ever seen. One Central player described the fray as "a rough-and-tumble battle with plenty of slugging, kicking, and gouging." They played without substitutions—Central had only eleven players—and, as this player recalled, wore baseball uniforms. When asked if he was hurt during the contest, he replied, "Oh, hell, yes." Centre won that game by one point but fell to Central the next year by the same margin. In 1892 State College fielded a team for the first time, with geology professor Arthur Miller as the first coach, "on the assumption that because he had attended Princeton, he knew something about the game." When engineering students enclosed a field on which to play this new, somewhat mysterious game, they had to relocate the "cows belonging" to President Patterson. Later in the year, State College's new coach, who had played at Purdue, participated in one game as a player because no rule prohibited him.[68]

In 1893 the Kentucky Intercollegiate Athletic Association was formed. That year Central defeated Centre, Kentucky University, Georgetown, and State College, winning the mythical state crown. State College's campaign the same year included a 56-0 win over the University of Tennessee, beginning a long rivalry. Central also played out-of-state teams, including Vanderbilt and Sewanee, as part of the Southern Inter-Collegiate Athletic Association. The rivalries between Centre, State College, and Central sometimes led to ill will, charges of using "ringers," and on- and off-field fisticuffs. State College faculty nearly disbanded the football team in 1896 but eventually relented while asserting their control. By far the best Kentucky college team of the nineties was the 1898 State College squad. Nicknamed "The Immortals," it defeated all its instate rivals en route to a perfect 7-0 season, outscoring its opponents 181-0. That same year, in another first for Kentucky, the description of Central's game with Centre in Danville was sent back to the Richmond campus via telephone. During that game Central's supporters may have used a favorite cheer: "Chew tobacco, eat tobacco, drink lager beer! Cen-tral Uni-ver-si-ty! We're all here!" Football was here to stay, with slogans, nicknames, and cheers becoming commonplace as well as fancy uniforms and the adoption of school colors. "Who knows," queried noted education historian John R. Thelin, "what rationale led Georgetown College of Kentucky to imagine itself in pink and gray, with the peculiar nickname of 'The Flying Parsons'?" Other sports, including baseball and track for men in the 1890s and the beginning of women's basketball after the turn of the century, all added to the athletics boom in Kentucky colleges. Moreover, athletics began to catch the interest of college officials, who slowly began to view sports as important for public relations and a method to connect with alumni. In 1899 the Centre board of trustees protested that both the baseball and football teams "have been beaten badly. Our men are physically light and unable to cope with the robust representatives of other institutions." The next year they hired a professor who, in addition to his modern language classes, coached football. President Patterson at State College in the 1890s opposed sports, but they caught on in spite of his disdain.[69]

In the late nineteenth century, Kentucky colleges reacted to the changes taking place in curricula, emphasizing technology and new courses. At State College, President Patterson encouraged curriculum change. After the school moved to South Limestone Street, the establishment of the Agricultural Experiment Station and of a department of mechanical engineering brought State College closer to the land grant school trends across the nation. Faculty increased more rapidly than enrollment. New majors in English, ancient languages, and history replaced "the old classics curriculum," with anatomy and physiology added in the nineties. However, the agricultural program, despite adding a master's degree, developed very slowly at State College, which did not confer its first B.Agr. degree until 1898. The Department of Veterinary Science, created in 1891, had to be abolished five years later because of a lack of student and public interest. During this period the study of civil and mechanical engineering proved much more successful than the study of agriculture at State College.[70]

Hopkins, in his history of the University of Kentucky in its early years, maintained that "Patterson's relationship to his staff was that of a high school principal to his teachers, rather than that of a college President to a Senate of professors." Most faculty members were loyal to Patterson, whom the students (behind his back, of course) called "He Pat," to distinguish him from his younger brother Walter Kennedy Patterson. The latter the students called "She Pat," because the younger brother "had once held the position of assistant matron of the girls' dormitory and had served as principal of the Academy and the Preparatory Department." The older Patterson, who most often appeared proactive, took preemptive measures to support the special tax for his school, writing editorials and appearing before the legislature. His vision of State College extended beyond Bowman's. Patterson thought State College should become a true "comprehensive" university, one that encompassed higher learning beyond that of a liberal arts college. As noted, the study of agriculture at State College got off to a slow start. Patterson wanted the scientific study to extend to graduate programs. Soon after he took over from Bowman, he ended the student labor program, arguing that it did nothing to educate students for a career in scientific agricultural pursuits.[71]

Patterson fully supported and worked for federal legislation beyond the first Morrill Act. He visited other land grant schools and hired agriculturalist Melville Amasa Scovell to head the experiment station at State College. Two years before passage of the Hatch Act of 1887, to fund experimental farms, Patterson had helped organize one at State College. The Kentucky Grange, a farm organization, opposed Patterson's plans, wanting a completely independent experiment station. It was not long before tension developed between Patterson and Scovell. "Patterson's goal for the station was to introduce science into the agricultural curriculum that would improve the life of the everyday farmer, whereas Scovell seemed to see agriculture as a business and thus the role of the station as making farmers better businessmen," claimed Kiesel. A special state tax on fertilizer for upkeep of the experiment station came under the control of Scovell for a time and created even more tension, setting up "a rivalry between the two men for the title of true champion of the commonwealth's farmers. This rivalry created an unbridgeable rift between the two men," one that continued into the first decade of the twentieth century. Nevertheless, the experiment station served a vital function in agricultural education in the latter nineteenth century.[72]

The second Morrill Act, of 1890, extended more aid to land grant schools, "in some cases nearly $50,000 within twelve to eighteen months of the bill's passage." Furthermore, over a period of years, "an annual endowment of $15,000" was increased until it reached a "permanent annual payment of $25,000." This money could be used for hiring in all areas, "from English to engineering." Patterson supported all of this legislation and urged its passage in Congress, and he was one of the first land grant college presidents to make studies of other schools. By the end of the nineteenth century, he had led State College through some tremulous times: through the divestiture from Kentucky University and the expansion of curricula and toward the new century. He was wise enough to follow if not always lead in the development of the land grant movement.[73]

Other colleges also reacted to the changing times. President Manly at Georgetown also championed change, in 1872 adopting the new "free" elective system sweeping the country. Mathematics, physical science, history, and the social sciences were added with the hiring of new professors. After the Civil War, Centre began adding "more utility" to its curriculum, including courses in astronomy, geology, and botany, with French, German, Spanish, and Italian as electives. Transylvania continued to be more grounded in the old classical system, although by the beginning of the twentieth century there was a modified elective system in place. These schools still required the study of Latin, but Greek was losing favor to the study of the modern languages French and German. By 1893 Kentucky Wesleyan College offered a "classical A.B. course and the Bachelor of Science curriculum." Like most other colleges of the time, Wesleyan also had one- and two-year programs for teaching and commerce.[74]

Kentucky higher education reacted to the new scientific ideas of the age. Darwin's theory of evolution reverberated in American higher education in the later nineteenth century, but the controversy arrived in Kentucky a bit later. At Central University, Professor J. L. Howe caused a bit of a stir. "The theory of the Evolution of life I understand to be the most satisfactory working hypothesis," he said, "which best explains the facts and phenomena as we find them." A committee of Central's Board of Curators studied complaints about Howe's teaching and found him to be "a fit and safe instructor." Kentucky University faculty reflected an "anti-Darwinian attitude," with Alfred Fairhurst, professor of natural sciences, in 1894 "energetically" attacking Darwin in a chapel address titled "The Origins of Man," much to the delight of both faculty and students.[75]

Professional training in Kentucky also survived the tumult of the Civil War, and such opportunities even expanded in the latter part of the nineteenth century.

Seminaries struggled in the postwar period. The moving of Southern Baptist Theological Seminary from Greenville, South Carolina, to Louisville in 1877 proved to be a boon not only to that city but to Kentucky Baptists as well. Although the school struggled for financial assistance, it began to grow in its downtown location. After the purchase of land at Fifth and Broadway in 1888, a campus began to develop. New York Hall, named for "significant contributions" from the Empire State, became a downtown landmark. Espousing a belief in Darwin's theory of evolution led to the forced resignation of Old Testament professor Crawford H. Toy in 1879. When President William Heth Whitsitt questioned the origins of old Baptist ideals, Baptist fundamentalists known as "Landmarkists" forced his resignation. Edgar Young Mullins, a graduate of SBTS, became president of the school in 1899. Contentiousness among Southern Baptists bedeviled the Louisville school well into the new century.[76]

The Disciples of Christ also had a school of theology, the first for the denomination; the College of the Bible began in 1865 as part of Kentucky University. John W. McGarvey led in the founding of the school. Like many other theologians of the era, he was "self-righteous and inflexible in his encounters with any who differed from him." There was little ecumenism among Protestants of the day. And the Disciples of Christ fought among themselves as much as did the Baptists and others. In the midst of the pressure to separate A&M from the Kentucky University umbrella, McGarvey and others campaigned against Bowman's continued dominance of KU, as its financial woes intensified. The Kentucky Christian Education Society campaigned to fund a "separate and independent" College of the Bible. In the fall of 1877, only three students enrolled at the old school still connected with KU, while forty-one students participated in the new College of the Bible, which met in the basement of the Main Street Christian Church in Lexington. McGarvey and Bowman continued their battles. Finally, the Board of Curators of Kentucky University, left with only the College of Arts and a small law department, dismissed Bowman as regent and elected Henry White as KU's first official president. Bowman's dream of a great public western university, encompassing all realms of knowledge and study, had faded away. "When John B. Bowman left Kentucky University he was a broken man," declared Idus Wilmer Adams. However, his legacy left behind, according to a church historian, "not one institution, but three—a thriving church related college (now Transylvania), a growing state university, and a promising theological seminary. Forces which at the time had appeared so destructive had been truly creative."[77]

The battle between "Southern" and "Northern" Presbyterians that led to establishment of their own schools of higher education at Central University and Centre College divided them over theological education as well. With the northern wing controlling Centre College and Danville Theological

Seminary, the southern faction founded Louisville Presbyterian Seminary in 1893 as an adjunct of Central University. The staunch Northern Presbyterian and Union warhorse Rev. Robert J. Breckinridge continued to teach at Danville Theological Seminary until 1869. He mellowed only slightly in old age, finally reconciling with his southern-leaning children before his death in 1871.[78]

The oldest theological school in Kentucky, St. Thomas Seminary, began in 1811. Founded by Bishop Benedict Joseph Flaget, St. Thomas moved on several occasions, "sometimes barely limping along," according to Catholic historian Clyde F. Crews. "The original St. Thomas Seminary was much more to Bishop Flaget than a place of instruction. For all its modesty of size and curriculum, it was the matrix from which would come the next generation of clerical leadership, beginning a vital tradition of native priests." The original regimen of St. Thomas included a daily round of meditation, prayer, study, and other spiritual exercises beginning at four thirty in the morning. St. Thomas remained open during the Civil War, and Bishop William McCloskey transferred it in 1871 to Newburg Road in Jefferson County, where it was popularly called "Preston Park Seminary." From then until 1888, St. Thomas operated as a "major seminary" of the Catholic faith. As a "minor seminary" thereafter, St. Thomas continued off and on at other locations until it finally closed in 1969.[79]

Law education continued in its infancy in Kentucky; Central University and Kentucky University had only small classes. The Commonwealth of Kentucky even had its own Columbia Law School, which operated briefly at Columbia in Adair County in the mid-1870s. Many lawyers still received their only education by "reading law" in a law office. After former governor J. Proctor Knott came to Centre in 1890, that school began a law course, and Knott, known as one of the commonwealth's best lawyers, became dean of the School of Law in 1894. The University of Louisville, whose College of Liberal Arts did not begin offering undergraduate education until 1907, had perhaps the best law education in the state. The American Bar Association, founded in 1878, established higher standards of law study and practice and eventually modernized Kentucky law education, but not until the early twentieth century. The U of L law school boasted of having practicing lawyers as professors, including James Speed, Lincoln's attorney general. In the eighties Dean William Chenault pushed for increased professionalism. One of the school's most famous graduates, Reuben T. Durrett, made a fortune in private practice and then became a collector of historical documents. Even law students enjoyed a prank, as when they "substituted beer for the brownish Ohio River water Professor Charles B. Seymour used to quench his thirst during lectures. The victim of the prank, who claimed to never consume liquor in any form, took one sip of the brew, spewed the beer toward the class, and launched into a temperance lecture."[80]

Unlike law education, medical training began to take on an even more modern form in the late nineteenth century. In 1874 the Kentucky General Assembly passed landmark legislation requiring that all physicians thereafter be medical school graduates. As the largest city in Kentucky as well as a transportation hub on the Ohio River and the L&N Railroad, Louisville became a center of medical schools before the Civil War. Between 1835 and 1900, by one estimate, "the city of Louisville harbored no less than eleven medical schools of one sort or another." Some were good, some not so good. These schools included the Louisville National Medical College for African Americans (established in 1879) and the Southwestern Homeopathic Medical College (1892). In the beginning these schools depended on lectures and a typical education lasted only two years. They slowly adopted laboratory and clinical studies in the latter part of the nineteenth century and moved toward a four-year training course in the nineties.[81]

The three major medical schools in Louisville in the latter nineteenth century came from different origins. The city's first medical school resulted from the defection of Dr. Charles Caldwell and others from the Transylvania University medical department; they formed the Louisville Medical Institute in 1837. LMI became the medical department of the newly founded University of Louisville in 1846. The Kentucky School of Medicine, founded in 1850, drained off more Transylvania faculty. Further medical intrigues and mergers led to Louisville Medical College, founded in 1869, which merged with the Kentucky School of Medicine in 1875. From 1898 to 1907, the Kentucky School of Medicine operated as the Medical Department of Kentucky University (Transylvania). The third major Louisville medical school came with the founding of the Hospital College of Medicine as part of Richmond's Central University in 1873. The latter also had a program for the training of dentists.[82]

These schools competed against each other, sometimes rather ruthlessly, for students and funds. Cutting fees and other ploys led to hard feelings. Standards were not high. The somewhat rough river-town atmosphere of Louisville added to the mix as "contemporary accounts reported that students drank, gambled, and engaged in public brawls. Some even carried firearms." Students still occasionally robbed graves for laboratory cadavers. One time, "irate Hoosiers gunned down one member of a University of Louisville grave-robbing excursion into southern Indiana." Finally, the Kentucky General Assembly passed a law setting "the maximum penalty for disinterring bodies at a $1000 fine and six months in jail." Medical school education in Louisville progressed slowly after the Civil War. By the end of the nineteenth century, such training had expanded from two to four years of study. "Between 1860 and 1910, the University of Louisville alone produced four thousand doctors," maintained the historians of that school. As standards improved, the number of graduates annually decreased. Despite the improved standards, the American Medical Association "described Louisville in 1907 as one of 'five especially rotten places' responsible for most of the abuses in the nation's medical education. That fall some local officials reportedly warned an AMA inspection team that they would not be welcome in the city." But change was on the way. Finally, the rivalry ended in 1908, when the University of Louisville, which had already taken over the Kentucky University Medical Department, absorbed the recently merged Louisville Hospital College of Medicine and the Kentucky School of Medicine. Medical school education in Kentucky improved steadily in the twentieth century under the guidance of the AMA.[83]

While Central University's medical and dental schools in Louisville and its preparatory schools prospered, the Richmond campus failed to grow. As in all other Kentucky colleges, during the Panic of 1893 and the continuing depression, conditions worsened and investments faltered. Competition with State College and other schools finally overcame Central's meager finances and its will to survive. Talks about a merger of Central and Centre began, unofficially, as early as 1898. Finally, Chancellor Blanton admitted that consolidation with Centre College could not be avoided, declaring rather sarcastically: "If we combine with Centre, you will not have to change the names on your football suits. You might as well try to stop the Kentucky River as try to stop this movement." Realistically, both schools needed each other to survive in the new century. If Central had a larger student body, Centre had more money. A combination of Madison County residents, Central alumni, and southern Presbyterians tried to forestall the merger. Old Confederate veteran Henry Watterson, editor of the *Louisville Courier-Journal*, lauded merger as "another step in wiping out sectional feeling." Once the blessing of the northern and southern synods of Kentucky Presbyterians was secured, assent by the Central Alumni Association remained the only stumbling block to consolidation. During a night-long meeting, some southern-leaning alumni used filibustering tactics, but to no avail. Two weeks later Central's alumni voted 59-41 to consolidate. Under the terms of the agreement, the consolidated college in Danville would be called Central University of Kentucky. In another sign of peacemaking among Kentucky Presbyterians, the old seminary in Danville merged with the newer one in Louisville, becoming Presbyterian Theological Seminary of Kentucky (renamed Louisville Presbyterian Theological Seminary in 1927).[84]

Kentucky higher education in the period 1860–1900 made strides in facing the realities of the postwar world. Feeding on the increasing high school graduation rate, Kentucky colleges began to add more courses, moving toward four-year degree programs. Old schools such as Georgetown and Centre survived. New schools like Kentucky Wesleyan College, Union College, Asbury College, and Bethel College added to the mixture. Except for State College, née A&M, all the colleges owed their allegiance to a religious base. Religious passions often ran high, and rivalries between as well as within denominations often did little to advance the cause of higher education in Kentucky. The brief experiment in racial integration at Berea College, the final admission of women to all male colleges, and the slow development of State College as a true land grant school demonstrated signs of progress in Kentucky higher education. Presidents came and went, administrations changed, students matriculated, some dropped out, and some graduated, as Kentucky colleges began to develop a momentum, an inertia, that would carry them through the rough times of economic, social, and political upheaval. Being a relatively poor state, Kentucky lacked the funds, either public or private, to develop a truly great university in the nineteenth century. The history of Bacon College/Kentucky University and the dreams of John Bryan Bowman to found a great egalitarian western university were destroyed by sectarian strife, pettiness, and the political realities of Kentucky. But all things considered, the effort was laudable. The spinoff of State College proved to be the only way it could survive in the new century as higher education modernized. Moreover, Transylvania survived all of this turmoil to eventually prosper in the twentieth century.

Thomas D. Clark's critique of education in Kentucky, in this case the lack of investment in higher education, rings true for this period: "Too little—almost none—of the tobacco money has flowed back into Kentucky to endow universities such as Duke, Wake Forest, Davidson, and Furman, nor is there a state hospital or medical service which has benefited materially from a tobacco capital endowment." Without a large industrial base, except perhaps in Louisville, and with an agricultural base "so heavily populated by subsistence farmers," the tax base remained abysmally low. Clark might have added that Kentucky's vaunted horse and coal industrialists failed by the same measure. Because the state lacked great philanthropy, particularly in the late nineteenth and early twentieth centuries, education at all levels limped along in an increasingly competitive age.[85]

Part 3

1900 TO 1941

Chapter 5

Elementary and Secondary Education from the Progressive Era to World War II

In the latter decades of the nineteenth century, the United States continued its chaotic, almost irrepressible, growth, becoming the industrial leader of the world and creating enormous wealth. With massive immigration and completion of the westward movement, the United States blossomed into a world power. Victory in the Spanish-American War, the spoils of war, and the annexation of Hawaii—all in the last decade of the nineteenth century—catapulted America toward the beginning of an American empire. The twentieth century became the "American Century."[1]

The period from the 1890s to 1920 is often called the Progressive Era, for good reason. Although the presidencies of Theodore Roosevelt and Woodrow Wilson in the opening decades of the century promised more than they delivered, national legislation attempted to rein in the monopolies and improve the lot of common people. Many people were concerned about the fate of America's public schools. Of course, educational reform during the Progressive Era included the ideas of John Dewey, who became the best known of the proponents of change. While the normal school movement expanded across the nation, Kentucky remained one of only two states without publicly financed normal school education. The commonwealth faced new challenges but at the same time had many opportunities to influence lasting changes in its public schools.[2]

Harrison and Klotter, in *A New History of Kentucky*, found some reason for optimism about education in Kentucky at the beginning of the twentieth century. Daily attendance in the public schools had risen to 36 percent by 1900 after passage of a compulsory attendance law. In *Kentucky: Portrait in Paradox, 1900–1950*, Klotter reiterated that the commonwealth "was the only southern state" with a compulsory attendance law at the onset of the twentieth century. However, children in the rural areas were always behind their urban counterparts, attending school terms on average two-thirds as long as city children and being "about two and one half years behind" in nationally scaled achievement. The poorest counties, mostly in eastern Kentucky, could not or would not tax themselves to provide basic public school education. Among the southern states—Kentucky had cast its lot with that region after the Civil War—the commonwealth "stood fourth in expenditures per pupil," and, with an average school term of 115 days, ranked third in that category. However, outside the South and even in the old Confederate states, educational progress accelerated in the first decade of the new century. Would Kentucky be able to keep up?[3]

Part of the mood for optimism soon after the turn of the century could be traced to the atmosphere of reform and uplift. In 1908, at a time when industrial America appeared to be dominating the nation, President Theodore Roosevelt appointed the Country Life Commission. Valerie Roddy Summers, in "A New Rural Life: Kentucky Education Reform and the Country Life Movement, 1905–1920," offered a more sanguine view of education reform. She argued that Kentucky reformers were part of a well-defined educational reform movement centering around the "Country Life Movement" of the late nineteenth and early twentieth centuries, one that was never as isolated or as unsuccessful as conventional historical wisdom declared.[4]

However, Thomas D. Clark got it right when he said that "education was Kentucky's cross" at the turn of the new century. "Running through the whole tapestry of Kentucky educational history is the dominant thread of agrarian rurality," declared Clark. He was not as generous as Harrison and Klotter in his estimation of Kentucky public schools in 1900. Though weakened, "the black beast" of education, as he termed the district trustee system, continued to inefficiently and often corruptly mar the educational landscape. He gave some credit to the fourth constitutional convention of 1890 for an educational article mandating that the General Assembly "provide for an efficient system of common schools throughout the state." But in the end, Clark condemned public school education from 1865 to 1910 "as being of shabby, backwoods, log cabin–era quality" and improving only at a "snail's pace." The reluctance to adequately fund the public schools, particularly at the local level, and slothfulness in curriculum change in the county schools, indicate a lack of foresight and direction. Furthermore, by joining the South after the Civil War, economically, racially, and even spiritually, Kentucky cast its lot with nostalgic defeatism, rather than aspiring to the rising standards of the Midwest.[5]

Moses Ligon, a historian of Kentucky public education, a bit more charitably called the period from 1860 to 1900 one of "marking time"; there were some signs of progress since the Civil War, however. County superintendents were now elected for four-year terms with some qualifications added, the trustee system had been reduced to one trustee per district, and teacher certification was now being established at the state level, with an examination controlled by a board of examiners. Most teachers continued to be paid based on the number of students in their district rather than those actually attending, but teachers were a little better trained than in 1860. There was hope for better things in the new century because of a groundswell of opinion, urging improved teacher education with annual institutes and public normal schools.[6]

During the administrations of superintendents Harry V. McChesney (1899–1903) and James H. Fuqua (1903–1907), while J. C. W. Beckham was governor, there appeared to be progress on several fronts. But was it really progress? For example, choosing a better method of textbook adoption proved again Kentucky poet James H. Mulligan's old adage "And politics— the damnedest in Kentucky." The 1904 legislature passed the Chinn School Book Law, aimed at establishing uniformity of textbooks and a maximum price. The best thing about the law was that it took textbook selection away from the district trustees. The law created the State Book Commission and a book commission for each county. The real power lay in the County School Book Commission, which would review books, sending its recommendations to Frankfort. The State Book Commission was required to "adopt any book for which a majority of the county commissions had voted." Although the law appeared to democratize the selection process, it only intensified the politicization of the process. The textbook companies fought this legislation, and each other, tooth and nail. State senator J. Campbell Cantrill of Georgetown pushed through the measure, which many school superintendents opposed and which Governor J. C. W. Beckham did not sign. No one appeared satisfied, except perhaps the American Book Company, which received a near monopoly. No doubt, book publishers lubricated the political system in the interim. A new law in 1908 allowed "Ginn and Company to bid competitively." In 1914 the General Assembly continued to tinker with the issue and created a new state commission. Two years later the legislature increased the amount of state money available for books for "indigent children." The issue of free textbooks became the mantra of some Kentucky politicians, who demagogued the issue into the 1920s.[7]

However, there was progress on other fronts. In 1904 the legislature mandated that all schools meet for a minimum of six months. This law particularly impacted rural schools; many urban schools were already in session for seven to eight months. Another law in this session required children between ages seven and fourteen to attend school for the full term in urban areas. McChesney also pushed the idea that schools should hold graduation exercises, thus encouraging students to complete their educations. For several generations, well into the post–World War II era, graduation from the eighth grade meant much to education-starved Kentuckians as a sign of success.[8]

Just below the surface of the apparent civility in Kentucky was the overarching heritage of violence illustrated by incessant mountain blood feuds, the assassination of William Goebel, and the suppression of African Americans. The county nicknamed "Bloody Breathitt" became nationally known for its feuds, as did other counties. Violence in Rowan County in the 1880s, for example, included twenty murders without a single conviction. To quell the mayhem, Governor James Proctor Knott (1883–1887) sent in the state militia on two occasions. The General Assembly even toyed with the idea of abolishing Rowan County, breaking it up and including its parts in other counties. In western Kentucky, "Night Riders" tried to enforce a boycott against the tobacco monopoly during the "Black Patch War" in the first decade of the new century. Despite the name "Progressive Era" for the period 1890–1920, rampant racism in Kentucky humiliated and degraded blacks. Lynchings and other outrages continued well into the twentieth century with little abatement. Could Kentucky make any progress in public education against such odds?[9]

Violence as part of the political process in Kentucky operated at the state level with the Goebel assassination and all the way down to the local level in school board and trustee races. After a particularly "heated trustee election" in Wayne County, someone torched the Greenbriar School. The story of Ike Short's family in Clay County echoed throughout eastern Kentucky in the early twentieth century. Short recalled:

> My grandfather ran for school trustee. A bunch of drunks didn't like him. They just thought they would get rid of him. He had won. I think my grandfather was shot six or seven times. My mother said if they could have got the crowd away, I had an uncle there who was dodging the law. He was a very mean guy and he had killed three or four men. Every time he would raise his gun to shoot [from an upper story window], one of these women would step in. He would have stopped it right now. These women were just hollering and screaming.

Transported by boat down the Kentucky River and then by train to Lexington, Short's grandfather died of gangrene a week later. Short's father later killed one man in self-defense and narrowly escaped mountain revenge.[10]

Harry Caudill reported another much more famous incident in *Night Comes to the Cumberlands.* "The trifling but coveted office of school trustee inspired many battles which went beyond the ballot box and voting booth," he said. One of the "bloodiest" episodes in Kentucky history took place at Clay-hole on Troublesome Creek in Breathitt County on election day, November 8, 1921. The infamous "Battle of Clayhole" began when one side challenged Aunt Lisa Sizemore's right to vote. Gunfire erupted, leaving nine men dead and six others wounded.[11]

Only the coordinated efforts of educators, political figures, and the general citizenry would be able to shake Kentucky from its education doldrums. That would be a tall order, considering the commonwealth's political climate, with its feuding Democratic Party factions, its oppressive racial divide, and its agrarian economy, the "rurality" that Clark saw as omnipresent. However, there would be occasions when the time would be right for reform and change, and Kentuckians would step up to the challenge.

Kentucky's common schools of the nineteenth century slowly evolved into the graded public schools of the early twentieth century, as in most other states. Education had come a long way since the pre–Civil War days when just about anyone could teach. At the turn of the twentieth century, during the term of State Superintendent Harry V. McChesney (1899–1903), school law required a prospective teacher to pass an examination to obtain a teaching certificate: a state diploma, a state certificate, or a county certificate. The requirements for the state certificate were rigorous: the teacher had to be at least twenty-four years of age, with two years of teaching experience. The examination included sections on spelling, reading, writing, arithmetic, grammar, composition, geography, history, physiology, theory and practice of teaching, literature, and algebra.[12]

The two-day state diploma exam in Frankfort was difficult (the author doubts he could pass it today), requiring an average of 90 percent for passage. A sampling of items from various exams is instructive. For example, the teacher was asked, "How would you overcome stammering?" On the issue of classroom control, the teacher was quizzed about "your remedy for whispering." Words the candidate was asked to spell included "gherkin, singeing, cymling, daguerreotype, and kaleidoscope." In the category of theory and practice, one item stands out: "Discuss plans for enlisting interest of patrons and general public in the work of the school." On one examination the teacher was asked to write a one-page composition on the subject "The Value of an Education." A geography item asked the teacher to draw an outline of Kentucky, "locating three principal rivers and five cities," and to name all the countries of South America. If the teacher answered successfully the questions I have seen, I have no doubt that he or she would have been a proficient candidate for a teaching certificate.[13]

Teachers who passed the examination for the state diploma received a certificate good for eight years of teaching anywhere in the state. At the lowest level, though, that of the county certificate, the problem of the "question peddler" persisted well into the new century. The "question peddler" either stole or bought the questions used at the county or district level and sold them to a prospective teacher so that she or he might easily pass the examination and qualify for a certificate. "The nights before the examination found these persons going around to the candidates, peddling their wares," said one observer. One teacher taking part in the exams recalled, without apology or the pangs of conscience, "The best way to do it was steal the questions if you could." Another time, he traded examinations with another applicant during an examination and made $100. Once he got called on the carpet before the state superintendent in Frankfort and barely escaped punishment. A female teacher freely admitted, "My daddy bought my first school job for me. Paid a trustee for it. The trustee told him, '. . . give me fifty [dollars] and it's yours.'" No critic of public school education in eastern Kentucky surpassed Harry Caudill, who claimed the good teachers were pushed aside "as the sons and daughters of local citizens assumed their duties," because of the corrupt trustees and superintendents. This led to a slothful education system. Slowly the system was reformed, but only on a piecemeal basis, being replaced first by holding all examinations in Frankfort and second by ending testing completely in 1920.[14]

An observer of common school education in 1860 and again in 1900 would have found much familiar ground on the latter date. One-room schools still predominated in the rural areas. No public county high schools existed in eastern Kentucky. There were good teachers as well as bad. Younger teachers often had students older than themselves. It was possible to get a good education in a one-room school with a little initiative and a willing teacher. In 1900 salaries were low, with white teachers in the commonwealth making on average $34.10 a month and black teachers $29.95. The school itself had improved somewhat. Taxes levied by counties ranged from none at all in twenty-six counties to $2,033, the total received for a year in Woodford County. "Subscription" paid by individuals and tuition ($33,000, taken together) made up a larger amount than the total paid for all county taxes in the state ($30,504). Indeed, there were counties that could only be described as "pauper counties," those that could not or would not tax themselves adequately to fund public schools. They depended entirely on state funds for schools. In 1890, for example, even well-positioned Hardin County spent more on school services than it collected locally, "thus placing it in that humble position designated by later state finance commissioners as a 'pauper' county." A majority of Kentucky counties at the turn of the century followed the same path as Hardin, and their schools suffered as a consequence. Clearly, local taxes were lacking in supporting the public schools. In the last twenty years of the nineteenth century, the number of frame school buildings increased from 2,138 to 6,752 while the number of log structures decreased from 3,360 to 1,238. Brick structures increased in number only slightly, from 145 to 150. School consolidation slowly began to change the nature of rural education. The elimination of the excessive district schools, with their omnipotent trustees, and consolidation became part of the "modernization" of education in the commonwealth. The Country Life Movement of the late nineteenth and early twentieth centuries encouraged consolidation, particularly in such "southern" states as Kentucky, and was very successful in spreading the word across the country.[15]

The obstacles for pupil and teacher alike were formidable, particularly in the rural schools. Kentucky was still predominantly agrarian and rural in 1900, with 234,667 farms recorded in the census of that year. Whereas 467,688 Kentuckians, or 21.8 percent, lived in cities and towns, 1,679,506 inhabited the farms, tiny villages, and recesses of the mountains and innumerable hills. Thomas D. Clark described the trials and tribulations of the teacher well when he said, "Teaching a Kentucky country school prior to 1930 often required the wit of Solomon, the courage of David, the fortitude of Job, and the self-sacrifice of the widow and her mite."[16]

Virginia P. Carrithers began her education in a one-room school in Jefferson County at the age of five. That year she attended school for only five days, and the next year for two weeks, because the school was more than three miles away. When the family moved closer to the school, she began to attend regularly, but one year she attended for only two and one-half months. Finally, at the Old Kennedy School on Taylorsville Road, she began to excel. "In those days very few students went further than the fifth or sixth grade," she recalled. "In fact, in the history of the school, only one student had passed the eighth-grade examination." Because there was no opportunity for Carrithers to finish a high school education at that time, a favorite teacher helped her prepare for her first certification examination, and she began teaching in 1907. She later finished high school and went on to complete A.B. and B.S. degrees. Her experiences would have been similar to those of thousands of public school teachers, male and female, black and white, in the early twentieth century.[17]

Cora Frazier's school at Mayking in Letcher County became the "hub of the community," with its pie suppers and PTA meetings that she organized. "We gathered at the schoolhouse and had a good time," she recalled. Believing that sparing the rod spoiled the child, "Sometimes, if they used bad language or had fights on the school grounds," Frazier reported, "I whipped them. It might have been wrong, but I did. Turn them across a desk, paddle them good, and they'll learn. The parents generally made me [a paddle], bored holes in it, and sent it to school to me." One time, after finding a moonshine still in a "willow bed" near her school, she persuaded "the boys" to ask their parents to remove it, which they summarily did. When the county superintendent found out about the incident, he jokingly asked why she had not told him about it. With typical eastern Kentucky pluck and understatement, she said: "Well, I didn't know it needed telling."[18]

Throughout its history, education in Kentucky often seemed to take nearly as many steps backward as forward. Education suffered another blow in 1904. After becoming president of Berea College in 1892, William Goodell Frost changed the direction of the school by emphasizing the education of "Appalachian Americans." By 1903, black enrollment had decreased to only 16 percent of Berea's students. To the present day, a controversy exists over Frost's intentions. Arguing that whites should be educated before blacks, Frost forced Berea's only black teacher to resign. At best, he appeared to be "a lukewarm friend of Black students and community," according to one of his biographers. Was he complicit in segregating Berea, or only reacting to perhaps the inevitability of early-twentieth-century Kentucky racial mores?[19]

In November 1903, Representative Carl Day of Breathitt County visited Berea and sounded an alarm after seeing blacks and whites "living together." Aiming at Berea College, the only school in the state permitting biracial education, Day introduced House Bill 25, "An Act to prohibit white and colored persons from attending the same school." Eight hundred white citizens of Madison County signed a petition supporting the bill. Although Berea was not a state-supported school, most legislators quickly lined up on the side of segregation. Superintendent McChesney testified in favor of the bill, claiming that segregation would "increase the value of Berea College as an institution." Overwhelmingly passed by the General Assembly, the Day Law went into effect in July 1904, with substantial fines of fifty dollars for each offending teacher or student and $1,000 for each offending school.[20]

A Madison County grand jury indicted Berea in October of that year for violating the law, initiating court cases that went all the way to the highest court in America. The Kentucky Court of Appeals in *Commonwealth v. Berea College* upheld the Day Law, declaring "the purity of racial blood" to be "deeper and more important than the matter of choice." The U.S. Supreme Court concurred in 1908, with Kentuckian Justice John Marshall Harlan dissenting. Relying on the "separate but equal" dictum of *Plessy v. Ferguson*, the highest court in the land declared that the Commonwealth of Kentucky had the right to require that the races be educated separately.[21]

Apparently reconciled to eventual defeat even before the court cases unfolded, Frost worked to create a new all-black school. Berea graduate James Bond and other black graduates of the school joined in the movement. The effort raised $400,000 in state and national pledges, including a donation from industrialist-philanthropist Andrew Carnegie. Incorporated in 1910, Lincoln Institute opened near Simpsonville in Shelby County as a high school and added a normal school program two years later. The majority of the first teachers were white, including Lincoln's first principal, Rev. A. E. Thomson of Berea. In the early years, Bond served as an anchor for blacks on the faculty. Whitney M. Young Sr. became the first black president of Lincoln Institute in 1935.[22]

Although the Day Law meant a step backward for Kentucky education, a groundswell grew for improving teacher education. As far back as 1830, educational commissions and successive state superintendents had urged the founding of state-supported normal schools. Private normal schools of one type or another abounded in Kentucky in the nineteenth century. Before the Civil War, the two-year normal school experiment at Transylvania was the only state-funded attempt at expanding and improving the teacher pool. However, a General Assembly that had dedicated funds for the school in 1855 repealed the law two years later by large majorities. This vote "has given a retrograde movement to State education, which cannot be retraced for at least a quarter of a century," claimed State Superintendent John Daniel Matthews (1853–1859). Unfortunately, Matthews's prediction proved more than true. While the development of state normal schools flourished in most states, only in Frankfort at the State Normal School for Colored Persons did the commonwealth have a state-sponsored school at the turn of the twentieth century.[23]

After the Civil War, the movement for state-supported normal schools in Kentucky languished. However, most colleges soon added teaching programs or normal education, providing a service as well as producing revenue. In its nineteenth-century form, a normal school operated as a high school. Such schools as Central University added teacher education as a way of increasing enrollment. By one count at least twenty-five normal schools were founded in Kentucky between 1870 and 1905. Beginning in 1871, the city of Louisville operated its own normal school but limited the enrollment mostly to women in a program that included internships. Kentucky Normal and Industrial Institute for Colored Persons, founded in 1886 in Frankfort, served as the major teacher-training school for African American teachers in the state well into the twentieth century. After the federal government provided for land grant colleges for blacks in 1890, the school also began to include education in the agricultural and mechanical arts. Southern Normal School, which started operations in Glasgow under Professor A. W. Mell in 1875, moved to Bowling Green in 1884. Coming under the direction of tireless educator Henry Hardin Cherry and his brother, by 1899 the school had nearly seven hundred students attending at one time or another during the year. After separating from Kentucky University in 1878, the Agricultural and Mechanical College in Lexington moved to its own campus. In 1880 the legislature passed enabling legislation creating a Normal Department at A&M. It took some strong arguments by President James K. Patterson and Judge W. B. Kinkead to convince the board of trustees that because women made up a majority of teachers in the state, they should be admitted. Enrollment in the Normal Department grew steadily and "opened the doors of State College to Women." Soon A&M expanded its offerings to include a four-year bachelor of pedagogy program as well as the basic normal course.[24]

But this was not enough, and momentum built for change. The Kentucky Education Association, the state's primary education interest group, had been urging the development of a state normal school program since its inception just before the Civil War. In June 1904 the KEA annual meeting appointed a "committee of three to devise a plan for the organization of the teachers of the state into a federation." In effect, leaders in KEA and others wanted the organization to be more aggressive in pursuing goals. The committee of three reported the next year to the KEA meeting at Mammoth Cave, which appointed another, larger committee that included Patterson, H. H. Cherry, and Superintendent of Public Instruction James H. Fuqua (1903–1907). Out of that committee came a recommendation that led to formation of the Kentucky Educational Improvement Commission. The executive committee of the commission recommended the establishment of "professional schools for teachers." The commission also raised funds in the fall of 1905, nearly $1,500, for a publicity campaign and circulated petitions urging enactment of a law "to provide for the establishment and maintenance of an efficient system of State Normal Schools." Commission members and others made speeches across the state and flooded newspapers with stories and editorials in preparation for the meeting of the General Assembly in January 1906. The *Southern School Journal,* the official publication of the Kentucky State Board of Education, encouraged "every friend of education" to urge his or her representative in Frankfort to pass normal school legislation.[25]

A personal and professional conflict played an important role in the forming of Kentucky's first normal schools. After coming to the Normal Department of State College in 1889 as a faculty member, native Kentuckian Ruric Nevel Roark became its dean in 1891. Enrollment increased under his watch, surpassing that of other departments of the college. "However, the good news of increasing enrollments only tended to overshadow the schism that was building between President Patterson and Professor Roark," according to Terry L. Birdwhistell. The "status" of the "Normal Department within the college remained low," increasing the "personal antagonism between Roark and Patterson." One professor of the time recalled that it was "said that the President was jealous of Roark's popularity." Moreover, they were of different generations. In this test of wills between the old Scottish educational warrior, who took no prisoners, and the much younger, ambitious, and forceful normal school advocate, who exuded personality and confidence, there had to be a parting of the ways. Patterson wanted State College to gain a substantial appropriation to expand its offerings. Roark wanted separate state-funded normal schools. One historian of education in Kentucky, Nelda Wyatt, succinctly summed up this denouement: "In spite of James K. Patterson, the normal schools came into existence."[26]

Another savvy educator, Bowling Green's Henry Hardin Cherry, added his own personal and institutional ambitions to this mixture. Something else was obvious: Kentucky was one of only two states, Arkansas being the other, that did not have state-funded normal schools. Although Kentucky was overdue to enter the field, the outcome was still in doubt. While many legislators visualized that the time had arrived to act, Governor J. C. W. Beckham (1900–1907) expressed doubts that the money could be found for such a venture. Roark resigned at State College in May 1905 and threw himself into pressing for the normal school legislation. Patterson hoped that with Roark gone, the Normal Department of his college could receive extra funding from the legislature. The state's educators and school superintendents began to line up either in the State College camp or for creation of new normal schools. The setting for the debate was the incessantly political Kentucky milieu with its annual elections as well as regional antagonisms.[27]

Representative Richard W. Miller of Madison County introduced a bill on January 9, 1906, proposing three normal districts, each with a school. The contest was on to name sites for the schools before passage of the bill. Cherry, president of the proprietary Southern Normal School in Bowling Green, and boosters in Richmond offered their cities and existing educational facilities for the effort. Political intrigues in Frankfort abounded, along with the irreconcilable conflict between Patterson and Roark.[28]

Civic boosters in Richmond, including Mayor Clarence E. Woods and lawyer Jere A. Sullivan, promised to turn over to the state the old Central University campus, valued at $150,000 and now occupied by the Walters Collegiate Institute. State senator Curtis Field Burnam of Richmond pushed the bill. Cherry and his Bowling Green allies did also. Other cities also asked to be considered, but only Richmond and Bowling Green were unrelenting in their quests for the normal school sites. President Cherry of Southern Normal in Bowling Green once estimated that he spent "seventy-one days in Frankfort in 1906 lobbying for the normal school measure at his own expense."[29]

When it appeared that Bowling Green's bid was gaining more support than Richmond's, lawyer Jere Sullivan set to work. First, he drafted a substitute bill specifying only two sites. Second, knowing the antipathy between Richmond politico and former governor James B. McCreary and Governor Beckham, Sullivan arranged for an ally to persuade the governor to commit to the two-site bill. While Beckham agreed to the latter, he threw a monkey wrench into the machinery by proposing that a committee, appointed by him, choose the two locations. With faith in the merits of their proposal, the Richmond contingent agreed, and the amended bills went to the floors of both houses. Most of the opposition to the normal school bills came from State College and the private colleges in the state.[30]

After more minor intrigues, the bills unanimously passed the House on March 2 and the Senate on March 9. Governor Beckham immediately signed the measure into law. Understanding the importance of the moment, the General Assembly announced in the law that "an emergency is therefore declared to exist and this act shall take effect from and after its passage and approval of the Governor." The law specified a normal school in the western district and one in the eastern district, a board of regents for each, and, most important, appropriations of money. When Louisville did not pursue selection as a normal school site, Bowling Green and Richmond became the only candidates and were chosen by the location commission. Beckham appointed a board of regents for each of the new schools, and the regents in turn appointed a president. Henry Hardin Cherry became president of District 2, Western Kentucky State Normal School, and Ruric Nevel Roark became president of District 1, Eastern Kentucky State Normal School. Western took over the Southern Normal School function and the Potter College campus, and Eastern took over the Walters property that had earlier been the nucleus of Central University.[31]

Opponents of the normal school movement refused to give up, challenging the constitutionality of the new law. They sought an injunction to prohibit appropriation of $5,000 for equipment and repairs for each normal school campus. Meanwhile, the Eastern and Western regents ignored the lawsuit and spent the funds, assuming that the statute would be upheld. In April 1907 the Kentucky Court of Appeals ruled in favor of the normal schools by upholding a lower court opinion.[32]

The Eastern and Western normal schools had one purpose: to take students without a high school education and mold them into teachers as effectively, efficiently, and quickly as possible. Those who entered with the least qualifications took a review, or remedial course, which prepared them to pass the county examinations needed for teaching in the typical one-room schools in the state. The curricula of the two schools were much the same: students would take the same courses they would later teach to schoolchildren. Initially, the schools were no more than high schools, not adding "college" level courses until the early twenties. Meanwhile, the Normal Department at State College offered a higher level of public school preparation than did Western and Eastern. And after State College became State University in 1908, the Normal Department became the Department of Education. That year as part of more legislation, along with negotiations and compromises between the three state institutions, State University received $200,000 and Eastern and Western $150,000 each from the General Assembly for capital improvements.[33]

One of the first students to enter the new Eastern Kentucky State Normal School, Jennie Jeffers Ashby, represented a transitional figure in Kentucky public school education. After graduating from Greenville High School in 1901, she studied for a year in order to gain county certification and then began her teaching career when she reached the mandatory age of eighteen. After she completed fifty hours at Eastern and received a "Normal Life Diploma," allowing her to teach anywhere in the state, she returned to teaching in 1907 and retired in 1954. Like many others of her generation of teachers, she did not complete a degree program. However, Ashby led in developing the School Fair in Muhlenberg County in 1914 and was continually innovative.[34]

Education in Kentucky appeared to be on the march, the state finally recognizing the need for a state-funded normal school program. But even though public school education in Kentucky ranked high in the South at the turn of the century, it lagged seriously behind Kentucky's northern neighbors. In another groundswell, like the one that led to the founding of Western and Eastern, reformers looked toward improving high school education in the commonwealth. Now appeared to be the time to act. Moreover, several other states, including Virginia, began to double their education expenditures in the first decade of the twentieth century. The Richmond Education Association, led by prototypical "southern" female progressives, and the Cooperative Education Association of Virginia, worked with the Southern Education Board and pushed the Virginia General Assembly until it passed reform legislation.[35]

The Kentucky Federation of Women's Clubs was one of the leading advocates for educational reform from 1903 to 1909 and played a key role in Kentucky's version of progressivism. After several clubs organized into the KFWC in 1894, they began to look for ways to improve life in the commonwealth, including funding traveling libraries and improving education among mountain youth. In 1903 Martha Stephenson of Harrodsburg took the lead in urging support of statewide education reform. At state and local meetings, members of the KFWC publicized the need for change and even brought the *Louisville Courier-Journal* and other state newspapers into the fray. These women combined their concerns about the state's educational problems with their own need for a public voice and full suffrage rights. Mary Creegan Roark, the wife of the Eastern president, who later served briefly herself as leader of the school, and Madeline McDowell Breckinridge, a Lexington reformer and wife of the editor of the *Lexington Herald*, led the way. These and other women, most of them suffragists, demonstrated great concern for child labor and school attendance problems.[36]

The suffrage issue proved to be a motivation and a stumbling block for both women and educational reform. The twists and turns of the issue went all the way back to 1838, when the right to vote in county trustee races was granted by state law to unmarried women owning property. Although few women either qualified for or used this limited suffrage, it was the first granting of the vote to American women. The 1891 constitution further empowered the General Assembly to sanction the vote for all women in school elections and other races. The efforts of the Kentucky Equal Rights Association led to the enactment of a suffrage law in 1894, giving women the vote in school races in second-class cities, including Lexington, Covington, and Newport. An incident in Lexington again proved Mulligan's adage about politics being "the damnedest in Kentucky." When more women, many of them black, registered as Republicans (1,997 Republicans to 662 Democrats), race became paramount to Democrats, who feared they might lose control of the city. The Democrats won the election, but Democratic representative William A. "Billy" Klair and Senator J. Embry, of Lexington, led a successful battle in Frankfort in 1902 to repeal the 1894 law, against the efforts of Breckinridge and others. Again, Kentucky could claim a first: this was, ignominiously, "the only instance in the history of the American suffrage movement, when the franchise, once won, was taken away by the action of a legislature." In an effort to ally the sensibilities of racist Kentuckians, white suffragists renewed their battle for the vote with the thinly veiled argument that only literate women, like themselves, should have the right to vote, thereby denying suffrage to illiterate African American women. Against this blatant subplot also played out the KFWC effort to bring about educational reform.[37]

Leadership in Frankfort also proved crucial in educational reform. In 1907, a year when Democratic forces were divided, Republican Augustus Everett Willson, after losing five straight races for public office, narrowly won the governorship. Hamstrung by a Democratic Party–controlled legislature, Willson had difficulty getting his agenda across. Furthermore, he got caught up in trying to suppress violence during Kentucky's tobacco wars in western Kentucky. Yet he fully supported his fellow Republican John Grant

Crabbe, state superintendent of public instruction (1907–1909), in his efforts on behalf of badly needed education reform.[38]

A native of Ohio with a master of pedagogy degree from Ohio University, Crabbe came to Kentucky as superintendent of the Ashland public schools in 1890. Under his direction Ashland High School became one of the leaders in the commonwealth in the development of a comprehensive high school program. He soon became one of the leading educators in the state, won the state superintendency in 1907, and, after two years, resigned to become president of Eastern (1909–1916) after the untimely death of Roark.[39]

In the first decade of the twentieth century, Kentucky faced numerous educational issues, listed by Fred Engle as "public support of educational programs, favoritism in teacher selection, county administration, financing the schools, census padding, the school term, teachers' salaries, certification, the question peddler, textbooks, attendance, grading the schools, teacher training, school buildings, teacher security, consolidation, recodification [of school law], vocational education, Negro education, and long-range planning." These were more than enough to tackle, and Crabbe chose his battles wisely.[40]

Governor Willson and Superintendent Crabbe lost no time after their election in setting up an educational reform agenda for the 1908 meeting of the General Assembly. Willson sent a special message to the body. It is time, he said, for "better schools, better school houses, better teachers, better teaching, longer terms, better courses of education, better pay, first class normal schools, and a complete change in the whole school system to bring it up to the necessities of the people and to the first modern school standards." Most of the specifics he listed were passed by the legislature.[41]

The support of the KFWC and key legislators such as Senator Jere Sullivan of Richmond became essential. The "Sullivan Law," or County School District Law, mandated "almost complete reform of the Kentucky public school system." The law ended the one-room-school district. Each county became a single district, possibly containing one or more independent urban districts. The part of the county outside urban districts was organized into "subdistricts" containing between forty and fifty white children. A county school board would be made up of an elected trustee from each subdistrict. By 1910 each county was to organize a high school of one of the following types: A first-class high school would offer a four-year standard program, established by the State Department of Education; a second-class high school would have a three-year program; and a third-class high school a two-year program. The law mandated that each county levy a school tax, between twenty and twenty-five cents, on each $100 of assessed property value. "All laws and parts of laws in conflict with this act are hereby repealed," the Sullivan Law ordered.[42]

And education legislation in 1908 did not end there. To further attack the problem of school attendance, the legislature added to child labor laws passed in 1890, 1902, and 1906. A Compulsory Attendance Law of 1908 provided for a "truant officer" to enforce attendance of children ages seven to fourteen in cities of the first four classes. Children in urban areas still had a much better chance for a public school education in Kentucky than in the rural areas. To support higher education in the commonwealth, State College became State University, and then the University of Kentucky in 1916, and the Eastern and Western normal schools received large appropriations. A separate law provided improvements at Kentucky Normal and Industrial Institute for Colored Persons in Frankfort. By statute, Kentucky University reverted to its original name, Transylvania University.[43]

Owing to the cost of all this legislation, Governor Willson seriously considered a veto, but Crabbe and the KFWC leadership persuaded him to relent, and he signed these bills. Lexington suffragist Madeline McDowell Breckinridge cooperated with the KFWC and spoke before the House of Representatives advocating education and suffrage reform. Perhaps no "reformer" of the era was as indefatigable as she in pursuing the goals of Kentucky progressivism in the first twenty years of the new century. Much of the credit for passage of legislation must be given to Sullivan and other Democrats. What is most amazing is that all this legislation passed a Democratic Party–controlled legislature seriously divided over other issues. Democrats "brought the work of the General Assembly to a virtual standstill" as they battled over a U.S. Senate election and the liquor question. Divided by the wet-dry issue, enough Democrats defected in the General Assembly to the Republican aisle to elect former governor William O. Bradley over former governor J. C. W. Beckham to the U.S. Senate seat after twenty-nine exhausting ballots. Undeterred by all this political folderol, Crabbe initiated what became known as the "whirlwind campaign" to publicize and build support for public school education. Actually, there were two campaigns, one beginning on November 28, 1908, and the other on June 27, 1909. The Southern Education Board fully supported these efforts.[44]

The November 28, 1908, "Whirlwind Campaign," as described by Crabbe, "was a continuous cyclone bombardment against illiteracy and ignorance for a period of nine days. Twenty-nine speakers, forceful, sensible, well-informed, intelligent, enthusiastic, were in the field. Nearly three hundred public set addresses were delivered. The entire state was covered, with a speaker or by speakers visiting every county. Nearly 60,000 people heard these addresses."[45]

On June 27, 1909, designated "Public School Sunday" by Crabbe, the second of the "Whirlwind Campaigns" began with sermons or addresses in an estimated five thousand churches, attended by perhaps as many as five hundred thousand people. With a slogan of "For the Boys and Girls and the Commonwealth," Crabbe and his coworkers sent out publicity releases all over the state in a campaign that lasted until July 4. Crabbe's organizational skills were impressive. This time one hundred speakers, including Governor Willson, Governor William H. Cox of Ohio, Mrs. Charles P. (Anna) Weaver of the KFWC, Cherry, Sullivan, and dozens of school superintendents fanned out across the state. For example, superintendents George Colvin of Springfield and Lee Kirkpatrick of Paris, two of the most important "schoolmen" of the early twentieth century, took part. Richmond held a "Rally Day" on June 28, one like those planned for each county, on the campus of the new normal school, where a cornerstone was laid for the Ruric Nevel Roark Building. Crabbe estimated he disbursed about $5,000, using private sources, on the expenses for the crusade. "This campaign has had a wonderful effect in bringing the gospel of public education nearer to the hearts of the people," he said.[46]

To maintain this momentum, the legislature also created an Educational Commission of eighteen members to keep on top of the education issues of the day, study other states, and make recommendations at the next meeting of the legislature. With the state superintendent as ex officio chairman, the committee included presidents of the state normal schools and colleges, members of the House and the Senate, Dr. Virginia E. Spencer of the KFWC, and several county and city superintendents. In the report of commission secretary George J. Ramsey, professor of education at Central University (Centre), was listed improvement after improvement due to the passage of the County Board Law of 1908. With 25,000 trustees controlling 8,000 schools, something had to be done to change what had been developing for a century. The commission's critique of the present system was explicit and emphasized creating an "efficient system." First, the composition of the State Board of Education needed a change: the secretary of state and the attorney general should be replaced by teachers and administrators. Second, teacher examinations for certification should be held only in Frankfort. Third, the role of the state superintendent should be expanded. Fourth, the county superintendent position should be made a full-time job with added responsibilities. Moreover, the commission suggested minimum and maximum salaries for each level of teaching certification. As with many other such studies, it was going to take years of effort to get its recommendations accepted into law and practice.[47]

Similar reform was sweeping the states adjacent to Kentucky. In Tennessee, the General Education Law of 1909 modernized the public school system as well as mandated that "25 percent of the gross revenue of the state" go toward public education. In the next decade the state raised the support level to one-third of the state budget. To the North, Indiana public schools made even more progress in the early twentieth century. Though ranking below most midwestern states, Indiana made some outstanding strides. In 1905 its legislature passed a law toward equalizing funding for rural schools and began consolidating and closing one-room schools at a faster rate than in Kentucky. Gary City School Superintendent William A. Wirt introduced a new style of education for an industrial city by developing a comprehensive vocational-academic program, "providing efficient, practical, mass education much as the Gary Works produced steel." No one in Kentucky matched this kind of innovation except perhaps Crabbe. In another southern state, North Carolina educational reform mirrored that of Kentucky in the early twentieth century. As in Kentucky, urban schools continued to do better than rural ones and black education received short shrift. In 1929 the Bowling Green school system reported spending $96.08 for each white student but only $64.89 for each "colored" child.[48]

"The educational winds seemed to be blowing strong," Harrison and Klotter concluded about the 1908 educational reforms, in *A New History of Kentucky*. The plethora of new laws appeared to have an immediate impact: school attendance increased, and in the first year, the amount of money available to the public schools produced by the new county taxes brought about an increase from $180,000 to $1 million. While 48 percent of Kentucky children attended school in 1900, ten years later the percentage had increased to 57. Only 106 public high schools existed in Kentucky during the 1909–1910 school year. By the advent of the Great Depression in 1930–1931, amazing growth had taken place, with 733 high schools housing 3,268 teachers and 60,315 students. That year 9,422 students graduated. Accreditation of Kentucky schools really began with the formation of the Association of Kentucky Colleges in 1905; the idea was to have some uniformity among high school education standards to aid in admitting students into higher education. Schools were divided into Class A and Class B, with graduation from the former automatically allowing entry into college. To achieve Class A recognition, a high school had to require fifteen credits, have a school year of not less than thirty-six weeks, and maintain at least three teachers. Accreditation by the Southern Association of Colleges and Secondary Schools took more time. In 1909–1910, no Kentucky high schools were accredited, but by 1930–1931, the Southern Association had accredited 82 public and 41 private high schools in Kentucky.[49]

The 1908 General Assembly, "the Education Legislature," according to Thomas D. Clark, "enacted a fresh blueprint for Kentucky Public School education in the Sullivan Law, as well as other landmark legislation." Nearly everyone writing about this era, including James Klotter, Fred Engle, Nancy K. Forderhase, Moses Ligon, and Frank L. McVey, has hailed this as one of the premier periods in the history of education in the commonwealth.[50]

However, Keith C. Barton in "The Gates Shut Quickly: Education and Reform in Kentucky, 1903–1908," offered a nearly opposite interpretation. First, he saw a conflict between those who wanted to centralize the county systems, "the reformers," and those who preferred the old decentralized trustee-controlled district schools. He maintained that the district schools were not as deficient as the reformers claimed. Second, although the KFWC pushed for education reform, its primary ambition was to secure suffrage. As it turned out, suffragists got educational reform but not full suffrage when the 1912 General Assembly passed limited suffrage for school elections. Barton's interpretation underscored the fact that subdistrict trustees still controlled the most vital factor in the local school; that is, they appointed the teachers, and many did so by bribery. Unfortunately, the sometimes tyranny of the local school trustee did not end but lingered into the Great Depression. It was replaced by the sometimes tyranny, cronyism, and nepotism of the school superintendent. By linking county taxation with more centralization in empowering the county superintendent, more money should be available for the schools. The poverty of the rural districts continued to contrast with the relative affluence of the towns and cities. In effect, there was simply, then and now, more money available in the urban areas than in the rural areas. The ongoing struggle in the twentieth century was over "equalization," giving compensatory funding to the poorer schools. Barton is correct that "the story is not so simple, and the changes not so progressive, as contemporary reformers and subsequent historians have described." However, Kentucky educational reformers were caught up in a regional and national movement of progressivism. Kentucky's professional educators, often called "educationists" by their detractors, followed a scripted reform rubric that had worked in other states. As had happened before and has happened since, educational reform was sporadic and difficult to maintain over a long period of time. Barton is basically wrong in asserting that "administrative centralization effectively destroyed community involvement." The latter depended on local interest in the schools, improvements in transportation, and the changes of the twentieth century. Moreover, he overlooked the importance of the Sullivan Law in finally pushing counties to form high schools.[51]

If the legislation of 1908 moved education forward for white Kentucky schoolchildren, it did nothing for African Americans. Because the new law did not specifically place "restrictions on black voters in the election of county board members," some whites feared black board members might be elected in areas "where blacks outnumbered whites." Bowing to the racial mores of the day, both John Grant Crabbe and Jere Sullivan went out of their way to "calm the fears of some Kentuckians who believed" that the new law "opened the door for the eventual mixing of the races in the state's public schools." Crabbe said the Kentucky Constitution ensured separation of the races. "If the colored voters in any school district in the county outnumber the white voters therein, that district can be changed by the local authorities, and thereby such result can be prevented," maintained Sullivan. Or, if worse came to worst, the whites could "establish a white graded school." After the first school elections under the new law, Sullivan boasted that "not a colored trustee was elected in the State, and in our judgment none will be." Black county high schools would have to fend for themselves in the rush to create more white county high schools.[52]

Two years after the passage of reform legislation in 1908, Crabbe reported that many county superintendents had seen real "progress." The Adair County superintendent said, "People are beginning to rally from the shock of new school law!" Many counties reported opening, or plans to open, at least one high school, including Bell, Boyle, Breckinridge, Caldwell, Campbell, Fleming, Grant, Hardin, Henderson, Lewis, Madison, Montgomery, Muhlenberg, Nelson, Oldham, Owen, Pendleton, Robertson, Rowan, Todd, Warren, Webster, and Wolfe. Shelby County reported opening four new county high schools. Several superintendents reported that their teachers were attending the new normal schools in Richmond and Bowling Green. The Whitley County superintendent said, "Forty teachers attended the State Normal in Richmond this year." Crabbe concluded in his report to the legislature that for the most part the new laws were working.[53]

The reform spirit of the early-twentieth century encouraged more urban areas to take the initiative and build new high school structures, as Maysville did in 1909. Other buildings evolved from one educational use to another. For example, the Hardin Collegiate Institute became a city high school building until Elizabethtown built its own high school. In the county systems, high schools were usually located in small towns and villages. By 1920 the little village of Bagdad had a new high school building and its first four-year graduates, five girls. (My mother, her brother, and her sister attended Bagdad High School in Shelby County, first organized in 1912.) Another interesting school was organized in the first decade of the twentieth century. For forty-one years, beginning in 1904, Rhoda C. Kavanaugh oversaw the Kavanaugh School in Lawrenceburg. Though coeducational from its beginning, the school became known as a topnotch preparatory boarding school for men. Called "Little Annapolis," Kavanaugh educated 150 men who became students at the U.S. Naval Academy as well as 15 who attended West Point. The school also operated as Anderson County High School from 1909 to 1920 and as Kavanaugh High School from 1920 to 1949.[54]

Change in the large urban districts and counties of the commonwealth in the early twentieth century outstripped change in the more rural areas of Kentucky. The Louisville and Jefferson County schools demonstrated all the ideals of Progressive Era education by expanding opportunities to more children. Louisville led the state in providing kindergarten education for the youngest children. By the turn of the century, the work of Patty Smith Hill and others had become nationally recognized. The biggest change was making kindergarten free and part of the Louisville public school system. John Dewey and other progressive educators were impressed by the Louisville experience. The Louisville Kindergarten Association became a national leader. In 1915 Male High School moved to a fine building located at Brook and Breckinridge Streets. Male and Manual merged for three years, 1915–1918, separated again, and did not become coeducational until 1952. Female High School officially became Louisville Girls' High School in 1912. Two additional high schools, Atherton, which opened in 1924 for girls, and Shawnee, which opened in 1929 as a boys' school, testified to the growth of the city. Known as du Pont Manual Training High School until 1950, Manual continued to grow in the early decades of the twentieth century. Theodore Ahrens Trade School, founded in 1925, evolved from an earlier vocational school. Theodore Ahrens, president of the Standard Sanitary Manufacturing Company, donated nearly $1 million to the school, which became a city high school in 1939. The Louisville system grew at the expense of the county as the city of Louisville annexed more of the county region. For example, in 1906 the Portland Elementary School became part of Louisville and its school system.[55]

The Louisville Board of Education evolved over time. A long-fought reform movement eliminated the twenty-four-member system, elected in districts, and replaced it by a five-member board in 1910. The pre-1910 Louisville Board of Education was highly politicized, as Democrats and Republicans openly vied for school board membership as part of their battle to control the city. The old board often sparred over individual teacher employment. Some board members brought concerns of the black community to the full board from time to time before 1910. Such groups as the Louisville Board of Trade, the League of Women Voters, and the Louisville Women's Club controlled who ran for the new school board seats into the Depression decade of the 1930s.[56]

The Jefferson County Board, being a county system, changed more slowly than did Louisville's board; it followed the old plan of one trustee for each school well into the new century. Small schools and independent districts predominated in such communities as Fairdale, Fern Creek, Middletown, and Shively. In 1928 five small districts consolidated and built the new Fairdale Grade and High School. During the 1923–1924 school year, Fern Creek added a two-year high school curriculum to its schools. The little Anchorage Graded and High School, building on the traditions of earlier private schools in the community, organized in 1911 as an independent district. Though generally prosperous, the residents of Anchorage still struggled to offer all the amenities needed in a small high school, and finally in the early 1950s, that school joined the county system.[57]

In the late nineteenth century, Fayette County, which had had forty-one rural districts at one time, slowly began consolidating the smaller schools. The five black districts in the county were located in the "new freedmen communities" at Bracktown, Maddoxtown, Cadentown, Uttingertown, and Fort Springs. Superintendent Nannie Faulconer (1905–1921) pushed consolidation of the white schools, and Greendale became the first in the county. Horse-drawn wagons transported children to the new consolidated schools until the county began acquiring motor vehicles in 1916. As happened in many county systems, some Fayette County youth, whose parents paid tuition for them, attended the city high schools. Massilon A. Cassidy, a Lexington school superintendent and one of the educational reformers in the state, also pushed for consolidation of one-room schools. Under his leadership Lexington opened its first consolidated elementary school at Picadome in 1888 and the first public high school at Morton in 1905. In 1917 Lexington High School opened. Responding to the growth of Lexington, the new Henry Clay High School opened in 1928.[58]

The effort to build a new African American high school in Lexington proved to be daunting. The Fourth Street Colored School opened on Fourth and Campbell Streets in 1889. Eventually it turned into Lexington's first high school and was named for Green P. Russell. By the early twenties that school had become outdated. William Henry Fouse and a committee of blacks advised the white school board on the location for a new school on North Upper Street. Paul Laurence Dunbar High School, built at a cost of $175,000, opened in 1923. "The erecting of Dunbar's building reflects one of the finest moments in the history of Blacks in Lexington," claimed the historian of the school. Moreover, Dunbar offered a comprehensive program of studies. Fouse, principal of the school from 1923 to 1938, encouraged students to attend college. Because it was a neighborhood school, "the community had a sense of ownership." Dunbar and the adjacent annex served as meeting places for women's groups such as the Kentucky Federation of Colored Women, as well as other organizations.[59]

The University of Kentucky provided some guidance to the Fayette County system, as did local Better School leagues. As a result of a 1930 study of the schools made by the system itself with assistance from UK's Bureau of School Service in the College of Education, Fayette County became a leader in reorganizing its county system by concentrating on consolidation. In 1930 the county board merged all subdistricts into one county system. Two years later the board constructed Bryan Station High School and planned for more change. A further study led to closing the high school at Athens and building Lafayette High School in 1939, funded with a Public Works Administration (PWA) grant. Just as important were curriculum modernization and providing more services to students. Moreover, UK personnel continued to consult with both city and county boards in Fayette County in attempts to educate all students more efficiently.[60]

A school of another kind filled an urgent need in Lexington. Witnessing the poverty of Irish immigrants in Irishtown and Davis Bottom, Lexington reformer Madeline McDowell Breckinridge initiated a project to provide both childhood and adult services in these areas. The Lexington Civic League coordinated with the school board to plan a school and settlement house facility. With donations from the Lexington Board of Education as well as $30,000 from the sixteenth president's eldest son, Robert Todd Lincoln, the Abraham Lincoln School opened in 1912. Originally called the West End School, this facility provided services based on the "model" of Chicago's leading settlement house, Jane Addams's Hull House. The school included shops, a laundry, showers, an assembly hall, and even a swimming pool.[61]

Catholics, devoted to education as part of the Americanization process, continued to expand their parochial education throughout the state. With the largest concentration of Catholics in the commonwealth located in Louisville, Louisville parochial schools prospered. St. Xavier High School for boys, founded in 1864; Ursuline Academy for girls, opened in 1858; and Mercy Academy for girls, founded in 1885, rivaled the public high schools of the city in providing a creditable education. Bishop William McCloskey established the Catholic School Board in 1887. The Louisville Archdiocese also enlarged its black school, Saint Augustine Catholic Elementary School, by adding high school classes. The school became known as Catholic Colored High School in 1929. Operated by the Sisters of Charity of Nazareth, this school, though always small, provided a basic education in "classical studies." When the General Assembly mandated higher certification of all teachers by 1926, Louisville Catholic colleges such as Nazareth College, Sacred Heart Junior College and Normal School, and Ursuline College provided the training. Bishop John A. Floersh reorganized the Catholic School Board in 1925, appointing Father Felix N. Pitt as executive secretary. Pitt led the board from 1925 until 1967 and mirrored the position of superintendent throughout his tenure. He oversaw a whole range of schools, including such elementary schools as Holy Rosary, and Cedar Grove Academy, later called Loretto High School.[62]

Wherever there was a sizable Catholic population, a parish school soon was built. In Maysville, St. Francis de Sales Academy for females prospered in the early twentieth century. The Visitation Sisters founded Cardome Visitation Academy, a boarding school outside Georgetown in the former estate of Governor James F. Robinson, in 1875. Cardome thrived in the early twentieth century; it had eighty-five students in 1937. From the "Rising Bell" at 6:30 A.M. to "Lights Out" at 9:20 P.M., the girls of Cardome followed a rather spartan regimen under the "Sister Directress." The Benedictine Sisters founded schools in Covington, in northern Kentucky. Other Catholic schools in Marion and Nelson counties formed a nucleus of communities in that area south of Louisville where Catholics first settled in Kentucky. In the northern Kentucky cities of Covington and Newport and along the Ohio River in Owensboro and Paducah, Catholic schools evolved into systems with high schools. Several Catholic parishes in western Kentucky, such as St. Jerome's at Fancy Farm in Graves County, began a tradition of holding community political gatherings and barbecues in the early twentieth century. Most were large enough to build elementary schools and perhaps even sustain high schools until they were overtaken by the merits of public school consolidation.[63]

Other nonpublic schools also flourished in the early twentieth century. Louisville Hebrew School, established in 1908, though founded by Orthodox Jews, also served Conservative and Reform families. Originally conducting classes only in Hebrew, the school changed over the years and eventually admitted girls. Military schools were popular in the wake of the Spanish-American War. Millersburg Military Institute, founded in 1893, occupied the old Kentucky Wesleyan College campus after that Methodist school moved to Winchester. MMI served a student body from several states and competed with Kentucky Military Institute, which in 1896 had moved to Lyndon in Jefferson County from Mt. Sterling. Though closing twice briefly in its early history and changing ownership several times, beginning in 1906 KMI wintered in Venice, Florida, for many years. Its enrollment often topped three hundred students.[64]

If Kentucky was to keep up its educational advancement in the United States, its culture needed to change. Even before women received full civil rights in the suffrage, they took on roles of leadership in a state beset by seemingly insoluble problems. At the age of four, Cora Wilson Stewart told her parents she wanted to be a teacher. Becoming certified to teach at age seventeen, she taught in the Rowan County schools and then received normal school education, including attendance at the renowned National Normal University in Lebanon, Ohio. Stewart became superintendent of Rowan County schools in 1901, married a teacher, and later divorced. Elected the first woman president of KEA in 1911, she took on the task of attacking one of the commonwealth's greatest educational problems, adult illiteracy.[65]

As the twentieth century opened, one of the commonwealth's biggest problems continued to be adult literacy. The overall illiteracy rate was 16.5 percent in 1900, a rate ranking "second best in the South." In the Kentucky state prisons, 60 percent of the inmates could neither read nor write. Kentucky had improved statewide to 12.1 percent ten years later. Beginning in 1911 Stewart initiated a plan to attack this problem at its base. She explained its origins in *Moonlight Schools for Emancipation of Adult Illiterates*, published in 1922. "They [Moonlight Schools] were designed, primarily, to emancipate from illiteracy all those enslaved in its bondage," she declared. "They were also intended to afford an opportunity to those of limited education who desired to improve their store of knowledge. . . . It was decided to have the schools on moonlight nights, and let the moon light them on their way to school." Between ages eighteen and eighty-six, they "came singly or hurrying in groups, they came walking for miles, they came carrying babes in arms, they came twelve hundred strong," Stewart exulted. Volunteers supplied most of the early teaching, and she published a newspaper, the *Rowan County Messenger*, with reading lessons in history, literature, and mathematics. Stewart reasoned that by learning to read a newspaper, illiterates would be saved the "embarrassment of using an elementary primer."[66]

The teachers used drills in history, instilling a few basic facts, and English, even teaching the correct pronunciation of words ending in "ing." School trustees, postmasters, and preachers, among others, learned to read and write. In the second year, Stewart reported that out of an enrollment of 1,600, 350 had learned to read and write. "The children were wonderful recruiting officers for the moonlight schools," said Stewart. "They worked and reported their success with the keen enthusiasm of childhood."[67]

Stewart's crusade appeared to be headed toward finally ending the ignominy of Kentucky's illiteracy problem. She lobbied the governors and the legislature for support and in 1914 received a grant of $5,000 for the newly created Kentucky Illiteracy Commission. The KFWC and other groups lent their support. Stewart's arc of leadership grew wider with her initial success in Kentucky and her penchant for promotion. The Rowan County superintendent led in organizing national illiteracy groups, including commissions founded by the National Education Association and the World Federation of

Education Associations. Among her books Stewart published adult readers, including *Soldier's First Book, Country Life Readers,* and *Mother's First Book.*[68]

However, by the time the legislature ended its support of the KIC in 1920, Kentucky's illiteracy rate had only fallen to 8.4 percent, or by about as much as it had between 1900 and 1910, 16.5 percent to 12.1. Meanwhile, Stewart's role in national education organizations widened. She was elected to the executive committee of NEA in 1923, and President Herbert Hoover appointed her chair of the executive committee of the National Advisory Committee on Illiteracy in 1929. Honors came to her. In 1924 she received a five-thousand-dollar achievement prize from *Pictorial Review* for her work and six years later the Ella Flagg Young medal for contributions in the field of education. Although progress appeared to be made, a 1943 study by the Committee for Kentucky revealed that the commonwealth ranked forty-seventh in literacy among the forty-eight states.[69]

For all the tumult and shouting, did Stewart ultimately fail? Was she a prophet without honor in her own state? While some saw her as a courageous woman fighting the good fight, apparently others viewed her as a meddlesome female who had forgotten her place. Did she make a mistake in personifying the crusade into a nearly one-woman show? Did Kentuckians numbingly tire of her incessant crusading spirit? "The crusade had failed," James Klotter declared in *Kentucky: Portrait in Paradox.* However, Stewart's most recent biographer, Yvonne Honeycutt Baldwin, comes to almost the opposite conclusion. "Stewart was strong-willed and determined, well organized and capable, and, above all, charismatic," Baldwin claimed. Moonlight schools taught "more than 700,000 Americans to read and write," of which "more than 100,000" were in the Commonwealth of Kentucky. Baldwin considered the reduction of illiteracy in Kentucky and the other states Stewart influenced, including Georgia, Alabama, South Carolina, Louisiana, and Arizona, highly significant. "If she failed to eradicate illiteracy, Cora Wilson Stewart nevertheless made an important contribution." Baldwin faulted "professional educators" for disparaging Stewart's programs. Moreover, the Moonlight School programs were handicapped from the start, owing to "only sporadic government backing." In the long run, Stewart inspired adult "literacy practitioners" and "a generation of volunteers" who "continue to look to her crusade for both wisdom and example." In the end, it was the fight that mattered, not necessarily the short-term results. Stewart stands out as a crusading Progressive Era reformer.[70]

With passage of the 1906 Normal School Law forming the new schools in Richmond and Bowling Green, a flurry of activity swept the state. Roark and Cherry began a rivalry, good-natured most of the time, and they cooperated in tweaking the nose of President Patterson. Roark died after a brief illness in early 1909 and was replaced on an interim basis for one year by his wife, Mary Creegan Roark. Governor Willson supported his fellow Republican State Superintendent Crabbe for the presidency of Eastern, and the Board of Regents unanimously voted their approval on April 9, 1910. Crabbe determined to build Eastern into a first-class normal school as quickly as possible. "We must teach teachers to teach," he declared in the *Eastern Kentucky Review* in 1915. Eastern and Western competed against each other for state funds and continually sparred over the boundaries of their districts.[71]

After Crabbe moved on to Eastern, Governor Willson appointed Ellsworth Regenstein (1909–1911), former superintendent of the Newport city schools, as state superintendent to fill out the unexpired term. Regenstein had some experience in Frankfort circles, having been appointed by Crabbe to the Board of Examiners, the body that governed state certification. After a brief study, Regenstein won a grant from the Southern Education Board to fund two new positions, a rural school supervisor and a high school supervisor. By this time, the General Education Board, established by the John D. Rockefellers, junior and senior, had begun to channel funds into the SEB, soon subsuming the latter. Thomas Jackson Coates became the rural supervisor and McHenry Rhoads the high school supervisor. Both Eastern and Western promised to support Coates's efforts. Coates received a joint appointment at both Eastern and Western normal schools to encourage their cooperation. The trustees of State University appointed Rhoads a professor of secondary education and supported his work. SEB/GEB funds also paid the salary of Anna Weaver as School Improvement League Organizer within the State Department of Education. The KFWC also helped support the work of Weaver. During his short time in office, Regenstein encouraged the efforts of the KEA to finalize a legislative agenda for the 1911 meeting of the General Assembly.[72]

The Progressive Era intensified in Kentucky during the administrations of two Democratic governors from 1911 to 1919, James B. McCreary, who had served a previous term from 1875 to 1879, and Augustus Owsley Stanley. They caught the crest of a wave of reformism sweeping America in the early twentieth century. While some historians view progressivism as being more sham than substance, because it appeared to be a reaction of white urban middle-class America against the rise of immigrant America, needed reforms did take place at the national and state levels. Regulation of railroads, utilities, and corporations came out of the growth of rural populism of the post–Civil War period. Middle-class reformers pushed for direct election of U.S. senators, a workable civil service, and control of lobbyists. Ending the worst abuses of child labor, creating a progressive income tax, and extending the suffrage to women all became important Progressive Era reforms. Coalitions of supporters on one issue, child labor reform, for example, might divide over another issue, such as Prohibition. Women's suffrage and the liquor question became so controversial in Kentucky that they divided progressives. Even Kentucky reformers could not always agree on the best way to bring about reform. For example, while Madeline McDowell Breckinridge supported a national amendment for suffrage, Laura Clay, a state's rights advocate, initially wanted suffrage laws to be passed by individual states. Eventually, the "wet-dry" issue irrevocably divided progressives, particularly in the Democratic Party, into warring camps. It is also important to remember that the Progressive Era was regressive about the racial divide in Kentucky, the South, and the rest of the nation generally. The period from 1890 to 1920 witnessed lynchings and other abuses of the black race in record numbers.[73]

McCreary's win in 1911 over Republican Judge Edward C. O'Rear occurred to some extent because of the support of the wealthiest man in the commonwealth, John C. C. Mayo, who had made his fortune with land options in eastern Kentucky, using the broad-form deed. So, would McCreary be beholden to the wealthy interests of the state, the liquor, tobacco, and other oligarchs? Called "Bothsides" by some of his detractors because of his continual testing of the political winds and waffling on issues, McCreary, a seventy-three-year-old Confederate veteran, seemed to sense the will of the people and adopted a surprisingly progressive agenda.[74]

The old governor, who dyed his hair and allegedly wore elevated shoes, urged new measures and improvements that paralleled progressivism in other states. The General Assembly created new regulatory commissions, including the State Board of Forestry, the Department of Banking, and the State Insurance Board. Following a national trend, the legislature also restricted a woman's labor outside the home to sixty hours a week.[75]

Elected along with fellow Democrat McCreary in 1911, State Superintendent Barksdale Hamlett (1911–1915) came to the office with experience as a teacher, as principal in Hopkinsville, and as superintendent of the Henderson City Schools; he had also served a term on the State Board of Examiners and had been president of the Kentucky Education Association, which had continued to grow and become an important political force in the commonwealth.[76]

McCreary's agenda for his first legislative session of 1912, and Hamlett's agenda too, included progressive educational measures. One of the best ways of improving school attendance in the rural areas was by improving roads. In 1912 the legislature passed a highway-improvement law creating the Department of Public Roads and the Road Fund. "There was a close parallel between consolidation and compulsory school attendance, on the one hand," said Clark in his piece on public education in the *Kentucky Encyclopedia*, "and the condition of Kentucky's roads on the other." In 1906 the General Assembly had passed a law limiting child labor to ten hours per day and sixty hours a week up to the age of sixteen. In McCreary's term the legislature lowered those limits to an eight-hour day and forty-eight hours per week. During school hours in the regular school term, no child under age fourteen would be allowed to work.[77]

The Legislative Committee of KEA, which included a blue-ribbon cross-section of the state's education leaders, worked hard to come up with a plan for the legislative session. Boone County superintendent Edgar C. Riley chaired the full committee; included were such influential Louisvillians as businessman John M. Atherton and John B. McFerran of the Louisville Commercial Club. Thomas Jackson Coates, state rural school supervisor, chaired a subcommittee. The committee reported to the annual KEA meetings of 1911, 1912, and 1913, proposing a consensus of what was needed to improve Kentucky's schools. Its list of seventeen recommendations included a panoply of ideas, from improving the rural districts, teacher certification, and teacher pay, to empowering the county superintendent, the state superintendent, and the State Board of Education. Specific progressive measures pushed by Hamlett included inspection of schools, changing the method of using the School Fund, a new compulsory school law, school suffrage for women, a county superintendent law, and a new county bond law.[78]

Laws passed by the 1912 General Assembly and signed by McCreary provided Kentucky with impetus in public school education. First, the state superintendent received more power to inspect schools, particularly for "gross frauds . . . perpetrated by the management of the school affairs of the State." In his first report after passage of the law, Hamlett reported the saving of $200,000 in state funds. The addition of a rural school supervisor in seventy counties was a start toward improving efficiency. A new law codified the minimum pay for the county superintendent ($600) and the maximum ($2,500). Hamlett claimed that the county superintendent had been raised to the same level as other county officials and that the holder of that office in a poorer county should no longer need to have other employment. A new teachers' salary schedule attempted to do away with the old corruption of paying a teacher for the total number of children in her or his district rather than the actual number of pupils taught. Now a teacher would be encouraged to get students into school and keep them there. However, the salary range, $35 to $70 per month, was shameful. The new compulsory attendance law, though receiving limited enforcement, increased attendance by 25 percent in rural districts, Hamlett reported. Suffrage in "school matters" was owed to women, Hamlett reasoned, because they historically took so much interest in the welfare of their children. However, this law, allowing women to vote in school trustee and board races, applied only to literate women. The County Bond Law permitted a county to sell bonds in order to build "school houses."[79]

Hamlett, an ambitious politician as well as an educator, undoubtedly padded the last part of his contribution to *History of Education in Kentucky*, published during his term. Nonetheless, his critique of the current situation in 1912–1914 and that of the KEA committee was realistic and farsighted. Kentucky children needed a longer school term. Whereas "almost every" urban area had a school term of "at least eight or nine months," he explained that "in only two or three counties of the State does the term extend beyond six months." While the two normal schools and State University now issued many of the life certificates, county examinations still existed, and enlightened Kentuckians saw the need to centralize certification even more. Acknowledging that the "question peddler" persisted in some areas, Hamlett vowed "that this nefarious business shall cease, and I shall use all the power of my office and the State to put a stop to it." Moreover, "census padding" continued in some areas. There was still work to do. "A great State must have vision, purpose and unity of effort," Hamlett said. "It must have moral, intellectual and industrial ideals and work to accomplish them. It must be affirmative and fearless. These qualities depend upon the people composing the State." The rhetoric that Hamlett used in his pronouncements perfectly fit with the uplifting ideals of progressivism in reforming education in America. "Progress" and "efficiency" were the watchwords.[80]

With the recommendations of the KEA committee and Hamlett's publicity, the education agenda of McCreary's second biennial General Assembly session in 1914 included more progressive-minded legislation. However, Kentucky Democratic Party factionalism was already rearing its ugly head as the Beckham and Stanley cliques maneuvered for the next battle. Nevertheless, the 1914 General Assembly passed some needed progressive laws, covering disclosure of campaign contributions and a uniform system of accounting, for example. Education legislation appeared even more successful.[81]

The education legislation of 1914 included laws encouraging the consolidation of graded and rural schools into a single county school district, creating a textbook commission for uniformity in county districts, refining the examination of teachers and increasing the penalties for "selling examination questions," increasing the school term when the per capita increased, giving more power to the State Board of Education over certification, and creating "the Kentucky Illiteracy Commission." School attendance also received an added boost by improvements to the child labor restrictions. Child labor laws, even in a state like Kentucky, which was not heavily industrialized, still had as much to do with keeping older children in school as school attendance laws did. Amending the law of 1906, the new law imposed a forty-eight-hour week and an eight-hour day, with the provision that no child under age fourteen should be working during school hours. Unfortunately, the first Kentucky child labor laws required notice of inspections, and businesses would often give children time off on the day inspectors were to arrive. Such organizations as the National Child Labor Committee had supporters in Kentucky and kept the issue before the public during the Progressive Era. Extending the mandatory school term to seven months briefly made Kentucky a leader in the South, but even that was not enough in the coming years to keep up with southern and national trends.[82]

Illustrating that partisan politics dominated Kentucky, former state superintendent (1899–1903) and secretary of state (1903–1907) Harry V. McChesney, "an ardent prohibitionist," ran in the Democratic primary for governor as an ally of J. C. W. Beckham against the leader of the wet faction, A. O. Stanley. After soundly defeating McChesney, Stanley faced Republican Edwin P. Morrow of Somerset in the 1915 gubernatorial race. To say "The Stanley-Morrow campaign was one of the most colorful and memorable in Kentucky history" is an understatement. While Stanley and Morrow publicly attacked each other at every turn, "in private they enjoyed dining and drinking together, and they were once observed walking with their arms around each other's shoulders." Stanley's win by only a 471-vote plurality was the narrowest victory margin in Kentucky gubernatorial election history. He carried along with him the entire Democratic ticket, including Virgil O. Gilbert as state superintendent.[83]

The Prohibition issue bedeviled Kentucky politics, as well as that of the nation, in the late teens. Although much of Stanley's first legislative session, in 1916, was taken up with bickering between wet and dry legislators, the General Assembly did produce progressive-minded laws, including "a corrupt practices act, an antitrust law, a workman's compensation measure, and a convict labor bill." Wanting to reform the taxing structure and system of Kentucky, Stanley called a special session in 1917. After "sixty days of often rancorous debate," the General Assembly passed several laws, including one establishing a three-member tax commission given the task of supervising tax laws and property assessments. The State Tax Commission and the new law brought substantial change, increasing land assessments and tangible property taxes significantly. While it would seem that with more tax revenue Kentucky's schools would receive more support, that did not happen immediately. Other issues took first place. The Prohibition question persisted, and in 1919 Kentucky, "the home of bourbon became officially dry before the nation did," by way of the Eighteenth Amendment, passed in 1920.[84]

Elected along with Stanley in the election of 1915, State Superintendent Virgil O. Gilbert had come up through the teaching ranks in the late nineteenth century, obtaining a normal school education in Glasgow. He became superintendent of the Simpson County Schools, then the Franklin City Schools, and served briefly as an instructor at Western Kentucky State Normal School before moving on to be chief clerk in the office of the state superintendent in Frankfort. Gilbert encouraged recodification of school laws, except for city schools. The measures he proposed included taking the school census every two years rather than annually and increasing from $100 to $200 annually the amount that could be spent for "textbooks for indigent children" in each county. Railroad and bridge taxes were to be paid directly to the county superintendent. All graded schools—and there were many independently created within county districts in small towns and villages—were to either provide for a high school or pay tuition for their students to attend a "standard high school." Eventually, this law encouraged many of the smaller district schools to consolidate into county systems. Teacher certification became better defined as normal school education became more available after the creation of the normal schools at Eastern and Western. An elementary certificate would be issued after one year of normal school education, an intermediate certificate for two years of work, and an advanced certificate for three years of normal school study. Finally, legislation passed by the 1916 General Assembly changed the name of State University to the University of Kentucky.[85]

The 1918 session of the General Assembly took place while the United States was engaged in the "Great War." That legislative session raised the maximum county school levy from twenty to thirty cents per $100 of evaluation. The school census age range was changed from 6–20 to 6–18. An agriculture course was to be added to all schools except in the town and city independent systems. Owing to World War I, the whole country became caught in an inflationary spiral. Unfortunately, cash-strapped school systems were allowed to issue interest-bearing warrants when the state School Fund did not have sufficient funds. These warrants were sold at a discount, sometimes substantial, in order to raise money at all levels of government. This system bedeviled Kentucky government for generations.[86]

World War I, the "war to make the world safe for democracy," placed a great stress on the nation. Male teachers as well as older students went into the armed forces or the war industries in large numbers. From 1916–1917 to 1917–1918, Superintendent Gilbert estimated that the number of male teachers in the state declined by 40 percent. Many were replaced by instructors with lesser credentials. On top of the stress of the war came the great influenza pandemic in the fall and winter of 1918–1919. The outbreak of the "Spanish Lady" (influenza) began at Camp Zachary Taylor in Louisville in September and then spread across the state. Although the city of Louisville rallied to help, eventually fifteen hundred men died at Camp Taylor. As the malady quickly spread across the commonwealth, the State Board of Health on "October 7 ordered all schools, churches, and places of entertainment closed until further notice and [ordered] that Kentuckians refrain from travel." These restrictions ended in late October, but the flu continued to reach all parts of Kentucky. Eventually, as many as sixteen thousand Kentuckians died, young and old, parents and children. One Eastern alumna, Mabel G. Pullen, lost five of her elementary school students to the dreaded disease. By the spring of 1919, the number of cases had abated, but the economic repercussions and family hardships continued for many years.[87]

During the era of World War I, an incident added to Kentucky's colorful history with an eventual fillip for education. Louisville lawyer Robert Worth Bingham married wealthy heiress Mary Lily Kenan Flagler, the widow of Henry Flagler of Standard Oil fame, on November 15, 1916. On June 27, 1917, just after the United States entered the war, the new Mrs. Bingham, billed as the "richest woman in America," died. The circumstances of her death are still debated, but the outcome for the commonwealth proved fortuitous. Everyone scrambled to get part of her estate. The state governments of Kentucky and New York, where she owned extensive property, as well as prominent political figures in Kentucky, such as governors Stanley and Morrow, became involved in extended court cases and proceedings. After years of wrangling, the bulk of her estate went to her North Carolina relatives, but Bingham ended up with $5 million through a codicil to his wife's will, the federal government received $6 million, and eventually the commonwealth got $3.3 million, which was divided among the road, general, sinking, and common school funds and small amounts for the University of Kentucky and the Western and Eastern state normal schools. Former state senator Jere Sullivan, who sponsored the 1908 law bearing his name, somewhat callously and cynically summed up the event in a letter to Robert Worth Bingham: "At the time, I had no idea that that important event, to wit; your said marriage, could possibly mean as it now seems it will mean to the State of Kentucky and its taxpayers."[88]

During Stanley's term "the Progressive Era reached its apex in Kentucky," according to Harrison and Klotter in *A New History of Kentucky*. But if there was progress on some fronts during the so-called Progressive Era in Kentucky, race relations appeared at a standstill at best. Education for African Americans in Kentucky continued to be a considerable uphill battle.[89]

After the Civil War, race relations in the South, with which most white Kentuckians identified, inexorably ground toward nearly complete separation of the races in any public arena. An 1882 law, ratified overwhelmingly at the polls, authorized taxation to equalize education for white and black children, but it also completely separated black and white public school education. This law, however, required only equality of state funds; neither taxation nor funding at the local level for black education was included. The 1891 Kentucky constitution mandated "separate schools for white and colored children" in public education in Section 187, and the Day Law of 1904 completed the segregation of private school education. Although Kentucky supposedly practiced "separate but equal" education, declaring in its constitution, "In distributing the school fund no distinction shall be made on account of race or color," in the first two decades of the twentieth century African American youth received short shrift. In a state with poor school housing, black schools were among the worst, and black students often received "the worn-out leftover" textbooks. As late as 1939, a study of curriculum in Kentucky also pointed to a dearth of educational material for African American students. "The Negro graduate of the public-school system is practically made an orphan from his racial heritage," said Rolfe Lanier Hunt. "The Negro has been practically ignored in the textbooks, normally prepared by white men for white students who have constituted the bulk of the book market. The Negro has been practically ignored by the creators of courses of study, for the most part impressed by the needs of the greater numbers of white students." Furthermore, the Sullivan Law of 1908 made no mention of creating high schools for blacks.[90]

Louisville, the largest city in the state, with the largest black population, remained a focal point for the aspirations of African Americans. Black students, teachers, and administrators, as in the rest of the state, had to struggle to get adequate funding and salaries. For example, in 1900 principals of white schools in Louisville received $250 monthly while blacks got $165. Black teachers received at least sixty dollars less per month than their white counterparts. While Central High School lacked the depth of courses at the Male, Manual, and Girls' high schools, under principal A. E. Meyzeek Central had a mostly standard academic program, like the white high schools. Throughout the early part of the twentieth century, the Louisville School Board pushed black children at all levels into "domestic science and manual training" more than white students. African American leaders in Louisville urged that a separate vocational school like Ahrens be built, but instead, vocational courses were added at Central and other schools after World War I.[91]

An infusion of private support aided African American Kentucky educators and their institutions in the early twentieth century. The Jeanes Fund provided money to the Negro Rural School Fund, which primarily supplied teachers for industrial training. The John F. Slater Fund aided the development of black high schools, particularly those that offered vocational education. Between 1911 and 1919, five black high schools were established, including Maddoxtown in Fayette County, Pembroke in Christian County, Little Rock in Bourbon County, Mt. Sterling in Montgomery County, Providence in Webster County, and Campbellsville in Taylor County. While the Slater Fund contributed $500 annually toward teaching costs, funds from the General Education Board, originally endowed by John D. Rockefeller Sr., went toward equipment purchases and housing for teachers. The GEB in effect reinforced segregation by helping fund a division for "Negro" education within the State Department of Education. In a more "southern" state, such as North Carolina, the results were the same, with the GEB following the strictly segregated "color line" of southern racial mores. The GEB funded annual African American summer schools in several Kentucky counties, including Jefferson, Madison, Daviess, and Todd, cooperating with State Normal in Frankfort and the West Kentucky Industrial College for Colored Persons in Paducah. One of the biggest problems continued to be building and funding school buildings for African Americans. Beginning in 1912, Julius Rosenwald, president of Sears, Roebuck, and Company, joined with Booker T. Washington in developing a program to build and equip badly needed school buildings for blacks. Of 5,300 buildings in fifteen southern and southwestern states, 158 "Rosenwald Schools," or buildings, were constructed in Kentucky. Without these programs, the education of black children in Kentucky would have languished under even more deplorable conditions. However, the generosity of the Rosenwald, Jeanes, and Slater agencies allowed the Commonwealth of Kentucky to divert funding to white schools from monies that should have been expended on African American education.[92]

The Julius Rosenwald Fund disbursed "seed" money for the construction of schools, paying a sometimes small but important part of the overall cost. For the 158 schools built in sixty-four Kentucky counties from 1917 to 1932, most of the funding ($878,748 of a total expenditure of $1,081,710) came from state and local taxes. The significance of the Rosenwald Fund was the impetus it gave to the building of black schools that otherwise might never have been built. For example, for the building of the appropriately named Rosenwald School in Harrison County, in 1924–1925, the local African American population contributed $100, the "public" contributed $1,650 through taxation, and the Rosenwald Fund paid $400 of the total of the $2,150 construction cost. Most of the schools were one-, two-, or three-teacher schools. The Madisonville School, a ten-teacher high school with a shop and a library, built in 1930–1931, was an exception. With no "Negro" or "White" contributions for construction, the "public" paid $27,500 and the Rosenwald Fund $7,500 of the total cost of $35,000 for the Hopkins County school. Because many of the old Rosenwald schools were abandoned after the beginning of desegregation in the 1950s, an effort is presently being made to save such schools, including the Hickory Colored School in Graves County. Of the total cost of this one-teacher school built in 1925–1926 for $2,010, the "Negro" contribution was $50, the "public" contribution $1,560, and the Rosenwald Fund contribution $400.[93]

Rosenwald helped fund the construction of the Middletown Elementary School in southern Madison County. From 1927 to 1963, this school, led by principal "Professor" Robert Blythe (male elementary and secondary teachers were often given this title in the nineteenth and early twentieth centuries) throughout its history, became a focal point of black rural education of the area. Aided by nearby Berea College with a grant of four acres to the Madison County schools, Middletown also received from the college a school bell that had once belonged to John G. Fee. With some sacrifice, the school built a tower to contain the bell, which announced to the surrounding community the beginning and ending of the school day. Blythe received his schooling at Kentucky State in 1922 and a bachelor's degree from the University of Cincinnati in 1938. Along with his sister, he bucked the trend and emphasized academic over vocational education.[94]

Against amazing odds, more and more African American youth obtained a high school education. A declining black rural population made it difficult to fund county African American high schools under segregation. Only a few public high schools for blacks existed. The first one opened in Louisville in 1874, and by the 1890s public high schools operated in Frankfort, Covington, Lexington, Owensboro, Paducah, Paris, and Winchester. Black high schools usually emphasized practical and industrial skills more than academic coursework. However, by 1900, 714 students attended high schools and 93 of them graduated, statistics that led the segregated South. Seven years later a higher percentage of blacks actually attended school on a daily basis than did white students. When Douglass High School opened in Henderson in 1905, adding one class at a time, rural students "came on foot, by bicycle, and in horse and buggy" to take advantage of the opportunity. The efforts of black educators, their white allies, and the Jeanes, Slater, GEB, and Rosenwald funds began to make great changes. However, the results were mixed. As the twentieth century progressed, black males tended to drop out of high school at a higher rate than females. By 1938 females accounted for 64 percent of enrollment by the twelfth grade. Black illiteracy rates in Kentucky steadily declined, from 56 percent in 1890 to 28 percent in 1910. After its founding in 1912, Lincoln Institute became the leading black residential school in Kentucky, emphasizing traditional skills as well as home economics and "the building trades."[95]

The Bond-Washington School in Elizabethtown, named for Dr. James Bond and Booker T. Washington, evolved from a graded elementary school into a school offering all twelve grades by the mid-twenties. Originally called the East Side School, the new building, dedicated on October 1, 1923, was one of the four-room Rosenwald model structures. The school became a magnet for black students from not only Hardin County but adjacent LaRue and others. Out-of-town students boarded with black families or worked for their room and board. Lydia Beller Wells worked for a white family for her room and board and received a salary of four dollars per week until she graduated. David Cleaver Sr. roomed with other male students from out of town, and the group prepared their own meals. He told an interviewer many years later that "he ate so many pork and beans he cannot face a bean to this day." Early basketball games were played on an outdoor dirt court. Occasionally, the Bond-Washington High School team received permission to play in the Elizabethtown High School gymnasium. Kentucky's early-twentieth-century racial mores and prejudices were never far below the surface. Once when the bus carrying the basketball team had a flat tire in the late evening, some players asked for help at a nearby house. A man came to the door carrying a shotgun and shouted: "You niggers get away from here." After sleeping on the bus through the night, the team found assistance at a garage the next morning and made their way back to Elizabethtown later in the day.[96]

Because fewer opportunities for black educated professionals existed in Kentucky and the nation at large, well-qualified and well-educated African Americans were drawn into long-time teaching careers. "For many [black] women, teaching became a kind of sacred calling, rather like that of the celibate priest," maintained a historian of black education. "Many never married. Others subordinated husbands and children to their driving commitment as teachers. Frequently their marriages and families suffered. Either way, they acted as if God had called them to teach and expected their husbands to either help them or not interfere." For generations white northern missionaries in the South "viewed teachers as bearers of religion and morality. Booker T. Washington saw them as agents of economic progress." The advent of progressivism reinvigorated these roles. The Jeanes Teacher Program, aimed at encouraging and improving education for rural blacks in the South, was among several groups that aided Kentucky African Americans. Between 1919 and the late 1940s, forty-three Jeanes-sponsored supervisors labored in black Kentucky schools. Black teachers tended to stay in the profession longer than their white counterparts because they had fewer opportunities elsewhere, and on the whole they were better trained. Whereas in 1921 only 23 percent of white Kentucky teachers had one or more years of college education, 46 percent of black teachers had such training. However, they generally received less pay. A study in 1916 showed that white teachers averaged $322.76 annually and black teachers $310.05. Nevertheless, the efforts of black teachers and parents and their children, encouraged by the GEB, Rosenwald, and Jeanes funds and leadership, encouraged "black agency": gaining some control over their destiny in a still blatantly segregated society.[97]

From 26 high schools and 1,054 students in 1915–1916 to 73 high schools and 4,083 students in 1929, African Americans in Kentucky appeared to make advancement in this era. In 1929, 40 of the high schools were in cities, 31 in counties, and 2 were state schools. However, only 25 of the city high schools provided a full four-year education. Most were small schools with a very limited curriculum. In 1929, 65 percent of them enrolled fewer than fifty students. Fourteen schools had only one teacher. A study by Myrtle R. Phillips, published in the *Journal of Negro Education* in 1932, revealed the promise and the problems of black high school teachers and pupils. Even though black high school teachers, on average, had more college education than their white counterparts, and although Kentucky had a nondiscriminatory law, in 1929 black high school teachers averaged $741.68 annually, compared with $1,023.98 for white high school teachers. Phillips summarized the problems facing the education of black high school students as a need to add more four-year high schools, increase the size of schools, improve teacher salaries and pupil retention, move toward accreditation of all schools, and reach more students. As in all small communities, black schools were the center of attention in black communities in the early twentieth century. The "Boston" area of Georgetown "is still a community within a town," said one resident in 2008. In 1884 the Chambers Avenue School opened there, in 1929 renamed Ed Davis High School for its first principal.[98]

In 1939 President Rufus B. Atwood of Kentucky State College realistically assessed the state of African American education in Kentucky. Although progress had been made, glaring "inequalities" still existed as more and more black families left rural areas for the city. Atwood believed that local school boards did not always channel state funds equally to black and white students and that an equalization law was needed not only for black students but also to help whites in the poorer county districts. A law passed in 1936 required that each school district provide for "a twelve grade school" for all African

American students. However, 61 of Kentucky's 120 counties had only an average of seventy black students, making it nearly impossible to maintain a high school. A study by the Department of Education found seven hundred black children in the state with "no school service provided." A 1938 law addressing this problem offered some promise. Thereafter, any school district that did not provide a black high school was to pay for and transport students to another district for an education. All was not bleak. In the larger towns and cities, black students attended school on a par with the average white child and their teachers were well trained. However, blacks' school facilities were of lower quality and their teachers' salaries were below those provided for whites in the late interwar period. There appeared to be valiant efforts to better educate black Kentuckians, particularly by philanthropic groups, but it is difficult to dispute the conclusions of Timothy J. Jackson in a study of vocational education in Kentucky: "Black vocational education in Kentucky and throughout the South was designed and implemented by middle and upper class whites for the specific purpose of keeping blacks in the lowest positions in economic and social hierarchy." Historian James L. Leloudis also found that in North Carolina from 1880 to 1920, white educationists supported a policy of limiting the "Great Migration" of African Americans out of that state by improving black schools, but only just enough to create a plentiful and subservient supply of black labor.[99]

Like the lives of teachers, those of schoolchildren often go unrecorded. An insight into the life of African American schoolchildren in the early twentieth century can be found in *The Dark Side of Hopkinsville: Stories of Ted Poston.* Poston, who later had a long career in journalism, including thirty-five years at the *New York Post,* fictionalized his childhood experiences, claiming that "someone should put down the not-always depressing experiences of a segregated society like the one I grew up in." The son of a teacher who labored at Kentucky State Normal and Industrial Institute for Negroes in Frankfort at one time, Poston worked hard to become educated himself. In a series of ten delightful, insightful, often funny stories, he describes black culture of the time from the perspective of an observant black child. The book's hero, "Rat Joiner," was based on a real person, as were many other characters in the book.[100]

There was another underserved student population in Kentucky. "As late as the early twentieth century, the Appalachian region of eastern Kentucky was still physically isolated from the mainstream of American life," maintained historian Nancy Forderhase. "Few roads penetrated the area, and the people living in the remote hollows and narrow valleys had limited access to public schools and health care." Although the "Moonlight Schools" of Cora Wilson Stewart made a slight dent in the region's illiteracy rate, too few children found access to the public schools. To fill this void, reformers followed the rationale of the urban settlement-house movement and began filtering into the recesses of Kentucky's mountains. Some of these ventures were undertaken by religious organizations, but even the secular reformers had a missionary zeal for their work.[101]

Religious groups tried to fill the educational void in Kentucky's Appalachia on a broad front. Oneida Baptist Institute, on the South Fork of the Kentucky River in northern Clay County, opened in 1900. Baptist minister James Anderson Burns believed that education would alter the feuding nature of the region. Claiming to have started with but twenty cents and a willingness to work, he helped create a school in an otherwise barren educational region. Like many other such schools, Oneida operated as a boarding school to exert a wider influence. Another Baptist mission field, outside of Appalachia, developed at Campbellsville in the form of Russell Creek Academy, founded by the local Baptist association in 1906. Williamsburg Institute, another Baptist school, and Sue Bennett Memorial School, a Methodist one, also demonstrated the vitality of the religious-oriented mountain institution. Williamsburg Institute opened in 1889 and evolved into Cumberland College in 1913. Sue Bennett Memorial School, sponsored by the Woman's Parsonage Missionary Society of the Methodist Episcopal Church, South, opened in London in 1897. It also moved toward college status, becoming Sue Bennett College in 1922; like early Cumberland College, it first offered a junior college curriculum. Beginning in 1924, Campbellsville Junior College grew out of Russell Creek Academy while the institution still offered elementary and secondary education. Frenchburg Presbyterian College functioned as a high school in the county seat of Menifee County; it was an educational mission of the Women's General Missionary Society of the United Presbyterian Church of North America from 1910 until just after World War II.[102]

Presbyterian minister Sam Vandermeer came to Appalachia on a summer mission trip in the early twenties, stayed into the fall to teach at the Buckhorn School in Perry County, and fell in love with the people and culture. He taught briefly in other places but ministered mostly at Morris Fork in Breathitt County. He married a missionary nurse, Nola Peace, and they moved to an area described by Robert M. Rennick in *Kentucky Place Names* as "a remote and disreputable section" of Breathitt County. They wound up staying for more than fifty years in a place Vandermeer described, originally, as "a tired country. The mothers were tired, the children were tired, the men were tired trying to make out a living on those steep hillsides. . . . And the land itself was tired because it had raised corn year after year after year with no crop rotation." The Vandermeers not only ministered to the souls of their community but also encouraged education and economic change. Missionaries like the Vandermeers made great personal sacrifices to bring hope and change, if only limited, to small communities in Appalachia.[103]

Forderhase summed up the progressive impulse of the first wave of female reformers to come to Kentucky. "By the early twentieth century, adventurous, well-educated, idealistic young women, nurtured in reform ideas of the era, turned their attention from the urban scene and began working in the remote regions of southern Appalachia," she noted. "They were drawn to the mountains because the hill country had attracted national attention." As Henry D. Shapiro explained in *Appalachia on Our Mind*, the region became popularly known by the late nineteenth century, and northern missionaries turned their attention to the area. Many of these religionists shifted the thrust of their outreach from blacks to poor whites "in Appalachia, where they believed a hardy pioneer breed could be uplifted by educational and religious endeavors." Apparently many reformers, of either a secular or a religious resolve, became disillusioned with uplifting America's black population. This coincided with "increasing racism and northern disappointment over Reconstruction."[104]

Hindman Settlement School and Pine Mountain School were two of the earliest and best known of the secular mountain settlement schools. Katherine Pettit, born in Fayette County, attended Sayre School before becoming a teacher. May Stone, born in Owingsville, attended private schools in Kentucky before leaving the state for Wellesley College. Between 1899 and 1901, Pettit and Stone taught summer schools near Hazard and Hindman. They believed the urban settlement-school model could be applied to the mountains. "Encouraged by those experiences," and sponsored by the Women's Christian Temperance Union (WCTU), they founded a settlement school in Hindman in Knott County at the forks of Troublesome Creek in 1902.[105]

In her book *Challenge and Change in Appalachia: The Story of Hindman Settlement School*, Jess Stoddart described the school as a prototypical institution that "grew out of the great reform impulse called Progressivism." Hindman holds an important place in women's history. "Pettit and Stone's work reflected the special concerns of southern reform, the conservative cultural context in which southern women reformers operated, and the attitudes and beliefs common to the first generation of women who entered roles in the public sphere," Stoddart maintained.[106]

Early teachers at Hindman came from prestigious eastern women's colleges, including Smith, Mt. Holyoke, Vassar, and Wellesley. Hindman Settlement School reached out to the surrounding community by helping other rural schools and providing medical clinics. After thirteen years Hindman Settlement School ended its relationship with the WCTU and struck out on an independent course. Pettit left Hindman to found Pine Mountain

Settlement School, in an "even more remote location" in Harlan County in 1913. While she concentrated on construction and farming at Pine Mountain, her coworker Ethel de Long Zande "managed academic and fund-raising activities."[107]

These mostly eastern college graduates found the Appalachian experience unusually positive. "They viewed Appalachia as a remote, almost foreign, land, and they saw their experiences in the rugged hinterland as a great adventure," explained Forderhase, "perhaps *the* most important adventure of their lives." Catherine Rittenhouse, who arrived at Pine Mountain from Minnesota in 1914, thought of Oberammergau, explaining, "I almost expected to see the cross on the mountain top when the mists lifted or to meet long haired Bavarians going to early mass." Another worker found the hills and mountains "intoxicating." "I find it hard to stick to my job and yet I realize how fortunate I am to have my job in such surroundings," she said. Zande, principal of Pine Mountain, in her promotional material for the school fund-raising, stressed the idyllic nature of the region: "To us grown people, Pine Mountain seems almost like a Utopian place, where the children's work is not slavish but joyful—where their thought and their play are shot through with imagination and their courtesies are unfailing and sweet." However, the settlement-school women "were shocked and dismayed by the squalor they witnessed in some of the mountain homes." And they were sometimes worn down by the work, the poverty, and the lack of progress.[108]

In 1916 Alice Geddes Lloyd came to Knott County at Pippa Passes on Caney Creek and began a community center. A Massachusetts native and a graduate of Radcliffe College, Lloyd received land from a Knott County landowner in return for educating his children. Her husband, Arthur Lloyd, returned to the East after only one year. Wellesley graduate June Buchanan arrived in 1919 to become a lifelong worker in the school. Their school, Caney Creek Community Center, at first offered the elementary grades but began adding high school courses in 1919. In 1923 the effort evolved into Caney Junior College, later called Alice Lloyd College. Buchanan served nearly seven decades at the school, and grades one to twelve at Pippa Passes became the June Buchanan School. Unfortunately, the educators of Appalachia did not always present a united front. The clash of Lloyd with Hindman was one example. P. David Searles in *A College for Appalachia: Alice Lloyd on Caney Creek* admitted that the "record strongly suggests that Alice Lloyd started the whole fuss by her aggressive fund-raising, by the way she positioned her own work as unique in the mountains, and by the way she implicitly and explicitly called into question the value of the work performed by other groups, by her unwillingness to join with other benevolent workers in common cause, and by her sharp, public criticism of denominational missionaries." Stone and

Lloyd also disagreed about how to best educate mountain youth. This conflict is perpetuated somewhat by the contrasting interpretations of Searles, in his book on Lloyd, and Stoddart, in her book on Hindman, over which was the more conservative, industrial education or "purely academic education."[109]

Other mountain settlement schools founded in the early twentieth century include Hazel Green Academy (1895) in Wolfe County; Henderson Settlement School (1925), at Frakes in Bell County; Red Bird Mission School (1921), also in Bell County; Stuart Robinson School (1913) and Kingdom Come School (1924) in Letcher County; and Lotts Creek Community School (1933) in Knott County. Hiram Milo "Parson" Frakes, a Methodist minister, founded Henderson as an elementary school and community center to serve nearby coal camps. A high school was soon added. Like other such boarding schools, it depended on a substantial farm operation as well as donations from Methodists and other sources. Lotts Creek, founded by Alice H. Slone, was one of the last such schools started in Appalachia. A native of the region, she attended Ohio State University and returned home to teach one year at Caney Creek Settlement School before founding Lotts Creek in 1933. She was associated with the school for more than a half century. Annville Institute, formed by the Women's Board of Domestic Missions of the Reformed Church in America, opened in 1910, under the leadership of Rev. William A. Worthington and closed in 1978. Over the years its mission changed from time to time. Beginning as an elementary school, Annville in 1923 added a high school with commercial and vocational training to fit the area of its service. Students worked on the campus farm. As in other schools of this type, religion was always a priority. "I will attend and cooperate in the religious program of the Annville Institute" was the first item in the "Student's Pledge" upon enrollment. Annville remained the only accredited "A" high school in Jackson County until after World War II.[110]

Unfortunately, in order to raise money for their efforts in these places of obvious need, the settlement workers perpetuated "stereotypes of the region." As James Klotter explained, "ironically, they had to present the worst picture in order to get the most money" for their institutions. Although they were perhaps too romantic in their thinking and even elitist, they provided needed services during the time, services the public schools could not or would not provide. Pettit and Stone encouraged conservation of mountain culture, including folklore, music, and crafts. Pine Mountain sponsored trachoma, tonsil, and dental clinics. Many people learned for the first time about healthful living. Some of the women courageously attacked the scourge of mountain moonshining. Forderhase found that in the end, the mountain settlement-house effort was indeed worthy of the efforts of these progressives. These were not pie-in-the-sky reformers. For example, after years of experience Zande had matured "from a misty-eyed idealist to a practical, yet optimistic professional." One historian of the Pine Mountain Settlement School, James S. Greene III, described its founders as "realists who clearly perceived the dangers of doing too much for the people, who abhorred the effects of pauperization and patronization, and who sought no self-gratification from their efforts."[111]

There has been much scholarly debate over the motivations and outcomes of the mountain settlement-house movement and "the do-gooders" of the early twentieth century. Among others, John Fetterman, Gerald Jones, and David E. Whisnant attacked the founders of such schools as Hindman and Pine Mountain, saying they were disrupters of original mountain culture who, perhaps more inadvertently than overtly, prepared the way for industrialization of the region. Whisnant argued that these reformers tried to radically change the cultural context of the region for the worse. Rodger Cunningham places what he calls the "infantilization" of Appalachians in a larger context of Celtic and Scots-Irish heritage. The youth of Appalachia would have been much worse off if not for the efforts of these educators and their local supporters and fellow workers. All in all, most if not all of the mountain settlement workers, religious and secular, performed admirably. They did not always have the best of intentions, but most all of their work in education filled a void that could not at the time be filled in any other way. They were living out the theories of John Dewey's progressive education, improvising and working to develop the whole person. The final question is this: If they had not educated these people, who would have? Public education was not able to do so for years. Even Whisnant did not deny that. "What it [Hindman] did do for a time—very well indeed—was to provide a superior basic education for hundreds of Knott County youngsters, along with food, clothing, shelter, and medical care for many of them." Questioning the intentions of these reformers does little good except to give scholars an opportunity to write books and ruminate at conferences decades after these reformers, mostly women, entered the breach. James C. Klotter, Kentucky state historian, said: "I am aware of all those criticisms of the settlement schools and agree with those at a certain level, but there were no educational opportunities in some areas without those schools." The charge of "cultural imperialism" against them is specious, because all levels of education indoctrinate. "For that reason I give them [the settlement schools] pretty high marks," Klotter concluded. The final word and judgment should be that of Loyal Jones, an Appalachian expert, who believes that these "women were readily accepted and even revered by the mountain people" for their devotion to "a whole range of social programs."[112]

There were others laboring on behalf of Appalachian youth. Mountain communities that contained coal prospered in the best of times and suffered during an economic downturn or when the coal seams ran out. Coal camp schools, funded by the coal companies, were among the best in the mountains. Even in the segregated coal camps, black schools served their students well. Lynch and Benham in Harlan County, and Jenkins in Letcher County became showplaces of what company towns could become. In Wheelwright, founded in 1916 by the Elkhorn Coal Company in Floyd County, the company even paid for the uniforms of the football and baseball teams and the band instruments. Black children living in Lynch and Benham began attending Lynch Colored High School, also called West Main High School, in 1923. This school closed in 1963 when integration came to the community. There were problems in the eastern Kentucky highlands. An early-1920s study by the National Child Labor Committee discovered serious neglect of school structures as well as of the education of children. In Magoffin County one of the NCLC's investigators found three rural schools where, because the parents were off tending onion fields in Ohio, no students attended. At one dilapidated school, "sitting in the doorway," he discovered a teacher "fulfilling his part of the contract by being at the school although no children came." When the Great Depression hit in full force, many coal camps cut back production or completely closed, ending the educational progress they had brought as well. Only Wheelwright, as a company coal town, survived into the postwar years.[113]

Teachers, public and private, no matter where they worked, faced a daunting task educating Kentucky youth in the early twentieth century. The hours were long, the work hard, the schoolrooms crowded. A front-page notice in a Powell County newspaper about a young teacher personified the problems faced by many a teacher and school in this period. "Miss Wash, teacher of intermediate grades in the city Graded and High School, resigned with her last week's work. Her room was overcrowded, thus rendering her duties so onerous, that she could not do justice to the grades, so she resigned, and the school board is now looking for a teacher or two to fill the vacancy. The position pays $65.00 per month."[114]

Most Kentucky educators of the early twentieth century grew up in the same educational milieu they entered as teachers in their late teens and early twenties. Many received a modicum of teacher education at Eastern or Western or summer teaching schools before entering the profession.

Born to Greenup County tenant-farming parents in 1906, Jesse Stuart had a life that illustrated much about the educational struggles of the time. He became a teacher himself and grew into one of Kentucky's best-known and undoubtedly most prolific writers. At age eighteen, the minimum legal age for a beginning teacher, he taught all eight grades in a one-room school, not finishing high school himself until two years later. In semifictional style, he immortalized his early life and, albeit brief, teaching career in *The Thread That Runs So True*.[115]

"As a teacher in a one-room school, where I taught all eight grades, and then high school, as a principal of rural and city high schools and superintendent of city and county school systems," Stuart said, "I learned by experience that teaching is the greatest profession there is, and that the classroom can be made one of the most exciting places on earth for young, middle-aged, and older people to improve themselves for more useful and richer living." Although he said "my heart was always in the classroom," Stuart admitted leaving the profession "because I thought I could not make enough money to live." His statement points to an obvious problem in Kentucky education: many teachers stopped teaching because of low salaries. But thousands of Kentucky teachers over the years stuck it out, accepting a lower salary than they could have commanded elsewhere.[116]

The life and teaching career of Thelma Beeler also illustrated much of the evolution of Kentucky education from the early twentieth century to the advent of the twenty-first century. Born in 1904 in Canaan Land in Mercer County, Beeler began teaching in 1922 in a two-room school near Shakertown. For sixty-five years she labored in Kentucky schools, ending her career at Lafayette High School.[117]

Beeler's duties included "getting up very early in the morning in order to get to school to build a fire in the potbellied stove so the room would be warm before the children got there." She often brought a "huge pot of vegetable soup to keep hot on the big stove" to feed the students at lunchtime. Teaching could be a real adventure for the new teacher. Knowing that one boy in her first class had pulled a knife on the previous teacher, driving her off, Beeler was ready. "Well, true to form, on my second day in the classroom, the bravest of the bullies, Cal, tried the same knife trick with me," Beeler recalled. "I grabbed the knife, threw it up front against the blackboard, knocked him out of his seat onto the floor, grabbed him, shook him, and flopped him back down into his seat. Things were very peaceful after that. I was told that, during recess, he warned the other boys, 'Don't fool with that hyena; she'll kill you.'" The next day the boy's father came to school, not to fight, but to thank Beeler for "straightening out my son."[118]

Renowned Appalachian scholar Cratis D. Williams got his first teaching job because his father persuaded the local school trustee that Cratis, only eighteen years old, should take over the Boggs School on Caines Creek in Lawrence County. Williams's memoir, *I Become a Teacher: A Memoir of One-Room School Life in Eastern Kentucky*, describing his early education at Cumberland College and his first year of teaching, is a classic. Because of his slight stature, he was mistaken for a student by a visiting health officer one day. A highlight of this year of teaching, he said, was a "pie mite," or pie supper. Dancing, a cake walk, and a pie-eating contest preceded the bidding on and sale of pies. "Young men" competed for the pies of their favorite "young women," and Victorian mores were observed. After sampling their pies, "they departed, young men walking beside young women and leading their horses." Williams used the thirty-one dollars gained that evening to purchase phonetic flash cards, reading books, and a duplicator and supplies. He described with great pride as well as nostalgia the experience of celebrating Christmas at the Boggs School with a small cedar tree and homemade decorations. Life was simple at the school but rewarding for Williams and his students: "All thought we had had a good school [year]. They were proud that it had not been necessary for me to whip anybody for misbehavior."[119]

Stuart, Beeler, Williams, and thousands of other early-twentieth-century Kentucky teachers had similar experiences. In 1918–1919 there were more than seven thousand one-room schools dotting the Kentucky landscape. Teaching in such a school required management skills and sheer grit, and it still seems daunting today. Requirements for an elementary school teacher changed over time, but in the early twentieth century all you had to do was pass a county test or complete a minimum of one term in a normal school. Most of these country schools held classes only from July through December or early January.

"You had to be janitor and everything," remembered Ethel Merritt Lisle. "You got there at eight o'clock and you were off at four. But sometimes you had to carry the water and make the fires, and clean the windows and the floors." For all that, she received the grand sum of forty-two dollars a month.[120]

After finishing a spring term at Eastern Kentucky State Normal School, Raymond Layne borrowed enough money to get him through his first few weeks of teaching in a Harlan County coal camp. Digging pits for outhouses was among his duties, as well as teaching the "three R's" and handling discipline. One incident made his reputation in that community. Not knowing that a mischievous boy had matches in his back pocket, the young teacher administered a healthy swat to the miscreant's backside. "The matches ignited and burned a hole in his pants and blistered his hip," Layne recalled many years later. "The word got around that 'Mr. Layne sot a boy on fire at school.'"[121]

Many teachers, like Katie Carpenter and H. E. Richardson Sr., were only eighteen when they entered the classroom. Carpenter had sixty-two students in her first school and was paid only $35 a month. Salaries were this low or even lower because some local school trustees expected to be paid part of the salary, what today would be considered a "kickback." In many mountain counties, particularly during the difficult economic times of the twenties and thirties, teaching positions were bought and sold with alacrity. Henry Scalf recalled that a local doctor paid a trustee $150 to buy a teaching job for his sister in the Floyd County school system.[122]

Richardson took over the Webb School in southeastern Madison County, near the Jackson County line, after only one year at Berea College and having reached the minimum age of eighteen. He described the building as a "dirty old schoolhouse, inside and outside, with paint scaling." How much support did he receive from officials for this school of sixty-five students? "They gave me a water bucket, a dipper, a box of chalk, two erasers, and a roll book," he recalled many years later. "We didn't have a map, didn't have a globe, a book, a dictionary, nothing." People in the community wanted a pie supper, another great rural tradition, in order to raise money for the school. "I was afraid to," Richardson said, "I was afraid the drunks would come and shoot the school house down." Sometimes a guardian angel comes out of nowhere. "I guarantee they won't," said "Humpy" John Webb, who lived across the road from the weather-beaten school. "I'll be right there with a double-barreled shotgun and a box of shells." In a community where many men made their money making moonshine during these early Prohibition days, "there were drunks falling all over each other" at the pie supper, Richardson recalled. "They'd sold that whiskey and they had wads of twenty-dollar bills. They'd stagger up and roll out that twenty-dollar bill. Well, I had a sack of money when that thing was over. They never said a loud word. Old man Webb came there before anybody and sat there in a corner with his shotgun."

With school supplies now in hand, the students progressed beyond anything Richardson could have imagined. One of his students scored highest in the county on the eighth-grade exam. Moreover, as "a big stout fellow," weighing about two hundred pounds, Richardson had no discipline problems. However, outside the school, the community still demonstrated some of the lawlessness of the Appalachian foothills variety. "I was sitting at my desk teaching history," Richardson recalled. "I heard a loud commotion and I was sitting where I could look out the window. Two men were coming up the road. One man had a big .45. Just as I looked up that .45 went off. I thought he had shot through the window and I fell in the floor. I pretended like my chair slipped. I thought I was looking right down that muzzle. Though most people carried guns around there, they were nice to me. They treated me like I was king." Richardson taught for only two years before going into business. "It was quite an experience," he said.[123]

A generation later another one-room school teacher, Pauline Moore of Pike County, said: "I taught all subjects. I taught as long as I had a room full of kids, and books, and a chalkboard, and some chalk. That's all I needed." In the decades from 1930 to 1960, the changes in Pike County mirrored what occurred across the state. As transportation improved, one-room schools consolidated into two- or three-room graded schools and eventually into schools offering all twelve grades. This was still too slow for those who wanted radical change, but the impediments to education remained many, including distances to school, fluctuations in the economy, local politics, and national and international events. One teacher said it best: "That's just the way it was." From 1930 to 1960, Pike County superintendent Claude Farley led in the consolidation of the system from 203 schools to fewer than 50 and in the building of several high schools in the largest county in the commonwealth.[124]

The one-room schools in which Richardson, Moore, and thousands of others labored slowly declined until only 146 existed in 1968–1969. The State Department of Education began authorizing specifications for one-, two-, three-, and four-room schools in 1909. By then the School Improvement League had initiated a campaign to "establish and maintain efficiency in the schools." Some buildings were in terrible condition. School trustees closed down one school in Wayne County and, fearing its collapse, issued an order that children were not to climb on the roof. Proving that "boys will be boys," ten young males took the dare. Luckily they survived unscathed when the roof collapsed. Although school buildings improved slowly in the state, it was at nearly a snail's pace. Not until after World War II did the pace of change accelerate.[125]

Sometimes teachers gave up the profession to make more money in another field. In 1919 two enterprising Frankfort teachers, Ruth Hanley and Rebecca Gooch, decided to enter the candy-making business full time. The next year they opened what became the Rebecca-Ruth Candy industry in a Frankfort hotel's barroom that had been closed because of Prohibition. Eventually their Kentucky Bourbon ball candy became a sensation, and the company still flourishes. Others left teaching for other professions. At least two of Kentucky's finest female writers, Harriette Simpson Arnow and Elizabeth Madox Roberts, taught briefly before finding their "voice" and a wider classroom by evoking Kentucky and its culture in immortal fiction.[126]

Public school education in Kentucky reacted to the changing times of the early twentieth century. John Grant Crabbe and others supported, in varying degrees, the addition of vocational education to the curricula of Kentucky's public schools. Urban schools began to add home economics and manual arts to their offerings. Even rural schools began offering "practical studies in gardening, sewing, cooking, and drawing." School Improvement leagues and Homemaker Clubs aided these efforts. Roark endorsed his idea of "manumental" training in *Economy in Education*, published by the American Book Company in 1905, as a "democratizing influence." In the first decade of the new century, KEA moved from urging manual training to recommending vocational education. Except for the Louisville school district, the mountain settlement schools, and black high schools, the effort stopped far short of fully accepting the trade school concept. However, high schools in Frankfort, Maysville, Owensboro, Somerset, Bellevue, and Richmond soon added courses in the manual arts modeled on the Louisville system, particularly at Manual High School. For example, manual arts were introduced in the Richmond City Schools in 1910, and eventually a separate building was built and used for training in mechanics and woodworking.[127]

The Smith-Lever Act of 1914 initiated a program employing the University of Kentucky, the commonwealth's land grant school, to coordinate agricultural extension work. With passage of the Smith-Hughes Vocational Education Act in 1917, formal vocational education began in the United States. At first designed to give job training to members of the armed forces returning from World War I, Smith-Hughes provided programs in agriculture, home economics, and vocational and industrial education in the nation's high schools. To take advantage of this law, the Kentucky Department of Education named its first director of vocational education, McHenry Rhoads, in 1917. Federal money was used to pay teachers and supervisors and also to provide for their further education. The study of agriculture in particular gained impetus in the high schools; schools offering such courses, and enrollment in the courses, grew from 8 schools and 171 students in 1918 to 124 schools and 4,340 students by 1932. By 1940 more than seven thousand students were taking vocational education courses in Kentucky. The residential West Kentucky Vocational Training School for blacks in Paducah and the Mayo State Vocational School for whites in Paintsville by 1941 were both implementing the National Youth Administration and National Defense Training programs.[128]

As the nation entered the Jazz Age of the 1920s, Kentucky still languished in the "rurality" that Thomas D. Clark described. With the big push for school consolidation reducing the exorbitant number of village graded schools and consolidating them into a county system, the need for transportation became crucial. Mason County made the first effort to transport students. By 1920 Warren County could report that in its rural schools the "horse sheds in the well-appointed school" were being "almost supplanted" by modern transportation, the bus and the auto. However, the old way died hard. In the midtwenties Woodford County transported students to its newly consolidated Millville school by "two conveyances," for which the drivers furnished "their own teams and harness," each receiving sixty-five dollars a month. State support for transportation lagged, and only slowly did the "motor bus" replace the "horse-drawn vehicle."[129]

After his narrow defeat in the 1915 gubernatorial race against Stanley, Republican Ed Morrow, using the slogan "Right the Wrong of 1915," came back to win the race four years later by a substantial margin over Democrat James Dixon Black. Fellow Republican George Colvin rode Morrow's coattails, as did the rest of the Grand Old Party ticket. The administration of State Superintendent of Public Instruction George Colvin (1919–1923) came at a crucial time in the history of Kentucky education. Trained in law, Colvin had become a principal and then the superintendent of the Springfield City Schools. Some friends pushed his candidacy for public office, and he was chosen in the Republican state convention to run for the state superintendency in 1919. The 1919 election in Kentucky was a precursor to the 1920 presidential election and the advent of Warren G. Harding and Republican ascendancy for the next twelve years. Republicans also controlled the Kentucky General Assembly.[130]

Morrow is better known for putting down a mob that attempted to lynch African American Will Locket by calling in the National Guard in Lexington than for his legislative agenda. However, he still had a somewhat progressive record. During the 1920 and 1922 sessions of the General Assembly, education legislation proved to be more successful than legislation in other areas. Much of this record had to do with Superintendent Colvin's preparation for these sessions.[131]

In 1920 the General Assembly, with the strong urging of State Superintendent Colvin, changed the county superintendent position from an elective one to an appointed one and reduced the number of school districts. The law also required that a five-person county board at large be elected by the people. The reconstituted county board now had the power to appoint the county superintendent for a four-year term, the subdistrict trustees, and the teachers. The State Department of Education took over the task of certifying teachers, ending forever the old county examinations and the reign of the "question peddler." Some opposition developed over the at-large election of the school board. The School Act of 1922 divided each county into five districts, each district with an elected board member under the regular November election cycle. This law also mandated that no new independent school district could be created. With 120 county and 388 independent units at the time, there were still too many hands in the pot, draining it of funds. School consolidation became an increasing necessity for modernizing the Kentucky system. When the county systems were reinforced by law in 1908, some villages opted out. The number of independent grade schools in smaller towns and villages had mushroomed from 102 in 1900–1901 to 353 in 1918–1919. As increasing costs became prohibitive, many of the smaller village-type graded schools gave up and accepted consolidation into a county system. By 1930–1931, the number of independent grade schools had decreased to 191. In a mid-twenties thesis at the University of Kentucky, Hattie C. Warner claimed that consolidated schools became "social centers," providing entertainment and meeting places for the community. "Parents do not have to worry about how their children spend their spare time when they know they are attending some social function at the school house instead of loafing in pool-rooms in some near by town," she maintained.[132]

The 1920 General Assembly created the Kentucky Educational Commission and instructed it "to make a survey of the public educational system of the State including all schools and educational institutions supported in whole or in part by public taxation." With a $15,000 grant from the General Education Board and $10,000 from the General Assembly, the commission conducted the survey. Its 1921 published study, *Public Education in Kentucky*, gave legislators and educators valuable suggestions for improving public school education in the state. In perhaps the most comprehensive study up to this time, Dr. Frank P. Bachman directed a survey of sixty-six counties, which included 222 graded school districts, more than 136,000 students, and hundreds of teachers.[133]

Part 1 of *Public Education in Kentucky*, "Present Condition of Schools," realistically assessed the public schools of the time. Kentucky had "steadily fallen behind, going from a ranking of thirty-fifth in 1890 to forty-fifth in 1918," the study declared. All the old handicaps of the past were enumerated. From the office of the state superintendent on down, the system was weak. The state board was cited as inefficient, if not incompetent. The city schools, obviously, were far better on average than the rural ones. "The schoolhouse situation is . . . extremely bad," the study said. Teachers' salaries, though increasing, were still far below national averages. Everywhere, there was vast room for improvement.[134]

Part 2, "Needed Improvements," made specific recommendations, beginning with "better state organization and administration." First, the commonwealth should replace the "ex-officio" state board with "a non-partisan board of education." Praising the county unit law of 1920, the report urged better administration of the county schools, including substantially raising taxes. City school codes should be made into a single code for all sizes of urban areas. The tiny independent graded schools scattered about many counties needed to be consolidated into the county units. Teacher education was problematical. For example, in 1920–1921, the public and private colleges and the state university did not turn out enough high school teachers to replace those quitting the field each year. States like North Carolina and Maryland had recently passed legislation to improve teacher education. "What these states have done, Kentucky can do," the study concluded. Of course, this report asked for better management of school finances, tweaking the taxing system, and improving accountability at all levels.[135]

Statistics from the exhaustive surveys appended to *Public Education in Kentucky* enumerated the problems facing public education in the state. Among white educators, the rural elementary teachers had the least education. For example, nearly 30 percent of them had only an elementary education themselves. In the city schools, more than 25 percent of the elementary teachers had at least two years of education "above high school." The average length of the school year varied widely, from an average low of 129 days in the rural schools to 190 days or more in some of the city schools. Many students were too old for the grades they were in, and this situation contributed to a high dropout rate. In rural schools nearly one-third of the students dropped out after the fifth grade. School achievement also lagged. While the average rural fifth-grade student was a year and a half "below the standard reached in other states," the average city student was a half year below standard. Although in recent years new laws had extended the school term and compulsory attendance laws had been strengthened, poor attendance in the rural schools was "almost prohibitive of good school work," the report concluded. And to illustrate the continued problems of literacy in Kentucky, the commission stated, "It is not surprising that Kentucky stands among the states today [1922] practically where it stood twenty years ago in the relative amount of illiteracy."[136]

Kentuckians had their work cut out for them if they were to improve the commonwealth's public educational system and do so quickly. Progressive educational legislation in the Morrow-Colvin years, though impressive, again demonstrated signs of retreat as well as improvement. The County Administration Law provided for a modernized county board of five members elected at large, but two years later the legislature, pressured by localism and ruralism, went back to the old arrangement, whereby school members were elected in districts. The original law also gave the county board the duty of electing a superintendent and setting the minimum salary at not less than $1,200. The maximum allowable county tax rate was raised from the thirty cents allowed in 1918 to fifty cents. Colvin argued that this increase would offer the only hope of equalizing opportunities for county schools with the city systems. Wartime inflation also had added to the woes of teachers and the schools. The minimum salary for Kentucky teachers was set at $75 per month.[137]

Extending the minimum school term from six to seven months and transferring complete responsibility for certification from the county superintendents to the State Department of Education in Frankfort also showed the progressive nature of early-twenties legislation. Certification laws were also strengthened and began to require more schooling, particularly increasing the time needed in a normal school setting. In 1922, as a result of both political logrolling and true educational reform, the General Assembly authorized creation of two new normal schools in Murray and Morehead.[138]

Other legislation in the Morrow-Colvin years addressed the problems of the city schools. New charters were authorized for third- and fourth-class cities, allowing a taxation maximum of one dollar per $100 of property evaluation. Even more important was legislation forbidding the creation of any new independent districts, a vital step toward school consolidation. A much-needed nepotism stricture passed the legislature but did little good. There were two other failures as well. Two very progressive measures went to the voters in 1921 for their approval, and both went down to defeat. A constitutional amendment to make the state superintendent an appointive post rather than elective failed, as did a provision to equalize state distribution of school funds on other than on a per capita basis by setting aside as much as 10 percent of the state appropriation to be "apportioned" to poorer districts.[139]

In the middle of the Morrow-Colvin terms came one of the most crucial legislative battles in Kentucky history, perhaps in the entire history of all the nation's state legislatures, when the General Assembly considered the first antievolution bills in America. After the turn of the twentieth century, a growing fundamentalist movement in America coalesced against what were considered antireligious ideas. The advent of World War I encouraged even more hypervigilance against things considered foreign. The teaching of evolution in the public schools proved to be a convenient whipping boy for conservative Christians. Nationwide, the antievolution movement received the support of "the Great Commoner" William Jennings Bryan. The World Christian Fundamentals Association chose Kentucky as a testing ground in 1922, because it was one of only six states having legislative meetings that year. The whole affair appeared to originate with what I called "Porter and the Baptist Conspiracy" in my 1967 M.A. thesis at Eastern Kentucky University, titled "The Kentucky Evolution Controversy." J. W. Porter, pastor of the Lexington First Baptist Church (1908–1922) and editor of the Baptist statewide weekly, the *Western Recorder*, actively campaigned in his editorials against evolution. His immediate successor, Victor I. Masters, pushed even more for legislative action in the last months of 1921. Rev. O. O. Green of Richmond First Baptist Church warned President Frank L. McVey of the University of Kentucky about the growing danger and urged that McVey secure the assistance of President E. Y. Mullins of the Southern Baptist Theological Seminary in Louisville. Sure enough, the University of Kentucky became the specific target of the antievolutionists. The general public, the newspapers, and the commonwealth's educators began choosing sides as rumors of legislative action circulated.[140]

On January 17, 1922, the Kentucky Senate adopted a resolution inviting Bryan to speak before the General Assembly. During the second half of his speech, two days later, Bryan staunchly advocated a law to prohibit the teaching of Darwinism, believing such instruction to be "anti-Bible." Four days later Representative George W. Ellis of Barren County introduced House Bill 191: "An act to prohibit the teaching in public schools and other public institutions of learning, Darwinism, atheism, agnosticism, or evolution as it pertains to the origin of man." The bill included a stiff fine for both the teacher and the institution. On January 25, Senator James R. Rash of Madisonville introduced a less stringent bill, Senate Bill 136, which forbade the teaching of "any theory of Evolution which derives man from the brute or any other lower forms of life, or that eliminates God as the creator of man by a direct creative act." The proposed bills were aimed at public and private educational institutions at all levels. Immediately, the press was full of both support and condemnation of the bills. In particular, President McVey of the University of Kentucky became the focus of the attacks. Neither Governor Morrow nor Superintendent Colvin chose to get involved; they were completely mum about the pending legislation.[141]

Over the next several weeks of legislative action, those for and against the antievolution bills tried to influence the outcome. McVey took the offensive by publicizing replies to telegrams he had sent to the state's leaders and by releasing "A Letter to the People of Kentucky" to the press. "As president of the University of Kentucky," McVey declared, "I desire to say as emphatically as possible that the charge that there is teaching in the University of atheism, agnosticism, and Darwinism (in the sense that man is descended from baboons and gorillas) is absolutely false. . . . The University, however, does teach evolution." He went on to explain that evolution was the basis of all modern science and that UK could not serve the state without teaching modern science.[142]

With the editorial support of the *Courier-Journal*, the *Louisville Evening Post*, and the *Lexington Herald*, McVey built a stalwart defense. First, Dr. E. L. Powell, pastor of Louisville First Christian Church, and then Mullins came into the fray. A battle-scarred veteran of battles with fundamentalists in his own denomination, Mullins, a leading moderate in the Southern Baptist Convention, added a vital link in defusing the situation. McVey, Powell, and Mullins all offered substitute bills, saying they were against strict antievolution bills but "took this course as the best way out." For example, Mullins's suggestion would prohibit teaching any theory that would "undermine the religious beliefs" of students in tax-supported institutions. During the spirited debates in both houses, one antievolution advocate trampled an offending textbook underfoot and one representative called a colleague a "monkey." While such antics did the Rash and Ellis bills little good, the Commonwealth of Kentucky's reputation for anti-intellectualism received reinforcement nationwide.[143]

The Rash bill in the state Senate died in committee after failing to muster enough support for a floor vote. When the Ellis bill was reported out of committee for a floor vote, heated debate and voting pressures mounted. When the tally reached 41-41, one observer compared it to "a neck and neck horse race, and Kentuckians do dearly love a horse race." Representative Bryce Cundiff from Breathitt County, who identified himself as a "hardshell Baptist," cast the deciding vote against the bill, thus "ending the first ballot in the nation on legislation to suppress the teaching of evolution." Although the issue surfaced again in the 1924 and 1926 sessions of the Kentucky General Assembly, none of those antievolution bills came to floor votes.[144]

In the early twenties, high school biology teachers in Kentucky undoubtedly taught about evolution, but to what extent is unknown. Many used George William Hunter's *A Civic Biology: Presented in Problems* (1914), a book that prominently addressed evolution, with a full discussion of Darwin in one chapter. While the book was quite cutting-edge about the implications of evolution, it was also openly racist. There is no doubt that University of Kentucky biologists taught the theory of evolution. With Morrow and Colvin not taking a stand either way on the issue, it was imperative that other leaders step into the breach. In Tennessee, Arkansas, and Mississippi, where leaders like McVey and Mullins did not emerge, antievolution legislation was passed in the twenties. While the pressure on McVey lessened, that on Mullins intensified. Though never an evolutionist, the Louisville seminary president always maintained that the teaching of evolution should not be restricted by state statue.[145]

During the 1922 antievolution controversy, the University of Kentucky's undergraduate population included John T. Scopes, who became the defendant in the famous "Monkey Trial" in Dayton, Tennessee, in the summer of 1925. Repression of the teaching of evolution occurred in Kentucky. In 1923 "Kentucky Wesleyan College suspended a faculty member for his support of evolution." The Paducah School System fired Scopes's sister Lila when she followed her brother's lead in teaching evolution openly. One year after the Scopes trial, a new edition of *Civic Biology* dropped the use of the word *evolution*, substituting "The Development of Man" for "The Evolution of Man." However, the open racism of the book remained, portraying the Caucasian race as "the highest type of all."[146]

The state of the teaching of biology in the public schools was the focus of a 1929 thesis at the University of Kentucky. The author of that study found that only 213 of 640 high schools in Kentucky taught biology and that many more students took general science or home economics. Interestingly, the teachers of biology were better trained than most other teachers, nearly 90 percent of them having a bachelor's degree. It is difficult to know the extent of the teaching of evolution in the twenties, but most Kentucky schools that taught biology used Hunter's *Civic Biology*. However, the author of the 1929 thesis unabashedly proclaimed, "The evolutionary point of view that one almost invariably gets from biological study is invaluable in gaining a broad outlook on all questions involving achievement and progress. Improvement in economic status, in social, industrial and political relations, in art, in education, or even in ethics and religion is an evolutionary process. It proceeds by variation, selection, and elimination, by continuous adjustment, and by survival of the fit."[147]

The winds of educational change in America blew across the Kentucky landscape with varying degrees of change and continuity in the early twentieth century. The curriculum of Kentucky public schools around 1920 included, of course, the Bible. In 1905 the Kentucky Court of Appeals, in *Hackett v. Brooksville School*, "ruled that the King James Version of the Bible was not a sectarian book and might be read, and prayer be said if unsectarian." Pressure mounted to adopt the progressive education ideals of John Dewey. The Progressive Era mantra, "efficiency," became a watchword. In particular, educationists like Ellwood Cubberley attacked the "hidebound nature of the rural school curriculum." Lawrence Cremin perhaps had said it best by stating that the Progressive Era manifested "reform *through* education and the reform *of* education." Both rural and urban Kentucky schools fought a constant battle between those who wanted change and those who did not.[148]

In Louisville, Male and Manual high schools represented the older view that traditional and vocational schools should be separate. Owing to the influence of John Dewey and other progressive educators, the modern "comprehensive" high school, which included vocational industrial and commercial courses along with academic courses, emerged in urban areas. Urban high schools also moved away from the old classical English rubric. In 1918 an NEA report, *Cardinal Principles of Secondary Education*, became widely circulated, first entering Kentucky normal schools and then the high school classroom. Principal author Clarence Kingsley, a former high school teacher, maintained that schools, like any other institutions, resisted change. Noting that only about one-third of ninth-graders finished high school nationally, the *Cardinal Principles* proposed that high schools should provide for "individual differences in capacities and aptitudes." That could be accomplished only by relying on scientific study and applications to "promote broader social goals and practical outcomes." With seven stated principles, this document remained the leading educational topic in teacher-preparation classes well into the lifetime of the author, who recalls memorizing these principles as his "mantra" in a Georgetown College education class.[149]

Two years before the NEA report, the *Elementary State Course of Study and Teacher's Manual,* written by Coates to be used primarily in the rural school, and published by the Kentucky Department of Education in 1916, asserted that "the individuality of the pupil should be carefully considered to the end that he may be instructed in the light of his limitations and capacity; and we recommend to all local authorities the necessity of a greater care in the arrangement of courses of study, that they may be adapted to the pupils to be instructed, rather than the pupils should be adapted to fixed courses of study and an inflexible system of grading." Like many such educational pronouncements, *Cardinal Principles* became controversial and the source of both good and bad changes in American education. In the wake of the debates, some asked which was more important, for example, the study of Latin or physical education? Moreover, the battle between those who championed high school vocational education always faced the opposition of traditionalists.[150]

John Grant Crabbe, as superintendent of Ashland City Schools, state superintendent of public instruction, and president of Eastern Kentucky State Normal School, influenced a generation of Kentucky school officials. His curriculum changes fitted the city school movement of the early twentieth century. Over time manual training and home economics replaced most of the older classical education courses. Trigonometry, biology, and solid geometry also became standard in most Kentucky high schools by the time of World War I.[151]

The Paducah school system offered a good example of an urban Kentucky school in the early twentieth century. As in the rest of Kentucky, white and black schools were completely separate. By 1919 that school system was moving toward a white junior high school of grades seven to nine. A comprehensive report of that year, prepared by George Peabody College for Teachers for its faculty, pointed to needed improvements. Based on the Cleveland Arithmetic Tests, Paducah fourth- to eighth-graders, both black and white, were well behind students in the St. Louis, Missouri, and Grand Rapids, Michigan, schools, averaging more than a two-and-one-half-year deficit. The course of study in the white Paducah high school, an example of a "comprehensive" institution at the time, included a wide range of classes; required were four years of English, mathematics, science, and several history courses. All things considered, the Paducah system appeared healthy though ready for improvement.[152]

A similar study of the county system of Madison County a decade later did not paint as pleasant a picture. There were too many one-room and two-room schools and an abysmal salary schedule. For example, a teacher with one year of high school (or one year of normal school) and no experience would make a beginning salary, probably in a one-room school, of $76 a month. At the highest level, a teacher with four years of college and more than three years of experience would make only the ceiling of $90 a month. Attendance problems plagued Madison County elementary schools. Teacher training lagged. In a county with normal schools and college training at Eastern and Berea, "fifty percent have little training above high school." How could the schools be providing an adequate educational experience when, for example, "the average child in the one-teacher schools was absent 58 out of 137 days"? School facilities also were poor, the "school toilet or school privy" in particular being "a criminal insult to the fair name of the county and Kentucky. They are breeders of ill health, physically, mentally, morally, socially and spiritually." In a study of achievement on standardized tests, Madison County elementary pupils scored well below norms. This impressive, realistic study concluded with a "Standard for Teachers in Service," aimed at improving instruction. Quite obviously, Madison County had a long way to go in providing an adequate education for its children in the first third of the twentieth century. Another study found continuing problems in the mid-thirties, particularly with school facilities. The majority of the nine rural white high schools were still lighted by kerosene lamps, "outdoor pit toilets" and cisterns were the norm, and there were no central heating systems.[153]

Kentucky followed most national trends in the new century. The early twentieth century also brought more organization to sports, including high school athletics as more and more Kentucky high schools, especially city schools, began fielding athletic teams. Football and baseball were already well established by the time basketball, both girls' and boys' versions, gained popularity. Unfortunately, many schools cheated by using nonstudents, the "ringer" famous in Kentucky sports lore. A movement developed to clean up and organize high school sports. After a Kentucky Education Association committee made recommendations to rein in the lack of rules and coordination, the Kentucky High School Athletic Association was organized in 1916.[154]

High school basketball tournaments began in 1918 for boys and in 1921 for girls. At first basketball at both the high school and college levels for girls and young women outpaced that for males, but beginning in the twenties, administrators and some coaches, mostly men, argued that the game was "too strenuous" for women and girls. In 1924 the University of Kentucky fielded its last female team, and by the mid-thirties most Kentucky high schools stopped sponsoring the game for girls. Meanwhile, boys' high school basketball flourished. Little Carr Creek High School, a boarding school founded in 1920 by Massachusetts natives Olive V. March and Ruth E. Watson, gained great national acclaim in 1928. After the team won the regional tournament in Richmond, the crowd pitched in to buy the "Creekers real uniforms," replacing their cut-off overalls. Four thousand fans attended the 1928 state tournament finals matching Ashland and Carr Creek at the University of Kentucky's Alumni Gym. The Ashland Tomcats' Ellis Johnson scored the final basket in the fourth overtime, defeating Carr Creek 13-11. Both teams received invitations to the National High School Basketball Tournament in Chicago. From a student body of only forty-one, including eighteen boys, the Knott County "barefoot boys" caught the attention of the nation. Ashland won the tournament, ending a perfect, undefeated season with thirty-seven victories. Three of the "Carr Creek boys" went on to play college basketball at Eastern Kentucky State Teachers College from 1928 through 1933. Requiring a minimum of equipment and often played on or at least practiced on outdoor courts, basketball became the overwhelming favorite of the small county high schools.[155]

High school football became more and more important. One western Kentucky enthusiast complained when a game was canceled. "A wonderful team at Mayfield . . . had to be wasted due to a football armistice during the first World War." The author's father-in-law, like many a Kentucky farm lad, actually played in the first football game he saw, after entering the freshman class at Mayfield High School in the mid-twenties. Rivalries soon developed. The Male-Manual game in Louisville took on mythic charm as the oldest rivalry in Kentucky, beginning with the first game in 1893, which Male won 14-12. Held on Thanksgiving Day for many years, the annual event drew thousands of spectators. Within a few blocks of each other in the early days, these schools hazed each other, including the prank of painting each other's school using their own colors. The "Victory Barrel" for the game became a prized possession and often the object of kidnapping. One Louisvillian observed: "Some reported that more blood was spilled off than on the field." Urban African American high schools also began fielding athletic teams. On Thanksgiving Day, Louisville Central High School also played rivals, for example defeating Douglass High School of Henderson, 33-0, in 1924. Owing to the cost of equipment and practice and game facilities, football became more prevalent and popular in city schools than county schools in the early part of the twentieth century.[156]

Public school education in Kentucky also made gains against old impediments to progress in the county systems. While Thomas D. Clark disapproved of "the black beast of Kentucky educational history," Jesse Stuart, in his semifictionalized memoir *The Thread That Runs So True,* railed against "the abominable trustee system." As a young teacher, he urged school consolidation, but Stuart reported that trustee John Conway "said my thought was dangerous, and, as for me, if I wanted to be a good teacher and stay healthy, I had better stop having such crazy talk." "Why should I, a teacher, be at the mercy of John Conway? Why should John Conway have more power than the superintendent, elected by the members of the Greenwood County Board of Education, and they, in turn, elected by the people?"[157]

The experiences of Cora Frazier were those of many a mountain school teacher. "The first school I ever taught was on Bottom Ford at Mayking in Letcher County," she recalled in *Our Appalachia.* "A trustee recommended me to the county superintendent and whoever he recommended that superintendent had to hire." The school trustee races "were hotter than the President's because there were so many teachers that didn't have jobs. The ones that had the biggest number of votes and relatives could vote in their behalf" to elect a favorable trustee.

The local district trusteeship persisted far longer than it should have. Trustees, a remnant of excessive localism and ruralism in the guise of true democracy, proved difficult to eliminate. During the second "Whirlwind Campaign" of 1909, Superintendent Crabbe minced no words in condemning the trustee system. "The old cumbersome, iniquitous trustee system is as bad as any school system in the world," he argued. "No system could be worse. The witnesses bear testimony. The new school law [1908] under the county board offers us a sane, progressive system which is as good as any modern school system." However, "each district would continue to elect trustees, but only the district chairpersons would sit on the county board."[158]

The school trusteeship system lingered into the Jazz Age and the Great Depression era. A 1928 study, *Rural Education in Madison County,* made by two Eastern Kentucky State Normal School and Teachers College professors, further indicted the old trustee system. "The schools of Madison County can never be what they should be until the Superintendent and the Board of Education have the right to determine who shall teach in the schools," the report concluded. "The naming of a teacher to teach children is not the job of the trustee, but the job of a person who knows good teaching." Soon afterward, Herman L. Donovan, president of Eastern (1928–1941), joined forces with other progressive educators in the state to try to end, once and for all, what he saw as a corrupting influence, the old "kickback" system still rearing its ugly head, particularly in the mountains, where a teaching job often went for $100 to $150. Using anecdotal information, gathered from a survey of the commonwealth's school districts, he armed himself for a crusade. He approached the major newspapers and political and educational leaders for one last effort to get rid of the trustees. Arguing that rural teachers made such low pay anyway, he asked, "What will be the effect if they are forced by a nefarious system to hand over to a sub-district trustee from $25.00 to $150.00 of their meager salaries?" The effort paid off when the *Courier-Journal* and other state papers editorialized against the subdistrict trustee system. Finally, the 1934 General Assembly passed a new school code that did away with the trustees forever and reduced the six categories of local school districts to only two, the independent district and the county district.[159]

In the mid-twenties, a study by Donovan of the state's elementary teachers found that Kentucky did not adequately train and place teachers. As expected, the amount of training varied greatly across the state, with city schools having better-trained teachers than rural areas. "The Louisville teachers represent the most adequately trained group of teachers in the state," his study determined, with "practically 84 out of each 100 teachers" having an advanced certificate. Of elementary teachers in the state, only about 15 percent had "adequate training." Teacher turnover, or "transiency," continued as a major problem. Moreover, both urban and rural teachers were paid much less than the national averages. African American teachers were slightly better educated than their white counterparts in rural areas. In the view of Donovan and other educators, Kentucky needed to reinforce its normal school programs to include more teachers and expend more money to up-grade schools. Finally, Donovan suggested the need for "a sound certification law."[160]

Donovan was part of the Kentucky Education Association establishment, school men and women who were also part of the larger national "Education Trust." In the early twenties, KEA began publishing, monthly during the school year, the *Kentucky School Journal* as its "Official Organ." The periodical included departments for city and rural schools; news about meetings, the opening of schools, and new programs; and, most importantly, continuous calls for change and "reform." There were advertisements for the state's colleges, for school equipment, and for almost everything else related to education. More and more of Kentucky's educators came under the influence of the Teachers College of Columbia University, including Donovan; Lee Kirkpatrick, superintendent of the Paris City Schools; and more than twenty others who became Kentucky superintendents. There were so many Kentuckians at the school as to warrant the organization of a "Kentucky Club." Many of these students, particularly the women, studied during the summers only. Alfred Leland Crabbe took an M.A. in 1921 at Teachers College and became dean at Western before joining the faculty at Peabody Teachers College. More female Kentucky educators attended Teachers College of Columbia than men, but most women did not rise above teaching to become principals and superintendents. Many of the men went into college administration, while the women continued as college teachers, "in their male-dominated world." Several women found better opportunities outside the state, including Sarah Gibson Blanding, who left the dean of women position at the University of Kentucky to become president of Vassar College. A master's degree at Teachers College had much prestige at the time, as did experiencing the contrasting lifestyle of New York City, even if only for a few weeks at a time. Peabody Teachers College in Nashville, where such educators as Donovan and Crabbe earned their doctorates, also had a growing influence on Kentucky education in the period before World War II.[161]

From the mid-twenties through the Great Depression, several battles were waged in public education, the most important being over free textbooks, equalization, and certification. Moreover, "opportunities" for the greatly increasing funds available for education were missed.[162]

Politics as usual in Kentucky in the twenties turned out to be the "damnedest." A tremendous struggle within the Democratic Party during the 1923 gubernatorial primary had all the best and the worst elements of a reform struggle. Congressman J. Campbell Cantrill of Scott County, backed by the Stanley faction, faced Congressman Alben Barkley of Union County, supported by a Beckham-Haly-Bingham clique. Barkley appeared the more progressive with his anti–race-track-gambling campaign, but both candidates and factions had similar visions of power dancing in their heads. Gaining the support of the coal lobby, Cantrill won a narrow race by nine thousand votes. When Cantrill died in early September, the Democratic State Central and Executive Committee, under the thumb of banker James B. Brown of Louisville, chose Congressman William Jason Fields as the substitute candidate. The election of "Honest Bill from Olive Hill," along with fellow Democrat McHenry Rhoads as state superintendent, again raised the question of what could be done to better public school education in Kentucky.[163]

Early in his administration, Fields accepted the findings of the state-funded Efficiency Commission and its study *The Government of Kentucky*. Moreover, in the 1924 legislative session, he urged the General Assembly to take a bold move and approve a $75 million bond issue, to be voted on by the people of the commonwealth. The bonds would be spread over educational and charitable institutions, including public education, prisons, public health, and new roadways, to be paid for with an automobile license tax, a gasoline tax, and an increase in the property tax. After the measure passed the General Assembly, Fields signed the bill, which now specified $50 million for highway construction and $25 million to be divided among educational, penal, and charitable institutions. The fate of the $75 million bond issue was in the hands of the people. As often occurs in Kentucky, a good idea got bound up in politics, personalities, and pettiness. Most Republican leaders, as well as Robert W. Bingham's *Courier-Journal,* opposed the plan vociferously, charging that Fields and his administration could not be trusted to spend the money wisely. While the "Good Roads Association" supported the measure, a "Pay-As-You-Go" counter group, heavily funded by Bingham, attacked the idea of such a large bond issue. On the general election day in 1924 that brought victory for Republican presidential candidate Calvin Coolidge, the bond issue was defeated by more than ninety thousand votes. State Historian Klotter concluded: "An opportunity for advancement had been missed." It was a "road not taken."[164]

Superintendent Rhoads fared better than Governor Fields, who was plagued throughout his term by continued party factionalism, charges of nepotism, and being saddled with political bosses like Brown. Working his way up through the ranks, Rhoads had gained experience as teacher, a principal, and a superintendent before joining the faculty of the University of Kentucky as professor of secondary education. The 1924 General Assembly passed some important measures. Reorganization of the Department of Education included streamlining the eight divisions: Certification and Examination, High School Supervision, Rural School Supervision, Vocational Education, Supervision of Negro Education, Inspection and Accounting, Music Supervision, and Teacher Training. Kentucky now had the bureaucracy needed for advancing its public schools. The question remained: could Kentucky continue to make educational progress in an increasingly competitive century?[165]

Other 1924 educational legislation included improving certification, revising qualifications for the superintendents to include at least two years of college work, and encouraging consolidation. The 1926 General Assembly increased the maximum allowable county school tax from fifty to seventy-five cents per $100 evaluation. An important new law required a "uniform budget system" for all public schools. One of the most crucial battles of the 1926 session dealt with a much-debated bill to return to electing the county school superintendents by popular vote. Rhoads and the growing education "establishment" in the state, including KEA, roundly opposed the measure, and it did not pass. The Fields-Rhoads administrations proved to be good years for public education in the state. The state school fund increased from about $4.65 million in 1924–1925 to nearly $5.6 million at the end of their watch. Teacher training at UK and the normal schools also received much-needed increased appropriations. Vocational education, home economics, industrial education, and even rehabilitation gained increasing attention at the state and local levels. Kentucky public education appeared to be modernizing.[166]

In 1927 the Kentucky Education Association adopted a new slogan, "An Equal Educational Opportunity for Every Child in Kentucky." The next governor and state superintendent would have some momentum for improving public school education in Kentucky and what appeared to be an ever-improving national economy. That political circus known as the Kentucky Democratic Party continued to be riven by factional fighting. Bingham backed his old ally former governor and senator John C. W. Beckham in the 1927 race against Republican Flem D. Sampson of Barbourville. Beckham took up former candidate Barkley's anti–race-track-betting cudgel, and several bosses in his own party worked hard for his defeat. The Jockey Club and the ominous "bi-partisan combine," composed of varying combinations of Democrats and Republicans, assured the victory of Sampson. While Beckham lost by more than thirty-four thousand votes, all other Democrats, including W. C. Bell, the candidate for state superintendent, won rather handily. "And politics—the damnedest in Kentucky," as Jim Mulligan said, continued.[167]

Governor Sampson faced a strongly entrenched Democratic Party–controlled General Assembly and did not have a successful term in office. Because he was unable to ally himself with either of the Democrat factions, his tenure was "four years of bitterness and drift." Perhaps the highlight of his term was the legislature's adoption of "My Old Kentucky Home" as the state's anthem. Sampson's election in 1927 presaged that of fellow Republican Herbert Hoover for president in 1928.[168]

In Sampson's first message to the General Assembly, he called for several key educational measures; they included free textbooks, to be paid for with a tax on sand and gravel; higher pay for teachers; more funding for the normal schools; and an equalization fund to help out the poorer districts—none of which passed. Two years later he championed what today would be called a progressive "education package." Again he called for increased funding, equalization, and other stimulant measures, but everything got bound up in the usual imbroglio of Kentucky politics.[169]

The free-textbook bill proved exceptionally controversial during Sampson's term. "I can think of no one thing that will do more to advance the interest of the children of the free schools than free textbooks," claimed Sampson. Superintendent Bell "opposed the idea as impracticable," believing "that the money would be better spent on improving school buildings, raising teachers' salaries, providing better teacher training, and other programs." Textbooks were a great source of income for the book companies, and they competed fiercely. Publishers could at times be unethical in their efforts to get a book adopted; one state official characterized their efforts as "damnable." Rumors of bribes to politicians and educators were rife. A Frankfort grand jury even indicted Governor Sampson "for receiving gifts from textbook manufacturers, but the indictment was dismissed." While the legislature passed a free-textbook law, it did not fund the measure. A KEA-sponsored bill to abolish the State Textbook Commission and establish one for each county failed to pass muster when the state's leading newspapers voiced opposition. KEA then switched to an eight-man board plan, which was used as part of so-called ripper legislation to "strip" Sampson of his appointive powers.[170]

Equalization of funding remained one of the ambitions of the education establishment in Kentucky, including KEA, the State Department of Education, and educationists at the University of Kentucky and the normal schools. In the mid-twenties, a 268-page bulletin published by the Bureau of School Service of the University of Kentucky exhaustively explained the major problems of public school education in the commonwealth. The study ranked county school systems, showing "inequalities," and suggested solutions. Many of the statistics were predictable. Most mountain counties did not "hold" their students well, in other words keep them in school for long periods. For example, comparing the eighth grade with first grade, Meade County's retention of its enrollment was "ten times as great as . . . Breathitt County." "Measures of school efficiency," including rates of illiteracy and teachers' qualifications, showed that the poorer counties in eastern and also western Kentucky faced serious deficits. The poorer the county, and the less taxable property it had, the more it depended on state funding and the less on its own. The state paid 70 percent of the cost of education in Jackson County but contributed only 15.2 percent in Clark County, where the county spent more on its children. Mason County had ten times as much wealth per pupil in its county school system as did Menifee County. Such states as North Carolina, South Carolina, Tennessee, and even Mississippi, by one measure, spent more of their wealth on elementary and secondary education in the mid-twenties than Kentucky did. Finally, the study suggested that each county must tax itself to the limit, thirty-nine cents on each $100 of assessed tangible wealth. Added to this would be the "old state aid" amount and the "new state aid," an equalization fund. If passed and funded by the General Assembly, and if all counties taxed themselves to the limit of the law, Kentucky would become a leader in funding public school education, particularly in the South.[171]

Education legislation of the Sampson-Bell era showed some foresight. Teacher retirement, compulsory attendance, consolidation, and textbook uniformity all received attention. Significantly, based on the study mentioned above, the legislature passed and the governor signed an act for the

"Equalization of Educational Opportunities" at an initial annual sum of $1.25 million. An equalization appropriation made for school year 1931–1932 went for naught when the Kentucky Court of Appeals declared the law unconstitutional on June 24, 1932. Therefore, the period from 1927 through 1931 was again years of disappointment for educational progress in the state.[172]

The election of a Democrat, Ruby Laffoon, as governor in 1931 portended the national election of a president, this time a Democrat, Franklin D. Roosevelt in 1932, as many people blamed President Hoover and his Republican cohorts for the economic downturn. The stock market crash and the onset of the Great Depression stressed education as it did all other institutions in Kentucky and the nation at large. As in most of the nation, soon more than 25 percent of Kentucky workers were out of a job. In addition, the terrible drought of 1930 left many Kentucky farmers devastated, and conditions did not soon improve. Bank deposits vanished, and the national banking crisis hit the state. The failure of BancoKentucky, the linchpin of James B. Brown's economic empire, spread fear all across the South. These catastrophes, coupled with the devastating Ohio River Valley flood of early 1937, left both rural and urban Kentuckians facing challenges not seen since the Civil War or the economic crisis of the early 1890s.[173]

One sign of the economic downturn was that more men in Kentucky began entering the teaching profession. Here at least they felt they would receive a steady, if paltry, paycheck. Kentuckians were not alone in their misery. At one time during the Great Depression, the state of Georgia owed its teachers $5 million in back pay, "while Ohio, the mother of colleges and presidents, reported its school fund to be $17 million short." With state revenues plummeting, Governor Laffoon searched for ways to increase funding. He asked the General Assembly in 1932 to pass a sales tax measure. In opposition to the much-needed tax measure, an anti-administration faction developed around State Highway Commissioner Ben Johnson and Lieutenant Governor A. B. "Happy" Chandler. The debate continued after the meeting of the General Assembly ended. Just before the inauguration of Roosevelt, Laffoon declared a bank holiday, "reflecting the near collapse of Kentucky's economy." By the end of 1933, the governor also closed the burley tobacco market when prices fell, as threats of violence grew. To pay Kentucky's debts, Laffoon borrowed more and more by issuing interest-bearing notes, or warrants. Education took large cuts.[174]

Superintendent of Public Instruction James H. Richmond, elected in the Laffoon landslide in 1931, probably had the best credentials of any early-twentieth-century educator holding the post. Like several of his predecessors, he had been a high school inspector in the State Department of Education and also had a wealth of experience in public education. In the supercharged political atmosphere in Frankfort, teeming with Democratic Party factionalism, he proved to be an exceptional superintendent. Fred Allen Engle Jr. maintained that Richmond ranked "first in accomplishment" of the fourteen state superintendents he studied who served the commonwealth between 1891 and 1943.[175]

Laffoon kept pressing to get a sales tax passed. By using all the political skullduggery he could muster, he weakened Chandler and his allies while gaining allies for his taxing plans. The governor's strategy included cutting state property and automobile taxes, leaving a sales tax as the only alternative to the declining state revenues. School systems became desperate. With retailers and a host of others against it, a three-cent-per-dollar sales tax measure was passed by a special session of the General Assembly in 1934. The sales tax gave some hope of increased revenue for the benefit of all Kentuckians.[176]

The regular session of the 1934 General Assembly passed some important school legislation, much of it based on a study by the Kentucky Educational Commission, created by the General Assembly in 1932. Meanwhile, a decision by the Kentucky Court of Appeals in January 1933 had suggested that "no body of our statutory law is in a more confused state than our school laws." Superintendent Richmond, supported by KEA, developed the *Report of the Kentucky Educational Commission*. "The New School Code of 1934" built on this study and brought about sweeping change that included important reorganization and recodification of Kentucky school law. The new Division of Teacher Education and Certification combined the work of three former divisions into one. The State Board of Education became the only agency with the power to certify teachers. Certificates for elementary, secondary, administration, and supervision were simplified. For the first time, an effort was made to rein in the increasing competition between the state colleges and the University of Kentucky for state funds by forming the Council on Public Higher Education. New laws setting a minimum school term of six months for all schools and mandatory attendance to the age of sixteen appeared to modernize the state system of public education. One of the most important provisions of the laws of 1934 was the decision to accept one of the suggestions of the 1922 *Report by the Kentucky Educational Commission* and abolish the old "ex officio" state board composed of the state superintendent, the attorney general, and the secretary of state. Thereafter, the State Board of Education would comprise the state superintendent and seven lay members, each with four-year terms, appointed by the governor. The legislators also abolished the two independent governing boards of the state's two black schools, the West Kentucky Industrial College for Colored Persons in Paducah and the Kentucky State Industrial College in Frankfort, and gave that jurisdiction to the State Board of Education. Although the 1928 legislature had passed a free-textbook law, money was not appropriated in a substantial amount until 1934, when $500,000 was provided for each year of the biennium, covering the first five grades.[177]

Despite the lingering depression, Kentucky now seemed on the way, at last, to a progressive era in education. However, the personal whims of Kentucky political figures clashed with any hope for significant progress in the Depression decade. With Laffoon and Chandler now bitter political enemies, factionalism in the Democratic Party intensified. Laffoon's efforts to keep Chandler out of the governor's mansion ultimately failed. Chandler parlayed the public's disdain for the sales tax, his own popular electoral style, and the fatigue of the Laffoon faction to win the election and begin a brisk administration. First, he pushed the General Assembly into swiftly replacing the sales tax with liquor and cigarette "sin" taxes. Moreover, New Deal programs began to have a vital impact on the state.[178]

Superintendent H. W. Peters, elected on the Democratic ticket along with Chandler in 1935, had been the "only rural school member of the Kentucky Educational Commission, 1932–34." A graduate of Western Kentucky State Teachers College, he considered himself a protégé of Henry Hardin Cherry. With experience as a principal and a superintendent in western Kentucky, just prior to his election as state superintendent he served as director of free textbooks in the State Department of Education.[179]

For all the bombast of the Chandler years (1935–1939), Chandler's administration appeared progressive and took advantage of increased revenue. According to his biographer, Charles P. Roland, the young governor "sponsored significant improvements in the state's roads, schools, and health, welfare, and penal institutions." The Government Reorganization Act of 1936 "drastically reduced the number of departments and clearly defined the responsibilities of each." This aided in reducing the state debt. The state's rural roads received much-needed attention. The legislature also approved the building of the new penitentiary at LaGrange and creation of the Kentucky Highway Patrol.[180]

Education legislation during the Chandler-Peters years included increased funding at the state level. The Great Depression years placed a great stress on the state's finances, as property values decreased and more landowners failed to pay their taxes. Local revenue decreased from about $16.8 million in 1930–1931 to about $12.65 million in 1934–1935. Only an increase in state revenues during the Chandler administration kept the state's schools from completely faltering. By 1938–1939, local revenue had risen back to $14.7 million, and state revenue also continued to increase. The local and state finances were reflected in teachers' salaries. In 1930–1931, the average annual teaching salary stood at $896; it fell to $784.83 in 1934 and rose again to $826 in 1940. Meanwhile, school attendance rose, particularly in the high schools. Between 1930 and 1940, high school enrollments (enrollments for grades seven through twelve were totaled), both public and private, increased from 65,643 students annually to 144,447. The actual number of high schools (both public and private, black and white schools) declined from 832 to 738, as smaller schools were consolidated into larger schools between 1930 and 1940. Of these schools, 659 were fully twelve grades; 35 offered only grades seven to nine. (This story of educational advance is personal. My own mother and father were part of that flood of students entering Kentucky's high schools and graduating in the thirties.)[181]

Peters also secured a February 1936 grant of $65,000 from the U.S. Office of Education to fund a study of education in Kentucky. This study confirmed earlier studies. The disparity between poorer county districts and the wealthier city districts had not changed. The outcome of the new study proposed making "long-range" planning an ongoing enterprise. Another attempt at passing an equalization fund failed. Perhaps the highlight of the Chandler-Peters years in Frankfort was passage of a statewide teacher retirement law, although it did not go into effect until 1940.[182]

During the Great Depression, in mid-January 1937, the greatest natural disaster in Kentucky history hit the Ohio River Valley. An Army Corps of Engineers staff member, resorting to a little hyperbole, called it "a calamitous inundation of almost Biblical proportions." With more than half of the city of Louisville under water, thousands of residents were evacuated. Nearly $50 million in property damage struck the city. The Louisville public school system suffered more than $500,000 in damage. "One of the surest signs that life was turning to normal occurred on February 12 when the local high school basketball schedule was resumed." By February 22, forty-three public schools reopened. In the devastated west end, Shawnee High School did not reopen until the next school term. Other parts of the state suffered as well. Nearly 50 percent of Frankfort and 95 percent of Paducah were inundated, and numerous schools remained closed for weeks. (The principal of Second Street School on the Kentucky River in Frankfort in the thirties revealed to me in an interview the anxiety he felt being the only person in that school during the crest of the floodwater: at one time, he said, he would have sworn the whole building groaned and then lifted slightly.)[183]

Two years later a flash flood devastated the Kentucky mountains, in the early morning of July 5, 1939, cutting off roads at a time when most schools were not in session. Most of the damage was in Rowan and Breathitt counties, where a twenty-foot wall of water suddenly descended Frozen Creek. In Breathitt County, the Kentucky Mountain Bible Institute, affiliated with the

Kentucky Mountain Holiness Association, operated Mount Carmel High School. Founded by the legendary Lela G. McConnell, KMBI served a wide community. In the evening before the storm, the faculty, students, and families living there had celebrated the holiday with an ice cream social. About three o'clock in the morning, according to Lorene Rose, the storm hit in full fury, water roaring down the narrow valley. She recalled finally rushing to the attic of the main building and grabbing at the rafters of the building, but she soon floated in the raging stream, her leg gashed by a piece of careening farm machinery. Washed downstream two miles, she finally made it to the bank with only a fringe of a nightgown around her neck. Many more were not as fortunate. Horace Myers, the principal of the school, along with two of his young sons, died as he tried to take them to safety. Fifty-two people in all died in Breathitt County that night, and twenty-five in Rowan County. Many bodies, badly decomposed in the summer heat, were not found until days later. Rose recalled that Nettie Myers, the widow of Principal Myers, would sit weeping, repeating over and over, "'My arms are so empty.' It wasn't anytime until her hair was just as white as it could be." State government as well as secular agencies sent in aid. Survivor Dorothy Spencer said everybody was "stunned," but they went to work burying the dead and consoling the families of those lost. KMBI survived, building bigger and better buildings above the floodplain. Even Nettie Myers recovered and spent many more years teaching at the school.[184]

The New Deal of President Franklin D. Roosevelt had a positive influence on the educational institutions of Kentucky. National Youth Administration programs "allowed thousands of Kentucky youths to stay in high school and college," and the NYA also sponsored vocational workshops. As many as ten thousand students a year by the late thirties were being paid for school-related work as part of the NYA. Other New Deal programs, such as the Works Progress Administration and the Public Works Administration, "built hundreds of classrooms, gymnasiums, libraries, and laboratories that otherwise would not have existed until after World War II." Many of the buildings were made of native stone and survive to the present day. For example, the Perry Cline School in Pike County, built as a Civilian Conservation Corps project, "served black students for about 30 years" before being turned into a senior citizens center. WPA and NYA labor built the new Morgan County High School, which was dedicated on May 24, 1937, by Eleanor Roosevelt with rivals Senator Alben Barkley and Governor Happy Chandler in attendance. Unemployed teachers found work on WPA literacy projects across the state. Civilian Conservation Camps offered coursework taught by teachers who might not have found jobs anywhere else. These teachers attacked the literacy problems of many CCC campers, giving them a rudimentary education. "At the very least," claimed George T. Blakey, "the New Deal educational activities kept Kentucky from falling further behind, no mean achievement in the 1930s."[185]

Other agencies tried to help improve Kentucky public schools. In 1939 the Alfred P. Sloan Foundation began cooperating with the Bureau of School Services of the University of Kentucky to improve the diet of rural Kentuckians. New instructional materials were introduced into the first four grades of four schools in Estill and McCreary counties, to teach lessons in raising vegetables, poultry, and goats and in improving the worn-out land. *The Children Must Learn* and *And So They Live,* documentaries produced by the Educational Film Institute of New York University and Documentary Film Productions, Inc., "in cooperation with the University of Kentucky," touted this project. The films have the feel of typical thirties documentaries, with excellent narration and mountain background music. Shot in bleak wintertime with snow on the ground, the films have a dark, somber feel. Although the films depicted the hardscrabble lifestyle of the children and their parents, most of the children look relatively healthy, and the school scenes show children and teachers happily hard at work.[186]

Another study of education in Kentucky in the late 1930s, sponsored by the U.S. Office of Education, encouraged what would have been radical change for the state. The study concluded the obvious: Kentucky would benefit greatly by consolidating schools. There were too many small schools scattered across the Kentucky landscape. Average daily attendance in one-teacher schools was 69.7 percent of enrollment as compared with 80.12 percent for schools of four or more teachers. The project proposed that only high schools with six or more teachers could be efficient and offer enough variety of coursework for modern times. Only 26 percent of Kentucky high schools, or 222 out of 848, met this criterion in 1934–1935. Assessable wealth per student varied widely. A relatively poor county such as Breathitt assessed its property at the 75-cents-per-$100 maximum because of its low $539.13/census child. In Woodford County its low tax rate of 25 cents per $100 drew on $11,114.71/census child. Transportation costs had increased rapidly since World War I, but 87 "horse drawn" vehicles still operated in the state along with 898 of the "motorized" variety. Of 7,592 total school buildings in the commonwealth, 5,367 were "one teacher" buildings. State-wide in 1936–1937, per capita spending of $11.65 per student fell far short of the study's proposed expenditure of $25.00 per student. This study proposed higher local and state taxation, a mandatory nine-month school term, consolidation of elementary and secondary schools, and even reorganization to the point of combining county units into more efficient systems. However, poor roads, transportation costs, localism, resistance to loss of local schools, the increasing power of the county superintendent for good or ill, and the lingering effects of the Great Depression all militated against the reforms suggested in this study.[187] Kentucky produced some excellent "schoolmen" in the early twentieth century, perhaps none better than Whitney Young Sr. and Lee Kirkpatrick. Born in Midway in 1897, Young was among the first students at Lincoln Institute when it opened in 1912. After service in World War I and a brief career in the auto industry, he came back to Lincoln as a teacher in 1920. In 1935 he became the first African American to direct Lincoln. He soon had the school out of debt and developed it into one of the premier African American residential preparatory schools in America. He remained head of Lincoln until the school closed in 1964. Young was an early civil rights leader, and generations of Lincoln Institute graduates during his tenure became teachers and other professionals. Among these was Young's son Whitney Young Jr., who served as executive director of the National Urban League from 1961 to 1971.[188]

Kirkpatrick, who received training at Georgetown College and Columbia University, rose through the ranks to become superintendent of the Paris schools in 1918. From then until his retirement in 1953, he led an enlightened, progressive district. His book *Teaching School Day by Day* (1941) was written particularly for the young teacher entering the profession. This practical guide for the classroom teacher included everything from handling discipline problems to the necessity of individually developing "a philosophy of education." The Paris superintendent also coauthored a public school history textbook, *Exploring Kentucky*, with Thomas D. Clark. Kirkpatrick required the teachers in his system to travel, study, and take graduate courses. Paris High School became the first in Kentucky to be evaluated by the Southern Association of Colleges and Secondary Schools in 1922, when it earned an AA rating. In the 1920s all the teachers in the Paris system had college degrees, and in the 1930s 70 percent had master's degrees. During his tenure in Paris, Kirkpatrick kept in constant touch with the educational issues of the day and remained a confidant of other educational leaders, including Herman L. Donovan and Frank L. McVey.[189]

All Kentucky educational statistics just before the beginning of World War II paint a picture of lost ground and bungled opportunities in the early twentieth century. For example, even though state funding increased, between 1910 and 1940 the percentage of state funds going directly to public education decreased drastically, from 44.7 percent to 24.9 percent. While other states, including those in the South, increased their school funds substantially, Kentucky did so only incrementally. Kentucky dropped from fourth to eleventh in the South in spending per student from 1900 to 1920.

And the decline continued to 1940. Nationally, Kentucky fell from fortieth in expenditures per student in 1912 to forty-fourth in 1920 and rose only to forty-first in 1940. In 1940 Kentucky spent an average of $48 per student while the national average was $92. There was also great disparity in spending within the state. The independent Kentucky districts spent about $70 per student while the county districts spent about $40 per student. High school enrollment in the independent districts was substantially higher than in the county districts. Other states, including those in the Old South, were expending more and more to educate their youth.[190]

Discrimination of several kinds existed in Kentucky public school education. The Day Law rigidity handicapped both blacks and whites with duplicate and expensive dual systems of education. Rural teachers made less salary than their urban counterparts. Men made more than women. African American and white female teachers had an uphill battle to gain salary equity in the teaching profession. However, a 1939 National Education Association study found that Kentucky was one of a minority of states that did not refuse employment by law for married female teachers. Some local school districts did have such strictures, but others would hire married women because of the necessity of filling a position. In October 1937 the Louisville Association of Teachers in Colored Schools and the NAACP began a campaign to eliminate the discriminatory (and standard) 15 percent differential between white and black teaching salaries as well as the two-hundred-dollar difference between male and female compensation. The visit of Eleanor Roosevelt to several Louisville black schools "spurred many Negro citizens to redouble their efforts to achieve full and equal rights." Initially, Superintendent Zenos E. Scott and the school board denied the request. The Kentucky Negro Education Association appropriated $500 "toward a fund to prosecute" a case in the federal courts. On May 16, 1941, with the threat of a lawsuit and a scheduled hearing in federal court, the Louisville Board of Education voted to eliminate the pay differentials over a period of four years.[191]

Although Kentucky public schools remained rigidly segregated in 1940, 85 percent of African Americans, ages ten to fourteen, attended schools, while only 63 percent of white children did. Blacks attended an average of eight days longer each year than whites did. "Indicative of the decline in Kentucky schools, both figures were near the bottom of the sixteen southern states surveyed," observed James C. Klotter.[192]

Little seemed to be going right in the state's educational system. Whereas in 1900 Kentucky ranked first in the South in school attendance "for both white and black students; by 1940 it ranked last and next to last in the two categories." While 95 percent of American schoolchildren were getting an elementary school education in 1940, only 63 percent of Kentucky children were being so trained, Harry W. Schacter reported in *Kentucky on the March*. Correspondingly, Kentucky's "per capita income was 59 percent of the United States average in 1943." As Klotter stated in *Kentucky: Portrait in Paradox*, even with improvements in Kentucky education in the first decades of the twentieth century, "what were hailed as solutions to the commonwealth's problems turned out to be cruel mirages of hope." In 1940 Kentucky students attended school an average of nearly 130 days, the national average being 151 days. To the north, in Indiana, the attendance rate was 149 days, and in Tennessee it was nearly 138. However, there was always a bright spot to offset complete gloom. For example, as a sign of growing professionalization in Kentucky education, in 1926 the Kentucky Association of Secondary School Principals organized for the first time, the sixteenth such state organization to become part of the National Association of Secondary School Principals. The KASSP began meeting during the annual meetings of KEA with informational sessions, and soon regional groups for principals had been formed. In 1941 the KASSP became officially affiliated with KEA.[193]

Kentucky's educational system had been nearly studied to death from 1900 to the early 1940s. These mostly trenchant, if turgid, works included the Kentucky Educational Improvement Commission of 1905; the Kentucky Education Association studies of 1911, 1912, and 1913; a report of the Kentucky Educational Commission of 1921, published in 1926 as *Public Education in Kentucky: A Study of the Equalization of Educational Opportunities in Kentucky*; the *Report of the Kentucky Educational Commission*, published in 1933; and *A Study of Local School Units in Kentucky*, published in 1937. And yet, there appeared to be little if any progress, especially compared with national norms. Schacter's *Kentucky on the March* pointed to the economic consequences of a poor educational system. Furthermore, contemporaries such as Moses Ligon and Frank McVey and commentators Thomas D. Clark, James C. Klotter, and Harry Caudill found Kentucky's lack of educational progress distressing.

By the late 1930s the world appeared irrevocably turned toward war. First in Asia and then in Europe, the totalitarian dictatorships of the world turned on the free nations. The neutrality of the early Roosevelt years slowly evolved into a greater awareness that the United States of America could not remain out of the fight forever. Then on December 7, 1941, the Japanese attacked Pearl Harbor in the Hawaiian Islands. The insular world in which many Kentuckians lived was soon swept away as thousands of men and women went into the armed forces and off to work in war industries across the nation. The Kentucky educational system was placed under greater pressure than ever before. The first four decades of the twentieth century had been years of promise and struggle with only very limited fulfillment. The saying "Thank God for Arkansas" was on the lips of many Kentuckians, because in 1940 it was the only state with a smaller percentage of adults who had graduated from high school. Education flourished in some parts of Kentucky while it languished in others. For example, illiteracy ranged from 8 percent in Kenton County to a state high of 44 percent in Martin County, according to *Kentucky on the March*. "This was not the Balkans," Schacter exclaimed; "it was in the United States. It was not the eighteenth century—it was near the middle of the twentieth." A lingering problem continued to be Kentucky's lack of a culture that demanded education. In 1940 only 78 percent of the commonwealth's children were enrolled in school. Several studies and the work of commissions had made valuable suggestions to improve Kentucky's public school system since 1900, but little of substance had been accomplished. Meanwhile, other states bypassed Kentucky in educational attainment and effort. How would Kentuckians respond to the challenges of the war years and beyond?[194]

Chapter 6

Higher Education in the New Century

At the turn of the twentieth century, Kentuckians were influenced, indeed had been impacted for much of their history, by educational experiences beyond the classroom. In the broadest sense, education is "intergenerational, with adults teaching children." Acculturation is the process whereby a person is incorporated into the larger group, absorbing the culture of his or her surroundings from birth.[1]

Outside of the normal school setting, whether elementary, secondary, or college, there were opportunities to learn for the willing and able. After the Civil War print media became more available with the development of cheaper printing methods. While there had always been proper books, magazines, and newspapers, the "dime novel" became a democratizing influence in the late nineteenth century.

The church remained the center of not only worship but also learning in the nineteenth century. Those who attended were exposed to learned clerics in the larger urban churches, where some ministers had attended some of the finest colleges and theological seminaries in the country. If their doctrine was strict, they lent an air of sophistication to their flocks. In the country churches, the preachers may not have been as learned but were even more expressive. The Bible was the center of these churches and was also found in nearly every home. Children grew up reading the Bible if nothing else.[2]

Organized Sunday schools became a source of learning, first in urban areas in the East, then spreading eventually to rural areas of the South after the Civil War. Children and adults learned Bible lessons as well as a degree of reading skills in an evangelical Protestant setting. Forbidden to preach in most Protestant denominations, women found Sunday school work an outlet for their talents and religious zeal. Sunday school conventions of the late nineteenth century demonstrated the growing role of women in Kentucky, particularly in affairs religious. Whereas "women made up 30 percent of the delegates to Kentucky's 1875 convention," three years later their numbers had increased to 45 percent.[3]

The imagination of Americans for nonformal public education abounded. Beginning at Lake Chautauqua in New York in the 1870s, a movement swept the country that brought "enlightenment, education, and entertainment to thousands of people over the summer months." From June to September, Chautauqua circuits crisscrossed Kentucky by the late nineteenth century, and "lecturers brought ideas, world news, and culture to those who might not otherwise have been exposed to such informative refinement." Their events lasting from a few days to two weeks, such circuits as "The Redpath Chautauqua" came to perform and inform in special tents erected for the events. Those who attended could hear such political figures as William Jennings Bryan deliver speeches. Renowned composer and band leader John Philip Sousa even came to Elkton on one occasion. Educational leaders such as Henry Hardin Cherry often toured the western Kentucky region, helping develop "Rural Chautauquas." On one such tour in 1913, he proposed reform. "The policy for the development of Kentucky has been too indefinite, negative and vague," he said. "Our civic, social and industrial standards have been too frequently made by men who have appealed to the prejudice and ignorance of the people rather than by a consideration of the fundamentals of permanent and universal development." To be more specific, he argued that Kentucky had "too many elections and suffered too much politicking." Oratory of this type and intensity during the Progressive Era would have been the highlight of many a Chautauqua circuit.[4]

In some places Chautauqua exhibited a more religious emphasis. For example, an 1888 meeting at Woodland Park in Lexington highlighted workshops for Sunday school teachers. Other instruction included a lecture titled "In and about Shakespeare's Home," accompanied by "Stereopticon Illustrations." Chautauqua could also have an agricultural emphasis, as at one held in London, Kentucky, in August 1919. Shakespearean plays and demonstrations such as the "Wonders of Modern Science" were performed before packed crowds of Madison countians in the early 1920s. Separate programs for African Americans followed the strict segregation of the time in the commonwealth. For as little as $2.50 for a week's events, white patrons could take part in all the events of Chautauqua in Winchester and Ashland in the summer of 1915. However, a study of Chautauqua in Kentucky found that between 1920 and 1930, the variety of entertainment increased so rapidly, along with automobile transportation, as to render the old circuits passé. Once the "most American thing in America," Chautauqua retreated to the confines of its New York origins.[5]

Talking movies and radio also sounded the death knell of Chautauqua. With the coming of the telephone, electricity, and the automobile, Kentuckians were not as isolated as they had once been. Railroads now wound into the recesses of Kentucky's mountains. After WHAS radio went on the air on July 18, 1922, other stations soon followed in Lexington, Paducah, and Hopkinsville. The "commercial" was born, informing far-flung Kentuckians, like other Americans, of the merits of commercial products. Radio stations not only provided entertainment, news, and weather reports; they also began to offer public services. For example, WHAS and the University of Kentucky set up listening stations in forty eastern Kentucky locations. President Frank L. McVey often addressed the citizens of the state, as did other educational leaders.[6]

Libraries served a vital function in educating Kentuckians. The first library opened at Transylvania in 1784, and others formed as companies in the early nineteenth century. By the latter third of that century, Kentucky had seventy-five libraries. After construction of the first Carnegie Library in Covington in 1881, by 1935 the Carnegie foundation had built twenty-seven buildings in the state, nine of which were in Louisville. Carnegie grants built libraries on four Kentucky college campuses: the University of Kentucky (1909), Centre College (1913), Berea College (1906), and Kentucky Wesleyan in Winchester (1915). Beginning in the 1890s, the Kentucky Federation of Women's Clubs, in cooperation with Berea College, began bringing books into the Kentucky mountains by horseback. After the turn of the century, most large towns and cities established free libraries, and by the mid-thirties all high schools in the state had libraries. One of the most successful New Deal programs, the packhorse libraries of the Works Progress Administration, began operating in 1937. If Kentuckians in the first half of the twentieth century had the desire to read, books were available, including many by native writers.[7]

Kentuckians could read extensively about their own state in books written by Kentuckians. Considering its size, Kentucky has always produced some fine literature. The writers of the early twentieth century were no exception. In 1903 five of the top ten books on the best-seller list of *Publisher's Weekly* were penned by Kentucky authors. James Lane Allen and John Fox Jr. wrote about their native state in different ways, but always with attention to detail. Fox's *The Trail of the Lonesome Pine* is one of the greatest novels in Kentucky literary history. Other writers, such as Irvin S. Cobb, Robert Penn Warren, and Elizabeth Madox Roberts, also wrote about their state. Newspapers offered good writing as well, the editorials of Pulitzer Prize–winner Henry Watterson of the *Louisville Courier-Journal* being among the best in the nation. With more than 160 newspapers in the late nineteenth century, Kentuckians did not lack for local news and commentary. Some local editors, including H. A. Sommers of the *Elizabethtown News*, wrote particularly worthy editorials and usually espoused progressivism of the southern variety.[8]

Then there were always the experiences of sitting around the family hearth, hearing family history and stories, reading the Bible, and learning the rudiments of social life. Conversations and listening to adults talk far into the night provided special times for children growing up in the early twentieth century. The country store remained the cornerstone of life in rural areas; there conversation, a dialogue about everyday life, glued the community together. Court Day in many counties brought together hundreds if not thousands of people in a mass assembly for entertainment, commerce, and legal matters.[9]

Society, even in largely rural Kentucky, was unavoidably altered by the social, technological, intellectual, and economic movements of the late nineteenth and early twentieth centuries. The life of "vivacious, intelligent, and attractive" Fannie Morton Bryan of Russellville demonstrated some of the changing social mores of the late nineteenth century, as Bryan matured in the new century. A female had more choices than ever before. Bryan attended Logan Female College in Russellville, "a prestigious primary and secondary school for young ladies owned and operated by the Methodist Episcopal Church, South." In her diaries she traced the story of her life as a student and a young woman. As the nineteenth century drew to an end, her life reflected the tensions of the time, in which "young women were simultaneously being urged to be 'independent' and to adhere strictly to the codes of etiquette." Although she never married, Bryan did not lack for romances, as her diaries revealed. She had numerous serious suitors from nearby Bethel College and several marriage proposals, but for various reasons she chose not to accept any of them. Her name often appeared in Bethel College's yearbook, *The Blue and the Gold*, connected to some young man. In some ways her dalliances appeared the height of flirtation with no meaning. She wanted a career in education and cared for her aging parents until their deaths. And, perhaps even more important, she was among the first generation of women who, because of their increasing acceptance in the workplace and education, could choose not to marry. As author Sue Lynn McGuire concluded, "By the end of the last decade of the nineteenth century, numerous women from the 'better' southern homes were entering the teaching ranks." Bryan's career as teacher and principal of an elementary school in Russellville began in the late 1880s and lasted more than fifty years. She was active in church and civic organizations as well. There were untold numbers of women like Fannie Morton Bryan, "southern" to a degree, who kept schools in the commonwealth functioning well into the twentieth century.[10]

Just as public elementary and secondary education in Kentucky at the turn of the twentieth century appeared to have been marking time since the Civil War, higher education in the commonwealth struggled to keep pace with the nation. Kentucky, "southern" in many of its characteristics, particularly in following "the color line," blended the old with the new.

Some scholars maintain that "the South had a more rigid definition of the role of women than the North," because "the antebellum image of the Southern lady on a pedestal limited her freedom as she entered the twentieth century." The life of Fannie Morton Bryan demonstrated increasing possibilities for the "new woman" of the South. But was this a general trend in Kentucky or an anomaly? Southern women's colleges such as Randolph-Macon, Converse, Mississippi University for Women, and Sophie Newcomb became famous for their strong rules and discipline and were dominated by male faculty. These women's colleges, as well as those in Kentucky, such as Hamilton in Lexington and Bethel in Hopkinsville, faced a dilemma. Should they train women in domesticity or for the new age of work outside the home? How would they react to the growing fight for women's suffrage and other women's issues of the day? Although several Kentucky colleges became coeducational, or "mixed," according to the nomenclature of the times, in the latter part of the nineteenth century there still existed several all-female schools. The history of Potter College in Bowling Green illustrated much of the tension surrounding female education, particularly in the South, at the dawn of the twentieth century.[11]

Incorporated as a nondenominational private women's college in 1890, Potter College was named for Pleasant J. Potter, a local banker who helped raise $21,160 to construct a three-story building. The school had begun classes the previous September, with about two hundred students and eleven faculty members. Was there a need for such a school in Bowling Green? Lynn E. Niedermeier, the historian of Potter College, succinctly summed up the causes for its founding, when she said, "Bowling Green's male elite founded Potter College as a symbol of the town's 'liberal spirit,' but in the hope that it would perpetuate the jewels of the Old South's identity, its 'ladies.'" Perhaps the most characteristically "southern" part of Kentucky, and the site of Kentucky's Confederate capital, Bowling Green was fighting a rear-guard action against modernity. Ogden College, a Bowling Green men's school, founded a few years earlier by Methodists, like most Kentucky "colleges" of the late nineteenth century, had more students in the preparatory department than in higher education. For a time Ogden even closed all its college classes.[12]

Bowling Green then had two "colleges," one male and the other female, at the turn of the twentieth century, operating in tough economic times.

Other boundaries were being set. In 1891 President B. F. Cabell took the initiative of building a fence completely around Potter College as "a meaningful dividing line between commerce and culture, risk and safety, nature and civilization, male and female." Potter began offering one classical course, "Mistress of Arts," with content similar to that in Ogden's collegiate program. Potter College did not completely fit the view of higher education for women expressed by Smith College president L. Clark Seelye when he wrote, "The college is not intended to fit woman for any particular sphere or profession but to develop by the most carefully devised means all her intellectual capacities, so that she may be a more perfect woman in any position."[13]

Actually, Bowling Green was a center for education in the south central part of the commonwealth, with Potter and Ogden colleges offering separate female and male instruction and Bowling Green Business College and Literary Institute serving as a continuation of Southern Normal School. Proprietor Henry Hardin Cherry changed the name of the latter school to Southern Normal and Bowling Green Business College in 1894; it also included preparation in telegraphy. Cherry sold the school for $16,000 in 1906 when he became president of Western Kentucky State Normal School. Eventually becoming Bowling Green Business University, the school operated as a proprietary coeducational college from then until the early 1960s, when it became part of Western Kentucky University.[14]

Potter College and Ogden College limped along into the first decade of the twentieth century, exuding a southern "Lost Cause" aura that befitted schools located much farther south. To protect Bowling Green's "southernness," an Ogden College professor and graduate of Virginia Military Institute "declared that he had never been 'taught by a Yankee himself'" and said, "We should not let our girls be taught by them." But other leaders of the region questioned the southern social mores of the day, expecting that change was inevitable. The strongest force of change was that neither Potter nor Ogden could surmount the economic problems of the time. Potter's enrollment declined in its second decade, with only forty-one women in the college courses in 1907–1908. By this time the state had founded Western, providing a much less expensive opportunity for the education of women in Bowling Green. As President Cabell's health failed, Western, disregarding local protests, bought the property and buildings of Potter College in 1909. The rise originally known as "Vinegar Hill," where Potter had been located, became the center of the new normal school. Meanwhile, Ogden College puttered along for some additional years before succumbing to the same fate. With low attendance and failure to receive accreditation by the Southern Association, the school closed its doors on January 1, 1928, and was absorbed into Western.[15]

In 1900 there were enough colleges to educate Kentuckians, black and white, female and male. State College in Lexington taught both males and females. The Kentucky State Normal School for Colored Persons in Frankfort very slowly emerged as a college in the new century. However, Simmons University for African Americans in Louisville "gave blacks their best college instruction in the state" in 1900. At the turn of the century, Berea College offered the only desegregated education in the commonwealth. There were four-year denominational colleges aplenty, including Georgetown, Transylvania, Centre (which merged with Central University in 1901), Kentucky Wesleyan, and Asbury. In addition, institutions at Pippa Passes, Campbellsville, Cumberland, Columbia (Lindsey Wilson), Bethel, and Pikeville began their evolution from academies and high schools into junior colleges in the early twentieth century. Then there were the colleges that struggled: Potter, Ogden, Logan Female, and others, which hardly qualified as colleges and soon ended as institutions. Sandy Valley Seminary in Paintsville had transformed into John C. C. Mayo College, only to finally fail when the Methodist Episcopal Church, South, pulled its support. The University of Louisville did not reopen its Academic Department, or undergraduate program, until 1907.[16]

Kentucky students continued to find opportunities outside the commonwealth at the turn of the century. "A serious handicap in the improvement of schools in Kentucky was the fact that an astonishing number of college graduates had attended institutions of higher prestige outside the state," declared Thomas D. Clark. He went on to claim that "whatever the Kentuckian's local pride, it somehow did not include a warmness of affection for some of the local colleges. The law school in the University of Virginia was a training ground for Kentucky boys who studied law. Washington and Lee University rivaled Centre College for Kentucky students, as did Princeton, Harvard, and Yale. Too many doctors, theologians, and degree holders from graduate schools got their degrees outside the state." Perhaps the best example of such a student was Edward F. Prichard Jr., who had been chosen "one of the six brightest students in America" in 1931. That fall he went off to Princeton University, where he graduated at the top of his class before taking a law degree at Harvard Law School. His biographer concluded: "For any young man wishing to obtain the highest academic challenge in 1931, no school in Kentucky or, for that matter, the entire South, could meet his requirements." Katherine Graham, longtime owner of the *Washington Post*, "described Prichard as 'the most impressive man of our generation, the one who dazzled us most.'"[17]

Kentucky colleges, as they faced the challenges of the twentieth century, needed to appeal to a broad spectrum of students, those of Prichard's intellect as well as those who had poorer academic preparation. Just as today, retaining students for any length of time, thus continuing the revenue stream of tuition and fees, could be a serious challenge for college administrations. John R. Thelin, in his study of American higher education, found this true for State College at the turn of the century. Only 30 percent of the entering class of 1903 stayed on to receive a bachelor's degree four years later. During the same period at Transylvania, the problem was even worse: half of the freshman class dropped out, "with seldom more than 10 percent of an entering freshman class persisting to receive bachelor's degrees four years later." Transferring from one college to another continued to be important in the development of statewide student populations.[18]

At the turn of the century, the private denominational colleges in the state, while not growing expansively, continued, collectively, to educate more white middle-class students than State College did. Eleven such institutions had been founded before the Civil War. Those that survived the postwar years, those difficult economic times, were joined by a few others. These colleges were changing, as all such schools did in the new century. However, none of the private colleges in the commonwealth at the turn of the twentieth century had either enough endowment, student bodies generating large revenues, or freedom from denominational schism to rest easily in the new age.[19]

Georgetown College offered only one example of the roiling sectarian waters in the state. The relationship of Georgetown College to Kentucky Baptists changed around the turn of the century. After being completely under the control of the Kentucky Baptist Education Society from its founding in 1829, the school was brought under control of the General Association of Baptists in Kentucky in 1895 by Rev. T. T. Eaton. Thus began a controversy that continued for years over autonomy versus denominational control. An initial settlement was reached in 1906, when a new society formed, chaired by President E. Y. Mullins of the Southern Baptist Theological Seminary, and was given the responsibility of choosing Georgetown's trustees.[20]

The Georgetown campus changed slowly in the new century. Under Arthur Yager, a Georgetown graduate with a Johns Hopkins University Ph.D. who became president in 1907, academic life on campus improved to the point where two students, Allan Barnett and Tom Jones, received Rhodes Scholarships. After a career in private-school education in the East, Barnett returned home to Shelbyville and taught high school English at Shelbyville High School for a few years (I was fortunate to be in one of his classes). Yager instituted a comprehensive examination policy for senior majors that was in effect when I graduated from Georgetown in 1962 and continues to the present day. However, the future of Georgetown College reflected the economic times as enrollment fluctuated from as many as 192 in 1909 to 108 in 1912. The founding of nearby Eastern and increased state support for the University of Kentucky probably accounted for the decline in Georgetown's enrollment as well as challenges for Centre and Transylvania.[21]

After President Woodrow Wilson appointed Yager governor-general of Puerto Rico in 1913, Georgetown reverted to the usual procedure of appointing Baptist ministers as presidents, in this case, Rev. M. B. Adams, who served until 1925. During his watch enrollment increased from 112 to 400 and faculty grew from 10 to 31. Moreover, the college passed through the turbulent World War I years, including the terrible flu epidemic, and the early-1920s economic challenges. Baptists were not among the wealthiest denominationalists, though, and that fact proved nearly disastrous in the twenties. First, a General Education Board grant fell far short of what President Adams requested and did not materialize. Then Georgetown received only $200,000 of an originally promised $700,000 from the Southern Baptist Convention's 75 Million (Dollar) Campaign. Most of the money went to covering "operating deficits" during the agricultural depression of the early 1920s. A 1929 General Baptist Convention of Kentucky report presaged the terrible years of the Great Depression by noting that all Baptist institutions in the state were in dire straits and saying, "Georgetown is on the verge of bankruptcy."[22]

Baptists in Kentucky, although theirs was the most numerous denomination, had colleges like Georgetown and Bethel to support as well as other schools that had begun as academies with high schools and sprouted into colleges in the twentieth century. What is more, in the late nineteenth and early twentieth centuries, numerous junior and community colleges were founded across the nation as academies moved to offer the beginnings of higher education. Cumberland College had begun as Williamsburg Institute on January 1, 1887, a product of the local Baptist association. Renamed Cumberland College in 1913, it did not become a true "college" until it added junior college classes in 1918. Campbellsville College had begun as Russell Creek Baptist Academy in 1906, also founded by the local Baptist association. In 1924 the school began offering junior college courses. The question for Baptists was going to be how well they could support so many "colleges" with their limited resources.[23]

Presbyterians had their own problems. After the 1901 consolidation of Centre College and Central University, under the name Central University of Kentucky, "Northern" and "Southern" Presbyterians, with some trepidation, as well as old wounds, tried to make the consolidated school work. Actually, "Central University" was the name of the umbrella now extending from Louisville, with its medical and dental schools and theological seminary, to Danville and the old Centre campus and to the preparatory schools. Again in a compromising mood, a northern Presbyterian, William C. Roberts, the incumbent chief executive of Centre, became president of the merged school, while the old Central's Lindsay Hughes Blanton became vice president. In 1918 the school reverted to the venerable name Centre College.[24]

Centre College had no pretensions of becoming a university and remained an all-male school well into the twentieth century. "Centre was a man's world," concluded one historian of the school. In 1926 Kentucky College for Women, the old Caldwell College, became the "Women's Department" of Centre, but women did not move to the Centre campus until 1962, during the presidency of Thomas A. Spragens. Caldwell College/Kentucky College for Women had its own world, separate from the men of Centre. An annual "May Festival" highlighted the women's year in the early twentieth century. As many as twenty-five hundred spectators attended that event in 1930, which included not only the crowning of a May Queen but also "interpretative dancing based on the story of Keats' 'Endymion.'" Centre had very close ties to the community of Danville, with many students coming from the surrounding central Kentucky region. In the style of many colleges, Centre operated Centre College Academy, known locally as "Prep," which closed in 1918. Improvements had been made to public high school education, and Danville citizens had begun to feel that "Prep" was an "obstacle to a public high school."[25]

"There is no better place where a man can put his money to insure a perpetual good accomplished by it, than in a well-endowed Christian College," claimed a Centre College catalog. Even though Centre was better financed by its constituents than Georgetown and other private denominational colleges in the commonwealth, it also faced financial crises. To fill at least some of its needs, Centre developed a relationship with the newly founded Carnegie Foundation in 1905 that lasted until 1921. However, this "raised serious questions about the nature of Centre, its support from the Presbyterian Synods, its Christian character and the willingness of constituents to contribute to the institution during the time the Carnegie Foundation gave financial support and influenced its policies," according to Idus Wilmer Adams.[26]

The Carnegie Foundation began with an idea in 1902 of "assisting colleges and universities," secular rather than sectarian; the first objective was to provide pensions for faculty who were paid miserly salaries. Centre became interested in the plan because, though apparently sectarian, the school had an 1824 charge from the Kentucky legislature stipulating that Centre must impose no religious test on students and that "no religious doctrine peculiar to any one sect of Christians shall be inculcated by any professor in said college." Presidents William C. Roberts (1898–1904) and William A. Ganfield (1904–1922) avidly pursued a Carnegie connection. At first the southern and northern Presbyterian synods of the state acquiesced. The first Centre (the name still used for the undergraduate arm of Central University) professor received a retirement stipend in 1908. Retired chancellor Blanton of old Central University then received a pension, eventually raised to $1,800 per year. Some Presbyterian leaders opposed the arrangement with the Carnegie Foundation from the start. That tension grew as both synods moved toward a closer relationship with Centre. Centre enrollment suffered, falling to a low of 88 students in 1915. Ganfield became afraid that the northern Presbyterian move to "standardize" colleges might lead to a further loss of students and donations. Eventually, the Centre trustees succumbed to pressure in 1921 and amended the school's 1901 charter, which had consolidated Central University and Centre College. There would be no religious test of students, but the trustees required that thereafter Centre's president be a Presbyterian, or of the same doctrine, and that all faculty be evangelical Christians, with a majority of them Presbyterian. More important, the southern and northern synods asserted irrevocable control over the self-perpetuating board; each synod could name four of the twelve members of the board. The board severed the Danville school's relationship with the Carnegie Foundation on October 21, 1921. Centre would remain a small, elite liberal arts school, training leaders into the new century, but now it was firmly under the control of Presbyterianism. "Centre College found that it had to yield to the growing pressure from the Presbyterian Church from 1915–21 in order to survive," concluded a historian of central Kentucky colleges.[27]

The remnant of Kentucky University, operating on the old Transylvania University campus, had by 1900 become a liberal arts coeducational college under strong Disciples of Christ control. Gone were the days of Bowman's visionary university and all of the other appendages except for the College of the Bible, the Disciples' theological seminary. Transylvania had all the trappings of similar schools across the nation: fraternities and athletic teams, as well as the old traditions of literary societies. But it also faced economic crises, like most other small Kentucky private schools. James Lane Allen, a Transylvania graduate in 1872 and 1877, angered the orthodox of the Disciples of Christ when he published *The Reign of Law*, a novel "dealing with religious doubt and Darwinism" in 1900. The plot of the novel fictionalized the fate of William Benjamin Smith, a classmate of Allen's and later a Kentucky University professor who resigned when his religious-scientific views conflicted with that school's positions. President John McGarvey of the College of the Bible protested Allen's attacks as well as the honorary degree that Kentucky University had given him in 1898. The popular central Kentucky novelist famously retorted that KU was "a ruin which will stay a ruin."[28]

Whether a "ruin" or not, Kentucky University was, and remained, a liberal arts college within a sectarian, decidedly Disciples of Christ, context. In 1908 Kentucky University reverted to the name Transylvania University by legislative act in order not to be confused with the new title for the State College of Kentucky, eventually to become the University of Kentucky. In 1917 Transylvania had nearly two hundred students, of whom nearly one-quarter were women. Thirty-four ministerial students labored at the College of the Bible, which continued as part of Transylvania University. The old Lexington school was not without controversy. "It all began as a small tempest in a teapot," declared historian Wright. Richard Crossfield, president of both Transylvania and the College of the Bible, and three newer "liberal" members of the faculty came under attack by a conservative ministerial student and his cohorts. Disciples of Christ periodicals and pulpits became involved in the controversy and what ended in a famous "heresy trial." The theory of evolution and religious modernism became the points of contention. In a trial-like atmosphere, witnesses and some of the accused were examined and cross-examined. Although the Transylvania trustees "found no teaching in this College by any member of the faculty that is out of harmony" with the principles of the school, the controversy continued into the 1930s. These attacks led to some reduced donations to the College of the Bible and Transylvania.[29]

Like other Kentucky Protestants, Methodists also displayed divisiveness and contentiousness. After moving to Winchester from Millersburg in 1890, Kentucky Wesleyan College developed better facilities and became coeducational. However, competition arose among the Methodist faithful in Kentucky. Asbury College appealed to conservative/fundamentalist sectarian Methodists, while Union College in Barbourville catered to the mountains. There were newer Methodist "colleges" like Sue Bennett in London, which had begun as a high school and began offering junior college courses in 1922, receiving accreditation by the Southern Association ten years later. Lindsey Wilson in Columbia, founded by the Louisville Conference of the Methodist Episcopal Church, South, followed the same path and began offering college courses in 1923. The citizens of Columbia soon pledged $10,000 to the college.[30]

At the beginning of the twentieth century, Kentucky Wesleyan College, like most other "colleges" in the commonwealth, still operated academies to prepare students for the true college coursework. As the "senior" Methodist college in the state, supported by the Methodist Episcopal Church, South, Wesleyan suffered all the trials of other Kentucky schools, including the tenuous nature of the times. All colleges have their controversies. After the resignation of President C. H. Pearce in 1900, owing to declining enrollment and his increasing unpopularity, Professor David W. Batson, dean of the faculty, served briefly as interim. Never an advocate of intercollegiate athletics, Batson soon resigned over this issue. The coming of Rev. John Langton Weber in 1901 held great promise, particularly if he could unite "the two factions of Methodism," North and South. Then on a bitterly cold Valentine's Day 1905, a disastrous fire struck. "KY. WESLEYAN COLLEGE BURNED," blared a headline in the Winchester newspaper.[31]

When a college only has one main building, such a disaster can be impossible to recover from. However, supporters in Winchester, as well as others, including entrepreneur John C. C. Mayo, came to the rescue and a new, "superior building" was soon under construction. Wesleyan also received funds from the Carnegie Foundation to build a library. But all was not well. A turnover of presidents on the Winchester campus hurt student enrollment growth. Athletics continued to roil Methodists with an on-again, off-again program at Wesleyan. Eventually, Wesleyan received new life when the Louisville Conference, which operated Logan Female College in Russellville, and the Kentucky Conference, which controlled Wesleyan, began to talk merger of their resources. After the resignation of yet another president, Wesleyan nevertheless had made some progress and constructed new dormitories for men and women. Merger finally came in 1926, as the two conferences, under the leadership of Bishop U. V. W. Darlington, who served as interim president of KWC, voted to unite their educational boards.[32]

Meanwhile, conservative "holiness" Methodists went their own way. Revivalist Henry Clay Morrison's fiery preaching in Wilmore touched off a movement that led to John Wesley Hughes's founding of Asbury there in 1890, adhering to the doctrines of "entire sanctification" and "scriptural holiness." Hughes, who literally owned Asbury College, served as president from 1890 to 1905. After he transferred the school to a board of trustees, this group chose another president, apparently with his approval. Morrison, who served two terms as president of Asbury, 1910–1925 and 1933–1940, used his writings in the *Pentecostal Herald* as a bulwark against everything from religious modernism to mainline Methodism. Periodically, spontaneous as well as planned revivals swept the campus and the town. The strong personality of Morrison, known as "The Warrior" to his supporters, led the Asbury community until he died in 1942. The school even ambitiously added a master's degree program. Asbury Theological Seminary, founded in 1923, opened as a department of the college and separated in 1931. Perhaps no college in the state ever saw its place in the world and its mission as clearly as did Asbury.[33]

Berea College's challenges to the Day Law ended when the U.S. Supreme Court upheld segregation in 1908. This unique Madison County school became more and more known as a haven for poor mountain youth after the founding of Lincoln Institute for African American education in

Shelby County in 1912. William Goodell Frost continued in the Berea presidency, serving from 1892 to 1920. He refocused Berea's mission and oversaw a 1911 amendment to the school's constitution making "Appalachia Berea's special field." From then until his retirement, Berea's endowment grew from $100,000 to over $2 million and its enrollment from 350 to 2,400. Moreover, while still operating preparatory and normal departments, the school began developing college courses, which served only 25 students in 1893 but 215 in 1920. The normal department still drove enrollment, growing from 6 students in 1894 to 452 in 1920. Along with the Appalachian mission came the increasing sanctity of work. Although the work program was designed to help students pay expenses, it was also intended to "maintain equality on campus." The 1910 Berea College catalog stated, "We believe it better that all students should do some manual work, and have no room for young people who are too proud to share these duties."[34]

Frost believed that two-year vocational studies in "teaching, agriculture, home economics, carpentry, and other areas equipped mountaineers to meet the pressing problems of Appalachia." Extension work, teacher institutes, and other services he saw as important to Berea's mission. The "needs of less-elite students," those "of lesser means," continued to be Berea's raison d'être into the presidency of William J. Hutchins (1920–1938).[35]

During Hutchins's tenure, he had to contend with the semiretired Frost, who remained in Berea and continued to influence the school. Berea operated five departments: the Foundation School, offering basic education; the normal school, educating elementary teachers; a standard high school; a vocational high school; and the four-year college, which during Frost's tenure had no more than one-tenth of the total student body. While Frost believed that the solutions to the problems of the mountains should begin from the ground up, "for Hutchins the answer to Appalachia's situation was not a collection of schools with a college department, but a true college."[36]

The students of Berea themselves were changing between the wars, with more and more avoiding the vocational courses, particularly in the college department. Hutchins and the faculty instituted curriculum changes in the lower divisions that Frost deemed unacceptable. The retired president charged Hutchins with "stealing the millions [that Frost had raised] to help the poor people of the mountains." Frost was only slightly mollified by Hutchins's attempts at reconciliation. The new president faced a daunting task. The school was in debt and he had to rein in expenditures. Very soon Berea College did away with two-year degrees and settled on the B.A. as "the only appropriate degree Berea College should award." Frost disagreed, sometimes quite vehemently, with any changes in his old five-department arrangement. When the state required two years of college education for minimum teaching certification in 1922, Berea made adjustments, as it also did for its nursing program. Throughout his tenure, Hutchins continued to push for change of the old Frost model of mountain education. Although the college curriculum changed, it did so with some faculty dissent. These conflicts delayed accreditation by the Southern Association for Colleges and Secondary Schools.[37]

Higher education in the Kentucky mountains also received an added impetus when Alice Lloyd's vision of educating and uplifting Appalachian youth resulted in the founding of Caney Junior College in 1923. The school stated its purpose simply, "to train leaders," primarily teachers who would carry education into the hills and hollows. The school actually began teacher training as early as 1919. From a normal school setting to the beginning of two-year college training, Caney Junior College followed the dictates of the Kentucky General Assembly that in 1922 began requiring two years of training beyond high school for teacher certification. Students and teachers lived on campus under the watchful eye of Alice Lloyd. The circumstances were spartan, Victorian, and formal. Caney's work-study standards were even higher than those of Berea, owing to its lack of funding and endowment, and its isolation. Women wore uniforms and the men wore coats and ties to class. Because Lloyd believed part of Appalachia's problems were due to girls' marrying too young, the school's administration tried to enforce rigid separation of the sexes. Of course, it did not always work. One alumna recalled that "students entertained themselves by trying to break the rules and not get caught. . . . Making contact with a boy became a challenge." Lloyd's objective of training teachers who would "usually return to their own communities to teach" succeeded in the period before World War II.[38]

The Catholic community continued its separate sectarian path, much like Kentucky Protestants, in maintaining and founding schools of higher education scattered around Kentucky. In 1920 the Sisters of Charity founded Nazareth College (through a series of name changes it became Spalding University) in an old mansion at Fourth and Breckinridge Streets in downtown Louisville. By 1940 a wing had been added to the original building, a gymnasium had been built, and other buildings had been purchased to serve as dormitories, which were named for Catherine Spalding and Bishop Flaget. Many Nazareth women entered the nursing field. At the beginning of World War II, enrollment topped six hundred, and accreditation had been granted by the Southern Association. The elementary school and academy founded by the Ursuline Sisters in Daviess County prospered and led to "offering postsecondary courses" and the establishment of Mt. St. Joseph's College in 1925. The school moved to Owensboro and was renamed Brescia College in 1950. The Dominican Sisters of St. Catherine founded a school in 1931 in

Springfield that became St. Catherine College, first offering a junior college program. In another center of Catholic population, northern Kentucky, Villa Madonna College became a degree-granting institution in 1923. Through numerous consolidations of Catholic resources, the school became Thomas More College in 1968.[39]

After successfully operating medical and law schools from its 1846 chartering by the General Assembly, the municipally owned University of Louisville reactivated the academic department as the College of Liberal Arts in 1907. The name was changed to the College of Arts and Sciences in 1912. Higher education in Louisville presented special challenges. Because it was a border city, its residents who wanted higher education could just as easily attend schools in the midwestern states. Nevertheless, with several professional schools in the city, there came to be a pressing need for a bachelor's degree program. The college added new programs and was soon even competing in athletic events. The new college of the U of L grew slowly under the leadership of longtime dean John Letcher Patterson. President A. Y. Ford (1914–1926) reorganized the university and raised money for expansion.[40]

In 1912 the U of L College of Arts and Sciences began a two-year pre-engineering program. A 1923 study commissioned by President Ford indicated the need for an engineering school, and with funding from Mrs. William B. Belknap, the university purchased the old Louisville Industrial School; the area became known as Belknap Campus. William Shallcross Speed gave $250,000 from the James Breckinridge Speed Foundation to fund a school that became known as the Speed Scientific School. In 1928 Speed graduated ten engineers. The first new building for the school (the first building south of Eastern Parkway on the U of L campus) was completed in 1941.[41]

At the beginning of the twentieth century, African Americans seeking higher education in Kentucky attended Simmons University in Louisville. Starting as Kentucky Normal and Theological Institute in 1879 and funded by the General Association of Colored Baptists in Kentucky, the school went through several permutations, including being named State University in 1882. The only college controlled by blacks in the commonwealth, the school operated a liberal arts program as well as training for nurses. The Louisville National Medical College and Central Law School were affiliated with State University. When Rev. Charles H. Parrish Sr. became president in 1918, he had the school renamed in memory of William J. Simmons, its chief executive from 1880 to 1890. With little financial support, Simmons University struggled to find its place in the early twentieth century. Meanwhile, the University of Louisville began to expand, receiving funds from a bond issue in 1920. Because blacks could not attend the all-white school, the Urban League began urging that the city of Louisville also offer public higher education for African Americans by expending some funds earmarked for the University of Louisville. President A. Y. Ford and the U of L board of trustees promised to do something, but when Ford died the issue languished. Nothing was accomplished during the short presidency of George Colvin (1926–1928). Finally, University of Louisville president Raymond A. Kent took action just as the Great Depression arrived. Simmons, already insolvent, was purchased by the U of L. The site became Louisville Municipal College for Negroes in 1930. Simmons Bible College split off and became a separate private entity. A 1925 bond issue, General Education Board and Rosenwald grants, and city funds funded LMC. For the next two decades, LMC offered not only college courses but also extracurricular activities and a limited sports program. In the decade of the thirties, Louisville Municipal College enrollment expanded from 83 to 331, with as many as 43 students graduating in 1938. When a department of education was added in 1934, LMC began turning out better-qualified black high school and elementary school teachers.[42]

The twentieth century opened with two state-supported schools of higher education, the "white" land grant university, State College of Kentucky in Lexington, and the "black" land grant college, Kentucky Normal and Industrial Institute for Colored Persons, whose name was changed in 1902 from State Normal School for Colored Persons, its original (1886) name. The rest of the state's private and public schools at all levels were already following the southern "color line" when the Day Law ended Berea College's attempt at desegregation. According to historian John A. Hardin, "With both legal and informal racial caste structures in place, Kentucky's black leaders accommodated to racial segregation by rushing to open or enlarge their own educational institutions."[43]

Kentucky Normal and Industrial Institute in Frankfort had an unfortunate early history, owing to its location in the state capital. Because the governor had the sole right to appoint the board of trustees, which in turn appointed the school's president, the presidency of the school became a political football. For example, President Green P. Russell, a Democrat, ran afoul of the Republican administration of Governor Edwin P. Morrow (1919–1923). Russell was fired but then returned to the presidency, only to be asked to leave again in 1929 after charges of mismanagement. The school did not become a true college but continued to offer preparatory, agricultural, and normal courses, even after being renamed again, this time Kentucky State Industrial College for Colored Persons, in 1926. There was never enough money appropriated by an all-white parsimonious legislature to do much on the hill above Frankfort. Under the terms of the Morrill Act, State Normal received only one-twelfth of the income from Kentucky's sale of federal land.

Not until Rufus B. Atwood became the school's sixth president in 1929 did KSIC begin offering a college curriculum, gain some stability, and develop a clearer mission.[44]

A decorated World War I veteran, Atwood worked at Prairie View A&M College in Texas and Virginia State College before coming to Kentucky. He came to a school that had been demoralized by the previous administration and by charges of fiscal mismanagement. Although it was said to have junior college status, students' grades could not be transferred to other colleges. Atwood immediately met with Dean James Bond to develop a core college curriculum. Because the black high school movement was gaining momentum, just like that of white high schools, he reasoned that Kentucky State no longer needed to offer high school or preparatory studies. Of course, all these changes faced uneasy prospects, coming at the onset of the Great Depression. However, by 1932 Kentucky State had achieved a Class "B" for a "Standard Four-Year College." Seven years later the rating was changed to "A," a testimony to the hard work of Atwood and his administration and faculty. Understanding the political waters of Kentucky better than his predecessors, Atwood avoided "the political wars that raged around the Capitol," even registering as an independent. Moreover, he brought fiscal responsibility to the Frankfort campus.[45]

When the new century dawned in Kentucky, State College struggled to become a university in a time when some state and private schools were growing during the "Age of the University." Although President James Kennedy Patterson and other Kentucky leaders had hopes of projecting the State College banner across the state, it proved to be difficult. While other states increased state appropriations, those for the Lexington school languished. In 1904 State College, nearly starved to death by the legislature, received an appropriation of only $35,380. In that same year the state of Wisconsin spent $471,500 on its land grant institution. State Historian James C. Klotter found another "opportunity" for state advancement slipping away: "A few years later a similar comparison indicated that the renamed State University of Kentucky [1908] realized $130,000 in annual income; Ohio State University garnered $700,000, and the universities of Wisconsin and Illinois, $1.1 million each. In 1912, the city of Louisville devoted more dollars to Male High School than the Commonwealth of Kentucky did to its one state-supported university. The funds for one strong university simply were not allocated." The relative poverty of agrarian Kentucky compared with the expansive industrial midwestern states meant that the University of Kentucky continued to be undersupported.[46]

Nevertheless, State College of Kentucky had the largest single enrollment of any college in the state, and it had the potential to expand. It had no single constituency, as did the denominational colleges, but could draw students from across the commonwealth. How could State College become a true university while the denominational colleges still opposed it at almost every turn? Later president of UK Herman L. Donovan recalled as a youth hearing "many sermons condemning the Godless State College and attacking its atheistic professors" at the little country church he attended as a youth in Mason County. Consequently, each appropriation from the legislature became a fight against prejudice and misinformation.[47]

James K. Patterson continued as president of State College into the new century. "He Pat," as cantankerous as ever, while amassing a "small fortune," according to one historian of UK, "was none too sympathetic towards his subordinates' demands for higher pay." Patterson tolerated athletics only because of increasing alumni, student, and public interest. Moreover, the antipathy between Ruric N. Roark at Eastern and Patterson did not lessen in intensity. If the older educator chafed at the thought of some power being taken from his school, the younger one relished the idea of striking out on his own. After passage of the normal school law, Patterson "could not resist the opportunity to take yet another swipe at his old nemesis Roark." "Instead of a loss," the crusty president told a correspondent, "we have gotten rid of an incubus which retarded" the growth of State College's normal department. Roark saw his school as being in direct competition with Patterson's in 1907. To Henry Hardin Cherry he warned: "I am still very distrustful of our friends in Lexington. . . . By so much as they get, by that much we lose." A short while later Roark had not changed his mind. "I am certain that President Patterson and all under his control will seize and use any advantage they may get, no matter how slight to block the State Normal schools, now or at any other time."[48]

One of the biggest changes in the history of the Lexington school began in December 1907, when State College paid Kentucky University a sum of $5,000 to cover the expenses of "advertising and printing" as it reverted to its original name of Transylvania University in order that State College could officially became a university. Actually, Patterson had campaigned for more than ten years to obtain the "university" designation. After gaining the support of the board of trustees and the alumni, the legislature finally complied with his request during its 1908 session. Part of the legislation appropriated $200,000 for the newly styled "State University" and $150,000 each for Eastern and Western. The normal school would now become the Department of Education. Patterson and the administration set about reorganizing the departments into a university. Agricultural studies were organized into a college, a new law school was immediately planned, and State University was divided into six "colleges." However, the hope of having a new medical college did not materialize until decades later.[49]

Approaching forty years of service to the commonwealth, Patterson began considering retirement in 1909 and officially retired the next year. He gave State University his extensive library, worth approximately $10,000, as well as other bequests. However, he exacted what would be considered "a golden parachute" today. He demanded that he be allowed to have a "semi-official connection with the University," have a voting place on the board of trustees, participate in faculty "deliberations," be recognized "as an adviser and auxiliary to the Vice-President and later to the incoming President," and represent the institution at national and state educational associations. In addition, he said, "I should like the privilege of continued residence on the University grounds." The board of trustees and Governor Willson accepted these conditions. Judge Richard C. Stoll praised Patterson, stating, "There is nothing that this University can do for President Patterson that President Patterson has not earned." President Emeritus Patterson got all that he requested, including 60 percent of his annual salary. The only concessionary stipulation was that, while he could participate in trustee meetings, he could not vote. The lengthy shadow of James Kennedy Patterson continued to influence the University of Kentucky for yet another decade.[50]

After due consideration of his oppressive leadership style and self-promotion, one should, in the words of University of Kentucky professor John R. Thelin, give the wily Scotsman "his rightful place in the history of American higher education." A definitive study of Bowman and Patterson concluded with these words: "Patterson deserves this examination because his administration, despite such formidable obstacles to the school's survival as the devastating fall-out from divestiture and the state's checkered history of funding for education, was a triumph for the land-grant institution and a tribute to his leadership." Patterson moved State College toward being "a comprehensive university." As a "Jeffersonian Agrarian" he helped lead the school into an important role in Kentucky agriculture. However, one study of the UK presidency from 1903 to 1940 found that Patterson "no longer fit the mold of the contemporary higher education president" in the early twentieth century because the American university had changed greatly in his last years. His cocksureness often ran afoul of others, and he had little forgiveness in his soul. For example, his successor, Henry Stites Barker, maintained that Patterson "hated" the director of the Experiment Station, M. A. Scovell, because of the latter's closeness with Kentucky farmers, as well as F. Paul Anderson, dean of the College of Mechanical Engineering. "President Patterson hated those two men worse than the devil hates holy water," Barker said. And Patterson worked hard to see that neither was considered as his successor. Having given Patterson his due, few faculty members were sorry to see him go, particularly since the president, being financially well off himself, apparently thought little about their needs.[51]

Patterson also participated in the selection of his successor, a process that took an inordinate amount of time. Vice President James G. White became acting president. Meanwhile, Patterson remained on campus, "unwilling to go into actual retirement." A member of the State University board of trustees, Henry Stites Barker, "a former judge of the Kentucky Court of Appeals but a man of limited background in education and in administrative experience," reluctantly became a candidate for president. Barker became the favorite of Republican Governor Willson. Even the qualms of the head of the Carnegie Foundation, which was considering funding retirement pensions for the university, did not deter a subcommittee that eventually recommended Barker, with Patterson demurring. Although accounts of the participants differed, Patterson finally came around to Barker's appointment, and on June 1, 1910, Barker accepted the presidency. In 1916 President Barker stated that "James K. Patterson is alone responsible for my acceptance of this office." However, thinking back about how he had approved Patterson's retaining power as president emeritus, he also said, "Oh, yes, I was a big fool in those days."[52]

Like President William J. Hutchins at Berea College, who endured the constant sniping of President Emeritus William Goodell Frost, Barker could never escape the omnipresence of Patterson on the UK campus and his insinuation into every facet of campus life.

The administration of Barker at UK from 1910 to 1917 was somewhat progressive. The presence of the College of Arts and Sciences, the College of Agriculture, three separate engineering schools, and the new College of Law gave all the appearances of a true "university." On the minus side, the "General Education Board and the Carnegie Foundation for the Advancement of Teaching officials weren't pleased with the 1911 selection of Barker for the presidency," according to Michael J. McCorkle, a historian of the UK leadership from 1903 to 1940. CFAT summarily turned down the university's application for membership. As a matter of fact, in the first place, the president of the Carnegie Foundation had urged Barker not to accept the Kentucky presidency. However, there were other signs of progress. Women continued to play an increasing role at UK; the school was one of only seven southern universities that were coeducational in 1912. Enrollment also nearly doubled during the Barker years. The number of degrees grew by 50 percent, and the faculty and staff expanded from 104 to 153. More land was added to the campus, particularly to the Experiment Station, as well as the Mulligan tract that contained what became Maxwell Place, the home of the president. Graduate studies lagged, but the university reacted positively to passage of the Smith-Lever Act of 1914 and the Smith-Hughes Act of 1917. The Smith-Lever Act developed the statewide program of cooperative extension services, while the Smith-Hughes Act began public school agricultural vocational programs. Carl Cone, longtime professor of history at the University of Kentucky and the author of a history of the school, found another positive note. "At State University under Barker, the atmosphere was lighter and less oppressive than at Patterson's State College." Barker, unlike his predecessor, delegated authority to departmental heads and deans. Moreover, finally the name changes came to an end on March 15, 1916, when the General Assembly changed the school's name from State University to the University of Kentucky.[53]

Unfortunately, Barker faced an array of problems during his tenure, many the result of Patterson's scheming and some only natural to a growing, maturing university. First, Barker ran into "vested interests" when he recommended that the three engineering colleges merge into one. Second, the faculty squabbled over salaries. Third, leadership of the College of Agriculture was problematical. Fourth, some wanted the university to be more aggressive in funding. Fifth, owing to his lack of educational credentials, many outside sources such as the General Education Board and Carnegie leadership opposed him from the start. Finally, all these issues came to a head. In January 1917, Governor A. O. Stanley appointed a subcommittee of the trustees to make recommendations ending this impasse.[54]

The findings of the "Survey Commission" were blunt. Although Barker was praised for "a largeness of soul" and other qualities, he was pronounced an ineffective university leader. While admitting that Patterson had made a "nuisance of himself, the commission nevertheless said that Barker should not have been appointed in the first place," owing to his lack of education and administrative experience. The roles of the College of Agriculture and the Extension Service were better defined. To erase one issue, the board of trustees agreed with Barker and recommended that the three engineering colleges be merged and a new dean be appointed from outside the university. Barker was asked to resign and he immediately did so. Other recommendations had to do with improving faculty quality and student discipline. The final part of the report urged that a new, well-qualified, president be found quickly and that Patterson be removed from the board of trustees and from campus residency. Of 69 total recommendations, the full board accepted all except removing Patterson from the campus. On August 15, 1917, the UK board appointed Frank L. McVey, then the president of the University of North Dakota, who held a Ph.D. in economics from Yale University. The state's land grant university now had someone in charge who had all the attributes and credentials lacking in Barker. However, McVey faced the same challenges his predecessor had faced.[55]

As the University of Kentucky went through the final years of the Patterson administration, the struggles of the Barker years, and the election of McVey, Eastern and Western normal schools continued to mature in the new century. "The Best Is Not Good Enough" became the Eastern motto; Henry Hardin Cherry chose "The Spirit Makes the Master" for Western. Both Eastern and Western produced new teachers, operating as state-sponsored high schools for the first few years. While Eastern experienced rapid changes in leadership with the untimely death of Ruric Roark, the interim service of his wife Mary, and then the appointment of State Superintendent John Grant Crabbe in 1910, Western's Henry Hardin Cherry served continuously from 1906 to his death in 1937. Thomas Jackson Coates became president of Eastern in 1916 after Crabbe left to accept the presidency of Colorado State Teachers College. The Western president's longevity gave him an advantage in leveraging money out of Frankfort. Cherry sometimes displayed more political savvy than his Eastern counterparts and even had aspirations for the governorship, falling out of the 1915 and 1919 Democratic Party primary races when he failed to garner much initial support.[56]

With his background as proprietor of Southern Normal School and Bowling Green Business College, Cherry had somewhat different ambitions for his school than the presidents of Eastern had for theirs. From the beginning he aspired to add vocational and business classes as soon as possible. Moreover, being at a greater distance from Lexington than Eastern, he was not looking over his shoulder all the time. "President Cherry ran the school with a firm, paternalistic hand, and faculty seemed content with that arrangement," concluded Lowell Harrison in his definitive history of Western. But regarding the contented faculty, he added parenthetically, "(Those who were not did not remain long on the faculty.)"[57]

President of Eastern from 1910 to 1916, John Grant Crabbe was an energetic administrator and a worthy competitor of Cherry and Barker. Crabbe was inspirational, driven, and something of a martinet. As classes changed in the Roark Building, he would stand on the steps, repeating rhythmically, "All right, students, file and to the right, single file and to the right," all the while chapping his hands. Crabbe usually wore a tuxedo to chapel and musical presentations, often playing the piano himself. Slowly, the notion grew that even elementary school teachers needed at least some college instruction, and both Kentucky normal schools reacted to this trend. Eastern and Western were supposed to respect each other's territory, Eastern being District One, and Western District Two, but they often conflicted over transfers of students and recruitment. Thomas Jackson Coates was not aggressive at all, and in the generally prosperous early twenties, he did not push for expanded expenditures as Cherry did. Western grew ahead of Eastern in student numbers. Cherry worked the legislative halls far more effectively than his Eastern counterparts. For example, in the early twenties, a new state inheritance tax was routed so that one-half went into the general fund and one-half was divided among the state's schools: "one-fourth for the University of Kentucky, three-sixteenths for Western, and one-sixteenth for Eastern."[58]

Higher education in Kentucky followed national trends in the early twentieth century as the 1906 General Assembly finally, if belatedly, created and funded public normal schools at Western and Eastern. The dream of James Kennedy Patterson became reality when State College evolved into the University of Kentucky, also following the national trend. But world events continued to intrude into the lives of Kentuckians, often in unexpected and calamitous ways.

Not long after Coates went to Eastern and McVey to UK, the United States became directly involved in World War I. "The world is afire," Coates wrote. "The German must and will be beaten. The world of democracy expects every Kentuckian to do his duty." Western's enrollment dropped abruptly when war began, as most colleges' did. To keep up enrollment, Eastern began accepting students with a county superintendent's recommendation, "whether they sign the agreement to teach or not." State campuses formed Student Army Training Corps (SATC) units. At Western 150 men lived in "hastily constructed" two-story barracks. SATC units also formed at Transylvania University, Kentucky Wesleyan College, Georgetown College, and the University of Kentucky. Emotion ran high as many former students and alumni entered the armed forces. President E. Y. Mullins of Southern Seminary encouraged Georgetown College cadets in a commissioning ceremony "to make the world safe for democracy," using Woodrow Wilson's famous phrase. About the time the SATC programs began to produce officers, the war ended with an armistice on November 11, 1918. Already the first soldiers were dying of influenza in army camps like Camp Taylor in Louisville. A son of the Roarks died at an army camp in Wisconsin. Kentucky college men fought and died in World War I. Victor Strahm, the son of German-born Western professor Franz Strahm, "became an American air ace." Lee Shearer, Eastern class of 1916, president of the YMCA and editor-in-chief of the *EKSN Student,* died in the Battle of Chateau-Thierry.[59]

The post–World War I years were initially prosperous ones for higher education in Kentucky, particularly public institutions. In a scenario seen throughout America, the old "independent liberal arts college," such as those at Georgetown, Centre, Wesleyan, and Transylvania, faced a stiffer challenge from the University of Kentucky as it grew at their expense. Moreover,

Eastern and Western evolved into teachers' colleges, also following a national pattern. Public higher education, being funded at the public trough, had a great advantage over the private schools that had no such access.[60]

McVey at the University of Kentucky, unlike his predecessor Barker, enjoyed initial success without a carping ex-president snapping at his heels. The new president immediately proposed a new constitution for the university, which reorganized the school and gave him more power. The coming of new dean Thomas P. Cooper to the UK College of Agriculture gave needed stability to that post. A year later Cooper also became director of agricultural extension. McVey also pushed to add more Ph.D.s to the faculty while increasing salaries, personally hiring such up-and-coming academics as Thomas D. Clark in 1931. UK also followed through on the findings of the Barker-era Investigating Committee by combining the three engineering schools into a single college with F. Paul Anderson as dean. Although Kentucky still lagged behind other states in funding public higher education, periodically there came a surge of support. UK, as well as all other levels of public education in the state, received some aid in 1917 when Governor A. O. Stanley called for a special session for tax revision. The recommendations of special tax commissions in 1912 and 1916 were followed, and the General Assembly raised the general property tax to 40 cents, out of which UK got 1¾ cents and Eastern and Western ⅝ cent each, with 18 cents going to the common schools. However, with one state university, four budding state colleges after 1922, and the African American institution in Frankfort, the question always remained: was there enough support for higher education in Kentucky to adequately fund all these schools?[61]

The training of teachers at UK remained an important task, and choosing a dean for the newly created College of Education presented McVey with challenges. McVey had come to his post as an outsider, chosen perhaps for that reason among others, including his academic credentials and experience as a university president. However, being a nonnative Kentuckian, he had to quickly learn the ins and outs of not only the political structure of the commonwealth but its educational environment as well. He was well connected with the national education establishment: the GEB and CFAT "national network." For McVey's plans for the College of Education to be successful and for UK to reach into the recesses of Kentucky, he needed to become part of the Kentucky network of "schoolmen." That group, "educationists" one might call them, included the leadership of the Kentucky Education Association (KEA), prominent school superintendents, the state superintendents, personnel at the normal schools, and professors of education at UK, particularly McHenry Rhoads and Cotton Noe. To a lesser extent McVey needed to address the likes of George Colvin and Henry Hardin Cherry.[62]

Upon the basis of several recommendations, McVey pushed expanding the Department of Education into a separate college, receiving authorization from the trustees in 1923. There was some speculation that Colvin might become dean or that Rhoads might move up. However, Rhoads left university employment and ran successfully for state superintendent in 1923. McVey, hoping to combine both national and Kentucky educational networks, chose William S. Taylor, a Kentucky native who had attended UK but also the University of Wisconsin and Columbia University, where he had just finished his doctorate. Therefore, he was an insider but at the time working outside the state, giving McVey what he wanted: someone with knowledge of Kentucky but an understanding of the national scope of education. Taylor readily accepted the post. One of his first tasks was naming Moses E. Ligon as the new principal of the University High School.[63]

McVey had ambitious plans for the University of Kentucky, and in the twenties he strengthened his control and influence. He pushed development of the graduate school and encouraged the growth of the law school, expansion of the library, and the creation of new departments. McVey also worked to add more Ph.D.s to the faculty. Oral historian Terry L. Birdwhistell has recounted how the wife of Thomas D. Clark recalled that older instructors "were concerned about the Ph.D.'s being hired, but they may have been more concerned about the number of them who were Yankees!" When maintenance and campus planning became crucial, McVey brought in an employee from his University of North Dakota days to become the first superintendent of buildings and grounds. Campus planning for the first time became the centerpiece of an administration. McVey took personal charge, not always following the plans laid out by the firm of Olmstead Brothers, and chose "contemporary" style for all new buildings rather than the "monumental," in order to save money. During a time of relative prosperity in the twenties, UK built Alumni Gymnasium and new dormitories and classroom buildings as well as adding new experiment stations at Quicksand in Breathitt County and near Princeton in Caldwell County.[64]

Although public normal school education in Kentucky evolved at a slower pace than in the rest of the nation, it now appeared to be on the move. While UK, Western, and Eastern sometimes cooperated in their quest to better educate the commonwealth's citizens, they more often than not saw one another as competitors for the public funds. Sometimes Western and Eastern would gang up on UK. "The state schools competed for limited funds, and the University of Kentucky tended to view the other schools as unwanted siblings who should never have been conceived and who should certainly be satisfied with a distinctly inferior role," determined Western's historian Lowell Harrison. Even after Western graduate and Cherry protégé

Herman L. Donovan became president of Eastern in 1928, the relations between the two older colleges could be soured by the beginning of another legislative session or, increasingly, even in athletic contests. Both Eastern and Western matured and evolved like other normal schools by adding college curricula. They were already technically junior colleges. Momentum and political pressure built to develop more state teacher training colleges. With more and more high schools developing in the state, the need lessened for traditional normal education, which offered a high school curriculum to prepare elementary school teachers. In 1922 the Kentucky General Assembly authorized the renaming of both schools; they now became Western Kentucky State Normal School and Teachers College and Eastern Kentucky State Normal School and Teachers College. Both schools began requiring fifteen high school units for admission to take the college curriculum. Eastern and Western, along with many other normal schools, followed a pattern observed by Jurgen Herbst: either become a multipurpose college or cease to exist. Meanwhile, President McVey at UK had taken the advice of the GEB and authorized a College of Education.[65]

The year 1922 proved to be a pivotal year in the history of Kentucky higher education. A report prepared by the GEB found that public school education in Kentucky still seriously lagged behind the standards of the nation. An educational commission appointed in 1920 suggested two more normal schools for the commonwealth, one in the west and one in the east. On March 8, 1922, Republican governor Edwin P. Morrow signed legislation creating new normal schools for the state. He soon charged a commission with determining locations, touching off a good deal of politicking, like that of 1906. Eight cities vied for the location to be chosen in western Kentucky while five competed for a school in the eastern part of the commonwealth. Judge Allie W. Young worked hard for a normal school to be placed in Morehead. Having the Morehead Normal School, founded in 1887 by the Christian Women's Board of Missions, headed by Frank C. Button, worked to that city's advantage. Towns seeking a school had to raise at least $100,000 to qualify for a bid. Murray beat out eight other western Kentucky sites by raising $117,000. On September 17, the State Normal School Commission, with support of the General Education Board, chose locations in Murray and Morehead. After the appointment of boards of regents and presidents, both schools prepared for opening in September 1923.[66]

The 1922 meeting of the Kentucky General Assembly also witnessed one of the most crucial legislative battles of the early twentieth century when both houses considered the first antievolution bills in the nation. As described in chapter 5, the state of Kentucky became the focal point of the controversy between those who supported quashing the teaching of evolution in both public schools and colleges and those who supported academic freedom. Although the bills failed to pass the legislature, the fallout resounded throughout higher education, both public and private, in the commonwealth.[67]

Antievolutionists applied pressure at the state schools of higher education. At the University of Kentucky, McVey continued to play an important role not only in the state but in giving advice to educators outside Kentucky. Meanwhile, President E. Y. Mullins at Southern Seminary in Louisville began to take considerably more heat from Baptist fundamentalists. McVey had to rein in some of his more outspoken faculty. When the *Courier-Journal* reported that Professor Edward Weist had said that in a conflict between science and religion, science should take precedence, McVey reacted quickly. He and Weist issued statements immediately. Weist claimed that he had been misquoted and had really said, "The teacher of science should confine his teaching to the sciences and not flounder around in theology." Having already received an increased appropriation in 1922, the UK president knew he would have to walk a tightrope in conservative Kentucky to obtain another in the 1924 legislative session.[68]

Several Kentucky colleges experienced adverse reactions to the early evolution controversy. At Kentucky Wesleyan College, popular professor Ralph G. Demaree, who "had already accepted a position at the California College of Technology for the following year," in an April 7, 1923, chapel address maintained that "the modern theories of organic evolution do not contradict the Bible, since two truths cannot conflict." Temporarily suspended by Wesleyan president Will B. Campbell, Demaree met with a Methodist Conference board of education and then issued a conciliatory statement, saying, "I hereby agree not to discuss the subject under controversy in any official capacity . . . during the remainder of my stay at this institution." Of course, he soon left for California. At the more conservative Asbury College, biology professor David W. Nankivel, holding a UK master's degree, and four other teachers ran afoul of college officials and all were fired. The ostensible reason was to cut expenses. In late 1922 the Kentucky General Association of Baptists condemned evolution and vowed to withhold funds from any of its schools that taught the theory. Two years later, in 1924, the Kentucky Baptist Mission Board sent questionnaires to all teachers in its colleges requesting their views of the Bible as well as of the theory of evolution; as a result two faculty members at Georgetown College resigned. No doubt other Kentucky college professors felt the sting of fundamentalist/antievolutionist ire and possibly downplayed their belief in and teaching of evolution. There is no evidence of such controversies at Eastern, Western, Murray, and Morehead.[69]

The seminaries in Kentucky also faced new challenges and issues in the early twentieth century. All reacted to the rise of not only such scientific views as Darwinian evolution, but higher criticism of the Bible as well. After the settlement between northern and southern Presbyterians in 1901, the Louisville Presbyterian Seminary operated a successful school at First and Broadway. Presbyterians were a small but economically privileged denomination in Kentucky. Southern Baptists, relatively poor and quite combative at times, constituted a large faction among Kentucky Protestants. While Southern Baptist Theological Seminary president Mullins was tussling with his fundamentalist brethren over the evolution issue, SBTS was in the process of moving from downtown Louisville to the "The Beeches," a $2 million campus on Lexington Road. When Mullins died in 1928, the school entered the Great Depression owing a large debt that took some time to retire. The "heresy" trial at the College of the Bible, as discussed earlier, ignited controversy among Kentucky Protestants. Henry Clay Morrison at Asbury Seminary, which separated from the college in 1939, led the formation of the holiness Methodist theological school. "Meant to be an antidote to liberalism" from its beginning, Asbury Seminary remained a bulwark against modernism in the interwar period. Morrison excelled at raising funds for both the college and the seminary in Wilmore by means of his publication *The Pentecostal Herald*.[70]

By far the greatest changes in professional training came in the early twentieth century with the encouragement of studies made by Abraham Flexner, a Louisville native. After matriculation in Berlin, Flexner wrote *The American College: A Criticism* in 1908, in which he maintained that German higher education was far superior to that in the United States. The Carnegie Foundation for the Advancement of Teaching, headed by Henry S. Pritchett, then funded Flexner's study *Medical Education in the United States and Canada*, published in 1910. Flexner had little good to say about the medical school at the University of Louisville. The only American medical school that received any plaudits at all was Johns Hopkins. Flexner also "labeled U of L's new liberal arts college 'a people's institute,' unworthy of its name and incapable of providing academic leadership for the university." Through some strenuous efforts, the University of Louisville reorganized the graduate and undergraduate programs and received accreditation by the Southern Association in 1915. With the demise of local proprietary medical schools, the medical program at the U of L improved and modernized, becoming one of the leading schools in the region and, of course, the only medical school in Kentucky. Moreover, the city of Louisville began to make modest appropriations to support its municipal university. The opening of City Hospital in 1914, dubbed the "Million Dollar Hospital," became the U of L's teaching facility. The U of L law school continued to educate a larger number of lawyers than UK. Supreme Court justice Louis Brandeis, a Louisville native, supported the law school "through gifts and frequent advice." In 1918 the U of L took over the independent Louisville College of Dentistry.[71]

In the 1920s, one of the most bitter instances of executive-faculty conflict in the history of higher education in the commonwealth took place at the University of Louisville. After the death of U of L president Ford, the school's trustees appointed George Colvin, then superintendent of the Louisville and Jefferson County Children's Home. Colvin, who had been elected as superintendent of public instruction on the Republican ticket of Governor Edwin P. Morrow (1919–1923), had a somewhat progressive education record during his tenure in Frankfort. His political ambitions took a downturn when he failed to receive the 1923 Republican nomination for governor. After the University of Louisville reinstated the Academic Department and the College of Arts and Sciences, the school developed quickly in those fields. Colvin soon came into conflict with faculty. While he wanted to push undergraduate curriculum development, a sizable portion of the faculty wanted to "strengthen graduate programs." Moreover, without a terminal degree himself, he did not place emphasis on hiring more Ph.D.s. Seeing himself as "not a professional educator," as well as an outsider in educational circles, Colvin apparently valued his training as a lawyer more.[72]

A nephew of Colvin, renowned Kentucky historian Hambleton Tapp, maintained that "what Colvin wanted was to broaden the university's scope— perhaps to make it a school for the masses rather than concentrating upon developing a limited number of bright students." A test of wills developed between Colvin and the University of Louisville trustees on one side and what was now called the College of Liberal Arts and some key professors, on the other. The former argued that with limited resources—the U of L was a municipal institution—undergraduate enrollment was the overriding priority; graduate work must be secondary. The latter dug in their heels, being led by history professor Louis R. Gottschalk and Dean Warwick Anderson, who was soon dismissed by Colvin. Everyone on the campus and many in the city of Louisville chose sides in the conflict. The embattled first-year president worsened the problem by "issuing one year contracts during the second semester," appearing to "purge the faculty" of his opponents. The suicide of the head of the mathematics department added to the uncertainty and turmoil.[73]

All of the issues came quickly to a head when, after historian Rolf Johannesen delayed in signing his one-year contract, Colvin dismissed him. Gottschalk then resigned and requested that the American Association of University Professors investigate. The university also conducted an investigation as some students lampooned "King George Colvin" for "educational crimes." The AAUP censured the school. In the midst of a complicated series of studies, one by UK president Frank L. McVey, the U of L began to get back on track. Then Colvin died after complications of a delayed operation for appendicitis, having completed only two years at the U of L. The university lost some talented faculty, including Gottschalk, who went on to an important career at the University of Chicago. The historians of the school concluded, "The Colvin years at the University of Louisville were marked by rancor and public embarrassment. His administration destroyed the endowment campaign planned by President Ford." However, the office of the presidency and the authority of the board of trustees were strengthened in the end; this was a national trend also ongoing at the University of Kentucky. The next president of the U of L, Raymond A. Kent, an outsider, led the school from 1929 to 1943. Inheriting a stronger presidency, he built the U of L into a finer-tuned institution and developed both undergraduate and graduate programs into regional leaders.[74]

The young women and men, black and white, attending segregated schools of higher education in Kentucky from the beginning of the twentieth century to the outbreak of World War II came of age during a time of great change. The United States passed through one world war and stood on the precipice of another. The economy of the country moved from growing affluence into the worst depression in the nation's history. Transportation evolved from horse-and-buggy days through the days of the Model T "Tin Lizzie" to commercial air travel. In these forty years, American higher education also became more democratized as high schools turned out more and better-trained students, increasing numbers of whom entered colleges and universities. If usually behind the times, Kentucky nevertheless showed some improvement in higher education. The students who matriculated in the state's private and public institutions of higher education were part of the changing world.

The famous and the not-so-famous attended Kentucky colleges and universities. For all of the fine education that Ed Prichard received outside the Commonwealth of Kentucky, he fell into temporary, if not permanent, ignominy when convicted in a vote fraud conspiracy. Other Kentucky politicians of note remained in the state for most if not all of their education. Bert T. Combs grew up in Clay County and spent a few semesters at Cumberland College before moving to UK to pursue a law degree, received in 1937. "Legend has it I arrived at Transylvania with no resources other than a red sweater, a five dollar bill, and a smile," claimed Albert B. "Happy" Chandler. Chandler had a much more conventional college experience than Combs, who was not able, because of finances, to stay in the classroom for extended periods. Chandler played on several athletic teams, became a singer of some fame, graduated, and went off to Harvard for one year before returning to take a law degree at UK in 1925. Both became important Kentucky Democratic Party figures and governors with differing philosophies.[75]

Kentucky students not only cooperated with college authorities but also rebelled, on occasion, as students have always done. Even at serene, isolated Caney Junior College at Pippa Passes in Knott County, where males wore coats and ties and females had a standard uniform, there were ways to show independence. A female student in the early days recalled spending "one week on the dish line in Hunger Din [the student name for the dining hall] for writing a 'three-corner' [a note folded into a triangle] to a boy. . . . Boys and girls were not allowed to pass notes. This made 'three corners' even more fun. Making contact with a boy became a challenge. But I didn't pass any more notes after that one-week experience on that dish line!"[76]

Students at Berea College rebelled against the strict rules where and when they could. Although there was a ban on radios, some male students kept one in the janitor's room in the gymnasium. Despite all the efforts of the "No-Tobacco League," a few students were able to indulge their habit. Berea officials also tried to keep males and females at arm's length. By the thirties couples would walk "together across campus after meetings of the Christian Endeavor Society, a coeducational organization." In doing so, students were asserting "a modicum of control over their own leisure time, a control that educators feared and fretted over, but were powerless to co-opt for themselves." Nevertheless, Berea continued to have strong YMCA and YWCA units, ever searching for the modernization of "Christian servanthood."[77]

While student activities at the University of Kentucky may have been somewhat modern in the "Jazz Age" of the 1920s, at the other state schools students were a bit more subdued. If this was the "Age of the Roaring Twenties," one alumna of Eastern noted, "we didn't roar so much, we didn't have the opportunity." Many students at the state colleges had to work part-time to pay for their schooling, so they had less time for frivolity. And many students at the state colleges continued the pattern of teaching during the academic year, then returning to school in the summer terms to work toward finishing their degrees. "Lawsy me," one alumna said, "I would teach awhile and then go to summer school." Sometimes this process would take nearly two decades before the college degree was completed.[78]

However, even at conservative women's colleges, the times changed. In the Women's Department of Centre College, still rigidly segregated from the men's campus, "during the thirties, black serge bloomers were replaced by short gym suits." Of course, by this time Centre's women had given up any pretense of playing intercollegiate sports; all of their sports activities had become intramural. Just as in high school athletics, women's intercollegiate sports were considered unladylike and strictly forbidden by the thirties.[79]

At the University of Kentucky as well as at other coeducational colleges in the state, women matriculated as long as they accepted their role, which was always subordinate to that of males on the campus. Only slowly did UK and other colleges accept women into traditional male strongholds like engineering, mathematics, and science. The Department of Domestic Science at UK gave women an alternative to library work or teaching. By the end of the twenties, as a sign of the times, the choosing of a beauty queen became "increasingly important at the University."[80]

The dean of women's position at Kentucky's schools of higher education became more and more important. At UK, dean of women Sarah Gibson Blanding built on the work of Frances Jewell McVey to institutionalize her office. During her tenure, female enrollment at UK doubled from 566 to 1,165. Eastern Dean of Women Marie L. Roberts—"Miss Strict," some students called her—represented an older scheme of Victorian control over female students. When Roberts first came to the Richmond campus in 1915, women where strictly chaperoned. For example, to view a movie they had to walk hand and hand to a downtown theater, and if that motion picture became too racy, "a chaperone rang a bell and then whisked the ladies from the iniquitous scene." Emma Case, who replaced Roberts in 1932, eased the rules within limits, in what she called "allowance of great personal freedom in as much recognition of small details as is possible."[81]

College life did not exist in a vacuum, being part of a larger community. Centre College not just coexisted but became a vital part of Danville, a small central Kentucky town. In Lexington, Transylvania and the University of Kentucky were important elements of the cultural context of Lexington, as described by Kolan Thomas Morelock in *Taking the Town: Collegiate and Community Culture in the Bluegrass, 1880–1917*. Beginning in the late nineteenth century, college literary societies blossomed, leading the "high culture" intellectual life of Lexington. The community was enthralled by oratory in the Gilded Age, before the advent of mass communication and transportation. Town and gown melded, in other words, as literary society events became great public spectacles. Oratorical contests between competing colleges in central Kentucky became extremely popular. Slowly and then with increasing momentum, things began to change. First, literary societies gave way to the growing popularity of dramatic clubs. Finally, both activities became part of the "formal curriculum" of institutions of higher education in Lexington. The same thing happened elsewhere. For example, after the turn of the century, on the Centre College campus, the YMCA and literary societies began to fade as fraternities became the centerpieces of the all-male campus. The Centre board of trustees began to fear a decline in "religious engagement" on campus. The Literary Societies declined as debate, being seen as more utilitarian, became popular. While fraternities and literary societies "co-existed" at the Danville school for more than eighty years, one member of the class of 1933 recalled that by the time he entered Centre the latter "almost did not exist." "The twentieth century students were more candid, direct, and fun loving," declared a historian of student life at Centre.[82]

In the early twentieth century, college athletics grew almost exponentially as students and alumni became a greater and greater base of interest. While football gained the greatest popularity, collegiate basketball also came of age, particularly after World War I. Both sports became modernized with rule changes. All of the state's colleges played the "major" sports, basketball and football, and most also fielded baseball and track teams. Rivalries intensified. The coming of Adolph Rupp to the University of Kentucky in 1930 led that school into a new era of athletic excellence. After winning the Southeastern Conference tournament in 1933, his reputation was made as a winner, even if sometimes controversial and arrogant. The exploits of Western's Ed Diddle, waving his red towel and emitting occasional "malapropisms," also became the stuff of legends. His teams were almost unbeatable in the "Big Red Barn" on Western's campus, where he would sometimes tell his players to line up "alphabetically according to height." Both coaches became firmly established before 1940. The will to win seemed to grow even stronger in Kentucky inter-collegiate athletics. When Herman Donovan came to Eastern as president in 1928, he had no intention of the school's fielding anything but representative athletic teams, but that changed as the Richmond school absorbed loss after loss to Western. Donovan brought in Ohioan Rome Rankin and Eastern entered a "golden age" in both basketball and football from 1935 into the war years. Art Lund, one of his best footballers, went on to fame as a singer and actor, starring in the 1956 Broadway musical *The Most Happy Fella*, as well as other shows.[83]

Perhaps the greatest athletic event of all time in Kentucky sports, at least of the human variety from 1900 to 1940, has been immortalized in the cryptic phrase "C6-H0." In 1919 the Centre College football team recorded a perfect 9–0 season. Harvard University, then national champions and in the midst of a string of what became five undefeated seasons, scheduled the Kentucky squad. Playing on the Cambridge, Massachusetts, campus for the first time in 1920, Centre was defeated 31–14, with Centre's quarterback, Bo McMillin, gaining over 280 yards rushing. Then on October 29, 1921, before forty-five thousand fans in Harvard's stadium, McMillin scored the only points of the game with a thrilling run of 32 yards. "Many people that day believed that they had seen David defeat Goliath. The Associated Press in 1950 and the *New York Times* in 1971 agreed the Centre victory was the football upset of the century," concluded Charles R. Lee Jr. in the *Kentucky*

Encyclopedia. Attending Harvard Law School in 1921, Happy Chandler, who had played in an earlier lopsided loss to Centre while on the Transylvania squad, always maintained that his scouting of the Harvard Crimson eleven had added to the victory. That magical year Centre went undefeated, defeating the University of Kentucky, 55–0. After a couple more outstanding seasons, including close losses to Harvard, Centre lost coach "Uncle Charley" Moran to Bucknell University and began a slow decline into a small college football program.[84]

Earle Combs, arguably the greatest Kentucky athlete of the first half of the twentieth century, grew up in Owsley County, playing baseball with homemade bats and balls. He played baseball as well as basketball at Eastern, receiving a teaching certificate in 1919, and went on to teach in one-room schools for a while. But his prowess on the diamond had already caught the eyes of scouts as he played in summertime semiprofessional leagues. The Louisville Colonels signed him to a contract, and he played with them for a couple of years before joining the New York Yankees in 1924. Combs played center field, where he often covered ground for the slow-footed right fielder Babe Ruth. Known as the "Gray Fox," Hall-of-Fame inductee Combs (1970) had a lifetime batting average of .325 and led the Yankees in their glory days of the twenties and early thirties. "The introspective, religious Combs was considered one of the few real gentlemen on a series of great Yankee teams noted for their fun-loving boisterousness," concluded Bill Marshall in the *Kentucky Encyclopedia.* Combs's great speed in the outfield and on the base paths was cut short by terrible injuries after crashing into a wall in a game in St. Louis. He coached for several years and then settled in Madison County, where he served on the Eastern Kentucky University board of regents for two decades.[85]

Intercollegiate athletics became so big a part of the expansionist twenties that the Carnegie Foundation for the Advancement of Teaching made a "detailed study," producing a report in 1929. Most of the abuses of the system would have been found at the larger universities in the country. While President McVey opposed overemphasis of athletics and placing "too much stress on winning," UK fielded good teams. Forest "Aggie" Sale, a graduate of Kavanaugh High School in Lawrenceburg, became Rupp's first All-American in the early thirties. Charles T. "Turkey" Hughes, who lettered in four sports at UK in the twenties, for many years held the school record for the longest return of an intercepted pass for a touchdown. He went on to become a longtime coach and athletic administrator at Eastern, beginning in 1929. One of UK's legendary football players of the early thirties, John Sims "Shipwreck" Kelley, appeared to score with abandon, and the school had continuing winning records. Perhaps the greatest "scholar-athlete" of all time in the commonwealth, Albert D. "Ab" Kirwan captained the 1925 UK football team as an all-conference back. He went on to become UK head football coach, serving from 1938 to 1944, and then for many years held UK positions of dean of men, professor of history, and president (1968–1969). By 1940 only the University of Kentucky played football at the highest level, as a member of the Southeastern Conference.[86]

The Great Crash on Wall Street in 1929 and the subsequent downturn in the American economy soon impacted Kentucky's campuses. One of the first signs of trouble was reports of more "dishonored checks" than usual at Eastern, for example. All schools in the state suffered. The low point for UK enrollment came in 1934: enrollment dropped by 1,000 students to 3,822, while the state appropriation fell from a record $1,315,462 to half of that. Conditions on the Louisville campus got so bad and the budget so tight that even obtaining a "new set of harness for the campus mule" required the personal approval of President Kent. At Western, President Cherry cut expenditures to the bone, including removing telephones from several buildings and personally "turning off unneeded lights." "When Western entered the 1934–35 fiscal year, the 'cash on hand' balance was just six cents," observed Lowell Harrison.[87]

The conditions at Eastern were typical of many schools across the state and the nation. More and more students turned up at President Donovan's door asking for loans and part-time work. As at UK and other schools, declining state appropriations necessitated raising student fees. With an estimated cost of $250 to $300 for nine months of education on the Richmond campus, including room, fees, books, and meals, a college education began to be beyond the reach of many of the commonwealth's aspiring students. People knew there were tough times at Eastern, and the nation generally, when even the daughter of a prominent banker had to plead for a student loan. While teachers took pay cuts, students moved into cheaper rooms if possible. Eastern alumni of the era recalled in oral history interviews seeing coeds passing out in the cafeteria lines. Having fasted for a time, because of a lack of money, they would be overcome by the smell of hot food. Working in the cafeteria was considered the best job on campus, especially cleaning up in the evening, when a little innocent pilfering of food, such as ice cream, would be possible. Students worked when and where they could to support their schooling. Hiram Brock Jr. worked during summer breaks in Harlan County coal mines. For six dollars a day one summer he labored removing an obstruction using a "pick and shovel" in knee-deep water. "I worked in that darn job two or three months cleaning it out to where the water could drain back out of that mine," he said.[88]

All the state schools faced the same economic issues, plus their own individual problems. In 1931 the economic crisis became so bad that Morehead forced students to buy meal tickets to keep the cafeteria from a deficit, but some students simply did not have the money. The school also noticed that the number of cold checks increased. Rather than declining, enrollment almost tripled between 1929 and 1935, from 440 to 1290. However, enrollment dropped to 955 the next year, when the registration fee increased from $15 to $25, proving the shaky nature of students' finances. A lack of funds or students contributed to other problems on the Morehead campus. A study by the Southern Association in 1934 indicated a lack of "minimum standards," including too little expenditure on students, too high a student-faculty ratio, and extremely poor library facilities. Morehead also went through a succession of presidents in the thirties and forties—John Howard Payne (1929–1935), Harvey A. Babb (1935–1940), and William H. Vaughn (1940–1946)—in part because of a state statute of 1934 permitting the governor to fire anyone from a board without cause. Babb proved to be particularly unpopular with faculty and students. On one occasion, students "padlocked classrooms" briefly, and another time, drama instructor Lucille Caudill publicly challenged Babb on his efforts to push the football program. Governor Chandler, a Democrat, also gave no support to the Republican Babb.[89]

The hard times struck the private colleges as well. New president Arthur Braden (1930–1941) at Transylvania had to cut seven faculty members as well as reduce salaries of the remainder of the staff in the early thirties. At Kentucky Wesleyan, enrollment actually improved during the years of greatest crisis and a successful fund drive. Then student numbers fell precipitously in 1938, from 368 to 203, dealing "a severe blow to the budget." Fortunately for the Winchester school, enrollment rebounded in 1939. The canceling of intercollegiate football at Wesleyan became one of the first casualties of the economic crisis in 1931.[90]

The threat of Baptist schism compounded the impact of the Great Depression at Georgetown College. President M. B. Adams, in his seventeen-year tenure, witnessed the tragedies of World War I, accreditation by the Southern Association in 1919, the discontinuation of the old academy/preparatory school, and construction of a multipurpose building housing a "chapel, gymnasium, offices, classrooms, and the 50,000 volume library." In 1930 this building burned, and "Dr. Adams, seeing his presidency burdened by the fire plus other financial problems brought on by the depression, resigned from office." The Georgetown trustees even considered "closing the school permanently," but the state Baptist convention allowed the college to "solicit directly from churches instead of depending [entirely] on the statewide budget of the convention." After the brief presidency of Eugene Watters (1931–1934), whose idea of converting Georgetown into a student industries program similar to Berea College's failed, Indiana University Ph.D. Henry Noble Sherwood became the Georgetown school's chief executive.[91]

Sherwood faced a difficult situation. With faculty salaries in arrears and with large college deficits, "many faculty members and their families ate in the college dining room for months while taking promissory notes for part of their salaries." Salaries were cut and maintenance deferred, but the financial crisis continued. However, after two years Sherwood stabilized the school during the depths of the Great Depression. With the closing of Bethel College in Russellville and the transfer of its endowment to Georgetown, the future of the college appeared more secure. Meanwhile, there developed what came to be known among Kentucky Baptists as the "Sherwood Affair."[92]

Not long after Sherwood arrived in Georgetown, conservative denominationalists, "so-called fundamentalists," questioned his Baptist credentials. The controversy began when it became public knowledge that Sherwood had been accepted into the Highland Baptist Church of Louisville from the Disciples of Christ denomination without being "re-baptized," a sin among conservative Baptists known as "alien immersion." When the conservatives found they had no power over the trustees of Georgetown College except by withholding funds by action of the General Association of Baptists in Kentucky, they did precisely that, beginning in 1935. In time, enrollment fell from 340 students to 175. Sherwood offered to be baptized Baptist-style, by full immersion, but the fundamentalists would not accept that. Finally, after receiving no funds from the state organization for more than five years, the pressure built on the trustees to end this impasse. Only one day before Pearl Harbor, December 6, 1941, the trustees refused to renew Sherwood's contract, in effect firing him from his post and succumbing to the will of fundamentalist Baptists. Although the embattled president had throughout the turmoil received both overwhelming student and faculty support, he eventually had to concede defeat. In the end, Georgetown lost its semi-autonomy to growing conservative/fundamentalist insurgency.[93]

When funds through New Deal programs became available to Kentucky colleges after the election of Franklin D. Roosevelt in 1932, conditions started to improve. Public Works Administration funds paid for construction of a dormitory at Kentucky State, an enlarged library at Eastern, a new classroom building at Western, a student union at UK, and other badly needed structures on Kentucky college campuses. Both high school and college students also received support, first through federal Emergency Relief Administration funds and then through the National Youth Administration. All schools of higher education in the state participated in NYA funding except for Southern Baptist Theological Seminary in Louisville, which refused to cross the barrier it saw as separating church and state. Students worked part-time in college libraries and labs, mowed grass, and did other essential jobs, keeping their schools functioning and themselves in school during these tough times. George Blakey in his history of the commonwealth during the Great Depression concluded, "The NYA programs allowed thousands of Kentucky youths to stay in high school and college."[94]

The colleges and universities in the Commonwealth of Kentucky followed the national pattern, suffering the most in the early thirties. Initially, many colleges and universities across the country experienced enrollment declines. Faculty salaries suffered. Thomas D. Clark recalled that in March 1932, President McVey held a special faculty meeting in Memorial Hall. "That assembly was more funereal than academic," Clark said. "The president said that it had become necessary to reduce salaries, that in fact for some members of the faculty salaries would be reduced below the subsistence line. In my case it meant a hundred dollars a month, and in time not even that amount." At one time in 1932, Lexington businessmen came up with $40,000 to loan UK faculty because of their smaller paychecks. After Roosevelt took office in March 1933, and the New Deal programs were implemented, recovery was evident by 1935–1936. New Deal programs then helped stabilize higher education. One historian of higher education, in a study from 1915 to 1940, concluded: "American higher education fared better than most social institutions during the Depression." However, "thousands of students were forced to withdraw from school." Some students drew on family resources and their own savings in order to stay in school. Others placed their education on hold. Public higher education, with its lower tuition, fees, and other costs, fared better than private schools. In the late thirties, Kentucky college enrollments, including state and private—the latter continued to suffer—increased from 18,862 in 1936 to 19,997 in 1938 and then jumped to 22,414 in 1940.[95]

Nationally, women fared worse than men during the Great Depression as their numbers at colleges and universities declined and their career paths became more restricted as a result. Financial problems for women were more difficult to overcome. Even the NYA seemed to be against women: they did not receive as many campus jobs, proportionally, as men. However, at the University of Kentucky, female enrollment remained constant during the thirties, varying from 40 to 44 percent of total students. Female students sought grants and scholarships, loans, and money from their families, and they worked when they could. Women at the Lexington school met lesser resistance by choosing fields such as library science rather than engineering or the sciences, according to longtime UK librarian and alumna Jacqueline Bull. She "noted that advisers 'signed you up for what they thought you should have.'"[96]

Competition among the state's institutions of higher education continued unabated during the Depression decade, and it even intensified because of declining state dollars. The meetings of the 1932 and 1934 General Assembly cut budgets, frightening all the college administrators. The economic conditions placed the state colleges at a disadvantage because they had fewer funds to dole out to students to keep them in school. Donovan at Eastern and Cherry at Western carried on a sometimes none-too-friendly competition for students and state funds but then united only to stave off what they saw as a rapacious University of Kentucky. Schools like Eastern, Donovan maintained, "are the poor man's colleges." Donovan told the president of Murray, "I do not think that we should always have to go to the University [of Kentucky] to secure their consent to achieve what may be desirable for the teachers' colleges." Some critics in the state even suggested the closing of one or more of the state colleges. One critical legislator in 1932 introduced a bill to close both Murray and Morehead and convert them into mental hospitals. Both the *Courier-Journal* and the *Lexington Herald* supported the move as a good cost-saver for the state. To a friend at Peabody College, Donovan wrote, with obvious alarm: "You have no idea of the attacks being made on the Teachers Colleges of Kentucky. The very existence of these institutions is at stake." To another colleague he exclaimed: "I have never seen such a chaotic condition as is to be found at Frankfort at the present time. Nobody knows what is going to happen." At a national meeting he attended, Donovan declared that even the venerable John Dewey had had nothing good to say about the teachers' colleges.[97]

Owing to the Great Depression, the General Assembly, at the behest of Governor Chandler, commissioned a study of state government that included higher education, published in 1933, the first of several done by Griffenhagen and Associates of New York City. Chandler took advantage of the study's recommendations to push the General Assembly into passing the Government Reorganization Act of 1936, "streamlining" state departments, finances, and expenditures, while using the law to increase his power. The 1933 Griffenhagen study included recommendations about the physical plants as well as the instructional programs of the state schools. Developing graduate courses and degrees at the state colleges only increased the tensions. By the early thirties, pressure mounted to offer master's degrees in education at the state colleges, with the UK College of Education opposing it. Cherry champed at the bit to begin a program, but Donovan was a bit more cautious. Beginning in 1931, Western offered graduate school courses, and apparently the Griffenhagen report gave "a qualified endorsement in 1933." However, the Southern Association then stepped into the fray and "questioned the validity of the program" at Western. Meanwhile, Donovan positioned Eastern into offering graduate courses to compete with Western. Murray began offering some graduate courses in 1935, while Morehead, beset with accreditation problems, concentrated on keeping its undergraduate programs intact.[98]

From the creation of the normal schools in Richmond and Bowling Green in 1906, a Normal School Council included the presidents of Eastern and Western, with the state superintendent, also a member of the boards of these schools, as chairman. In 1924 the council was enlarged to include the new schools at Murray and Morehead. The council helped coordinate these schools' programs, courses, calendars, and other functions but, as "a semi-official body," did little to keep down the competition. The Kentucky Educational Commission created by the General Assembly in 1932 prepared a report that suggested creation of another oversight group. Governor Chandler also believed that greater coordination was needed for the state's colleges and pushed creation of the Council on Public Higher Education in 1934 as part of a new school code of that year. Membership of the CPHE (the name was changed to Council on Higher Education in 1977) included the president and one regent from each of the five state colleges; the president, three trustees, and the dean of the College of Education of the University of Kentucky; the members of the State Board of Education; and the state superintendent. The GEB refused to fund the salary for an executive secretary of the CPHE, and there was no state money in the thirties to pay someone to coordinate the state's campuses. A 1950 study of the CPHE, by Adron Doran, who became president of Morehead four years later, indicated that up to 1950 the council had been ineffective in coordinating higher education in the commonwealth. Doran recognized that "conflicts in interests" between the members were interminable. In the absence of strong independent leadership, sometimes members intentionally missed meetings, issues languished, and the CPHE achieved little beyond its primary role of coordinating teacher education and setting fees.[99]

Chandler took an adamant stand in 1936 against the competition between the state colleges and UK. The governor called the presidents into a closed meeting and asserted his ideas. At the March 24, 1936, meeting of the CPHE, the young governor's impact began to be felt. "After considerable discussion," the council agreed to charge students $25 per semester or $50 per year, at the governor's suggestion. Although he did not attend this part of the meeting, Chandler had declared it was time for the state teachers' colleges to discontinue all graduate work. UK, in return for discontinuing its freshman and sophomore education courses, would be the only school to have a graduate program. With the stick came the carrot. Because of the reduction of "duplication," more money would become available for higher education in Kentucky. With a strong governor's insistence, the CPHE complied. Governor Chandler then joined the meeting and watched while his proposals passed.[100]

The "implied" carrot of better appropriations for higher education in Chandler's meeting with the higher education president brought results. Chandler kept his promise and forced the General Assembly to revoke the state sales tax and develop a state income tax as well as new "sin" taxes on whiskey, beer, and cigarettes. Money flowed back into the state schools' coffers. The March 24 meeting represented perhaps the greatest personal defeat in the lifetime of Western president Henry Hardin Cherry; he initially did not vote but finally relented to make the vote "unanimous." Western regent Judge F. J. Pentecost informed Cherry that Chandler had told him "that he was not open for any persuasion at this time." Donovan obediently wrote the governor, saying, "During my life time, no governor of Kentucky has ever served this state so successfully." McVey also gushed: "In the year in which you have been in office much more has been accomplished than would have thought possible." A "strong" governor in difficult economic times had carried the day.[101]

Although rumors circulated for several years about Cherry's retirement from the Western presidency, he continued in the post into his sixties. Somewhat erratic at times, Cherry was even arrested in Louisville in 1931 for public drunkenness while operating a vehicle. Quite a furor hit the press, as old friends like Donovan did their best to give him support and hush up the incident. Cherry soldiered on through the tough early Depression years, although he did give up some of his duties. Clearly the years had taken their toll. In July 1937 Cherry fell in his home and, after appearing to recover, died on August 1. Plaudits poured in for his more than three decades as president of Western, leading it from its normal school form into the late thirties. Cherry Hall, a classroom building, opened soon after his death, and "Teachers College" was also dropped from the name of the four white state colleges. Western Kentucky State College and the Commonwealth of Kentucky owed much to Cherry and his longtime leadership. If not always on the right side of an educational issue, he always kept the debate stirring.[102]

Initial speculation about Cherry's successor centered mostly on Western professor M. C. Ford, who held a University of Wisconsin Ph.D. as well as being a Western alumnus. Into the picture immediately stepped Governor Chandler, aptly described by Lowell Harrison as a "consummate politician who believed in rewarding friends and punishing foes. He had resented what he saw as Cherry's arrogant attitude toward governors, and he was convinced that some key people at Western were members of the Tom Rhea political faction that had so often opposed him." At Cherry's funeral in Bowling Green, Chandler brought Paul L. Garrett with him, "possibly with the idea of having the regents elect him that day." While they did not do that, the governor introduced Garrett to one faculty member as Cherry's successor. While the "Hill" was still grieving over the death of Cherry, Chandler moved to settle the issue. He called a special meeting of the Western regents in his office in Frankfort on September 1, one month after Cherry's death. In a discussion that included the names of other possible candidates, Chandler strong-armed the Western regents into accepting Garrett. One regent later revealed that Chandler had declared he would replace the whole board if they did not bend to his will. While the state's newspapers complained, Chandler said flatly, "There has been no secret of my endorsement of Mr. Paul Garrett for the Presidency." A longtime friend and political ally of Chandler, Garrett came to his new post with educational experience as a school superintendent of Versailles, Chandler's adopted hometown. In contrast to the intense, full-steam-ahead Cherry persona, Garrett was low-keyed with an "unimpressive appearance and personality." He had his work cut out for him in leading Western and had to depend greatly on other administrators of that school.[103]

Chandler's pressure to keep the state colleges from teaching graduate courses worked only briefly. By the next year, after the death of Cherry, Donovan took the role of pushing for graduate work. He enlisted the support of Garrett and the other state college presidents. The course was easier this time, with Chandler no longer at the head of state government. Chandler had lost his 1938 bid to unseat incumbent Senator Alben Barkley in the Democratic Party primary and was able to enter the U.S. Congress as Kentucky's junior senator in October 1939 after the death of Senator M. M. Logan. First, Chandler resigned as governor, his place taken by Lieutenant Governor Keen Johnson, and then Johnson appointed Chandler to fill the senate slot. Johnson won the governorship handily a few weeks later. The owner of the *Richmond Daily Register*, Johnson was a close friend of Donovan. Therefore, he did not oppose the effort to obtain CPHE approval of graduate work at the state colleges. The council accepted the proposal on September 7, 1940, and soon Western and Eastern began offering graduate coursework.[104]

After coming to the University of Kentucky in 1917 and weathering the repercussions of the Barker years, the improving economy of the twenties, and then the challenges of the Great Depression, Frank L. McVey began considering retirement in the late thirties. Under his leadership student enrollment and faculty numbers had grown. The training of UK faculty was upgraded, more doctorates coming to the Lexington campus. All of the professional schools improved rapidly. Although McVey was not a great fan of athletics, UK sports rose to the national level of importance as part of the Southeastern Conference. Twenty new buildings were constructed on the campus, and UK extended itself out into the state as never before during his presidency. McVey took advantage of radio to reach as many citizens of the commonwealth as possible. Thomas D. Clark cited McVey's encouragement of graduate education, library expansion, and founding of a university press as highlights of his presidential career. "In my own private opinion, he was one of the best-educated and most thoughtful university presidents I've served under on this campus. . . . He had a vision of what he wanted for the University of Kentucky to be."[105]

The retirement of McVey touched off what one historian has called "another unique University of Kentucky presidential selection process," one similar to that of Barker. Dean Cooper of the College of Agriculture was named acting president while rumor swirled about who would be favored by Governor Johnson, who had won the governorship in his own right in November 1939, and who served as chairman of the UK trustees. McVey and others prepared lists of possible candidates. Cooper apparently had the favor of Johnson but declined to be considered. The UK Senate and AAUP wanted some input, but they failed to gain any attention. The UK board of trustees met in April 1941 in the president's office with Governor Johnson presiding. Judge Richard C. Stoll offered a resolution that offered reorganization of the university, one adopted before the selection of the new president. The newly created position of controller of the university had responsibilities over all business functions of UK. The board immediately elected Frank Peterson, currently in the Johnson administration, to that post. A new dean-of-the-university post was also created, although no one was appointed that day. The greatest change was the creation of the Faculty of the University, a body consisting only of administrators, which replaced the Faculty Senate. Although some students and faculty protested the latter change, apparently there was no consideration of their pleas by the board. The meeting ended with Judge Stoll recommending Herman L. Donovan, president of Eastern, as the new president of UK. The board unanimously approved the appointment. Donovan officially became president of the University of Kentucky on July 1, 1941.[106]

With Donovan going to UK, the presidency at Eastern became open. Here the final lines of James Mulligan's immortal poem "In Kentucky" come to mind again: "And politics—the damnedest in Kentucky." In this case education politics melded with the body politic in Kentucky. According to several similar versions of the story, Governor Johnson "owed" both Donovan and William Francis O'Donnell, superintendent of the Richmond Public Schools, for their efforts in his gubernatorial election campaign of 1939. Apparently Donovan had supplied Johnson with a list of Eastern alumni, and O'Donnell, in his leadership role among school superintendents

Robert Jefferson Breckinridge is rightfully given credit as "the father of the public school system" in the Commonwealth of Kentucky for his efforts in the 1850s. (Courtesy of the Kentucky Historical Society)

The faculty of A&M College, 1885. President James Kennedy Patterson is in the middle of the front row. (Courtesy of the University of Kentucky Archives)

A group of South Elkhorn Colored School students with teacher H. G. Owisly, 1901, in Fayette County. (Courtesy of the University of Kentucky Archives)

A schoolteachers' conference held at Kings Mountain, Lincoln County, September 1906. (Courtesy of the Eastern Kentucky University Archives)

Richmond lawyer Jere A. Sullivan helped negotiate passage of the Normal School Law of 1906 and wrote the Sullivan Law of 1908. (Courtesy of the Eastern Kentucky University Archives)

The Central Point county grade school class of Jennie Jeffers Ashby rides an elaborate float during School Fair Day in Greenville, the seat of Muhlenberg County, in 1914. (Courtesy of the Eastern Kentucky University Archives)

Students in an early school "wagon" in Fayette County with Superintendent Nannie G. Faulconer and a wagon driver, ca. 1920. (Courtesy of the University of Kentucky Archives)

Athens School, ca. 1920. Nannie G. Faulconer, superintendent of Fayette County Schools (1905–1921), is standing on the extreme right. Note the Colonial style of the building, which was new at the time. (Courtesy of the University of Kentucky Archives)

The opening of a new school for African Americans in Bracktown, ca. 1920. (Courtesy of the University of Kentucky Archives)

the Centre versus Harvard game, on October 29, 1921, a Harvard player attempts a pass against the Centre defense. Notice the large Cambridge, Massachusetts, crowd. Centre won by a single touchdown, immortalizing the cryptic "C6-H0" for Centre students. The Centre fight song of the era included the lines, "We'll bite 'em on the elbow, kick 'em on the shin, Until they want to fight no more . . . Keep up the steam, steam, steam, Old Centre, Give 'em hell." (Courtesy of the Centre College Archives)

Forest "Aggie" Sale, a six-foot, five-inch center, was Adolph Rupp's first All-American. Sale won the Helms Foundation player of the year award in 1933. (Portrait Print Collection, University of Kentucky Archives)

Transylvania students and faculty on a trip to Quebec in the early 1930s, with tents for camping the background. L. P. Howser, fifth from the left in the front row, served as principal and then superintendent of the Kentucky School for the Blind in Louisville from 1957 to 1974. (Courtesy the Kentucky Historical Society)

Students on their way to Church Grove School pause on a dirt road in Marshall County, ca. 1930. (A Kentucky Progress Commission photograph; courtesy of the Jillson Collection, Kentucky Historical Society)

An unidentified man sits on the threshold of Dogtown Schoolhouse, a one-room school six miles west of Williamsburg near the village of Jellico Creek in Whitley County, ca. 1930. (A Kentucky Progress Commission photograph; courtesy of the Jillson Collection, Kentucky Historical Society)

Rufus Atwood (*front row, center*), president of Kentucky State, with high school teachers and students after a graduation ceremony in 1931. (Courtesy of the Cusik Collection, Kentucky Historical Society)

On High School Day at Eastern Kentucky State Teachers College in 1937, several
hundred students fill Hiram Brock Auditorium. (Courtesy of the Eastern Kentucky
University Archives)

At the unveiling of Auguste
Rodin's *The Thinker* on
March 25, 1949, in front of
the University of Louisville
Administration Building,
Louisville mayor Charles
P. Farnsley holds the hand
of Nancy Speckman, a
member of the family that
donated the statue. (Pho-
tograph by Norris Mode;
courtesy of the University
of Louisville Archives and
Records Center)

A graduate of Central High School, Lenny Lyles helped to integrate the University of Louisville football team in the mid-1950s. He still holds the school record with forty-two touchdowns. Lyles went on to a professional football career with the Baltimore Colts (where he joined Johnny Unitas) and the San Francisco 49ers. (Courtesy of the University of Louisville)

Left to right: presidents John W. Oswald of the University of Kentucky, Carl M. Hill of Kentucky State University, Robert R. Martin of Eastern Kentucky University, Kelly Thompson of Western Kentucky University, Ralph H. Woods of Murray State University, and Adron Doran of Morehead State University observe the signing of House Bill 238 by Governor Edward T. Breathitt on February 26, 1966. (Courtesy of the Eastern Kentucky University Archives)

Since 1967, Eastern Kentucky University students have rubbed the left big toe of the bronze statue of Daniel Boone for good luck. This copy of Enid Yandell's famous *Daniel Boone*, a pub. piece in Louisville, stands in front of the Keen Johnson building on the Eastern Kentucky Un. versity campus. (Courtesy of the Eastern Kentucky University Archives)

Officers D. A. Conrad of the Kentucky State Police and Ben Wethington of the
Louisville Police Department escort black students as their school bus returns from
Fairdale High School to Shawnee High School at the height of the desegregation-
merger controversy in September 1975. (© *Louisville Courier-Journal*)

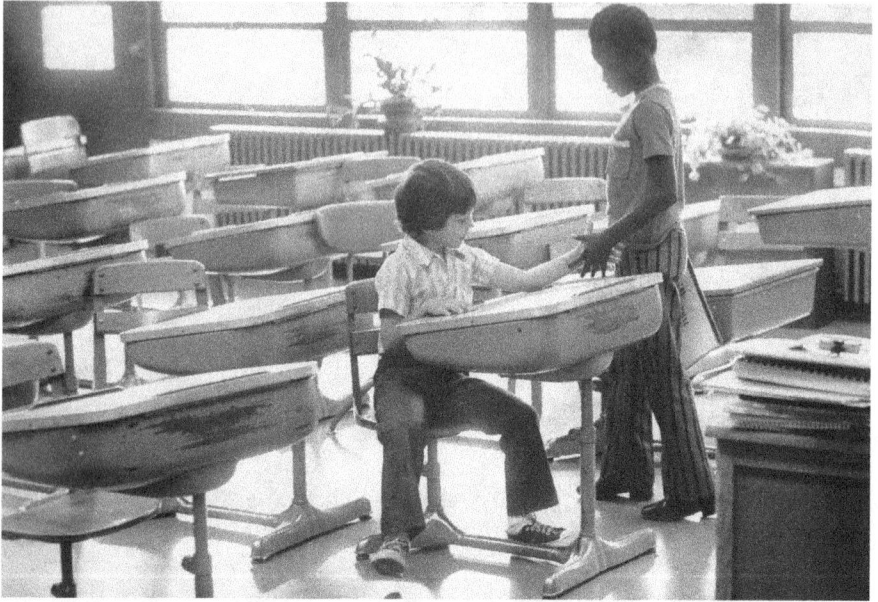

Eight-year-old Greenwood Elementary student Mark Stewart and new classmate Darrell Hughes, also eight, greet and shake hands in September 1975. (© *Louisville Courier-Journal*)

as well as in KEA, had worked even harder for hometown favorite Johnson. Both were working in league with the Kentucky educational establishment of "schoolmen" in favor of Johnson in his primary race against John Young Brown Sr. and then against Republican King Swope, whom he defeated by more than one hundred thousand votes in the November 1939 general election. In effect, Johnson was able, because of the retirement of McVey and his own election as governor, to pay off both of his close Richmond friends for their support. "And so I've been told that Keen wanted to move Donovan out so that he could move O'Donnell in"; this was how Tom Clark succinctly summed up the matter.[107]

Kentucky higher education in the thirties showed other signs of stress and division, the ferment of the radicalism of the time. During the Harlan County coal strike of 1932 against the Samuel Insull interests, college students from outside the state, including students from New York colleges, Smith, Cincinnati, and Harvard, came to support the miners. It is not known whether any Kentucky students joined the effort. As the world of the thirties turned ever more toward war, Kentucky college students reacted by joining peace organizations in mid-decade. Students at Berea and the University of Louisville took part in one-day strikes, supporting the Oxford Pledge by refusing "to support the United States government in any war it may conduct." Perhaps the most radical of Kentucky student newspapers in the mid-thirties, the U of L *Cardinal*, "promoted isolationism and argued against military preparedness." Louisville honor graduate George Lighton joined the Loyalist forces in Spain and was killed in early 1938. Others on the U of L campus following "leftist ideologies" in reaction to fascism included professors Harvey Curtis Webster, who later renounced his Communist views when Germany and Russia signed their nonaggression pact in 1939, and Ellis Freeman, who ran into opposition from President Kent. "Eventually," concluded U of L historians Cox and Morison, "Freeman left the University of Louisville, perhaps unwillingly, with a year's salary." Nationally and in Kentucky, the majority of students were basically conservative-minded, more worried about personal economic problems than about the world at large during the Great Depression years.[108]

Moreover, Kentucky's racial mores remained constant in Kentucky higher education from 1900 to 1941. Still solidly "southern," neither the University of Kentucky and the state colleges nor the private colleges did anything to display any movement against racism and the educational caste system they shared with their southern counterparts. Efforts were made to keep the educational color line intact. Governor Chandler led and white Kentucky educators followed in quashing any idea of allowing blacks to enter the University of Kentucky graduate school in 1936. When pressed by a Negro educator,

Chandler replied, "Such will not happen in your time nor mine." McVey chaired the Governor's Advisory Committee on the Equalization of Higher Educational Opportunities for Negroes, appointed by Governor Chandler in June 1939. Eastern's Donovan, a member of the committee, expressed the sentiments held by most white educated Kentuckians of the time. While he supported "the Negroes having educational opportunities equal to those of the whites," Donovan said, "I think that there should always be in our region separate schools for the two races. I am unalterably opposed to the idea that Negroes should be admitted to the professional schools or to the Graduate School of the University [of Kentucky]." The solution supported by McVey, Donovan, and Chandler was to upgrade graduate studies at Kentucky State College and to pay for black graduate education outside the commonwealth. While Kentucky's white higher education establishment all displayed some social criticism evident in the Progressive Era, neither McVey, Donovan, Cherry, nor their faculties strayed into critiquing racial relations in America. Neither were there any Kentucky scholars approaching the stature of North Carolinians Rubert Vance and Howard Odum in "explicating southern 'folk-ways.'" It took another world war and its aftermath to begin to budge Kentucky from its segregated past.[109]

Neither did Kentuckians' penchant for violence seem to change in the early twentieth century. Although lynching in the state appeared to lessen by the time of World War II, black Kentuckians still suffered from discrimination. And the Ku Klux Klan continued to have an impact in the commonwealth. The KKK operated openly, influencing elections. In 1933 Kentucky's murder rate ranked eighth in the country. "The commonwealth was a violent place," concluded the authors of *A New History of Kentucky*. College campuses could not escape the mayhem. On a warm evening in August 1937, George E. Wells, a native Kentucky mountaineer, confronted Opal Sturgill, a Berea College student, and her most recent boyfriend in front of Lincoln Hall on the college campus. A brief argument between these three ended in a terrible crime. Wells drew a pistol and fired three shots, one of which struck Sturgill fatally in the heart. The assailant then struck the other man and fled into the gathering darkness. Passersby tried to help but to no avail. With "feeling running high" in the community, posses searched for several days for the young murderer but found no trace. Eventually they gave up. Wells disappeared into the fastnesses of the Kentucky mountains, never to come to justice. In various places and times, residents claimed to have seen him. One person saw him hiding under a house, another saw him dressed in women's clothes, and still another glimpsed him wandering the streets. The event sounded much like a recurring theme of Appalachian folk music, as in

"Pretty Polly," "Tom Dooley," and "Poor Pearl" Bryan, but it had occurred on a small Kentucky college campus.[110] As the world appeared to move inexorably toward war in the thirties, Reserve Officers Training Corps (ROTC) programs became more commonplace. One of the requirements of the original Morrill Act of 1862 for a land grant school was to maintain a military training unit. The all-male Kentucky University had been under strict military organization but later changed as the school evolved. Initially, the modern ROTC program at UK evolved out of the short-lived Student Army Training Corps program, begun in the haste to train officers for World War I. After World War I ended in Europe, the pressure for such a program lessened but continued at UK into the twenties. By early 1941 more than 1,100 men at UK were enrolled in a voluntary ROTC program. At Western, the ROTC initially had difficulty keeping the 100-student minimum, but it prospered and won several national rifle-team competitions in the twenties and thirties. As war intensified in Europe and Asia, Murray State Teachers College became the first state college to host a new government program, in this case, the Pilot Training Program, begun on October 7, 1940. Eastern did not have an ROTC unit until 1936, when the Department of the Army approved an ROTC field artillery unit for the campus. When students did not sign up in sufficient numbers, Donovan had to fight to keep the program and used some congressional help in doing so. None of the private colleges or the University of Louisville had ROTC units before the beginning of World War II.[111]

By 1939–1940, Kentucky college students and faculty had begun joining the armed forces. Eastern professor George Hembree, a National Guard officer, went on active duty, as did Murray campus physician Dr. A. Fount Russell. Eastern demonstrated a divided mind about the growing tensions in the world. While the ROTC drilled, the *Eastern Progress* urged the forming of a peace club. The editor of the student newspaper declared that "war would bring a dictatorship to the United States," and he warned of "false propaganda" from both sides in the European war. While it still appeared that there was time to worry about college dances and complain about mandatory chapel services, war crept ever nearer. In early 1941 Eastern men were accepted for Army Air Corps training. War was still not foremost in people's minds on the Richmond campus. It was major campus news when Rex, the campus mascot dog, had to be retired to the Eastern farm. The *Eastern Progress* declared that although "Rex was sort of a nuisance," he "was such a lovable old pooch." Into the fall of 1941, Eastern faculty and students became increasingly uneasy. Bill Bright, a recent alumnus, wrote back from an air base, "Here I am, 'way down here in Texas, trying to learn to fly Uncle Sam's way, but I wish I was back in the [Eastern] Student Union, having a real time before and after the games, seeing all my old pals who have come back for the tilts." Two weeks later the senior editor of the campus paper, Claude Rawlins, predicted that if the United States entered the war, "We will be ruthless because others are ruthless."[112]

Part 4

WORLD WAR II TO THE MID-1980s

Elementary and Secondary Education from World War II to the Threshold of Major Reform

FROM THE BEGINNING OF World War II, elementary and secondary education in the Commonwealth of Kentucky struggled to keep up with national trends. Casting its lot with the South after the Civil War handicapped the state educationally, particularly in "following the color line." As throughout Kentucky's educational history, there were, from time to time, moments of reform followed by regression.

In 1941 the United States, its first peacetime draft already in place, had been supplying war material to those fighting the Axis Powers for several years. Yet, even with more and more men in the armed forces and war production increasing each month, the majority of Americans still hoped to remain isolated from the world at war. The Japanese attack on Pearl Harbor on December 7, 1941, changed the United States forever, from holding an isolationist "America First" stance to that of a world power.[1]

Kentuckians responded as other Americans did during the war. More and more men as well as women went into the armed forces. Rationing of gasoline, food, and other products became a way of life, but most Americans had already learned the lessons of frugality during the Great Depression. Now anyone who could work found jobs, and women entered into war industries as "Rosie the Riveter" became an image of wartime necessity. Fort Knox, Camp Breckinridge, and Fort Campbell, as well as other smaller military bases, added jobs and importance to the commonwealth's role in the war effort. "Victory Gardens" supplied many Kentucky families with an adequate diet. By the end of the war, nearly 8,000 Kentuckians had died, out of the almost 307,000 who had entered the armed forces.[2]

State Superintendent of Public Instruction John W. Booker (1940–1944), elected in 1939 on the Democratic ticket along with Governor Keen Johnson, improvised as the war deepened. When Johnson became governor, the state still faced a $7 million debt, but he left office four years later with a $10 million surplus, thanks to wartime prosperity. Money for education was not the main problem during the war years; finding teachers and shifting resources were the main concerns. Booker also served on the Committee for Kentucky, chaired by Harry W. Schacter, in the forties, and later he became executive director of KEA. One of the most important measures of the time was the first tenure law, which provided some protection for continuing employment for public school teachers, passed by the 1942 General Assembly.[3]

A highlight of Booker's tenure was the first realization of a longtime dream, funding of a modest equalization. Although the 1930 legislature had passed an equalization bill, only one minor distribution took place before the Kentucky Court of Appeals declared the law unconstitutional. The legislature reacted by raising the allowable county school tax rate to 75 cents per $100 evaluation and the independent-district rate to $1.50. After few school districts took advantage of the new rate limits during the Great Depression, another education reform effort was mounted in the late thirties. The General Assembly passed a new equalization amendment to Section 186 of the state constitution, and the voters of the commonwealth overwhelmingly confirmed the measure in 1941. Though inadequate, allowing only 10 percent of the state school fund to be distributed "according to need" in the poorer districts, the measure was a step in the right direction; the General Assembly appropriated $400,000 for each year of the 1943–1944 biennium. Initially, the 10 percent portion was to be used to bring the per-pupil per-year expenditure up to thirty dollars in the poorer districts. Moreover, for the first time, after passage of a law in 1938, beginning in 1940, the teacher retirement system began operation, with the state matching the contributions of teachers. By 1944 state appropriations had increased per biennium from $1 million to $1.62 million.[4]

World War II once again stretched Kentucky's educational institutions to the limits. A shortage of teachers and administrators soon developed, not only because men were going into the armed forces, but also because teachers were leaving for higher-paying civilian jobs. By 1943 Booker stated that because male "teachers have not been exempted from the selective service," they had to be replaced with "emergency teachers." Most of these teachers were not qualified, many of them lacking any college preparation whatsoever. Some were given funds out of an emergency state appropriation of $27,000 to attend summer school in 1943. Other areas of education in Kentucky showed improvement in the war years, as transportation of students, vocational education, and free textbooks received increased state funding. There was progress on other fronts too. Early in his administration, Governor Johnson went before the State Textbook Commission, urging it to be a good steward of state funds and not repeat history, where "there have at times been circumstances which did not smell right. . . . You are dealing with cunning, adroit men who are trying to make money by selling books. It is your obligation to protect the schoolchildren and the state." By the end of his tenure in 1943, free textbooks were being provided in all public schools for all courses through the eighth grade. Even though the School for the Deaf in Danville was closed during most of 1943–1944 for needed repairs, both that school and the School for the Blind in Louisville, which celebrated its centennial in 1942, continued to receive increasing appropriations from the state legislature.[5]

The improved economic conditions of wartime prosperity, coupled with manpower shortages, ended the need for New Deal programs such as the PWA, the WPA, the CCC, the NYA, and others, many of which had enhanced education in Kentucky. However, new government programs aided the home-front effort. Young people in "war training" courses became an important part of vocational education programs, beginning in 1940. For the first time, adult education became a significant Department of Education function. More than $2.5 million in federal funds poured into wartime Kentucky vocational education programs. Some trade schools in larger Kentucky towns and cities operated twenty-four hours a day to meet the demand for defense workers. As part of the Food Production War Training Program, the Department of Education facilitated the building of 156 "community canneries." As many as fifty thousand Kentucky families, including my grandparents and my mother and myself (my father was in the U.S. Army in the Philippines), used these canneries, in our case, at the Bagdad school in Shelby County. The Food Production program also trained more than 141,000 adults during the war years.[6]

Education in Kentucky continued to be studied, in both general and specific ways, during and immediately after World War II. As usual, these studies proved time and again that the state was behind the rest of the nation. The Committee for Kentucky project, headed by Harry Schacter, president of Kaufman-Straus Department Store in Louisville, operated between 1945 and 1950, studying all aspects of Kentucky life and work. *Kentucky on the March*, published in 1949, presented the findings of the study. It painted a bleak picture of educational backwardness in the Bluegrass State, but one that demonstrated a great range of educational opportunity, from the least effective school districts, usually in the mountain and western county districts, to some quite efficient schools, usually in the larger urban areas. The report and its publicity efforts urged that more state money, particularly equalization funds, be supplied to upgrade the poorer districts.[7]

Of course, Kentucky politics remained at the forefront of any change, positive or negative, in the commonwealth. The Republican Party surged again in Kentucky in 1943, electing Simeon Willis as governor after the Democrats suffered through a bruising and divisive primary. Republican John Fred Williams (1944–1948) swept into office as state superintendent, as all but one candidate on the GOP ticket were elected. Willis had begun his working career as a teacher before becoming a lawyer. Williams had worked his way up from a one-room school to a principalship in Paintsville and then to superintendent of the Johnson County schools before coming to Frankfort. Though faced with a General Assembly controlled by Democrats, Willis approached his legislative sessions with a reform agenda.[8]

Meanwhile, yet another study of the commonwealth, this one set in motion by the University of Kentucky, came out of the abbreviated celebration of the state's sesquicentennial in 1942. President Herman L. Donovan initiated conferences of the university's professors to brainstorm about the future of the commonwealth. The resulting report, *Kentucky: Designs for Her Future*, based on thirty radio addresses on WHAS, was edited by professor of rural sociology Howard W. Beers and published in 1945 by the University of Kentucky Press, which had just been formed in 1943. Maurice F. Seay, dean of the college of education, wrote the chapter on education. Noting the great disparity of educational opportunities, based on population density and relative wealth of county and city districts, Seay urged greater efforts for equalization, transportation funding for rural districts, increased teachers' salaries, appointment of the state superintendent, improvements in leadership at the local and state levels, and reduction of the number of teachers with emergency certificates. The latter problem had become serious during the war: "one-fifth of Kentucky's children" were being taught by unqualified teachers. Kentucky also still needed to expand the school term. Many rural one-teacher schools still operated for only seven months. While Professor Beers cheered a 50 percent increase in the common school fund in 1944, he asked for even more. Governor Willis also appointed the Postwar Advisory Planning Commission, which was to try its hand at suggesting ways to improve the commonwealth. The "Program for Action for Kentucky," prepared by this group, called for sweeping changes, including improving education. Most important, of course, was funding of the public schools, where the national expenditure average per student was $94.03 in 1940 versus only $48.09 in Kentucky. Money always seemed to be the major problem in educating Kentucky's children, particularly in the poorer rural districts.[9]

Within the Department of Education during the war years, efforts were made to improve instruction in elementary school reading. A grant from the General Education Board funded a program study that found that most first-graders did not learn to read readily enough because they were being exposed to a primer that was too advanced. As a result of workshops for teachers and the use of new "pre-primers," many children advanced more quickly, breaking a logjam; these steps reduced first-grade enrollments by making it possible to promote students to a higher grade sooner. Moreover, the study offered other suggestions adopted by the state, including funding a full-time elementary school supervisor. And a grant from the W. K. Kellogg Foundation funded a program to improve the health of schoolchildren.[10]

The Willis-Williams years were indeed progressive ones for education. The average salary of a teacher increased from $792 to $1,325 statewide, the state school fund was nearly doubled, the school term was lengthened from seven to eight months even for the poorer districts, and the allowable county school tax rate was doubled. This was an outstanding record, considering the turmoil of the war years and the usual Kentucky political milieu. Not only did Willis have to contend with a Democratic Party–controlled legislature led by Earle C. Clements and Harry Lee Waterfield, but his relationship with Republican School Superintendent Williams was not always coopera-tive. Perhaps the Commonwealth of Kentucky was indeed "On the March." The Willis administration, owing to flush economic times, even ended with an $18 million state surplus.[11]

Earle C. Clements roared into office as governor in the election of 1947, carrying with him the entire Democratic Party ticket, including State Su-perintendent Boswell B. Hodgkin. A powerfully built man, the intimidat-ing Clements outworked and out-organized his opponents and remained a political force in the state for many years. Moreover, he allied himself with important local politicos such as Circuit Judge Ervine Turner and his wife Marie, superintendent of Breathitt County schools. Hodgkin came to his post after serving as superintendent of the Winchester City Schools. The Clements administration faced most of the same educational issues as previ-ous ones, including funding of the poorer districts and, significantly, renewed challenges to racial segregation.[12]

Superintendent Hodgkin, as one of the leaders of the Kentucky Educa-tion Association's "schoolmen" network, followed the standard KEA line of proposing educational uplift in the state. Included were increasing equaliza-tion, now being called "a minimum foundation program," lengthening the school term to nine months for all schools, improving school plants, and addressing the teacher shortage. Governor Clements also had a progressive agenda of moving the state forward, including passage of a bill creating the Legislative Research Commission, replacing the old highway patrol with a modernized state police agency, and new taxes on distilled spirits and gasoline that would help fund the common schools. More money went into building county roads, what Clements called getting Kentuckians "out of the mud," a move that aided school transportation. Between 1939 and 1949, the number of students being transported increased from around 101,000 to more than 187,000, and daily miles traveled by bus increased from nearly 68,000 to more than 136,000. Building of school facilities also received an impetus. In the 1948–1949 biennium, more than $20 million was expended on 245 building projects statewide. Two constitutional amendments approved by the commonwealth's citizens affected education. The first amendment, after the fifth attempt to pass it, increased the maximum salary possible for state employees from $5,000 to $20,000, making it possible to hire and keep "the most skilled officials and administrators." Another amendment, which was supported by most newspapers, including the widely read *Courier-Journal*, raised to 25 percent the allowable assistance to "the very poorest school districts," as part of the equalization program. This second amendment passed by an eighty thousand–vote majority, demonstrating that perhaps Kentuckians were finally getting serious about improving education in the state.[13]

Clements in some ways was considered an "education governor." He also called a special session of the General Assembly to consider improving the inequity of property tax assessments in the commonwealth. However, even this governor needed a bit of prodding during the 1950 legislative session, and teachers did something they had never done before. With tacit KEA approval, they organized "a troublesome protest march" in Frankfort in March 1950. Called "The Frankfort Committee of Teachers" and consisting of one teacher from each of the 236 school districts, the group urged a united front against the sometimes rigid governor. In the background was always the growing dissatisfaction of classroom teachers with the dominance of KEA by administrators. After the strong-willed Clements made feeble attempts to ridicule the teachers, that ploy backfired, giving teachers even more support. Although the number of teachers actually "striking" was small, most local superintendents apparently supported them. "The Frankfort Committee of Teachers" dissolved and left Frankfort only after Governor Clements relented and agreed to push the General Assembly into substantially increasing the state school fund. Eliza Clark, a teacher in the Russell City Schools in Fleming County and one of the revolt's leaders, in which as many as five thousand teachers came to Frankfort at one time or another, won the KEA presidency in 1950–1951.[14]

Other major changes were taking place in Kentucky education. The Department of Education, with General Assembly authority in 1950, began a statewide program of annual mandatory two-day in-service meetings. Certification of teachers also became more standardized through centralized control by the Council on Public Higher Education and the State Board of Education. Postwar education appeared to have a renewed impetus. For example, in November 1946, Louisville voters approved an $8 million bond issue by a 6-1 majority to improve school facilities. Even more important was the beginning of the end of legal racial segregation in Kentucky, but that change began in higher education, not elementary and secondary. Hodgkin also reported more and more school consolidations, part of a national trend. While the number of teachers on emergency certification decreased ever so slowly, by 1948–1949, 49 percent of Kentucky teachers met the national standard of having four years or more of college preparation.[15]

Clements resigned from the governorship in November 1950 in order to run for the U.S. Senate and easily defeated Republican Charles I. Dawson. Lieutenant Governor Lawrence W. Wetherby took Clements's place and soon called an "Extraordinary Session of the General Assembly" in March 1951, with education an important part of the agenda. With a $10 million state surplus, Wetherby pushed a willing legislature into raising teachers' salaries and also gave increasing aid to the elderly, the blind, dependent children, and others. Teachers received an average of $300 more per year for 1951–1952, and $6 million was added to make a final total of $30.5 million for education. Moreover, the education bill increased the per-pupil minimum annual funding to more than thirty-eight dollars.[16]

Wetherby, a native of Jefferson County, ran for a term in his own right in 1951, and he was elected along with the entire Democratic Party ticket, including Wendell P. Butler as superintendent of public instruction. Although the Kentucky Constitution of the time did not allow public officials to succeed themselves, Butler went on to serve two more terms as state superintendent and two terms as agriculture commissioner by alternating terms in each office every four years. He was the consummate "insider," not only in Kentucky Democratic Party politics but also among the education establishment. Wetherby, whose years as governor coincided with generally prosperous years in the state and the nation, and Butler, who had followed the KEA mantra of increasing appropriations for public education, worked well together in a state dominated by their party in Frankfort.[17]

Though "often overlooked for its record of solid progress," according to historian John E. Kleber, Wetherby's tenure was a good period for the commonwealth, particularly in education. Wetherby also worked hard to broaden the state's economy by encouraging industrialization and improving transportation. Something of a liberal, he encouraged the first strip-mining legislation and killed a right-to-work bill. Wetherby urged the development of a statewide educational television network as well as bookmobiles to reach the undereducated parts of the commonwealth. With the support of the Friends of Kentucky Libraries, eighty-four bookmobiles went into service in 1954, administered by the Kentucky Department of Libraries and Archives.[18]

The funding of public school education, particularly for the poorer districts, continued to bedevil the Commonwealth of Kentucky even in the apparently flush times of post–World War II America. With passage of the 1941 constitutional amendment, 10 percent of the school fund became available to distribute to the poorer districts. The 1949 equalization law increased this proportion to 25 percent. When Butler came into office, he immediately set about to further amend Section 186 of the Kentucky Constitution "so that the legislature could distribute educational funds on any basis it deemed fair and efficient." "I had preached in the hollers and highways and byways—anyplace people would listen," Butler maintained later in his folksy way, about his efforts to get the measure passed. Butler and his allies, including the KEA establishment, the Kentucky Congress of Parents and Teachers, the State Department of Education, the *Courier-Journal*, Governor Wetherby, and most Kentucky "schoolmen," pushed the General Assembly into allowing the citizens of the commonwealth to amend the constitution. Supporters held meetings across the state and distributed forty thousand copies of the proposal. Not everyone was in favor of the change. In districts with substantial numbers of students attending Catholic schools, some public school officials favored keeping the old method of money distribution on a per-pupil basis because that way they received more money. Nevertheless, on November 3, 1953, the voters overwhelmingly passed the amendment by a 2–1 vote. The *Courier-Journal* opined that this "was merely the beginning"; the burden was now on the next meeting of the General Assembly to fully fund the "minimum foundation."[19]

Two methods of administration were developed: all schools received funds from a per-capita account, and "districts in need" could qualify for extra funds from the equalization account. In 1954 the legislature established the Minimum Foundation Program, but it was not fully funded until the meeting of the 1956 General Assembly. Extending the school term to nine months, funding the Teachers Retirement System, encouraging school consolidation, reducing the number of one-room schools, and improving elementary and high school standards marked the Wetherby-Butler years as crucial to Kentucky education reform.[20]

World War II and its aftermath moved the United States and Kentucky toward inexorable change in racial relations. Integration of Kentucky classrooms began after a successful lawsuit against the University of Kentucky by Lyman Johnson in 1949. Two years later the General Assembly passed a statute modifying the Day Law, permitting colleges to voluntarily integrate. Catholic colleges in Louisville, including Bellarmine, Nazareth, and Ursuline; Berea College; and the University of Louisville, the only public school of higher education in that city, immediately opened their doors to African Americans. The landmark *Brown v. Board of Education* decision, handed down by the U.S. Supreme Court in 1954, directly affected public educa-tion. Chief Justice Earl Warren said, writing for the unanimous court, "We conclude that in the field of public education the doctrine of 'separate but equal' has no place. Separate educational facilities are inherently unequal." *Plessy v. Ferguson*'s "separate but equal" ruling no longer had the sanction of law in public school education.[21]

Governor Wetherby reacted positively to the *Brown* decision. "We will do whatever it takes to obey the law," he said in the immediate aftermath of the decision, while most "southern" governors and politicians decided to dig in their heels and fight any semblance of desegregation. Not that all white Kentuckians rushed to end segregated schools once and for all. While Wetherby took a courageous stand at the Southern Governors' Conference by "refusing to sign a statement against integration," Lieutenant Governor Emerson "Doc" Beauchamp supported the old "southern" mores. Biographer Kleber maintained that Wetherby's "urban orientation" brought him down on the side of desegregation. When the Supreme Court in the *Brown II* decision in 1955 ruling urged that schools desegregate "with all deliberate speed," many segregationists saw this as a pretext for even more temporizing. Furthermore, according to education historian William J. Reese, "President Dwight D. Eisenhower only encouraged more resistance when he made it clear that he was unhappy with the Supreme Court, saying that laws could not change men's hearts."[22]

Brown v. Board of Education abolished Section 187 of the 1891 Kentucky Constitution as well as the Day Law of 1904. At the advent of desegregation in Kentucky, the state had 301 black elementary schools, 6 separate high schools, and 52 schools combining grades one to twelve. There were about 12,000 African American students taught by 1,453 black teachers. Integra-tion did not come as easily by many white Kentuckians as it is often viewed. Even at such state institutions as the School for the Deaf in Danville, "full integration" of dormitories and dining halls did not take place until 1963.[23]

As a "border state" with both "southern" and "midwestern" traits, Kentucky stood at a crossroads of America. The NAACP filed lawsuits to integrate several Kentucky school systems, visualizing that "successful school integration in Kentucky would be a positive example to the South of peace-ful desegregation," observed George C. Wright. The first of these lawsuits in Louisville had the support of the Bingham newspapers and the implied consent of Louisville School superintendent Omer Carmichael. "Some suits were quietly invited by school officials who wanted to desegregate but sought full backing by the courts," according to Gifford Blyton and Galen Martin in the *Kentucky Encyclopedia*. However, there were always numerous local citizens who opposed any change in racial mores, and other issues, such as the integration of teaching staffs, also served to slow, deter, or completely stymie desegregation efforts, at least in the short run.[24]

The KEA and the State Department of Education reacted slowly but positively to the fact that desegregation was now the law of the land. The *Kentucky School Journal*, published by the KEA, began publishing articles preparing teachers and administrators for the realities of the desegregation process. In one piece, UK librarian Azile Wofford explained how a State Department bulletin encouraged including books about African Americans in school libraries. Praising black school librarians for their suggestions, she suggested that biracial committees in each community work on adding titles to the bookshelves. In another article Dean W. C. Lappin of Morehead State College encouraged principals to prepare for desegregation by learning more about blacks and their culture. He warned principals that while they could control classrooms, school social activities and bus transportation would be more problematical. "Probably the most troublesome problem of all, however, will be that of dealing with the adult public," he prophetically cautioned.[25]

Factionalism returned with a passion in the Democratic gubernatorial primary in 1955, when Albert B. "Happy" Chandler sought a second term. Senator Clements "handpicked a long-shot candidate, eastern Kentuckian Judge Bert T. Combs." The effervescent Chandler had a great advantage over the reserved Combs. "Be like your pappy and vote for Happy," shouted his ads. Robert R. Martin, a political ally of the Clements faction and head of the Bureau of Administration and Finance in the State Department of Education, became a candidate for state superintendent. Chandler and Martin both won handily in the 1955 Democratic primary and then in the general election, along with the rest of the Democratic Party ticket.[26]

In the beginning of his term, Chandler affirmed he would not oppose integration of the public schools. It remained to be seen how much he would be willing to use his office to push desegregation. In 1955 the Kentucky Court of Appeals followed the dictates of *Brown v. Board of Education* and ruled in *Willis v. Walker* that the Day Law was unconstitutional in a case involving the Columbia school system in Adair County. Desegregation began. Lafayette High School in Lexington admitted a black girl, and several African American students entered the Wayne County system in the fall of 1955 without incident at the Griffin School.[27]

Superintendent Martin had come up through the ranks of Kentucky education and politics. After World War II interrupted his teaching career, he returned from military service in 1946 to become a principal in Lee County before joining the State Department of Education as an auditor. All the while he played his role, at first minor, as a Democratic Party stalwart, allied with the Clements-Combs faction in opposition to that of Chandler. Martin clashed with Governor Chandler when the governor tried to remove the Division of Surplus Property from the Department of Education. The new state superintendent acquiesced when Chandler wanted to "dump Wendell Butler" and two others from the Department of Education because of their support of Combs in the primary. Edward F. Prichard Jr. referred to this as the "decapitation of Wendell Butler," in an oral history interview in 1977. This action created a rift not only between Martin and Butler but also between Martin and others in the public school establishment of the commonwealth. Apparently it was the price Chandler exacted to push education, allowing Martin to lead efforts to increase teachers' salaries. Chandler and Martin kept a wary distance between themselves on patronage matters. Prichard found the Department of Education to be, like the rest of the agencies in state government, highly "politicized." The Chandler administration was complicated by continual machinations within the state Democratic Party, in which the governor sometimes allied himself with Republicans. Meanwhile, in the general election of 1956, incumbent Dwight D. Eisenhower won the presidency; Republican Thruston B. Morton defeated incumbent senator Clements, with Chandler's support; and incumbent senator John Sherman Cooper defeated former governor Lawrence Wetherby.[28]

After World War II, the advent of the cold war and the civil rights movement caused an increasing federal response in education. The launching of the first Sputnik by the Soviet Union intensified the fear that the United States was falling behind in education and brought passage of the National Defense Education Act of 1958. Supporting curriculum development in mathematics, science, foreign languages, and to a lesser extent in the humanities and social sciences, the act brought money into the public schools as never before. Although conservatives fought the movement, President Johnson's Great Society programs not only encouraged desegregation but also directly assisted education in such programs as the Elementary and Secondary Education Act of 1965, which included such programs as Head Start and other initiatives. In 1965 alone, the federal government spent $4 billion on education. Beginning in the Martin years, these programs began to have a great impact on Kentucky public school education.[29]

During Martin's term, the continuation of mergers into consolidated schools further reduced the number of districts from 223 to 216. The consolidation-merger juggernaut marched on in Kentucky education as it did across the nation. With new money going into school construction, mergers eliminated 750 one-room schools during Martin's tenure. The state also began making headway against issuing the Temporary Elementary Certificate and other expedient measures to address the teacher shortage. Beginning in 1960, for the first time, a four-year program and a degree were required for all elementary teaching certificates. A five-year program was required for all superintendents, principals, and guidance counselors. Kentucky teachers, like teachers elsewhere, were becoming more professional. The teacher retirement program received improved benefits, for the first time providing survivor benefits and death benefits and liberalizing disability retirement. During the Martin years, the first National Defense Education Act supplied funds under Title V-A to train guidance counselors. With the Minimum Foundation now an intrinsic part of school funding, the Chandler-Martin administration had to find ways to fund the program. Chandler, unalterably opposed to a sales tax, pushed through the General Assembly increases in state income and corporate taxes and other excises, including taxes on the production of whiskey and the sale of gasoline for trucks.[30]

Salaries for teachers continued to be a paramount problem; the commonwealth ranked forty-sixth nationally in 1956–1957, with an average salary of $2,900. This caused a continued exodus of some of Kentucky's best-trained teachers to such states as Ohio and Florida, where salaries were thousands of dollars higher. In 1954, when the median Kentucky teacher's salary was $2,311, a starting salary in Ohio averaged $3,975 and in Florida $3,725. Martin estimated that in the single year 1955–1956, 971 teachers left the state "for employment in other states." The shortage of teachers in Kentucky continued as school populations increased. One study demonstrated that more teachers left the state or left teaching altogether than were being graduated from all of the colleges in the state in 1955–1956. Martin, with Chandler's approval, pushed fully funding the Minimum Foundation Program, which reached eighty dollars per student during their last year in office. Improving the Teachers' Retirement System would increase teacher retention. Training of teachers did improve in the Martin years near the end of his term; two-thirds of the state's teachers had at least a four-year degree. The push to improve teacher education at state and private institutions of higher education appeared to be paying off. Martin also encouraged curriculum change, particularly in light of the Russian challenge of firing Sputnik into orbit in 1957. And the Department of Education increasingly emphasized development of "the comprehensive high school" as the answer "to serve the needs of all." As he was leaving office, Martin succinctly described the perennial problem facing education in the Kentucky: "We have made progress but we are so far behind we didn't make enough progress."[31]

The greatest challenges as well as changes during the Chandler-Martin years were, of course, following the dictates of *Brown v. Board of Education*. Schools in western Kentucky, Lexington, and Louisville, as well as others, became focal points in the beginning of the battle for desegregation.

Superintendent Martin preferred to allow local districts "a large degree of autonomy" over how and when they integrated.[32]

Following the first halting steps of desegregation in the Wetherby administration, the Chandler/Martin years became a time of more heated turmoil, particularly in western Kentucky. On the positive side, in 1955 eighty-five schools across Kentucky "integrated without incident." Most of those schools were in small districts with small numbers of blacks. Black athletes played on integrated teams for the first time. For example, in Powell County, black students who had previously been bused to Clark County from their homes in West Bend were integrated into the county high school without incident. Coach Bill Orme welcomed several African Americans to his basketball team. Although there was statewide discussion of integrating black teachers as well as African American students, in the mid-fifties little was done to assure black teachers continued employment. State Superintendent Martin hoped for the best in the fall of 1956, "but you can never tell," he said. By the time school opened in the fall of 1956, there had been much progress: 92 of the 160 districts in the state reported having "mixed enrollments," and Louisville was apparently a beacon of what could be accomplished in racial integration of public schools. However, stout resistance developed in some western Kentucky communities. Often thought of as the most "southern" area of the commonwealth, that region, stretching from Bowling Green to Henderson westward and bounded by the Ohio River and the Tennessee border, had a mixed record of complying with court-ordered desegregation in the fifties and sixties.[33]

In September 1956 the good will, good sense, limits of government, and intentions of both integrationists and segregationists were tested. Sturgis in Union County, Henderson in Henderson County, Madisonville in Hopkins County, and the Clay city schools in Webster County became crucial tests of the will of the governor and the intent of Kentuckians to follow the Supreme Court's *Brown v. Board of Education* decision. When segregationists in Henderson County voiced their disapproval of the district's integration of black children before any formal plan had been offered, Assistant Attorney General Robert Matthews ruled that a board "has no legal right . . . to abandon these plans" and go back to a segregated system. On September 4, 1956, nine local black students, who had been attending Dunbar High School in Morganfield, tried to enroll in the previously all-white Sturgis High School. They were confronted by a mob of whites. That same day Lafayette High School in Fayette County peacefully integrated, although there was a cross burned on school grounds. The entire Larue County system also successfully desegregated. At first, it appeared that Frankfort would allow the locals at

Clay and Sturgis to prevail, but then Governor Chandler acted. Over the first school weekend, he ordered National Guard units to mobilize and enter Sturgis. Troops were also sent into Clay, only eleven miles from Sturgis, after crowds blocked nine black students from enrolling and "forced newspapermen from the town for a time." Adjutant General J. J. B. Williams took personal charge of the troops.[34]

At Sturgis on Monday, September 10, 1956, only a small number of white students showed up as National Guard troops escorted seven black students into the school. In Clay, Mayor Herman Z. Clark became combative, claiming that only Kentucky law applied to his town, not that dictated by a Supreme Court decision. Chandler took "responsibility for the decision" to send in troops and said he "acted on good advice." M-47 tanks were brought in, and soldiers patrolled the streets with fixed bayonets. White demonstrators and students liberally used the "N" word in denouncing the attempt to integrate the schools of Sturgis and Clay. In Clay, General Williams took two black children "by the hand" and escorted them into the school. The tense situations in both towns drew national and even some international attention. For example, an English reporter protested to Chandler over his rough treatment by irate whites. Kentucky attorney general Jo M. Ferguson ruled that the *Brown* decision did not apply to Sturgis because the law gave school officials, and "not parents or students, the right to decide when and where integration would take place." Therefore, since there had been no plans made to integrate these schools by the school boards, blacks should not be admitted. However, he also said that if the black parents went to court, they could undoubtedly prove that the school boards were not acting in good faith and adopting plans "with all deliberate speed" as ordered by the Supreme Court in the *Brown II* decision of May 31, 1955. As a result, both the Sturgis and Clay school boards voted to keep blacks out of their schools. Black parents decided to give up the fight, at least in the short term, and white teachers and students returned to the Clay and Sturgis schools. There appeared to be little goodwill in some white communities in western Kentucky as White Citizens Council members, local and from outside the commonwealth, as well as local newspapers, including one in Henderson, supported the old order. Mayor Clark exulted: "There will be no integration here this year, next year, or ever." However, Sturgis mayor J. B. Holeman stated that his constituents had not "faced facts" and would have to do so sooner or later. Within a few days, General Williams pulled out his troops and the contingent of state police left as well from Sturgis and Clay. It was not until the next year that tempers cooled and black students could peaceably attend Sturgis High School. During the fall of 1956 the Hopkins County schools also rejected integration, while a boycott of the Henderson Schools encouraged by the White Citizens

Council was ruled illegal by the attorney general's office. James Dumas of the state White Citizens Council branded Governor Chandler "a traitor" who had "sold out the state to the National Association for the Advancement of Colored People."[35]

In an oral history interview after his retirement from active political life, Chandler explained that his actions as governor were the result of simply following the law. When "black people came to see me in '36 and wanted to go to school with the white folks, I said 'you can't do it. There is a constitutional provision that says schools have to be separate and there's the Day Law.'" Twenty years later, Chandler said, the *Brown* decision had made all the difference. "Some of the white folks they told me, I never will forget, 'Albert, ain't no Nigger is going to school here.'" Chandler said he told the mayor of Clay, one of his old western Kentucky political cronies, "I don't know if they show up or not, but if they show up they are [going to school]. The law's in their favor now." Although Chandler may have overstated his conversion, he did pragmatically follow, in 1936 as well as in 1956, what he believed to be the current law of the land. He had traced the same path in accepting integration of baseball in 1947 when he was commissioner of the major leagues.[36]

Desegregationists, realizing they had the Supreme Court rulings on their side, took the legal route. Louisville attorney and Kentucky NAACP president James A. Crumlin had already begun to file lawsuits in the federal courts during the fall of 1956. Federal judges Henry Brooks, Mac Swinford, H. Church Ford, and Roy Shelburne, successively in their terms, forced compliance. In an article about school desegregation in the western Kentucky counties, David L. Wolfford pointed out that, as in the Deep South, there were cross-burnings, intimidation of black families and students, and reprisals leading to loss of employment in some places. At the same time, desegregation in Russellville, Madisonville, and a few other western Kentucky school districts occurred with "little fanfare" or negative publicity in the national press. Although only "token integration" existed in some places, according to the studies of Wolfford, statewide, at least by 1964, more than 90 percent of Kentucky school districts had "some black students attending classes with white students." That did not mean all classes were integrated. "Roughly sixty-two percent of Kentucky's African Americans attended school with whites, while only two percent of black residents of the old confederacy did so," Wolfford concluded. The passage of the federal Civil Rights Act in 1964 and a state Civil Rights Act in 1966 soon accelerated desegregation efforts in the remaining districts.[37]

The larger cities of the South became the bigger stories of the 1950s and 1960s. While Governor Orval Faubus in Little Rock, Arkansas, fulminated along with other southern demagogues and resisted integration, President

Eisenhower initially refused to use federal troops to enforce the law at Little Rock Central High School. "The Louisville Story" became an example of how a border state city could provide leadership in peaceful integration. The Bingham newspapers fully supported following the dictates of the *Brown* decision and urged the Louisville school system to become a leader. Superintendent Omer Carmichael, a native of Alabama, had worked his way up in school circles, becoming head of the Louisville system in 1945. When the 1954 decision came down, Carmichael and the Louisville board began a two-year planning process.[38]

For decades the move toward desegregation had appeared stymied in Louisville, where, as in most "southern" cities, neighborhoods had been rigidly segregated since the Civil War by "de jure" (legal) restrictions. In 1914 the Louisville Board of Aldermen passed a segregated-housing law, which, though overturned by a 1917 Supreme Court case, continued to operate "as a fact of life" in practice. Beginning with World War II, the black population shifted dramatically from rural Kentucky to urban centers, with African American growth in Louisville showing the greatest increase. Significantly, while blacks represented only 16 percent of the total population of Louisville, they accounted for almost 27 percent of the public school enrollment. For more than a decade, the Louisville Urban League and the NAACP campaigned to open Louisville parks and swimming pools to both races. Integration of colleges and universities resulted from the efforts of many individuals and organizations, including black Louisville legislator Charles W. Anderson, who introduced legislation in 1946 to allow black nurses to receive training in previously all-white hospitals. That measure passed the General Assembly in 1948, and two years later the initial "death blow" to the Day Law came with legislation to allow all colleges to desegregate if they desired. Before the *Brown v. Board of Education* decision, the only substantive change in the racial mores in Kentucky's largest city had been the integration of the University of Louisville in 1951 by absorbing Louisville Municipal College, the all-black school founded in 1931.[39]

Carmichael followed the dictates of the *Brown* decision but also agreed with the *Brown II* ruling of "all deliberate speed," temporizing to develop a plan that would be acceptable to most of Louisville's citizens. More particularly, he wanted a peaceful solution, fearing the turmoil and violence seen in many southern cities. He had reason to suspect the dangers that school integration might bring. Just a few weeks after the Supreme Court handed down the first *Brown* decision, racists planted dynamite at the suburban home of a black couple who had integrated a previously "all-white subdivision" outside Louisville. Carmichael got input from numerous sources, but mostly he wanted the "Louisville Program" to be indigenous to the city. He was afraid "outsiders," either supporting or opposing desegregation, would lead to trouble.[40]

First came Carmichael's and the Louisville elite's acceptance of the two *Brown* decisions in 1954 and 1955. Ministers and other leaders voiced their approval. Accused of stalling, Carmichael vowed that time would be needed to successfully integrate his schools. The Bingham papers, the *Louisville Times* and the *Courier-Journal,* backed Carmichael and urged compliance. The "Louisville Plan" included "twelve points," the most important being redistricting of schools "without regard to race" at all levels. However, a parent could be permitted a "safety valve," to transfer a child under certain conditions. Such transfers would be limited. This "freedom of choice," or "free-choice transfer," allowed both black and white parents and students an alternative to integration. Woodford Roy Porter Sr., the first African American on the Louisville School Board, elected in 1958, refused to ask for transfers of his children to keep them in all-black schools. His oldest daughter recalled that he said, "No. We wanted desegregation. We worked on this plan. We want to live by this plan." When desegregation went into effect on September 10, 1956, more than forty-five thousand students attended integrated schools in Louisville, the largest number in any city of that size that year to desegregate without violence. There were White Citizens Council pickets at the Louisville Board of Education Building and at City Hall, but little else occurred that day to warrant fear that the plan would fail. In the coming months, the Louisville community was praised for its efforts to integrate its schools and its apparent success. Carmichael received immediate accolades. The *Courier-Journal* applauded the Louisville superintendent for his "wise preparation." "I think Mr. Carmichael must be a very wise man," said President Dwight D. Eisenhower. "I hope to get some advice from him as to how he did it." Invited to the White House, Carmichael pleased the president with his views and, when challenged by the national press, defended what was taking place in Louisville as "real integration."[41]

Coming hot on the heels of the 1954 and 1955 *Brown* decisions, exactly how successful was "The Louisville Story" in the late fifties? Carmichael admitted initially that of seventy-five elementary, middle, and secondary schools, fifty-five had "mixed student bodies," eleven had all-white classes, and nine had African American students only. Central High School had no white students, but the previously all-white high schools all had some black students. With integration of students as his first priority, Carmichael placed no emphasis on integrating the teaching cadre of the Louisville system. While he claimed that elementary schools were the most integrated, he admitted that the high schools were the least. Conversely, a modern critic of "The Louisville Story," historian George C. Wright, found that many whites avoided integration when they could. "Though the Louisville system was widely heralded in 1957 for peacefully desegregating its schools," Wright contended,

> very little integration occurred, with only a few blacks enrolling in white schools and no whites going to the black schools. It seemed, to many observers, that Afro-Americans attending the white schools had been carefully selected. The black students at Male High School, for example, had high intelligence scores and were very strong scholastically—which came as a surprise to many whites. Also, a significant number of the first black students at white schools were outstanding athletes, a pattern that would become all too common in Louisville. Again, it is a reflection of American society of the 1950s that the moderate plan initiated by Superintendent Carmichael was praised by educators and politicians in Kentucky and all over the nation.[42]

Integration also meant a loss of black control over their institutions. As Kentucky schools began to desegregate, other changes came to the commonwealth. Black teachers first organized in 1877 under the name of Colored Teachers State Association; the name changed to Kentucky Negro Education Association in 1913 and to Kentucky Teachers Association in 1954. In 1957 black teachers merged their organization with KEA, which in reality subsumed the KTA. Integration brought the closing of black schools, often without regard for the loss of a sense of community that followed. Examples abounded. Lynch Colored High School, also called West Main High School, opened in 1923 and closed in 1963 along with the black elementary school. Bond-Washington School's students went into the Elizabethtown system in 1959. The integration of black teachers took a backseat to integration of African American students into previously all-white schools.[43]

Amid all the tumult and shouting about racial integration across the country came one of those tragedies that so often marks a decade. Public transportation was first used for students in Mason County in 1911; by 1958, 169 school districts operated 3,500 buses. On a cloudy and cold February 28, 1958, occurred one of the worst tragedies in the history of Kentucky. Three miles east of Prestonsburg on old Highway 23, on its morning run, a school bus struck a wrecker removing a pickup truck that had slipped off the road. The bus ran off the roadway, through a willow thicket, and into the swollen Levisa Fork of the Big Sandy River, where twenty feet of water swirled in a stream that ordinarily held no more than two feet. The causes of the crash remain a mystery and remain controversial. Twenty-one children survived that day, the *Courier-Journal* reported, "before the heavy current swept the bus like a log into the deeper water, and closed over the screams of the children trapped inside." Twenty-six children and the bus driver died. Governor Chandler sent in National Guard units, and the Army Corps of Engineers lent their expertise in the recovery efforts. The last victim was not found until sixty-nine days after the accident. The worst school bus accident in American history, this tragedy continues to scar the community more than a half century later.[44]

These turbulent years were a period of personal growth for me. I grew up in the rigidly segregated community of Shelbyville and graduated from high school in 1958 without ever feeling the true effects of early desegregation efforts in the state. Shelbyville had a sizable black population but resisted desegregation, even in the face of NAACP challenges, while I was in school. I do not recall having many contacts with African Americans except at my father's place of business. I do remember the separate restrooms and water fountains in the Shelby County Courthouse. I played on an all-white high school football team at Shelbyville and also at Georgetown College from 1958 to 1961. My sheltered life in racially divided Kentucky came to an abrupt halt when I went to Harrodsburg High School in 1962 as a callow twenty-two-year-old history teacher and head football coach. About one-fourth of the members of the first football team I coached there were African American kids. The Harrodsburg system had rather successfully and peacefully integrated a few years earlier. Reality struck me early in the year when, returning from a scrimmage in Irvine, we stopped in Richmond for a meal on the way back to Harrodsburg. A prominent locally owned restaurant refused to admit us because we had black players. I was informed that the white players could come inside but the black players would have to eat on the bus. When I told the players what had been said, they shouted to go on to another place. We found refuge at a Jerry's Restaurant that welcomed us. I had received my first, needed dose of realism about Kentucky racial mores. While our experience in Jerry's was fine, we were confronted by a couple of local Richmond thugs outside as we walked to the bus. Fortunately, no blows were struck, but to this day I recall the rage I felt that evening and the difficulty of not lashing out. The next year I moved on to Shelby County High School, which was all white until the system desegregated in my second year. There desegregation began in the elementary grades, ostensibly because black Shelby County high school students could go to Lincoln Institute, which closed in 1966.[45]

Integration of high school athletics came with desegregation of education. In 1955 the first African Americans, John "Pie" Liveious and Jim Beck of Louisville Central High School, were named to the Kentucky All-Star team, which competed against Indiana in a two-game series. Since 1932 separate black and white state tournaments had been held in the commonwealth. The remaining all-black schools became eligible for district and regional tournaments in 1957, although they could not compete in the state tournament until the next year. In 1957 Goebel Ritter's integrated Hazard High School team became the first to have black players in the state tournament. Central High, Lexington Dunbar, and Bowling Green High Street, the latter defeating an all-white Shelbyville High School team, all made it to the 1958 tournament. Cynthiana's Louis Stout, who later became commissioner of the Kentucky High School Athletic Association, and Dunbar's Julius Berry became the first African Americans to be named to the all-tournament team. The road to integration was not always easy. Stout later recalled: "I'm not saying everything was smooth and easy, but we had a motive. We ignored a lot of stuff. We had to. When we went to play, [hecklers] attempted to intimidate us. We were prepared to play basketball."[46]

The political milieu in Kentucky at the advent of integration followed patterns that reflected both the state's "southernness" and the changing times. The 1959 general election in Kentucky proved to be a divisive one for the Democratic Party. Judge Bert T. Combs, who had lost the 1955 Democrat Party primary to Chandler, swamped his Republican opponent in the general election. Wendell Butler, elected state superintendent for the second time, was carried along in the Democratic sweep of state offices. The new governor took an avid interest in improving the state's educational institutions. "Just as one can talk about the weather and do nothing about it, for too many years Kentuckians could only talk about their problems in education. Too long our state sat in the back of the classroom," Combs told a meeting of the Fayette County Teachers Association in 1961. "Too proud to whitewash, too poor to paint," was an old mountain adage that Combs used on numerous occasions to encourage Kentuckians to aspire to higher goals.[47]

Combs wanted to improve all aspects of Kentucky life and found a much-needed source of revenue in the recently passed veterans' bonus, approved by a referendum, which was to be funded by a sales tax. While the original sales tax was only 1 percent, Combs persuaded the legislature to increase it to 3 percent in order to pay for capital improvements, human services, and education. "The result was one of the most progressive gubernatorial administrations of the century," claimed State Historian James C. Klotter. A new merit system and the newly created Human Rights Commission added to the progressive image of the Combs years, as did the state's first billion-dollar budget, one that increased state school funding by 50 percent and began a statewide community college system. The *Courier-Journal* praised the governor and the legislature for giving teachers "the largest lump-sum pay increases ever given Kentucky teachers."[48]

During the meeting of the 1960 General Assembly, Representative Harry M. Caudill chaired a committee in the House to study the state of education in Kentucky. A rather "scathing" report at the end of that biennial session concluded that, overall, "a great deal is wrong with school administration at the local level in much of Kentucky." Generally, the Caudill Report criticized the intrusion of politics in school affairs. According to John Ed Pearce, long-time *Courier-Journal* reporter and editor, the report bore the obvious imprint of Caudill's biting rhetoric. In his "indignant voice," the state representative denounced "self-serving paragons of mediocrity who can twist to their ungodly advantage the best laws ever written." With a broad brush Caudill denounced just about everyone from top to bottom, including "professional educators in the Department of Education, the 212 school superintendents, the ruling clique of the Kentucky Education Association and the presidents and deans of the state's colleges." The report claimed, "Many teachers have written to this committee about matters pertinent to its inquiry, but in most instances the writer was unwilling to sign his name, explaining that to do so would cause him to be fired or transferred to a remote and inconvenient teaching assignment." Of the twenty recommendations of the committee, several stand out: (1) electing county school boards at large; (2) giving power to the Department of Education "to compel" consolidation "where districts or schools are inefficient or uneconomical to operate"; (3) changing tenure laws and providing a system using merit and job performance for teacher salary increases; (4) centralizing purchase of school buses; and (5) encouraging a "back to basics" approach, with an emphasis on traditional coursework. Although none of these were adopted during the Combs administration, they continued to be points of discussion in the years to come. Caudill soon left the legislature, becoming a noted critic and author with a national standing.[49]

In 1960 Combs appointed to the Kentucky Commission on Public Education a group of members that included the types of leaders criticized by Caudill. Booz, Allen & Hamilton of Chicago conducted the Program Evaluation Study, and the Associated Consultants of Meridian, Mississippi, did the Minimum Foundation Program Study. These studies were more complete and more positive than the Caudill report, praising the efforts of most, if not all, superintendents, other administrators, and schools. However, there was room for vast improvement. The Booz, Allen & Hamilton report concluded: "Competent teachers are the chief determinant of excellence in the public schools." Some of the recommendations, which echoed those of the Caudill report, included appointing the state superintendent; changing the structure of the state school board and the method of appointing members to it; electing county board members at large; improving the auditing of school expenditures; and, most importantly, authorizing "the State Board of Education . . . to obtain price contract agreements, through the Department of Finance, for items on which the board [believes] substantial savings could be effected." The Booz, Allen & Hamilton report criticized the "school districts with problems," specifically those with "questionable political activities" and "relatively low average personal income" and again centered on the issue of county boards elected by divisions. Like the critique of the Caudill committee, these reports took years "to percolate to the top" of the debate over how to improve education in the Commonwealth of Kentucky. Also on the Kentucky Commission on Public Education, Caudill, who had a low regard for teacher education in the state colleges, strongly recommended in a "minority statement" that prospective teachers be tested for proficiency in "mathematics, science, history, literature, and composition," Moreover, he declared, many Kentucky teachers had a poor command of English that needed immediate remediation.[50]

Notwithstanding all of these critical studies of the state's public school system, specific educational developments during the Combs-Butler years built on those of the previous administration. Consistent with Butler's status as a Democratic Party insider, his second term as state superintendent was part of a string of successive state offices: he had terms as commissioner of agriculture (1964–1968 and 1972–1976) alternating with terms as state superintendent of public instruction (1960–1964 and 1968–1972). Once Robert R. Martin not-too-charitably remarked about the importance of Butler's election to the agriculture post, claiming, "He'll do less harm to a pig than he can a child." Like any other institution, the Department of Education operated upon inertia in a merit system that protected professional staff and followed national and regional trends in education. "Safeguarding gains and moving forward" became the slogan of the second Butler administration. The Minimum Foundation and the sales tax made it possible to significantly increase state funding, particularly to poorer districts. The creation of Kentucky Educational Television in 1962 as a state-funded authority offered another educational advance in the state. Governor Combs appointed the first members of the KET board. Significantly, free textbooks were now being provided for all grades of the public schools. Services for blind, deaf, and other special-needs students in special education programs were improved. Consolidation of schools, including elimination of one-room and other small schools, continued. High school enrollment continued to increase, rising from 151,025 in 1959–1960 to 189,466 in 1962–1963 as the number of fully accredited "comprehensive" high schools increased. The latter included a wide range of subjects in their curricula, including academic, or college preparatory, coursework as well as vocational courses. The number of teachers with "emergency" certification also decreased.[51]

Federal money made an increasing difference in public school education in Kentucky. The National Defense Education Act in Title III allowed for the expenditure of matching federal and state funds for new science and math projects; included among eligible projects were the development of better instruction and teaching materials and opening up additional foreign language classes. My personal recollection of these years as a high school teacher is that for the first time we had spirit master and thermal copying machines, some specialists available for remedial work, and visual aid equipment. I was able to use an overhead projector in my classes.[52]

The reformers hailed closing down the remnants of the old trusteeship system in 1934, but the growing importance of the local school superintendent did little to eliminate politics, nepotism, and other abuses from local education in Kentucky. After 1920 county and city superintendents were elected by school boards and not by districtwide popular election. Coming from the old rural subdistricts or villages, or urban neighborhoods, school board members often looked after their local constituencies to the detriment of the remainder of the district, in effect displaying just as narrow a perspective as the old trustees did. Once a superintendent gained office, she or he could use the power of the position for good or ill. Often controlling the largest number of jobs in a county and consequently a considerable bloc of votes, these educational fiefdoms radiated throughout the commonwealth, but nowhere more than in the mountains. Harry M. Caudill, in *Night Comes to the Cumberlands*, published in 1962, excoriated the power of that region's school superintendents. "As a rule the school clique is interwoven with the courthouse political machine which spends funds and discreetly oversees the local management of the State Aid programs," Caudill averred. In Breathitt County, Marie R. Turner wielded a strong hand in league with her husband, Circuit Judge Ervine Turner, whom she succeeded as superintendent in 1931. Marie Turner became adept at gaining federal funds, and she often became a spokesperson for the poverty-stricken areas of eastern Kentucky. During the presidency of Lyndon B. Johnson, she obtained "War on Poverty" funds to build the ultramodern Lyndon B. Johnson Elementary School. (While I was teaching at Lees Junior College in the late sixties, my son attended the Head Start program one summer and my daughter attended the second and third grades at what was locally called "LBJ." They both received what my wife and I considered a good education.) Marie Turner also used her position to help her own family, though. When she resigned on June 22, 1969, her "administration was accused of conflict of interest and mismanagement of funds." Although she was charged with misusing federal dollars to "enhance her political power," nothing came of these allegations, and the Turners continued to be regional political powers.[53]

In contrast, the case against Carter County superintendent Heman McGuire became a cause célèbre for educational reformers in the state, beginning in late February 1960, after a local citizens group raised questions. They charged that McGuire manipulated school funds and personnel illegally. The *Courier-Journal* vilified McGuire in editorials and news exposés, asking, "How Many Other Kentucky Baronies [Are] Like Carter County?" According to inimitable Kentucky political observer John Ed Pearce,

> Heman McGuire could play a county school system the way a country man can play a banjo. He rewarded those who supported him with purchases, contracts, or jobs. School board members who opposed him were not reelected. Teachers who questioned his orders found themselves in remote and difficult schools, while those who did as they were told and asked no embarrassing questions got good assignments. When the teachers were given a holiday on election day so that they could work at the polls, they did not have to ask for whom they were working. Heman told them.

A friend and ally of State Superintendent Wendell Butler, McGuire worked with both political parties but primarily with Republicans. When Butler refused to investigate the charges against McGuire, Governor Combs asked the combative county superintendent to resign. McGuire refused, and Combs sent in Attorney General John Breckinridge to investigate. Breckinridge found that the county had actually paid for more buses than were in service. These charges of impropriety led to another investigation, which resulted in the dismissal of four Carter County school board members. Their state-appointed replacements fired McGuire. The episode ended in March 1963 with the conviction of McGuire for evading federal income taxes. He was sentenced to a year and a day in prison, fined $5,000, and forced to pay the Carter County school system "some $36,000 in misappropriated funds." Pearce, in his summation of this episode, was not sanguine. "It was still possible for a Heman McGuire to get control of a county school system and use it for his own power and profit. The superintendent of public instruction could still refuse to remove a McGuire, and still had so much power that he could defy the governor's reform efforts." Perhaps Thomas D. Clark best summed up the danger of McGuire and his ilk by declaring that in order for the commonwealth to advance educationally, "we must keep off the front pages of the daily press stories of political finagling and partisan activities by state superintendents, county superintendents, and school board members. Sadly, this has never been the case in the past."[54]

Fortunately, there were many more good than bad superintendents. Lee Kirkpatrick in Paris, Claude Farley in Pike County, and Talton K. Stone in Elizabethtown, among many others, represented the best class of school leaders. Even the better, honest superintendents understood the political nature of their positions. With a five-person board of education, often the shift of one or two votes could mean dismissal. Therefore, it was always paramount for a city or county superintendent to keep on top of the politics of his or her district. Sometimes superintendents recruited people to run for board seats. Farley lost his post in Pike County when in 1966 and 1968 new school board members were elected who opposed him. With experience as a school superintendent in two counties, Robertson and Jackson, John W. Smith admitted, "The politics was the thing I hated worst," but "politics is a necessary part of the process." Both superintendents and board members, he declared, are by nature "political animals." The five school board members, whether elected in county or independent districts, represented divisions, or subdistricts, and many acted much as the old trustees did. Forniss Park, a Madison County school board member from 1952 to 1964, recalled how important it was to keep alliances on the board. Early in his school board tenure, he seconded the vote for a new school that an older member proposed in his division, knowing that he would later need votes to build elementary schools needed in other parts of the county. Each time the schools were accepted by narrow 3-2 votes. Another time a board member verbally attacked him after a meeting for voting to build a new school in an area rather than refurbishing an older one that that member had an interest in. When Park displeased a superintendent with his votes, he had to defeat an opponent handpicked by the superintendent. Such conflicts and patterns were common all over the state.[55]

The quality of education in Kentucky has always been considered substandard compared to the rest of the nation and its students suspect in educational attainment. Yet the post–World War II era proved to be years of increasing expenditures for public school education and improvement of teacher salaries in the commonwealth. From only 51 percent in 1950, by the mid-1960s 94 percent of Kentucky teachers had a college degree. In the decade after 1964, "state aid to education more than quadrupled," a rate of increase greater than the national rate at that time. From 1963 to 1969, expenditures per student increased from 65 percent of the national average to 79 percent. However, it almost proved to be a case of "the faster we go the behinder we get." Even though it was a national leader in teacher salary increases, the commonwealth ranked forty-second overall nationally in 1968 and slid to forty-sixth in 1976 before rebounding to fortieth place in 1978. Educational attainment still floundered. In 1970 Kentucky "stood last in median years of schooling (9.9 years versus the U.S. average of 12.1) and tied for forty-eighth in the years of high school completed." Ten years later, the state "ranked last in the nation in the percentage of high school graduates (53.1 percent as opposed to the national average of 66.3 percent)." As State Historian James C. Klotter characterized this era, "the state cowered at or near the bottom in almost all educational categories."[56]

Individual experiences varied widely, however, and there were always good places to learn and grow, even in the small schools. Jackie Couture moved from tiny Glencoe in Gallatin County to Fresno, California, in the middle of the school year, transferring to a seventh-grade class. "The first day of school my English teacher asked me to read aloud," she said. "When I finished the boy in front of me turned around and asked [incredulously] where I learned to read. The teacher immediately sent me to the office and had me transferred to Honors English class. There wasn't an honors math class, so in the regular math class I tutored other students while my teacher taught me Algebra." Couture recalled having good teachers in the Glencoe elementary school, which had only four classrooms, where classes were combined for grades one through six. Was it necessary to have a full-service library? "Our school library consisted of a cupboard with doors about sixteen feet long in the cafeteria. Many of the books were biographies and other nonfiction titles and by the time I left Glencoe Elementary I think I had read everything in their library. I hear all the time about how poor Kentucky's educational system is, but in my case, I got an elementary education much superior to that of many California students," Couture concluded.[57]

The post–World War II one-room school experience could also be quite positive for Kentucky elementary school students. Even though there was a concerted effort to consolidate small schools into larger ones, the Department of Education considered the one-room school still important. A 1947 bulletin, "Building a Program for the One-Teacher School," emphasized grouping of students and—characteristic of the times—stressed Bible teaching. "Groups could be multi-age and multi-grade," said the experts in this bulletin. Particularly eastern Kentucky mountain counties and the more rural areas of the state continued to have most of these schools in the postwar period. One postwar one-room-school teacher in rural Pike County explained how she got the most out of her students. "My philosophy is I loved my students," explained Lola Doan Tackett. "I loved them and they knew it, and they returned it." There were always plenty of critics of small rural schools, particularly in Appalachia. Jack E. Weller in *Yesterday's People* and John Fetterman in *Stinking Creek* echoed Harry Caudill's bleak picture of the educational landscape in eastern Kentucky.[58]

Though often viewed with the nostalgia of "yesteryear," the combination of an inquisitive student and a competent teacher worked just as well in the one-room school as in the larger consolidated schools. At the end of World War II, Adell English Martin attended a one-room school at Stice in rural Marshall County, near where her father labored on the construction of Kentucky Dam. Her father had attended the same school. The school was much like her home, having a pot-bellied stove, an outhouse, and a well as the source of water. "There was no play equipment and no supervised play, so we'd make up our own games," Martin recalled. "I was the only student in the first grade that year. I remember standing in front of all the students to recite the alphabet and other assignments. I don't recall ever feeling afraid or unhappy at school. That 'one room school' was an extension of a loving and caring community." Martin admitted to learning one of "life's lessons" when she was enticed one day during recess to take a puff from a homemade pipe filled with tobacco. "I remember getting choked and coughing and to this day I have never taken another puff of any kind of smoke."[59]

Marshall Myers at the Oolite School in rural Meade County, in a company town on the Ohio River, also had a positive small-school experience in the 1950s. The school even had indoor restrooms, although drinking water had to be brought in. "We boasted a warm furnace below in the basement that the eighth-grade boys built a fire in before the chill of a cold, winter morning caught us unaware," he recalled. One of the highlights of school was when Mr. Grisso, the teacher, read aloud from children's classics like *Huckleberry Finn, Tom Sawyer,* and *Oliver Twist* "that for a few minutes took us away from that company town, and its safety, to places that soared with adventure, giving us a glimpse of life at other times and other locales. . . . The words of those books teased our imaginations and drew us into a time that seemed out of time, somewhere we had never traveled to before, somewhere that we conjured up in our own minds when he would read to us." Grisso also took his charges on nature hikes when the weather cleared in the spring. "We always were left with the impression that Mr. Grisso cared as much about this world outside of books as he cared about the books themselves."[60]

At the Story School House near "76 Falls" in Clinton County, Rodney B. Piercey also received a more-than-adequate education in the late fifties and early sixties. "Filled with well-engraved, old-styled chair-desks," the school had "a single coal-burning stove exposed in the middle of the room." "We never had more than one teacher for all eight grades and just keeping up with everybody was a full time job," Piercey said. "The teacher would regularly recruit 7th and 8th grade students to teach the lower grades reading and math. Older students were assumed to take some responsibility for educating the younger ones." Learning was enriched with spelling bees and game competitions with other schools. The coming of the bookmobile was a special event. Piercey, former provost of EKU, recalled: "I graduated from the 8th grade with two other students and was excited about going to high school. The idea that I would be going to town everyday [to Clinton County

High School] was as profound to me as going to college is to kids today." The practicality of Jerry Cook's one-room school experience in rural Knott County left him with a love of learning and teaching that gained expression in his career as a physics professor at Eastern Kentucky University. He was the winner of a 2008 Acorn Award.[61]

The experiences of Couture, Martin, Myers, Piercey, Cook, and thousands of other Kentuckians testified to the virtues and even the efficiency of the education they received in the one-room and other small schools of Kentucky after World War II. As these schools declined, other trends also modernized Kentucky education. From the early 1930s, the number of one-room, or one-teacher, schools decreased from more than five thousand to none in 1990.[62]

The gubernatorial election of 1963 brought out all the old antagonisms of the Kentucky body politic. Edward T. "Ned" Breathitt easily defeated former governor Chandler in an acrimonious Democratic primary in which the sales tax was the major issue. While Breathitt promised to continue the initiatives of the Combs administration, Republican nominee Louie B. Nunn vowed to "abolish" Governor Combs's "executive order concerning open housing." Chandler bolted his old party, carrying along his diehard supporters. "Segregationists in western Kentucky stayed home," according to historian Kenneth E. Harrell in *Kentucky's Governors*. Therefore, Breathitt narrowly defeated Nunn by thirteen thousand votes. Elected in an otherwise good year for the Democratic Party, Harry M. Sparks became the new state superintendent. A holder of a doctorate in education, Sparks had come up through the education ranks, with experience as a teacher, a principal, and a superintendent, and at the time of his election he was a professor at Murray State College. He continued the tradition that longtime educationists and KEA stalwarts, and usually loyal Democrats, won the state school superintendent post.[63]

Though a committed Democrat, Breathitt represented "a new breed" of southern politician who wanted to bridge the racial divide. Moreover, in his inaugural address he stressed "educational disadvantage" as being the biggest factor in keeping Kentucky from progressing like the rest of the nation. Breathitt's first legislative session proved to be rancorous, and there was little to show for it except improving teachers' benefits and the passage of a $176 million bond issue to be sent to the people. Through all of this, Lieutenant Governor Harry Lee Waterfield and his ally, former governor Happy chandler, contested most issues, even opposing the bond issue, which passed 3-1 in a state referendum. With federal matching dollars, the bond issue money was used chiefly for highway construction; a limited amount went to education. To gain more of a voice in Frankfort, the KEA worked the legislative aisles and teachers staged a one-day walkout to emphasize their needs. The General Assembly responded by increasing teachers' salaries based on rank and experience.[64]

The Breathitt administration generally followed a progressive racial course. In 1966 Breathitt signed the state Civil Rights Act, whose directness and clarity contrasted with the usual obfuscations produced by Kentucky's southern neighbors at that time. Meanwhile, integration of Kentucky public schools slowly built momentum. Two school systems as diverse as Somerset and Paris desegregated. In 1963 Paris began integration by bringing four black students into the formerly all white Paris High School. The next year all-black Paris Western High School closed and its students all transferred into Paris High. As happened in many places, black males were readily accepted if they were good athletes. Paris resident Melva Fields recalled that at first other black students were ignored, but slowly things changed. "By the mid-sixties, most of Kentucky's black students no longer attended all-black schools, though a few schools in the state remained all-white," according to historian George C. Wright. "In the school year 1964–65, 95.2 percent of the school districts had integrated." The Shelby County, Graves County, Montgomery County, Glasgow, and Mount Sterling school districts dragged their feet, sometimes sending their black students to other districts. As happened in most school systems, the Shelby County district assigned black teachers to library or remedial positions after the closing of the all-black schools. In Lexington, school officials received an upbraiding from the U.S. Office of Education in 1966 for the slow pace of integration in that central Kentucky city. If slowly and with some timidity, integration was continuing in the Commonwealth of Kentucky. In 1965, 40 of the 200 school districts in the commonwealth had no "biracial" student bodies, or had so few blacks that black students were sent to other districts.[65]

If black schools were being closed and their students slowly but surely integrated, the same could not be said for black teachers and administrators. At first, many black teachers believed their positions would be folded into the integration process as their schools closed. Apparently, educationists at the state level had given little thought to integrating faculties. By the late fifties, the situation had become so acute that the NAACP began to file lawsuits and make the inequity publicly known. Even in Louisville, where integration proceeded under the guidance of Superintendent Omer Carmichael, the strategy appeared to be to just ignore the plight of black teachers. Carmichael, without any data for his claims, explained that black teachers were not as well trained as white teachers. Actually, statewide, black teachers had, on average, higher levels of training. All the while, Louisville and other school systems across the state hired white teachers on emergency certificates before retaining or employing black teachers with certification. Black teachers with tenure had a better chance of keeping their jobs, but often they had to go to court to retain their positions. When confronted by black Louisville high school teacher Lyman Johnson at a school board meeting about the failure to hire African American teachers, Carmichael, obviously frustrated by being questioned, blurted out, "I'm through with you," according to the black press.[66]

When something is gained, something is often lost. While Adam Fairclough, in *A Class of Their Own: Black Teachers in the Segregated South*, also decried the initial loss of teaching positions that blacks suffered in the South during the earliest days of desegregation, he understood that the closing of black schools represented a serious challenge to the black community. In the days before integration of public and private housing, blacks experienced a meaningful sense of place in their churches, businesses, and schools. When the schools were taken away, part of the underpinning of the African American sense of community was eroded. Without integration of black teachers, particularly black males, African American students in primarily white school systems also lost valuable role models. The merging of black teacher associations into their larger white counterparts, such as the folding of the Kentucky Teachers Association into the KEA in 1957, also diminished blacks' control over their affairs. Just as there is generally a sense of nostalgia and loss in mostly white, small communities and rural areas when schools are closed because of consolidation, many black Kentuckians reacted with sadness to the loss of their schools. Fairclough declared that while the quest to follow the law of the land may have been well-founded and democratic, "the closure of so many black high schools, on the other hand, was cruel and unnecessary. The malice of white southerners, the insensitivity of the federal government, and the fixation of liberal integrationists on percentages and quotas all conspired, inadvertently, to destroy something valuable. Denied even symbolic recognition of their worth, the black high schools disappeared leaving scarcely any physical trace, their existence preserved only in the memories and reunions of former students and teachers." If this appears a bit strong, it comes from a realization that integration of education, with blacks still living in segregated housing communities, did not integrate society. Did black children receive a better education than they would have received in their old schools? Or were they pawns of sociological experimentation?[67]

Analyses of desegregation in Kentucky, particularly from 1964 through 1968, indicated that one of the greatest failures came not with integration of students but with blending black teachers into the school systems of Kentucky. Though Kentucky was far ahead of the majority of southern states in school desegregation, a "black gap" in teacher integration persisted well into the latter part of the twentieth century. The largest towns and cities, particularly Louisville, had the largest numbers of black students and teachers. For example, Louisville had 26 percent of the total number of black teachers in the commonwealth. The problem in integrating teachers into the school systems reflected the continuing racial mores of the commonwealth. White parents, as well as most white administrators, were uneasy with having black teachers in charge of integrated classes, even those with substantial numbers of black students. Integration of faculties generally proceeded slightly better in the elementary schools, but the tendency was for the black teachers to become assistant librarians. The Kentucky Council on Human Relations protested the loss of black teachers. Although KRS 161.800 required that school boards "give preference to teachers on continuing contracts and to teachers who have greater seniority," the public schools' form of tenure, some black teachers lost their jobs outright. After passage of the 1964 Civil Rights Act, those Kentucky school districts that had not desegregated did so with urging from the U.S. Department of Education.[68]

Some black teachers who lost their jobs in Kentucky went to other states or dropped out of the profession entirely. In Louisville, Superintendent Carmichael dismissed black teachers and hired white replacements. If not for the stand of Lyman Johnson, investigations by the *Louisville Defender* (the local African American newspaper), and pressure from civil rights groups and officials in Frankfort, who moved only after federal pressure, little would have changed in the commonwealth's largest city. Title VI of the 1964 Civil Rights Act prohibited the distribution of federal money to any institution that practiced racial discrimination, which included teacher-hiring practices. Finally, the State Board of Education declared on December 16, 1964, that all schools must comply with *Brown v. Board of Education*. Putting teeth into the order, the state board used the Minimum Foundation as a lever to force compliance. The next year the numbers of blacks "placed on desegregated faculties nearly doubled." The nine largest school districts in the state had the largest numbers of black teachers and black students. From 1954 to 1968 the number of black teachers increased in the "Big Nine," while the numbers of black teachers decreased in the other districts. The conclusions of a paper by Linda Cornett are striking: "From 1955 to 1968, the number of black teachers across the state increased by some *90* teachers or 6 percent, but the number of black students increased by 60 percent. What is disturbing is the fact that while there were 90 'new' black teachers in the state, the "Big Nine" had *increased* their black employment by some *370* teachers. All of the other school districts in Kentucky (189) had *reduced* their black teachers by *49 percent* from

1955 to 1968." When I taught at Harrodsburg High School in 1962–1963, there were no black faculty members, although the school had a substantial number of black students.[69]

Economically, the Breathitt years were prosperous ones for the average Kentuckian, except for "the poverty of Appalachia," and the state coffers appeared full. During the second meeting of the General Assembly of the Breathitt administration, teachers again received raises. Republican Louie B. Nunn, who had narrowly lost to Breathitt in 1963, won his party's primary by again going for the viscera; he attacked opponent Marlow Cook as a "'liberal, former New Yorker,' from the urban area [Louisville], then struck out at what he saw as Cook's weakest point, his Catholic religion." Democrat Chandler supported Nunn. Promising he would never raise taxes, Nunn won rather easily over Democrat Henry Ward, while Democrats swept other offices, including the lieutenant governor position, where Wendell H. Ford was elected. Wendell P. Butler won this third and last term as state superintendent in his cycle of political "musical chairs." Like other "southern" states, Kentucky "was turning Republican," and presidential candidate Richard Nixon carried the commonwealth the following year.[70]

With a revenue shortfall, Nunn faced the dilemma of either drastically cutting the budget he had inherited or raising taxes. To his credit, Nunn accepted the necessity of increasing the sales tax from three to five cents, often referred to as "Nunn's Nickel." "He knew he was cutting his own throat politically," said *Courier-Journal* editor David Hawpe, who praised Nunn for making the hard decisions that others might have avoided. Although racked by a continuing racial divide, the 1968 riots in Louisville, and the trauma of the Vietnam War, which included a student riot that ended with the burning of the old ROTC building at the University of Kentucky in 1970, the state generally prospered during the tumultuous years of President Richard Nixon. Nunn took strong action against rioters, calling in the National Guard.[71]

There were numerous interest groups clamoring for a voice in the late 1960s and early 1970s, and public school teachers were among them. Beginning in 1951, teachers could elect a delegate for each fifty members, giving even smaller districts better representation at the annual delegate assembly of KEA. The challenge of the Kentucky Federation of Teachers in the larger urban areas added to the urgency for KEA to change its nature. During the Nunn years, the KEA's domination by administrators and the "old boys" network in Frankfort continued to operate as classroom teachers organized themselves into political action committees. In effect, Kentucky teachers over this decade and later chose to make KEA their voice, and in rejecting the leadership of KFT, an affiliate of the American Federation of Teachers, opted for a professional interest group over unionization. Though accused by its detractors of being a "union," KEA took this route along with other state teachers' associations. Some of this change was in response to the influence of the Louisville Federation of Teachers, an affiliate of the AFT, which was a labor union affiliated with the AFL-CIO. During the Nunn administration, KEA raised its dues to five dollars a year and added a UniServ Program to assist teachers in eleven district offices across the state.[72]

Since the late 1950s, the National Education Association had been planning for "collective bargaining," or professional negotiation, in response to the challenge of the American Federation of Teachers. Kentucky teachers began to talk about professional negotiation, particularly in areas of the state that had strong unions, setting up conflict between KEA and the Kentucky School Boards Association and the Kentucky Association of School Administrators. In 1970, during the meeting of Nunn's last legislative session, teachers staged another "strike," to influence the governor and the General Assembly. KEA executive director Marvin Dodson and the old KEA establishment opposed the strike, in which an estimated 25,000 classroom teachers out of about 30,000 total walked out. Lawsuits finally brought all such work stoppages to a halt. In the end, education got an additional $16 million out of $18 million put "up for grabs" in Nunn's budget presentation. Hard feelings were present on both sides as teachers believed they had not been fully represented and were forced to take such action. Administrators, the governor, most legislators, and many in the general public remained fearful of the newfound power of classroom teachers. All things considered, education prospered during the Nunn years. The sustained revenue of "Nunn's Nickel," along with an increase in the motor vehicle licensing fee, increased the state revenue, and overall, $82 million went into teachers' salaries and public education; higher education received an increased appropriation of 34 percent. The University of Louisville came into the state system, and with Nunn's influence, Northern Kentucky University developed from a community college into a regional university.[73]

The Nunn years also witnessed yet another study of public education in the commonwealth. In January 1967, KEA published a landmark study of the first years of the Minimum Foundation Program along with its recommendations for the future. The study originated in a December 12, 1964, resolution passed by the KEA delegate assembly. "The Committee for the Study of the Foundation Program" included a study committee, an executive committee, a citizens' advisory committee, a technical advisory committee, and consultants. In the latter group were educationists Edgar L. Morphet, retired from the University of California, Berkeley, and W. Monfort Barr, of Indiana University, as well as several Kentuckians. The researchers-writers-coordinators on the project included Kern Alexander and Charles Whaley of Louisville. Several important school superintendents across the state, one of them Richard Van Hoose from Jefferson County, sat on committees along with higher education representatives Robert R. Martin of Eastern Kentucky University and Robert Mills of Georgetown College. Employing the expertise of these educationists as well as a survey questionnaire sent to select groups, national and state studies, and statistics, the KEA-sponsored group came up with an interesting, though predictable, study and set of recommendations.[74]

Although the resulting report, *Beyond the Minimum*, declared that educational progress had been made since 1954, including a rapid decrease in the number of one-room schools; higher certification of teachers, 94 percent then having a "bachelor's degree or higher"; and other positive signs, much remained to be done to bring Kentucky education up to national standards. Kentucky still lagged badly in relation to national averages, and, tellingly, the report stated the crux of the problem succinctly: "The economy of a local school district determines its ability to support its share of the cost of its school system." State and federal programs, including Head Start, the Economic Opportunity Act, and federal elementary and secondary legislation, could not do it all. Statistics did not lie. Overall, the state averaged 71 percent of the national personal income average. In a comparison of nearby states, Illinois had twice the personal income per capita of Kentucky. The commonwealth ranked forty-first nationally in per-capita property tax revenue, with the national average more than double that of Kentucky ($111.02 compared to $47.54). Kentucky remained a relatively poor state, particularly eastern Kentucky and the still mostly rural counties. Seen another way, Kentucky ranked forty-eighth nationally "in percent of ninth graders graduating from high school."[75]

This KEA study claimed that although the number of schools had decreased from 4,241 to 2,057 in about ten years, there were still too many and more consolidation was warranted. The foundation formula was based on average daily attendance (ADA) in classroom units. (Those statistics were kept by homeroom teachers in an attendance book with a picture of the state bird, the Kentucky Cardinal, on the cover. The book was [not always humorously] referred to by teachers when I was teaching in high school as "the bird book.") *Beyond the Minimum* also emphasized that the most "desirable characteristics of local financial support of schools are missing in Kentucky"; that is, most school districts did not receive nearly enough local property taxes to adequately support their schools. Most property owners paid only a small percentage of the value of their property. Then the state's highest court threw the whole school taxing system into turmoil. In 1965 the Court of Appeals ruled in *Russman v. Luckett* that real property had to be assessed at

100 percent of its true value. Governor Breathitt, under great pressure, called the General Assembly into special session and won "a reduction in property tax rates in proportion to the increased assessment ratio," called a "rollback." In effect, taxes increased only minimally and most of the additional revenue went to the public schools. Local school districts had to rely too much on bonded indebtedness and paid high interest rates, particularly for capital improvements. Increasing needed funds for special education, vocational education, and transportation stretched school revenues even more. Statewide, 90 percent of the school districts were so poor as to be unable to "operate even a minimum program without supplementation from state revenues." Further, Kentucky had too many small counties among the ridiculous total number of 120 for such a small state. Over the years, the process of creating new counties to honor officials and placate local "elites" had broken up larger areas into smaller ones that had too little taxable land to support public schools. For example, the creation of Lee County in 1870 reduced the size of Owsley County by one-half. The latter ended up with fewer resources, poorer land, and a smaller tax base for the support of education and local administration. Moreover, county and independent districts statewide were not imposing other permissible taxes, such as poll taxes and building funds, to raise revenues.[76]

Admitting that the Minimum Foundation Program had turned out to be precisely that, accentuating the "minimum," *Beyond the Minimum* called for much more effort to improve the public schools of Kentucky. Better training and salaries for teachers ranked at the top of the wish list. "Capital outlay" included raising the classroom-unit expenditure from $600 to $1,400 per year and initiating kindergarten classes for all districts. Much more funding would be needed for transportation and to reduce pupil-teacher ratios from 27:1 to 25:1. The KEA report also repeated the consolidation mantra as a necessary move to improve education efficiency in the commonwealth. With a ranking of forty-second in the nation in classroom time, Kentucky needed to extend the school year to 180 days out of a total of 190. Finally, *Beyond the Minimum* argued, the restriction on local school tax rates imposed by the 1965 special session on property taxes should be lifted and all available revenue from occupational, utilities, and excise taxes should be used.[77]

The recommendations of *Beyond the Minimum* had far-reaching effects in the long run, but not in the short run, certainly not in the administration of Governor Nunn. The Kentucky political caravan ground forward with the end of the Nunn-Butler years and the coming of a new election in 1971. Former governor Bert T. Combs tried to resume his political career after serving as a federal judge. For Kentucky education he promised, if elected, to raise revenue and push for professional negotiation measures. By a surprising margin, Lieutenant Governor Wendell Ford defeated "his former mentor" Governor Combs in the 1971 Democratic gubernatorial primary and went on to defeat a weak Republican opponent in the general election. Lyman V. Ginger, dean of the University of Kentucky College of Education from 1956 to 1966, won the state superintendent post, having easily defeated his Republican opponent. As the only Kentuckian who had served as president of the National Education Association, Ginger had a national reputation as well as being a traditional KEA insider; he had been president of KEA in 1957. Ford, who seemed ready to go to work, said, "Winning an election is like nothing else. . . . And the day after the election you get right to work, because you don't want any of that adrenalin to go to waste."[78]

Throughout Kentucky's history, its schools had labored to keep up with national trends and norms. In addition, a wide variation in educational opportunity existed across the state. Louisville and other urban areas always had longer school terms and generally had better public schools, both black and white, than other parts of the state. The county schools struggled into the post–World War II period. In no place was education more problematical than in Appalachia, as poverty, out-migration, low local tax revenues, transportation problems, and sometimes corrupt school officials worked against the possibility that mountain youth would have the same opportunities as other Kentucky children. As explained in chapter 5, in the early twentieth century settlement-school institutions filled some of the gap and continued into the early post–World War II years. Moreover, other groups such as the Council of the Southern Mountains, headed by Perley F. Ayers, worked to improve education in the 1950s. Building on the promise of President John F. Kennedy to work on the problems of Appalachia, President Lyndon B. Johnson visited eastern Kentucky in April 1964. The administration of Governor Bert T. Combs, a native of Clay County, also drew renewed attention to the problems of the area. Studied to an extreme, Appalachia became a centerpiece of the War on Poverty of the Great Society programs of the Johnson and later administrations. The Volunteers in Service to America, Appalachian Volunteers, and the Appalachian Regional Commission, among other groups, focused public and private efforts to address the problems of the region. Outsiders were not always welcomed into eastern Kentucky, touching off conflicts with local power elites. Already a champion of his region, U.S. Representative Carl D. Perkins became even more influential and active when he assumed the chairmanship of the House Education and Labor Committee in 1967.[79]

Improving education in the mountains of Kentucky as well as in other areas, particularly the larger urban areas, became an objective of the War on Poverty, as experts in several social fields developed a view that a "culture of poverty" prohibited the children of poor families, both black and white, from benefiting from the gains of modernity. Therefore, the problems of inner-city youth and those of the hollows in eastern Kentucky were thought to be basically the same. Michael Harrington, author of *The Other America*, was joined by others in defining the problem, while such programs in the Office of Economic Opportunity as the Jobs Corps appeared to be quick fixes. The Appalachian Regional Commission (ARC) adopted the strategy of applying most of its aid and influence to improving urban Appalachia rather than the rural areas. The ARC combined with other government programs and local initiatives to lower the poverty rate in Appalachia. It was the cities of Appalachian Kentucky that demonstrated the most change, while the rural areas were still mired in poverty. But everyone realized that a change in education from top to bottom was needed for long-term success. Individuals who came from outside to help often ran into local resistance and did not understand mountain culture. One critic even argued that mountain-born teachers are better able to teach in the region. "Teaching in familiar circumstances provides a better understanding of students," claimed Constance Elam, a Pike County native.[80]

In the post–World War II era, the old eastern Kentucky mountain settlement schools went into an eclipse as public school education and transportation improved. Alice Lloyd evolved first into a junior college and then a four-year college. By the early twenty-first century, the Annville Institute, Hazel Green Academy, Henderson Settlement School, Kingdom Come Settlement School, and Stuart Robinson School had closed, although some settlement institutions still served as community centers. Hindman Settlement School provided education for special needs, including a program for children with dyslexia. Pine Mountain Settlement School ran environmental education programs. Red Bird Mission School, Oneida Baptist Institute, Riverside Christian Training School, and Mt. Carmel High School still operated as K-12 schools into the first decade of the new century.[81]

Another set of schools that had filled an important gap in Kentucky elementary-secondary education also changed in the post–World War II period. Several private/sectarian schools, Cumberland, Campbellsville, Union, and a few others, evolved from primary-secondary schools into junior colleges and then into four-year colleges. With the exception of the Model Laboratory School at Eastern Kentucky University, all the state institutions of higher learning closed their demonstration schools. Most of these schools had been of great importance when normal school education was in its infancy in the early twentieth century. Berea College, a nonsectarian school with a long heritage of educating mountain youth, began a process of changing part of its mission in the early 1960s. Its Training School and Foundation

School became increasingly expensive to maintain and had in reality outlived their usefulness in training elementary and secondary students. Berea College officials had to decide whether to join either the Madison County school system or that of Berea, which itself faced the likelihood of being forced into a merger with the county system. With the backing of President Francis S. Hutchins, who wanted to finalize the issue before he retired, negotiations proceeded with the city system. In the end, Berea College's K-12 programs and the Berea City Schools merged, with each accepting a sizable bond issue in order to build a new school. Berea College, like all of the other colleges in the state, now depended on placing teacher-education students in the public schools for their practical student teacher training.[82]

The Ford-Ginger years (1971–1975) continued what appeared to be the same old story, making progress but never enough to catch up with national averages. Education did well in the governor's budgets. Although Ford vetoed the first statewide collective bargaining bill for teachers passed by the legislature, several of the largest urban school systems were already in the early stages of professional negotiations. Ginger worked hard to increase the number of vocational schools in the state. Even with the energy crisis beginning, Kentucky prospered, particularly with renewed emphasis on coal mining. An adept politician, Ford resigned just after his second legislative session as governor and rather easily defeated incumbent Senator Marlow Cook. Lieutenant Governor Julian Carroll took over for Ford and won a full term in his own right in the 1975 gubernatorial election.[83]

Superintendent Ginger cooperated fully with Governor Ford but had his own agenda, which was that of KEA, for improving education in the commonwealth. The General Assembly approved funds for one hundred pilot programs for kindergarten units in the state, the beginning of such classes in most schools. Title IX, passed by Congress in 1972, forced schools to begin offering school sports for females, if they were not already doing so, or lose federal aid; it also prohibited sex discrimination in hiring. It took lawsuits to equalize opportunities for girls in such sports as basketball. Renewed efforts to change the 1891 Kentucky Constitution to make the office of state superintendent of public instruction appointive failed again in the general election of 1973. Meanwhile, the momentum of educational change built because of the growing federal influence. New federal laws and regulations changed education in the state. In 1973 federal legislation and regulations broadened the role of vocational schools. The federal Rehabilitation Act of that year expanded opportunities for handicapped individuals. The next year, a class-action lawsuit on behalf of exceptional children pushed local districts to offer more opportunities for the handicapped. In 1974 state legislation provided for home instruction for children who could not attend the public schools, and the next year a new federal law, the federal Education for All Handicapped Children Act, made this form of education free. Almost all of the federal legislation bore the imprint of the efforts of Congressman Perkins, who never lost touch with his district. Perkins also worked to get appropriations to fund vocational schools through the Appalachian Regional Development Act.[84]

Education advocates in the 1972 meeting of the General Assembly asked Superintendent Ginger to initiate yet another study of education in the commonwealth. As part of this process, the Office of Research and Planning in the State Department of Education sifted through more than one hundred thousand questionnaires filled out by "thoughtful citizens." More than a thousand high school and college students added their own ideas to the study, and ten citizen conferences were held across the state. The goals of the study, published in 1973, included three general areas: general education; economic understanding; and creative, constructive, and critical thinking. Governor Carroll appointed the Governor's Task Force on Education in 1976, with Don W. Stephens as executive director. Though no longer state superintendent, having been succeeded by James B. Graham in the election of 1975, Ginger helped lead the task force. Two years later, during the second biennial session of the General Assembly under Governor Carroll, the legislature passed the School Improvement Act in 1978. According to Ginger, Superintendent Graham "was not on the best of terms with the governor [Carroll]. . . . As a result, he was not included in the deliberations that led to the development of the School Improvement Act." The new law encouraged the development of "academic excellence," which mandated for the first time statewide testing for grades three, five, seven, and ten. Governmental agencies, such as the Legislative Research Commission, the Advisory Committee for Educational Improvement, and the State Board of Education, were to use the results for "long-range planning for academic excellence." More than $270 million for public education was in the next budget. Governor Carroll had all the advantages of an improving economy, increasing sales tax receipts, and momentum for educational progress. And he ruled with an iron hand; his foes named him "Emperor Julian." Teachers' salaries were increased substantially in the commonwealth, and the statewide average rose from forty-sixth to thirty-eighth place nationally. The free-textbook program was expanded to include all grades, K-12. The newly created School Building Authority was given the responsibility of funding badly needed schools in the poorer districts. However, state-mandated collective bargaining for teachers, or professional negotiations, failed again to gather much support, and a bill died in committee after the Kentucky School Boards Association adopted a resolution flatly against any such measure.[85]

Kentucky school districts continued to consolidate at an ever-increasing rate. With the county district as the basic district within which an independent town or city district existed, the trend was for the smaller towns to merge their districts with the county districts, particularly as the suburbs grew. Small independent districts could continue to exist only if the local taxpayers remained committed to fund their schools. Small independent school districts including Burgin in Mercer County, Augusta in Bracken County, Eminence in Henry County, and Silver Grove in Campbell County, as well as a few others continued to serve students into the twentieth-first century.

An American institution faded quickly in the late twentieth century as the one-room schools continued to be merged and consolidated into larger elementary schools. While James M. Gifford claimed in a piece in the *Kentucky Encyclopedia* that the last one-room school in the commonwealth closed in 1989 in Perry County, Daniel Tysen Smith in a University of Kentucky dissertation conducted a case study of what he considered to be the last such school at Jacobs Creek in Floyd County. "The climate of Jacobs Creek School was a warm, open and caring one on the part of all participants," he observed. Older students tutored the younger ones, there were few discipline problems, and the children played well together. However, although the school appeared to be functioning well, with students learning and apparently well-adjusted to the environment, when they graduated from the eighth grade they did not do well in high school; most of them dropped out. Most pupils were one or two years behind "appropriate grade levels." In July 1987, the Floyd County School District closed Jacobs Creek School. Because only nine students had attended there the previous year, the superintendent said the cost per pupil was "just much too high" and the students would benefit from "the multitude of programs offered at the consolidated schools, which just weren't possible at Jacobs Creek." With the closure of Jacobs Creek School, yet another hub of an Appalachian community had been lost. Improving transportation routes and increased funding, the growth of urban areas, and increasing stress on accreditation and evaluation intensified the pressure to merge and consolidate schools into larger and larger units. Consolidation of schools continued to be a much-debated issue in the late twentieth century, but one that seemed unstoppable.[86]

Added to the consolidation decisions in Kentucky in the 1970s was the increasing pressure to comply with court-ordered desegregation. Louisville–Jefferson County school issues had been simmering for years even without the challenge of racial integration. For example, there had always been the issue of taxation, because the county's lower property taxes pulled residential and industrial development from the city. Both districts tried to retain as many distilleries as possible because these were lucrative sources of revenue.

Louisville annexed more land, such as Shively in 1942, at the expense of the county. In the forties, many county students still wanted to attend the Louisville high schools, and county officials were upset when the city system raised its tuition rates for out-of-district students. After World War II, the Louisville system still seemed supreme, having more money and students than the county. In 1950 Louisville had about 45,000 students and there were about 16,000 in the county. However, merger talks between city superintendent Omer Carmichael and county superintendent Richard Van Hoose took place from time to time. While the League of Women Voters supported merger, Louisville mayor Charles Farnsley actively opposed it during his term (1948–1953). Because city teachers made higher salaries, they did not want to merge. Just when both boards appeared to be on the same page, fully supporting merger, Carmichael died unexpectedly in 1960, the same year the General Assembly took no action on a plan of enabling merger legislation. Farnsley, meanwhile, continued to oppose merger vehemently. As the Louisville city schools declined in students and had increasing money problems, the Jefferson County system grew, with many schools operating on double sessions in the 1960s. A "Charter Committee" of the mid-1960s, representing city and county leaders, also pushed merger in the state legislature, only to be disappointed. Every time merger seemed about to occur, something broke the momentum.[87]

Beginning with World War II, Lexington and Fayette County rapidly grew in population and developed into a commercial center in central Kentucky. The county system doubled in students from 1950 to 1960 while the numbers of students in the Lexington system also increased. Voters in the county resisted increasing taxes to improve their schools, forcing officials to shut down the kindergarten program in 1960. After Guy Potts became county superintendent, a well-planned effort brought about an increase in the school levy. The federal Civil Rights Act of 1964 forced both school districts to renew integration efforts. By 1966 Fayette County had won approval for its desegregation efforts. However, the city of Lexington continued to maintain neighborhood schools and faced increasing federal and state pressure to fully integrate. In July 1967 the Kentucky Court of Appeals mandated a merger of the two systems with Potts remaining as superintendent.[88]

The newly merged Fayette system followed the usual pattern of closing black schools. "Deep resentment in the black community" resulted from the closing of the Dunbar Senior High School, an African American landmark, and dispersing its students among four other high schools. Even when integrated, black teachers received less pay than their white counterparts. While integration of high schools appeared to satisfy federal officials, elementary and middle schools in Fayette County remained predominantly all black or all white. At first, Potts and the Fayette Board offered a "freedom of choice" option, which had been tried in other "southern" school systems, including Louisville. But very few students and teachers took this option. Meanwhile, in 1971 the U.S. Supreme Court ruled in *Swann v. Charlotte-Mecklenburg* that district judges could use "mathematical ratios as a remedial tool" in integration, which soon translated into busing both black and white students.[89]

Robert Jefferson and other black parents in Lexington were able to gain the support of Robert A. Sedler, a University of Kentucky law professor and chair of the Kentucky Civil Liberties Union, to lead their legal challenge. In *Robert Jefferson et al. v. Fayette County Board of Education*, federal district judge Mac Swinford followed the dictates of the *Swan* decision and asked that the Fayette board develop a plan to integrate rapidly so that no schools would have "below 15 or above 30 percent enrollment of black students." Although two members of the school board opposed the decision, Superintendent Potts and the school staff worked to comply with the court order. Opposition came both from whites, who did not want any integration at all, and from blacks, who understood that their children would face the most change and be forced to travel the longest distances to new schools. Several black schools were closed, the rationale being the generally poor conditions of the older buildings. No violence accompanied these new orders to integrate by using busing as the primary means of transporting students to schools away from their neighborhoods. The "good-faith" efforts of the Fayette board did not create a perfect system. Nevertheless, David L. Wolfford concluded: "The system has not fully met Swinford's ideal, but it has integrated to a level that would never have resulted without the suit, without the order, or without the unpopular plan."[90]

The challenge of racial integration of the public schools continued to reverberate in the 1970s. By then most of the smaller school districts in the state had desegregated. Where the numbers of African American students were small, generally the task had been completed to the satisfaction of the courts and most advocacy groups, as well as of local citizens, black and white. A few school districts, such as Rockcastle County and Corbin for example, did not face integration because they had no black students. For many years Corbin was known as a "Sundown" community, owing to adamant, sometimes violent efforts to remain totally segregated. There are also other examples of completely white Kentucky communities. In the 1950s and early 1960s, Shively, a suburb of Louisville, remained totally white when efforts by Carl and Anne Braden to move in a black family in 1954 failed. Andrew and Charlotte Wade moved out after their house was dynamited. The larger urban areas of Lexington-Fayette County and Louisville-Jefferson County faced more turmoil because of large black populations.[91]

In Kentucky's most populous urban area, the path to integration proved to be troublesome. By the early 1970s, the Jefferson County system had overtaken the Louisville system in numbers. "White flight" to the suburbs of Jefferson County and, to a lesser extent, into the surrounding counties, took a toll on the Louisville system, draining the system of students as its tax base steadily eroded. Louisville and Jefferson County became the focal point of national attention again, just as in the mid-1950s, when Louisville had apparently quickly and painlessly desegregated. While there had been some initial success in desegregating the Louisville system under Carmichael in the mid-1950s, with black students doing most of the moving to previously all-white schools, "by 1968 90% of the city's students were attending schools predominantly black or white." Or, seen another way, "ten schools remained either all-black or all-white; in twenty-five others, over 95 percent of the students were of one race," according to *A New History of Kentucky*. As the Louisville system continued to decline in student population owing to white flight to the suburbs, the Jefferson County system ballooned. By the mid-seventies the Louisville school system had about 48,000 students, about 52 percent of them black, and the now-much-larger Jefferson County system had "only 4 percent blacks in its more than 95,000 students." The NAACP, the Kentucky Civil Liberties Union, and other groups filed lawsuits claiming that integration was being evaded in those districts.[92]

Integration of schools statewide did not occur in a vacuum. Although the schools in Louisville had apparently desegregated under Superintendent Carmichael's direction in the 1950s, historian George C. Wright maintained that the Derby City had a "reputation (which, of course, it never deserved) as a liberal community regarding race relations." In spite of passage of the Civil Rights Act in the Breathitt administration and passage of a "comprehensive Fair Housing Act" in 1968, the first in the South, violence broke out in the Parkland section of Louisville after the assassination of Dr. Martin Luther King Jr. that summer. The situation was calmed down only after Governor Nunn sent in the National Guard. Violence spread across Kentucky in the summer of 1968; two whites were killed near normally placid Berea in a confrontation between blacks and a white supremacy group. Kentucky and Kentuckians could not be isolated from the general turmoil sweeping America in the late sixties and early seventies. In May 1970, after the bombing of Cambodia, Governor Nunn called the National Guard onto the University of Kentucky campus following an antiwar demonstration.[93]

As the time approached for massive desegregation, many blacks in Louisville did not have a positive view of such change. Valerie Stringer, a student reporter in a 1969 article for the Russell Junior High newspaper, found that many of her interviewees were "against racial integration of Central [High

School]," the traditionally all-black school. One student said that if white students were forced to come to Central, "it would make the white kids feel that they were doing us blacks a favor," while another said she would quit school if Central were closed. After admitting both sides of the issue were emphatic in their views, Stringer urged, rather optimistically, "Let's get together. We are all the same under the skin, regardless of race, color, or creed." African American parent Betty Jo Manning maintained: "I am against busing children merely to achieve school integration, for there is a vast difference between integration and desegregation. Racial mixing does not automatically mean social acceptance or a better education for black people."[94]

After the early implementation of *Brown I* and *Brown II* and passage of federal and state civil rights legislation and an open-housing ordinance, Louisville in effect "resegregated": only a few (by one estimate, 150) black families moved into formerly all-white Louisville neighborhoods. As urban renewal wiped out old black neighborhoods, African American families had no choice but to seek admission into previously all-white areas. Whites left west Louisville and other areas after a block was "broken" by sometimes unscrupulous real estate "sharks" who reaped big profits. During the administration of Carmichael's successor, Samuel Noe, federal investigators argued, "There are vestiges of a dual school system in Louisville." By the time Noe resigned in 1969, Louisville had a student population of 53.3 percent white and 46.7 percent black. Three years later, the black student population surpassed the white for the first time in the Louisville system. Total enrollment continued to decline in the public schools as private and parochial education numbers increased. Noe's replacement, former Paducah superintendent Newman Walker, came to the troubled Derby City with a reputation for innovation and soon instituted the Focus-Impact program, trying to cut Louisville's horrendous dropout rate. All the while, efforts by the Jefferson County delegation to merge the two systems by legislative act of the General Assembly failed.[95]

This period of Kentucky history coincided with the ascendancy of conservatism as the administration of President Richard Nixon weakened the Health, Education, and Welfare Department (HEW), the arm of the federal government charged with enforcing school desegregation. Nixon's "Southern Strategy" was to go slow on civil rights to please Senator Strom Thurmond and his cohorts. Moreover, the chief executive voiced disapproval of enforced busing. Nixon had the opportunity to change the structure of the Supreme Court with the appointment of Warren Burger as the chief justice. The Supreme Court did take a more conservative turn, but not as far to the right as Nixon had hoped. More important, somewhat surprisingly, the Burger

Court did not radically alter the Warren Court's desegregation directives. Meanwhile, Galen Martin of the Kentucky Commission on Human Rights took the initiative by filing suit to disperse Jefferson County's Newburg School's African American enrollment and bring in white students.[96]

Robert A. Sedler, who had led the successful litigation desegregating the Fayette County school district, became the lead lawyer for the Kentucky Civil Liberties Union in the effort to remedy the Louisville-Jefferson school racial disparity. The KCLU began calling for cross-district busing for racial integration. From his post as a University of Kentucky professor, Sedler did not have to depend on either outside employment or funding as did other litigants. The Louisville system had two black school board members and a sympathetic superintendent in Walker; therefore many African Americans voiced concerns about merging with the predominantly white Jefferson County schools. Eventually, all the litigants, the KCLU, the NAACP, and the Kentucky Human Rights Commission, joined the same team and urged merger of the two districts to desegregate the Louisville and Jefferson County school systems.[97]

The busing of students, black and white, became the instrument to remedy the situation in Kentucky's largest metropolitan area, because housing patterns had not significantly changed. The Kentucky Human Rights Commission declared that integration in Louisville "failed—either by design or by lack of effort—to deliver on the promise of full student and faculty desegregation. The myth of 'neighborhood schools' has been put forward to conceal this basic failure." In *Newburg Area Council, Inc. v. Board of Education of Jefferson County* (1971), litigants initiated the push for integration. The Louisville–Jefferson County environment proved to be particularly contentious. Newburg School in Jefferson County and Central High School in Louisville "remained practically all black after city and county schools were desegregated in 1965." Both became the center of lawsuits in the Sixth U.S. Circuit Court, filed by integrationist interests with Sedler as the lead lawyer. U.S. District Judge James F. Gordon of the Western District of Kentucky became the focal point of the legal maneuvering on both sides of the issue. In 1973 he ruled that housing patterns rather than public school policies kept the local school districts segregated. Therefore, there could be no relief for the plaintiffs. The Sixth Circuit Court of Appeals in Cincinnati overturned Gordon, which almost everyone expected, in the summer of 1975 and "ordered him to implement a desegregation plan by the start of the fall term."[98]

Gordon took his role seriously, having said he received his "marching orders" from the Sixth Circuit. Although a judicial conservative, he attempted a group effort in adhering to the Sixth Circuit's determination to heed the direction of the Supreme Court. Other city-county districts, such as Charlotte-Mecklenberg in North Carolina, had been merged, and cross-district busing of students for racial integration had already been forced by federal court decree. Therefore, Gordon appeared to have very little choice. After both school districts produced proposed merger-desegregation plans, Gordon refused both the city's Plan A and the county's Plan C and ordered that his own Plan X be implemented as soon as possible, preferably for the opening of school in the fall of 1974. The situation became even more complicated when the U.S. Supreme Court in *Milliken v. Bradley* voted 5-4 that cross-district busing was not a legal remedy, sending the Louisville–Jefferson County case back to the Sixth Circuit in Cincinnati. Understanding that it would cease to exist if merged with the county, the city as an independent district tried but failed to get special legislation in the General Assembly to keep a semblance of city representation. More importantly, Superintendent Lyman Ginger got behind the merger issue, and the State Board of Education voted unanimously to merge the two systems beginning April 1, 1975. When the merged schools opened the fall of 1975, the personnel of the most recent years had changed; Jefferson County superintendent Richard Van Hoose had retired, Walker had gone off to Palo Alto, California, as school superintendent, and Sedler had taken a position at Wayne State University. The coming months were some of the most shameful as well as heroic in Kentucky history.[99]

The order to bus students in the merged Jefferson County system followed by a year the same kind of order in Boston, where there had been massive resistance, turmoil, and violence. Judge Gordon planned for about an 80 percent white to 20 percent black ratio in the merged schools. The county board continued to drag its feet as the summer of 1975 wore on. Black parents worried about the safety of their children as radical groups such as the KKK announced rallies. Organized labor, the Union Labor against Busing, Concerned Parents Incorporated, Citizens against Busing, Spirit of Seventy-Six, Stop Tyranny and Busing, Independent Parents and Taxpayers against Busing, and several other groups all came out against Gordon and his plan. Some antibusing advocates called for a boycott of schools while others recommended demonstrations. Efforts of the Jefferson County Board of Education to get a reprieve from the Supreme Court were rebuffed by Justices Lewis F. Powell Jr. and Harry F. Blackmun. The Sixth Circuit also denied a request for a delay.[100]

Southwest Jefferson County became a hotbed of protest against busing. Judge Gordon, fearing for the safety of schoolchildren and personnel, ordered that demonstrations for the opening day of school take place only at the Kentucky State Fairgrounds between the hours of 9:00 A.M. and 3:00 P.M. New county superintendent Ernest Grayson prepared for the opening of school on September 4, 1975, by purchasing 570 buses and hiring monitors. County Judge Todd Hollenbach did his part by preparing off-site jail holding facilities. On the opening day of school, protesters disobeyed Gordon's order and marched downtown; many white students stayed home. Minor protests took place at some schools, and black students were taunted the first few days. While most protestors only ranted and raved, some turned violent, burning three buses at Southern High School in Okolona, where police had to use teargas to disperse a mob. In that first week of busing, more than thirty police officers were injured, one struck in the eye with a fishing weight launched from a slingshot. National KKK leader David Duke came to Louisville, and Kentucky Klansmen marched. Things quieted somewhat when Governor Carroll sent in state policemen and nine hundred National Guard troops. Judge Hollenbach, Louisville mayor Harvey Sloane, and Judge Gordon cooperated in imposing more rules, and Gordon placed the buses under federal jurisdiction. During one point in this civil unrest, Judge Gordon later recalled, "I was absolutely in a rage . . . I was trembling," that "grown people would threaten little children, black or white." If things had not settled down as quickly as they did, Gordon claimed he was prepared to go to nearby Fort Knox and ask for federal troops. Gordon, Sloane, and the *Courier-Journal* became convenient targets for the antibusing advocates.[101]

Antibusing agitation lessened in intensity so that by mid-September the public schools reported attendance of over 80 percent. However, a well-planned boycott cut attendance again in October. Antibusing foes vilified Judge Gordon, burning him in effigy on more than one occasion. No amount of reasoning could persuade his foes that he was just following the law of the land and the dictates of the Sixth Circuit. The issue lingered into the fall as even Governor Carroll voiced his disapproval of busing generally. Carroll barely carried Jefferson County in the fall gubernatorial election but took the state handily in defeating his Republican opponent Robert Gable. For all the furor, dozens of marches, and acts of violence, eventually the schools got back to what they should have been doing, teaching students. Given his background, his inherent conservatism, Gordon stayed the course, even under all the constant threats on his life. Retired Louisville attorney Glenn Schilling, in a 2005 *Courier-Journal* interview, recalled that Gordon "was as cool as anyone could be. He knew exactly what his obligation was, and he was absolutely unswerving." Sedler said he "had the highest respect for his [Gordon's] ability and integrity." Gordon closed the Louisville–Jefferson County desegregation case in 1980, finding that his job had been completed. When a reporter asked for his assessment of his role, he characteristically replied: "Oh, with all modesty, I'd give myself an 'A.' I don't know of anybody that would do it any better than I did it."[102]

For those who were bused, both black and white, the reality of busing could be wrenching. After one year of busing, Jeanne McCutcheon put her son in a private school because he was being transported to an unkempt downtown elementary school. Steve Vest was bused from his home in southwest Jefferson County to what had been a mostly black Shawnee High School in his freshman year because his last name began with a "V." "I was interviewed by the *Courier-Journal* at the time and said that I saw going to Shawnee as a chance to meet people I might not normally meet. The result was someone driving through my parents' yard while screaming offensive names. This was quite an accomplishment since my parents lived on a court. I did meet people from other schools and other parts of town, but before any of us had a chance to develop any friendships—with blacks or whites—we were uprooted again," Vest recalled. City kids got transported often to better county school buildings and vice-versa. "When I returned to my home school [Doss] as a sophomore," Vest continued,

> many of my friends replaced me at Shawnee. This game of musical chairs was hardest on the Bs and Fs, who were bused during their junior and senior years. . . . It's hard enough in high school to fit in, but when you find your place—and then are removed from it—it's almost impossible to fit back in where you left off. This lack of continuity left us so disorganized that we didn't even attempt things that other schools simply take for granted. No senior play. No senior trip. Not even a powder-puff football game.

Chris Atzinger had much the same experience when he was bused in the fall of 1978 to Central High School. "I feel that busing took away my friends and my school away from me," he said. "My class at Ballard had black students in it and my class at Central was all-white. No one wanted to be there. All of our friends were at different schools." In a limited study of "interracial" student reactions and attitudes in a southern Jefferson County middle school during the first year of busing, a University of Louisville graduate student found some room for hope. A questionnaire was administered to about six hundred seventh-to-ninth-grade black and white students. The fact that there was no deterioration of attitudes during the school year was regarded by the author as offering a chance for future improvement. However, it was going to take a concerted effort on the part of administrators, counselors, teachers, and students to create a "positive" atmosphere for change. A study of busing in Nashville and Louisville in the late seventies confirmed the obvious: "White parents do not seem to mind blacks coming to their local suburbs as long as it is just for school. The rub comes for white people when their children are transported into a black neighborhood."[103]

In a 2005 retrospective in the *Courier-Journal*, several interviewees noted the omnipresent fear, uncertainty, and difficulties of that time. Timothy Hopewell recalled sitting alone in class on September 4, 1975, as an eight-year-old. All other whites boycotted that day. Black parent Benetha Ellis helped form United Black Protective Parents, which opposed busing. She maintained that racially mixed schools were unnecessary: "I don't think it matters where the kids go, as long as we teach them the basics." White busing protester Martha Zoeller voiced the same complaints as she did in 1975. "You have more loyalty to a neighborhood school." Sharri Bailey recalled, "A black girl that had been bused to my school walked into my class at PRP [Pleasure Ridge Park] High School and was so scared she had been crying. I felt so sorry for her that I went against my parents' instructions and spoke to her anyway. Denise or I never told our parents that we had become best friends that year because we both knew our parents would not understand." There is no doubt that the busing of white and black students in the fall of 1975 and in subsequent years radically changed education, and to an important extent society in Louisville and Jefferson County. Initially, the merged system lost money because of the average daily attendance issue in the Minimum Foundation Program. Not only did many students miss school, but in that first year of busing, "the private school population increased by 22 percent from the previous year," according to the *Encyclopedia of Louisville*. However, as pointed out by David V. Hawpe, longtime editor of the *Courier-Journal*, that was actually a very small increase considering the small number of such schools in Jefferson County.[104]

Catholic parochial school education also faced problems in the post–World War II era. In the first years after the war, Catholic schools were crowded. A 1946 Kentucky Court of Appeals decision allowed Catholic children to be bused at local public expense. When the Kentucky General Assembly partially repealed the Day Law in 1950, allowing voluntary desegregation, the Catholic schools of Kentucky immediately began integrating. All-black Catholic schools in the commonwealth began closing; Catholic Colored High School in Louisville ended its sessions in 1958. The 1950s was a period of rapid growth, with the building of new parochial elementary and high schools, six in Jefferson County alone. As fewer Catholics entered traditional teaching orders, the numbers of sisters and brothers declined, as did priests at Trinity High School, and they were being replaced by lay teachers in the 1960 and 1970s. Although they were paid lower salaries than public school teachers, the hiring of more and more lay teachers forced Catholic schools statewide to raise tuition and increased other costs, often more than 400 percent in a short time. The percentage of Catholic children in Catholic schools in Jefferson County reached its peak at 95 percent in the early 1950s and began a slow decline, while nationally, from 1960 to 1995, the percentage of Catholic students in Catholic schools "dropped by more than 50 percent." Because Catholic families were shifting to the suburbs, Flaget High School in the west end of Louisville lasted for only a short time after the founding of Trinity High School in suburban St. Matthew's. Beset with non-Catholic white parents attempting to transfer their children to the parochial schools of Jefferson County, the Archdiocese of Louisville finally declared a "no haven" policy in the mid-1970s. Into the mid-1980s, Catholic schools in Kentucky remained vibrant; fund-raising efforts and tuition kept them among the best schools in the commonwealth. The Catholic high schools in the commonwealth continued to have much higher percentages of graduates attending institutions of higher education than the public high schools.[105]

Added to the Catholic parochial system and the few other private schools of the mid-1970s was a new phenomenon, the "Christian" school movement. These schools opened because of what Protestant parishioners considered to be the moral decline of public education as well as the integration and busing issues. One woman declared that her young son in the second grade "needs the prayer and the Bible in the classroom," which the public schools would not provide. Beth Haven Christian School in southwestern Jefferson County opened in 1971 and the Christian Academy of Louisville in 1975. Perhaps the most outspoken of the antiestablishment organizers was John Thoburn, the son of a Virginia pastor, who came to Jefferson County in October 1975 to lend advice on founding Christian schools. "We want the public schools abolished," he said, describing himself as a "Christian reconstructionist." "We believe they are immoral." That fall, the Baptist Tabernacle in Shively organized a school that, like several other Christian schools in Jefferson County, was begun as a direct result of busing. From the mid-1970s into the late 1980s, the Christian school movement in Kentucky more aggressively pushed its goals, which included opposition to the intrusion of the state into their affairs. They denied that their schools needed state accreditation because they were accredited through the Kentucky Association of Christian Schools (KACS). The purchase of textbooks at state expense came before the legislature in 1978 and failed. In the late 1970s there was little state oversight for these new Christian schools, owing to court rulings and legislative timidity. KACS schools refused to use any of the state-adopted texts "because of their handling of the creation of man," said Rev. Guy Goodell, head of the Tabernacle Christian School in Frankfort. In October 1979, the Kentucky Supreme Court upheld a Franklin Circuit Court ruling that Christian schools had the right to operate outside the state system because of Article 5 in the Kentucky Bill of Rights, which dealt with the "right of religious freedom," specifically in the clause stating, "Nor shall any man be compelled to send his child to any school to which he may be conscientiously opposed." While Christian school advocates applauded the decision, Lexington Baptist minister Rev. Bob Brown, vice chairman of the state school board, took the view that "now it'll be impossible to enforce compulsory attendance because you can't compel attendance until you say what a school is. It's important to understand that the state board wasn't trying to say what a church is, we were trying to say what a school is. Now, without any regulation or control, anyone in the name of religion will be able to teach children anything at all." By one estimate at least five thousand students, other than those in parochial Catholic schools, attended Christian schools in Jefferson County, and the movement appeared to be growing statewide in the 1970s and early 1980s. As education historian William J. Reese concluded for this era: "By the late 1970s, then, far from being an anomaly, Christian schools were becoming a small but permanent and growing part of the educational landscape." The home-schooling movement became another alternative to public education.[106]

Nonsectarian private "day" schools in Louisville, Lexington, and a few other towns also grew in these volatile times. In Lexington, the Sayre School and the Lexington School prospered. Other private schools did not fare as well. Kentucky's military schools, Kentucky Military Institute and Millersburg Military Institute, fell out of favor during the Vietnam War era. KMI, ending its more than 130-year run as a distinctly military school, merged with Louisville Country Day School to form the new Kentucky Country Day School. MMI soldiered on into the early twenty-first century in several permutations. Though not always specifically founded to negate *Brown v. Board of Education*, most private schools continued to have nearly all-white student bodies into the 1980s. However, Kentucky, unlike most of the states of the Deep South, did not have a proliferation of "segregationist academies" during this era, according to former *Courier-Journal* editor David V. Hawpe.[107]

Did court-ordered desegregation work in Kentucky? Robert A. Sedler maintained that the lawsuits he directed were essentially successful. Although the results appeared to be in doubt when the Louisville and Jefferson County school systems merged and court-ordered busing set off resistance and some violence, and although to a lesser extent there was turmoil in Lexington, Sedler explained that "both communities accepted desegregation, the school systems worked hard to implement the court-ordered desegregation plans, and the basic structure of the plans, with some modifications, remains in effect today [2004]. According to the recent study of the Harvard University

Civil Rights Project, Kentucky leads the nation in school desegregation, with 80.9 percent of its African American students in majority-white schools and virtually none in 90–100 percent African American schools." As it turned out, because whites made up 80 percent of students in Jefferson County, they stayed in the community rather than fleeing. "In Kentucky, then, school desegregation has worked," Sedler maintained.[108]

In 1979, a new face appeared on the Kentucky political horizon. John Y. Brown Jr., the son of a famous Democratic politician, entered the 1979 Democratic Party primary with less than ten weeks before the vote. He parlayed a media blitz with a whirlwind campaign, taking a brief time-out to marry TV personality Phyllis George, into defeating his closest rival, Louisville mayor Harvey Sloane, by a small margin in the Democratic primary. He then swept into the governor's mansion by soundly defeating former governor Louie Nunn. Raymond Barber, the candidate for state superintendent, like all other Democratic Party candidates, rode the young Kentucky Fried Chicken millionaire's coattails into office by a wide margin. Barber had worked his way up in the Allen County School System as well as serving in the state House of Representatives from 1964 to 1968.[109]

During the Brown-Barber years, several issues came to a head. Church-state issues, regarding the establishment clause, continued to be controversial in the post–World War II era, creating difficulties for public education. A mid-1950s study of religion in Kentucky schools presaged what was developing in state and federal court cases. Interviewing 120 teachers in five mostly small communities and rural settings, Jack Jones Early found that most teachers did not understand that they were violating state and federal law and court dictums and did not comprehend the meaning of the separation of church and state. For example, many went beyond the law to "comment on" or "interpret" Bible verses read in class. Protestantism dominated these communities, and their values were propounded in prayers and religious instruction, including religious assemblies, for "the development of moral and spiritual values." This study concluded that the school districts themselves and teacher educators needed to clearly instruct teachers on these vital issues. Early's findings most likely fit the majority of schools in the commonwealth. In the early days of the Brown administration, church-state issues in the Kentucky public educational system became more prominent. After the U.S. Supreme Court in *Engel v. Vitale* (1962) declared that an "official state prayer" was unconstitutional, local school boards and the Kentucky Board of Education were left in a quandary as to what constituted such a prayer. The next year the Supreme Court declared in *Abingdon School District v. Schempp* that a Pennsylvania law requiring the reading of Bible passages was unconstitutional. Kentucky school law wrestled with these issues as advocates of prayer and Bible reading argued that both were acceptable if done on a "voluntary" basis. The posting of the Ten Commandments and religious art in schools and other public places also became controversial and contentious. For example, after a court ruling to remove of the Ten Commandments from public spaces, Superintendent Frank R. Hatfield of the Bullitt County School System did so. At the next school board meeting, proponents of the posting became so agitated that for the only time in his more than twenty years as superintendent, "I really felt threatened," declared Hatfield. For his own protection and a return to civility at the meeting, he had an assistant call the sheriff's office.[110]

Periodically the teaching of evolution in the public schools roiled the educational waters as well. Although antievolution laws had been rejected in the Kentucky General Assembly in the early 1920s, the issue never completely died. In 1968 the Supreme Court appeared to settle the issue once and for all by declaring in *Epperson v. Arkansas* that state laws outlawing the teaching of evolution were unconstitutional. Antievolution forces then shifted their approach by claiming that "creation science," or "creationism" was a viable alternative to evolution or, at a minimum, could be taught alongside evolution in biology instruction. As a competing idea, creationists claimed that the "fairness doctrine" should allow them "equal time" to present their views. In 1974 a creationist "equal time" bill languished in a Kentucky House of Representatives committee and died as the session ended. Creationism, however, gained a foothold in Kentucky's largest school system, Jefferson County, in 1975, when the guidelines for the high school biology course allowed the creationist theory to be taught alongside evolution. The next year KRS 158.177, "Teaching of evolution—Right to include the Bible theory of creation" sped through the General Assembly with little notice. The law stated that in public school instruction that involved "the theory thereon commonly known as evolution, any teacher so desiring may include as a portion of such instruction the theory of Creation as presented in the Bible." Furthermore, a student could choose to be tested on the Genesis 1 account rather than the theory of evolution for class credit. It is not known whether any teachers at that time took this avenue of instruction.[111]

In the next four years, creationist strategy shifted. House Bill 889 in the meeting of the 1980 General Assembly got more attention. This piece of legislation carefully defined both the "theory of evolution" and "scientific creationism" and provided that "references to any theory of evolution shall be presented only with reference to scientific creationism which are equal in content and context." This law would cover all levels of public school education and would require the State Textbook Commission to adopt scientific-creation textbooks. Democrat House Majority Leader Bobby Richardson used his position to oppose the bill, claiming, "I support the separation of church and state." Representative Bob Heleringer, a Republican from Louisville, said this was a matter of academic freedom and if passed, the bill "will come back to haunt us." The supporters of the bill used some parliamentary maneuvering, attaching it to a dissimilar Senate bill, but the creationist bill was separated out and went down to defeat. Creationists in Fayette County began asking for school board action. Superintendent Barber stepped in and declared, based on his understanding of KRS 158.177, that individual districts "may voluntarily choose to present a theory of scientific creationism and purchase necessary teaching supplies."[112]

I had a dog in this fight: professionally, because of my interest in antievolution as an intellectual/cultural/educational issue, and personally, because of my belief in the separation of church and state, a precept grounded in an old-fashioned Baptist fear of government intrusion into the public sphere. Because there were no studies of how much or how little evolution was actually taught in the public high schools in the Commonwealth of Kentucky, I determined to come up with a survey instrument. With input from colleagues in the social and behavioral sciences at Eastern and benefiting from conversations with a few high school teachers and others, I designed a survey form. I sent a questionnaire to all the high school biology teachers in the state from a list provided by the State Department of Education. After the results came in, I also sent a similar questionnaire to a random sample of high school biology teachers in Indiana and Tennessee, the former because it represented a midwestern state, and the latter because it represented a more southern state. Forty-four percent of Kentucky's high school biology teachers responded, and nearly 53 percent of them claimed to place a "moderate" emphasis on evolution, meaning they taught "at least one unit about the theory of evolution and never avoided usage" of the term. Thirty-one percent said they placed "little" emphasis on the theory of evolution. The written comments of teachers also proved to be enlightening. The overwhelming majority had never faced any pressure not to teach evolution, and most also, voluntarily, mentioned the Creation story from Genesis 1. The reports from the Tennessee teachers indicated that they were a little more conservative than the Kentucky teachers, and the Indiana teachers were a bit more liberal. I concluded that "in Kentucky, Indiana, and Tennessee—and in all likelihood across the country—evolution is moderately emphasized in the average high school biology classroom." I shared this information with the press, where it was reported in several major southern newspapers, and spoke in a session at a national convention of the National Association for the Advancement of Science on the subject and in other venues. I also wrote several articles on the subject. While "moderates" on the subject applauded my study and its results, both conservatives (religious fundamentalists) and liberals (who demanded that no mention of the biblical account be permitted) refused to accept either the conception of the study, the results, or the implications. The vast majority of the teachers surveyed opposed a creationist law, believing that they served the best interests of both students and science. I was very impressed by these science teachers, who often labored under trying conditions.[113]

I became more deeply involved in this controversy than I had intended when creationists chose Fayette County as a test for their efforts in 1980. One school board member proposed integrating creationism into the Fayette County school system. Superintendent Guy Potts openly opposed any such intrusion. Both sides of the issue formed interest groups, and "outsiders" for and against visited Lexington. With preliminary results of my survey in hand, I contacted Potts about my work, and he invited me to attend an open meeting of the board. On the evening of October 19, 1981, a crowd of more than six hundred packed the old Henry Clay High School auditorium. I spoke first for the opposition, to be followed by several others, pro and con, in a meeting that lasted more than four hours before the board voted. With two school board members on record for and two against, the deciding vote was cast against sanctioning creation science by member Harold Steele. This vote appeared to dampen the resolve of creationists in the short term, as the issue did not arise in another Kentucky school board meeting for some time. Moreover, in 1982 an Arkansas federal judge declared an equal-time statute in that state unconstitutional, and a year later a Louisiana federal judge issued a summary decision blocking enforcement of a similar law. KRS 158.177 was repealed by the General Assembly in 1990.[114]

Superintendent Barber, through all this "sound and fury," took no stand for academic freedom. Meanwhile, the 1980 census indicated that Kentucky was last among all the states in the level of education of adults over age twenty-five, with 47 percent of Kentuckians lacking a high school diploma. Governor Brown thought of himself as the chief "salesman" for the commonwealth. He brought to Frankfort many "new faces," eschewing the "usual party-connected, old-buddy appointments." Owing to an economic downturn during the Reagan years, Kentucky lost federal money, but Brown was able to balance the state's budget by cutting the number of state employees. His "no meddling" policy toward the General Assembly gave the state's lawmakers their most independence ever. He presented his first budget and then left the state on a vacation. Although the governor favored professional negotiation for teachers, his hands-off approach meant its defeat. In both legislative sessions of Brown's governorship, public education received increased appropriations, but there was no money for growth or true reform. In one rather comical situation, Brown even proposed selling his state-owned helicopter to help raise teacher's salaries, "a gesture he later regretted when he decided to keep the craft." Even though there were no major educational initiatives during the Brown-Barber years, the state budget for education improved somewhat, and the State Department of Education increased the number of high school credits needed for graduation from 18 to 20. Beginning in 1979, kindergarten programs became available for all five-year-old children in the commonwealth.[115]

Throughout the post–World War II era, consolidation and merger of the public schools of the commonwealth proceeded at an increasing rate and scale. Kentucky educationists into the 1980s argued that consolidation offered an economy of scale because schools would be able to save money by transporting students to more central locations and offer more subjects in the high schools. However, consolidation also seriously disrupted local communities. The removal of a high school and then later elementary schools caused many local villages to lose a central focus and pride. In my home county, small village high schools at Waddy, Bagdad, and Simpsonville were consolidated into Shelby County High School in 1960. Already the old village high schools at Finchville, Henry Clay at Clay Village, Gleneyre, and Mt. Eden had been folded into the first three. "Bigger is better" became a mantra for the state education establishment. Eventually, nearly all of the old community schools were eliminated as mergers and consolidations rationalized the school systems of Kentucky. An oral history project on the Buckeye School in Garrard County in 1987 chronicled the rise, decline, and fall of a small community school. Beginning in the early twentieth century, Buckeye School grew, eventually even adding a high school. In an isolated part of Garrard County, this "once-flourishing farm trade center" began to decline with the advent of more modern transportation and the closing of a ferry on the Kentucky River. Alumni, teachers, and residents made a valiant effort to save the school but eventually gave up as the consolidation movement, which also absorbed the Lancaster school system, swept Garrard County.[116]

In a series of articles and books, Alan J. DeYoung, professor of educational policy studies and evaluation at the University of Kentucky, has been critical of school consolidation. He has expressed doubts about the argument of increasing efficiency as well as that of improving education, particularly for rural Appalachia. "The net result of school consolidation in much of Appalachia has been to disenfranchise local citizen groups from control of their schools while enabling school officials to carve out a niche as educational experts at the county level," according to a coauthored piece by DeYoung and Tom Boyd. "Consolidation has continually eroded the school as a location for community activity and has made the yellow school bus a symbol of modern education." According to DeYoung and Barbara Kent Lawrence, rural parents know that supposedly better schools or consolidated ones will lead their children away from the community.[117]

Regardless of the critiques of scholars like DeYoung and others, or the outcries of local residents, consolidation became a fact of life for Kentucky education. With a dropout rate twice the national average in Appalachia in the late 1970s, is it any wonder that state and local officials sought any measure to keep more children in school? In another study, DeYoung and his colleagues found: "School district scores on Kentucky's Comprehensive Test of Basic Skills show that children in most Appalachian school districts in Kentucky perform significantly more poorly than children in non-Appalachian districts." In Appalachian Kentucky, independent school districts scored better than the county, more rural ones. Clearly, the age-old problems of education in what was becoming known as Kentucky's "Problem Crescent," all of the eastern mountain region and stretching to the Mississippi River, as opposed to the "Golden Triangle," the more generally prosperous area encompassed by Lexington, Northern Kentucky, and Louisville, continued into the late twentieth century. Whether the forced merger of Jefferson County and Louisville school districts in 1975 or the more benign merger of small-town districts into county districts, the results were the same. Schools and school systems became larger and larger. Sometimes the effects of a winning basketball or football team in a newly consolidated district would raise the spirits of the local population, but this also meant that fewer boys were participating in school athletics or, overall, that fewer female and male students had opportunities to excel in other extracurricular activities. Whereas in 1920 there had been 508 school districts in the commonwealth, by 1990 that number had been reduced to 176, or 56 independent and 120 county districts. Did consolidation of Kentucky schools work to benefit the children of the commonwealth? That question was not answered in the time frame of this chapter. Into the late 1980s, critics of the Kentucky educational system argued that much needed to be done to uplift the state, and consolidation was a continued thrust of the educational establishment in Kentucky.[118]

One of the most far-reaching developments of the early eighties was the forming of a new educational advocacy organization. In 1980 the Kentucky Council on Higher Education appointed thirty people to an advisory committee, the Committee on Higher Education in Kentucky's Future. The next year the committee presented a report, *In Pursuit of Excellence*, and became known as the Prichard Committee, because Edward F. Prichard Jr. was its chairman. The committee's report called for improving funding and access to higher education, establishing a Fund for Academic Excellence, and improving coordination of the system. The committee kept meeting and urged other reforms such as Centers for Excellence and higher standards. In 1983 the group became privately funded and adopted a new name, the Prichard Committee for Academic Excellence, with Prichard as chairman and Robert F. Sexton as the executive director.[119]

During the same year, 1983, *A Nation at Risk,* a report by the National Committee on Excellence in Education, sponsored by the U.S. Department of Education, was published. This study blamed an American descent into mediocrity and economic decline on the failure of the public schools to keep up with international competition, particularly from Japan. "If an unfriendly foreign power had attempted to impose on America the mediocre educational performance that exists today," *A Nation at Risk* claimed," we might well have viewed it as an act of war." The head of the Carnegie Foundation, Ernest L. Boyer, wrote *High School: A Report on Secondary Education in America,* published that same year, a scathing study criticizing secondary schools as failing because of poor teaching, declining "academic standards," and a "smorgasbord curriculum." Though perhaps rightly named a "famous conservative manifesto," promulgated by the administration of Ronald Reagan, *A Nation at Risk* joined other studies, liberal and conservative, state and national, that declared quite openly that the American public schools were failing. As developed by William J. Reese in several books, Henry J. Perkinson in *The Imperfect Panacea: American Faith in Education, 1865–1990,* and many other critics, Americans have always depended too much on public schools for solving America's ills, and then they have railed against the schools when their dreams have not been realized.[120]

In this milieu of educational criticism and condemnation, Prichard and his committee seemed to fit the age and the well-worn American pastime of blaming many, if not all, of the nation's ills on the public schools. The efforts of the Prichard Committee in publicizing the education shortcomings of the commonwealth appeared to be making headway in the early 1980s. Moreover, the gubernatorial election of 1983 promised to be a referendum on education. Lieutenant Governor Martha Layne Collins, a former high school teacher, worked her way up in the Democratic Party machinery and had the support of party regulars. With 33.97 percent of the primary vote, she narrowly defeated Harvey Sloane's 33.28 percent and Grady Stumbo's 30.34 percent. The Democratic Party then united behind its first female gubernatorial candidate. In the face of a major economic recession, Collins campaigned on a message of no new taxation while pushing educational reform. She easily defeated her Republican opponent, state senator Jim Bunning, by more than one hundred thousand votes. Not only did Kentucky have its first female governor; it also had its first female state superintendent of public instruction with the election of Democrat Alice McDonald, a former teacher and guidance counselor in the Jefferson County schools. McDonald also had experience at the state level as head of the Office of Federal Programs in Frankfort and as a deputy superintendent of public instruction. "The reputation of both Mrs. McDonald and Mrs. Collins will hinge on their ability to bolster the schools," the *Courier-Journal* editorialized, trumpeting the election results. Immediately after the election, McDonald pledged to work hard for "more accountability and better academic performance in Kentucky schools." "The public wants to know what the schools are doing," she claimed.[121]

Some leaders both within the Department of Education and across the state believed that the inequity of school finance had not changed enough with passage of the Minimum Foundation Program and "power equalization" funding. Three employees in the Department of Education, Arnold Guess, James Melton, and Kern Alexander, soon left their posts after the election of Collins and McDonald. Because Guess had openly worked for McDonald's Democratic Party primary opponent, former state superintendent James B. Graham, he saw the impossibility of staying on and resigned before she took the oath of office. He and others began talking about ways to improve educational funding. The question remained, how Kentucky's first female governor and state superintendent of public instruction would fare in the traditional man's political world and what impact they would have on education as well as other pressing issues. Professional educators in KEA were a bit suspicious of Governor Collins because she had voted against professional negotiations legislation for teachers while president of the Senate in 1980 as lieutenant governor.[122]

Collins presented an education agenda to the legislature in early January 1984, which carried a hefty price tag of $324 million in additional state funds. A few younger members of the House of Representatives, known as the "Young Turks," had their own agenda and went their own way in developing an education program. With most of the members of the House of Representatives up for reelection in 1984, most incumbents did not want to vote for a tax increase. Ultimately, Collins withdrew her "tax package" and called for a "continuation budget." However, even with the limited funds available, the General Assembly passed bills to encourage the growth of kindergarten programs, testing programs for new teachers, and remedial programs for the elementary grades.[123]

Collins and most education advocates were disappointed in the outcomes of the meeting of the 1984 General Assembly. The governor considered it a personal defeat and set her sights on education change by touring the state and appearing at state meetings. She appointed yet another "blue ribbon" education committee, The Governor's Council on Educational Reform, on July 2, 1984. Al Smith, journalist and moderator of KET's *Comment on Kentucky* program, served as chair of a commission that included several legislators, educators, and businesspeople. Superintendent McDonald also had a study group, "New Directions in Education," one "focusing on community involvement in public schools." "Teachers must demand improved education," Collins told a town forum. "Administrators must do their part to ensure that we get the most out of our education dollars, to make sure they correct what problems they can locally." Meanwhile, the Prichard Committee redoubled its efforts. The Council on Educational Reform presented a report in early January 1985, recommending more money for education and supporting the governor's idea of a "career-ladder plan for teacher compensation." The council also suggested more money for the poorer school districts. To encourage academic excellence, the council and the governor proposed the beginning of what became the Governor's Cup competition for students. With KEA, the Prichard Committee, and legislative leaders like House Speaker Don Blandford on board, the climate for reform looked bright.[124]

To this apparent growing consensus for education change in Kentucky was added a new and more radical approach. Arnold Guess began talking with several school superintendents about a renewed effort to gain adequate funding for the poorer districts. On May 14, 1984, the Council for Better Education (CBE) incorporated and began to function outside the usual state organizations and even outside the confines of the Prichard Committee. Guess, Jack Moreland, and superintendents Frank R. Hatfield of Bullitt County, Eugene Binion of Elliott County, Alex Eversole of Jenkins Independent, and Tony Collins of Wolfe County were the early organizers of the committee; Hatfield was president. Soon they were considering filing a lawsuit against the state for breaking the intention of the Kentucky Constitution, Section 183, which provided "for an efficient system of common schools throughout the state." Governor Collins, Superintendent McDonald, and most members of the General Assembly, in varying degrees of intensity, opposed the idea of a lawsuit. Nonetheless, the council began gaining some headway by asking school districts to voluntarily join and fund the effort. Kern Alexander added his knowledge of school finance to the council's efforts and suggested, "You'll have to get someone with some stature to represent you." Guess and Hatfield went to former governor Bert T. Combs, who said, with typical understatement, "I don't know if I qualify but I would love to represent you." The biggest coup of the council was adding Combs to its legal efforts in October 1984. By then, about sixty school districts had signed on, paying "a quarter a student" in fees. Although Superintendent McDonald "tried to scare us out of it," maintained Hatfield, "we went ahead with it."[125]

By late 1984 and early 1985, there were contending forces urging some sort of educational reform. The Prichard Committee seemed to be going in one direction while the Collins administration went in another. Ed Prichard did not have a high regard for Collins, and he had supported Louisville mayor Harvey Sloane in the 1983 Democratic gubernatorial primary. Prichard and Collins apparently never completely reconciled their differences, but Prichard Committee executive director Robert F. Sexton did develop a working relationship with the governor. Meanwhile, the Council for Better Education pursued its goal of forcing the issue through the courts. The CBE received support from the *Courier-Journal*, the *Lexington Herald-Leader*, the *Kentucky Post*, and other smaller, regional newspapers.[126]

The Prichard Committee pressed the issue into the fall of 1984, calling for statewide meetings as well as a special session of the General Assembly specifically for education. Longtime Prichard Committee executive director Robert F. Sexton explained this new strategy as a way to pressure Collins. "We felt we needed something to create a parade," he said, by planning statewide forums and a KET broadcast and then inviting the governor to participate. Collins had already been giving speeches in favor of education, so she joined the effort. The bandwagon gained momentum as school superintendents, editors of many state newspapers, and others pushed the idea. Dr. Thomas D. Clark added his personal gravitas in letters to the state's newspapers, reiterating what he had been saying for decades. "Failure now to materially raise the standards of education in Kentucky will once again consign Kentucky to the unhappy status of being a 'bypassed' state," he argued. The Prichard Committee's Sexton organized "Town Forums" across the state, with a KET broadcast as the anchor on November 15, 1984. More than twenty thousand Kentuckians showed up that night. By one count, only five school districts did not host meetings, while groups met in about 140 locations. Governor Collins, Judge Combs, and McDonald spoke on the KET telecast, touting the efforts to unite the state for education reform. The next day the *Lexington Herald-Leader* charged the governor with the responsibility of putting together a statewide campaign. "Only the governor can supply the decisive leadership necessary to build a better future for the children of Kentucky," the paper asserted. Meanwhile, the Council for Better Education continued plans to place a lawsuit before the courts, arguing that Section 183 of the Kentucky Constitution was being violated.[127]

The forums built a momentum for improving education that had not been felt for years, at least since the mid-1950s and the development of the Minimum Foundation Program. Robert F. Sexton believed that at the time, the mid-1980s, Kentucky was far behind several other states in educational reform, including Tennessee, Mississippi, North Carolina, Texas, Mississippi, and Arkansas. "We were not even close to being one of the leading states in education reform in the 1983 to 1987 period," Sexton said in a 2009 interview. The governors of these other states had taken a position of strong leadership. "The constant pressure and this buildup of media interest, business interest, community interest, government interest, and parent interest in improving schools" began to bear fruit, he mantained.[128]

Early in 1985, the Prichard Committee issued its first report on elementary-secondary education, *The Path to a Larger Life*, calling for better teacher training and incentive pay. "Good teaching and good teachers are keys to good schools and good education," the committee declared. Improved working conditions and "continued professional growth" were keys to providing for better educational opportunities. To address the issue of lagging teacher morale, the committee asked for class size reduction, better in-service training, elimination of permanent certification, a "career ladder" approach tied to salary increases, and improved teacher education in the colleges of the state. The report urged the elimination of "patronage politics" from the public schools. Meanwhile, Collins embarked on a mission to visit all 120 counties in the state, urging educational reform. "Everywhere I go these days I carry this message: Teachers are the most important part of any formula for sound education," she told the annual meeting of KEA. "I tell audiences that whatever we do, teachers remain the key to better schools. Higher standards, tougher curriculum, more math and science—all of these are of limited value unless we also recognize that teachers make the difference." "I think Martha Layne Collins deserves credit" for education reform, said *Courier-Journal* editor David Hawpe. "She literally went to every county to sell educational reform during her term. She prepared the groundwork for education reform, she raised the issues, and she did a great public relations job."[129]

All the pieces began to fall into place. The Prichard Committee, the Council for Better Education, Governor Collins, KEA, and other friends of education, including the Kentucky Chamber of Commerce, all appeared to be ready for moving public school education forward. In early July 1985, Governor Collins called for a special session of the legislature with the aim of appropriating $287.7 million for school improvement, to be paid for through higher taxes on business and a five-cent increase in the motor fuel tax to bolster the road fund. The latter ultimately failed to pass muster in the legislature. "I think the legislature is ready, and I think we're ready," the governor said. House Speaker Don Blandford voiced his desire to "get the legislation through as expeditiously as possible." "But we also want to make sure everybody and everything gets a hearing." If Shakespeare had been quoted, he would have replied, "There's the rub." Lobbyists were already active. Collins expanded the agenda to include prisons and foster care. The *Courier-Journal* editorialized for quick action. One pundit predicted a short legislative session because neither the House nor Senate chambers were air-conditioned for the predictable July heat and humidity. Since the session would cost $40,000 a day, many Kentuckians hoped it would be a short "extraordinary" session.[130]

The special session began with a televised address delivered by Collins before a joint session of the General Assembly. "The choice is ours," she said in her challenge. "You and I cannot escape this responsibility. We can only act, or refuse to act. I am confident that we are ready to act." A large part of her tax proposal would go to poorer districts in the power-equalization program, a plan that had become the primary thrust of the Council for Better Education. Five former governors were on hand for the opening speech, and overall response appeared positive. The *Courier-Journal* supported the governor's proposal but went even further in urging support for "the poorer counties." In its early deliberations, the House dropped three of Collins's proposals: increasing local school boards by two members, the creation of a commission to study early childhood development and preschool education, and the establishment of an Education Management Institute at one of the state's colleges. More importantly, the "Young Turks" who had scuttled Collins's plans in early 1984 and who had KEA and teacher backing, mostly supported her package. In what promised to be a "long, hot session," the House threshed through House Bill 6. One important addition to the bill was the requirement that at least forty-two districts would have to raise local taxes in order to qualify for grants. Money for new school buildings as well as reduction of class size added to the improvements. After heated debate the House accepted a career-ladder pilot project as well as increasing teacher pay by 5 percent annually for 1986–1988. Representative Harry Moberly of Richmond argued that "this issue is not going to go away." "There's a great deal of public sentiment for some kind of career ladder," he said. On July 19, after the usual last-minute ironing out of House and Senate differences, a $305.9 million "education package" passed both houses. The self-congratulations were widespread, but more than one legislator voiced an opinion that the forty-two districts that already fell below the "required 25-cent rate" would not be able to raise more revenue in order to quality for more power equalization funding. "Selfless spirit may be session's greatest legacy," said the *Lexington Herald-Leader* editorialist at the end of the July 1985 special session. It remained to be seen if this truly was a step forward. Or, as had happened so many times in the past, would this be the usual scenario of waning enthusiasm and the inability to sustain change across the state?[131]

The Council for Better Education continued on its course, appearing to be even more energized by passage of the mid-1985 legislation. More and more school districts joined in the effort, even as some politicians in the state continued to pressure them not to do so. Governor Collins did not lend her support, saying that a lawsuit might hurt the effort to lure the Toyota Motor Manufacturing Company to the state. President Frank Hatfield and other leaders, however, pushed the lawsuit. Its primary thrust was simple: if Section 183 was to provide an "efficient" school system across the entire state, Kentucky schools were not being funded adequately, and the students in the poorer parts of the state were being hurt the most. On November 20, 1985, the council filed its suit, *Council for Better Education, et al. v. Martha Layne Collins, Governor, et al.*, Civil Action No. 85-CI-1759. The *Courier-Journal* and other papers immediately voiced their support. Others were not so happy. The Education Committee in the Kentucky Senate filed a bill to forbid school districts to use public funds to pay for suing the state. Superintendent McDonald proved just as contentious. Her political ambitions got in the way of her work. Already she had politicized the Department of Education for her own political benefit by firing those who were not helpful to her and hiring others who would promise to advance her career. Late in her term, ethics questions surfaced that led to her retirement from the political arena. As it turned out, perhaps the best thing that McDonald did for Kentucky education was, ironically, pushing Arnold Guess out of the Department of Education. This allowed him to provide leadership to the Council for Better Education at a crucial time. Moreover, McDonald's behavior and political machinations persuaded many Kentuckians that having an elected chief of Kentucky's public schools had long since outlived its usefulness or purpose.[132]

The public and private debates over the efficacy and necessity of a lawsuit testing Section 183 continued. Those in opposition pointed out that many of the poor districts had not even tried to tax themselves. However, Superintendent Hatfield of Bullitt County maintained, "We were kid rich and property poor," compared with the high tax rates and revenue sources of adjacent Jefferson County. Judge Combs used his influence to get the Prichard Committee to support the lawsuit and file an amicus curiae brief. Now the future of Kentucky education lay in the hands of the Kentucky justice system, first in Franklin Circuit Court and then, finally, in the Supreme Court of the commonwealth. Would the courts find for the Council for Better Education or for its opponents? Kentucky public school education again stood at a crossroads in the mid-1980s.[133]

Chapter 8

Higher Education

Most Americans heard about the Japanese attack at Pearl Harbor in the afternoon of Sunday, December 7, 1941, while listening to the radio. That's how future governor Louie B. Nunn found out, while he was a student at Bowling Green Business College. Eastern senior ROTC student Ken Perry was lying in bed recovering from a broken leg suffered in the Morehead football game when he heard the broadcast. "My first reaction was, they can't be that stupid," he recalled. "I think everybody's reaction was the same. We all thought we'd end up in Europe." Across America the next day, most college students and faculty gathered in auditoriums, dormitories, and student unions to listen to President Roosevelt's message to Congress, in which he excoriated the Japanese Empire for the "day which will live in infamy." As at the time of the Great Depression, Americans were caught up in events over which they appeared to have no control. Life was changed quickly by this war, and Kentucky higher education soon adjusted to the exigencies of wartime.[1]

Kentucky college students were already leaving for the military, government posts, or civilian jobs long before Pearl Harbor and the formal declaration of war. Higher prices for wartime goods eventually brought rationing and price controls, but faculties, administrators, and staff faced the privations of war like everyone else. "Victory Gardens" appeared in faculty members' backyards and on college campuses.[2]

With an increase in draft notices, an upwelling of volunteers, and more rapid deployment of ROTC students, male enrollment in Kentucky higher education rapidly plummeted. Most colleges in the state quickly shifted from a semester system to a quarter system. The men entering the armed forces could finish the shorter quarter courses more easily than the longer semester coursework. Morehead enrollment dropped to a low of nine males at one time; total enrollment was only 166 in the fall of 1944, and that included 50 students placed in student teaching. At all of the regional schools of education, teacher education numbers dropped. Because fewer new teachers were being trained, more emergency staff were hired in the public schools, further dampening educational achievement in Kentucky. By the summer of 1943, the undergraduate enrollment at the municipally controlled University of Louisville faced "virtual extinction," according to the *Courier-Journal;* dental school enrollment dropped from the normal 62 to only 14 students.[3]

The University of Kentucky did not suffer as rapid a male depopulation as the other schools. Appointed only six months before Pearl Harbor, President Herman L. Donovan still waged an uphill battle to win over the faculty after his inauguration on May 6, 1942. The professional schools, including engineering, prospered, and the Lexington school added several new departments and augmented others during the war. The College of Agriculture and Home Economics was already intent on increasing and preserving food for the war effort. Nevertheless, Donovan took a strong stand for the liberal arts. "Technical education may be essential to winning the war," he said. "But it is liberal education that will win the peace."[4]

A "win-the-war spirit" permeated the nation's campuses. As a result of World War II, Kentucky colleges and universities took a world view more than ever before, placing greater emphasis on foreign languages, geography, and foreign policy courses. Many colleges, particularly the smaller ones, either halted or severely curtailed their athletic programs. Except for the University of Kentucky, all Kentucky schools gave up football during the war years, and Transylvania never revived the sport afterward. After the 1943–1944 basketball season, except at UK, most sports were completely suspended at both private and public institutions, since most of the athletes entered the armed forces. With the cancellation of basketball, Eastern lost the services of promising six-foot-nine freshman Arnie "Shorty" Risen, who went on to fame at Ohio State University and in the National Basketball Association. Maroon coach Rome Rankin at first helped out with the armed forces physical training being conducted at Eastern and then spent a year as an assistant to Adolph Rupp at the University of Kentucky. The Navy V-12 program at the University of Louisville actually improved intercollegiate basketball tremendously, making it a "major" sport; the 1943–1944 team of new coach Peck Hickman had a successful year with only one civilian on the temporarily renamed "Sea Cardinals" team.[5]

With the exception of Kentucky State College, all of the state colleges and universities received direct federal aid, including military training units. Army Specialized Training Programs (ASTP) and other units came to several campuses. ROTC units were also strengthened, but their members soon went off to war. At UK an Engineers Specialist School operated for a year, training 3,174 men, as well as another ASTP school. Newly appointed history department chairman Thomas D. Clark recalled in his memoirs that it was hard to find instructors to teach courses for the military units. One UK coed, Betty Tevis Eckdahl, had another experience: "Those soldiers were the best prospects for dates," she remembered, even though the administration tried to keep the civilians and military personnel at arm's length by building "wooden barriers" on a bridge between Patterson Hall, which housed soldiers, and Boyd Hall for women.[6]

In 1941 UK's Wenner-Gren Aeronautical Research Laboratory, the money for which came from the Viking Fund of Swedish industrialist Axel Wenner-Gren, began to play an increasing role in engineering research. However, the effort soon became enshrouded in controversy. Wenner-Gren, who was the owner of Electrolux and other companies, was accused of being pro-Nazi when he tried to broker peace in Europe. After he was blacklisted by the U.S. government, his name was removed from UK's research building. Then Colonel James H. Graham, dean of the College of Engineering, became controversial when he accepted outside employment. Lawsuits ensued as well as an investigation mandated by the General Assembly. All ended well, as Donovan and UK were given "a unanimous vote of confidence" by the legislature. The State Department also finally cleared Wenner-Gren of any wrongdoing, and his name was returned to the aeronautical laboratory. As he had done during his years at Eastern, Donovan took a proactive course in such controversies and ably defended UK.[7]

The regional state colleges also answered the call and sought military training units during World War II. For them the units meant an infusion of federal money that paid the bills and kept their campuses from declining beyond repair. Each college received federal funds for the housing, instruction, and feeding of military personnel. Moreover, ordinary faculty supplemented the military instructors, enabling the colleges to retain teachers. At Morehead, a Navy College Training program trained second-class seamen in a system that produced 150 graduates each month, a total of 600 students. Although President Paul Garrett at Western appeared less concerned about such programs than his cohorts, the 321st College Training Detachment, an Army preflight program, began at the Bowling Green campus in April 1943. Murray's contribution to the war effort included housing a Naval Pre-flight Training Unit initially and later a Naval Academic Refresher Unit.[8]

The Eastern campus was enlivened with the arrival of a Women's Army Auxiliary Corps training unit, which trained secretarial workers in six- to eight-week courses. The campus bustled even more when an ASTP engineer training unit came, overlapping the female unit by several months. President

O'Donnell admitted that "fraternizing" with the locals was a bit of a problem. "I am told that when study hall is dismissed at 10:00 in the evening the town girls descend upon the campus like paratroopers," he explained, tongue in cheek. "We are taking steps, however, to put a stop to that. Military guards are being placed around the campus and the State Patrol is lending its service." Everyone seemed to get along, and dances, swimming parties, and other activities were planned for the young people. Necessities of war struck the campus. First, the War Department decided to consolidate all WAC programs in a single location. Then, more ominously, men were leaving the program at Eastern and other campuses for combat.[9]

Asbury, Kentucky Wesleyan, and Georgetown did not have wartime programs to supplement their enrollment and income. All three suffered seriously declining enrollments. At three private colleges, Transylvania, Centre, and Berea, as well as municipally operated University of Louisville, military training units had an immediate impact. The Navy V-12 program at Berea College brought to the campus a different clientele. With only a hint of understatement, President Francis Hutchins said, "The Navy brought Berea College kicking and screaming into the twentieth century," as smoking on campus and in town was allowed for the first time and "the latest tunes and dance steps" pushed aside country dancing. An Army Air Corps training unit on the little Transylvania campus revived a small school that teetered on the brink with operating deficits and a civilian enrollment of only 115 in the spring of 1944. At Centre in Danville, the Army Air Corps Twentieth College Training Detachment literally took over the campus. The few regular male students at Centre moved over to the separate women's campus for a short time. Even President Robert L. McLeod went off to war, becoming a navy chaplain in the Pacific theater.[10]

During World War II higher education faced not only the pressures of wartime but also the usual stresses of educating students. The growing number of junior colleges in the state had many of the same problems as the senior colleges. They lost numbers without being able to tap government programs. For example, Cumberland College in Williamsburg sputtered through the Great Depression and the war and had only two hundred students enrolled when James Malcolm Boswell became president in October 1945. When the Georgetown College trustees decided not to renew the contract of beleaguered president Henry N. Sherwood just before Pearl Harbor, that Baptist college suffered from a budget deficit and a declining enrollment. After the inauguration of President Samuel S. Hill in November 1942, the General Association of Kentucky Baptists began again channeling funds to Georgetown. Like most other colleges during the war years, Georgetown had fewer and fewer male students. Three-quarters of the student body was female, and only fourteen students graduated in 1944. Georgetown came under direct control by the denomination in 1949 when the General Association assumed total control of electing trustees. At the University of Louisville, President Raymond A. Kent died in 1943 and was replaced by Einar Jacobsen. In 1944 the U of L renamed the Division of Social Administration the Kent School of Social World in honor of the president who served from 1929 to 1943 and led the school in the difficult Depression years.[11]

The administrations of Presidents O'Donnell at Eastern, Garrett at Western, Vaughn at Morehead, and Richmond at Murray survived the war years with hardly a ripple of disruption. The funds from the training of military personnel undoubtedly saved these colleges from even further reversal brought on by the Great Depression, and General Assembly appropriations did not substantially increase during the war years. Called "more or less fairly tight" by one longtime faculty member and coach, O'Donnell at Eastern was well known for hoarding his funds. He even paid off some of the school's debt with "$225,000 in cash" at the end of the war. Also known as being tightfisted, Western's Garrett dealt out faculty raises sparingly, losing some valuable teachers who found greener pastures elsewhere during and after the war, according to Lowell Harrison.[12]

The challenges to Kentucky State College during the war years were compounded by the constant refrain of racism in Kentucky and the nation at large. Apparently, President Rufus Atwood did not have a favorable relationship with Governor Keen Johnson; he even offered to resign after an embarrassing overspending incident. In what historian John A. Hardin called "tacit approval to black subordination to white authority" by "black leaders and educators," Atwood was caught in a conundrum of trying to break these old bonds. For example, during the war he attempted to get a government program that would teach welding to African American males but was denied the request, being told that industry would not hire black welders. Neither would the War Department allow an ROTC program. Without government programs, male enrollment dropped to only thirty-one in 1943. Atwood's pleas to the State Finance Department through the General Assembly increased the state appropriation only slightly by the war's end. He was able to gain a minor civil defense program and, in cooperation with UK, an engineering war training program. However, nothing seemed to substantially raise enrollment and income. Atwood tried every lobbying trick, on one occasion sending a supply of "Old Pepper 20 year old Kentucky Whiskey" to a state senator in order to win his favor. Even a favorable report for support of Kentucky State prepared by UK's Donovan had little effect in the short run; the Frankfort school had to wait until after World War II for any hope of advancement.[13]

While the Allies fought for the freedom of the people of Asia and Europe, segregation continued in most of the United States. With the 1891 constitution and the Day Law mandating segregation, the state colleges and universities followed "the color line" as closely as the commonwealth's southern neighbors did. Black Kentuckians attended either Kentucky State College or the Louisville Municipal College or none at all in the commonwealth. The U.S. Supreme Court in the *Gaines* decision of November 1938 ruled that an African American litigant in Missouri could not be admitted to the all-white University of Missouri Law School. However, the court claimed that the plaintiff had the right to attend law school under a "separate but equal" mandate. The implications for Kentucky and the segregated South were that in some way professional education, equal to but not necessarily in desegregated classes, must be available to that state's black citizens. When Alfred Carroll of Louisville applied to the University of Kentucky Law School, he was denied access. Moreover, mirroring his view of public school desegregation, Governor Chandler flatly declared, "I see no immediate prospects for completely equalizing opportunities for higher education [for blacks] at this time." A committee of black and white educators from the state-supported schools of higher education displayed the bifurcation of the racial divide. While all agreed that the black higher education needed more state aid and that the Day Law should be modified over time, the solution of the white faction was to increase out-of-state tuition to pay for the education of Kentucky's blacks in professional schools. Therefore, nothing substantial came of the committee's work. Wartime governors Keen Johnson and Simeon Willis and the white elite of Kentucky showed little indication that they would work for integration at any level of education. Meanwhile, the NAACP, the Kentucky Negro Education Association, and other African American support groups laid the groundwork for desegregation.[14]

World War II also taught lessons of hope and understanding in a war-torn era. James Oshiro, a Hawaiian of Japanese ancestry, came to Western in September 1940, only to be caught in the maelstrom and tensions of the war and be unable to return home. Most of the folks of Bowling Green and at the college accepted the predicament of the young Japanese American, and he graduated in December 1943. At Berea College the school also accepted to the campus Nisei, or second-generation Japanese Americans, who were also unable to return to Hawaii. Even in the face of local Civilian Defense Council opposition, President Hutchins insisted that Berea could host both Japanese American students and the navy unit. Most students and faculty knew more was at stake than a war. While the student newspaper *Eastern Progress* touted a scrap metal drive with the slogan "With Scrap—Slap a Jap," the same editors looked around them. "Ignorance, prejudice, poverty, and disease are in Richmond in alarming proportions. And these are both the causes and effects of war. In Richmond people live in homes which provide inadequate shelter from the cold and which are unsanitary." Without mentioning African Americans, the editors sensed the coming social, economic, and political struggles of the postwar period. A few months later a reviewer of a book about blacks concluded, "Can we continue that program [segregation] and still have any real growth of liberalism?"[15]

With its status as the white land grant institution in the commonwealth, the University of Kentucky was better poised to weather the war years. Money was not UK's primary problem in the early war years, because the General Assembly in 1942 gave the school its "largest increase in appropriations in the school's history up to that time." Also funds began coming to UK on a regular basis from the Keeneland Foundation. Although enrollment did not drop as precipitously as at the other state colleges, student numbers fell from 5,145 in the fall of 1941 to 3,156 by the fall of 1944. However, internal problems festered. The board of trustees meeting that named Donovan president also created "an enormously powerful department of business management and control, naming Frank Peterson, a state financial official, as controller." The trustees also replaced the Faculty Senate with the University Senate, consisting entirely of administrators. All of this reorganization was done without Donovan's knowledge, and he later said he would have not accepted the UK presidency if he had known of such abrupt changes. In a two-year campaign Donovan worked to overturn the administration-only body with one that again reflected a faculty majority. After the trustees turned down his first proposal for change, Donovan lobbied the members to get his message across. In this way Donovan began to win over a faculty that had been highly skeptical of his appointment.[16]

World War II had a profound and lasting impact on higher education in Kentucky. The schools struggled as did the rest of the nation to not only contribute to the war effort but also hold onto the old idea of what higher education should be. They were challenged with declining enrollments even as many had military programs that helped pay the bills. The numbers of Kentucky collegians killed, missing, and wounded increased during the last months of the war. The University of Kentucky built Memorial Coliseum in honor of 334 war dead and to accommodate the ever-increasing fans for Adolph Rupp's winning Wildcats and other public functions. With $3 million in state appropriations and another $1 million in bonds sold by the UK Athletic Association, UK was able to open the new structure in 1950. Eastern commemorated its war dead with a new Memorial Science Building in 1952, while Georgetown College named the street in front of the campus Memorial Drive. All of the colleges in the state suffered the deaths of former students and alumni. There were 53 Bereans lost, at least 53 from Eastern, 39 from Centre, 111 from the U of L, and 50 who had been students at Murray. The numbers of killed, missing, and wounded affected every school and community. Eastern faculty member George Hembree survived the war only to be killed in an accident during demobilization.[17]

As the war progressed into the final battles in Europe and Asia, one of the most important pieces of legislation in American history progressed through Congress. Public Law 346, the Servicemen's Readjustment Act of 1944, more commonly known as the GI Bill of Rights, opened the doors to many men and women who, under different circumstances, would probably never have had the opportunity to attend a college. By means of this law, "higher education was democratized," according to one historian. As an omnibus bill, the new law included benefits for acquiring loans for housing and the "52–20" clause, which paid servicemen looking for work twenty dollars a week for up to fifty-two weeks. This legislation not only stimulated the economy—many, including President Franklin D. Roosevelt, feared another business downturn and another Bonus Army March on Washington—it also expanded the middle class. By the time the first GI Bill of Rights ended in 1951, paying for tuition, fees, books, and living expenses, nearly 4 million veterans nationwide had been provided with a higher education or vocational training that most would not have received otherwise. Moreover, the rapid increase in postwar higher education enrollments continued for the most part into the latter twentieth century.[18]

The impact of the GI Bill on higher education in Kentucky was immediate. Even before the war ended in the summer of 1945, veterans began entering college in the fall of 1944. All together, if they qualified for the maximum benefits, veterans received up to $500 a year for tuition, fees, books, and supplies, as well as $50 a month for a single veteran and $75 a month for a married veteran. The education benefit ran for as long as forty-eight months. Some veterans joined what many called the "52–20 Club." But Norman Deeb, the son of Lebanese immigrants, recalled that his father had adamantly told him that America had been too good to his family to accept what seemed to him to be charity. At the first opportunity, Deeb headed back to Eastern, using other G.I. benefits, where he had played on the football team before entering the U.S. Army. Many other veterans whose collegiate days had been interrupted by the war also returned to college, usually to the same campus. Like Deeb, some veterans resumed their athletic careers.[19]

The GI Bill in Kentucky suddenly changed higher education in the state forever. Colleges that had been teetering on the brink revived and grew. Transylvania continued to have a large "operating budget deficit" during the war. By January 1946, President Raymond F. McLain was back on campus after service in the navy, and the Lexington campus began to recover. The infusion of federal money through the GI Bill allowed colleges and universities to build new structures and rehabilitate old ones. More important, thousands of Kentucky youth received an education that otherwise they would never have had. The veterans returned to college or attended for the first time as mature adults, most of them with a disdain for the usual frivolity of college life. At Eastern, for example, 120 veterans petitioned the administration for exemption from "Hell Week" for freshmen, claiming they would avoid it anyway. "We have decided that we took enough (Hell) in the service and this is no time to start it again," read the petition. At Georgetown College, ministerial students, many of whom were veterans, protested against the Greek social fraternities.[20]

Generally, World War II veterans were a serious lot, making better grades than other students and wanting to complete their studies as soon as possible. They ballooned classes in business, engineering, and teacher preparation. For several years male enrollment increased each year, overtaking the numbers of females on campus. By the fall of 1948, men outnumbered women at Western, 1,305 to 540. At Kentucky Wesleyan, where "cash-flow problems" of the war years developed when enrollment bottomed out at 99, student numbers "soared to 304" in 1946–1947. Veterans also returned to become administrators. John W. Taylor, who had served in the army, served as president of the University of Louisville from 1947 to 1950 and brought his firsthand perspective to that campus. U of L enrollment, bolstered by returning veterans, grew to nearly ten thousand by 1948–1949. From a low of 3,156 in 1944–1945, UK grew to 10,169 students, graduate and undergraduate, by 1950. Of that number only 27 percent were women. At Kentucky State in Frankfort, the veterans "proved a great stimulant to athletics," allowing that school to improve its schedule. Owing to the influx of veterans, men outnumbered women on most college campuses into the 1960s.[21]

On nearly every Kentucky campus, a "Vets Village" soon appeared, usually consisting of surplus housing from armed forces bases in the nearby area. While the buildings might be free, the colleges and universities had to pay for transferring and reconstructing them on their campuses. In these housing areas, called Shawneetown and Cooperstown at UK and Warrendale at Georgetown, whether barracks or single family dwellings, the living conditions were spartan. Married couples sometimes used common bathrooms in the barracks. The college provided their "central heat": a stove placed strategically in the middle of the "apartments." "Four families with a big black coal stove in the living room," one couple at Eastern recalled. "The school furnished all the utilities and a coal pile at the end of the building." If the accommodations lacked space and privacy for the young married couples and often a child or two, the rent was cheap, usually less than twenty-five dollars a month in the immediate postwar era. The thirteen steel-framed surplus buildings erected at Kentucky Wesleyan in Winchester housed twenty-six families. It was named "Reynolds Village" in honor of Major John Russell Reynolds, a 1939 alumnus killed in Europe. Because of the veterans' identity as separate from the "regular" students, most campuses had veterans' clubs, and some vets even organized minigovernments for their villages. The "Mattoxville" veterans' organization at Eastern included a mayor and eight councilmen "to control speeders and check prowlers." "Peepers" were apparently a problem, so one veteran took on the role of "special deputy." Some of these "temporary" structures did not completely disappear from Kentucky campuses until the 1970s.[22] The units at Georgetown continued for many years, serving veterans and nonveterans alike. When first married, my wife and I had a three-room unit, cold in winter, hot in summer. One of the first signs of spring was that the east wall parted enough for the morning sun to be viewed through a crack. We paid thirty dollars a month rent in 1960–1962.

In what historian John R. Thelin has called "the Golden Age" of higher education from 1945 to 1970, it appeared that, at last, democracy had come to the entire educational process in America. Kentucky followed many of the national trends. However, as a rather small state, it could not emulate the California model. Lacking one of the largest cities in the country, it could not imitate New York. Absent a well-endowed large university such as Harvard, it could not follow that course. Instead, Kentucky adjusted to the national trends. First, a result of higher high school graduation rates was that more young people attended college than ever before in American history as the baby boom generation came of age. Though in an uneven pattern, all Kentucky colleges and universities grew in enrollment and campus facilities. Two-year community colleges, also called junior colleges, were placed in strategic locations in the state and expanded rapidly. Programs in more diverse fields were added at most schools. A campus building boom, aided by the generally expansive economy, was evident on every campus. The federal government also became a more intrinsic part of higher education as the cold war, the civil rights movement, and the higher expectations of all Americans encouraged change. Although private colleges also grew during this era, the greatest rate of growth in the commonwealth came in public higher education.[23]

At the end of World War II, three studies were conducted that suggested change in the public higher education system of the commonwealth. The Postwar Advisory Planning Commission, created by Governor Simeon Willis, designed the Program of Action for Kentucky and made numerous suggestions about how to improve elementary and secondary education. As far as higher education was concerned, the commission urged "that all state institutions of higher learning be placed under a single administrative board." Concern about "better coordination" of the state system was also reflected in the Public Higher Education in Kentucky study made by Griffenhagen and Associates of Chicago. Although the Council on Public Higher Education had been created by legislative act in 1934 to coordinate all of the state schools, it had little authority except to act as a sounding board and to "regulate teacher training." The Griffenhagen report claimed what most everyone in Kentucky knew, that "the work of the Council has been largely ineffective." Both studies called for closer control in order to eliminate "costly duplication" and competition. The question remained whether the Council could improve the efficiency of the Kentucky system of higher education within the framework of the existing system or, as the *Courier-Journal* and others began suggesting in the postwar years, whether "a single governing board" should be created. During the 1948 meeting of the General Assembly, Senate Bill 343, which would have established such an all-encompassing board, never came up for a vote. The Committee for Kentucky, headed by businessman Harry W. Schacter, took even a broader view and sustained a program well into the 1950s. That group called for reforming the state from top to bottom, saying education and government both needed major change.[24]

Higher education also received more and more study at the national level. Not only did the GI Bill immediately begin to democratize higher education nationally; in July 1946 President Harry Truman formed the Commission on Higher Education to study how more opportunities might be extended to American youth. When issued a year later, the Truman commission's report "presaged" many of the issues of the coming years, For example, it argued for "social justice" by using federal legislation to ensure that black Americans had better educational opportunities and more development of "community colleges" to democratize higher education. Up to this time, based on traditional interpretation of the Tenth Amendment, little had been done by the federal government to put money into any other educational institutions than the public schools. However, the report languished, owing to Truman's uneasy relations with the Republican-controlled Congress.[25]

The postwar boom in Kentucky higher education particularly affected the University of Kentucky. The Lexington school became the commonwealth's only "multiversity," a university with associated schools and appendages. As the land grant institution in Kentucky, UK historically reached out to all 120 counties through the agricultural extension program and the experiment stations. The postwar era also built on the Wenner-Gren laboratory's work by UK's increasing research-oriented programs. Much of the impetus for research came through working closely with the Southern Regional Education Board. Each state paid a fee of $25,000 to become a functioning part of SREB. UK committed itself first under Donovan and then under later presidents to the "pooling of resources" concept, whereby the region's resources would be used more efficiently in higher education. For example, because Kentucky did not have a veterinary school, veterinary students from the commonwealth could attend Auburn University "under SREB auspices." Other cooperative programs soon developed. UK took advantage of the SREB programs to improve graduate and research efforts. Moreover, adding to the few junior colleges in the state, which were private, the University of Kentucky also began to follow the ideal of the Truman Report of 1947 and develop a system of public community colleges throughout the state. The direction of this program came not from the Council on Public Higher Education but mostly from internal decisions made at UK and in the political milieu of Frankfort. In 1948 the UK trustees approved the opening of the Northern Extension Center in Covington. That school, renamed Northern Community College, became the template for the creation of other public community colleges in later years by first offering college courses that would be part of a freshman-sophomore general education curriculum. Vocationally oriented courses were added later. In the ensuing decades, the control of the community college system by UK became a contentious point in the "turf battles" between UK and the developing regional colleges. The University of Kentucky continued at the top of the pecking order of public higher education in Kentucky.[26]

Above even the prestige of UK remained the control of the governor of the commonwealth over higher education in the state. The General Assembly and the governorship were usually in the hands of the Democratic Party, and public college and university presidents and administrators had to lobby the governor for their cause. Frankfort had become more and more oppressive with new laws in the thirties and forties. A 1934 law gave the governor the power to dismiss members of state boards, including those of UK and the state colleges, without cause. More power became entrenched in the governor when in 1936 all budgets had to be presented to the Department of Finance, controlled by the governor, rather than to legislative committees. Beginning in 1948, the State Building Commission decided on all projects. That same year, with Governor Earle C. Clements firmly in control, the legislature reduced the terms of the members of boards from six to four years, thereby giving the governor the power to immediately change the composition of boards to his liking. Then, to top it all off, in 1950 an even more ominous measure came before the General Assembly. Over the protest of Donovan and the other presidents of the state colleges, the legislature passed a bill giving the Division of Personnel within the Department of Finance control over all salaries.[27]

What appeared to be the meddling of the governor in higher education came from several sources from 1947 to 1950. First, Clements had attended the University of Kentucky briefly before entering the service in World War I. As chairman of the UK trustees because he was governor, he had an important role and a physical presence at the board's meetings. He also had a specific agenda for what he thought was beneficial to the state. His governorship proved to be a time of important change. For example, during Clements's three years as governor, new highways and infrastructure were built, public school funding increased, the state raised its maximum salary for salaries of public officials from $5,000 to $20,000, and he worked to "stave off disaccreditation of publicly funded colleges," particularly pushing Morehead State Teachers College to reaccreditation. To say that Clements was a "hands-on" chief executive is no exaggeration. He had his hand in everything and was the epitome of a "strong governor." On occasion, as observed by Democratic Party insider Ed Prichard, Clements bullied individuals into submission. "He had a terrible temper," recalled Prichard. "He'd shake people." A state legislator was accosted when he made a joke about supporting a Clements-backed measure. John Ed Pearce of the *Courier-Journal* also received a Clements thrashing: the governor lifted him "up off the floor and banged his head against that marble wall. . . . Sounded like a watermelon. Oh listen, he was rough," Prichard said. Pearce remembered that with each slam against the wall, the burly governor "growled," "You sonofabitch!" UK president Donovan also received the Clements strong-arm treatment when he came to Frankfort to lobby against the measure allowing the governor to remove trustees. As Prichard recalled, "Donovan came over there lobbying to get it repealed, and Clements didn't really give that much of a damn about it, but he thought they were attacking him, thought they were intimating that he wanted to fire trustees and so forth. So he and Donovan got into a little argument, and Clements shook him."[28]

The war years and those immediately afterward also revived the hope of desegregation of the public and private colleges and universities in the commonwealth. The U.S. Supreme Court's *Gaines* decision of 1938 notwithstanding, the Kentucky tradition of segregation lasted through the war years and into the immediate postwar era. Provisions in the 1891 Kentucky Constitution, as well as the Day Law, appeared to place Kentucky firmly in the segregationist camp. Kentucky State College for Negroes and Louisville Municipal College were the only institutions of higher learning for blacks in Kentucky, and the West Kentucky Industrial College in Paducah served as the only school of its type in the state. For twenty years the western Kentucky school had taught some junior college courses, but after 1938 that responsibility had been shifted to Kentucky State. The Kentucky Negro

Education Association, the NAACP, and some white allies faced up to the task of improving the education of African Americans in the commonwealth by challenging the state's segregationist past. The black population of Kentucky had been dwindling as African Americans left rural areas and moved to cities in the state and elsewhere. During the war years, the suit of Charles Lamont Eubanks to gain entry into the UK College of Engineering "plodded through the Eastern Kentucky federal district court in Lexington." A feeble attempt at starting a two-year engineering program at Kentucky State, encouraged by Governor Keen Johnson and the State Board of Education, failed to pass muster. In 1944 black Louisville Republican Charles W. Anderson Jr. introduced a bill in the House of Representatives of the Kentucky General Assembly to allow blacks to attend professional and graduate schools in the commonwealth, conforming to the *Gaines* decision, without dismantling the Day Law. Some blacks opposed Anderson's bill, supporting another that would have increased state support of Kentucky State. Although the Anderson Bill did not pass ultimately and the Eubanks suit was thrown out on a technicality, historian John A. Hardin claimed that the "commotion" caused UK to declare itself segregated, stirred internal debate with the black community about how best to advance higher education, and established this issue as one that would soon return.[29]

Momentum for change in American racial mores built toward the war's end with the publication of Swedish sociologist Gunnar Myrdal's *An American Dilemma* in 1944. This study charged that all facets of American life, including higher education, placed blacks at a disadvantage. However, compounding the problems of Kentucky blacks was a very public disagreement between Representative Anderson and Kentucky State President Rufus B. Atwood. While Anderson wanted to push hard for desegregation, Atwood appeared less willing to take on the challenges of the new era, wanting first and foremost to protect Kentucky State. Although the Committee for Kentucky brought together black and white leaders of the commonwealth in some of its meetings, the white community faced the new era tentatively. Chairman Harry W. Schacter devoted a chapter of *Kentucky on the March* to the race issue, titling it "For a Better Understanding between the Races." He noted an open discussion of the segregation in public meetings, but nothing of substance, particularly legislative initiatives, was adopted, because "we had agreed in advance to include such planks as were approved unanimously. A number of the groups could not yet cut themselves away from age-old prejudices on the race question."[30]

John Wesley Hatch applied for admission to the UK Law School in 1948. Instead he received instruction at Kentucky State from some UK professors who traveled to Frankfort, where he studied for only one semester. On

March 15, 1948, Lyman Johnson, a history teacher at Louisville Central High School and president of the Louisville NAACP, applied for admission to the Graduate School at the University of Kentucky. With an undergraduate degree from Virginia Union University and a master's degree from the University of Michigan, Johnson appeared to be the perfect candidate. UK resisted, and the case went to court.[31]

Federal judge H. Church Ford heard the case in Lexington. Thurgood Marshall argued for plaintiff Johnson, emphasizing that any program not available at Kentucky State should be opened for African Americans at the University of Kentucky. Donovan as well as history professors Thomas D. Clark and Bennett Wall were called to testify. Tom Clark in his memoirs recalled that in his testimony he stated that Johnson could not receive the same education at Kentucky State that he could in Lexington, which was precisely what Marshall wanted to hear. Donovan apparently made the same comments. Ford ruled that the Graduate School and the Law School must be opened to black applicants. At the next meeting of the board of trustees, Donovan recommended that UK not appeal the decision; ex officio member Governor Earle C. Clements agreed. In his memoirs Donovan reported a heated discussion. "Men who had always been serene, cool, and deliberate in their meetings became excited, vehement, and explosive." On the first ballot, the trustees voted 7-5 to appeal the case. Governor Clements and trustee Judge Edward C. O'Rear, who proposed appealing to the Supreme Court, got into a heated argument when the latter proposed spending state money to fund a school for blacks on a par with UK. Tom Clark recalled hearing Democrat Clements challenge Republican O'Rear to a round of fisticuffs outside the meeting room. But cooler heads prevailed. Judge Richard C. Stoll, who served on the board for fifty years with one brief hiatus and had voted for appeal on the first ballot, asked that the matter be addressed again. Stoll announced that he was changing his vote to not appealing the case, and after further discussion the trustees voted 10-2 not to appeal. Johnson and twenty-nine other African Americans entered the UK rolls in the summer of 1949.[32]

At the time Johnson did not have a high regard for UK.

After I had attended graduate school at the University of Michigan and the University of Wisconsin, I wasn't too thrilled about enrolling at Kentucky. When I went on campus, I said: "Isn't this some school? It's a dump. It's beneath me to even come to this place." But I stuck it out for the summer. Some people said: "Lyman now that you're in, why don't you go on and get your doctorate at Kentucky?" I said: "I wouldn't cheapen my master's degree from Michigan with a doctorate from the

University of Kentucky. If I did get a Ph.D., I would want to get it from a school I have respect for."

Johnson recalled that several crosses were burned near the campus protesting the black presence at UK that summer. He also received death threats. Johnson completed his summer classes, never to return to the Lexington campus. "Most of the faculty treated me decently if not cordially," he said. "Dr. Thomas D. Clark, who was head of the History Department then, was as courteous to me as he could be." When Clark took exception to a remark by Johnson that UK was "a dump" back in 1949, Johnson retorted, "until I won my case in federal court and came over here, you raised not one finger against the status quo. Like everyone else you went along with the mores. I repeat: Until the university was forced to do right by us blacks, the place was a dump. I'll even say it was a goddamn dump."[33]

Clark's perspective on the Lyman Johnson case was somewhat different. First, Clark believed that Donovan was fearful of a backlash against UK. He provided documentation in a 2005 *Register* issue devoted to his career, proving that he thoroughly concurred with the court decision. Clark claimed that he personally encouraged Johnson to complete a doctorate at UK. "I assured him that while most of the departmental staff favored the court decision, they expected good work from him," Clark maintained. "Later when I saw his record from Michigan State [actually, the University of Michigan], I wished it were more reassuring." After the summer of 1949, "he never came back. To me the Johnson case seemed timely and just, but I was disappointed that he failed to complete his studies and set a good precedent for other black students. It seemed to me that he was morally and intellectually obligated to carry through in order to fully prove the entire thrust of his court case and the judge's decision." Fittingly, when Johnson received an honorary doctorate at UK in 1977, he and Clark appeared to reconcile their different perspectives on that landmark summer of 1949. In an oral history interview, Clark reiterated his thought that Johnson was not a very strong student during his summer at UK. In Clark's words: "I got the report that Johnson was a very weak brother; that it was going to take some doings to get him moving in serious graduate study. That was not a racial remark, either. . . . That was par for the course. That sort of thing was said about many students. . . . We were sadly disappointed that he didn't come back."[34]

The next year, after Lyman Johnson and other African Americans entered a Kentucky public university or college for the first time, the Kentucky General Assembly passed legislation modifying the Day Law. Representative James P. Hanratty of Hopkinsville told his colleagues: "Even if you don't like it, it's the thing that's coming. It's developing right along." The new statute changed the Day Law, allowing colleges to voluntarily integrate. Catholic colleges in Louisville, including Bellarmine, Nazareth, and Ursuline, as well as Berea College, immediately opened their doors to African Americans. Although the University of Louisville board of trustees had voted to continue to follow the "Negro Ban" of the Day Law in November 1949, the next year the U of L board of trustees and city fathers voted to absorb Louisville Municipal College. Forty black students enrolled in U of L in the fall of 1950. However, Murray, Morehead, Eastern, and Western chose to remain closed to black students. George C. Wright, himself a UK graduate, in the second volume of *A History of Blacks in Kentucky*, summed up the primary reason for the lack of turbulence in initially integrating the Lexington campus. "One of the obvious reasons for the 'success' was the very small number of Afro-American students involved in the desegregation of the University of Kentucky; by 1956 only eighty-three of the 7,200 students were black," he averred. "Most were natives of Lexington, coming to the campus for classes only and not participating in extracurricular activities. They were, in other words, no threat to the status quo of the university." Another study of the first black undergraduates also found that they were restrained by an "invisibility policy" of the UK administration. Most UK faculty accepted black students. And, though "the University of Kentucky experienced little racial violence or civil unrest compared to other southern campuses," the "superficial integration" did not alarm the latent racism in Lexington. Only when African American numbers became a substantial proportion of UK students did the administration make more effort to truly integrate the campus and develop programs for minority students.[35]

The white state colleges did not integrate until after the Supreme Court decision in *Brown v. Board of Education* in 1954, and they did so reluctantly. Morehead and Western accepted black students for the first time in 1956. President O'Donnell at Eastern chose to ignore the 1950 Kentucky statute softening the Day Law. Andrew Miller, a local teacher, broke the color barrier at the Richmond school by entering graduate classes in the summer of 1958. Anne Peyton Spann was the first African American to attend four years at Eastern and graduate. "The first year I was there I was the only black on campus," she recalled. As at other colleges and universities, black athletes were accepted before the schools or local communities welcomed increasing numbers of African American students. Ironically, as black students began to join Eastern athletic teams in growing numbers, the college nickname was changed from Maroons to Colonels, complete with a stereotypical antebellum colonel mascot. Racial integration also proceeded slowly in Bowling Green. Apparently Western officials were prepared to admit black students, but they could not always control outside sources and white hegemony. For example, in 1959 the "first black graduate feared snipers" might attack him during the graduation ceremonies. The municipally owned Paducah Junior College desegregated only after repeated attempts by local authorities failed and court-ordered integration came in June 1953, one year before the *Brown* decision. Just as in the public schools, integration of the college and university faculties in Kentucky came at even a slower pace than did allowing black students to attend those same schools. It took federal legislation and affirmative action to close the hiring gap between whites and minorities. While Berea College and the Louisville Catholic colleges desegregated early, the other private schools dallied. For example, the first black students at Georgetown College were Nigerian students in the late fifties and early sixties. In 1964 Scotty Edwards from Princeton, Kentucky, became the first African American to attend Georgetown College.[36]

The University of Kentucky solidified its role as the premier school in the commonwealth in the immediate postwar years. It was still possible for a young person to complete an education, all the way from nursery school, kindergarten, and elementary and secondary schools operated by the College of Education to undergraduate and graduate degrees, including the Ph.D., entirely on the UK campus. Growth in undergraduate and graduate school numbers pushed UK into unprecedented growth. As temporary old war surplus buildings outlived their usefulness, new buildings replaced them. Memorial Coliseum was only the best-publicized example of construction; other projects completed were expansion of the football stadium, the soon-to-be-renamed Margaret I. King Library, and a new fine arts building. As Donovan had learned at Eastern in the prewar years, success in athletics drew support from legislators for his other concerns. A strong supporter of the semi-autonomous UK Athletic Association, Donovan admitted in his memoirs that UK reached new heights as Adolph Rupp's basketball teams and newcomer Paul Bryant's football Wildcats gained a national stage. Even a point-shaving gambling scandal involving some players on the 1948–1950 basketball teams did little to dampen fan reverence for the indomitable Rupp and University of Kentucky athletics. "The involvement of our basketball team in the athletics scandal was the greatest humiliation we have ever experienced," Donovan claimed in his memoirs, speaking for the entire university. "It is easy to see why I hold that the most trying problem of a college administrator is the athletics program." Thomas D. Clark in his memoirs did not have a high regard for Rupp and what Clark considered to be the overemphasis on sports at UK. Later, when UK faced the threat of not being allowed to play in the still rigidly segregated Southeastern Conference if it desegregated, the longtime UK history professor, then a member of the University Athletic Council, claimed, "I sowed the seed of discord by suggesting that we drop the university's membership in the conference. I might as well have advocated removing the Henry Clay obelisk from the Lexington Cemetery."[37]

Just after the war, the municipally owned University of Louisville continued its unique role in Kentucky higher education. With the medical and dental schools in downtown Louisville, the Speed Engineering School still dominated the Belknap Campus. There was little building in the immediate postwar years at the cash-strapped campus. The Speed family continued to donate to the engineering school and funded some construction there. In memory of President Raymond A. Kent, the Division of Social Administration became known as the Kent School of Social Work. Einar Jacobsen, president for only three years, left under something of a cloud. Apparently he had offended the Jewish community and others at the university. From 1947 until 1950, John W. Taylor held the U of L presidency. A veteran himself, Taylor encouraged U of L's participation in the GI Bill and also worked in outreach programs such as the Neighborhood College Program and the use of radio broadcasts to reach nontraditional students. Mayor Charles Farnsley, in office and out, continued as a major booster of U of L and tried to find new ways to financially support the school, because the city contributed only about 10 percent of U of L's "total budget." After a succession of short-term and acting presidents, Philip Davidson, who held a doctorate in history from the University of Chicago, served as the twelfth president of U of L from 1951 to 1968.[38]

Situated in the largest city in Kentucky, the University of Louisville could not help but grow in the postwar era, even though it sustained a brief drop of enrollment "as the veteran surge receded" in the early 1950s. The campus remained divided, with the Health Sciences campus downtown and Arts and Sciences and the law and engineering colleges on what was now commonly called the Belknap Campus. The medical, dental, engineering, and law schools continued to expand their offerings against the inherent disadvantages of low municipal support. Money was tight. For example, new biochemistry professor John W. Brown in 1957 felt the immediate impact of "budgetary constraints." When he found that the sink in his laboratory had never been connected to either a drain or a water supply, he had to go through both the departmental chair and his dean. After finding out that the hookup might cost $100, the dean exclaimed, "Where in the world are we going to get that kind of money?" "Well, they did somehow find the money," recalled Brown. "A new and larger sink was installed, and it wasn't too long before I started my research." Both Brown and the historians of the University of Louisville agreed that the Davidson years were the "Golden Age" on the campus. Without state support, Brown and other science researchers avidly sought and won federal research grants. "It wasn't long before almost all of the new young faculty had major research grant support," he said. "I view those years as the time when we helped the university take a major step forward in its development." Although many local students commuted, because the school had neither dormitories to house them nor funds to build dormitories, more and more students came from outside the Louisville urban area. A 1952 $4 million bond issue made it possible to begin expansion of the Belknap Campus.[39]

In many ways the fifties and sixties were also a "golden age" of sports at U of L. Although it appeared that U of L sports always played second fiddle to UK sports, these were the years when Hickman's Cardinals beat Rupp's Wildcats in the 1959 NCAA tournament and Johnny Unitas and Lenny Lyles led the football Cardinals. Moreover, while UK athletics remained rigidly segregated, U of L integrated its teams in the early 1950s. UK appeared to be "wooing" senior Wesley Unseld of Louisville Seneca High School as its "1st Negro athlete" in March 1964, but some doubted Rupp's enthusiasm. Unseld went on to become an all-American standout at hometown U of L.[40]

Intercollegiate athletics in all the Kentucky colleges and universities, public and private, followed the national trend of growth in the postwar era. While U of L and UK might field the dominant "major" sports teams in the state, the smaller schools participated just as enthusiastically. After World War II, the regional state colleges left the Kentucky Intercollegiate Athletic Conference, formed in 1923, and joined the Ohio Valley Conference, which also eventually included several Tennessee schools. UK remained a staunch member of the Southeastern Conference, and U of L remained an independent for many years. Only at UK and U of L did athletic programs substantially pay for themselves, making it unnecessary for administrators to delve into university resources. The other schools fought a constant battle to compete and at the same time fund scholarships, pay coaches, and cover all the other expenses of fielding teams. Except for football and basketball, all sport teams, such as track, baseball, golf, tennis, and softball, were "non-revenue" sports. Title IX mandated that any school that received federal monies have equal numbers of men's and women's sports beginning in the seventies; this requirement added even more expense to already thinly stretched college and university budgets. Just as in the public schools, integration of athletics often prepared the way for greater desegregation of the student body. This was not without controversy. For example, the loss of the all-white UK team to an all-black Texas Western University squad in the 1966 NCAA basketball tournament finals foretold what would happen eventually at UK with an integrated team. At the time this game placed the University of Kentucky in a very poor light. Adding African American athletes to their teams prepared the way for further integration at all Kentucky colleges and universities. By the 1980s, many Kentucky private colleges that had never fielded football teams before added this expensive sport to their athletic programs. Some supporters of this move claimed that it enhanced a full athletic program, including encouraging alumni to attend games and an annual homecoming.[41]

The private, independent colleges in Kentucky could not help but grow in the post–World War II era; the GI Bill immediately raised enrollments, as it did in the public sector. Back in the good graces of the Baptist Association, Georgetown College built a new chapel with some classrooms, a badly needed new library, and dormitories. Like all other schools after World War II, except for Transylvania, Georgetown College switched back to a semester system. There was never enough space for students, as dormitory space was limited into the 1950s. I attended there from 1958 to 1962, when dormitories and classrooms were packed. As on many other campuses, surplus government buildings served as classrooms after the war when the curriculum expanded. After the troubles of the Sherwood presidency, Georgetown's next two presidents were Baptist ministers. The year 1957 was a turning point in Kentucky Baptist higher education. First, Cumberland and Campbellsville were given the go-ahead by Kentucky Baptists to become four-year colleges. Second, for several years a group of Louisville Baptists, the Committee of Fifteen, and their allies, including Georgetown president H. Leo Eddleman, pushed for the removal of Georgetown to a more cosmopolitan area. When the Georgetown trustees, by only one vote, and the Kentucky Baptist Convention by a wider margin, voted to retain the Georgetown location, businessman V. V. Cooke and others funded the creation of Kentucky Southern College on the outskirts of Louisville. Some were already dreaming that it would become another Baylor University at its 238-acre Shelbyville Road campus. Bethel College in Hopkinsville became the victim of the newer urban-college idea, as Kentucky Baptists cut their support. The founding of a public community college in that western Kentucky location further doomed the old Baptist school. Kentucky Southern, which opened its doors in 1963, grew to about 900 students and 100 faculty and staff in its first two years. However, financial difficulties plagued the school. An innovative interdisciplinary focus and other experimentation failed to save Kentucky Southern. In 1969 the campus, its few assets, and its debt were absorbed by the University of Louisville, and it became the Shelby Campus. Reality struck Kentucky Baptists with the fact that their denomination could not sustain four senior colleges in a state the size of Kentucky. Educator and layman Dr. Robert Mills led Georgetown into its continued growth from 1959 to 1978. For example, he was one of the first leaders of a denominational college to push for acceptance of federal dollars, which to some, Baptists in particular, smacked of violating the old dictum of separating church and state.[42]

The move of Cumberland and Campbellsville colleges toward becoming four-year baccalaureate-granting institutions in the 1960s and 1970s required great effort. First, Cumberland, Campbellsville, and Georgetown competed for students and funds within the same milieu. The Kentucky Baptist Convention doled out funds to these three as well as other educational institutions, including Oneida Baptist Institute. Non-self-perpetuating boards made up of Baptists appointed by the KBC offered little room for expanding and thinking outside a Baptist mind-set. Intramural skirmishing among Kentucky Baptists followed quasi-ideological/theological themes. According to longtime Georgetown College history professor Lindsey Apple, "Campbellsville and Cumberland enjoyed painting Georgetown with a 'liberal' brush" in the competition for funding in the second half of the twentieth century. After the turn of the twenty-first century, amid worsening relations between Georgetown and the increasingly fundamentalist-controlled state convention, Georgetown exited the system, relying on a self-perpetuating board of trustees. Both Campbellsville and Cumberland, becoming universities, adhered strictly to the directions of the Southern Baptist Convention, which had been in fundamentalist hands since in 1979. Second, these institutions drew students from the same student clientele, meaning there would be increased competition for student numbers. Third, room for growth would only come, as it did, from an increase in the number of Kentuckians and others graduating from high school. Fourth, one thing that aided Georgetown in holding the line on enrollment, and Cumberland and Campbellsville in expanding, was the relative distance from each other. Fifth, all had to depend on an increasing number of non-Baptist students to improve student numbers. Sixth, they had to use sources outside historical Baptist circles in order to survive. For example, students could begin to draw on National Defense Student Loans, as I did at Georgetown, beginning in the late fifties, because this money went to students and not directly, or so the reasoning went, to the colleges.[43]

As Cumberland and Campbellsville expanded their curricula to include four-year liberal arts and then more technical courses, they also built new buildings. Both schools had begun as efforts to implant Baptist denominationalism in their regions, supported by a local Baptist association, to fill a void not filled by public education around the turn of the twentieth century, and then to educate elementary teachers. As public school education improved and the state developed normal schools, both Cumberland and Campbellsville lost their original reasons for being. By allowing both to become "senior" colleges, the state Baptist convention followed a state and national trend. In particular, most denominational junior colleges either developed four-year curricula or went out of business. From 1947 to 1980, when President James Malcolm Boswell presided over the Cumberland campus, enrollment grew from just over 400 to more than 2,000 students. Similar growth took place on the Campbellsville campus into the early 1980s.[44]

Students at Kentucky's colleges and universities many times struggled to pay their expenses. The efforts of Ron Murphy at Cumberland College provide an example of how students from a farming background paid for college in the early 1960s. When the pigs that Murphy raised on the family farm reached approximately 225 pounds, he sold them before each semester in order to pay for his tuition. "During my junior year we had a very difficult winter," Murphy explained.

My pigs were not ready to go to market in time to pay my tuition for the spring semester. One day I was sitting with a small group of friends under the old gym in a small restaurant called the Wigwam. President Boswell [1947–1980] came in and sat down with us. He began asking each of us what classes we would be taking the following semester. When he asked me the question, I told him that I would have to sit out for a semester due to the fact that my hogs would not be going to market in time for me to pay my fees. Before he left he asked me when I thought the hogs would be going to market and I told him that my Dad said it would be around the first of February. Dr. Boswell proceeded to take a napkin and begin to write on it. He then handed it to me and told me to go ahead and register and that I could pay my tuition when I sold my hogs. I am sure that Dr. Boswell thought that if I sat out a semester that I might not continue my education.

Sometimes the efforts and kindness of an administrator like Boswell meant that a student could stay in school. "I have always been very indebted for his generosity and concern for my education," Murphy said. "His actions made me a much better teacher and administrator as I dealt with my students and teachers during my 27 years in public education."[45]

At Eastern a student in the 1950s could make it through a semester for as little as $300 a semester, including $50 in fees (the word "tuition" was not used), room and board, and books. Fifty-dollar scholarships were crucial to many students. One mid-fifties student from Shelbyville, Donald R. Swindler, had a $50 scholarship to pay all his fees. On Friday afternoon he returned to his hometown to work all weekend at a grocery store, then very early on Monday morning caught a ride back to Richmond, catching up on sleep. Other students worked on campus or off campus to make not just spending money but money to pay their college expenses. Like most other colleges, Eastern paid the one-ninth matching sum to make its students eligible for National Defense Student Loans in 1959.[46]

All of the denominational and private colleges faced a new age with increasing competition from public higher education. Slavery had divided Baptists, Methodists, and Presbyterians in the late pre–Civil War era. Methodists were the first to reunite, when the major white northern and southern Methodist organizations came back together in 1939. Methodists had their hands full in providing higher education at Kentucky Wesleyan College and Lindsey Wilson College, operated by the Louisville Conference, and Union College, controlled by the Kentucky Conference, in the immediate postwar years. Kentucky Wesleyan College, which had moved to Winchester from Millersburg in 1890, under President Paul Shell Powell, had struggled to survive the Great Depression and the war years with few students, little endowment, and little local support. With Wesleyan and Lindsey Wilson in the greatest financial distress, Bishop William Turner Watkins of the Louisville Conference in August 1945 urged that Wesleyan and Lindsey Wilson merge and relocate to Louisville. In a committee composed of representatives from both conferences, the issue was debated and apparently everyone was in agreement. Then Winchester citizens, as well as the KWC Alumni Association, began raising objections. Whereas the Kentucky Conference voted for the merger because it would solidify Lindsey Wilson's position, "after a session marked by great acrimony on both sides of the question and countless parliamentary moves the question of merger was finally put to a vote and defeated by a vote of 98 for the adoption and 100 against." Bishop Watkins immediately announced that the merger issue was dead.[47]

Nevertheless, Wesleyan faced an uphill battle for survival, needing to add money to the endowment, increase enrollment, and make other improvements in order to receive Southern Association of Colleges and Secondary Schools accreditation. Veterans returning to the Winchester campus helped increase enrollment, and the situation improved enough for the school to begin playing sports again. KWC felt the impact of inflation, as did all other Kentucky colleges and universities, and corners were cut when possible. President Paul Shell Powell, whom veterans on campus dubbed "Peashell," was a man "not accustomed to having his ideas questioned." Powell ordered that all lights on the Winchester campus be turned off at 10:00 P.M. for economy. Looking for a reason to demonstrate against "Peashell," veterans confronted him when they noticed that electricity illuminated the president's home in the late evening. Not only did veterans and others on campus begin petition drives against the austerity of KWC life, but conservative Methodists touted Asbury College as the best college for the Methodist faithful.[48]

A group of KWC supporters and alumni in Owensboro, along with the Owensboro Chamber of Commerce, began a concerted effort to bring the school to that city on the Ohio. They argued that the school would face less competition than in central Kentucky and that they could raise the money necessary to give KWC a secure future. Owensboro supporters raised $1 million. With declining health as well as prestige, Powell resigned on June 1, 1950. In a spirited meeting of both the Louisville and Kentucky conferences, held in Louisville, both voted by secret ballot to accept the offer of moving to Owensboro. Winchester supporters kept up the pressure to keep the school by arguing that Owensboro's offer was too low to fund the move of Wesleyan, but to no avail, as another meeting of the Kentucky Conference in Richmond also supported the move. Powell's successor, Rev. John Foster Baggett, "like all his predecessors, struggled with the day-to-day-problems of paying the bills." The move was difficult, but in the fall of 1951, KWC classes opened at several locations in Owensboro. Three years later a new campus opened on South Frederica Street. As is pointed out by the historians of Wesleyan, for all the growth of a new campus and support of the city, "it was basketball that gave the Wesleyan community its greatest sense of unity," because Coach "Bullitt" Wilson's teams began to win consistently.[49]

Union College in Barbourville served a mountain clientele primarily in its early days, but in the second half of the twentieth century more students came from outside the region. President Conway Boatman (1938–1959) presided over the rejuvenation of the school, and Union moved into the postwar era as a fully accredited four-year college. Under the Forward Program, Union, like other Kentucky schools, built much-needed buildings to augment a growing student population. Besides progressing academically, Union also participated in the Kentucky Intercollegiate Athletic conference of small colleges, and Coach "Pete" Moore's teams were very successful in the 1960s and early 1970s. Although World War II interrupted the football program for several years, Union added the sport back later, not only to enhance its athletic program but to also draw male students. Because the school was in an economically depressed area, Boatman found many problems. "To employ and to hold a faculty of superior quality had been really the most acute difficulty of these twenty years," he said at the end of his tenure as president.[50]

Lindsey Wilson College in Columbia and Sue Bennett College in London had similar origins and purposes, being organized to offer education and normal school training in an area that lacked these advantages. Founded by a Methodist's women's group in 1897, Sue Bennett, named for one of two founding sisters from Richmond, began, like many other schools of this type, as a elementary-secondary school and then began offering junior college courses later, dropping the high school courses as the public schools improved. In Sue Bennett's case, college courses were first offered in 1922. However, the school could not sustain growth as it expanded into a four-year curriculum, and it closed in 1997. Lindsey Wilson College received more direct support from the Louisville Conference and made a more successful move from a junior college to a senior college, receiving the right to grant the baccalaureate degree in 1986. When John B. Begley became president of Lindsey Wilson in 1977, the school had about 300 students, "an annual budget of $600,000, deficient academic programs, and a campus in embarrassing disrepair." "He was the right man at the right time for Lindsey Wilson," claimed one study of the school. By 1997 the school had grown to 1,400 students, with new buildings, a $15 million budget, varsity sports, and graduate programs; it had also found a regional niche as an educational, cultural, and athletic center.[51]

Asbury College and Asbury Seminary, with self-perpetuating boards, operated outside United Methodist Church circles as independent schools in the "Wesleyan-Holiness tradition." Actually nondenominational, Asbury appealed to conservative students, faculty, and constituencies. President from 1940 to 1966, Z. T. Johnson succeeded Henry Clay Morrison and led Asbury in a new age. Although World War II depleted male enrollment, Asbury grew after the war to over a thousand students by the mid-sixties. Unlike other Kentucky private colleges, Asbury did not field intercollegiate athletic teams until late in its development. However, as Coach Will Shouse explained in 2009, "Everything [at Asbury] is bigger than basketball. You're at this school for a different reason. Just to find God and get done with your major." More important than sports to this conservative school, periodic religious revivals, often spontaneous, sometimes swept the campus and community. Nevertheless, Asbury followed the pattern of offering more and more undergraduate majors other than just religious instruction.[52]

Caney Junior College was renamed Alice Lloyd Junior College in 1962 upon the death of its founder and did not become a four-year college until 1980. Alice Lloyd continued to concentrate on educating teachers. At some nearby elementary and high schools, up to fifty percent of teachers were alumni of that college. Like Berea College, Alice Lloyd continued its mandatory work-study program as a way of providing students both a means of paying for their education and work experience in the college community. The school steadily grew, having as many as five hundred students in the 1980s.[53]

Transylvania, the oldest school of higher education in Kentucky, blundered along into the war years. Recurring financial crises and World War II brought Transylvania "to the brink of disaster." The GI Bill increased the school population just after the war. Postwar presidents Raymond McLain and Frank Rose argued that Transylvania must "play a unique role in American education." Small private colleges no longer had a dominating role in Kentucky higher education, as they had in the nineteenth century, because public education now had overwhelming funding sources. Therefore, the small private colleges had to find a niche. President Rose, described by Transylvania historian John D. Wright Jr. as "one of the most handsome, energetic and popular presidents the college ever had," became head of the school in 1952. A minister of the Disciples of Christ denomination and a Transylvania and College of the Bible graduate, Rose successfully gained support of the church. The beginning of a successful campaign to pay off old debts and construct new buildings even brought President Dwight D. Eisenhower to the Lexington campus for a ceremony in 1954. After Rose left for the presidency of the University of Alabama, Irvin E. Lunger became president of Transylvania and served from 1957 to 1976. Under Lunger Transylvania continued to grow, with enrollment increasing to more than one thousand students. Another Disciples school, Midway College in Woodford County, founded in 1847, had begun as Kentucky Female Orphan School. It came under Disciples of Christ authority, primarily to offer normal course work, but grew into a junior college and then a baccalaureate-granting institution after the war as Kentucky's only college for women. By 1990 it had more than five hundred students. The more conservative wing of the denominations generally called the Christian Churches had founded their own school in Grayson in 1919 as an elementary, secondary, and normal school. Kentucky Christian College, affiliated with the Christian Church/Church of Christ, followed the familiar pattern of evolving into a junior college and then a senior college in the post–World War II years. However, unlike Transylvania, this Christian school continued to concentrate on religious studies and vocations into the 1980s.[54]

The Presbyterians also sought to maintain their place in the state's higher education mixture. President Walter Groves of Centre presented his case to President Raymond McLain of Transylvania and others just after the war. From 1921 to 1946 the enrollment numbers of tax-supported colleges and universities in the commonwealth nearly tripled. While in 1921 the private colleges enrolled 50 percent of the state's students, by 1946 the percentage had dropped to about 20. Even though Centre College in Danville, the oldest Presbyterian college west of the Allegheny Mountains, came through World War II better off than its denominational competitors in Kentucky, Groves argued that his school and similar ones had to continue to seek distinctiveness in order to survive. Centre had always trained a somewhat "elite" clientele. Centre professor Hardin Craig, class of 1897, in his eccentric and personal history of the school, decried what he saw as the decline of higher education owing to its proliferation in America. While he found that "the debasement of education" typified most colleges and universities, he criticized his school's abandonment of Latin and Greek for more modern studies. In October 1967 Craig declared that "Centre College had apparently lost the art of creating eminent men at least of any conspicuous degree." Though "Presbyterian-affiliated," Centre went to a "self-perpetuating" board in 1958.[55]

President Thomas A. Spragens (1957–1981) pushed Centre into the new age; enrollment doubled to eight hundred and there was a concomitant increase in faculty. The Fund for the Future campaign, begun during his presidency, raised about $34 million. In 1962 women moved from the old Kentucky College for Women site to the Centre campus, making the school totally coeducational. Seven years later Centre made another historic change by cutting ties to the Presbyterian synods. Spragens and later presidents Richard L. Morrill and Michael F. Adams worked diligently to increase the school's endowment, and Centre soon led the nation in the percentage of contributing alumni. Centre continued to lead the state in producing Rhodes scholars and Fulbright scholars, contrary to the pessimism of Professor Craig in his book, as well as providing a most prolific Greek social life on campus. In the eighties Centre students demonstrated the frivolity of youth by starting the tradition of "Running the Flame." A large metal sculpture on campus, "The Flame," became the quest of occasional nude male students running from their residences, particularly as they neared graduation.[56]

Two other eastern Kentucky Presbyterian institutions, Pikeville College and Lees Junior College, followed much different paths than the more prestigious and well-endowed Centre College. Both began as missionary efforts of the church. Founded as Pikeville Collegiate Institute in 1889 by Presbyterian ministers William C. Condit and James P. Hendrick, the mountain school grew slowly. Isolated in a coal-bearing area, the school found its fortunes tied up in improving transportation into the region. During most of its early history, Pikeville focused on developing an elementary and high school and then soon adding teacher education courses. Fearing the "outsiders" who ran the school, someone at the turn of the twentieth century planted dynamite under the school's only building. Fortunately, President James F. Record, a Minnesota native, found the explosive in time to save the building. Pikeville began adding a few college classes in 1918 and graduated its first junior college students in the twenties. The high school curriculum was not dropped until 1957. Like many other such mountain schools, it was multipurpose in an era of limited opportunities for both high school and college education. It became a tradition to climb the "ninety-nine steps" from the town to the campus. In the early years, all students worked. On "Potato Day," all classes were called off to plant vegetables on the college farm.[57]

The institution that originated as Jackson Academy in Breathitt County in 1883 to bring elementary and secondary education to the region became S. P. Lees Collegiate Institute in 1897 and began offering junior college coursework in 1927. Rev. Troy R. Eslinger, president from 1961 to 1988, oversaw an expansion of the student body to more than three hundred students and the construction of several buildings. I taught history at Lees Junior College from 1967 to 1970, when the school was caught up in the expansion of higher education in the mountain region. Eslinger "was a tireless worker and totally committed to energizing the college and getting the college on its feet," according to Fred Landrum, former Lees executive vice president. As at many other such schools, too much depended on the president's personal efforts and prestige, and the school went into an abrupt eclipse under the next president. Lees soon ended its days as a Presbyterian school and became the Jackson campus of the Hazard Community and Technical College. In contrast, Pikeville College continued to grow in the postwar era, awarding its first baccalaureate degrees in 1957, and, like all other Kentucky colleges, expanded its curriculum to appeal to a more diverse student body.[58]

The Catholic colleges of Kentucky followed many of the same patterns of private school education, concentrating their efforts in the Catholic population centers of Louisville, northern Kentucky, Owensboro, and Washington and Nelson counties. Bellarmine College, modeled on Catholic University's liberal arts core, opened in 1950 on Newburg Road in Louisville as a college for men and merged in 1968 with Ursuline College for women. Bellarmine developed a College of Arts and Sciences as well as nursing and business schools. By 1989 the school enrolled more than twenty-five hundred undergraduate and graduate students. Nazareth College of Louisville and Nazareth College of Nelson County merged at the Louisville location in 1960. Nazareth College for women changed its name to Catherine Spalding College in 1963, shortened it to Spalding College in 1969, and became coeducational in 1973. Spalding developed several master's degree programs and doctoral programs in psychology and education in the 1980s. Accordingly, it took the name Spalding University in 1984. Founded, like many other such schools, as an elementary-secondary school, St. Catherine College, near Springfield in Washington County, evolved into a junior college, converted from women-only to coeducational, and struggled through the eighties to maintain enrollment. As seen in the accounts of Lees Junior College and Sue Bennett College, the postwar pattern for sectarian junior colleges became one of either moving to a four-year program or closing, owing to the growth

of the UK-controlled community college system. In Owensboro, Brescia
College evolved from Mt. St. Joseph College and received accreditation as a
four-year school in 1957. Villa Madonna College, in Covington, also demonstrated the postwar changes affecting sectarian higher education. Beginning
as a college for women in 1923, the school became coeducational in 1945. On
a new campus in the Fort Mitchell area, the school was renamed Thomas
More College in 1968, and a dedication address was delivered by President
Lyndon B. Johnson. By the mid-1980s the school enrolled more than fifteen
hundred students.[59]

Theological education in the commonwealth also prospered in the post–
World War II era, but not without reacting to the pressures of the times, as
Baptists, Methodists, Presbyterians, Catholics, and Episcopalians continued
to be served by well-established seminaries. There were controversies as serious and divisive as those of the nineteenth century. Southern Baptist Theological Seminary remained the largest theological school in the state as well
as one of the largest in the United States. Beginning in 1979, fundamentalists
began taking control of Southern Baptist Convention institutions in a battle
over "inerrancy" of the Bible and other issues. Ten years later that dominance
became complete when fundamentalists gained a majority on the SBTS
board of trustees. Then began the expulsions and resignations of moderate
professors from that old institution on Lexington Road in Louisville.[60]

Other seminaries in Kentucky did not go through such crises. In 1965,
celebrating its centennial, the College of the Bible changed its name to
Lexington Theological Seminary, reflecting its evolution into a modernist
Disciples of Christ institution. LTS developed a reputation for cooperating
with other denominations, even offering a master's degree in religious education for Catholics. Asbury Theological Seminary had separated from Asbury
College in 1931 and remained on a separate campus. Both schools represented a conservative brand of Methodism in the holiness tradition. In 1963
Louisville Presbyterian Seminary relocated from downtown to Alta Vista
Road. Representing one of the smaller but more well-to-do denominations
in the state, this seminary, like LTS, often reflected a liberal stance in the
late twentieth century. After the closure of the Hopkinsville College of the
Bible, Simmons Bible College in Louisville was the only African American
seminary in the state.[61]

The constancy of politics in Kentucky higher education also affected the
health of Kentuckians. Although President Frank McVey (1917–1940) of the
University of Kentucky had advocated the building of a medical school in
Lexington, there had never been enough support for the effort. Governor
A. B. Chandler, during his first term in office (1935–1939), supported estab-
lishment of a UK medical school, but Depression conditions ended any hope

for such a costly project. The talk about a medical school continued into the war years with no action taken, although UK continued to grow in other areas. In 1947 UK took over the assets of the private Louisville College of Pharmacy, promising to move the school to Lexington when a new building could be built. However, it was not until eight years later that the General Assembly appropriated the necessary funds to complete the building. There was more and more talk of a medical school in Lexington. In the last year of his administration, Governor Lawrence W. Wetherby told a constituent that "our present tax structure" could not "bear" the expense of a new public medical school. Meanwhile, the Legislative Research Commission continued to study the issue.[62]

Much of the credit for keeping the issue alive belongs to Dr. John S. Chambers, who as director of the Kentucky Department of Hygiene and Public Health in the early 1930s began advocating for another medical school. He argued that the University of Louisville Medical School did not produce enough physicians for the needs of the commonwealth, and he kept up this crusade into the postwar years. In 1948 bills came before the General Assembly to provide state aid for the University of Louisville Medical School as well as to build a new school at UK. The legislature "narrowly approved SB 105," for the first time giving state funds for "medical research" for the U of L, but providing no funds for UK's proposed medical school. University of Kentucky interests continued pressing to add a UK school, even as Louisville president Philip Davidson (1951–1968), fearing the loss of accreditation, argued that U of L greatly needed new buildings and resources for its medical and dental schools.[63]

The pressures to build a new school, as well as the competition between U of L and UK to control the movement, continued. In 1952 the UK board of trustees issued a booklet encouraging Kentuckians to push for more medical education and more trained doctors for the commonwealth. The Legislative Research Commission studied the matter and found that the state did indeed need more medical education. And, as sometimes happens in Kentucky, all the political stars seemed to finally come into alignment. In the 1955 Democratic Party gubernatorial primary, both candidates, Bert T. Combs and A. B. Chandler, voiced support for a new medical center at UK as well as for more funding for the U of L schools. In the general election, even the Republican candidate, Edwin R. Denny, supported UK's expansion into the medical field. The victorious Chandler kept his promise to push for the UK medical school.[64]

The UK trustees took the initiative with this enabling legislation and established a medical school. Chandler recommended that the General Assembly appropriate $5 million for a medical school as well as build a university hospital, for a total of about $28 million, $9 million of it to come from the federal government through the Hill-Burton Act for construction of the hospital. In May 1956 colleges of dentistry and nursing joined the new medical college as building of the facilities proceeded on the old Experiment Station Farm on Rose Street. Although U of L president Davidson kept a low profile and stayed out of the fight, the U of L medical and dental schools also received increased state aid. As UK gained increasing state support, the U of L continued to search for revenue. In 1960 Louisville voters "soundly rejected a U of L bond issue."[65]

Just after the landmark UK medical school legislation passed the General Assembly, Donovan announced his retirement. Tom Clark later recounted, "I've been told, on good authority, that UK Vice President of Business Administration Frank Peterson [who came to UK as controller, jointly appointed by Governor Keen Johnson along with Donovan in 1941], Donovan, Frank Dickey [dean of the College of Education]," and Governor Chandler "met at breakfast in Maxwell Place [UK's presidential residence], and that's where the decision was made to appoint Frank Dickey." And, as a fait accompli, the UK board of trustees soon appointed Dickey president, at age thirty-eight the youngest one in the history of the Lexington school. Dickey presided over a rapidly expanding campus, with the Medical Center as the centerpiece of a $21 million annual budget and with an enrollment of more than seven thousand. The future looked bright and limitless for the new president and the commonwealth's land grant university.[66]

With the exceptions of Presidents Ralph Woods of Murray (1945–1968) and Rufus Atwood of Kentucky State, new leaders, somewhat more vigorous than those two, emerged at the other state schools. Kentucky politics was always deeply involved. In 1954 Adron Doran, a former state legislator and educator, with a UK doctorate in education, became the prime candidate for the presidency of Morehead State College after "Governor Lawrence W. Wetherby orchestrated the selection from Frankfort." There was some dissension on the board, and State Superintendent of Public Instruction Wendell Butler cast the deciding vote, making it 3-2 for Doran's appointment. The personable Doran, who was also a Church of Christ minister, took over a school that had deteriorated somewhat during World War II, had added only one new building since 1937, and had lost its accreditation over political interference in 1948. He immediately set about the task of winning favor in Frankfort. In his UK dissertation on the Council on Public Higher Education, Doran had argued for centralized control of all institutions of higher education in the commonwealth, agreeing with the Griffenhagen and other studies of the mid-forties. However, once Doran became president of Morehead, he took an individualistic course and became very effective in getting money from Frankfort. "No one could play the game of politics better than he," according to the historian of Morehead. The school caught onto the growth pattern typical of the time, expanding its offerings to a growing student body. During Doran's tenure, "enrollment grew tenfold," reaching more than seven thousand by the early seventies. The strong-willed Doran tried to rule with an iron hand and clashed with some faculty immediately, prompting insertion of an academic-freedom clause in the Faculty Handbook in 1956.[67]

In Bowling Green, Kelly Thompson, a longtime Western administrator, became president of Western in 1955. "He had few equals in dealing with people on a one-to-one basis, and he was already an accomplished public speaker," opined Western's historian. From that time until Thompson's retirement in 1969, enrollment increased from just under 2,000 to more than 11,000. In his first ten years as president, the faculty more than trebled. With the closure of the private Bowling Green Business College, Western added a more extensive business curriculum. At Morehead, Western, Eastern, and Murray during the fifties and sixties, older faculty began to be replaced by younger instructors, most of whom had terminal degrees. Although these schools continued to train teachers, in keeping with their normal school origins, now the majority of students took degrees in other fields.[68]

Early in his term (1955–1959) as state school superintendent of public instruction, alumnus Robert R. Martin avidly sought to replace Eastern president O'Donnell, who was nearing the mandatory retirement age of seventy. The Kentucky body politic again played a key role in the appointment of a new president at Eastern, a process that all came down to timing and who would have a majority of votes on the Eastern Board of Regents. Governor Chandler appointed four new regents to the board in his term, and if O'Donnell retired before the next governor took office, Chandler could encourage the board to appoint his favorite, political ally John E. Robinson. Or, if a Chandler ally won the next governor race, Chandler could still influence whom the board chose. When O'Donnell refused to retire early, Chandler tried an end run by appointing someone before the venerable Eastern president stepped down. Attorney General Jo M. Ferguson, a Combs-Martin ally, shot down that idea quickly in a summary opinion. Martin and Governor Chandler had locked horns over several issues during their concurrent terms from 1955 to 1959. Thrown into this mixture of strong political personalities was the ever-present Wendell P. Butler, who had preceded Martin as state superintendent and won again in 1959. Bert T. Combs, who had lost the 1955 Democratic primary to Chandler, chose Martin (still in the superintendent position) as his campaign manager, much to the displeasure of the *Courier-Journal* and Governor Chandler, both arguing that Martin should resign his state post. Martin refused. Martin then brokered a deal whereby Louisville mayor Wilson Wyatt dropped out of the Democratic gubernatorial primary and instead joined the Combs ticket as the candidate for lieutenant governor. Combs won the primary against Harry Lee Waterfield, Chandler's surrogate, and went on to a landslide victory over Republican John M. Robsion Jr. in the general election.[69]

Martin received an immediate political plum in the form of a Combs appointment as commissioner of finance. Then in the new year of 1960, O'Donnell announced his pending retirement. Although Martin was the apparent leading candidate, others were mentioned. The April 13, 1960, Eastern regents meeting promised to be interesting, and there were intrigues afoot. Before the meeting, Butler, as chairman of the board, and three Chandler appointees met in downtown Richmond for a "strategy conference." Just after the Board of Regents came into session, O'Donnell announced his intention to retire on June 30. Butler immediately called for nominations for Eastern's next chief executive. Three candidates were put forward, and to be chosen, one of them would need a majority of the seven votes. On the first ballot, Martin received three of the seven votes while the other candidates split three votes with one abstention. Butler then burned the votes. On the second ballot, Martin was elected with four votes and three abstentions. Butler later claimed that he had changed his vote on the second ballot to elect Martin, who had the support of a sitting governor. "Bob needed four votes and I gave him the vote that elected him president," Butler claimed in an oral history interview. He perhaps had little choice, not wanting to upset the governor. "Well, there is no question that I wanted the Board of Regents to appoint him," Combs later recalled, "and I let that be known. . . . Intelligent people know what the score is without having their arms twisted." While most of the state's press editorially praised Martin's appointment, Barry Bingham Sr. and the *Courier-Journal* still held a grudge and remained silent.[70]

Meanwhile, Governor Combs encouraged two major studies of higher education: one to study the community college issue and the other a long-range study of higher education. Of course, the Council on Public Higher Education also continued to play a role, acting as a "coordinating body and not a controlling body." Some critics of the competitive method that UK and the other state colleges used every two years to obtain their state appropriations continued to urge that more power be given to the CPHE or that a "superboard" be developed, with UK in control. The issues of higher education in Kentucky were further complicated when greater pressures developed in the sixties to give more state support to the University of Louisville. As long as the presidents of all the state schools remained on the CPHE as voting members, the CPHE directly reflected their thoughts, which usually translated into attempts to achieve gain for their own school over that for others. However, the state colleges often "ganged up" on UK when new programs and state appropriations were discussed.[71]

While O'Donnell had been fiscally conservative to the core, often forgoing increases in state support in the spirit of collegial equanimity, Martin intended to go after any dollars wherever he could find them as he pushed Eastern to expansion. Some critics charged that while commissioner of finance he was already routing money to his alma mater. "He was a genius at getting money," said Tom Clark of Martin, adding that Martin "was the most astute of astute politicians." The Eastern president was one of the first college presidents in the state to take the lead in extensively using revenue bonding and consolidating debt for new buildings. Martin "more or less invented the whole concept of the consolidated bond issues and the system of financing capital outlay through bond issues," recalled Ed Prichard. Like Doran at Morehead, Woods at Murray, and Thompson at Western, Martin began a serious push to diversify his campus, placing it on a course to become a regional comprehensive university, thus mirroring the national trend for the old normal schools that had evolved into state colleges. Upon becoming president, Martin first pushed to develop an overall building and refurbishment plan, but he soon initiated programs characteristic of a comprehensive college, with schools of nursing and law enforcement as added incentives for students to attend the Richmond campus. The beginning of law enforcement coursework competed with the older Southern Police Institute at the University of Louisville, while UK appeared slow to take up this task. Eastern also developed a nursing program, with UK opposition. In the beginning Lexington hospitals would not accommodate Eastern's nursing students in their clinical work, so the Richmond school had to use hospitals in the surrounding area. In the sixties enrollment grew on the Richmond campus from about three thousand to nearly ten thousand. From only a $7 million plant, the Martin years witnessed a growth to $120 million overall value. In some ways rivals, Martin and Doran took relish in ganging up on UK on occasion in CPHE meetings. Reporter Dick Wilson of the *Courier-Journal* once compared them this way: "If the two men were orchestrating a parade, Martin would be satisfied with planning it flawlessly. Doran would insist on being the grand marshal."[72]

As UK and the regional colleges grew in the fifties with aggressive leadership, the role of Kentucky State College in the mix of state-supported institutions of higher education became even more problematical. With the *Brown* decision in 1954, as well as earlier state laws that began the overturn of the Day Law, the question became whether a historically black institution could survive in the age of integration. If so, what role should it play when higher education was diversifying more and more? President Rufus B. Atwood, representing an older black leadership, wanted to protect Kentucky State but appeared uncertain how best to do that. In these early years of desegregation, the traditionally white state colleges, UK, U of L, and the private colleges, had few black students.[73]

In the late fifties and early sixties, the NAACP, the Congress of Racial Equality (CORE), and other advocates of black civil rights took the offensive in Kentucky, as they did elsewhere. The desegregation of the public schools, as discussed in chapter 7, was only one facet of the movement. Tension on the University of Kentucky campus resulted in the departure of white CORE activist political science professor William O. Reichert, who realized that achieving tenure would be difficult after receiving a dressing down by President Frank Dickey, as the professor recalled in a letter to historian George C. Wright. The efforts of CORE in Frankfort and at Kentucky State College came to a crucial impasse in 1960. Integration of the Frankfort and Franklin County school systems and public accommodations in Frankfort restaurants became a focal point of some Kentucky State professors and students. Kentucky State itself was desegregating, with 69 white students enrolling in night classes but only 7 whites in day classes in the fall of 1959. White and black students on some campuses were becoming restive, not only asking for major civil rights change but also seeking a greater role in college and university governance.[74]

In this climate of uncertainty and change, the spring semester of 1960 at Kentucky State College proved crucial. "Sit-ins" were occurring all over the South. During the fall semester, students had "met with President Atwood to discuss concerns about poor student/faculty relations." However, when the administration appeared to be "unresponsive," on April 29, 1960, three hundred students responded by dumping their uneaten breakfast food in the cafeteria. Then some demanded that college officials meet with them. Atwood countered by calling a student convocation, where he asked for peace and announced that CORE was no longer welcome on the campus. As the situation escalated, KSC expelled twelve students and dismissed two faculty members. Atwood called in the state police, and more than half of the students returned home. The burning of Bell Gymnasium on May 2 only exacerbated the problems on campus. Although it was apparently a case of arson, no one was ever prosecuted. "The turmoil on campus had left President Atwood shaken and puzzled," according to a UK dissertation. Atwood said: "The whole thing was unexpected." Calm returned to the KSC campus in 1960, but on April 2, 1968, the Jones building was destroyed by arson. Overall, the sixties were turbulent times on the Frankfort campus. The author of the school's centennial history, John A. Hardin, noted that as Kentucky State

College integrated, "KSC's black students began to express mild resentment at the growing white presence on campus." Some Kentuckians, including the editor of the hometown *Frankfort State Journal*, argued that the campus should be closed. A study of KSC commissioned by Governor Combs advised that the school should continue as a four-year liberal arts college but also become more "multipurpose" by offering junior college work and courses for state government employees. White enrollment increased to 40 percent of the sixteen hundred total enrollment in 1970. Many of the white students were state employees who took evening courses. In effect, the KSC campus remained nearly all black during day classes and nearly all white at night. With the decision to save Kentucky State by legislative fiat, the General Assembly soon realized, according to longtime CPHE official Gary S. Cox, that "extraordinary" funding would be needed to keep it functioning because of its relatively small size.[75]

Kentucky followed national integration trends while attempting to comply with Title VI of the Civil Rights Act of 1964, which prohibited discrimination at any institution that received federal funding. Complying with Title VI, especially the spirit of the law, was not always easy. Although the traditional white schools increased black enrollment in the sixties and seventies, retention of those students lagged. By the end of the seventies, historically white colleges and universities had greater success in integrating black students than in hiring black faculty. Historically black colleges had greater success in integrating white faculty into their campuses, because the numbers of black doctorates was limited during this time. The traditional black schools had to hire whites to keep up with accreditation efforts.[76]

The junior or community college movement also had an impact on Kentucky higher education. Private denominational junior colleges like Campbellsville, Cumberland, Lindsey Wilson, and a few others moved to become four-year schools. Others, like Sue Bennett, Bethel, and eventually even Lees, folded. Kentucky, as usual, followed a little behind the major trend encouraged by the Commission on Higher Education of the Truman years, in founding and supporting a statewide system of "community" colleges. Although junior colleges in Paducah and Ashland had dissimilar origins in the Great Depression years, both became successful municipally owned junior colleges funded by citizens' taxes. Proprietary schools such as Spencerian and Sullivan came through the war years as training schools for business and, like many other such schools, later expanded their offerings to accounting and other associate degrees. Moreover, they began to enter other "markets" in the state. Sullivan evolved into a four-year college and began offering graduate work in business on its six Kentucky campuses.[77]

Governor Bert T. Combs, well aware of the current trends in American higher education, came into office in 1959 committed to improving educational opportunities for Kentuckians at all levels. The advent of the Kentucky sales tax added revenues that could be used to increase funding for public school education. Everywhere public colleges and universities were expanding, and the movement struck Kentucky in full force during the meeting of the 1960 General Assembly. During that session several legislators, including Harry Caudill, introduced measures to create in their communities junior colleges controlled by the University of Kentucky. When these passed, both the governor and President Dickey urged that the matter be further studied before any action was taken. At Combs's insistence, the legislature authorized the Commission on the Study of Public Higher Education. The 1960 General Assembly also asked the Legislative Research Commission to make a study of the need to expand opportunities by approving more schools in the commonwealth. In *Some Aspects of Higher Education in Kentucky*, published in 1963, the Council on Public Higher Education suggested that there indeed was much room for expansion. With all the state's public and private colleges and universities growing at unprecedented rates because of the onslaught of the baby boom generation, the question remained how to implement a bold plan and where to get the money for such expansion at the public level. And there was no consensus about the matter. "The Commission report was viewed by President Adron Doran and other council members as too bold and audacious to suit them," reported Neil Cook Ward in a dissertation on studies of higher education in Kentucky. The combination of politics and higher education was inevitable. "If we do not establish an extension in Prestonsburg," Regent H. D. Fitzpatrick Jr. told President Martin of Eastern, "someone else is going to do it for us." Ellis F. Hartford, longtime UK professor of education and a leader in the development of the UK Community College System, found that even his good friend Robert R. Martin reacted negatively to the control of UK over this educational enterprise.[78]

With Combs's leadership, the General Assembly, in addition to the usual public school funding issues, considered two important education measures in 1962: creation of Kentucky Educational Television and of a community college system to be administered by UK. Legislators from communities that did not have junior or senior colleges, including Elizabethtown, Prestonsburg, Somerset, and Whitesburg, led the way in pushing for such schools. The *Courier-Journal* supported the move, as did many business leaders in Kentucky. One battle took place over whether the system should be freestanding or part of the University of Kentucky. Even President Frank Dickey seemed uneasy, owing to the expense of adding such a role to the state's land grant university; he reported that it cost more money to educate a student at the UK centers than it did on the Lexington campus. The *Lexington Herald* opposed adding more "University extension centers" as well as a "master board to control all the institutions" of the state as urged by the report of the Commission on Study of Higher Education. The Republican *Lexington Leader* echoed these same sentiments, arguing that money should be spent "to provide adequately for what we have first, rather than set up a system that would give second-rate education to everybody." Eastern's Martin and Morehead's Doran believed that their schools should be offering junior college coursework both on their campuses and at their own off-campus centers and did not want what was later called a "superboard" overseeing them. Both let it be known that the community colleges would provide UK with a "power base" that diminished their own resources. Nevertheless, on March 6, 1962, Governor Combs signed into law the bill creating the UK Community College System. Alaska, Nevada, and Hawaii were the only other states in which the state universities "organized community colleges under their egis."[79]

Frank Dickey, perhaps worn-out and overwhelmed by the controversy, left in 1963 for a post with the Southern Association of Colleges and Schools. The new UK president, John W. Oswald, coming from the California system of state control of public education, including a vast system of community colleges, had the opportunity to implement the new system. The University of Kentucky had extension centers in Ashland, Covington, Cumberland, Fort Knox, and Henderson that automatically became "community colleges," to be joined by Elizabethtown and Prestonsburg in 1964. The Community College System of the University of Kentucky came under the governance of the UK board of trustees, with its own chancellor "directly responsible" to the UK president. Each college had its own director, later designated president, with typical administrative and support groups. By legislative mandate the community colleges offered two-year vocational programs, a two-year baccalaureate program, and programs for local citizens. The clientele of these schools tended to follow national trends. By 1989 more than half of enrollees were women (by one estimate as many as 65 percent) and nearly half were twenty-five years old or older. In addition, "44 percent were enrolled in technical or career programs, 35 percent in transfer programs [meaning they could go into a four-year baccalaureate program], and 21 percent were nondegree" students. Thus, the community colleges were fulfilling their mandated role. These schools replaced regional private junior colleges and accelerated the pace of others in becoming four-year colleges.[80]

Owing to the presence of Spencerian and Sullivan, as well as the offerings of Catholic colleges in Louisville in business and other typically "junior college" coursework, Kentucky's largest city did not organize a municipal community college until relatively late in the movement. In the early sixties, after passage of the 1962 community college legislation, there had been discussion and maneuvering by both the U of L and UK in consideration of jointly organizing such a college in Louisville. Although the negotiations resulted in seemingly joint responsibility, soon UK dominated, with the city of Louisville providing a site for the school and Jefferson Community College being placed under the centralized control of UK. JCC opened in 1968 on a downtown campus, at the old Presbyterian Seminary Building on First and Broadway. By that time, the University of Kentucky Community College System had been functioning for four years. The Southwest JCC campus opened at Jesse Stuart High School four years later. Like all other schools, JCC experienced some growing pains; it never had enough money, teachers, and infrastructure to serve the fast-growing student population in the age of the baby boom. Similarly, it served the dual purpose of offering "terminal" technical and vocational coursework leading to associate degrees and offering liberal arts courses for those who would go on to a four-year program. Unfortunately, although it was situated in a metropolitan area with the most concentrated African American population in the state, JCC had difficulty appealing to and retaining black students.[81]

If enrollments were the major test of accomplishment, the UK Community College System appeared successful: public junior college enrollment in Kentucky from 1956 to 1970 increased from 1,430 to nearly 10,000. By 1983 the enrollment of the UK community colleges exceeded that of the Lexington campus, 24,059 to 21,616, and community college enrollment climbed to 33,000 by 1988. It was easier for community college students to transfer to Western or other schools than to UK, according to James P. Chapman, a longtime UK administrator who also worked at Madisonville CC. "There was an assumption that these were inferior students. . . . The only time we [UK] seemed to notice them was during the legislative years and then we would go out and ask them to call upon all of their board members and all their contacts to get things for Lexington we wanted. So this was just a problem in that relationship. I don't think we treated them [the community college system] with the respect we should have. And then we lost them." The UK Community College System remained a lightning rod for complaints of the regional universities about the grasping nature of the school in Lexington.[82]

After the initial construction of the UK Medical Center complex, the passage of legislation, and action by the UK trustees implementing the Community College System, President Frank G. Dickey announced his resignation in September 1962. During his tenure the Patterson School of Diplomacy and International Commerce had come into being in 1960. The acquisition of Coldstream Farm, Spindletop Farm, and other properties added to the increasing diversity of the land grant university. Although UK experienced rapid growth in the Dickey years, Thomas D. Clark, then chairman of the Department of History, did not find Dickey successful. "He was an honest and decent man who perhaps should never have been president," Clark said in his memoirs. "Power brokers," including Governor Chandler, Frank Peterson, who came to UK as controller in 1941, and others made it difficult for Dickey, according to Clark. In addition, "matters academic were secondary to other concerns," including the difficulty of obtaining university approval of a new pension plan under TIAA-CREF coverage. Dickey "was well-motivated. . . . The thing that defeated him was that he should have been about 90 percent rougher, tougher than he was," concluded Clark.[83]

For the first time, with Bert Combs as governor, the chief executive of the state, as chair of the board of trustees, did not have a heavy hand in the naming of a UK president. A faculty-trustee committee recommended, and the full board of trustees appointed, John W. Oswald, vice president for administration at the University of California, Berkeley. Coming from a well-defined state system of higher education, Oswald "thought in big terms," according to UK historian Carl Cone. First, he would have the responsibility of developing the Community College System, with the presidents of the state colleges opposing his every move. Second, the state colleges were on the move to increase their undergraduate and graduate offerings, with Martin, Thompson, and Doran being especially aggressive. Third, Oswald intended to push UK into the national spotlight in research, initially receiving great support from research-oriented professors like Tom Clark. As an "outsider," Oswald came to UK with experience under President Clark Kerr, when the California model of higher education evolved into "specified and clear mission responsibilities" for each campus. His vision included a "multiversity," in which UK would be the centerpiece, controlling research as well as the community colleges, with the regional colleges mainly offering undergraduate work.[84]

In his memoirs, perhaps with too much hindsight, Tom Clark had little good to say about Oswald. The whole process of proposing Oswald by trustee Ralph Angelucci and others seemed precipitous to Clark, but then they appeared to get along, at least in the beginning. Oswald sought Clark's counsel, and the longtime UK professor warned the new president about the "dead wood" that existed on campus that should be expunged if UK was to become a major research university. Apparently this group even included College of Education dean Lyman Ginger as well as other older faculty members and some deans. However, Oswald soon pushed two faculty initiatives that caused controversy. First, UK became more of a "publish or perish" institution with new tenure measures. More controversially, UK moved to a process of rotating college deans and department heads. Clark did not take kindly to his dismissal as chair, criticizing not only Oswald but some of his younger history department colleagues as well. Irritated by the whole affair, Clark reflected that at a party celebrating the elevation of the new chair, "Beth and I were treated almost as coolly as if we had just escaped from a leper colony." Clark soon left UK and spent the next few years at Indiana University, writing a multivolume history of that institution.[85]

Soon after taking the helm at UK, Oswald went on the offensive. David V. Hawpe, student managing editor of the campus *Kentucky Kernel* at the time and later longtime reporter and editor of the *Louisville Courier-Journal*, caught the spirit of the times. At a meeting of the state college presidents and before the board of trustees, Hawpe declared in the *Kernel*, "President Dr. John Oswald has set the stage for his initial offensive maneuver in the battle over control of Kentucky higher education." Oswald was already clashing with Eastern's Martin and others over graduate programs at the regional schools. The four regional presidents communicated and met often. Doran wrote to Martin that he doubted that a "peace pipe smoking" session with Oswald would do much good. In a letter to Martin about forming a united front, Murray's Woods derisively referred to Oswald as the "garage man," for the latter's urging of such improvements at UK.[86]

Governor Combs commissioned a study of public higher education in Kentucky soon after becoming governor. It was during the first stages of this study that Oswald came to UK. The initial conversations and meetings in 1963 appeared civil enough. At a meeting chaired by Centre College president Thomas Spragens, who called for a wider-ranging study of higher education, both public and private, the battle lines were clearly drawn. Oswald wanted a California system of higher education stratification, with UK at the "apex." Although the Council on Public Higher Education had been given some responsibility for coordinating the state system since 1934, in the early sixties it still had little clout, being little more than a sounding board for the presidents of the state schools.[87]

At issue was what type of system would come out of the studies and debates. The UK Community College System gave Oswald a larger statewide constituency than his rivals had, and, whether it was true or not, they said he was trying to impose a California style of higher education on the Commonwealth of Kentucky. An "empire-builder," his enemies called him. Early on, the *Courier-Journal* argued for UK's dominating any move of the smaller regional schools toward university status. "The danger is that, under current conditions, the evolving system will be no system at all," the Louisville paper said, with each school using "the necessary political support" to "become a university" and without central planning and coordination. Even in a smaller city with a UK community college, the *Paducah Sun-Democrat* took the same view as the Louisville paper, arguing that "the unfettered ambitions of the individual and independent college administrations threatens to turn them into degree-mills, wasting great sums of tax money while cheapening their academic programs which may already be starved by being spread too broadly, and not being deep enough."[88]

In neighboring Tennessee, that state's higher education system in the sixties evolved into three tiers, with "regional" universities such as Austin Peay and five others, a separate system of ten colleges, and then the University of Tennessee System with the central campus in Knoxville and four other urban campuses. Although there was talk of merging the traditional black college in Nashville with another school, it remained, like Kentucky State, a separate entity. In the Commonwealth of Kentucky, the system had evolved into two tiers, the largest being the University of Kentucky system, including the Community College System, administered by the president of the university and the board of trustees. The regional colleges, Eastern, Western, Morehead, and Murray, plus Kentucky State, founded as the black land grant school, all operated independently of each other, with separate boards. The Council on Public Higher Education, founded in 1934, had the unenviable task of coordinating this contentious lot.[89]

Combs and later Governor Ned Breathitt worked to keep all these forces under control while guiding them toward some compromise position that would fit the political climate of the state. The state colleges continually pressured the CPHE to allow them to provide master's work in the arts and sciences. Now that they were growing apace with UK, their reasoning was that they could offer this service while UK concentrated on doctoral programs and higher research. UK Graduate School dean A. D. Albright, at a council meeting in 1963, pointedly spoke against the state colleges' ambitions, citing duplication and other problems. "They will be turning out students with master's degrees of inferior quality," he charged. "It's simply absurd for them to start master's programs in such things as history, physics, chemistry and mathematics." When told that UK had difficulty filling some of its graduate classes, Eastern's Martin, with a twinge of folksy sarcasm, retorted, "I'm right distressed they've had so little success with their graduate program at UK that classes are not full." Although the CPHE, with the regional college presidents as voting members, approved graduate classes in some arts and sciences fields in 1963, they did not immediately open the courses. The wrangling over funds continued on other fronts as well. Beginning in 1963, with implementation of the federal Higher Education Facilities Act, closer coordination of the state and private colleges and universities became more essential. With substantial funds in the offing and public administrators unable to cooperate within the confines of the CPHE, Governor Breathitt assumed leadership. In March 1964, Breathitt appointed a fifteen-member

commission of public and private college officials and laypersons to adminis-
ter the money in Kentucky, beginning with $3.6 million in fiscal 1964–1965.[90]

M. M. Chambers presented a state-mandated report in 1965, "Higher
Education in Kentucky, 1965–1975: A Program for Growth and Develop-
ment," at the conclusion of a detailed study for the state and the CPHE.
The study suggested that four of the regional colleges, Eastern, Western,
Morehead, and Murray, were now ready to be elevated to university status.
"All four, having become successively state teachers' colleges and multipurpose state colleges, were ripe in 1966 to become regional state universities,"
Chambers wrote. These schools were following the national trend of many
such schools that had originated as normal schools in the late nineteenth
and early twentieth centuries, becoming multipurpose colleges while still
maintaining a prominent teacher education function. Such schools in the
surrounding states were moving in the same direction. They also had their
own interest/lobbying group, the American Association of State Colleges
and Universities, to look after their interests, just as the land grant universities had the National Association of State Universities and Land-Grant
Colleges (changed in 2009 to the Association of Public and Land-Grant
Universities).[91]

The introduction of House Bill 238 in the 1966 meeting of the Kentucky
General Assembly drew the support of University of Kentucky graduate
Governor Breathitt, although UK tried to rally its forces to defeat the bill.
In the end the bill sailed through the House, 83-0 and the Senate, 32-5. In
a widely distributed picture of Breathitt's signing the bill, the bulky Martin
hovered over the governor with the other regional presidents and Kentucky
State's Atwood. A somewhat morose-looking Oswald stood at the extreme
right. What did everyone get from this legislation? The state colleges, given
this name in 1947, were now officially designated universities, which they
had been for some time anyway. With the granting of university status in
1966, the new regional universities began offering master's-degree-level
courses in the fields of history and English. (I might add that I was in the
first class at EKU offering a master's degree in history, graduating in 1967.)
Kentucky State College was not given the same designation in 1966, but its
continued existence as a separate entity was assured, and it too was granted
university status in 1972. The University of Kentucky received increased state
appropriations and continued to be the premier university of the state system.
Moreover, the CPHE (the word *Public* was dropped in 1977) changed with
the new law, becoming a lay council with nine voting members, appointed by
the governor, one of whom was Ed Prichard. University presidents remained
on the council as advisors and nonvoting ex officio members. Now that the
CPHE had nine lay members and six university presidents, its center of power

had decidedly tipped toward being a truly public board. And the 1966 law specifically added that all university budgets had to go through the council and not be presented individually before the legislature. While it appeared that the presidents now would be rather secondary to the council decisions, at the first of meeting of the new council, Martin made a successful motion that the nonvoting members be given the right to make and second motions and discuss them. However, the times were changing from when the council only discussed and made policy for teacher education. Furthermore, there were those who were already working to entirely remove the presidents from the CPHE, making them a separate advisory council. Just as important, a student and a faculty member now joined the boards of the regional universities as nonvoting members.[92]

The newly designated universities, as well as UK, continued to grow in the late sixties and early seventies. However, the relative prosperity of the Breathitt years did not last. When Louie B. Nunn, the first Republican elected since Simeon Willis in 1943, became governor in 1967, the state coffers were nearly empty. Despite a campaign pledge not to raise taxes, he won approval from the Democratic Party–controlled General Assembly to raise the sales tax from three cents to five cents. Because the governor now appointed members of the CPHE and retained the usual prerogatives of the office, Nunn still was a powerful governor. Lifelong Democrat Martin, who had worked for the election of Nunn's opponent, Henry Ward, told a friend how he approached the new governor soon after the inauguration in December 1967. "Hell, I put my hat in my hand and walked in and said 'here I am.'" Other public university presidents also had to make their peace with the new governor.[93]

The late sixties and early seventies were tumultuous for the entire country, higher education included, because of the growing rifts among Americans over civil rights and the Vietnam War. At all the colleges and universities in the state, particularly the public ones, students as well as some faculty took to the streets. Many students were also anxious to have more of a say in campus affairs. Faculty wanted a bigger role in university governance. Outside of campuses, civil rights issues erupted in the summer of 1968, with riots breaking out in Louisville. Governor Nunn sent in the National Guard. Louisville and the rest of the state were spared the much more violent affairs that occurred elsewhere. Nevertheless, two black youths died in the melee in the state's largest city.[94]

While panty raids might have been the height of student assertiveness in the fifties and early sixties, by the midsixties student movements became more serious. Civil rights and antiwar demonstrations occurred on most college campuses across the nation. Students began demanding more participation in university affairs and an end to in loco parentis, or at least more liberal dorm hours for university women. AAUP chapters on Kentucky college campuses became more aggressive. Campus student newspapers also took on a more independent role. Portents of things to come in Kentucky could be seen in student demonstrations against the Vietnam War at the culmination of UK's Centennial on Founder's Day in 1966. ROTC requirements at Kentucky's public universities became a point of contention as the war in Vietnam wore on in the late sixties. At Eastern President Martin dug in his heels and tried to forestall change, but concessions were made to the new age. ROTC was made optional on that campus. One ROTC alumnus, David Wainscott, who retired as a U.S. Army colonel, found that a student had to be careful joining a group of campus males. One evening he joined in a group of young men locked arm and arm but was soon told its mission was to protest the war, not conduct an impromptu panty raid. "I didn't think Col. Smith [the ROTC commander] would like that," he said with a laugh in an interview many years later, "so I dropped out."[95]

The sixties were years of expanding enrollments and faculties, as well as new construction on most campuses, public and private. The Commonwealth of Kentucky increased its spending on public higher education during this period. For example, compared with other states, Kentucky ranked a respectable twenty-seventh in investments in higher education based on population; however, the state still did not reach the nationwide average. Yet all was not well. Administrative changes came to some public universities in the late sixties. When President Ralph H. Woods retired at Murray State University in early 1968, he was replaced by Harry M. Sparks, a former state superintendent. Longtime Western administrator Dero Downing replaced Kelly Thompson in 1969. Though buoyed by rapid growth of the UK campus, the blossoming of the Community College System, and a successful Centennial, President John W. Oswald, fatigued by the fractious university system and the apparent lack of support from Nunn, resigned in early April 1968. The university spent a year under the leadership of interim president A. D. Kirwan before Otis Singletary became president. Some students were still protesting the dismissal of four of their cohorts for drug infractions. Doran at Morehead and Martin at Eastern remained in their posts and, although they often sparred with each other over state funding, remained ever committed to protecting their schools against intrusion by UK. Carl M. Hill, who had succeeded Rufus Atwood at Kentucky State in 1962 and survived the attempts of the editor of the *Frankfort State Journal* and one or two legislators to change the nature of the Frankfort campus, remained in office. Gary S. Cox, longtime CPHE official, found all these men to have strong personalities. Even though they could no longer vote on council affairs, "others seemed to wither under their power," and the tall, graying Singletary "could take over a room." "Singletary was so charming," Harry M. Snyder, director of the council from 1976 to 1986, recalled in a 2009 interview. "He could blow you out of the water."[96]

Thrown into this mixture was another strong personality. Governor Nunn exhibited an avid interest in the Kentucky system of higher education at a time when campus upheaval had come to the commonwealth. He took a hard line against protesters, on campus or off, and appreciated the way Martin "kept his finger on the pulse of the situation." Nunn pushed the elevation of Northern Kentucky Community College into becoming a college, created by legislation in 1968, as well as the addition of the Salmon P. Chase Law School. Especially Martin and Doran opposed Northern's inclusion into the state system, becoming another regional school, because they knew that the higher education pie would now have to be further divided with Northern. Highland Heights was selected as the site for the new campus, and Frank Steely became Northern's first president in 1970. Nunn also supported the transfer of the Salmon P. Chase College of Law, a night school, from its Cincinnati base to the Northern campus. Now the commonwealth had three law schools; those at U of L and UK continued to serve into the twenty-first century.[97]

Singletary, who came to UK during the Nunn governorship, brought outstanding credentials as a historian and administrative experience in Texas and North Carolina. UK enrollment exceeded twelve thousand in 1965, and the new president was adamant about keeping the Community College System firmly controlled by UK. He often humorously retorted that "he did not, to paraphrase Winston Churchill, become president of the University of Kentucky to preside over the diminution of the university or any of its prerogatives," and that included losing the Community College System. Singletary saw the struggle with Martin, Doran, and others as a natural battle over education dollars. To charges by Martin that the community colleges "tainted" the system, Singletary humorously replied, in an oral history interview, that what Martin really meant was, "T'aint mine." Nonetheless, Singletary said he had respect for Martin, finding him a "very delightful man"; it was "a pleasure to be in a meeting with him." "I never made the mistake of taking him lightly," the UK president said, knowing he was in for a battle on most issues. Strange bedfellows, Martin and Singletary agreed on the issue of adding more universities to the state coffers, both realizing that Northern Kentucky State College would take funds from them. In the late sixties they also agreed that the coming of the University of Louisville into the state university system would further diminish the already "inadequate resources" of the commonwealth and increase the "turf battles." The question remained how much the Council on Public Higher Education could do to restrain these strong university presidents and create a more cooperative system.[98]

Although the University of Louisville continued to grow in the sixties, it became increasingly clear that such momentum could not be maintained as debt accumulated and the university was forced to continually raise tuition. Those interested in aiding the Louisville school, especially the Jefferson County legislative delegation, began probing for more state support or even a state takeover of the U of L. Former mayor Charles Farnsley, who sat on the U of L board from time to time, led the effort to keep the school completely independent. The CPHE studied the problem, as did the General Assembly. Legislation in 1966 encouraged the U of L and UK to study the feasibility bringing the former into the system. Presidents Davidson and Oswald established a joint committee to make recommendations. Soon afterward Davidson retired, to be replaced by longtime Louisville administrator Woodrow Strickler in early 1968. The University of Louisville also hired a high-profile consulting firm to make recommendations. The joint U of L–UK committee could not agree on a single plan, and eventually the University of Louisville took a more aggressive stance. For the short term at least, UK and the regional universities appeared irrevocably united against admitting the U of L to the state system. Into this admixture of higher education intrigue and competition emerged another pressing issue. What would happen with the bankrupt Kentucky Southern College, the Baptist school in eastern Jefferson County? After it appeared that Western might be interested in taking over the campus, the University of Louisville, with Governor Nunn's approval, absorbed the Shelby Campus instead. This move left U of L as the primary school of higher education in Jefferson County. Meanwhile, Council on Public Higher Education member Ed Prichard pushed his group to become more active in the resolution of the U of L–UK impasse.[99]

The University of Louisville consultants, after mulling over at least six alternatives, suggested that the U of L and UK come together "on an equal and parallel basis," with a single president, even suggesting a new name, "Commonwealth University of Kentucky." With U of L supporters working the legislative halls, the General Assembly in 1968 passed a unanimous joint resolution "that called for U of L's entrance into the state system in 1970, regardless of progress in the merger talks." The departure of UK president Oswald brought in first interim president Kirwan and then in 1969 new president Singletary, neither of whom appeared to be in any hurry to settle the issue. Furthermore, although the U of L and UK at first cooperated on the opening of the new Jefferson Community College, that school immediately came under the control of the UK system. U of L president Strickler began attending meetings of the CPHE in July 1969. Soon the UK board of trustees passed a resolution decrying the idea of adding another new school to the state system without more study about "impairing" higher education funding. The blame for the lack of action was put squarely on the shoulders of Singletary, who declared negotiations at an impasse. Apparently Singletary wanted nothing short of the presidency of the combined campuses. The *Frankfort State Journal* declared that UK was the "reluctant bridegroom in the merger talks," while the *Louisville Times* ran a headline, "UK Trustees derail plans for early union with U of L." The CPHE appeared unable to lead, never being called on by the governor to mediate the U of L entry problem. The presence of Ed Prichard on the CPHE complicated the whole situation because of his prickly relationship with Governor Nunn. Prichard charged Nunn with weakening the council by not appointing three new members at a crucial time when a quorum was needed. In a 1977 oral history interview, Nunn countered, "Until they get people like Ed Prichard off of it [the CPHE], it will never amount to much. . . . That fellow's not solid in any sense, and I don't care if you play this back to him." Never reconciled, "they went to their mutual graves hating each other," said longtime education observer and Prichard Committee official Bob Sexton.[100]

The University of Louisville went ahead as if entry into the state system was assured. Strickler presented a biennial budget proposal to the CPHE, while Professor Dee Akers of the U of L law school drafted legislation "to bring the University into the state system as an independent member." Jefferson County senator Scott Miller introduced Senate Bill 117 to carry out the entry. Meanwhile, Farnsley continued his campaign to keep Louisville independent by proposing substantial tuition hikes. Eventually the Democratic Party–controlled General Assembly and Republican Governor Nunn agreed to the measure, and on July 1, 1970, the University of Louisville became part of the Kentucky system of higher education. The old U of L board dissolved, ending the school's history as "a semi-private, semi-municipal institution." The historians of the University of Louisville concluded, "The University of Louisville scored a significant victory by retaining all of its programs upon entrance into the state system, but the question of future funding remained unsettled." In the short term, the U of L could lower its tuition, that being set by the CPHE, and avoid bankruptcy by being able to tap state funding. Within five years, enrollment at the Louisville campus rose from 10,000 to more than 15,000, proving the wisdom of the effort to join the state system. UK, the U of L, the regionals, and Kentucky State knew that each would now have to compete even harder for state dollars. With their supporters in the legislature, both Northern and Louisville became formidable competitors for state dollars, according to State Historian James C. Klotter. The Kentucky

Government Council, founded in 1961, which studied various state problems, issued a report in 1969 that made some suggestions about how to improve higher education in Kentucky. One of its consultants suggested strengthening the CPHE or even forming "a single governing board," even styling it the "Kentucky Board of Regents." This form of centralization began to be called a "superboard" by its enemies, particularly at the regional universities. Such boards were growing in number across the county after 1950. Clearly something was needed, since between 1959 and 1969 enrollment in all public institutions (excluding the U of L) had tripled, growing from about 20,000 students to more than 62,000. Was the Council on Public Higher Education to become a state-level agency of "coordination or control"?[101]

Before the late sixties, the height of campus unrest on the UK campus occurred during the Dickey years. When Governor Chandler, the Wednesday before Thanksgiving, called a state holiday after a rare UK victory over the University of Tennessee football Volunteers, the Dickey administration declared that classes would be held. Three thousand UK students protested, arrests were made, and a few "rioters" were taken to the hospital. Times soon changed. Student unrest at UK in the late sixties was more intense, more complicated, and more dangerous. Nunn admitted to a strained relationship with Oswald. "Dr. Oswald and I had a talk . . . and I insisted that he clean up the place or do something but I wasn't going to sit there and see the university victimized by politicians over the filth and smut that was coming out." Then Oswald resigned and Singletary did not have enough time to "get a handle on the thing," according to Nunn. In an oral history interview in 1990, Singletary noted that at the beginning of his tenure his first priority was "merely holding the institution together."[102]

In the spring semester of 1970, "a minority of activists among the student body" at the University of Kentucky began protesting, among other things, the "irrelevancy" of the curriculum. The continuing war in Vietnam remained a cause of sit-ins and marches. A local chapter of Students for a Democratic Society and other groups sponsored demonstrations that spring. Governor Nunn as well as former governor Chandler, who was a new UK trustee, promised to keep a lid on the situation at UK. After President Nixon announced that American troops had attacked inside Cambodia, the antiwar movement heated up on college campuses. A May 4 protest on the campus of Kent State led to the deaths of four students and the wounding of nine others by National Guard troops who felt threatened. Although there were minor protests at the other Kentucky universities and colleges, only at UK did the tensions heighten. At the board of trustees meeting just before graduation—board chairman Nunn was not in attendance—several hundred students crowded into the Patterson Office Tower. After taking no action on the students' demands, the board adjourned from its meeting on the top floor. Because of a problem with the elevators, the board members moved toward a stairwell. A confrontation occurred when a female student asked Governor Chandler a question. As he answered her, the former governor "patted her cheek." A male student touched the governor's face, and Chandler grabbed him and punched him in the face. Police separated the two and neither was arrested. Chandler told the press, "I shouldn't have done that, but some of those students shouldn't be at this school—they're filthy and dirty and have long hair." After President Singletary met with the dissident students, the affairs of the day appeared to be settled and tempers cooled.[103]

That Tuesday evening about five hundred students demonstrated on campus, wandering around apparently without leadership. At the Buell Armory, an ROTC facility, students demonstrated with singing and speeches. At that point the campus safety director called in city and county police. While the police gathered and students milled around, flames suddenly broke out in an old Air Force ROTC office building on Euclid Avenue, endangering the nearby women's dormitory, Blazer Hall. Governor Nunn watched the fire from his auto, coming to the campus "after receiving reports about a deteriorating situation." No one was ever successfully prosecuted for the obvious arson. Although Singletary apparently quieted the campus, the next day Governor Nunn declared a curfew and called in National Guard troops. "There exists a clear and present danger to the lives of students and the University of Kentucky," he said in an executive order. After a confrontation on the UK campus, several hundred students walked over to the Transylvania campus. Because the end of the semester was so near, Singletary suggested that graduation be called off but that the campus schedule, including final examinations, go on as usual. After another confrontation, in which National Guard troops sprayed tear gas on demonstrators on Thursday, the campus quieted as many students went home. A few arrests, including that of Student Government Association president Steve Bright, were made on Friday. Called a "moderating influence" by one historian, Singletary helped calm the restive campus and kept both Governor Nunn and former governor Chandler from further enflaming students. In the end, campus student leaders, the UK administration, and, perhaps lastly, Governor Nunn, backed off from what could have been a rapidly deteriorating situation ending in violence. Gloria Singletary, the wife of the UK president, summarized: "We came at a terrible time. We came at the height of Kent State and it was rough on both of us."[104]

There were similar, if less confrontational, incidents on other Kentucky college campuses. At the University of Louisville, war protests were supplemented by a Black Student Union peaceful occupation of President Strickler's office for a short time and the removal of demonstrators by police from the office of the Arts and Sciences dean. Out of this came the development of the Office of Black Affairs on the University of Louisville campus. At Eastern, Martin kept a vigilant eye on both students and faculty, declaring that his campus would "not become a haven for hippies, beatniks, and others of the unwashed." Nevertheless, there were student demonstrations against ROTC. The wily Martin was not above a bit of chicanery. One time word leaked out that protesters were going to disrupt a review of ROTC students. "We knew what their plan was," admitted a longtime dean of students at EKU in an oral history interview. Ed Prichard recalled, "If Bob was going to err it would always be on the side of a tight ship." When time came for the ROTC review, members of the Eastern Veterans Club sat beside several of the suspected demonstrators, keeping them from leaving their seats during the ceremony. Student government president Steve Wilborn in 1969 became the bête noire of Martin, when they locked horns over campus student rules. However, that crisis passed as well, and some years later they both served in General Assembly at the same time. At Western an attempt by the administration to control invited speakers on the Bowling Green campus touched off a furor when civil rights leader Carl Braden came to town. A temporary restraining order quieted the situation. At most campuses the American withdrawal from Vietnam "defused one of the main causes of student discontent," according to Western historian Lowell Harrison. The battles of the sixties and the early seventies for greater student rights ended with students on most Kentucky campuses gaining more control over their lives. Student government associations gained ground, women's hours were liberalized, black student organizations became recognized, and faculty, as well, were able to gain more say in university governance. The Congress of Senate Faculty Leaders developed to coordinate efforts by faculties in the state universities to gain a controlling, or equitable, vote in the typically administration-dominated university senates, a process that took several years to complete.[105]

In the 1970s, the greatest challenges in public higher education in Kentucky arose from the increased number of mouths at the public trough, now that Northern Kentucky and the University of Louisville had joined the system. Moreover, in order to keep Kentucky State functioning, according to longtime Council on Higher Education official Gary S. Cox, the school needed increased support because of years when it had been underfunded. Then there was the burgeoning Community College System bound up within the UK budget requests. All of the public universities had their political constituencies with representation in Frankfort. UK, the U of L, and Northern Kentucky University, because they were located in heavily populated areas, had more representation in the General Assembly in Frankfort than the regional universities had. Moreover, with its more numerous alumni and the presence of UK agricultural and extension services in all the counties, the Lexington campus had more of a statewide appeal. Inflation, rapid growth of student enrollment, compliance with state and national laws, and increasing competition for the education dollar made it increasingly imperative to rationalize the system. There were never enough dollars to go around.[106]

The question was how to change the Council on Public Higher Education so that all would be represented at the table in the highly charged political environment in Kentucky. The reforms of 1966 under Governor Breathitt allowed the four regional schools to become universities while strengthening the council. UK under Oswald appeared to have lost its primacy, but actually, with the regional presidents losing their votes, which could be combined against UK, the Lexington campus was strengthened. The question of the seventies was how to continue this momentum. Should the council be given more power? In a 1977 interview, council member Ed Prichard said he wanted a

better degree of cooperation. I don't know anybody in the state council on higher education even among the members or staff that really believed in higher centralized control such as you have, for example, in Florida or some other states. I think they have the feeling that resources are limited and we have got to have a better coordination in order to make sure that those resources are used in a most productive way. This may imply some little bit greater degree of scrutiny over some of the activities of the institutions than there's been before.

It was this "scrutiny" that caused much debate during the seventies and beyond.[107]

Under the governorships of Wendell Ford, Julian Carroll, and John Y. Brown Jr., from 1971 to 1983, public higher education in Kentucky began to fall under greater "scrutiny" by legislators as well as the governors. Ford did not make personal attempts to rein in the increasing costs of higher education. However, he did give his assent to changes being wrought by the General Assembly. The state appropriation for higher education increased from the end of the Nunn administration into the early Ford years from $95.9 million in 1968–1970 to $107.4 million in 1970–1971 and $117.1 million for 1971–1972. All legislation needed Ford's imprimatur in a time when governors exercised nearly total control over legislation and state budgets. With the entry of U of L into the state system, Ford pushed for the inclusion of a new teaching hospital at that school, thereby keeping in touch with his urban base. Serving only three years as governor, Ford defeated Marlow Cook for a seat in the

U.S. Senate in 1974, and Lieutenant Governor Julian M. Carroll took over. He, in turn, was elected to a full term as governor in 1975.[108]

Carroll was also a "strong" governor, dominating the legislature. The Cumberland Presbyterian lay minister had been called "Saint Julian" by his Republican opponent Robert Gable in 1975, but some of his political enemies now unhappily referred to him as "Emperor Julian." The Carroll administration had full "coffers" as a result of the energy crisis in the country. The coal industry, prosperous because of the Arab Oil Embargo, in the short term at least, brought in tax revenue and added jobs in the state. Carroll took a great interest in improving the public schools. Teachers' salaries during his administration increased substantially, raising the state in that category from a rank of forty-sixth in the nation to the "low thirties" by the end of his term. The old dream of free textbooks for grades K-12 was finally realized, as was the creation of a School Building Authority for badly needed construction in poorer districts. Everything seemed to be on the upswing for the public schools; Minimum Foundation money even flowed into the less affluent districts.[109]

Carroll took a harder line on higher education. "We are no longer in the golden age of higher education growth," he said in his 1976 budget message before the Kentucky General Assembly. Ominously, enrollment growth nationwide and in Kentucky began to slow by the mid-seventies; it even dropped at some schools. New strategies would have to be developed to increase the appeal of a college education, including attempts to attract the "non-traditional" student, an older adult who either had dropped out of higher education or never entered the system. With Louisville and Northern Kentucky now part of the state system, Carroll demanded that the council take a greater leadership role. The council responded by mandating a moratorium on new programs. Nearly everything now would be required to go through the council. The universities responded by asking for more money, citing increased costs.[110]

In the late sixties and the seventies, particularly in the Carroll years, the higher education political milieu in Kentucky began to change with the retirements of Eastern's Martin in 1976, Murray's Woods in 1968 and his successor Sparks in 1973, Louisville's Strickler in 1972, Western's Downing in 1978, and Morehead's Doran in 1977. Martin, Woods, Sparks, Downing, and Doran had come of age in the days of World War II and were political to the core. Governor Nunn enjoyed the old political give and take with "two pros" such as Martin and Doran. "You knew exactly what they were doing," Nunn said. Once when the *Courier-Journal* published a picture of Martin, Doran, and Sparks sitting in the Senate gallery overseeing a vote, Nunn responded that they looked like "Winkin', Blinkin', and Nod." Nunn's witty remark made it to the press. "I was the one that said it," Nunn admitted, "just aggravating them." (One version of this story is that Lieutenant Governor Julian Carroll, who was presiding over the Senate session, had made the comment.) To them all, governor as well as university president, it was all part of the game to try to get a leg up. Then, during the negotiations over the entry of the University of Louisville into the state system, the governor was left off the board of trustees. When Doran and Martin arrived at the Governor's Mansion, where Nunn was recovering from a broken leg, he knew something was up. Both told him how mad they were that he had not been included on the U of L board, as he was on the board of trustees of UK. Nunn, who in an oral history interview said he cared nothing about being on another such board, knew that they were trying to get him to derail the merger. After they left to return to the capitol, said Nunn, "I could see Bob laughing. They were both chuckling to each other, I'm sure, about how they'd prejudiced my mind on that bill." Martin and Doran returned that evening and had dinner with the governor. At the proper moment, Nunn asked which of them had written the bill to leave him off the U of L board. Doran blurted out, "Ha, Ha, Bob, he's caught us, you might as well admit it." "You could be in a meeting and see them make moves and go over others' heads," Nunn continued. "But you knew exactly what they were doing. They were looking down the road a lot farther than most of the other people."[111]

Carroll's ideas of economy and centralization had the full support of the *Courier-Journal,* which editorialized in favor of a "superboard." The Louisville paper predicted that if tight control did not take place, the politicization of the system would reemerge, what it called the "dark political route." Meanwhile, the CPHE encouraged the universities and Northern to update all their planning. For the 1974–1976 biennium, the Council now had the power to force the state schools into a "common format" to use for requesting funding. The Council staff itself had grown with legislative approval, to allow for an increased budget and staff. In 1973 Harry M. Snyder Jr. came on board with special responsibilities in administration and finance, under Executive Director A. D. Albright. Administrators at the state universities began to complain more about incessant demands for studies and paperwork.[112]

With all of this newfound coordination, Kentucky higher education did not expect a shocking pronouncement that they received in 1976. When the council presented a united budget through the Finance Department, Carroll cut it by 40 percent. The governor also pushed the council into increasing tuition rates at all the state schools, except for Louisville, studying a quota system for the professional schools, and other measures to increase efficiency. For the first time a bill, which turned out to be unsuccessful, was introduced to establish specific regions of service for each school. The lines were being drawn, regardless. All of the regional universities had reached what appeared to be static enrollments in the mid-seventies. The exception was Northern Kentucky State College, which matured quickly under President Frank Steely and had more than six thousand students attending in 1975. Many students from northern Kentucky who had traditionally attended other colleges, such as Eastern, now stayed at home. A. D. Albright succeeded Steely in 1976 as the Highland Heights campus was given university status, being renamed Northern Kentucky University. On the council, Snyder replaced Albright as executive director in 1976.[113]

Over the next few years, the council became more assertive under the leadership of Snyder. President Dero Downing, the last of the old guard at the state universities to retire, along with the new presidents, J. C. Powell at Eastern, Constantine Curris at Murray, and Morris Norfleet at Morehead, chafed at the increased centralization. Downing told the Western Faculty Senate that "campus autonomy" had now given way to control by "higher boards, councils or coordinating bodies designed to exercise control over all institutions." Carroll publicly stated that he wanted an end to unnecessary "duplication." Again in 1978 a bill was introduced in the Kentucky Senate to create a "superboard," but it did not pass. One study by Doug Whitlock, longtime EKU administrator and later EKU president, indicated that the public did not favor such an organization or even expanding the role of the Council. The public, that is, voters, while basically happy with higher education in Kentucky, wanted an efficient system of higher education, one that would "produce measurable outcomes." The University of Kentucky might have the largest amount of support in the General Assembly, but the regional universities and the University of Louisville had their champions as well. The partisanship could be comical on occasion, as when a state senator from Jefferson County, citing the dominance of the University of Kentucky in funding, added an amendment to a bill (which did not pass) to make members of the Council wear blue blazers with a white "K" and to change its name to "The University of Kentucky Council on Higher Education."[114]

Governor Carroll intended to change the direction of the Council, and he did so by supporting Snyder. He also renamed the council by executive order the Council on Higher Education (CHE), on April 15, 1977. Snyder declared that the name change better reflected the role that the council should play in all higher education in the state. Clearly, the private colleges now had a role that was subordinate to the state system. Moreover, the UK Community College System became dominant, as the private junior colleges either expanded to four-year programs or folded. The CHE began pushing all the state institutions to develop "mission statements," refining their roles in Carroll's and Snyder's view of what higher education should be doing in

Kentucky. Higher education became more newsworthy. The presidents of the regional universities, the U of L, and UK, were always being asked by the press for their opinions about an issue. How the University of Louisville and the University of Kentucky would coexist in the new order became the subject of news and commentaries. Council meetings also began to receive more press coverage, not only because of the incessant changes being discussed and the Council's new powers, but also because of the presence of the irrepressible Ed Prichard, now blinded by his diabetes. According to observer Gary Cox, "Prichard would sit with his chin on his cane and then he would suddenly erupt. He would sound off and wake everybody up."[115]

After the entry of the semiprivate, municipally owned University of Louisville into the state system, the friction between the two largest schools in the commonwealth intensified, even finding its way into athletics. When some criticized Carroll for promising to spend $1 million in state funds to build a football dormitory at UK, Singletary retorted with a hint of sarcasm, "I did not hear them when the University of Louisville was given $1.5 million to build an athletic facility [improvements at the Kentucky Fair and Exposition Center]. When the University of Kentucky gets in the picture, everything is different." UK could no longer ignore the U of L. Even Lexingtonians and some UK basketball fans began to question the UK Athletic Department's refusal to play the U of L. After the U of L won an NCAA basketball championship in 1980, sportswriter Billy Reed and others pushed for the event, and the state Senate "in semi-seriousness" attached to a bill an amendment (which did not pass) requiring at least one regular season game.[116]

After the retirement of Woodrow Strickler at the University of Louisville, his replacement, James Grier Miller (1973–1980), a Harvard-trained M.D. and Ph.D., immediately locked horns with UK's Singletary. In what the University of Louisville historians call "the fracas," the issue was which school would become the premier university in the state. While Singletary hailed UK as the "one REAL university" in the state, Miller asked for parity with the Lexington school. At stake were doctoral programs that both the U of L and UK wanted to emphasize as their raison d'être. Higher levels of research, as well as medical, dental, and law schools, hung in the balance.[117]

The regional universities also wanted to maintain what they had attained in the sixties, including the right to offer master's degree programs in addition to their education degrees. For example, Eastern's law enforcement and allied health programs had been pushed by Martin to be leaders in the state. A state higher education study, the Crane Report of 1971, argued that UK and the U of L should predominate in those fields. In the early seventies, Martin used all his influence in getting state approval for the building of a law enforcement building complex. He argued that since Eastern had already become a leader in the state and the nation, there was no reason to lose that momentum. Martin got the *Lexington Herald-Leader*, as well as Ed Prichard on the Council, to support Eastern's case. The bulk of the money for construction came from federal dollars, and the $7 million complex opened on August 7, 1975; it was later named the Robert R. Martin Law Enforcement, Fire Science, and Traffic Safety Center. At Western, Downing in the early seventies took on CPHE executive director A. D. Albright, defending his school and declaring, "We will resist through every avenue available to us any attempts which may be made to prevent Western from fulfilling the educational role and the mission of the University in the areas of teaching, research, and service."[118]

As always, there were incessant studies by the CHE and others to determine what public higher education should be. There was very little agreement on any single course of action. Singletary opposed the "Blee Report" of 1970, because it suggested that the Community College System was not doing its job and should be detached from the Lexington campus. Doran usually took the lead for the regional presidents in the campaign to strip UK of the community colleges; the issue would not die. The *Courier-Journal* stayed the course with UK, continuing in the seventies to defend UK's hold on the Community College System. In January 1976, the Council produced a "Comprehensive" plan for higher education, prepared by Booz, Allen, and Hamilton, which none of the state schools were entirely happy with. Murray wanted funding for a veterinary school, but without the full support of Governor Carroll, Murray had to settle for control of the Hopkinsville Animal Diagnostic Laboratory, later renamed the Breathitt Veterinary Center. Morehead, Eastern, and Western appeared satisfied with their programs in the seventies but wanted no one to tamper with them. Curris and Powell continually complained that the academic programs should not have to go through the Council but should be a matter of supply and demand under local control. Moreover, the regional universities into the seventies raced to develop outreach "university centers" in their service areas, expanding their offerings of off-campus coursework.[119]

Executive Director Snyder took a proactive stance soon after his appointment. His first effort became one that caused even more controversy: the determination of "mission statements." With the proliferation of degrees and courses, "duplication" became the hot-button issue for those who wanted more control of higher education in Kentucky. As Carroll charged and most others accepted, the "age of limitless resources" was over. While the regional universities mostly accepted their roles, the U of L and UK continued to cause debate. Louisville became Kentucky's "only urban university" and was given the responsibility for "urban studies." The CHE defined the University of Kentucky's mission as the "principal institution of statewide research and service program without geographical limitations." The banter went back and forth, UK claiming that it also served an urban function if it had no geographical limitations. Eventually, after an "all-night marathon discussion" involving Miller; Singletary; Snyder; and J. David Grissom, chairman of the council, the participants agreed to these roles. The University of Louisville agreed to limit its doctoral programs, although its status was something other than a "regional" university. UK continued to tout itself as the "flagship." The roles of the commonwealth's schools of higher education had been refined, at least on paper; now it remained to be seen how cooperative they would be. CHE executive director Snyder appeared to have had initial success in pulling back the competitive nature of the system. Council member Joy Bale Boone said in a *Courier-Journal* interview, "I think he's doing a good job. He's firm, and some people think he's kind of tough, but I believe he has to be."[120]

If money is any indicator, it would appear that Louisville came out best in the seventies, having raised its state appropriation during the Miller years 400 percent, from $16.7 million in 1973–1973 to $68.2 million in 1980–1981. However, UK still received twice the U of L appropriation, $122.7 million in 1979–1980 to the U of L's $61.4 million. Carroll's last legislature in 1978 treated higher education well, increasing the total appropriation for the CHE and the Kentucky Higher Education Assistance Authority from $241 million in 1977–1978 to $286 million in 1978–1979 to $315 in 1979–1980. The percentage of state appropriations for higher education to the University of Kentucky actually decreased in these years, from about 65 percent in 1970 to 42 percent in 1980. The regionals continually argued that they were getting the short end of the stick, not only reacting against the preeminence of UK and the U of L but also chafing at Snyder's leadership. For example, at a legislative committee meeting in late 1978, Murray's Curris complained that the two larger universities, "who fared so well at the table last time are already starting their campaign."[121]

In the seventies the CHE increased its control of public higher education incrementally, into every facet of the university system. In 1972 the General Assembly gave the Council the power to approve all graduate programs and any capital construction costing more than $100,000. Five years later, when the name of the group was shortened, its power was increased with added responsibilities: it was given authority to control all degree and certificate programs, the purchase or sale of property over $25,000 in value, and the initiation of renovation projects valued over $100,000. None of the university administrations were very happy with the new arrangements; they viewed the authority of the CHE no more favorably than they did the mandated mission statements for the schools. However, they would have to live with the new realities of public higher education in Kentucky.[122]

After a difficult Democratic Party primary, John Y. Brown Jr. swept into office in the general election of 1979, easily defeating former governor Louis B. Nunn. Coming from a business background, Brown promised to cut government jobs and expense. For the first time, a governor left the General Assembly to do its job without a heavy-handed chief executive controlling the agenda and the votes. The record of the "political maverick" Brown is difficult to assess, but he did balance the budget in increasingly difficult economic times. He supported the reform efforts of Snyder and the CHE. With the approval of Brown, the CHE appointed the Committee on Higher Education in Kentucky's Future in 1980. Appointed to the State Board of Tax Appeals, Prichard left the CHE but was soon named to the new committee, becoming its chair. When the committee presented its findings in 1981, the thirty-member group renamed itself the Prichard Committee on Higher Education. The findings of the Prichard Committee were not revolutionary but were the culmination of years of debate and research; the group proposed better funding, admission standards, ending duplication, improving faculty, even reducing the number of law schools. In the coming years there were battles over the "Centers of Excellence" funded at each of the universities as well as putting the other facets of the report into effect. In 1983 the Prichard Committee was renamed the Prichard Committee for Academic Excellence. Its role was broadened and it became an independent, privately funded citizens' organization.[123]

Budget shortfalls during the Brown years forced greater economy on public higher education in Kentucky. "The Bluegrass Plan," based on the mission statements, caused a furor in 1981 by giving UK and the U of L larger shares of the higher education budget. State senator Robert R. Martin, president of Eastern from 1960 to 1976, led the opponents in the legislature. Eventually Governor Brown, the legislature, and all the universities and their supporters settled on a compromise budget. With his business background, Brown insisted on following a fiscal plan that included using the CHE to rein in expenditures. In order to control costs in public higher education, Snyder introduced the idea of "formula funding." "Cutting out the fat" became a clichéd way of asking for sacrifice. These were lean years in which little if any money was available for construction and new programs. However, the CHE did make an effort to raise faculty salaries to a level approximating those at "benchmark" institutions in the surrounding states. Eastern's Powell complained to Snyder that the cuts were harmful. "Perhaps more fundamental, though is the truly erosive effect of two consecutive years of substantial reduction in state support to this institution with no apparent prospect for relief," he continued. With inflation, budget cuts, and higher energy costs, Powell found "an erosion of quality" to be Eastern's paramount problem. Western's president echoed the same sentiments. Administrators at the regional universities believed that UK and now the U of L received increasing funding, and they considered these years of retrenchment for their own institutions. When Snyder, with a UK law degree and coming from a UK administrative background, and the UK graduate Brown touted that Kentucky needed a "flagship" to compete with other states, it only intensified the "us versus them" mind-set.[124]

Brown countered by taking Snyder's suggestion and removing the university presidents from the CHE. Legislation in 1966, creating the state universities and modifying the CHE, had allowed their continued presence on the council, but without a vote. Now the "Conference of Presidents" would be advisory, separate from the full panel of lay persons on the CHE. With a mandate from the General Assembly to develop a "unified budget recommendation" for each biennium, the legislature in 1982 mandated "a funding formula." The changes encouraged the state universities to develop consensus on key issues. As in everything else, however, all the state universities pushed and tugged at the system, arguing their cases as exceptional. Many states now had such state-mandated public university organizations, so the comparisons with other states as "benchmarks" became the norm. Developing a method of arriving at "performance funding" for each university and the Community College System still brought out all the old political tendencies of the past. "We got ourselves absolutely beaten to death," said Gary Cox, at that time an assistant to Snyder, over the process of designing a formula for the state. "I got unshirted hell from the regional people," reported Snyder. "That was the thing that probably brought me down," he concluded. Up to 1990, Kentucky's funding average for all institutions never exceeded 90 percent of the appropriation as a percentage of the formula, with each individual school fluctuating well below that. For example, in 1989–1990, the statewide average was only 80.3 percent for all institutions. Moreover, Kentucky still ranked well below the benchmark states. To assuage some of the conflict, Funds for Excellence, eventually renamed Centers of Excellence, was a source of increasing competition for state dollars. These "special areas of expertise" eventually included law enforcement at Eastern. Each university eventually got one or more special funding appropriations for Centers of Excellence.[125]

Administrative changes of the late seventies and early eighties brought new actors onto the scene. The process of replacing the retiring Downing at Western turned into something of a circus in early 1979, when there were 179 nominations and applications for the post. Cutting the number down to a manageable size proved to a formidable and controversial task. The student regent on the search committee "reported threatening phone calls and the disappearance of files from his office," according to Lowell Harrison. There were rumors afoot of political influence peddling, particularly as charged by S. Kern Alexander Jr., who withdrew his name as one of the five finalists. Finally, Donald W. Zacharias was elected by an 8-2 vote of the regents. At Murray, Kala Mays Stroup, the first female university president in Kentucky, replaced Curris in 1983 and served until 1989. J. C. Powell remained in the Eastern presidency until 1984, when, worn-out by the constant strain of balancing budgets, fighting the inroads of CHE control, and trying to maintain quality, he retired. This time, in a mostly transparent process, the Eastern Board of Regents chose H. Hanly Funderburk, who had a long tenure as president until his retirement in 1998. Though a colorless administrator, the native Alabamian successfully carried out his pledge, "to make a good university a better one."[126]

The problems and promise of the administrations at all of the regional universities were much the same. At first, the Morehead administration of Morris Norfleet from 1977 to 1984 built on the success of Adron Doran. However, historian Donald F. Flatt in his history of that institution, said that Norfleet lacked the "charisma" necessary "to inspire people or command their respect." Furthermore, coupled with the economic downturn of the Brown years, "Draconian budget cuts" forced him to cut corners. Charges of minor financial malfeasance as well as the decision to close the University Breckinridge School, the campus laboratory school, caused controversy for the Norfleet administration. Then in 1983 the American Association of University Professors "censured" Morehead "for violating academic freedom" of two nontenured faculty members. Although enrollment also went into an eclipse, as at all of the other state universities during Norfleet's tenure, "both academic standards and private funding for the university rose," according to John R. Duncan in the *Kentucky Encyclopedia*. The controversial Norfleet resigned from the presidency in return for what Flatt called a "Golden Parachute," the chancellor of corporate relations position at Morehead.[127]

The search for a new president at Morehead proceeded with the now-standard practice of hiring a consultant firm. Professor Stuart Sprague and others argued that the faculty should be more involved in the selection process. To quell the arguments that the Morehead campus was too inbred, the regents chose Herb F. Reinhard Jr., an "outsider" who had been president of Slippery Rock University in Pennsylvania. Having impeccable academic credentials and administrative experience, Reinhard should have lasted long in the Morehead presidency. "Reinhard's ideas were impressive," declared Flatt. "But the baffling part is that someone so well-educated and widely-traveled never seemed to attain a glimmer of understanding of—nor appreciation for—Eastern Kentucky culture or the institutional background. Inept at handling people, he soon turned the campus into a sharply divided war zone." Immediately reorganizing academics did not help his case. Although Reinhard streamlined administration and procedures, he never seemed to catch on with the faculty. While a majority of students apparently supported him, the faculty was about evenly split. In early July 1985, *Courier-Journal* education writer Richard Wilson explained that the embattled president's "critics contend that his abrupt, sometimes aloof, manner is unnecessary and counterproductive on a campus where the personal touch has characterized previous administrations." After only a year, the Morehead Board of Regents chose not to extend Reinhard's two-year contract. Governor Martha Layne Collins then stepped into the breach in what seemed like an insoluble situation in early 1986. With Snyder and other political leaders involved, the governor persuaded the old regents to resign and asked Reinhard to go on a sabbatical. The appointments to the new board included former governors Nunn and Breathitt and soon quieted some of the furor, as did the interim presidency of A. D. Albright, former president of Northern Kentucky University. Not only did Albright provide "the tonic needed for this strife-torn campus," but enrollment increased slightly for the first time in several years. With budget-trimming and moving to a lower level of athletic participation, the financial outlook improved at Morehead. Just after Albright stepped down after one year at Morehead State University, the AAUP removed its censure of Morehead. In a noncontroversial process, the regents elected E. Nelson Grote to the Morehead presidency in 1987.[128]

Through most of the administrative changes at the regional universities and the University of Louisville, Otis Singletary had one of the longest tenures of a university president in Kentucky history; he remained at UK from 1969 to his retirement in 1987, a full eighteen years, much longer than the national average (six years) for a college or university president. This continuity over the seventies and most of the eighties gave UK an advantage in the pace of change in the CHE. While the U of L's James Miller appeared to hold his own against UK's Singletary, he was sometimes criticized for his leadership style. In 1976 most of the deans at the University of Louisville charged that Miller bypassed them and did not delegate enough authority. Miller weathered this storm while the campus expanded during the seventies; the U of L's share of state funds increased and construction continued. A historian like his counterpart at UK, Donald C. Swain became the new president of the University of Louisville in April 1981. Also like Singletary, Swain also enjoyed a long tenure, serving until 1995.[129]

Council on Higher Education executive director Snyder became increasingly, and conveniently, the bête noire of the regional universities. They all believed Snyder had it in for them and that he purposely favored the University of Kentucky. Hardly anything the embattled Snyder could do went over well at the regionals. Actually, Snyder favored separating the Community College System from the University of Kentucky. When he appeared at university forums, he usually got an earful of complaints. In early 1985 at Eastern, one professor, alluding to the second-class status of the Richmond campus, claimed he could not afford to get a tooth fixed. Referring to the fact that UK and the U of L got a bigger share of the education pie than EKU, professor of art Carroll Hale only half-jokingly argued, "Kentucky's a pretty small pond. Any chance of sinking one of the battleships?" Early in Funderburk's tenure, he took the offensive against CHE restrictions. With the CHE setting tuition rates, the new EKU president also chafed at the difficulty of getting approval for the Centers of Excellence. Lowell Harrison in his history of Western found that "Snyder had an abrasive personality, and some who saw him operate felt that he was sometimes petty and a bully when he could get away with it." Even those who worked with him understood Snyder's controversial nature. "Harry was one of the smartest people I have ever met," maintained Gary S. Cox, who replaced Snyder in 1986. "But he had some personality traits that eventually got him into trouble. He was too outspoken and fell out with too many people and wound up leaving." In Snyder's defense it must be said that he had a nearly impossible task. Singletary and the UK clique dug in their heels on the community college issue, and each university had its supporters in the legislature, making Snyder's task of coordination extremely difficult. The working out of details of formula funding for each biennium continued to be hotly contested. Relations of the regional universities improved somewhat when Cox replaced Snyder. However, even then, there continued to be as much competition for state dollars. If the university presidents felt that their schools were not being treated fairly in the formula funding, they retreated to the old, time-worn, tactics of lining up legislative allies and lobbying the governor.[130]

The battle between the U of L and UK continued into the eighties, and Singletary more than found his match in Swain. Eventually they arrived at what can best be called an accommodation, or détente, between the two largest and most powerful universities in the system. Both kept their law, dental, and medical schools. The University of Louisville, where President Swain recognized the need for reconciliation more than his UK counterpart, agreed not to offer as many doctoral programs as UK. As overall state support for each institution decreased, the U of L and UK increasingly depended on their own resources; they charged higher tuition costs than the regional universities and carried out more profound fund-raising efforts. The Chase College of Law also had its champions and remained steadfastly part of Northern Kentucky University. Increasingly in the 1980s, UK, the U of L, and the regional universities began to cooperate more, if grudgingly, with the Council on Higher Education at the will of Governors Carroll and Brown.[131] All the public universities now had their individual charges from the Council on Higher Education. However, the fate of Kentucky State University created a special problem. As it was the state's "traditional black" college, the question remained what should be done with a "high cost," small institution. Since it was strategically located in the state capital, everything that occurred there made statewide news. Though created as a state university by legislative act in 1972, Kentucky State University and the CHE searched for a unique role for the school in the 1980s. A 1981 decision by the federal Office of Civil Rights questioning the efforts of the state to desegregate its system of higher education brought a quick response from the Council. Executive Director Snyder argued that the state was indeed desegregated, owing to the fact that "over ninety percent (90%) of all black Kentuckians going to college attend traditionally white institutions." Moreover, efforts were being made to "enhance" KSU and to increase black student enrollment and African American faculty in all institutions. The resignation of President William Butts brought a crisis that appeared to be answered by the new president, Raymond Burse. Under CHE direction and that of Burse, KSU apparently found its niche in the Kentucky system of public higher education as a "small, public liberal arts oriented institution," with the Whitney M. Young, Jr., College of Leadership Studies as its centerpiece. It remained a training ground for state employees in night courses.[132]

With the completion of the changes made at Kentucky State University, by the late 1980s, each of the state universities now appeared to have a specified role, worked out with negotiations, within and without, of the Council on Higher Education. Through the administration of Governor Martha Layne Collins, coordination now seemed the order of the day. That is not to say that all of the actors were happy with the new reality of public higher education. University presidents and their associates still worked the legislative halls and committee rooms to get their agendas at the top of the list of the General Assembly. The old competition had not died. It even reared its head in campus histories. For example, Carl B. Cone, longtime UK historian, in his history of that school, argued, "Among the eight institutions, only the University of Kentucky is officially marked out to aspire to educational greatness. . . . The total educational endeavor of the University of Kentucky—undergraduate and graduate, professional, specialized, and community college—combine to make it the state's distinctive university, *the* state university of Kentucky."[133]

Everyone understood that the heyday of the post–World War II years was over. Enrollments continued to stagnate or at best grow slowly at the public universities. But enrollment in the Community College System increased to include about 25 percent of all students in higher education in the commonwealth by 1990. The private colleges continued to moderately hold their own in enrollment, with the Association of Independent Kentucky Colleges and Universities as their chief lobbying group. Moreover, many Kentuckians entering the state's public and private colleges and universities continued to need remedial work to bring them up to college standards. Clearly, not all of the high schools in the state were adequately doing their job in preparing their students for a college environment. Not only did reform of public elementary and secondary education in the commonwealth appear long overdue in the mid-1980s. There were also critics who wanted to overhaul the system of public higher education beyond what had been accomplished with the resurgent Council on Higher Education.[134]

Epilogue
Whither Education in Kentucky?

Education in Kentucky in the latter decades of the twentieth century could not help but change, owing to the forces both within the state and beyond that pushed for reform. Momentum built in the mid-1980s during the Collins administration, with the legislation of 1985 seemingly answering the cries of many for improvement in public school funding. The governor and most of the members of the General Assembly desired to improve Kentucky's public schools, particularly those in the poorer school districts. Although the Minimum Foundation Program had pumped some funds into these districts, mostly in the mountains and rural-oriented counties of the commonwealth, their students woefully lagged behind their peers in the more affluent urban and suburban areas. The question remained: could a state as diverse as Kentucky develop a truly equitable system of public education?[1]

It has often been demonstrated in the commonwealth that under the right conditions, the alignment of ideas, personalities, and forces can bring important change. As lawsuits slowly worked their way through the state courts, the Prichard Committee, the Council for Better Education (CBE), the state Chamber of Commerce, and other groups continued to push for reform. In particular, the Council for Better Education's lawsuit, as argued by Governor Combs, proved compelling. The lawsuit was based on the premise that the General Assembly and the governor were not doing their duty in providing for an "efficient" school system across the entire state as required by Section 183 of the Kentucky Constitution.[2]

Added to this mixture was again a colorful and critical gubernatorial election. The 1987 Democratic Party primary proved to be an old-fashioned political donnybrook. Candidates included former governor John Y. Brown Jr., Grady Stumbo, former governor Julian Carroll, and Lieutenant Governor Steven Beshear, who had the backing of the Collins administration.

Outsider Wallace G. Wilkinson, a forty-five-year-old self-made millionaire, coming late into the fray, made the lottery issue the centerpiece of his campaign. Wilkinson won the primary with 35 percent, or 58,000 votes, and then soundly trounced Republican John Harper, 504,674 to 273,141, in the general election. Upon taking office, the new governor immediately confronted the legislature with the lottery. The General Assembly concurred, passing an enabling lottery amendment that was approved by the citizens of the commonwealth. For the first time in more than a century, Kentucky now had a statewide lottery sponsored by the government.[3]

On May 31, 1988, Judge Ray Corns of the Franklin Circuit Court declared the state system of school finance unconstitutional based on his understanding of Section 183, agreeing with the CBE lawsuit and saying the General Assembly had not fulfilled its duty to implement and support the public schools of Kentucky. The next year the Kentucky Supreme Court in *Rose v. Council for Better Education,* upheld Corns's decision, even going beyond that decision to declare the entire system of public education to be in violation of Section 183. The supreme court also declared that the General Assembly must have remedial legislation in effect before school opened in 1990–1991. Within weeks the Education Reform Task Force (ERTF) was organized, made up of sixteen legislators and six other members appointed by Wilkinson.[4]

Thus began the efforts that led to one of those times in Kentucky history when education "reform" came to the forefront. Wilkinson had his own education agenda as well as a personal style that rubbed many people the wrong way. Nevertheless, the ERTF, with input from the Prichard Committee and others, began putting together a reform package. No one could deny that statewide only two-thirds of the students who entered the ninth grade graduated in four years. Only 58 percent of ninth-grade students in the Jefferson County system graduated.[5]

Governor Wilkinson, various legislative factions, including the so-called Young Turks, and KEA pushed their separate proposals. Eventually, they all came together in House Bill 940, a nine-hundred-page document, which worked its way through both houses of the General Assembly. Wilkinson eventually agreed to a new funding package, which included increasing the general sales tax to six percent. Out of the debate came landmark legislation, the Kentucky Education Reform Act (KERA). In the end, Frankfort politicians knew something had to be done. David Karem in the state Senate helped guide the measure. Karem later remarked, "One of the dynamics that made it happen was the tension between the executive and legislative branches. The tension became productive, because both sides wanted to be seen as doing the right thing." Speaker of the House Don Blandford, who was later disgraced by the Boptrot scandal, pushed his members into compliance. State Historian Jim Klotter summed up how the progress of this bill matched the usual way such laws wend their way through the Frankfort mélange: Wilkinson "and the legislature leadership also used a healthy number of promises of roads and projects in exchange for votes to pass the Kentucky Education Reform Act."[6]

The Kentucky Education Reform Act of 1990 included several important departures from the old system. The head of the state system would now be the commissioner of education, appointed by the State Board of Education. Local school councils of parents, administrators, and teachers would play important roles. Preschools would be developed statewide for disadvantaged children. Accountability became the watchword to "increase academic achievement" and focus on the success of all students. Family Resource and Youth Services centers were to be developed in schools with high poverty to increase learning opportunities. Antinepotism measures for local school systems were to be put in place. And efforts were to be made to tax property statewide at its full market value. The General Assembly authorized an extra $1 billion for public school education. The Kentucky Instructional Results Information System (KIRIS) began testing students in grades 4, 5, 7, 8, 11, and 12, using various types of questions. After some controversy in 1998, the Kentucky General Assembly passed a law mandating the Commonwealth Accountability Testing System (CATS), replacing KIRIS; it would include not only subjective items but also open-ended essay portions to test Kentucky students. Initially, cash awards were made to teachers whose schools showed improvement, but that incentive was abandoned after four years when the state developed budget problems. Money was also invested in improving technology in the schools.[7]

Although there were the usual naysayers, most of the Kentucky press, the state's educators and politicians, and interested parents believed Kentucky had arrived again at an important crossroads in the history of public school education. Plaudits came in from all over for the new legislation. The *New York Times* and even President George H. W. Bush congratulated the state on its foresight. While the Council for Better Education did not receive all the credit it should have, the Prichard Committee appeared at the height of its influence with the passage of KERA. Moreover, many Kentuckians remembered Edward F. Prichard Jr.'s efforts in helping launch the education reform movement. One of the greatest supporters of KERA, Thomas D. Clark, near the time of passage and then several years later, summed up the hopes of many Kentuckians. Calling KERA's passage evidence of "Sunrise in Kentucky," Kentucky's greatest historian exclaimed, "We're almost in the presence of a miracle." Clark, who died just a few weeks short of his

102nd birthday in 2005, maintained that KERA had helped Kentucky make "greater progress in education advancement during the past decade than in any comparable time in its history."[8]

From the time of KERA's passage in 1990 to the present, the question has continued to be asked: can Kentucky maintain the momentum promised by legislation? Much of the challenge is changing a culture that did not highly value education into one that does. Robert Sexton, executive director of the Prichard Committee for Excellence, perhaps said it best: "We were led to the unavoidable conclusion that implementation was more than changing schools; it required whole communities. If schools are to work well, communities need to do their civic business well."[9]

As the provisions of KERA were put into practice, one of the greatest changes was the appointment of the first commissioner of education, Californian Thomas Boysen (1990–1995). Ironically, until eliminated by constitutional amendment in 1992, the superintendent of public instruction post continued to exist, though without any real function or power. In the beginning Boysen may have been precisely what Kentucky needed to get the landmark reforms of KERA started. "Thomas Boysen was a very non-Kentucky kind of guy," explained *Courier-Journal* editor David Hawpe. The commissioner continually pushed testing to demonstrate the state of educational progress. "Accountability" became the educationist's buzzword. In addition to KIRIS and then CATS, there was site-based management that involved teachers and parents as never before in individual school decisions. From the beginning, a battle ensued between those who wanted to keep the old system intact, with local superintendents and school boards completely in control, and others who wanted power diffused and given to local school councils. One of the problems often cited for decades had been the difficulties of disadvantaged children entering the elementary grades. A preschool program for at-risk children from poor families promised to give them improved opportunities upon school entry. Moreover, family resource centers were aimed at counseling parents and children about services they could use in their communities. The newly created Education Professional Standards Board came into place to raise the level of performance and education of public school teachers.[10]

Governors Brereton C. Jones (1991–1995), Paul E. Patton (1995–2003), Ernie Fletcher (2003–2007), and Steve Beshear (2007–) generally supported the measures of KERA. There were lean budget years as well as those of largesse. Although in 1990 Kentucky teachers received the largest salary increases in the South, "bare bone budgets" offset those gains in other biennial budgets. In gubernatorial and General Assembly races, the merits of KERA many times became an issue. Republican candidates generally took a harsher view of KERA than their Democrat opponents. One of the most important provisions of KERA was the Support Education Excellence in Kentucky (SEEK) program to improve the funding disparity between the richer and poorer districts. Some districts, such as Fayette County, received lower state support than McCreary County, for example, because the former county was more willing to raise its taxes for school funding. The old problem remained: poor counties could not raise their taxes to the levels of the richer counties. Training of teachers and improving the schools' access to computer technology continued to be problems in the last decade of the twentieth century and the opening decade of the new century.[11]

Over time Boysen's "abrasive" style wore heavily on the state. Although the State Board of Elementary and Secondary Education "unanimously" extended his $125,000 contract in 1993 until the end of 1996, he had his detractors. "Instead of working with local school districts to bring about needed change," charged the *Richmond Register*'s editor Jim Todd, "he too often came off as someone who came to Kentucky to show ignorant hillbillies how to educate our children." Boysen ran afoul of leadership in the General Assembly, who then sought his ouster. The Kentucky School Boards Association went on record as "accusing him of trying to capitalize on the struggle between school boards and school councils to increase his power." In 1995 Boysen resigned and moved on to a position in the Michael Milken Foundation. Among the other commissioners since that time, Gene Wilhoit had the most success and the longest tenure; he left in 2006 to accept a position in Washington.[12]

In the early twenty-first century, Kentucky appeared to have the most integrated public school system in the nation. Robert A. Sedler, the lead attorney in desegregation cases that merged the Louisville and Jefferson County school systems in the mid-1970s, backed by a 2004 Harvard study, maintained that Kentuckians generally have accepted school desegregation. Most white parents stayed in Jefferson County and complied with court-ordered desegregation. There was even reconciliation in Frankfort. In 2004 Representative Teddy Edmonds of Jackson made an apology on the floor of the Kentucky House for the passage of the Day Law, which had been introduced by Representative Carl Day of Breathitt County one hundred years earlier. In 2006 *Courier-Journal* editor David Hawpe argued that an equilibrium now existed in Jefferson County, with 79 percent of the county's school-age children attending the public schools. "Both it [Jefferson County Public Schools] and parochial, religious, and independent private schools flourish here without the kind of backbiting that ruins the national debate," he claimed.[13]

Nonetheless, the integration of schools remained an issue, particularly in the larger urban areas of Kentucky. Because both Louisville and Seattle used race as one factor in determining school assignments, the matter simmered for several years. After the 1975 court order was removed in 2000, the Jefferson County School Board adopted the Student Assignment Plan the next year. In the Louisville plan, the aim was to have a black enrollment of at least 15 percent and no more than 50 percent in each school. Supporters claimed that diversity in school population contributed to a better community, integration, and racial harmony. "My racially diverse public school upbringing has become a source of pride for city people like me," said Ian McClure, who was bused from the eastern suburbs of Louisville to inner-city schools, including du Pont Manual High School. "It should be for every person who is a product of the JCPS system." However, other Jefferson County residents, primarily whites, were not as sanguine, arguing that their children were not allowed to enter schools near their homes. The administration of President George W. Bush sided with the latter, arguing that any kind of quota system was unconstitutional.[14]

After unsuccessful appeals in the lower courts, the plaintiffs arguing for ending the Student Assignment Plan took their case to the U.S. Supreme Court. In late June 2007, in a 5-4 decision based on ideological political lines, the nation's highest court demonstrated that America was still divided on how to approach the inequalities of public school education: it ruled that both the Seattle and the Louisville plans were unconstitutional. Chief Justice John Roberts, voting with the majority, remarked in *Meredith v. Jefferson County Board of Education*, "The way to stop discriminating on the basis of race is to stop discriminating on the basis of race." Dissenting Justice Stephen G. Breyer argued that "to invalidate the plans under review is to threaten the promise of *Brown*." One critic found Roberts's argument to be "dismissive of centuries of discrimination." The *Washington Post* declared the Louisville decision to be "A Blow to *Brown*," one that would allow "resegregation of schools by race." Jefferson County superintendent Sheldon Berman and his board now faced the task of complying with the Supreme Court decision while trying to retain a desegregated school system.[15]

There were also challenges in improving and diversifying Kentucky's classrooms, as well as in increasing the number of women in administrative positions. One study of gender patterns in public school administration found that although the number of female principals had increased since the 1980s, most were in elementary schools. African American Marlene Helm worked her way up through the system, becoming secretary of the Education, Arts, and Humanities cabinet in the Patton administration. She praised the efforts that had been made but pointed to much that remained to be done. "I still do not believe that Kentucky has really reformed its educational system," she explained. "We've still got a great achievement gap." Elaine Farris became superintendent of the Shelby County School System, the first African American superintendent in the state, after participating in the Minority Superintendent Intern Program. She later became the first African American and first female deputy education commissioner. She served briefly as interim education commissioner before becoming the current superintendent of the Clark County schools. The new century also opened opportunities for others to enter the teaching profession in Kentucky. For example, Marine Corps veteran Dan Sharrard came into the Oldham County School System by way of Troops to Teachers, a Department of Defense program that cooperates with states in transitioning military personal into teaching jobs.[16]

KERA appeared to be working in the early years of the first decade of the new century. There were plaudits and awards such as the Frank Newman Award for innovation, indicating that Kentucky appeared to be headed in the right direction. Students began to score above the national average on some standardized tests. The removal of three members of the Harlan County School Board by the state board and subsequent approval by the state supreme court gave hope that nepotism and old-fashioned Kentucky school cronyism was on the wane. However, for every gain there was a corresponding persistent problem. The commonwealth's high school graduation rate from 2002 to 2006 increased from 71 percent to 78 percent, a precedent-setting four points above the national average. From 1990 to 2007, Kentucky's ranking improved from forty-third to thirty-fourth, according to the Kentucky Long-Term Policy Research Center and other sources, including *Education Week*'s Quality Counts 2007 Achievement Index. Unfortunately, the school dropout rate continued to be a problem, particularly in the Jefferson County school system, the state's largest. Although Jefferson County ranked eleventh among the fifty largest cities in the nation in the percentage of students who graduated from high school, more than one-third (36.6 percent) of its students dropped out before finishing school. Conversely, the small Walton-Verona Independent School District in Boone County could boast in 2009 that, because of an aggressive program, no student had dropped out there in eleven years.[17]

Many of the old issues and controversies still plagued Kentucky public school education in the new century. Bible reading, public prayer, and the posting of the Ten Commandments remained hotly contested issues. Moreover, creationism morphed into the idea of intelligent design as its advocates pressured school districts to include creation science materials in their curricula. Contention also developed about textbooks. Changing from a B.C.–A.D.

designation for the world's chronology to B.C.E.–C.E. became an issue. The State Board of Education voted to retain the old designation even though many textbooks had already made the change to the newer system.[18]

Nationwide, school violence became an increasing problem in the 1990s. Kentucky could not escape this cycle. In late 1997, a male student at a Paducah area high school killed three students and wounded five others before being disarmed. The next year the General Assembly created the Kentucky Center for School Safety (KCSS) to channel state funds to the schools and provide information and training. The killing of even more students at Columbine High School in Colorado raised further safety concerns. Schools began hiring one or more "school resource officers" to keep the peace in the schools as well as taking KCSS advice and training to secure their buildings. Many public schools in the state also developed "alternative" programs for miscreants to take the place of the old measure of throwing troubled students out of school entirely.[19]

From the beginning of the reforms of KERA, critics argued that the CATS tests were costly and ineffectual, that "teaching to the test" was rampant, and that some schools even fudged on their testing and scoring. The inclusion of portfolio writing assignments for many courses had both its supporters and opponents. However, others wanted measurable criteria for judging schools. Liberals and conservatives sometimes agreed on national education policy, and that happened with the passage of No Child Left Behind (NCLB) early in the administration of President George W. Bush. With the support of Senator Ted Kennedy, the idea that a standardized test could be an instrument to gauge the success or failure of schools became law. Education historian William J. Reese has pointed out that such ideas and legislation were nothing new but only "reinforced the traditional view that testing and measurement are the sine qua non of education." With mandatory nationwide testing of grades three through eight in basic subjects, schools would be rewarded or punished based on student performance. Though oversimplified, the precept was that by 2014, 100 percent of all students should be performing at their grade level. Some critics argued that this placed an extra financial burden on inner-city districts and was aimed at attacking the public schools. Others claimed that overzealous testing harmed traditional learning.[20]

The merits and demerits of CATS and NCLB testing after 2005 became an increasing part of the education dialogue in Kentucky and throughout the nation. The pressure to surpass test scores of the previous year bedeviled administrators and teachers as they searched for ways to improve their students' scores. Pep rallies before testing became a common practice in some schools. Some teachers argued that too much testing and the preparation for tests took up time that would be better spent teaching. Testing near the conclusion of the high school experience also began to receive greater emphasis in the new century. The earliest form of standardized testing for entrance into college, the Scholastic Aptitude Test, developed by the College Entrance Examination Board, slowly gave way to the American College Test (ACT) as a measure of preparedness for entering higher education. For the first time in 2008, all high school juniors in Kentucky were required to take the ACT, as another measure of how Kentucky was progressing in preparing its young people for the world. The advocates of this measure believed it would also encourage more Kentucky youth to attend college and possibly reduce the number of students requiring remedial work. The results varied widely from school to school, but generally speaking, the higher average scores were recorded in the more affluent communities. The overall state average of 18.3 was three points below what ACT officials determined indicated that a student was ready to be successful in college. By the fall of 2008, only 8 percent of the schools in the commonwealth met the educational testing goals of 2014 as established by NCLB.[21]

Through all of this ferment of educational change, the Prichard Committee; the Council for Better Education; newspapers, including the *Lexington Herald-Leader* and the *Courier-Journal;* and other education advocacy groups kept up their efforts to improve Kentucky's education system. CATS became more controversial and the focal point of the critics of KERA. Mercer County High School teacher Erin Milburn, in a 2008 *Lexington Herald-Leader* opinion piece, voiced the frustrations of many a Kentucky teacher: "What has happened in the 18 years since KERA was introduced has moved beyond a paradigm shift into a full-blown paranoid slide into a sludge pit of indexes, calculations, punitive measures, debilitating demands on time and energy, threats, empty promises and above all, assessment, assessment and more assessment—assessment that has to be calculated, measured, graphed, analyzed and adjusted, looked at, shared, discussed, celebrated and wept over."[22]

The commonwealth could not sustain the funding gains promised by the passage of KERA in 1990. After the 9/11 tragedies, both the national and the state economies began a downward spiral that quickened in 2008–2009. The Prichard Committee pointed out the continual decline of SEEK funding adjusted for inflation. Legislative action in 2008 resulted in lower state funding, as the General Assembly and Governor Beshear did not increase taxation or add new taxes aimed at aiding education. For all the improvements in education owing to KERA, Kentucky in 2008 still spent less per student statewide on public school education than the national average. Reductions in the 2008 meeting of the General Assembly were followed by budget shortfalls in succeeding years. Nearly one thousand teaching positions were lost, as a result, for the opening of school in the fall of 2008. On the horizon there appeared to be little chance of holding the line against decreasing SEEK funding to the poorer districts.[23]

The controversy over the CATS test reached a climax in 2009, when opponents proposed scrapping the system and turning to a national standardized test. Senate president David Williams led the charge to eliminate CATS by introducing legislation in early 2009. Everyone seemed to agree that some form of testing was needed. Critics of the mostly analytical CATS test argued that it was too costly and could not be compared with other national standardized tests. Moreover, they believed that too much class time was taken up with the test preparation and the actual testing. The *Courier-Journal* and the *Lexington Herald-Leader* editorialized against changing or eliminating CATS. Both papers faulted Governor Beshear for opening up KERA for dismissal. "Wisely or unwisely, Mr. Beshear has opened Pandora's box," wrote the *Courier-Journal*. *Courier* editor David Hawpe maintained in an oral history interview that conservative opponents wanted to "basically dumb it down. . . . Many of these want the destruction of the public schools and the substitution of vouchers." The Kentucky Education Association supported Senate Bill 1, which required that the Department of Education develop new educational standards and a new test for the 2011–2012 school year. When the bill passed the General Assembly and was signed into law by Governor Beshear, it left in doubt the outcome of state testing for assessment both of the individual student and of the student's school. One idea was to have an end-of-course testing program; this plan was approved by the Kentucky Board of Education in late 2009. The *Lexington Herald-Leader*, with a hint of exasperation, admitted that the decades-long exercise in writing portfolios had been unsuccessful: "The National Assessment of Education Progress suggests that Kentucky's approach to teaching writing has not been particularly effective." Kentucky eighth-graders were woefully behind their peers nationally. If that was not frustration enough, NCLB testing, which hardly anyone approved of, was still federally mandated.[24]

KERA in its diminished form remained controversial. If KERA was working, its critics asked, then why did half of Kentucky high school graduates have to take at least one remedial course when they entered college? Everyone recognized that until high schools turned out better-prepared graduates, millions of dollars, $25 million annually by one estimate, would have to be expended for such training, making it nearly impossible to reach the goal of doubling the number of Kentuckians with bachelors' degrees by 2020. Editor Carl West in the *Frankfort State Journal* expressed it best: "This, of course, is the scandal of Kentucky secondary education. Kentucky high schools simply are not preparing a significant number of their college-bound graduates to study college-level courses." The "Task Force on Developmental Education," appointed by the Council on Postsecondary Education, made a series of recommendations in 2007 that, unless funded, will do nothing to solve this age-old problem.[25]

"What goes around, comes around," according to the old adage. This certainly continues to hold true for Kentucky education. In October 2009, Governor Steve Beshear announced the creation of yet another "task force" to study K-12 education. Consisting of thirty-one members, who represent the legislature, education cabinet officials, business, education, advocacy groups, and others, the Transforming Education in Kentucky Task Force was given the charge to reenergize school reform momentum. In February 2010, Kentucky became the first state to officially adopt the new national "common core content standards" for K-12 math and English language arts. The Kentucky Board of Education, the Council on Postsecondary Education, and the state Education Professional Standards Board voted unanimously in a joint session for the new venture. Standards for other subjects were to be developed soon. This move positioned Kentucky to obtain up to $175 million from the federal government in the Race to the Top program developed early in the Obama administration. Was this the beginning of a renaissance for public school education in Kentucky, energizing the state as in the early days of KERA, or just another cruel mirage of "reform"? Alas, Kentucky was not chosen in the first round of this program, ostensibly, among other reasons, because the state did not allow for charter schools. As with most issues regarding improving education, particularly in underperforming schools, the idea of charter schools touched off a continuing debate.[26]

Many if not all Kentucky students entering colleges were in a better position than their forebears. Most comprehensive public high schools as well as private schools taught advanced placement courses that prepared a student for college work and often counted for college credit. And academic competition between schools involved thousands of Kentucky students, encouraging academic excellence. The Kentucky Scholars programs joined the Governor's Scholars Program, which began in 1983, in tutoring a limited number of college-bound high school students. Private schools enjoyed an advantage over public schools in being able to choose their clientele, specifically those who could pay the fees. More than 90 percent of Catholic high school graduates, statewide, move on to college, winning scholarships and grants in record amounts. It is in the smaller community and county schools where students face a more daunting task. For example, Alexis Seymore, superintendent of the Dawson Springs Schools, pointed out in 2007 that her district would also send greater numbers to college, except that 63 percent of her students were eligible for a free lunch, 52 percent came from homes where neither parent had finished high school, and 28 percent qualified for special education services. Although nationwide more and more students from low-income families enter college, it is still the most affluent that can best afford a college education and follow through to graduation. One study indicated what is obvious, that the odds of graduating from college, not just attending, increase with family income. For example, the chances are 1 in 2 with family income over $90,000, descending to odds of 1 in 17 if the family income is less than $35,000. Too many Kentuckians fell into the latter category in the first decade of the twenty-first century. It takes more courage (as well as adequate income) for a first-generation Kentucky college student to take that step than for someone with a long family history of college enrollment and graduation.[27]

Public higher education in Kentucky, under the leadership of the Council on Higher Education from the mid-eighties into the 1990s, continued to search for a better way to fund an increasingly expensive system. Formula funding, worked out in the eighties, did not end competition for state dollars. Although the CHE under Executive Director Gary Cox appeared to coordinate the efforts of all the universities better than before, he recalled, "I remember Hanly Funderburk [of EKU] lecturing me at a council meeting 'that this is all well and good, but Eastern was going to do what Eastern was going to do.'" Cox also witnessed incessant "power plays" by one or more or more of the institutions.[28]

If Kentucky was to progress from its usual place in the bottom tier of states educationally, higher education faced many of the same problems as K-12 education. Commitment by the governors, the General Assembly, and the taxpayers to improve educational opportunity beyond the high school years became more and more important in the late twentieth century. The Council on Higher Education had tried to rein in the competition of the state's universities with a unified plan and budget, but in each legislative session, the regional universities, Kentucky State University, the University of Louisville, and the University of Kentucky and its community college appendages scrambled for every state dollar they could find. Clearly the system needed rationalizing so that tax dollars more efficiently served the needs of the state. The private colleges continued to play an important role, expanding their offerings and increasing their share of Kentucky's four-year-college enrollment.[29]

Over the years, the governor often set the pace for higher education leadership in Kentucky. At the time when Governor Wallace Wilkinson (1987–1991) and the General Assembly reacted to the Kentucky Supreme Court decision mandating radical change in public school education and ultimate passage of KERA, higher education appeared to take a backseat. Coming from a nongovernment background, and without a college degree, Wilkinson had difficulty getting along with higher education officials, particularly UK president David Roselle (1987–1989), who had replaced Otis Singletary in 1987. There was never enough money for all state responsibilities, and higher education continued to take almost annual budget cuts. It was difficult for the higher education community not to be cynical about the machinations of Wilkinson, who touched raw nerves when he chided university professors for their writings in "itty-bitty journals." Moreover, he created a firestorm in one of his last acts as governor by appointing himself to the University of Kentucky board of trustees. Perhaps UK political scientist Penny M. Miller best summed up Wilkinson's checkered record, when she called this "an affront to the academic world." She also scolded him for "influencing the resignation of President David Roselle and the appointment of his high school teacher and friend, Charles Wethington, to the presidency of the University of Kentucky." State Historian Klotter found that although Wilkinson had a somewhat positive governorship, "his style almost overcame his actions, and many found it hard to forget the first as they evaluated the second."[30]

The difficult funding times for Kentucky higher education continued during the administration of Governor Brereton Jones (1991–1995). Although the Kentucky Supreme Court upheld Wilkinson's right to appoint himself to the UK board, the legislature in the 1992 "trustees bill" dissolved all university boards as well as the Council on Higher Education and instituted a new system of nominating and choosing trustees and regents. Wilkinson was not reappointed to the UK board. During these difficult times, "the council's highest priority became maintenance of what we had," according to Cox, not new directions. Public higher education continued to be funded primarily through a formula based on full-time equivalency of students (FTEs), numbers of students graduating, hours taught, research efforts, and numbers of faculty and staff. From 1994 to 1998, "performance" funding became another key factor, and legislation required "accountability" to be measured and subsequently rewarded. Most of the universities fought the process, considering it just more paperwork that promised little in return.[31]

Governor Paul E. Patton (1995–2003) was the first governor to be able to succeed himself, owing to the passage of a constitutional amendment. A generally progressive governor and known as a hard worker, Patton excelled at "agenda setting," according to political scientist Paul Blanchard. His first term was successful in the main, especially the reform of higher education passed in a May 1997 special session. In that legislation, House Bill 1, which contained numerous "reforms," Patton proposed that the University of Kentucky shed its community colleges and concentrate on becoming a research university. He ran into strong opposition from the community colleges and their supporters. UK president Wethington, who had previously been chancellor of the Community College System, vociferously opposed the move. Former governor Ned Breathitt, chair of the University of Kentucky trustees, also disapproved the bill. The regional universities generally supported the governor, as did many others outside the UK orbit. "I will not be deterred by any kind of pressure or threats or possible adverse consequences," Patton averred. Kentucky "finally got a governor with the guts to separate the community colleges" from UK, said former CHE head Harry Snyder, who had encouraged the idea during his tenure from 1976 to 1986. Patton worked both sides of the political aisle and was generous to those legislators who supported his cause to push House Bill 1 through the General Assembly. The new law also contained a strengthened role for the U of L as a "metropolitan research university." Just as important, the law replaced the Council on Higher Education with the new, potentially stronger Council on Postsecondary Education (CPE). The governor and the General Assembly also promised to fund higher education at higher levels.[32]

The Kentucky Postsecondary Education Improvement Act of 1997 became law and encouraged the high hopes of not only Governor Patton but most of the state as well. While Wethington chafed at his defeat, UK was now being touted as on the way to becoming one of the top twenty public universities by 2020. But that can only happen if the legislature funds such an effort on a sustained basis. The community colleges and the technical schools of the state were merged into a separate Kentucky Community and Technical College System (KCTCS). A community college on the UK campus remained under UK aegis until 2004, when it became part of KCTCS and was renamed Bluegrass Community and Technical College. Initially, some KCTCS graduates protested not having the University of Kentucky imprimatur on their diplomas. The CPE and the KCTCS were each headed by a "president," equal in rank with the chief executives of the state's universities.[33]

The first president of the CPE, Gordon Davies, came to Kentucky from a similar post as director of the State Council on Higher Education in Virginia from 1977 to 1997. To UK historian John R. Thelin, Davies "represented a generation" of such administrators, who "truly believed that executive directors of the state agencies were going to be genuine influential players in the shaping of higher education." Marlene Helm, who served as secretary of the Education, Arts, and Humanities Cabinet in the Patton administration, maintained that "Gordon was what we needed at the time. He came with the right amount of knowledge. He really articulated the vision."[34]

The meeting of the 2000 General Assembly highlighted many of the unresolved issues in Kentucky public higher education. Davies and the CPE wanted to place tighter controls over the system. The question remained, as always, Who would get the biggest piece of the pie, UK, the U of L, or the regional universities? Each school had its own agenda and its own problems fitting into the new system. For example, because goals and performance were linked, Eastern, with its enrollment problems, faced stiff competition from its sister institutions. When the new funding package appeared to favor Northern Kentucky University, whose student population was increasing, Eastern president Robert Kustra (1998–2001) complained bitterly to the legislature and the CPE that his school was getting short shrift. The *Lexington Herald-Leader* called this "whining for dollars," and David Hawpe in the *Courier-Journal* chided the Eastern president for using "well-placed legislative help," that is, EKU official and state representative Harry Moberly, to seek favor with the legislature and thereby bypass Governor Patton's well-considered higher education budget.[35]

Whether a battle over appropriations in the General Assembly or for dominance of the CPE, politics is never far from the surface and the center of education in Kentucky. An old-fashioned political fight erupted in 2002 with CPE president Gordon Davies at the center. The reforms of 1997 began to unravel at the same time that Governor's Patton's powers diminished. The leaders of the General Assembly clearly did not favor Davies, while the *Courier-Journal* and the *Lexington Herald-Leader* argued that the regional universities continually set back the Patton reforms. The issues were wide and deep about how funds should be allocated. President Gary Ransdell of Western denied that "mission creep," in which the regionals kept increasing their roles, was at the heart of the debate. In the end, the CPE decided not to renew Davies's contract. According to former secretary Helm, Davies "and the governor [Patton] did not see eye to eye," and the CPE president had to go. The combative Davies never backed away from the flurry of charges against him. Claiming that reform had worked well under his direction, Davies snapped: "What the hell do I need to apologize for?" In contrast, Western Kentucky University English professor Joe Glaser, in an op-ed piece, criticized Davies for his "epic self-puffery" and for clearly siding with the "flagships," UK and the U of L, as well as NKU, at the expense of the other regional universities.[36]

With Davies gone, clearly relations among all involved, including the legislature, the governor, and the universities, needed to be mended. During Patton's second term in office, the political winds in Kentucky shifted yet again, as Republicans gained control of the state Senate. The admission of a sexual indiscretion as well as charges of ethics violations also damaged Patton's leadership. Thomas D. Layzell, the second president of the CPE, brought stability to the council and pushed for a continuation of the 1997 goals.[37]

Those objectives, including doubling the number of bachelor's-degree holders in the commonwealth from 400,000 to 800,000 by 2020, became increasingly difficult. To reach that goal, the public universities would have to expand their student enrollments. Eastern Kentucky University students and administration argued that the goal of twenty thousand students on the Richmond campus by that time was unreasonable because of a lack of space and inadequate funding. The other public universities and the community colleges also needed to increase their retention and graduation rates. First, the costly remediation to get many Kentucky high school graduates into mainstream college and university courses needed to be addressed. In the fall of 2006, 54 percent of entering freshmen needed extra work in one or more areas. Although Kentucky's public universities continued to improve their graduation rates, the commonwealth still lagged behind the nation. The University of Louisville, Eastern, and Western demonstrated higher increases in graduation than other schools by retaining more students. However, combined, the public and private colleges and universities in the state were not producing enough graduates to reach the 2020 goal.[38]

As if there were not enough problems clouding Kentucky higher education, the salaries of the presidents of public institutions became a source of controversy in the new century, particularly when faculty salaries did not rise and tuition increased annually. Kentucky apparently followed a national trend. In 2006 U of L president James R. Ramsey made a combined salary and support from the university's foundation of $489,433. University of Kentucky president Lee Todd made slightly less at $461,000. "Making Lee Todd one of the highest-paid presidents won't make the University of Kentucky one of the 20 best public universities," critiqued the hometown *Lexington Herald-Leader*. Not only were the salaries at issue, but the idea of giving a university president a "bonus" smacked of indifference to the plight of faculty and students. "Public confidence isn't bolstered when the top guys seem always to qualify for the near-maximum [bonus], while the state's fundamental higher education needs remain unmet," averred the *Courier-Journal*. In 2008 President Michael B. McCall of KCTCS topped not only all Kentucky college presidents with his remuneration package but also had the highest compensation, in total value, of all community college leaders in the United States at $610,000. Some controversy surrounded even the president's salary at independent Berea College in the wake of a "soul-searching" campus conversation about the old institution and the realities of the financial uncertainty of the second decade of the twenty-first century. One student suggested that President Larry D. Shinn's salary of $266,475, as reported in 2008, should be more like $120,000, to keep it only six times that of the lowest-paid college worker.[39]

The competition for state funds intensified in the early twenty-first century. Athletic competition remained an endemic part of the struggle for primacy in the state. Both the U of L and UK held the upper hand, owing to their large endowments; even their athletic teams' drawing power gave them an advantage in garnering private and public funds. The regional universities could not compete at the highest athletics level. Morehead even dropped from 1-AA competition in football to a lower division. Therefore, the state universities had to supplement athletic budgets from their general funds. However, as part of its ambitious plans, Western Kentucky University chose to raise its football team to the highest level of competition, Division 1-A, in 2006, now the BCS. Although there was some opposition from the faculty and criticism from the state's two largest newspapers, WKU continued on its course, charging students an extra seventy dollars a semester to help finance the sport. Critics of the vaunted University of Kentucky athletic program, particularly basketball, argued that more of the UK sports revenue should be allocated to UK's coffers. UK professor John Thelin, the author of *Games Colleges Play: Scandal and Reform in Intercollegiate Athletics* and *The Old College Try: Balancing Academics and Athletics in Higher Education,* continued to be a critic of his university's program, particularly since UK had not been invited to be a member of the Association of American Universities, "the most prestigious group of research universities in the nation." At UK and the U of L, as in Kentucky high schools, basketball was still almost like a religion to its devotees.[40]

The University of Kentucky's bid to become a top-twenty research public university advanced in fits and starts in the new century. Before the meeting of the 2006 General Assembly, the public universities reverted to the old practice of lobbying the governor and the legislature. The primacy of UK as the "flagship" became an issue in that meeting, where the General Assembly disregarded the budget recommendations of the CPE. Todd argued that all of Kentucky would benefit from UK's "Top 20 Business Plan." The legislature responded by increasing the higher education budget, providing particularly large increases for 2007–2008 and treating UK well, to the dismay of the other state universities. The *Lexington Herald-Leader* faulted Governor Ernie Fletcher (2003–2007) for ignoring the "CPE's funding recommendations." "If the CPE is irrelevant, if the governor and the legislature want to play a little politics, or a lot, with higher education, university presidents have no choice but to fight as hard as they can for their own institutions," the Lexington paper opined. "But that's not the way it was supposed to be." Editor David Hawpe of the *Courier-Journal* was even more blunt in an oral history interview. "CPE is a broken instrument," he said. "That its work prior to the last session was discarded proves that it's a broken instrument." Unfortunately, at the same time the CPE announced approval of tuition increases of 11–12 percent at all schools. Although the public university community generally had a favorable opinion of President Layzell's tenure, he announced his retirement in August 2006. The appointment of an interim head and then a permanent president turned into a comic opera of missteps from the last days of the Governor Fletcher's Republican administration into that of Governor Steve Beshear, the Democrat elected in 2007. With the appointment of Robert L. King in December 2008, the CPE appeared to regain some stability.[41]

The year 2006 may have been a high-water mark early in the new century for public higher education in Kentucky. Kentucky college classrooms, like most others in America, were going "high-tech," with computerization, podcasts, and other electronic mechanization addressing the age-old problems of communication. Both UK and Morehead had improved their diversity measures after decades of criticism by enrolling more black students. All of the state universities reported having more African American faculty members. The "Bucks for Brains" program, combining private and public funding, appeared to be working. Some universities received relatively high rankings nationally. In the fall of 2006, Kentucky colleges and universities reported record numbers, with a public enrollment of 207,498 (of which 87,286 was in KCTCS) and a private enrollment of 31,947, for a total of nearly 240,000. However, that figure was not on track to double the number of college graduates in the Commonwealth of Kentucky by 2020, particularly considering the persistent remediation and dropout problems.[42]

Tuition increased annually at most Kentucky colleges and universities, public and private, in the first decade of the twenty-first century. Ominously, Kentucky followed the national trend of pricing higher education out of the range of more and more students. As it turned out, the increasing number of graduating high school students in the state was offset by the increasing cost of attending college in Kentucky. In 2008 nearly one thousand fewer instate Kentucky students were attending college in the commonwealth than in 1997, the year of the passage of the Patton reform act. Also in 2008, Kentucky's tuition exceeded the averages of both the South and the United States for public two-year and four-year institutions. There appeared to be no good news nationally, as tuition costs increased four times faster than the rate of inflation near the end of the decade. In 2010 the CPE approved 4–6 percent increases for all the public universities as the presidents of these institutions decried their deficit problems.[43]

With increasing tuition and other costs of attending the private and public schools of higher education in Kentucky, including rising book prices, students were hard pressed to find the funds to cover these expenses. Although young people were told that obtaining a college education meant that they would earn substantially more during their lifetime, Kentucky remained near the bottom of the states in proportion of college graduates. In 2006 Kentucky's nearly 19 percent of college graduates in the general population was well below the nation's 28 percent average. There were many more opportunities to obtain college credits than ever before. Distance learning, or online courses, by the state's schools and from outside the state enrolled more and more students every year. Older proprietary schools such as Sullivan University, Spencerian College, and the National College of Business and Technology had several Kentucky locations. Increasingly, out-of-state, mostly proprietary, colleges set up satellite campuses in the state; Strayer University, McKendree College, and Indiana Wesleyan University led the way. Questions arose about their accreditation as well as the ethics of such online schools as the University of Phoenix and others.[44]

The Kentucky Educational Excellence Scholarship (KEES), funded with Kentucky Lottery proceeds, a scholarship that had begun two decades earlier, helped fund many college students' careers. This was the result of the successful gubernatorial election of Wallace Wilkinson in 1987, when first the General Assembly and then the people of the commonwealth accepted the lottery as an expedient to balance the state budget. Although I and other critics see the lottery as essentially "a poor man's regressive tax," many legislators consider such programs an alternative to tax reform (legislators love to tax "sin"). KEES scholarships were given to students who graduated from high school with a minimum 2.5 grade-point average and an ACT score of at least 15, neither of which was a particularly good indicator of college potential. The better the scores, the higher the amount received. However, in 2007 a report revealed that 40 percent of KEES recipients did not make the required 2.5 GPA in their freshman year in order to retain their scholarships. The student scores, the actual amounts given to students, and the general efficacy of the program were all being debated at the end of the first decade of the new century.[45]

The twenty independent colleges and universities in Kentucky had many of the same problems as public higher education. Enrolling more than twenty-nine thousand students in 2007, the private schools filled a vital need. Although they enrolled only about 11 percent of undergraduate students, including KCTCS in the total, the independent colleges and universities collectively graduated about 20 percent of all college and university graduates in Kentucky each year. The Association of Independent Kentucky Colleges and Universities, directed by Gary S. Cox, represented these schools. The private universities also have their plans for enlargement. Campbellsville and

Cumberland have moved to university status, and Asbury has plans to do so in the future. Pikeville College opened a new College of Osteopathic Medicine in the new century and added a high-profile president, longtime board member and former governor Paul Patton, as its chief administrator in 2009. Centre College, with its high rate of retention of students, annually graduated at least 80 percent of its students after four years of college work. In 2009 Forbes Magazine ranked Centre as the fourteenth-best liberal arts college in America. All of the private schools have better retention and graduation rates than the public universities in the state. Schools such as Alice Lloyd College fulfill their original purpose of educating mountain students. Transylvania, Berea, and Centre have proved particularly adept at raising their endowments. As a sign of its maturing, Lindsey Wilson College chose to add football to its expanding athletic program in 2010. Clearly, the independent colleges and universities in Kentucky will continue to play a major, perhaps even an increasing, role in higher education in the commonwealth in the new century.[46]

The seminaries of Kentucky in the first decade of the twenty-first century faced many of the same problems, particularly financial, as higher education everywhere. They offered a variety of theology and religious training, from the liberal to the conservative, in a graduate school setting. Asbury Theological Seminary in Wilmore, which remained true to its conservative independent roots, went through a crisis in 2006 when the school's board of trustees overruled the faculty and students and dismissed the president. Louisville Presbyterian Theological Seminary and Lexington Theological Seminary faced the daunting task of turning out religious leaders with their denominations declining in numbers. Both in 2009 cut their staffs owing to the financial crisis. The Baptists in Kentucky continued on their divisive course, which began with the fundamentalist takeover of the annual meetings of the national Southern Baptist Convention beginning in 1979. Southern Baptist Theological Seminary in Louisville turned ever more toward ultraconservatism when the fundamentalist-dominated board of trustees hired a likeminded president. With a reductionist blend of Calvinism and denominational political power in the guise of scholasticism, Southern Seminary tried to exclude others from fellowship. Moderate professors who did not resign or retire were pushed out. Wayne Ward, who began teaching there in the 1940s, found himself being "labeled a heretic" by the seminary's administration. Moderates founded the Baptist Seminary of Kentucky in Lexington in 2002, as a "Baptist alternative," in the words of founding president Greg Earwood.[47]

The role of African Americans in Kentucky higher education demonstrated some gains in the new century. Minority faculty hiring increased in the new century as Kentucky public universities attempted to meet goals set by the U.S. Department of Education's Office for Civil Rights since 1999. Moreover, black enrollment increased steadily, with the minority numbers surpassing 8 percent, the percentage of African Americans in the Kentucky population. The University of Kentucky worked particularly hard to raise its minority numbers and the retention numbers for all students. Kentucky State University, where more than half of the students enrolled were African Americans, developed programs under the direction of President Mary Evans Sias to retain students, helping them to continue on to graduation.[48]

Kentucky could not escape the controversies, scandals, and improprieties that sometime afflicted higher education. Some students still cheated, and even the professoriate could be devious. Northern Kentucky University exposed a research scandal in a "660 color-coded" page report where five professors of economics fraudulently produced papers. All left NKU employment. Athletic teams at the University of Kentucky, for all their success and revenue-producing ability, often faced sanctions from the NCAA in the post–World War II era, the most recent in the late 1980s. Although the University of Louisville escaped the results of athletic penalties, it had other problems. An investigation by New York attorney general Andrew Cuomo found U of L among major universities where loan officials encouraged students toward borrowing from a few loan providers and received something in return for their efforts. But this was nothing compared with "Felner's Follies," the way *LEO Weekly*, an alternative Louisville newspaper, referred to a sordid affair. Dean Robert Felner of the U of L College of Education became the center of a scandal for misuse of federal money, among other indiscretions. And a friend of Felner received a doctorate after only one semester. As Felner's case wound its way through the federal courts, he eventually received a sixty-three-month prison sentence, and the U of L College of Education successfully returned to respectability and accreditation. The University of Louisville Foundation also came under increasing scrutiny for its practices. The University of Kentucky was not without its controversies. UK professor of Islamic studies Ihsan Bagby defended himself against charges by conservative author David Horowitz that he was one of the "101 Most Dangerous Academics in America," for claiming that Muslims can never be "fully committed" to American citizenship. The controversy simmered for a while, and the UK administration defended Bagby as a valuable member of the faculty. In mid-2010 the question of priorities continued to reverberate in Kentucky higher education when a donation of $7 million by mining interests came to UK for construction of "Wildcat Coal Lodge," a plush dormitory for its basketball players. In protest, renowned Kentucky poet, novelist, and essayist Wendell Berry, who is also a leading environmentalist, requested that his personal papers be transferred from the commonwealth's flagship university to the Kentucky Historical Society.[49]

President Lee Todd's and the University of Kentucky's quest for top-twenty public university status appeared to be in crisis; even some UK faculty and students argued that the effort was off-track or counterproductive. The UK campus paper editorialized in 2009, "Pushing a plan people do not support is not only foolish and unadvisable, but could set UK further back than before it enacted the Top 20 Plan." Former UK administrator James Chapman believed that the school would have great difficulty reaching that goal, because the states that Kentucky is competing against "have a lot more money and they are moving ahead as well." Current UK historian of higher education John R. Thelin also doubted that UK could reach top-twenty status, owing to the "finite resources" of the state. "My own personal wish was that UK define itself as the university for Kentucky with more of a statewide focus than a national focus," he explained.[50]

Kentucky's colleges and universities have had difficulty balancing their budgets in the new century. With a full-fledged recession beginning in 2008, the task became more and more difficult as university and college endowments suffered nationwide. Although Berea's endowment had topped out at over $1 billion in July 2008, by the end of November of that year it had declined to $753 million. In May 2009, even the well-endowed Berea felt the economic crunch of the declining value of investments and was forced to eliminate 5 percent of its full-time positions. All of the public universities had the same problem, as their endowments dropped by 20 percent or more in 2008. Each institution tried to cut costs by cutting staff or freezing hiring, or giving no annual raises to faculty. All the schools struggled to rein in expenses. Utilities costs continued to rise, and schools resorted to such measures as shutting down most campus facilities during vacation breaks. Saving "energy" became more than an academic enterprise, as computers now monitored campus facilities. As economy measures, UK took telephones out of dorm rooms and the U of L cut back on window-washing. Governor Beshear appointed a task force in 2008 to make recommendations on how to make public higher education more affordable.[51]

Whither education in Kentucky? State Historian Jim Klotter said in 2006: "Currently, the state ranks fourteenth nationally in highway spending, but last in education spending per person. The will to build better roads, and to fund other things, still remains stronger than the will to build—and maintain—a better higher education system. Asphalt often seems more valued than a young mind." Was this too strong a condemnation of the Commonwealth of Kentucky's efforts?[52]

For all the pessimism about education, there have been in the past and are now signs of a vibrant educational atmosphere in most if not all of the urban and rural areas of the commonwealth. Most of the parochial Catholic schools and some of the private elementary and secondary schools offer as good an education as you can find in America. The majority of their graduates move on into higher education without missing a beat. In the public arena, there are many excellent elementary and high schools. The Oldham County schools, where three of my grandchildren attended, rank among the better schools in America. Several urban school systems have fine programs but still fall behind in schools where minority students predominate. Overall improvement on national standardized tests in the public schools gives tantalizing evidence that perhaps Kentucky education is indeed on the rise. For example, in the fall of 2009, Kentucky's eighth- and tenth-graders improved somewhat on national assessments in English, mathematics, reading, and science. With diligent application, a Kentucky student can get a good education in the state's private and public colleges and universities. Graduate study has improved in the larger public universities, and many of their programs rank nationally. The question is, as always, Is this enough to keep up in an ever-changing educational world?[53]

As it has happened throughout the history of Kentucky, education moves forward in fits and starts, regressing during difficult economic times or because of indifference by the citizens of the state. The challenges remain the same in the twenty-first century. To reach even the national average in most educational categories, Kentucky needs to drastically cut the public school dropout rate, produce more quality high school graduates and thus diminish the need for remedial noncredit college courses, and graduate more college and university students in order to reach the goal of eight hundred thousand Kentuckians with a baccalaureate degree by 2020. And can the University of Kentucky reach top-twenty public research university status? Will the Council on Postsecondary Education finally be able to control competition and better coordinate the public universities? Is there enough goodwill and equanimity among the Commonwealth of Kentucky's politicians and the Kentucky body politic to push the state into a new age of reform in public school and higher education? These and other stories will evolve in the coming years in the continuing saga of the history of education in Kentucky.

Notes

Abbreviations

EL   *Encyclopedia of Louisville* (Lexington: Univ. Press of Kentucky, 2001).
ENK   *Encyclopedia of Northern Kentucky* (Lexington: Univ. Press of Kentucky, 2009).
KE   *Kentucky Encyclopedia* (Lexington: Univ. Press of Kentucky, 1992).

Chapter 1. Tragedies, Blunders, and Promises

1. For a short overview of public education in antebellum Kentucky by Thomas D. Clark, see *KE*, 744–47; also see Clark, *A History of Kentucky* (1937; reprint, Ashland, KY: Jesse Stuart Foundation, 1988), 213–26; Edwina Ann Doyle, Ruby Layson, and Anne Armstrong Thompson, *From the Fort to the Future* (Lexington: Kentucky Images, 1987), 6; Lowell H. Harrison and James C. Klotter, *A New History of Kentucky* (Lexington: Univ. Press of Kentucky, 1997), chap. 1; Steven A. Channing, *Kentucky: A History* (New York; Norton, 1977), 75.

2. Stephen Aron, *How the West Was Lost: The Transformation of Kentucky from Daniel Boone to Henry Clay* (Baltimore: Johns Hopkins Univ. Press, 1996), 3, 184–200.

3. Adolph E. Meyer, *An Educational History of the American People* (New York: McGraw-Hill, 1957), 29; C. W. Hackensmith, *Out of Time and Tide: The Evolution of Education in Kentucky* (Lexington: College of Education, Univ. of Kentucky, 1970), 14–15; Harrison and Klotter, *A New History of Kentucky*, 148; Delta Kappa Gamma, *Well-Spring in the Wilderness: Delta Kappa Gamma, Project Pioneer Women Teachers, Kentucky* (Louisville: Gibbs Inman, 1955), 12–13.

4. Hackensmith, *Out of Time and Tide*, 15–16; William E. Ellis, H. E. Everman, and Richard D. Sears, *Madison County: 200 Years in Retrospect* (Richmond, KY: Madison County Historical Society, 1985), 78; James C. Klotter, ed., *Our Kentucky: A Study of the Bluegrass State* (Lexington: Univ. Press of Kentucky, 1992), 278.

5. *KE*, 894; John D. Wright Jr., *Transylvania: Tutor to the West* (Lexington: Univ. Press of Kentucky, 1975), 1–10.

6. Jesse LeRoy Miller Jr., "A History of the Academies and Seminaries of the State of Kentucky, 1792–1850" (master's thesis, Univ. of Chicago, 1926), 1–10.

7. *KE*, 894–95; Wright, *Transylvania*, 11–32.

8. Hackensmith, *Out of Time and Tide*, 18–21; Asa C. Barrow, "David Barrow and His Lulbegrud School, 1801," *Filson Club History Quarterly* 7 (April 1933): 88–93; Harriette Simpson Arnow, *Flowering of the Cumberland* (Lexington: Univ. Press of Kentucky, 1984), 178–79.

9. Doyle, Layson, and Thompson, *From the Fort to the Future*, 12–19; Robert B. McAfee, "The Life and Times of Robert B. McAfee and His Family Connections," *Register of the Kentucky Historical Society* 25 (May 1927): 118–32.

10. Susannah Johnson, *Recollections of the Rev. John Johnson and His Home: An Autobiography* (Nashville: Southern Methodist, 1869), 20–25; Robert M. Rennick, *Kentucky Place Names* (Lexington: Univ. Press of Kentucky, 1984), 243–44.

11. *KE*, 744–45; Harrison and Klotter, *A New History of Kentucky*, 148–50; Frank L. McVey, *The Gates Open Slowly: A History of Education in Kentucky* (Lexington: Univ. of Kentucky Press, 1949), 17–32.

12. Lewis Collins, *Historical Sketches of Kentucky* (Lexington, KY: Henry Clay Press, 1968), 295–96; Charles R. Staples, *The History of Pioneer Lexington* (Lexington, KY: Transylvania Press, 1959), 297–98; John D. Wright Jr., *Lexington: Heart of the Bluegrass* (Lexington, KY: Lexington–Fayette County Historic Commission, 1982), 8–9. Doyle, Layson, and Thompson, *From the Fort to the Future*, 9–11; Lewis Collins and Richard H. Collins, *History of Kentucky* (Frankfort: Kentucky Historical Society, 1966), 2:226.

13. Harrison and Klotter, *A New History of Kentucky*, 158; McVey, *The Gates Open Slowly*, 17–23; Wright, *Transylvania*, 6.

14. Harrison and Klotter, *A New History of Kentucky*, 63–64, 77–79, 250; *KE*, 224–25; Robert Ireland, "Politics of Kentucky Government," in *Kentucky: Its History and Heritage*, ed. Fred J. Hood (St. Louis: Forum Press, 1978), 75–87.

15. McVey, *The Gates Open Slowly*, 41; Edsel T. Godbey, *The Governors of Kentucky and Education, 1780–1852* (Lexington: Bulletin of the Bureau of School Service, Univ. of Kentucky, 1960), 110.

16. McVey, *The Gates Open Slowly*, 3–12, 33–46; Hackensmith, *Out of Time and Tide*, 24–35; Klotter, *Our Kentucky*, 278–79; Lowell H. Harrison, interview by author, March 20, 2005.

17. *KE*, 74, 489–90; James C. Klotter, "Promise, Pessimism, and Perseverance: An Overview of Higher Education in Kentucky," *Ohio Valley History* 6 (Spring 2006): 46; Hackensmith, *Out of Time and Tide*, 24–32; Harrison interview, March 20, 2005; William M. French, *America's Educational Tradition: An Interpretative History* (Boston: Heath, 1964), 94; Thomas D. Clark, "Kentucky Education through Two Centuries of Political and Social Change," *Register of the Kentucky Historical Society* 83 (Summer 1985): 177.

18. Hackensmith, *Out of Time and Tide*, 29–30; Ellis, Everman, and Sears, *Madison County*, 79.

19. *EL*, 150, 441; David Post, "From the Jefferson Seminary to the Louisville Free School: Change and Continuity in Western Education, 1813–1840," *Register of the Kentucky Historical Society* 86 (Spring 1988): 103–18; George W. Yater, *Two Hundred Years at the Falls of the Ohio: A History of Louisville and Jefferson County* (Louisville: Filson Club, 1987), 48, 51.

20. *EL*, 735; Henry J. Perkinson, *The Imperfect Panacea: American Faith in Education, 1865–1990* (New York: McGraw-Hill, 1991), 72.

21. McVey, *The Gates Open Slowly*, 28; William H. Townsend, *Lincoln and His Wife's Home Town* (Indianapolis: Bobbs-Merrill, 1929), 57, 60–62; Wright, *Lexington*, 33.

22. Gerald L. Gutek, *A History of the Western Educational Experience*, 2nd ed. (Long Grove, IL: Waveland Press), 220–52; Hackensmith, *Out of Time and Tide*, chap. 5; Ernest E. Bayles and Bruce L. Hood, *Growth of American Education Thought and Practice* (New York: Harper and Row, 1966), 92–113; Niels Henry Sonne, *Liberal Kentucky: 1780–1828* (New York: Columbia Univ. Press, 1939), 10, 78–107.

23. Hackensmith, *Out of Time and Tide*, chap. 5; Sonne, *Liberal Kentucky*, 95–105.

24. Hackensmith, *Out of Time and Tide*, chap. 5; *EL*, 327; Bayles and Hood, *American Education Thought and Practice*, 117.

25. *KE*, 803; Lulu Sutherland Hahn, "A History of Science Hill Female Academy" (master's thesis, Univ. of Kentucky, 1944), 145–47; Hackensmith, *Out of Tide and Tide*, 60–61; George L. Willis, *History of Shelby County, Kentucky* (Louisville: C. T. Deering, 1929), 107–9; James C. Klotter and Freda C. Klotter, *Faces of Kentucky* (Lexington: Univ. Press of Kentucky, 2006), 142; Otis McBride, *The Teaching of English in the Southern Antebellum Academy* (Nashville: George Peabody College for Teachers, 1941), 206–9; Delta Kappa Gamma, *Well-Spring in the Wilderness*, 62–65.

26. *KE*, 184, 475; Lindsey Apple, Frederick A. Johnston, and Ann Bolton Bevins, eds., *Scott County, Kentucky: A History* (Georgetown, KY: Scott County Historical Society, 1993), 109, 138, 157.

27. Clark and Ham, *Pleasant Hill and Its Shakers* (Harrodsburg, KY: Pleasant Hill Press, 1968), 64–65.

28. *KE*, 32, 351–52, 745; Ellis Hartford, *The Little White Schoolhouse* (Lexington: Univ. Press of Kentucky, 1977), 28–29; Hackensmith, *Out of Time and Tide*, 18–19; John Fox Jr., *The Little Shepherd of Kingdom Come* (New York: Scribner's, 1903), 41–53; Mabel Flora Mumford, "A Historical Sketch of Education in the Kentucky Highlands" (master's thesis, Univ. of Chicago, ca. 1920), 42; Arnow, *Flowering of the Cumberland*, 179–80.

29. McVey, *The Gates Open Slowly*, 63–65; *KE*, 696, 799; Hartford, *The Little White Schoolhouse*, 1–14.

30. McVey, *The Gates Open Slowly*, 63–74; Hartford, *The Little White Schoolhouse*, 38–49.

31. *KE*, 597–98; McVey, *The Gates Open Slowly*, 68–71; Perkinson, *The Imperfect Panacea*, 111–14.

32. McVey, *The Gates Open Slowly*, 38–46; Hackensmith, *Out of Time and Tide*, 31–33; *KE*, 74; Godbey, *The Governors of Kentucky and Education*, 14; Harrison interview, March 20, 2005.

33. *KE*, 793; Clyde F. Crews, *An American Holy Land: A History of the Archdiocese of Louisville* (Wilmington, DE: Michael Glazier, 1987), 58, 94–95; Philip Gleason, "From an Indefinite Homogeneity: Catholic Colleges in Antebellum America," *Catholic Historical Review* 94 (January 2008): 48–49; Felicity Allen, *Jefferson Davis: Unconquerable Heart* (Columbia: Univ. of Missouri Press, 1999), 45–50; Clement Eaton, *Jefferson Davis* (New York: Free Press, 1977), 4–5; William J. Cooper Jr., *Jefferson Davis, American* (New York: Alfred A. Knopf, 2000), 15, 17–19.

34. *KE*, 571–72, 793, 824–25; *EL*, 165; Crews, *An American Holy Land*, 89, 123–26.

35. Harrison and Klotter, *A New History of Kentucky*, 96–105, 168–69; Frank Mathias, interview by author, August 12, 2000; Mathias, "Slavery, the Solvent of Kentucky Politics," in Hood, *Kentucky*, 94–104; Harold D. Tallant, *Evil Necessity: Slavery and Political Culture in Antebellum Kentucky* (Lexington: Univ. Press of Kentucky, 2003), 13, passim.

36. Lowell H. Harrison, ed., *Kentucky's Governors* (Lexington: Univ. Press of Kentucky, 1985), 20–21; Harrison and Klotter, *A New History of Kentucky*, 90–95.

37. Harrison and Klotter, *A New History of Kentucky*, 149; *KE*, 745; McVey, *The Gates Open Slowly*, 50–51; Hackensmith, *Out of Time and Tide*, 36–39; Harrison, *Kentucky's Governors*, 22–25; Godbey, *The Governors of Kentucky and Education*, 39.

38. *KE*, 56, 745; Harrison, *Kentucky's Governors*, 26–28; McVey, *The Gates Open Slowly*, 51–53; *Kentucky Acts, 1821*, 351–52.

39. Doyle, Layson, and Thompson, *From the Fort to the Future*, 30–43; Hackensmith, *Out of Time and Tide*, 42; Miller, "A History of the Academies and Seminaries of the State of Kentucky," 64–70.

40. Doyle, Layson, and Thompson, *From the Fort to the Future*, 24–43; *Journal of the House of Representatives*, October 21, 1822; Hackensmith, *Out of Time and Tide*, 41–44.

41. *KE*, 745; Barksdale Hamlett, *History of Education in Kentucky* (Frankfort: Kentucky Department of Education, 1914), 4–7; Doyle, Layson, and Thompson, *From the Fort to the Future*, 6, 24–43; *Journal of the House of Representatives*, October 21, 1822; Harrison and Klotter, *A New History of Kentucky*, 149.

42. Harrison, *Kentucky's Governors*, 29–32, Harrison and Klotter, *A New History of Kentucky*, 109–12; Godbey, *The Governors of Kentucky and Education*, 59.

43. Harrison, *Kentucky's Governors*, 33–37; McVey, *The Gates Open Slowly*, 53–55; *KE*, 745; Doris Lynn Koch Moore, "Benjamin Orr Peers and the Beginnings of the Public School Movement in Kentucky, 1826 to 1842" (Ed.D. diss., Univ. of Kentucky, 1981), 3–4.

44. *KE*, 511–12; Doyle, Layson, and Thompson, *From the Fort to the Future*, 44–57.

45. *KE*, 511–12; James B. Beauchamp, *The Kentucky School for the Deaf Established* (Danville, KY: KSD Alumni Association, 1973), 1–14; Doyle, Layson, and Thompson, *From the Fort to the Future*, 44–57.

46. *KE*, 511; *EL*, 478–79.

47. Marion B. Lucas, *A History of Blacks in Kentucky: From Slavery to Segregation, 1760–1891* (1992; reprint, Frankfort: Kentucky Historical Society, 2003), 144–45; William J. Reese, *America's Public Schools: From the Common School to "No Child Left Behind"* (Baltimore: Johns Hopkins Univ. Press, 2005), 43–44; Lawrence A. Cremin, *Traditions of American Education* (New York: Basic Books, 1977), 73–80.

48. *KE*, 285–86, 312–13, 373–74; Harrison and Klotter, *A New History of Kentucky*, 151; McVey, *The Gates Open Slowly*, 143–47; Thomas C. Venable, "A History of Negro Education in Kentucky" (Ph.D. diss., George Peabody College for Teachers, 1952), 31–48; Lucas, *A History of Blacks in Kentucky*, 140–45; Shannon H. Wilson, *Berea College: An Illustrated History* (Lexington: Univ. Press of Kentucky, 2006), 9–21; Tallant, *Evil Necessity*, 193–219.

49. Harrison, *Kentucky's Governors*, 24; Harrison and Klotter, *A New History of Kentucky*, 149–50; Moore, "Benjamin Orr Peers," 84–87, 90, 93; Benjamin O. Peers, *American Education: Our Strictures on the Nature, Necessity, and Practicability of a System of National Education, Suited to the United States* (New York: John S. Taylor, 1838).

50. Harrison and Klotter, *A New History of Kentucky*, 150. Hackensmith, *Out of Time and Tide*, 65–67; McVey, *The Gates Open Slowly*, 190–94; Porter H. Hopkins, *KEA: The First One Hundred Years* (Louisville: Kentucky Education Association, 1957), 23–26.

51. Hackensmith, *Out of Time and Tide*, 67–68; Harrison and Klotter, *A New History of Kentucky*, 150; Harrison, *Kentucky's Governors*, 47–50; Miller, "Academies and Seminaries of Kentucky," 78.

52. Hackensmith, *Out of Time and Tide*, 68–69; Harrison and Klotter, *A New History of Kentucky*, 150; McVey, *The Gates Open Slowly*, 55–58; Hamlett, *History of Education in Kentucky*, 15–20; Klotter, *Our Kentucky*, 280–81.

53. *KE*, 745; Harrison and Klotter, *A New History of Kentucky*, 149–50, Hackensmith, *Out of Time and Tide*, 67–69; Harrison, *Kentucky's Governors*, 43–54; Hamlett, *History of Education in Kentucky*, 21–31.

54. Hackensmith, *Out of Time and Tide*, 69–70; Harrison and Klotter, *A New History of Kentucky*, 114; Harrison, *Kentucky's Governors*, 56–57.

55. U.S. Bureau of the Census, *Sixth U.S. Census: 1840* (Washington, DC: Government Printing Office, 1841); Post, "From the Jefferson Seminary to the Louisville Free School," 106.

56. *KE*, 745; Hackensmith, *Out of Time and Tide*, 69–70; Harrison and Klotter, *A New History of Kentucky*, 114; McVey, *The Gates Open Slowly*, 165–66; Harrison, *Kentucky's Governors*, 61; Hamlett, *History of Education in Kentucky*, 6–9.

57. *KE*, 746, 800–801; Klotter, *Our Kentucky*, 280.

58. *KE*, 451–52; Klotter, *Our Kentucky*, 280–81.

59. Harrison and Klotter, *A New History of Kentucky*, 150; *KE*, 872; Moore, "Benjamin Orr Peers," 5.

60. McVey, *The Gates Open Slowly*, 56–57; Hamlett, *History of Education in Kentucky*, 15–20; Doyle, Layson, and Thompson, *From the Fort to the Future*, 68–83; Klotter, *Our Kentucky*, 279; Reese, *America's Public Schools*, 17–18.

61. Doyle, Layson, and Thompson, *From the Fort to the Future*, 68–83; Hamlett, *History of Education in Kentucky*, 15–39.

62. Harrison and Klotter, *A New History of Kentucky*, 159; Harrison, *Kentucky's Governors*, 61; *KE*, 120, 746; James C. Klotter, *The Breckinridges of Kentucky, 1760–1981* (Lexington: Univ. Press of Kentucky, 1986), 51, 54–59.

63. Edgar W. Knight, *Education in the United States*, 3rd ed. (New York: Greenwood Press, 1951), 192–240; *KE*, 745–46; Hamlett, *History of Education in Kentucky*, 41–49; Klotter, *The Breckinridges of Kentucky*, 58–59.

64. Hamlett, *History of Education in Kentucky*, 42–44.

65. Ibid., 45–50; Harrison and Klotter, *A New History of Kentucky*, 150.

66. Harrison and Klotter, *A New History of Kentucky*, 117–19; Hackensmith, *Out of Time and Tide*, 70–71.

67. *KE*, 225; Harrison and Klotter, *A New History of Kentucky*, 117–19.

68. Harrison and Klotter, *A New History of Kentucky*, 117.

69. Clark, *A History of Kentucky*, 220–21; *KE*, 403; McVey, *The Gates Open Slowly*, 60–61; Thomas D. Clark, *Agrarian Kentucky* (Lexington: Univ. Press of Kentucky, 1977), 102–3; Harrison, *Kentucky's Governors*, 51–54.

70. Clark, *Agrarian Kentucky*, 102–4; McVey, *The Gates Open Slowly*, 61.

71. Harrison and Klotter, *A New History of Kentucky*, 117–19; McVey, *The Gates Open Slowly*, 167–68; Hackensmith, *Out of Time and Tide*, 71; Hamlett, *History of Education in Kentucky*, 53; Clark, *Agrarian Kentucky*, 104–5.

72. Harrison, *Kentucky's Governors*, 64–67; Harrison and Klotter, *A New History of Kentucky*, 115, McVey, *The Gates Open Slowly*, 166–67; Klotter, *The Breckinridges of Kentucky*, 59.

73. Hackensmith, *Out of Time and Tide*, 71, Harrison and Klotter, *A New History of Kentucky*, 117–19; Hamlett, *History of Education in Kentucky*, 53; Klotter, *The Breckinridges of Kentucky*, 59; Harrison, *Kentucky's Governors*, 69; William Hutchinson Vaughn, *Robert Jefferson Breckinridge as an Educational Administrator* (Nashville: George Peabody College for Teachers, 1937), 76–77; Godbey, *The Governors of Kentucky and Education*, 116.

74. Harrison, *Kentucky's Governors*, 71–73; Hackensmith, *Out of Time and Tide*, 71; Moses Edward Ligon, *A History of Public Education in Kentucky* (Lexington: Univ. of Kentucky Bureau of School Service, 1942), 90–103.

75. Hackensmith, *Out of Time and Tide*, 70–72; Harrison and Klotter, *A New History of Kentucky*, 150; Hamlett, *History of Education in Kentucky*, 49–50; Klotter, *The Breckinridges of Kentucky*, 59; McVey, *The Gates Open Slowly*, 168–70; Harrison interview, March 20, 2005.

76. *KE*, 120; Klotter, *The Breckinridges of Kentucky*, 59–60; Hamlett, *History of Education in Kentucky*, 54–57; Doyle, Layson, and Thompson, *From the Fort to the Future*, 84; Richard W. Griffin, *Newspaper Story of a Town: A History of Danville, Kentucky* (Danville, KY: Danville Advocate-Messenger and Danville Advocate, 1965), 39; Vaughn, *Robert Jefferson Breckinridge*, 107–9.

77. McVey, *The Gates Open Slowly*, 147; *Kentucky Acts, 1851–52*, 164, 168; Hackensmith, *Out of Time and Tide*, 72–73.

78. McVey, *The Gates Open Slowly*, 79–71; Doyle, Layson, and Thompson, *From the Fort to the Future*, 85–91; Hamlett, *History of Education in Kentucky*, 78.

79. McVey, *The Gates Open Slowly*, 70–72; Hamlett, *History of Education in Kentucky*, 78.

80. Klotter, *The Breckinridges of Kentucky*, 59–60; McVey, *The Gates Open Slowly*, 72–73; James Otis Lewis, "A History of the Kentucky Education Association" (master's thesis, Univ. of Chicago, 1927), 2–4.

81. Hamlett, *History of Education in Kentucky*, 62–78; McVey, *The Gates Open Slowly*, 87; Harrison and Klotter, *A New History of Kentucky*, 150.

82. Doyle, Layson, and Thompson, *From the Fort to the Future*, 84–91.

83. *KE*, 120; Harrison and Klotter, *A New History of Kentucky*, 150; Klotter and Klotter, *Faces of Kentucky*, 227; Klotter, *The Breckinridges of Kentucky*, 60; R. Freeman Butts, *Public Education in the United States: From Revolution to Reform* (New York: Holt, Rinehart, and Winston, 1978), 82; Jonathan Messerli, *Horace Mann: A Biography* (New York: Alfred A. Knopf, 1972), 298–301, 402, 432; Charles William

Dabney, *Universal Education in the South* (Chapel Hill: Univ. of North Carolina Press, 1936), 1:274–77; Brian D. McKnight, *Contested Borderland: The Civil War in Appalachian Kentucky and Virginia* (Lexington: Univ. Press of Kentucky, 2006), 147.

84. Harrison and Klotter, *A New History of Kentucky*, 171, 182; *Abstract of the Eighth Census, 1860* (Washington, DC: Government Printing Office, 1864), 36.

85. Meyer, *An Educational History of the American People*, 204–7; Hackensmith, *Out of Time and Tide*, 72–73; Travis Edwin Smith, *The Rise of Teacher Education in Kentucky* (Nashville: George Peabody College for Teachers, 1932), 108–16.

86. Wright, *Transylvania*, 179–84; Harrison, *Kentucky's Governors*, 76; Harrison and Klotter, *A New History of Kentucky*, 112–23; *EL*, 97; Tom Stephens, "Annotated Notes on Bloody Monday, Louisville, August 6, 1855," *Kentucky Ancestors* 41 (Summer 2006): 174–81, 210.

87. McVey, *The Gates Open Slowly*, 84–85; Wright, *Transylvania*, 179–84; Hamlett, *History of Education in Kentucky*, 82–87; Harrison, *Kentucky's Governors*, 76–77; Smith, *The Rise of Teacher Training in Kentucky*, 115–16.

88. McVey, *The Gates Open Slowly*, 47; Hamlett, *History of Education in Kentucky*, 82, 88; Hackensmith, *Out of Time and Tide*, 73–74; *Kentucky Documents, 1865–60*, no. 4, p. 27.

89. Hamlett, *History of Education in Kentucky*, 91; see Hartford, *The Little White School House*; *KE*, 696–97.

90. Miller, "Academies and Seminaries of Kentucky," 82–100, 140–48; Bettie Woodford to Martha Adams, February 14, 1858, Martha Adams Papers, Filson Club Historical Society, copy in possession of William G. Adams, Richmond, KY.

91. *Triennial Catalogue of the Officers and Students of Columbia Male and Female High School, at Columbia, Adair Co., Ky., under the Care of the Transylvania Presbytery* (Cincinnati: John D. Thorpe, 1858), 10–16; *History of Daughters College, 1856–1893, and Its Founder, John Augustus Williams, A.M., LLD* (n.p., n.d.), foreword, 10–11; both available in the Education File, Kentucky Library, Western Kentucky Univ.; *KE*, 64, 216.

92. *KE*, 905–6; Frank J. Williams, "Legend and Myth: Abraham Lincoln in Kentucky," *Register of the Kentucky Historical Society* 106 (Summer–Autumn 2008): 486–87; Elizabeth Cox Underwood to Joseph R. Underwood, January 3, 1852, Underwood Collection, Kentucky Library, Western Kentucky Univ.

93. James A. Johnson, Harold W. Collins, Victor L. Dupuis, and John H. Johansen, *Introduction to the Foundations of American Education*, 2nd ed. (Boston: Allyn and Bacon, 1973), 256–62; *8th Census of the United States, 1860* (Washington, DC: Government Printing Office, 1864), 174; Doyle, Layson, and Thompson, *From the Fort to the Future*, 5–9; *KE*, 744–46; Klotter, "Promise, Pessimism, and Perseverance," 46.

Chapter 2. The Early History of Higher Education

1. Sonne, *Liberal Kentucky*, vii–44.

2. Harrison and Klotter, *A New History of Kentucky*, 151; Klotter, "Promise, Pessimism, and Perseverance," 46.

3. *KE*, 894–95.

4. Wright, *Transylvania*, 1–9; Hamlett, *History of Education in Kentucky*, 290–91.

5. Wright, *Transylvania*, 10–12; Jurgen Herbst, *From Crisis to Crisis: American College Government, 1636–1819* (Cambridge, MA: Harvard Univ. Press, 1982), 193.

6. *KE*, 895; Wright, *Transylvania*, 21–25.

7. Wright, *Transylvania*, 13–25; Collins and Collins, *History of Kentucky*, 263–68; Thomas D. Clark, *Kentucky: Land of Contrast* (New York: Harper and Row, 1968), 55–68.

8. Wright, *Transylvania*, 25–30; Sonne, *Liberal Kentucky*, 31, 33–34, 46; Hamlett, *History of Education in Kentucky*, 292; Herbst, *From Crisis to Crisis*, 193.

9. *KE*, 894–95; Wright, *Transylvania*, 30–32; Sonne, *Liberal Kentucky*, 59, 62; Harrison, *Kentucky's Governors*, 8.

10. Wright, *Transylvania*, 33–36; Alan C. Ornstein and Daniel U. Levine, *Foundations of Education*, 8th ed. (Boston: Houghton Mifflin, 2003), 181.

11. Wright, *Transylvania*, 37–39.

12. Ibid., 38–45; Hackensmith, *Out of Time and Tide*, 118–20.

13. *KE*, 895; Wright, *Transylvania*, 45–47.

14. *KE*, 856–57; Wright, *Transylvania*, 47–64; Sonne, *Liberal Kentucky*, 17.

15. Wright, *Transylvania*, 47–64; Sonne, *Liberal Kentucky*, 10, 78–107; Clark, *Kentucky*, 64–65.

16. Sonne, *Liberal Kentucky*, 118–30, 135–39; Wright, *Transylvania*, 54–56; Hackensmith, *Out of Time and Tide*, 118–19.

17. *KE*, 436–47; Wright, *Transylvania*, 56–64; Sonne, *Liberal Kentucky*, 136–38, 153–59; Alvin Fayette Lewis, *History of Higher Education in Kentucky* (Washington, DC: Government Printing Office, 1899), 56–58.

18. *KE*, 436–37; Wright, *Transylvania*, 56–64; Harrison, *Kentucky's Governors*, 22–25, Moore, *The Frontier Mind*, 234; Herbst, *From Crisis to Crisis*, 208.

19. Sonne, *Liberal Kentucky*, 160–71; Wright, *Transylvania*, 66–67.

20. Wright, *Transylvania*, 67–68; John R. Thelin, *A History of American Higher Education* (Baltimore: Johns Hopkins Univ. Press, 2004), 46–47.

21. Wright, *Transylvania*, 70; Hackensmith, *Out of Time and Tide*, 121; Sonne, *Liberal Kentucky*, 172; Lewis, *History of Higher Education in Kentucky*, 58–64.

22. *KE*, 752–53; Leonard Warren, *Constantine Samuel Rafinesque: A Voice in the American Wilderness* (Lexington: Univ. Press of Kentucky, 2004), 53, 71–78.

23. *KE*, 752–53; Wright, *Transylvania*, 71–77; Warren, *Constantine Samuel Rafinesque*, 78–99.

24. Warren, *Constantine Samuel Rafinesque*, 78–99, 109–16, 199–200; Lewis, *History of Higher Education in Kentucky*, 59; Wright, *Transylvania*, 113, 353–56.

25. Harrison and Klotter, *A New History of Kentucky*, 152; Sonne, *Liberal Kentucky*, 68; Wright, *Transylvania*, x, 44, 93; Klotter, "Promise, Pessimism, and Perseverance," 54; Thelin, *A History of American Higher Education*, 46–47.

26. *KE*, 177, 973; Thelin, *A History of American Higher Education*, 60–62, Wright, *Transylvania*, 106–7; Herbst, *From Crisis to Crisis*, 194.

27. Walter A. Groves, "Centre College—The Second Phase (1830–1857)," *Filson Club History Quarterly* 24 (October 1950): 311–34; Hardin Craig, *Centre College of Kentucky: A Tradition and an Opportunity* (Louisville: Gateway Press, 1967), 1–29;

Louis B. Weeks, *Kentucky Presbyterians* (Atlanta: John Knox Press, 1983), 57, 105–7; Griffin, *Newspaper Story of a Town*, 34–35; Herbst, *From Crisis to Crisis*, 194.

28. *KE*, 248–49; Lewis, *History of Higher Education in Kentucky*, 323–24; Collins and Collins, *History of Kentucky*, 223.

29. *KE*, 42; Lewis, *History of Higher Education in Kentucky*, 312–16; William Warren Sweet, *Methodism in American History* (New York: Abingdon Press, 1961), 212–13; Sweet, *Religion on the American Frontier*, vol. 4, *The Methodists* (New York: Cooper Square, 1964), 67, 297, 458–60; Walter Brownlow Posey, *The Development of Methodism in the Old Southwest, 1783–1824* (Philadelphia: Porcupine Press, 1974), 68–69.

30. *KE*, 371–72; Carl R. Fields, *A Sesquicentennial History of Georgetown College* (Georgetown, KY: Georgetown College Press, n.d.), 1, 3; Robert Snyder, *A History of Georgetown College* (Georgetown, KY: Georgetown College, 1979), 1–11; Leland Winfield Meyer, *Georgetown College—Its Early History* (Georgetown, KY: Frye, 1929, 1962), 9–11, 37–44; William H. Brackney, *Congregation and Campus: North American Baptists in Higher Education* (Macon, GA: Mercer Univ. Press, 2008), 16–17, 257–58.

31. *KE*, 816.

32. *KE*, 199, 765, 780–81; Thomas C. Ware, "Camping Out with Theodore O'Hara," *Kentucky Humanities* (October 2006): 19; Crews, *An American Holy Land*, 94–107, 122–23, 162, 323; Lewis, *History of Higher Education in Kentucky*, 133–37, 318–22.

33. Gleason, "From an Indefinite Homogeneity," 50–52, 59, 63–64, 65, 67–69.

34. *KE*, 436; Sonne, *Liberal Kentucky*, 172–75; Wright, *Transylvania*, 75–87; Hackensmith, *Out of Time and Tide*, 121; Harrison and Klotter, *A New History of Kentucky*, 152.

35. *KE*, 55–56; Sonne, *Liberal Kentucky*, 175–76; Wright, *Transylvania*, 87–92.

36. Sonne, *Liberal Kentucky*, 176–90; Lewis, *History of Higher Education in Kentucky*, 62; Wright, *Transylvania*, 100–105.

37. Hackensmith, *Out of Time and Tide*, 121–22; Lewis, *History of Higher Education in Kentucky*, 61; Harrison, *Kentucky's Governors*, 26–28.

38. Lewis, *History of Higher Education in Kentucky*, 61; Wright, *Transylvania*, 109–17; Harrison, *Kentucky's Governors*, 31; Moore, *The Frontier Mind*, 234–35; Silas Lee McCormick, "Transylvania University: 'Public' Higher Education in Kentucky" (Ph.D. diss., Univ. of Illinois, 2007), 122–24.

39. Wright, *Transylvania*, 110–17; Sonne, *Liberal Kentucky*, 191–241; Hackensmith, *Out of Time and Tide*, 122–23; Romie D. Judd, *The Educational Contributions of Horace Holley* (Nashville: George Peabody College for Teachers, 1936), 75.

40. Wright, *Transylvania*, 99–117; Moore, *The Frontier Mind*, 210–37; Sonne, *Liberal Kentucky*, 191–241, 260; Hackensmith, *Out of Time and Tide*, 122; Harrison and Klotter, *A New History of Kentucky*, 152; Clark, *Kentucky*, 65; Charles William Hackensmith, *Ohio Valley Higher Education in the Nineteenth Century* (Lexington: Bureau of School Service, Univ. of Kentucky, 1973), 35; George M. Marsden, *The Soul of the American University: From Protestant Establishment to Established Nonbelief* (New York: Oxford Univ. Press, 1994), 72.

41. Harrison and Klotter, *A New History of Kentucky*, 152; *KE*, 436–37; Lewis, *History of Higher Education in Kentucky*, 63; Judd, *The Educational Contributions of Horace Holley*, 82–83.

42. Dwight E. Stevenson, "The Bacon College Story: 1836–1865," *College of the Bible Quarterly* 29 (October 1962): 7–11; McVey, *The Gates Open Slowly*, 95–96; *KE*, 43.

43. *KE*, 895, 913; *EL*, 561; Dwayne D. Cox and William J. Morison, *The University of Louisville* (Lexington: Univ. Press of Kentucky, 2000), 11–12; Wright, *Transylvania*, 145–55.

44. *EL*, 902–3; Cox and Morison, *The University of Louisville*, 12–16; Hackensmith, *Out of Time and Tide*, 164–70.

45. Harrison and Klotter, *A New History of Kentucky*, 153; Thelin, *A History of American Higher Education*, 41–42; *KE*, 615; *EL*, 593; McCormick, "Transylvania University," 3–4, 17, 211.

46. *KE*, 74, 569, 638; Lewis, *History of Higher Education in Kentucky*, 173–83, 233–36; Brackney, *Congregation and Campus*, 120.

47. *KE*, 296; W. Robert Insko, "The Kentucky Seminary," *Register of the Kentucky Historical Society* 52 (July 1954): 213–32; Hamlett, *History of Education in Kentucky*, 25.

48. *KE*, 942; Ira Birdwhistell, *Kentucky Baptists: 150 Years on Mission Together* (Middletown: Kentucky Baptist Convention, 1987), 57–58.

49. *KE*, 253; McVey, *The Gates Open Slowly*, 87; Walter A. Groves, "A School of the Prophets at Danville," *Filson Club History Quarterly* 27 (July 1953): 223–46; Weeks, *Kentucky Presbyterians*, 106–7; Vaughn, *Robert Jefferson Breckinridge*, 110–33.

50. Thelin, *A History of American Higher Education*, 58–60; *KE*, 506, 944; *EL*, 475–76.

51. *KE*, 506.

52. *KE*, 944; Mabel Altstetter and Gladys Watson, "Western Military Institute, 1848–1861," *Filson Club History Quarterly* 10 (April 1936): 100–115; Snyder, *A History of Georgetown College*, 30.

53. Jennifer R. Green, "Military Education and Social Mobility in the Late Antebellum South," *Historically Speaking* 9 (May–June 2008): 43–47.

54. *KE*, 895; Wright, *Transylvania*, 118–31.

55. Wright, *Transylvania*, 132–57.

56. *KE*, 895, Wright, *Transylvania*, 158–71.

57. *KE*, 372; Fields, *A Sesquicentennial History of Georgetown College*, 3–4; Stevenson, "The Bacon College Story," 14–18; Snyder, *A History of Georgetown College*, 13–22; Meyer, *Georgetown College*, 47–62.

58. *KE*, 372; Fields, *A Sesquicentennial History of Georgetown College*, 4–5; Snyder, *A History of Georgetown College*, 22–32; Meyer, *Georgetown College*, 63–73; Brackney, *Congregation and Campus*, 19.

59. Wright, *Transylvania*, 36–37, 50, 94–97; Sonne, *Liberal Kentucky*, 184–85; Griffin, *Newspaper Story of a Town*, 35; Snyder, *A History of Georgetown College*, 26–27; Meyer, *Georgetown College*, 72–73; Groves, "Centre College," 329; Cooper, *Jefferson Davis, American*, 26.

60. Robert F. Pace, *Halls of Honor: College Men in the Old South* (Baton Rouge: Louisiana State Univ. Press, 2004), 4–5, 17, 27; Peter S. Carmichael, review of Pace, *Halls of Honor, Southern Cultures* (Fall 2005): 109–10; Wright, *Transylvania*, 82–83; Margaret Newnan Wagers, *The Education of a Gentleman: Jefferson Davis at Transylvania, 1821–1824* (Lexington: Buckley and Reading, 1943), 29–30.

61. Wright, *Transylvania*, 36–37, 50, 93–96; Pace, *Halls of Honor*, 45. 48, 51–54; Wagers, *The Education of a Gentleman*, 24–25; Cooper, *Jefferson Davis, American*, 24–27.

62. Wright, *Transylvania*, 50; Snyder, *A History of Georgetown College*, 24–25; Hackensmith, *Ohio Valley Higher Education in the Nineteenth Century*, 43; Meyer, *Georgetown College*, 72–73.

63. Pace, *Halls of Honor*, 36; Snyder, *A History of Georgetown College*, 24–25; Wright, *Transylvania*, 94–96; Wagers, *The Education of a Gentleman*, 25; Hackensmith, *Ohio Valley Higher Education*, 38–39.

64. *KE*, 117; Klotter, *The Breckinridges of Kentucky*, 42–43, 95–98; Lowell H. Harrison, "A Young Kentuckian at Princeton, 1806–1810: Joseph Cabell Breckinridge," *Filson Club History Quarterly* 38 (October 1964): 285–315.

65. *KE*, 373, 569, 638, 932; Crews, *An American Holy Land*, 213; Hamlett, *History of Education in Kentucky*, 309, 312, 316.

66. *KE*, 293; Lewis, *History of Higher Education in Kentucky*, 325–27.

67. *KE*, 895–96; Wright, *Transylvania*, 172–89; Thelin, *A History of American Higher Education*, 46–47; McCormick, "Transylvania University," 187–88.

68. Harrison and Klotter, *A New History of Kentucky*, 153; *KE*, 43, 895; Wright, *Transylvania*, 190–201; Hackensmith, *Out of Time and Tide*, 132–33; Lewis, *History of Higher Education in Kentucky*, 83–88; Stevenson, "The Bacon College Story," 23–51; McVey, *The Gates Open Slowly*, 81.

69. *EL*, 902; McVey, *The Gates Open Slowly*, 81; U.S. Bureau of the Census, *8th Census of the United States, 1860, Population* (Washington, DC: Government Printing Office, 1864), 187.

70. *KE*, 42, 71, 942; Birdwhistell, *Kentucky Baptists*, 56–58; Wright, *Transylvania*, 168–71: Channing, *Kentucky*, 108–9; Tallant, *Evil Necessity*, 167–68.

71. Harrison and Klotter, *A New History of Kentucky*, 181–94; Klotter, *The Breckinridges of Kentucky*, 79–136; Channing, *Kentucky*, 109–21; Apple, Johnston, and Bevins, *Scott County*, 193.

72. Snyder, *A History of Georgetown College*, 42–44; Apple, Johnston, and Bevins, *Scott County*, 193–94.

Chapter 3. Elementary and Secondary Education

1. U.S. Bureau of the Census, *Eighth Census of the United States, 1860, Statistics* (Washington, DC: Government Printing Office, 1864), 505, 506.

2. Harrison and Klotter, *A New History of Kentucky*, 183–89; Harrison, *Kentucky's Governors*, 78–81.

3. Harrison and Klotter, *A New History of Kentucky*, 186–94; Lowell H. Harrison, *The Civil War in Kentucky* (Lexington: Univ. of Kentucky Press, 1975), 1–4; E. Merton Coulter, *The Civil War and Readjustment in Kentucky* (Chapel Hill: Univ. of North Carolina Press, 1926), 35–56.

4. Harrison, *The Civil War in Kentucky*, 54–55, 75, 101; Harrison and Klotter, *A New History of Kentucky*, 195–209; Clark, *A History of Kentucky* (1988), 301–36.

5. *KE*, 142, 158; Richard D. Sears, *Camp Nelson, Kentucky: A Civil War History* (Lexington: Univ. Press of Kentucky, 2002), 371–74; Darrel E. Bigham, *On Jordan's Banks: Emancipation and Its Aftermath in the Ohio River Valley* (Lexington:

Univ. Press of Kentucky, 2006), 229–31; Lucas, *A History of Blacks in Kentucky*, 155, 160–61, 170.

6. Lawrence A. Cremin, *American Education: The National Experience, 1783–1876* (New York: Harper and Row, 1980), 511; Harrison and Klotter, *A New History of Kentucky*, 209–10; Harrison, *The Civil War in Kentucky*, 103; Coulter, *The Civil War and Readjustment*, 254; *KE*, 394; Joe Nickell, *The Vanishing Schools: A History of Education in Morgan County, Kentucky* (West Liberty, KY: Nickell Genealogical Books, 1989), 6; McKnight, *Contested Borderland*, 145.

7. Hamlett, *History of Education in Kentucky*, 89–103; Caroline Carter to Martha Adams, June 20, 1861, Martha Adams Papers, Filson Club Historical Society, copy in possession of William G. Adams, Richmond, KY; Hackensmith, *Out of Time and Tide*, 73–76; *KE*, 65; Jean Calvert and John Klee, *Maysville, Kentucky: From Past to Present in Pictures* (Maysville, KY: Mason County Museum, 1983), 62.

8. Harrison, *The Civil War in Kentucky*, 78, 94–95, 102; Klotter, *The Breckinridges of Kentucky*, 80–91; John David Smith and William Cooper Jr., eds., *Window on the War: Frances Dallam Peter's Lexington Civil War Diary* (Lexington, KY: Lexington–Fayette County Historic Commission, 1976), introduction, 7–8, 38–39, 44, 50; *Lexington Herald-Leader*, February 12, 2009.

9. Channing, *Kentucky*, 120–21; Klotter, *Our Kentucky*, 203; Michael C. C. Adams, "The Historian Humbly Declines to Have a Nice Day: Thoughts on the Role of the Historian in Contemporary Society," *Register of the Kentucky Historical Society* 92 (Autumn 1992): 409; Harrison, *The Civil War in Kentucky*, 101–2; Thomas D. Clark, *A History of Kentucky* (New York: Prentice-Hall, 1936), 336.

10. Harrison and Klotter, *A New History of Kentucky*, 210–18; Clark, *A History of Kentucky* (1936), 354–55, 358, 417; Ross A. Webb, *Kentucky in the Reconstruction Era* (Lexington: Univ. Press of Kentucky, 1979), 25.

11. Klotter, *Our Kentucky*, 204; Hambleton Tapp and James C. Klotter, *Kentucky: Decades of Discord* (Frankfort: Kentucky Historical Society, 1977), 10–28; George C. Wright, *Life behind a Veil: Blacks in Louisville, 1865–1930* (Baton Rouge: Louisiana State Univ. Press, 1985), 20–28; Catherine W. Bishir, "Memorial Observances," *Southern Cultures* (Summer 2009): 74–84.

12. Meyer, *An Educational History of the American People*, 211–12; Harrison and Klotter, *A New History of Kentucky*, 219; Hackensmith, *Out of Time and Tide*, 80–82; *KE*, 746.

13. Harrison, *Kentucky's Governors*, 93–97; Harrison and Klotter, *A New History of Kentucky*, 240–42; Coulter, *The Civil War and Readjustment*, 278–311.

14. Hamlett, *History of Education in Kentucky*, 102–3; Hackensmith, *Out of Time and Tide*, 75–76; Harrison and Klotter, *A New History of Kentucky*, 380; McVey, *The Gates Open Slowly*, 171–72.

15. Tapp and Klotter, *Kentucky*, 26–59, 278–79; Channing, *Kentucky*, 149–51; Harrison and Klotter, *A New History of Kentucky*, 242–43; Daniel S. Margolies, *Henry Watterson and the New South; The Politics of Empire, Free Trade, and Globalization* (Lexington: Univ. Press of Kentucky, 2006), 25–43, n271; Wright, *Life behind a Veil*, 24–27.

16. Harrison, *Kentucky's Governors*, 98–100; Harrison and Klotter, *A New History of Kentucky*, 242–45.

17. Clark, *A History of Kentucky*, 359–61, 365; Tapp and Klotter, *Kentucky*, 185–87; Klotter, *Our Kentucky*, 284; Hamlett, *History of Education in Kentucky*, 105–17; Hackensmith, *Out of Time and Tide*, 80; Harrison, *Kentucky's Governors*, 99.

18. *KE*, 357; Bigham, *On Jordan's Banks*, 231, 276–85; Harrison and Klotter, *A New History of Kentucky*, 237; Lucas, *A History of Blacks in Kentucky*, 231–50; Webb, *Kentucky in the Reconstruction Era*, 56–57; Victor B. Howard, *Black Liberation in Kentucky: Emancipation and Freedom, 1862–1884* (Lexington: Univ. Press of Kentucky, 1983), 162–67; Yater, *Two Hundred Years at the Falls of the Ohio*, 110; Ligon, *A History of Public Education in Kentucky*, 251; Adam Fairclough, *A Class of Their Own: Black Teachers in the Segregated South* (Cambridge, MA: Belknap Press of Harvard Univ. Press, 2007), 65.

19. Harrison and Klotter, *A New History of Kentucky*, 237–39; Webb, *Kentucky in the Reconstruction Era*, 57; Coulter, *The Civil War and Readjustment*, 358–65; Tapp and Klotter, *Kentucky*, 49, 378–85; *KE*, 609; Fairclough, *A Class of Their Own*, 47.

20. Fairclough, *A Class of Their Own*, 43–44.

21. Kathleen M. Blee and Dwight B. Billings, "Race and the Roots of Appalachian Poverty: Clay County, Kentucky, 1850–1910," in *Appalachians and Race: The Mountain South from Slavery to Segregation*, ed. John C. Inscoe (Lexington: Univ. Press of Kentucky, 2001), 165–88.

22. Wilson, *Berea College*, 21–23, 51, 90; Lucas, *A History of Blacks in Kentucky*, 250–53; Ellis, Everman, and Sears, *Madison County*, 209–15; Sears, *Camp Nelson, Kentucky*, 337.

23. *KE*, 495; *EL*, 735; Bigham, *On Jordan's Banks*, 278–85; *72nd Anniversary and Dedication, State Street High School Souvenir Program* (Bowling Green), Education File, Kentucky Library, Western Kentucky Univ.; Yater, *Two Hundred Years at the Falls of the Ohio*, 110.

24. Tapp and Klotter, *Kentucky*, 187; *KE*, 799; "School Prospectus," September 1, 1869, Auburn, Kentucky, Education File, Kentucky Library, Western Kentucky Univ.; "Catalog of Powell Academy, Catlettsburg, 1868–69," *Kentucky Ancestors* 41 (Spring 2006): 148–50; Russell Dyche, *The Laurel Seminary, 1856–1906, London, Kentucky* (London, KY: Sentinel-Echo, 1943), 5–38; Ellis, Everman, and Sears, *Madison County*, 81, 241, 266, 284; Griffin, *Newspaper Story of a Town*, 35–50.

25. *KE*, 746.

26. Tapp and Klotter, *Kentucky*, 188; *Kentucky Documents, 1871*, II, no. 16, p. 105; *Annual Report of the Superintendent of Public Instruction, 1874* (Frankfort, 1874), 5.

27. Tapp and Klotter, *Kentucky*, 188–89; Hamlett, *History of Education in Kentucky*, 130–31, 171; Hackensmith, *Out of Time and Tide*, 89–90; Hartford, *The Little White Schoolhouse*, 16–17; Harrison and Klotter, *A New History of Kentucky*, 378–79; Carl E. Kramer, *Capital on the Kentucky* (Frankfort: Historic Frankfort, 1986), 205–6, 245–46.

28. Clark, *A History of Kentucky*, 360; Reese, *America's Public Schools*, 68; Gutek, *A History of the Western Educational Experience*, 465–66, 474–75.

29. Allen Anthony, *Pleasant Grove Grade School: Recollections of Bygone Days at an Early Two-Room Grade School in Jefferson County, Kentucky* (n.p.: Allen Anthony, 2004), 1–19.

30. Harrison and Klotter, *A New History of Kentucky*, 376–77; Klotter, *Our*

Kentucky, 278; Hartford, *The Little White Schoolhouse*, 50–57; Delta Kappa Gamma, *Well-Spring in the Wilderness*, 4.

31. Harrison and Klotter, *A New History of Kentucky*, 379; Hartford, *The Little White Schoolhouse*, 10–11; Tapp and Klotter, *Kentucky*, 190–91; Ligon, *A History of Public Education in Kentucky*, 129; Hamlett, *History of Education in Kentucky*, 110; Hackensmith, *Out of Time and Tide*, 84–85.

32. Harrison and Klotter, *A New History of Kentucky*, 379; Hartford, *The Little White Schoolhouse*, 10–11, 34–35, 61–72; Hackensmith, *Out of Time and Tide*, 84–85; Ligon, *A History of Public Education in Kentucky*, 131; Tapp and Klotter, *Kentucky*, 190–91.

33. *KE*, 943; *EL*, 658–59; Lowell H. Harrison, *Western Kentucky University* (Lexington: Univ. Press of Kentucky, 1987), 1–15; McVey, *The Gates Open Slowly*, 175–85; "Glasgow Normal Institute," School File, Kentucky Library, Western Kentucky Univ.; James F. Hopkins, *The University of Kentucky: Origins and Early Years* (Lexington: Univ. of Kentucky Press, 1951), 129–32.

34. Gutek, *A History of the Western Educational Experience*, 473–77; Hackensmith, *Out of Time and Tide*, 83–86, 123–24; McVey, *The Gates Open Slowly*, 181–82; *KE*, 873; Tapp and Klotter, *Kentucky*, 192, 207; Lucas, *A History of Blacks in Kentucky*, 262–63; John A. Hardin, *Onward and Upward: A Centennial History of Kentucky State University, 1886–1986* (Frankfort: Kentucky State Univ., 1987), 1–6.

35. Smith, *The Rise of Teacher Training in Kentucky*, 144–63.

36. Hackensmith, *Out of Time and Tide*, 83–84; *KE*, 872–73; Hamlett, *History of Education in Kentucky*, 113, 131–32, 146–47, 153–55, 168; Ligon, *A History of Public Education in Kentucky*, 126.

37. Hamlett, *History of Education in Kentucky*, 110, 179–80; Harrison and Klotter, *A New History of Kentucky*, 377.

38. Harrison and Klotter, *A New History of Kentucky*, 377; Doyle, Layson, and Thompson, *From the Fort to the Future*, 123–27.

39. Tapp and Klotter, *Kentucky*, 189–90; Clark, *A History of Kentucky*, 364–65; Hartford, *The Little White Schoolhouse*, 38–39; Meyer, *An Educational History of the American People*, 185–86; Ligon, *A History of Public Education in Kentucky*, 123.

40. Hamlett, *History of Education in Kentucky*, 108, 124–25; Tapp and Klotter, *Kentucky*, 190–91; Hartford, *The Little White Schoolhouse*, 39–41; Cremin, *American Education*, 390–97; Meyer, *An Educational History of the American People*, 181–86.

41. Harrison and Klotter, *A New History of Kentucky*, 378; Tapp and Klotter, *Kentucky*, 189.

42. *KE*, 746; Harrison, *Kentucky's Governors*, 101–7; Clark, *A History of Kentucky*, 361; Tapp and Klotter, *Kentucky*, 192–93.

43. Harrison, *Kentucky's Governors*, 101–4; Harrison and Klotter, *A New History of Kentucky*, 245–48, 378–79; Clark, *A History of Kentucky*, 358, 419; Tapp and Klotter, *Kentucky*, 37, 46–48.

44. Harrison, *Kentucky's Governors*, 105–7; Harrison and Klotter, *A New History of Kentucky*, 245–48, 257–59.

45. *KE*, 746; Tapp and Klotter, *Kentucky*, 38, 46, 132, 192; Clark, *A History of Kentucky*, 361–62; McVey, *The Gates Open Slowly*, 182–84; Hackensmith, *Out of Time and Tide*, 78, 89; Hamlett, *History of Education in Kentucky*, 119–47.

46. *KE*, 498; Doyle, Layson, and Thompson, *From the Fort to the Future*, 289–90; McVey, *The Gates Open Slowly*, 196–99; Hopkins, *KEA*, 21–32; Lewis, "A History of the Kentucky Education Association," 9–13.

47. Hamlett, *History of Education in Kentucky*, 125–26, 133.

48. Harrison and Klotter, *A New History of Kentucky*, 379–80; Klotter, *Our Kentucky*, 285; Bigham, *On Jordan's Banks*, 280–81; *Kentucky Acts, 1873–74*, 63–66; Lucas, *A History of Blacks in Kentucky*, 255–58; Tapp and Klotter, *Kentucky*, 205–6.

49. Lucas, *A History of Blacks in Kentucky*, 255–61; Ellis, Everman, and Sears, *Madison County*, 282–83; *KE*, 507; Tapp and Klotter, *Kentucky*, 206; C. L. Timberlake, "The Early Struggle for Education of the Blacks in the Commonwealth of Kentucky," *Register of the Kentucky Historical Society* 71 (July 1973): 223; Bigham, *On Jordan's Banks*, 283; Fairclough, *A Class of Their Own*, 311.

50. Harrison and Klotter, *A New History of Kentucky*, 380–81; *KE*, 203; Bigham, *On Jordan's Banks*, 282–84; Lucas, *A History of Blacks in Kentucky*, 255–62; Hackensmith, *Out of Time and Tide*, 97–102; Hamlett, *History of Education in Kentucky*, 158; Venable, "A History of Negro Education in Kentucky," 49–117; Howard, *Black Liberation in Kentucky*, 169–76; McVey, *The Gates Open Slowly*, 149–50; Reese, *America's Public Schools*, 75.

51. Tapp and Klotter, *Kentucky*, 164–71; Harrison, *Kentucky's Governors*, 111–12; Clark, *A History of Kentucky*, 423–24.

52. *KE*, 84; Harrison, *Kentucky's Governors*, 111–14; Tapp and Klotter, *Kentucky*, 163, 193, 461–62; Harrison and Klotter, *A New History of Kentucky*, 259–61.

53. McVey, *The Gates Open Slowly*, 76, 108; Hamlett, *History of Education in Kentucky*, 152–53; Tapp, and Klotter, *Kentucky*, 299; Clark, *A History of Kentucky*, 370.

54. Hamlett, *History of Education in Kentucky*, 156–58.

55. *KE*, 522: Harrison, *Kentucky's Governors*, 115–18; Tapp and Klotter, *Kentucky*, 193, 196.

56. James C. Carper, "William Morgan Beckner: The Horace Mann of Kentucky," *Register of the Kentucky Historical Society* 96 (Winter 1998): 34–37; *Louisville Courier-Journal*, December 30, 1882.

57. Carper, "William Morgan Beckner," 37–40; *Louisville Courier-Journal*, April 6, 7, 9, 13, 27; September 20, 21, 22, 1883.

58. *EL*, 838–39.

59. Tapp and Klotter, *Kentucky*, 193–96; Carper, "William Morgan Beckner," 40–41.

60. Hackensmith, *Out of Time and Tide*, 81, 87; Carper, "William Morgan Beckner," 41–42; Tapp and Klotter, *Kentucky*, 193, 196; Klotter, *Our Kentucky*, 208; Hamlett, *History of Education in Kentucky*, 158–59.

61. *KE*, 923; *EL*, 258, 259–60; Timothy James Jackson, "The Development of Vocational Education in Kentucky, 1890–1920: A Case Study in Curriculum Change" (Ed.D. diss., Univ. of Louisville, 1990), 46–52.

62. *EL*, 551, 558–59; Tapp and Klotter, *Kentucky*, 190–91.

63. *KE*, 431; *EL*, 386–87; Frances Farley Gwinn, "Patty Smith Hill: Louisville's Contribution to Education," *Filson Club History Quarterly* 31 (July 1957): 203–26.

64. *EL*, 781, 841; Crews, *An American Holy Land*, 127, 153.

65. *EL*, 33; Leone W. Hallenberg, *Anchorage: A Casual Gathering of Facts and*

Stories From the Past and Present of a Unique Kentucky Town (Anchorage, KY: Anchorage Press, 1959), 23, 40, 42–43, 89, 107, 109.

66. *EL,* 585; *KE,* 57–58, 306, 339–40, 842–43.

67. Gutek, *A History of the Western Educational Experience,* 465–67; Cremin, *American Education,* 389–90; Meyer, *An Educational History of the American People,* 189–93; Perkinson, *The Imperfect Panacea,* 134–36.

68. Hackensmith, *Out of Time and Tide,* 104–5; Ligon, *A History of Public Education in Kentucky,* 183; *Henderson: A Guide to Audubon's Home Town in Kentucky* (Northport, NY: Bacon, Percy, and Daggett, 1941), 66–67; Griffin, *Newspaper Story of a Town,* 40, 51; Wright, *Lexington,* 120; Stuart Sprague, *A Pictorial History of Eastern Kentucky* (Norfolk, VA: Donning, 1986), 48; Carl Henry Kardatzke, "The Origins and Development of the Public High School System in Kentucky" (Ph.D. diss., Univ. of Kentucky, 1933), 106–7.

69. Hamlett, *History of Education in Kentucky,* 161–72; Hackensmith, *Out of Time and Tide,* 81; Harrison and Klotter, *A New History of Kentucky,* 261–64; *KE,* 867–68; John Ed Pearce, *Days of Darkness: The Feuds of Eastern Kentucky* (Lexington: Univ. Press of Kentucky, 1994), 71–72.

70. Carper, "William Morgan Beckner," 44–45; Tapp and Klotter, *Kentucky,* 260.

71. Carper, "William Morgan Beckner," 45, 47.

72. Ibid., 52.

73. Ibid., 58–59.

74. *KE,* 225, 746; Clark, *A History of Kentucky,* 425–32; Tapp and Klotter, *Kentucky,* 266–67; Harrison and Klotter, *A New History of Kentucky,* 264–65.

75. *The Constitution of the Commonwealth of Kentucky* (Frankfort: Kentucky Legislative Research Commission, 1952), 30–31; *A Citizens' Guide to the Kentucky Constitution, Research Report No. 137* (Frankfort: Legislative Research Commission, 1989), 127–31, 193–94.

76. *The Constitution of the Commonwealth of Kentucky,* 1, 13–14.

77. Hamlett, *History of Education in Kentucky,* 161–69; Tapp and Klotter, *Kentucky,* 317, 319; Hackensmith, *Out of Time and Tide,* 79–81.

78. *KE,* 5, 407, 808, 809–10; Harrison and Klotter, *A New History of Kentucky,* 247–48, 348; George Brown Tindall, *America: A Narrative History* (New York: Norton, 1984), 2:719–23; George C. Wright, *A History of Blacks in Kentucky,* vol. 2, *In Pursuit of Equality, 1890–1980* (Frankfort: Kentucky Historical Society, 1992), 69–77; Anne E. Marshall, "Kentucky's Separate Coach Law and African American Response, 1892–1900," *Register of the Kentucky Historical Society* 98 (Summer 2000): 241–59; Howard, *Black Liberation in Kentucky,* 176.

79. *KE,* 514; Kramer, *Capital on the Kentucky,* 215, 245–46; Wright, *A History of Blacks in Kentucky,* 2:123–27; *Kentucky's Black Heritage* (Frankfort: Kentucky Commission on Human Rights, 1971), 55; Hardin, *Onward and Upward,* 1–15.

80. Tindall, *America,* 2:723–25; Gutek, *A History of the Western Educational Experience,* 507–9.

81. *EL,* 261, 822; Wright, *Life behind a Veil,* 66–67, 87–88, 101, 139; Wright, *A History of Blacks in Kentucky,* 2:112–13; Wyatt Wells, "The Reality of the Self-Made Man," *Historically Speaking* 8 (May–June 2007): 24–25; David Sehat, "The Civilizing Mission of Booker T. Washington," *Journal of Southern History* 73 (May 2007): 361.

82. Harrison and Klotter, *A New History of Kentucky*, 265–69; Ligon, *A History of Public Education in Kentucky*, 188–94; Tapp and Klotter, *Kentucky*, 348–55.

83. Hamlett, *History of Education in Kentucky*, 173–76; Hackensmith, *Out of Time and Tide*, 81.

84. Tapp and Klotter, *Kentucky*, 369; Harrison, *Kentucky's Governors*, 127–30; Hackensmith, *Out of Time and Tide*, 89.

85. Reese, *America's Public Schools*, 114–15.

86. Richard B. Drake, *A History of Appalachia* (Lexington: Univ. Press of Kentucky, 2001), 228.

87. *KE*, 459; Pearce, *Days of Darkness*, 146, 147, 149; Tapp and Klotter, *Kentucky*, 197–98.

88. *KE*, 425, 433, 719, 724, 810, 857; Jess Stoddart, *Challenge and Change in Appalachia: The Story of Hindman Settlement School* (Lexington: Univ. Press of Kentucky, 2002), 1–5.

89. *KE*, 696, 962; Doyle, Layson, and Thompson, *From the Fort to the Future*, 129–34; Samuel W. Thomas, ed., *Dawn Comes to the Mountains* (Louisville: George Rogers Clark Press, 1981), 6; Pearce, *Days of Darkness*, 125.

90. Jackson, "The Development of Vocational Education in Kentucky," 46–52.

91. Harrison and Klotter, *A New History of Kentucky*, 269–74; Harrison, *Kentucky's Governors*, 132–33; Ellis, Everman, and Sears, *Madison County*, 273.

92. Ellis, Everman, and Sears, *Madison County*, 272–75; *Lexington Morning Herald*, September 2, 1900; *Louisville Courier-Journal*, September 2, 1900; *Richmond Climax*, September 5, 1900.

93. Harrison and Klotter, *A New History of Kentucky*, 378; Hartford, *The Little White Schoolhouse*, 10; Ligon, *A History of Public Education in Kentucky*, 113, 135; Tapp and Klotter, *Kentucky*, 186, 196; U.S. Census Bureau, *Twelfth Census of the United States, 1900*, vol. 2, *Population* (Washington, DC: Government Printing Office, 1901–1902), part 2, pp. c, ciii, cx, cxi, cxv.

94. Harrison and Klotter, *A New History of Kentucky*, 381; Margolies, *Henry Watterson and the New South*, 199.

95. Tapp and Klotter, *Kentucky*, 294, 298, 313; Channing, *Kentucky*, 155, 174–75.

96. Channing, *Kentucky*, 155.

97. *KE*, 921; John Henry Hatcher, "Fred Vinson: Boyhood and Education in the Big Sandy Valley," *Register of the Kentucky Historical Society* 72 (July 1974): 243–61.

Chapter 4. Higher Education in an Age of Flux

1. *Louisville Courier-Journal*, August 8, 9, 1869.

2. Ibid.; "Solar Eclipse, 1869," *Harper's Weekly* 13 (August 28, 1869): 544–46.

3. *KE*, 816; Harrison and Klotter, *A New History of Kentucky*, 393; Kevin Collins, "Shelby College," in *The New History of Shelby County, Kentucky*, ed. John E. Kleber (Shelbyville, KY: Shelby County Historical Society, 2003), 274–78.

4. *Louisville Courier-Journal*, March 5, 2008; Cremin, *American Education*, 519; Jurgen Herbst, "Nineteenth Century Normal Schools in the United States: A Fresh Look," *History of Education* 9 (1980): 226–27; Klotter, "Promise, Pessimism, and Perseverance," 50–51.

5. Cremin, *American Education*, 519–20; Harris, *The Theory of Education* (Syracuse, NY: C. W. Bardeen, 1898), 32–35; Reese, *America's Public Schools*, 63–65.

6. Cremin, *American Education*, 511–13; Thelin, *A History of American Higher Education*, 74–75.

7. Harrison, *The Civil War in Kentucky*, 102; Snyder, *A History of Georgetown College*, 43; *KE*, 142; Apple, Johnston, and Bevins, *Scott County*, 190–91; Harrison and Klotter, *A New History of Kentucky*, 393.

8. Wright, *Transylvania*, 184–89; Coulter, *The Civil War and Readjustment*, 254; Craig, *Centre College of Kentucky*, 33–36; McVey, *The Gates Open Slowly*, 84–85; C. Thomas Hardin and Bob Hill, *Our Standard Sure: Centre College since 1819* (Danville, KY: Centre College, 2009), 28–36.

9. *KE*, 43; Stevenson, "The Bacon College Story," 44–46; Lewis, *A History of Higher Education in Kentucky*, 87; McCormick, "Transylvania University," 187–89.

10. Klotter, "Promise, Pessimism, and Perseverance," 47; *KE*, 43; Stevenson, "The Bacon College Story," 47–51; McCormick, "Transylvania University," 191; Idus Wilmer Adams, "Central Kentucky Colleges in the Age of the University, 1865–1917" (Ph.D. diss., Univ. of Kentucky, 1998), 22, 25.

11. Thelin, *A History of Higher Education in America*, 74–76; Hopkins, *The University of Kentucky*, 58–59; Ligon, *A History of Public Education in Kentucky*, 313–16; Linda Raney Kiesel, "Kentucky's Land-Grant Legacy: An Analysis of the Administration of John Bryan Bowman and James Kennedy Patterson, 1865–1890" (Ph.D. diss., Univ. of Kentucky, 2003), 30.

12. Merle Borrowman, "The False Dawn of the State University," *History of Education Quarterly* 1 (March 1961): 18; Wright, *Transylvania*, 193–97; Hackensmith, *Out of Time and Tide*, 133; Snyder, *A History of Georgetown College*, 46–47; Ligon, *A History of Public Education in Kentucky*, 316–17.

13. Carl B. Cone, *The University of Kentucky: A Pictorial History* (Lexington: Univ. Press of Kentucky, 1989), 3–5; Hopkins, *The University of Kentucky*, 61–67; Lewis, *History of Higher Education in Kentucky*, 89.

14. Stevenson, "The Bacon College Story," 50–51; Klotter, "Promise, Pessimism, and Perseverance," 47; Harrison and Klotter, *A New History of Kentucky*, 393–94; Kiesel, "Kentucky's Land-Grant Legacy," 30.

15. Tapp and Klotter, *Kentucky*, 198–202; Stevenson, "The Bacon College Story," 49–51; Lewis, *History of Higher Education in Kentucky*, 88–90; *KE*, 553; Ligon, *A History of Public Education in Kentucky*, 317–18.

16. Cone, *The University of Kentucky*, 4–6; Hopkins, *The University of Kentucky*, 70–72; Frederick Rudolph, *The American College and University: A History* (New York: Alfred A. Knopf, 1962), 252; Kiesel, "Kentucky's Land-Grant Legacy," 31.

17. *KE*, 713; Harrison and Klotter, *A New History of Kentucky*, 395; McVey, *The Gates Open Slowly*, 108–9; Tapp and Klotter, *Kentucky*, 200; Hopkins, *The University of Kentucky*, 136–61; Terry L. Birdwhistell, "Divided We Fall: State College and the Normal School Movement in Kentucky, 1880–1910," *Register of the Kentucky Historical Society* 88 (Autumn 1990): 433–35; Ligon, *A History of Public Education in Kentucky*, 318; Kiesel, "Kentucky's Land-Grant Legacy," 11–12.

18. Cone, *The University of Kentucky*, 7; Kiesel, "Kentucky's Land-Grant Legacy," 31–32.

19. Hopkins, *The University of Kentucky*, 83–93; Kiesel, "Kentucky's Land-Grant Legacy," 100.

20. *KE*, 516; Hamlett, *History of Education in Kentucky*, 297–98; Lewis, *History of Higher Education in Kentucky*, 125–31; Lee A. Dew and Richard A. Weiss, *In Pursuit of the Dream: A History of Kentucky Wesleyan College* (Owensboro: Kentucky Wesleyan College Press, 1992), 4–30.

21. Dew and Weiss, *In Pursuit of the Dream*, 31–40; Hackensmith, *Ohio Valley Higher Education*, 52–53.

22. Dew and Weiss, *In Pursuit of the Dream*, 31–63.

23. *KE*, 35; Dew and Weiss, *In Pursuit of the Dream*, 51, 63–71; G. Wayne Rogers, "A Study of Henry Clay Morrison and His Fund-Raising Technique in the *Pentecostal Herald* for Asbury Seminary, 1939–1942" (master's thesis, Univ. of Kentucky, 1981), 80, 114, 116–17.

24. *KE*, 907; Hackensmith, *Ohio Valley Higher Education*, 54–55; Richard Corwine Stevenson, "Daniel Stevenson and Union College," *Filson Club History Quarterly* 42 (October 1968): 340–45.

25. Jonathan Truman Dorris, "Central University, Richmond, Kentucky," *Register of the Kentucky Historical Society* 32 (April 1934): 92–95; *KE*, 177, 777, 973; *EL*, 962–63; Fred A. Engle Jr., "Central University of Richmond, Kentucky," *Register* 66 (July 1968): 279–305; William E. Ellis, *A History of Eastern Kentucky University* (Lexington: Univ. Press of Kentucky, 2005), 2–3.

26. *KE*, 177–78; Craig, *Centre College of Kentucky*, 34–48; McVey, *The Gates Open Slowly*, 86–87; Harrison, *Kentucky's Governors*, 118; Lewis, *History of Higher Education in Kentucky*, 120–25; Enos Swain, "Tribute to Danville as a College Town," *Filson Club History Quarterly* 43 (July 1969): 231; Hardin and Hill, *Our Standard Sure*, 42–44.

27. Sara Jane Montgomery, "Rackyte Cax, Cowax Cowax: The Student Culture of Centre College, 1865–1915" (Ph.D. diss., Univ. of Kentucky, 1996), 26–43.

28. Fields, *A Sesquicentennial History of Georgetown College*, 6–9; Snyder, *A History of Georgetown College*, 47–69; Lewis, *History of Higher Education in Kentucky*, 147–65.

29. Ellis, *A History of Eastern Kentucky University*, 3–5.

30. Ibid., 5–7.

31. *KE*, 71–72; Wilson, *Berea College*, 33–39.

32. "Meeting on Behalf of Berea College," from the *Kentucky Statesman*, February 4, 1869, reprinted in the Madison County Historical Society's publication *Heritage Highlights* 5 (Fall 2007): 26; Wilson, *Berea College*, 33–39; Lewis, *History of Higher Education in Kentucky*, 185–88.

33. Wilson, *Berea College*, 39, 69; Alice Allison Dunnigan, ed., *The Fascinating Story of Black Kentuckians: Their Heritage and Traditions* (Washington, DC: Associated Publishers, 1982), 216–20.

34. Harrison and Klotter, *A New History of Kentucky*, 395; Dunnigan, *The Fascinating Story of Black Kentuckians*, 175–77; *KE*, 609; Lucas, *A History of Blacks in Kentucky*, 213–17; Wright, *Life behind a Veil*, 127–29; Bigham, *On Jordan's Banks*, 249; Doyle, Layson, and Thompson, *From the Fort to the Future*, 249; *Kentucky's Black Heritage*, 41–42; *EL*, 562; Lewis, *History of Higher Education in Kentucky*, 301–3;

James Blaine Hudson III, "The History of Louisville Municipal College: Events Leading to the Desegregation of the University of Louisville" (Ed.D. diss., Univ. of Kentucky, 1981), 19.

35. Thelin, *A History of American Higher Education*, 96, 141–42; Hamlett, *History of Education in Kentucky*, 303–4, 317–18; Lewis, *History of Higher Education in Kentucky*, 133–40, 318–22; *KE*, 609, 765; Crews, *An American Holy Land*, 94–95, 97, 150, 163, 183, 192; Hackensmith, *Ohio Valley Higher Education*, 53.

36. *KE*, 688–89, 731; Harrison, *Western Kentucky University*, 34–35, 74–75.

37. *KE*, 74; "Bethel College Catalog, 1879–80," *Kentucky Ancestors* 40 (2004): 99–101; Lewis, *History of Higher Education in Kentucky*, 173–83, 239–43; Hackensmith, *Ohio Valley Higher Education*, 44–45.

38. *EL*, 845; John E. Kleber, "The Morse School of Telegraphy," in Kleber, *The New History of Shelby County, Kentucky*, 290–92.

39. Harrison and Klotter, *A New History of Kentucky*, 393–94; Hamlett, *History of Education in Kentucky*, 312, 318–19, 324–25, 328–29; *KE*, 64, 245, 293, 400–401, 723, 859; Lewis, *History of Higher Education in Kentucky*, 243–45, 250–52; Wright, *Transylvania*, 276–76, 288; "Annual Exercises of Eminence College, Eminence, Ky., Thursday and Friday, June 9 and 10, 1870," 8–17, Education File, Kentucky Library, Western Kentucky Univ.

40. Hopkins, *The University of Kentucky*, 199–204; Ellis, *A History of Eastern Kentucky University*, 3; Cone, *The University of Kentucky*, 23; Montgomery, "Rackyte Cax, Cowax Cowax," 34–54.

41. Tapp and Klotter, *Kentucky*, 198–99; C. Vann Woodward, *Origins of the New South, 1877–1913* (Baton Rouge: Louisiana State Univ. Press, 1951), 440–41; Engle, "Central University," 301; Ellis, *A History of Eastern Kentucky University*, 8; Montgomery, "Rackyte Cax, Cowax Cowax," 35–36; Kolan Thomas Morelock, *Taking the Town: Collegiate and Community Culture in the Bluegrass, 1880–1917* (Lexington: Univ. Press of Kentucky, 2008), 147–64.

42. Ellis, *A History of Eastern Kentucky University*, 7; Tapp and Klotter, *Kentucky*, 202; Hopkins, *The University of Kentucky*, 137–38, 166–78.

43. Ellis, *A History of Eastern Kentucky University*, 7; Snyder, *A History of Georgetown College*, 59; Tapp and Klotter, *Kentucky*, 200; Dew and Weiss, *In Pursuit of the Dream*, 33, 50.

44. Marion B. Lucas, "Berea College in the 1870s and 1880s: Student Life at a Racially Integrated Kentucky College," *Register of the Kentucky Historical Society* 98 (Winter 2000): 5–14.

45. Helen Lefkowitz Horowitz, *Campus Life: Undergraduate Cultures from the End of the Eighteenth Century to the Present* (Chicago: Univ. of Chicago Press, 1988), chap. 2; Ellis, *A History of Eastern Kentucky University*, 12–13.

46. Tapp and Klotter, *Kentucky*, 202; Ellis, *A History of Eastern Kentucky University*, 13–14; Snyder, *A History of Georgetown College*, 69; Wilson, *Berea College*, 44.

47. Montgomery, "Rackyte Cax, Cowax Cowax," 60–69, 75, 101–111.

48. Wilson, *Berea College*, 36, Lucas, "Berea College in the 1870s and 1880s," 17, 19–22.

49. Wright, *Transylvania*, 284–85, 288.

50. Horowitz, *Campus Life*, chap. 2; Ellis, *A History of Eastern Kentucky University*, 14–15; Hopkins, *The University of Kentucky*, 180.

51. Hopkins, *The University of Kentucky*, 169–70.

52. Wright, *Transylvania*, 289; Ellis, *A History of Eastern Kentucky University*, 14.

53. Ellis, *A History of Eastern Kentucky University*, 9–10; Wright, *Transylvania*, 299–301; Montgomery, "Rackyte Cax, Cowax Cowax," 109, 144–58; Cone, *The University of Kentucky*, 26; Hopkins, *The University of Kentucky*, 177–79; Snyder, *A History of Georgetown College*, 69; Fields, *A Sesquicentennial History of Georgetown College*, 12.

54. Hopkins, *The University of Kentucky*, 82–86; Cone, *The University of Kentucky*, 7–8.

55. *KE*, 5–6; Hopkins, *The University of Kentucky*, 94–127; Tapp and Klotter, *Kentucky*, 199–200; Hackensmith, *Out of Time and Tide*, 136–39; Wright, *Transylvania*, 234; Harrison, *Kentucky's Governors*, 106; Ligon, *A History of Public Education in Kentucky*, 321; McCormick, "Transylvania University," 202–3, 216–21; Kiesel, "Kentucky's Land-Grant Legacy," 149, 150; Henry Milton Pyles, "The Life and Work of John Bryan Bowman" (Ph.D. diss., Univ. of Kentucky, 1944), 133.

56. Kiesel, "Kentucky's Land-Grant Legacy," 11–12, 151, 152.

57. *KE*, 713; Tapp and Klotter, *Kentucky*, 200; Hackensmith, *Out of Time and Tide*, 135–42; Ligon, *A History of Public Education in Kentucky*, 322; *Session Acts, 1878*, chap. 424, p. 52; Birdwhistell, "Divided We Fall," 433–35; Geraldine Joncich Clifford, *The Shape of American Education* (Englewood Cliffs, NJ: Prentice Hall, 1975), 193; Lisa Phelps Collins, "Venturing Out: Students at Eastern Kentucky State Normal School, 1910–1924" (Ph.D. diss., Univ. of Kentucky, 2008), 1.

58. Ellis, *A History of Eastern Kentucky University*, 6–7; Hopkins, *The University of Kentucky*, 143–52; McVey, *The Gates Open Slowly*, 113–14; Ligon, *A History of Public Education in Kentucky*, 330–31; Kiesel, "Kentucky's Land-Grant Legacy," 174.

59. *KE*, 964; Thelin, *A History of American Higher Education*, 97–98; Meyer, *An Educational History of the American People*, 200–202; Klotter; "Promise, Pessimism, and Perseverance," 50–51; Snyder, *A History of Georgetown College*, 57, 67; Apple, Johnston, and Bevins, *Scott County*, 250; Lewis, *History of Higher Education in Kentucky*, 154–55; Dew and Weiss, *In Pursuit of the Dream*, 74; Griffin, *Newspaper Story of a Town*, 43, 48; Adams, "Central Kentucky Colleges," 46; Hardin and Hill, *Our Standard Sure*, 50–59.

60. Cone, *The University of Kentucky*, 27; Hopkins, *The University of Kentucky*, 130; Klotter, "Promise, Pessimism, and Perseverance," 50–51; Birdwhistell, "Divided We Fall," 433; *KE*, 120–21; Birdwhistell, "An Educated Difference: Women at the University of Kentucky through the Second World War" (Ed.D. diss., Univ. of Kentucky, 1994), 14–19; Klotter, *The Breckinridges of Kentucky*, 195.

61. Birdwhistell, "An Educated Difference," 17–35; Morelock, *Taking the Town*, 92.

62. Ellis, *A History of Eastern Kentucky University*, 8–9.

63. Tapp and Klotter, *Kentucky*, 202; Wilson, *Berea College*, 28, 44, 49, 63, 85; Cone, *The University of Kentucky*, 26–27; Wright, *Transylvania*, 292–301; Snyder, *A History of Georgetown College*, 66; Hopkins, *The University of Kentucky*, 135, 170–76; Ellis, *A History of Eastern Kentucky University*, 9–11, 13; Montgomery, "Rackyte Cax, Cowax Cowax," 121–44; Morelock, *Taking the Town*, 111–29.

64. Morelock, *Taking the Town, 1880–1917*, 1–11, 110–11.

65. *KE*, 339–40; Ellis, *A History of Eastern Kentucky University*, 11; Thelin, *A History of American Higher Education*, 177–79; Frederick Rudolph, "The Rise of Football," in *The American College and University: A History* (New York: Alfred A. Knopf, 1962), 373–93; Montgomery, "Rackyte Cax, Cowax Cowax," 159, 163–64.

66. *KE*, 339–40; Wright, *Transylvania*, 302–3; Tapp and Klotter, *Kentucky*, 112–13; Craig, *Centre College of Kentucky*, 105; Montgomery, "Rackyte Cax, Cowax Cowax," 164–66.

67. *KE*, 339; Ronald A. Smith, *Sports and Freedom: The Rise of Big-Time College Athletics* (New York: Oxford Univ. Press, 1988), 83–98; Ellis, *A History of Eastern Kentucky University*, 11.

68. Tapp and Klotter, *Kentucky*, 112; Dew and Weiss, *In Pursuit of the Dream*, 62, 77–78; Ellis, *A History of Eastern Kentucky University*, 11–12; Montgomery, "Rackyte Cax, Cowax Cowax," 159; Cone, *The University of Kentucky*, 29, 31; Gregory Kent Stanley, *Before Big Blue: Sports at the University of Kentucky, 1880–1940* (Lexington: Univ. Press of Kentucky, 1996), 9.

69. Ellis, *A History of Eastern Kentucky University*, 12–13; Cone, *The University of Kentucky*, 31–32, 34–35; Hopkins, *The University of Kentucky*, 181–83; Wright, *Transylvania*, 303–8; Tapp and Klotter, *Kentucky*, 113; Harrison and Klotter, *A New History of Kentucky*, 232; Stanley, *Before Big Blue*, 21–24; Thelin, *A History of American Higher Education*, 159; Richard A. Edwards, *Walters Collegiate Institute and the Founding of Eastern* (Richmond, KY: n.p., 1964), 6; Montgomery, "Rackyte Cax, Cowax Cowax," 174–75; Morelock, *Taking the Town*, 104–5.

70. Tapp and Klotter, *Kentucky*, 202; Cone, *The University of Kentucky*, 19, 25; Hopkins, *The University of Kentucky*, 217–42.

71. Hopkins, *The University of Kentucky*, 154, 159–60; Kiesel, "Kentucky's Land-Grant Legacy," 168–74, 180–81, 183–90, 192–207.

72. Kiesel, "Kentucky's Land-Grant Legacy," 168, 211, 215–16, 224–27; Hopkins, *The University of Kentucky*, 237–40.

73. Kiesel, "Kentucky's Land-Grant Legacy," 227, 230–35.

74. Wright, *Transylvania*, 326; Snyder, *A History of Georgetown College*, 50–51; Montgomery, "Rackyte Cax, Cowax Cowax," 81–87; Dew and Weiss, *In Pursuit of the Dream*, 75.

75. Ellis, *A History of Eastern Kentucky University*, 15; Wright, *Transylvania*, 241–43.

76. *KE*, 834; Bill J. Leonard, *Dictionary of Baptists in America* (Downers Grove, IL: Intervarsity Press, 1994), 195, 255, 268–69, 287; William E. Ellis, *"A Man of Books and a Man of the People": E. Y. Mullins and the Crisis of Moderate Southern Baptist Leadership* (Macon, GA: Mercer Univ. Press, 1985), 32–43; Lewis, *History of Higher Education in Kentucky*, 283–88; Birdwhistell, *Kentucky Baptists*, 89–91; Woodward, *Origins of the New South*, 443.

77. *KE*, 553, 596–97; Wright, *Transylvania*, 200, 203–6, 211, 219, 229–33; Dwight Stevenson, *Lexington Theological Seminary* (St. Louis: Bethany Press, 1964), 59; McCormick, "Transylvania University," 201–2; Adams, "Central Kentucky Colleges," 27–31, 40.

78. *KE*, 584, 737; Klotter, *The Breckinridges of Kentucky*, 87–91; Lewis, *History of Higher Education in Kentucky*, 275–79, 306–9.

79. *KE*, 793; Crews, *An American Holy Land*, 80–82, 95, 150, 162–64, 183.

80. *Catalogue of the Columbia Law School at Columbia, Kentucky, Session 1874–75* (Columbia, KY: Spectator, 1874), n.p.; Wright, *Transylvania*, 200; Craig, *Centre College of Kentucky*, 47–38; Tapp and Klotter, *Kentucky*, 204; McVey, *The Gates Open Slowly*, 134–35; Cox and Morison, *The University of Louisville*, 39–42, 44–45.

81. *KE*, 624; McVey, *The Gates Open Slowly*, 130–33; Tapp and Klotter, *Kentucky*, 203–4; *EL*, 603–4; Lewis, *History of Higher Education in Kentucky*, 301–6.

82. *EL*, 154–55, 603–4; Wright, *Transylvania*, 145–57, 259–61; McVey, *The Gates Open Slowly*, 132–33; Tapp and Klotter, *Kentucky*, 203–4; Cox and Morison, *The University of Louisville*, 33–38, 42–43; Yater, *Two Hundred Years at the Falls of the Ohio*, 157.

83. Cox and Morison, *The University of Louisville*, 31–38.

84. Ellis, *A History of Eastern Kentucky University*, 16–18; *EL*, 726; Hardin and Hill, *Our Standard Sure*, 43–46.

85. Clark, "Kentucky Education," 188.

Chapter 5. Elementary and Secondary Education from the Progressive Era to World War II

1. Tindall, *America*, 2: chap. 23.

2. Reese, *America's Public Schools*, 113–42; Jurgen Herbst, *And Sadly Teach: Teacher Education and Professionalization in American Culture* (Madison: Univ. of Wisconsin Press, 1989), 3–11, 109–39; Ellis, *A History of Eastern Kentucky University*, 21–22.

3. Harrison and Klotter, *A New History of Kentucky*, 378; Klotter, *Kentucky: Portrait in Paradox, 1900–1950* (Frankfort: Kentucky Historical Society, 1996), 145, 147–48.

4. Valerie Roddy Summers, "A New Rural Life: Kentucky Education Reform and the Country Life Movement, 1905–1920" (Ph.D. diss., Univ. of Kentucky, 2001), 1–3, 230–46; *KE*, 231.

5. Clark, *Kentucky*, 236–39; *The Constitution of the Commonwealth of Kentucky*, 180; Clark, *Agrarian Kentucky*, 54; Clark, "Kentucky Education," 183; *KE*, 746.

6. Ligon, *A History of Public Education in Kentucky*, 113, 135.

7. Fred Allen Engle Jr., *The Superintendents and the Issues: A Study of the Superintendents of Public Instruction in Kentucky* (Frankfort: Department of Education, 1968), 110–17; McVey, *The Gates Open Slowly*, 76–77; Hamlett, *History of Education in Kentucky*, 191; John Wilson Townsend, *"In Kentucky" and Its Author, "Jim" Mulligan* (Lexington, KY: John Bradford Club, 1935), 8–9.

8. Engle, *The Superintendents and the Issues*, 110, 183; Hamlett, *History of Education in Kentucky*, 190–91; Doyle, Layson, and Thompson, *From the Fort to the Future*, 361.

9. Klotter, *Kentucky*, 51–72; *KE*, 784–86; Hackensmith, *Out of Time and Tide*, 191–96; Donald F. Flatt, *A Light to the Mountains: Morehead State University, 1887–1997* (Ashland, KY: Jesse Stuart Foundation, 1997), 2–8; Wright, *A History of Blacks in Kentucky*, 2:79–84, 89–90, 101; *KE*, 784; see also Pearce, *Days of Darkness*, for a wider view of feuding.

10. Ira Bell, *History of Public Education of Wayne County, 1842 to 1975* (Monticello, KY: Lakeview, 1976), 14; Ike Short, interview by author, September 10, 1987.

11. Harry M. Caudill, *Night Comes to the Cumberlands* (Boston: Little, Brown, 1962), 135–37.

12. James L. Leloudis, *Schooling the New South: Pedagogy, Self, and Society in North Carolina, 1880–1920* (Chapel Hill: Univ. of North Carolina Press, 1996), xii–xiii, 20–21, 229; Doyle, Layson, and Thompson, *From the Fort to the Future*, 145–53; Hamlett, *History of Education in Kentucky*, 177–84; Reese, *America's Public Schools*, 32–33, 57, 61–62, 265–67.

13. Doyle, Layson, and Thompson, *From the Fort to the Future*, 145–53; Engle, *The Superintendents and the Issues*, 101–2; *Biennial Report of the Superintendent of Public Instruction of Kentucky, 1899–1901* (Frankfort, 1901), 21–51.

14. Engle, *The Superintendents and the Issues*, 100–102, 107; Harrison and Klotter, *A New History of Kentucky*, 377; Klotter, *Kentucky*, 146; Laurel Shackelford and Bill Weinberg, eds., *Our Appalachia: An Oral History* (New York: Hill and Wang, 1977), 250–52; Ligon, *A History of Public Education in Kentucky*, 118; Caudill, *Night Comes to the Cumberlands*, 135–36.

15. Hartford, *The Little White Schoolhouse*, 8–11, 17; *KE*, 696–97, 799–800, 801; Hackensmith, *Out of Time and Tide*, 90; *Biennial Report of the Superintendent of Public Instruction, 1899–1901*, 455, 460–61; Clark, *Agrarian Kentucky*, 53–55; Summers, "A New Rural Life," 95–96.

16. Clark, *Agrarian Kentucky*, 62, 106.

17. Doyle, Layson, and Thompson, *From the Fort to the Future*, 155–57.

18. Shackelford and Weinberg, *Our Appalachia*, 50–56.

19. *KE*, 359; Wright, *A History of Blacks in Kentucky*, 2:142–44; Klotter, *Kentucky*, 152–53; Wilson, *Berea College*, 75–76; Lee Edward Krehbiel, "From Race to Region: Shifting Priorities at Berea College under President William Goodell Frost, 1892–1912" (Ph.D. diss., Indiana Univ., 1997), 59–118.

20. Wilson, *Berea College*, 82–89; Patricia Rowland Bacon, "White Town / Black Gown: The Role of Kentucky State College in the Integration of Frankfort, Kentucky, 1940–1962" (Ph.D. diss., Univ. of Kentucky, 2004), 117, 162–66.

21. *KE*, 258; Wright, *A History of Blacks in Kentucky*, 2:144–48; Klotter, *Kentucky*, 152–54; Wilson, *Berea College*, 83–85; Richard A. Heckman and Betty J. Hall, "Berea College and the Day Law," *Register of the Kentucky Historical Society* 66 (January 1968): 39–49; John Arthur Hardin, "Hope versus Reality: Black Higher Education in Kentucky, 1904–1954 (Ph.D. diss., Univ. of Michigan, 1989), 15–18.

22. *KE*, 558; Harrison and Klotter, *A New History of Kentucky*, 381–82; Wright, *A History of Blacks in Kentucky*, 2:148; Wilson, *Berea College*, 88–90; Heckman and Hall, "Berea College and the Day Law," 43–52; George C. Wright, "The Founding of Lincoln Institute," *Filson Club History Quarterly* 49 (January 1975): 59–70; Krehbiel, "From Race to Region," 153–58.

23. Hamlett, *History of Education in Kentucky*, 82–87; Hackensmith, *Out of Time and Tide*, 175–76; McVey, *The Gates Open Slowly*, 175–82; Christine A. Ogren, *The American State Normal School* (New York: Palgrave Macmillan, 2005), 16–52, 56, 77, 218.

24. *KE*, 376, 514, 872–73, 943; Hackensmith, *Out of Time and Tide*, 177–79;

McVey, *The Gates Open Slowly*, 182–83; Birdwhistell, "Divided We Fall," 431–35; Hopkins, *The University of Kentucky*, 129–31; Nelda Wyatt, "Into the Promised Land: The Transformation of Eastern and Western Kentucky Normal Schools into Teachers Colleges, 1906–1922" (Ed.D. diss., Univ. of Kentucky, 1999), 9.

25. *KE*, 498; Hackensmith, *Out of Time and Tide*, 179–81; Hamlett, *History of Education in Kentucky*, 191–92; Ellis, *A History of Eastern Kentucky University*, 22–23; W. M. Beckner, "Normal Schools in Kentucky," *Southern School Journal* 16 (February 1906): 25–28; *Southern School Journal* 17 (March 1906): 25; Hopkins, *KEA*, 74–75; Smith, *The Rise of Teacher Training in Kentucky*, 175–81.

26. *KE*, 713, 775; Birdwhistell, "Divided We Fall," 435–40; Ellis, *A History of Eastern Kentucky University*, 24–28; Wyatt, "Into the Promised Land," 150.

27. Harrison, *Western Kentucky University*, 15–18; Birdwhistell, "Divided We Fall," 441–44; Ellis, *A History of Eastern Kentucky University*, 22.

28. Harrison, *Western Kentucky University*, 15–18; Hopkins, *The University of Kentucky*, 211–16; *Louisville Courier-Journal*, June 30, 1906; Birdwhistell, "Divided We Fall," 431, 437.

29. Ellis, *A History of Eastern Kentucky University*, 23; *Richmond Climax*, February 7, 1906; Hamlett, *History of Education in Kentucky*, 282–87; Jesse M. Pangburn, *The Evolution of the American Teachers College* (New York: Teachers College, Columbia Univ., 1932), 93; Harrison, *Western Kentucky University*, 11–17; Edwards, *Walters Collegiate Institute*, 45–67.

30. Hamlett, *History of Education in Kentucky*, 282–85; Hackensmith, *Out of Time and Tide*, 180–81; Ellis, *A History of Eastern Kentucky University*, 23; *Richmond Climax*, February 7, 1906; Kentucky General Assembly, *House Journal, 1906* (Frankfort, 1906), 92, 516, 585, 1173, 1183; Harrison, *Western Kentucky University*, 16.

31. *Louisville Courier-Journal*, June 3, 1906; Harrison, *Western Kentucky University*, 16–18; *Lexington Herald*, June 3, 1906; Ellis, *A History of Eastern Kentucky University*, 23–24; Smith, *The Rise of Teacher Training in Kentucky*, 177–80.

32. *Richmond Kentucky Register*, December 4, 1908; Ellis, *A History of Eastern Kentucky University*, 24; Birdwhistell, "Divided We Fall," 449.

33. Ellis, *A History of Eastern Kentucky*, 25–26; McVey, *The Gates Open Slowly*, 185–88; Hopkins, *The University of Kentucky*, 248–52; Birdwhistell, "Divided We Fall," 451–56, Cone, *The University of Kentucky*, 37–38; Collins, "Venturing Out," 12–13, 18.

34. Jennie Jeffers Ashby Papers, University Archives, Eastern Kentucky Univ.

35. Harrison and Klotter, *A New History of Kentucky*, 382; *KE*, 746; Raymond H. Pulley, *Old Virginia Restored: An Interpretation of the Progressive Impulse, 1870–1930* (Charlottesville: Univ. of Virginia Press, 1968), 133–45.

36. Nancy K. Forderhase, "'The Clear Call of Thoroughbred Women': The Kentucky Federation of Women's Clubs and the Crusade for Educational Reform, 1903–1907," *Register of the Kentucky Historical Society* 83 (Winter 1985): 19–35; *Louisville Courier-Journal*, June 22, 1906; February 4, 1907; *KE*, 499, 746.

37. *KE*, 965–66; Jackson, "The Development of Vocational Education in Kentucky," 138–39; James Duane Bolin, *Bossism and Reform in a Southern City: Lexington, Kentucky, 1880–1940* (Lexington: Univ. Press of Kentucky, 2000), 55–57; Wyatt, "Into the Promised Land," 26–34.

38. Harrison, *Kentucky's Governors*, 141–44; Harrison and Klotter, *A New History of Kentucky*, 280–84; Klotter, *Kentucky*, 211–17; Hamlett, *History of Education in Kentucky*, 193–94.

39. *KE*, 775; Hamlett, *History of Education in Kentucky*, 193–94; Hackensmith, *Out of Time and Tide*, 107; Ellis, *A History of Eastern Kentucky University*, 21–38.

40. Engle, *The Superintendents and the Issues*, 70.

41. Ibid., 57; *Lexington Herald*, January 24, 1908.

42. *KE*, 860; *Kentucky Acts, 1908*, 22–32, 133, 170–71, 198–205; Hackensmith, *Out of Time and Tide*, 105–7; Hamlett, *History of Education in Kentucky*, 205–6.

43. *KE*, 527; Forderhase, "The Clear Call of Thoroughbred Women," 29–30; Klotter, *Kentucky*, 148–49; Engle, *The Superintendents and the Issues*, 57–58; Hopkins, *The University of Kentucky*, 243–61; Wright, *Transylvania*, 312–20.

44. Klotter, *Kentucky*, 148–49, 212–17; *KE*, 860; Harrison, *Kentucky's Governors*, 144; Melba Porter Hay, "Madeline McDowell Breckinridge: Her Role in the Kentucky Woman Suffrage Movement, 1908–1920," *Register of the Kentucky Historical Society* 72 (October 1974): 346–48; Summers, "A New Rural Life," 78–80.

45. Engle, *The Superintendents and the Issues*, 72; Hamlett, *History of Education in Kentucky*, 200.

46. Engle, *The Superintendents and the Issues*, 72–75; *Richmond Climax*, June 23, 30, 1909; Hamlett, *History of Education in Kentucky*, 200–203; Hartford, *The Little White Schoolhouse*, 91–92; *EL*, 930.

47. Hamlett, *History of Education in Kentucky*, 206–10; Engle, *The Superintendents and the Issues*, 64–65.

48. Robert E. Corlew, *Tennessee: A Short History* (Knoxville: Univ. of Tennessee Press, 1990), 525–27; Stanley J. Folmsbee, Robert E. Corlew, and Enoch L. Mitchell, *Tennessee: A Short History* (Knoxville: Univ. of Tennessee Press, 1969), 415, 460–61; William J. Reese, *Hoosier Schools: Past and Present* (Bloomington: Indiana Univ. Press, 1998), 67–73; James H. Madison, *The Indiana Way: A State History* (Bloomington: Indiana Univ. Press, 1986), 180–84; H. Leon Prather, "The Public School Movement in North Carolina, 1901–1913" (Ph.D. diss., New York Univ., 1961), 468–71; "Forty-Seventh Annual Report of the Bowling Green Public Schools for the School Year Ending, June 30th, 1929," 10, Education File, Kentucky Library, Western Kentucky Univ.

49. Hamlett, *History of Education in Kentucky*, 201; Harrison and Klotter, *A New History of Kentucky*, 383; Hackensmith, *Out of Time and Tide*, 106; Ligon, *A History of Public Education in Kentucky*, 220–24; Kardatzke, "The Public High School System in Kentucky," 171–77, 266–316.

50. *KE*, 746; Klotter, *Kentucky*, 149; Harrison and Klotter, *A New History of Kentucky*, 382; Forderhase, "The Clear Call of Thoroughbred Women," 29–30; Hamlett, *History of Education in Kentucky*, 193–206; McVey, *The Gates Open Slowly*, 238–42.

51. Keith C. Barton, "The Gates Shut Quickly: Education and Reform in Kentucky, 1903–1908," 1–35, graduate paper, Univ. of Kentucky, copy in author's possession; Jackson, "The Development of Vocational Education in Kentucky," 140–41.

52. Jackson, "The Development of Vocational Education in Kentucky," 182–84; *Bulletin of the Kentucky Department of Education, 1909* (Frankfort, 1909), 8–9.

53. Hamlett, *History of Education in Kentucky*, 210–21.

54. Calvert and Klee, *Maysville, Kentucky*, 78. Daniel E. McClure Jr., *Two Centuries in Elizabethtown and Hardin County, Kentucky* (Elizabethtown, KY: Hardin County Historical Society, 1979), 332–35; Julian K. Wood, "History of Bagdad High School, 1920–1960," 1–3, mimeographed copy in possession of the author; *KE*, 483; Dianne Wells, comp., Melba Porter Hay and Thomas H. Appleton Jr., eds., *Roadside Kentucky: A Guide to Kentucky Highway Markers* (Frankfort: Kentucky Historical Society, 2002), 131, 164–65.

55. *EL*, 52, 19–20, 100–101, 259–60, 270, 483–84, 551, 558, 735; McVey, *The Gates Open Slowly*, 269; Ligon, *A History of Public Education in Kentucky*, 184; Brenda Feast Jackson, "The Policies and Purposes of Black Public Schooling in Louisville, Kentucky" (Ph.D. diss., Indiana Univ., 1976), 9, 141–44.

56. *EL*, 100–101; Jackson, "Black Public Schooling in Louisville," 12, 16, 24–31, 42, 84–85.

57. *EL*, 33, 100–101, 268–69; Hallenberg, *Anchorage*, 107–15.

58. Wright, *Lexington*, 118–20, 138–41, 175–76.

59. Cleophus Valentino Price, "Agents of Change: An Examination of Graduates at Paul Laurence Dunbar High School and the Fight for Equality from 1940–1954" (Ed.D. diss., Univ. of Kentucky, 2005), 18–24.

60. Teachers of Fayette County, *A Study of LaFayette and Other Fayette County Schools* (Lexington, KY: Fayette County School System, 1943), 3–22; Wright, *Lexington*, 176.

61. Wright, *Lexington*, 139; *KE*, 118; Jackson, "The Development of Vocational Education in Kentucky," 141–46; Hay, "Madeline McDowell Breckinridge," 343; Melba Porter Hay, "The Lexington Civic League: Agent of Reform, 1900–1910," *Filson Club History Quarterly* 62 (July 1988): 348–55.

62. *EL*, 164–65, 294–95, 395–96, 551–52, 781–82; Crews, *An American Holy Land*, 128, 230, 239, 247–61, 253, 261, 268, 270, 275, 277–78, 289, 303, 323; Father Clyde Crews, personal communication.

63. Calvert and Klee, *Maysville, Kentucky*, 62; Frederick A. Wallis, supervising ed., and Hambleton Tapp, author and ed., *A Sesqui-Centennial History of Kentucky* (Hopkinsville, KY: Historical Record Association, 1945), 683–86, 708–9; Apple, Johnston, and Bevins, *Scott County*, 251–52; *Cardome: Academy of the Visitation, 63rd Year, 1937–38* (n.p., n.d.), 24–32; *KE*, 308; *EL*, 164–66; Father Clyde Crews, personal communication.

64. *EL*, 475–76, 551–52; *KE*, 506, 638.

65. *KE*, 646; Doyle, Layson, and Thompson, *From the Fort to the Future*, 162; Yvonne Honeycutt Baldwin, *Cora Wilson Stewart and Kentucky's Moonlight Schools: Fighting for Literacy in America* (Lexington: Univ. Press of Kentucky, 2006), 7–36; Willie E. Nelms Jr., "Cora Wilson Stewart and the Crusade against Illiteracy in Kentucky," *Register of the Kentucky Historical Society* 74 (January 1976): 10–14.

66. *KE*, 646; Harrison and Klotter, *A New History of Kentucky*, 383; Klotter, *Kentucky*, 163–64; Doyle, Layson, and Thompson, *From the Fort to the Future*, 163–64; Baldwin, *Cora Wilson Stewart*, 37–69; Stewart, *Moonlight Schools for the Emancipation of Adult Illiterates* (New York: Dutton, 1922), 14–20; Nelms, "Cora Wilson Stewart" (1976), 14–16.

67. *KE*, 646; Doyle, Layson, and Thompson, *From the Fort to the Future*, 176–79; Baldwin, *Cora Wilson Stewart*, 41–47; Stewart, *Moonlight Schools*, 21–31; Nelms, "Cora Wilson Stewart" (1976), 16–22.

68. Harrison and Klotter, *A New History of Kentucky*, 383; Klotter, *Kentucky*, 164; Doyle, Layson, and Thompson, *From the Fort to the Future*, 162; Baldwin, *Cora Wilson Stewart*, 53–55, 86–87, 105, 108–9, 169–71; Stewart, *Moonlight Schools*, 70–80.

69. *KE*, 855; Harrison and Klotter, *A New History of Kentucky*, 383; Klotter, *Kentucky*, 112, 164; Baldwin, *Cora Wilson Stewart*, 144–45, 165; A. G. Mezerik, "Dixie in Black and White," *Nation* 165 (July 12, 1947): 41.

70. Klotter, *Kentucky*, 164; Baldwin, *Cora Wilson Stewart*, 184–93; Stewart, *Moonlight Schools*, 124–44; Nelms, "Cora Wilson Stewart" (1976), 27–29; Nelms, "Cora Wilson Stewart and the Crusade against Illiteracy in Kentucky, 1916–1920," *Register of the Kentucky Historical Society* 82 (Spring 1984): 164–69.

71. Ellis, *A History of Eastern Kentucky University*, 28–38; Hamlett, *History of Education in Kentucky*, 203; Harrison, *Western Kentucky University*, 19–40; Collins, "Venturing Out," 42.

72. Hamlett, *History of Education in Kentucky*, 223–26; Summers, "A New Rural Life," 40, 42, 44–46, 64; Wyatt, "Into the Promised Land," 58–61; Engle, *The Superintendents and the Issues*, 45–46.

73. Harrison and Klotter, *A New History of Kentucky*, 278–79, 282; Dewey W. Grantham, *Southern Progressivism: The Reconciliation of Progress and Tradition* (Knoxville: Univ. of Tennessee Press, 1983); *KE*, 118–19, 202–3; Hay, "Madeline McDowell Breckinridge," 358–63; Melba Porter Hay, "Suffragist Triumphant: Madeline McDowell Breckinridge and the Nineteenth Amendment," *Register of the Kentucky Historical Society* 93 (Winter 1995): 32–42; Wright, *A History of Blacks in Kentucky*, 2:79–85, 101; Woodward, *Origins of the New South*, 369–95.

74. Harrison and Klotter, *A New History of Kentucky*, 284; Nicholas C. Burckel, "From Beckham to McCreary: The Progressive Record of Kentucky Governors," *Register of the Kentucky Historical Society* 76 (October 1978): 297–300.

75. Harrison and Klotter, *A New History of Kentucky*, 282–83; Harrison, *Kentucky's Governors*, 107–10; Klotter, *Kentucky*, 220; Burckel, "From Beckham to McCreary," 300–303.

76. Engle, *The Superintendents and the Issues*, 46; Hamlett, *History of Education in Kentucky*, 233–34.

77. Harrison, *Kentucky's Governors*, 107–10. Hamlett, *History of Education in Kentucky*, 233–36; Harrison and Klotter, *A New History of Kentucky*, 284, 286; Klotter, *Kentucky*, 220; Burckel, "From Beckham to McCreary," 301–3; *KE*, 746.

78. Hamlett, *History of Education in Kentucky*, 236–48; *EL*, 52.

79. Hamlett, *History of Education in Kentucky*, 234–43, 258–61; *KE*, 965–66.

80. Hamlett, *History of Education in Kentucky*, 243–56; Reese, *America's Public Schools*, 121–22.

81. Hamlett, *History of Education in Kentucky*, 243–66; Harrison, *Kentucky's Governors*, 109; Burckel, "From Beckham to McCreary," 303–5.

82. Hamlett, *History of Education in Kentucky*, 265–66; Burckel, "From Beckham to McCreary," 303–4; *KE*, 527, 678–79; Harrison and Klotter, *A New History of Kentucky*, 284, 286; Tindall, *America*, 2:909–10; Klotter, *Kentucky*, 147.

83. Thomas H. Appleton Jr., "Prohibition and Politics in Kentucky: The Gubernatorial Campaign and Election of 1915," *Register* 75 (January 1977): 28–54; Engle, *The Superintendents and the Issues*, 43–44; Harrison, *Kentucky's Governors*, 146.

84. Harrison, *Kentucky's Governors*, 147; Appleton, "Prohibition and Politics in Kentucky," 28–54; Nicholas C. Burckel, "A. O. Stanley and Progressive Reform, 1902–1919," *Register* 79 (Spring 1981): 150–61; Harrison and Klotter, *A New History of Kentucky*, 286; Klotter, *Kentucky*, 230–32.

85. H. W. Peters, *History of Education in Kentucky, 1915–1940* (Frankfort: Department of Education, 1940), 13–20; Collins, "Venturing Out," 54–57.

86. Peters, *History of Education in Kentucky*, 21.

87. Ibid., 21–22; *EL*, 273; Nancy Disher Baird, "The Spanish Lady in Kentucky," *Filson Club History Quarterly* 50 (July 1976): 290–301; Klotter, *Kentucky*, 239–40; Mabel G. Pullen, interview by author, October 4, 1986.

88. William E. Ellis, *Robert Worth Bingham and the Southern Mystique: From the Old South to the New South and Beyond* (Kent, OH: Kent State Univ. Press, 1997), 55–63.

89. Harrison and Klotter, *A New History of Kentucky*, 286; Woodward, *Origins of the New South*, chap. 14, "Progressivism—For Whites Only."

90. Hackensmith, *Out of Time and Tide*, 100–101; Harrison and Klotter, *A New History of Kentucky*, 380–81; McVey, *The Gates Open Slowly*, 151; Myrtle K. Phillips, "The Origin, Development, and Present Status of Public Secondary Education for Negroes in Kentucky," *Journal of Negro Education* 1 (October 1932): 415; Rolfe Lanier Hunt, *A Study of Factors Influencing the Public School Curriculum of Kentucky* (Nashville: George Peabody College for Teachers, 1939), 204; *The Constitution of the Commonwealth of Kentucky*, 31.

91. Jackson, "Black Public Schooling in Louisville," 120–24, 144–64, 226; Ruby Wilkins Doyle, *Recalling the Record: A Documentary History of the African-American Experience within the Louisville Public School System of Kentucky, 1870–1975* (Chapel Hill, NC: Professional Press, 2005), 149–57, 206–23, 260–63; *EL*, 619; George D. Wilson, "A Century of Negro Education in Louisville, Kentucky," 81, 84–85, 100–101, typescript microfilm, 1941, Louisville Municipal College.

92. McVey, *The Gates Open Slowly*, 153–54; Doyle, Layson, and Thompson, *From the Fort to the Future*, 247; Phillips, "Public Secondary Education for Negroes in Kentucky," 418–20; H. Leon Prather Sr., *Resurgent Politics and Educational Progressivism in the New South, North Carolina, 1890–1913* (Rutherford, NJ: Fairleigh Dickinson Univ. Press, 1979), 214–15, 223–24, 239–41, 255–56, 280; Leloudis, *Schooling the New South*, 213–28; Summers, "A New Rural Life," 46–48, 141–42; *Richmond Register*, October 15, 2007; Peters, *History of Education in Kentucky*, 26–27; Price, "Agents of Change," 1–2; Hardin, "Hope versus Reality," 29–31.

93. Peter M. Ascoli, *Julius Rosenwald: The Man Who Built Sears, Roebuck and Advanced the Cause of Black Education in the American South* (Bloomington: Indiana Univ. Press, 2006), 135–54, 230–38; Alicestyne Turley-Adams, *Rosenwald Schools in Kentucky, 1917–1932* (Frankfort: Kentucky Heritage Council, 1997), 3, 8–9, 17–23, 25, 52, 54; *Richmond Register*, May 5, 2008; Joan Malczewski, "Weak State, Stronger Schools: Northern Philanthropy and Organizational Change in the Jim Crow South," *Journal of Southern History* 75 (November 2009): 983–84.

94. "History of Middletown Elementary School," unpublished manuscript, 1968, 6–7, 13, 21–22, University Archives, Eastern Kentucky Univ.

95. Wright, *A History of Blacks in Kentucky*, 2:110–11; Harrison and Klotter, *A New History of Kentucky*, 381; Fairclough, *A Class of Their Own*, 232–34; Doyle, Layson, and Thompson, *From the Fort to the Future*, 248; Venable, "A History of Negro Education in Kentucky," 118–83; Reese, *America's Public Schools*, 210–11; Frieda J. Dannheiser, editor-in-chief, *The History of Henderson County, Kentucky* (Henderson, KY: Henderson County Genealogical and Historical Society, 1980), 245–47; Jackson, "The Development of Vocational Education in Kentucky," 217.

96. Lottie Offett Robinson, *The Bond-Washington Story: The Education of Black People, Elizabethtown, Kentucky* (Georgetown, KY: Kreative Grafiks, 1983), 36–39, 48–49, 56–59.

97. Fairclough, *A Class of Their Own*, 234, 245; Harrison and Klotter, *A New History of Kentucky*, 381; Mildred M. Williams, ed., *The Jeanes Story: A Chapter in the History of American Education, 1908–1968* (Atlanta: Southern Education Foundation, 1979), 99–100, 134–35; Malczewski, "Weak State, Stronger Schools," 998.

98. Phillips, "Public Secondary Education for Negroes in Kentucky," 420–23; *Lexington Herald-Leader,* February 20, 2008; Apple, Johnston, and Bevins, *Scott County,* 338; Ligon, *A History of Public Education in Kentucky,* 254–55; Kardatzke, "The Public High School System in Kentucky," 194–203.

99. R. B. Atwood, "Financing Schools for Negro Children from State School Funds in Kentucky," *Journal of Negro Education* 8 (October 1939): 663–65; Jackson, "The Development of Vocational Education in Kentucky," 231; Leloudis, *Schooling the New South,* 212–13.

100. Kathleen A. Hauke, ed., *The Dark Side of Hopkinsville: Stories by Ted Poston* (Athens: Univ. of Georgia Press, 1991), xv, xvii, xx, xxiii, xxix.

101. *KE,* 810; Harrison and Klotter, *A New History of Kentucky,* 383.

102. *KE,* 245, 696, 859–60; Thomas, *Dawn Comes to the Mountains,* 6–11; Doyle, Layson, and Thompson, *From the Fort to the Future,* 98–103; J. Chester Badgett, *History of Campbellsville University* (Prospect, KY: Harmony House, 2005), 14–162; A. G. Weidler, ed., *First Fruits from Frenchburg* (Frenchburg, KY: Women's General Missionary Society of the United Presbyterian Church of North America, n.d.), 3–28; "Frenchburg Presbyterian College," Internet link abandoned, last accessed 2010.

103. Shackelford and Weinberg, *Our Appalachia,* 179–91; Robert M. Rennick, *Kentucky Place Names* (Lexington: Univ. Press of Kentucky, 1984), 203.

104. Forderhase, "Eve Returns to the Garden: Women Reformers in Appalachian Kentucky in the Early Twentieth Century," *Register* 85 (Summer 1987): 239–43; Henry D. Shapiro, *Appalachia on Our Mind: The Southern Mountains and Mountaineers in the American Consciousness, 1870–1920* (Chapel Hill: Univ. of North Carolina Press, 1978), 32–58; James C. Klotter, "The Black South and White Appalachia," *Journal of American History* 66 (March 1980): 884, 849.

105. *KE,* 433, 719, 857; Forderhase, "Eve Returns to the Garden," 246.

106. Stoddart, *Challenge and Change in Appalachia,* 2, 4.

107. *KE,* 719, 867; Stoddart, *Challenge and Change in Appalachia,* 4–5.

108. Forderhase, "Eve Returns to the Garden," 244–45, 249, 252, 257.

109. Harrison and Klotter, *A New History of Kentucky*, 384; *KE*, 135, 564; P. David Searles, *A College for Appalachia: Alice Lloyd on Caney Creek* (Lexington: Univ. Press of Kentucky, 1995), 122–23; Stoddart, *Challenge and Change in Appalachia*, 103–4; Patricia G. Hilton, "The Leaders Are Here: Teacher Education at Alice Lloyd College in Pippa Passes, Kentucky," (Ph.D. diss., Univ. of Akron, 1991), 220, 227–30; Carolyn Clay Turner, "Patterns of Educational Initiative, Reorganization and Decline in Eastern Kentucky, 1889–1940: Pikeville Collegiate Institute, Sandy Valley Seminary, and Caney Community Center" (Ed.D. diss., Univ. of Kentucky, 1987), 37–47.

110. Doyle, Layson, and Thompson, *From the Fort to the Future*, 129–34; *KE*, 352, 425, 460, 810; William Metcalf, "A History of Annville Institute" (master's thesis, Eastern Kentucky State Teachers College, 1946), 3–9, 45–49, 360–61, appendix; *Settlement Schools in Appalachia*, KET, 1995.

111. *KE*, 719, 810; Harrison and Klotter, *A New History of Kentucky*, 383; Klotter, *Kentucky*, 162–63; Forderhase, "Eve Returns to the Garden," 253, 255, 261; James C. Klotter, interview by author, February 28, 2008; James S. Greene III, "Progressives in the Kentucky Mountains: The Formative Years of the Pine Mountain Settlement School, 1913–1930" (Ph.D. diss., Ohio State Univ., 1982), 372.

112. David E. Whisnant, *All That Is Native and Fine: The Politics of Culture in an American Region* (Chapel Hill: Univ. of North Carolina Press, 1983), xvi, 90; Searles, *A College for Appalachia*, 145–47, 162; Stoddart, *Challenge and Change in Appalachia*, 225–31; Jess Stoddart, ed., *The Quare Women's Journals: May Stone and Katherine Pettit's Summers in the Kentucky Mountains and the Founding of the Hindman Settlement School* (Ashland, KY: Jesse Stuart Foundation, 1997), 323–27; Rodger Cunningham, *Apples on the Flood: The Southern Mountain Experience* (Knoxville: Univ. of Tennessee Press, 1987), xvi–xvii, 134, 157–58; Klotter interview, February 28, 2008; *Settlement Schools in Appalachia*, KET, 1995.

113. Klotter interview, February 28, 2008; Shackelford and Weinberg, *Our Appalachia*, 209–17; 223–25, 313–15; *KE*, 221–22; Rennick, *Kentucky Place Names*, 20, 153, 181, 315; *Lexington Herald-Leader*, February 13, 2008; Mark F. Sohn et al., *Education in Appalachia's Central Highlands* (Pikeville, KY: Mark F. Sohn, 1986), 155–57; Mumford, "A Historical Sketch of Education in the Kentucky Highlands," 57–62.

114. *Clay City Times*, September 11, 1919.

115. *KE*, 858; Doyle, Layson, and Thompson, *From the Fort to the Future*, 224–29; Stuart, *The Thread That Runs So True* (New York: Scribner's, 1949, 1958); William S. Ward, *A Literary History of Kentucky* (Knoxville: Univ. of Tennessee Press, 1988), 232–45.

116. Stuart, *The Thread That Runs So True*, 3–4; *KE*, 858–59.

117. Doyle, Layson, and Thompson, *From the Fort to the Future*, 188–99.

118. Ibid., 189–93.

119. *KE*, 956; Cratis D. Williams, *I Become a Teacher: A Memoir of One-Room School Life in Eastern Kentucky* (Ashland, KY: Jesse Stuart Foundation, 1995), 1, 20–21, 29, 38–43, 61, 67–68, 73.

120. Ethel Merritt Lisle, interview by author, July 17, 1986.

121. [Madison County] *School Bell Echo* (Winter 2001): 7–8.

122. Katie Carpenter, interview by author, November 24, 1986; Ellis, *A History*

of Eastern Kentucky University, 66; James C. Burnett, interview by author, October 9, 1977; Shackelford and Weinberg, *Our Appalachia,* 250–52.

123. H. E. Richardson Sr., interview by author, October 28, 1983; Robert E. Little, "History of Education in Madison County, Kentucky" (master's thesis, Univ. of Kentucky, 1933), 204.

124. Constance Elam, "That's Just the Way It Was: Teacher Experiences in Appalachian Kentucky, 1930–1960" (Ph.D. diss., Univ. of Texas at Austin, 2003), 41–43, 175, 178–80; Sohn et al., *Education in Appalachia's Central Highlands,* 417–39.

125. *KE:* 696, 799; Bell, *History of Public Education of Wayne County,* 14; Hartford, *The Little White Schoolhouse,* 50–72.

126. Kramer, *Capital on the Kentucky,* 310; Clark, *Agrarian Kentucky,* 85–90; *KE,* 32; Ward, *A Literary History of Kentucky,* 150, 216.

127. Perkinson, *The Imperfect Panacea,* 142–46; Jackson, "The Development of Vocational Education in Kentucky," 55–59, 76–98; Summers, "A New Rural Life," 154–55; Ruth Allene Hammons, "History of the Richmond City Schools" (master's thesis, Eastern Kentucky State College, 1949), 42.

128. McVey, *The Gates Open Slowly,* 119; Gutek, *A History of the Western Educational Experience,* 494; Doyle, Layson, and Thompson, *From the Fort to the Future,* 208–9; *KE,* 923; Hackensmith, *Out of Time and Tide,* 107–8; Ligon, *A History of Public Education in Kentucky,* 174; Summers, "A New Rural Life," 160–61; Meyer, *An Educational History of the American People,* 359, 416; *Biennial Report of the Superintendent of Public Instruction, June 30, 1941* (Frankfort, 1941), 624–27.

129. Peters, *History of Education in Kentucky,* 25; *Louisville Courier-Journal,* July 23, 1928; Louise Hatcher, "A Sanitary Survey of the School Plants of Rural Warren County, Kentucky, 1920," Education File, Kentucky Library, Western Kentucky Library; Hattie C. Warner, "Consolidation of Rural Schools in Kentucky" (master's thesis, Univ. of Kentucky, 1925), 52–54.

130. Harrison, *Kentucky's Governors,* 152–55; Doyle, Layson, and Thompson, *From the Fort to the Future,* 181–83; Klotter, *Kentucky,* 232–33, Peters, *History of Education in Kentucky,* 29–30.

131. Klotter, *Kentucky,* 267–69; Harrison and Klotter, *A New History of Kentucky,* 350–51; Doyle, Layson, and Thompson, *From the Fort to the Future,* 183–86.

132. *KE,* 746, 800–801; Hackensmith, *Out of Time and Tide,* 94; Ligon, *A History of Public Education in Kentucky,* 210–11; Little, "History of Education in Madison County," 203–7; Warner, "Consolidation of Rural Schools In Kentucky," 41–52, 55, 68.

133. Hopkins, *KEA,* 75–76; Doyle, Layson, and Thompson, *From the Fort to the Future,* 184–85; Peters, *History of Education in Kentucky,* 39–40; Clark, "Kentucky Education," 193; *Public Education in Kentucky: A Report by the Kentucky Educational Commission* (New York: General Education Board, 1922), v–ix.

134. *Public Education in Kentucky,* 3, 55, 76, 84, 136.

135. Ibid., 149–202.

136. Ibid., 101–2, 106, 110, 203–13.

137. Peters, *History of Education in Kentucky,* 40–42; Doyle, Layson, and Thompson, *From the Fort to the Future,* 184–85.

138. Doyle, Layson, and Thompson, *From the Fort to the Future,* 40–41; Flatt, *A Light to the Mountains,* 29–36; *KE,* 644; Harrison, *Kentucky's Governors,* 155.

139. Peters, *History of Education in Kentucky*, 38–45.

140. Klotter, *Kentucky*, 269–71; Harrison and Klotter, *A New History of Kentucky*, 356–47; Ellis, "The Kentucky Evolution Controversy" (master's thesis, Eastern Kentucky University, 1967), 5–7, 24–34; *KE*, 23, 730; William E. Ellis, "Frank LeRond McVey: His Defense of Academic Freedom," *Register of the Kentucky Historical Society* 67 (January 1969): 39.

141. Ellis, "The Kentucky Evolution Controversy," 7–10; McVey, *The Gates Open Slowly*, 221–28.

142. McVey, *The Gates Open Slowly*, 229–33; Frank L. McVey, *A University Is a Place . . . A Spirit: Addresses and Articles* (Lexington: Univ. of Kentucky Press, 1944), 17–20.

143. Ellis, "Frank LeRond McVey," 50–54; Ellis, "The Kentucky Evolution Controversy," 14–18.

144. Ellis, "The Kentucky Evolution Controversy," 17–19; Klotter, *Kentucky*, 269–71; McVey, *The Gates Open Slowly*, 234–35.

145. Ellis, "The Kentucky Evolution Controversy," 1–4, 40–41, 60–61; McVey, *The Gates Open Slowly*, 234–36: Ellis, *"A Man of Books and a Man of the People,"* 147–68, 185–208.

146. *KE*, 803; Ellis, "The Kentucky Evolution Controversy," 95–98; Harrison and Klotter, *A New History of Kentucky*, 346; Klotter, *Kentucky*, 271.

147. Mrs. Joe C. Grable, "The Status of the Teaching of Biological Science in the Secondary Schools of Kentucky" (master's thesis, Univ. of Kentucky, 1929), 56–57, 115–18.

148. McVey, *The Gates Open Slowly*, 73; Reese, *America's Public Schools*, 154–55; 190–92, 208; Lawrence Cremin, *The Transformation of the School: Progressivism in American Education, 1876–1957* (New York: Alfred A. Knopf, 1961), 85.

149. Reese, *America's Public Schools*, 190–93.

150. *Elementary State Course of Study and Teacher's Manual* (Frankfort: Bulletin of the Kentucky Department of Education, April 1916), 9; Summers, "A New Rural Life," 117.

151. Hackensmith, *Out of Time and Tide*, 107; Ellis, *A History of Eastern Kentucky University*, 28–38.

152. *Survey of the Public School System, Paducah, Kentucky* (Paducah, KY: Board of Education, 1919), 9–16, 73–85, 126–40.

153. R. E. Jaggers and W. C. Jones, *Rural Education in Madison County* (Richmond: Eastern Kentucky State Normal School and Teachers College, 1928), 9, 27, 36, 39, 43–44, 47–57; Challis Henry Warren, "Reorganization of Public Education in Madison County" (master's thesis, Univ. of Kentucky, 1935), 34–42.

154. *KE*, 57, 340, 843; Hopkins, *KEA*, 77; Charles T. Hughes, interview by author, February 23, 1978; Lewis, "A History of the Kentucky Education Association," 46.

155. *KE*, 340; Klotter, *Kentucky*, 99–102; Rennick, *Kentucky Place Names*, 50–51; Harrison and Klotter, *A New History of Kentucky*, 232; *KE*, 57–58; Dave Kindred, *Basketball: The Dream Game in Kentucky* (Louisville: Data Courier, 1976), 23–27; Ellis, *A History of Eastern Kentucky Univ.*, 72; H. D. Tartar, interview by author, August 2, 1990.

156. *KE,* 340; *EL,* 306, 595; Klotter, *Kentucky,* 101; Doyle, *Recalling the Record,* 288–89; Dannheiser, *The History of Henderson County,* 261.

157. *KE,* 746; Engle, *The Superintendents and the Issues,* 78–79; Doyle, Layson, and Thompson, *From the Fort to the Future,* 226–29; Stuart, *The Thread That Runs So True,* 34–37, 135–37, 336–37.

158. Shackelford and Weinberg, *Our Appalachia,* 50–56; *KE,* 746, 800; Hackensmith, *Out of Time and Tide,* 94.

159. Jaggers and Jones, *Rural Education in Madison County,* 9; Ellis, *A History of Eastern Kentucky Univ.,* 66; Burnett interview, October 9, 1977; Shackelford and Weinberg, *Our Appalachia,* 250–53; *Louisville Courier-Journal,* May 11, September 6, 1931; July 10, 1933; Herman L. Donovan, "I Remember Eastern," unpublished manuscript, 38–44, Donovan Papers, Univ. of Kentucky and Eastern Kentucky Univ. Archives; Hackensmith, *Out of Time and Tide,* 94.

160. Herman L. Donovan, *A State's Elementary Teacher-Training Program (Kentucky)* (Nashville: George Peabody College for Teachers, 1925), 32–33, 85–90; Lewis, "A History of the Kentucky Education Association," 53–54.

161. Lori Frances Kincaid, "The Influence of the Educational Trust on a State's Educational Movement: The Connection between Teachers College, Columbia University, and Education in Kentucky" (Ed.D. diss., Univ. of Kentucky, 1997), 73–121, 127, 139–40, 155–56; see issues of the *Kentucky School Journal,* vols. 4, 5, and 6, for examples.

162. Klotter interview, February 28, 2008.

163. Klotter, *Kentucky,* 271–75; Harrison, *Kentucky's Governors,* 156–59.

164. Klotter, *Kentucky,* 276–78; Ellis, *Robert Worth Bingham,* 115–22; Harrison, *Kentucky's Governors,* 157–58; Harrison and Klotter, *A New History of Kentucky,* 354–55; Nollie Olin Taff, *History of State Revenue and Taxation in Kentucky* (Nashville: George Peabody College for Teachers, 1931), 141–43; Klotter interview, February 28, 2008.

165. Peters, *History of Education in Kentucky,* 47–56; Harrison and Klotter, *A New History of Kentucky,* 353–55.

166. Peters, *History of Education in Kentucky,* 56–65; Engle, *The Superintendents and the Issues,* 48, Hopkins, *KEA,* 50; Lewis, "A History of the Kentucky Education Association," 55–56.

167. Klotter, *Kentucky,* 189, 284–88; Harrison, *Kentucky's Governors,* 160–63; *KE,* 660–61.

168. Klotter, *Kentucky,* 288–89; Harrison, *Kentucky's Governors,* 162.

169. Engle, *The Superintendents and the Issues,* 58–59; *KE,* 795–96; Harrison, *Kentucky's Governors,* 162–63.

170. Peters, *History of Education in Kentucky,* 71; Hunt, *Factors Influencing the Public School Curriculum,* 170; Harrison, *Kentucky's Governors,* 162; Harrison and Klotter, *A New History of Kentucky,* 356–57; Engle, *The Superintendents and the Issues,* 58–59, 109–10; Brooks Lynn Hargrove, "A Textbook Law for Kentucky" (master's thesis, Univ. of Kentucky, 1933), 26–27, 94, 100–102.

171. *A Study in the Equalization of Educational Opportunities in Kentucky* (Lexington: Univ. of Kentucky, 1926), 9–19, 44–73, 166–72, 189–90, 208–9, 234–68; Ira

Bell, "The Problem of Equalization of Public Education in Kentucky," *Kentucky School Journal* 2 (January 1939): 113–18.

172. Peters, *History of Education in Kentucky*, 74–82.

173. Harrison, *Kentucky's Governors*, 164–67; Harrison and Klotter, *A New History of Kentucky*, 359–62; George T. Blakey, *Hard Times and New Deal in Kentucky, 1929–1939* (Lexington: Univ. Press of Kentucky, 1986), 4–44.

174. Hunt, *Factors Influencing the Public School Curriculum*, 151; Meyer, *An Educational History of the American People*, 424; Harrison, *Kentucky's Governors*, 165; Klotter, *Kentucky*, 298–99; Harrison and Klotter, *A New History of Kentucky*, 362–63.

175. Peters, *History of Education in Kentucky*, 85–86; Engle, *The Superintendents and the Issues*, 49, 168–69.

176. *KE*, 529; Harrison, *Kentucky's Governors*, 166; Harrison and Klotter, *A New History of Kentucky*, 362–63, 367–68.

177. Hopkins, *KEA*, 76; *Report of the Kentucky Educational Commission* (Frankfort: Department of Education, 1933); Doyle, Layson, and Thompson, *From the Fort to the Future*, 272–73; Peters, *History of Education in Kentucky*, 91–108; Klotter, *Kentucky*, 301; Harrison and Klotter, *A New History of Kentucky*, 384; Engle, *The Superintendents and the Issues*, 106, 110, 117, 151–57; Clark, "Kentucky Education," 197.

178. *KE*, 179; Harrison, *Kentucky's Governors*, 168–72.

179. Peters, *History of Education in Kentucky*, 111–12.

180. Harrison, *Kentucky's Governors*, 170–72; Harrison and Klotter, *A New History of Kentucky*, 368–69; Klotter, *Kentucky*, 307–15.

181. Peters, *History of Education in Kentucky*, 144–45; *Statistical Abstract of the United States, 1942–1943* (Washington, DC: Government Printing Office, 1943), 136, 138; *Biennial Report of the Superintendent of Public Instruction of the Commonwealth of Kentucky, June 30, 1941*, 602–3.

182. Peters, *History of Education in Kentucky*, 95, 116–24, 128, 137; Engle, *The Superintendents and the Issues*, 56, 169; *Biennial Report of the Superintendent of Public Instruction of the Commonwealth of Kentucky, June 30, 1941*, 614–15; *Kentucky Educational Report* 8 (March 1940–February 1941): 390–417.

183. Yater, *Two Hundred Years at the Falls of the Ohio*, 200; Rick Bell, *The Great Flood of 1937: Rising Waters—Soaring Spirits, Louisville, Kentucky* (Louisville: Butler Books, 2007), 116, 120; Jerry Hill, *Kentucky Weather* (Lexington: Univ. Press of Kentucky, 2005), 58, 74–79; Kramer, *Capital on the Kentucky*, 321, 339, 341.

184. William E. Ellis, *The Kentucky River* (Lexington: Univ. Press of Kentucky, 2000), 117–20; *Louisville Courier-Journal*, July 6, 7, 8, 1939; Lorene Rose, interview by author, August 30, 1992; Dorothy Spencer, interview by author, August 21, 1992; Lela G. McConnell, *Faith Victorious in the Kentucky Mountains* (Winona Lake, IN: Light and Life Press, 1946), 142–47.

185. Nickell, *The Vanishing Schools*, 25, 31–32; W. Lynn Nickell, *The Morgan County Phoenix: A History of W.P.A. Schools in Morgan County, Kentucky* (West Liberty, KY: W. Lynn Nickell, 1994), 42–49, 85, 100–108; Blakey, *Hard Times and New Deal in Kentucky*, 199; Sohn et al., *Education in Appalachia's Central Highlands*, 63; Klotter, *Kentucky*, 250–53.

186. Charles Gano Talbert, *The University of Kentucky: The Maturing Years*

(Lexington: Univ. of Kentucky Press, 1965), 126; *The Children Must Learn* and *And So They Live*, videos, copies presented to the author by Richard Angelo, Univ. of Kentucky professor of education.

187. Project Staff, Federal Project, O.P. 5-119, *A Study of Local School Units in Kentucky* (Frankfort: Kentucky Book Manufacturing, 1937), vii–vii, 41–56, 59–70, 77–126.

188. *KE*, 974; *LE*, 963–64; Wright, *A History of Blacks in Kentucky*, 2:140–41; Klotter, *Kentucky*, 154.

189. *KE*, 519–20; Ellis, *A History of Eastern Kentucky University*, 60, 86; Lee Kirkpatrick, *Teaching School Day by Day* (Lexington: Hobson Press, 1941); Thomas D. Clark and Lee Kirkpatrick, *Exploring Kentucky* (New York: American Book, 1939).

190. Harrison and Klotter, *A New History of Kentucky*, 384; Klotter, *Kentucky*, 152; McVey, *The Gates Open Slowly*, 270.

191. George D. Strayer Jr., H. C. Brearley, Dennis H. Cooke, and Susan B. Riley, "Types of Discrimination against Teachers," *Peabody Journal of Education* 18 (September 1940): 97, 99–101; Wilson, "A Century of Negro Education in Louisville," 126–31.

192. Klotter, *Kentucky*, 155–56; *Statistical Abstract of the United States, 1942*, 138.

193. Harrison and Klotter, *A New History of Kentucky*, 384–85; Klotter, *Kentucky*, 145; *Statistical Abstract of the United States, 1942*, 135; Harry W. Schacter, *Kentucky on the March* (New York: Harper, 1949), 4–6; Willis G. Wells, "A History of the Kentucky Association of Secondary School Principals" (Ed.D. diss., Indiana Univ., 1966), 1–12, 145–50.

194. Tindall, *America*, 2: 1099–1145; Harrison and Klotter, *A New History of Kentucky*, 385; Schacter, *Kentucky on the March*, 5, 33–35.

Chapter 6. Higher Education in the New Century

1. Cremin, *Traditions of American Education*, 135.

2. Klotter, *Kentucky*, 84–86.

3. Anne M. Boylan, *Sunday School: The Formation of an American Institution, 1790–1880* (New Haven, CT: Yale Univ. Press, 1988), 123, 166–70.

4. Judith J. Phillips, "Enlightenment, Education and Entertainment: A Study of the Chautauqua Movement in Kentucky" (master's thesis, Univ. of Louisville, 1985), iii–iv, 23, 31–32, 47; Harrison, *Western Kentucky University*, 53; Clark, *Agrarian Kentucky*, 116; James P. Cornette, *A History of Western Kentucky State Teachers College* (Nashville: George Peabody College for Teachers, 1939), 149–51.

5. Phillips, "Enlightenment, Education, and Entertainment," 50–53, 55–59, 66–69; Ellis, Everman, and Sears, *Madison County*, 289, 304, 312; Klotter, *Kentucky*, 83, 88–89.

6. Klotter, *Kentucky*, 81–97; Harrison and Klotter, *A New History of Kentucky*, 338–41; *EL*, 935–36; Ellis, *Robert Worth Bingham*, 90–92; Terry L. Birdwhistell, "WHAS Radio and the Development of Broadcasting in Kentucky, 1922–1942," *Register of the Kentucky Historical Society* 79 (Autumn 1981): 33–46.

7. *KE*, 553–54; Zanne Jeffries, "Instant Landmarks," *Kentucky Humanities* (April 2006): 21–27.

8. Klotter, *Kentucky*, 169–78; Ward, *A Literary History of Kentucky*, 40–47, 57–61, 76–83, 150–59; *EL*, 925–26; Clark, *Agrarian Kentucky*, 58–60; Ellis, *Robert Worth Bingham*, 110.

9. Klotter, *Kentucky*, 87–88.

10. *KE*, 74, 569; Sue Lynn McGuire, "Fannie's Flirtations: Etiquette, Reality, and the Age of Choice," *Register of the Kentucky Historical Society* 93 (Winter 1995): 43–78.

11. Anne Firor Scott, *Making the Invisible Woman Visible* (Chicago: Univ. of Illinois Press, 1984), 223; Deborah A. Hall, "'Coming of Age' in the Progressive Era: The Role of Southern Women's Higher Education between 1900 and 1917" (Ed.D. diss., Univ. of Kentucky, 1991), 12, 36, 80, 82, 111–16, 122–23.

12. *KE*, 688–89, 731; Lynn E. Niedermeier, *"That Mighty Band of Maidens": A History of Potter College for Young Ladies, Bowling Green, Kentucky, 1889–1909* (Bowling Green: Landmark Association, 2001), 12, 34–38.

13. Niedermeier, *"That Mighty Band of Maidens,"* 47–49; Barbara Miller Solomon, *In the Company of Educated Women: A History of Women and Higher Education in America* (New Haven, CT: Yale Univ. Press, 1985), 49.

14. William M. Jenkins Jr., *Education for Achievement: The B.U. Story* (Bowling Green, KY: n.p., 1995), 1–36, 59–68; Harrison, *Western Kentucky University*, 180.

15. *KE*, 688–89, 731; Niedermeier, *"That Mighty Band of Maidens,"* 32–33, 53–54, 153–54, 180–208; Harrison, *Western Kentucky University*, 74–75.

16. Harrison and Klotter, *A New History of Kentucky*, 393–96; Klotter, *Kentucky*, 156–58, 164–67; Wallis and Tapp, *A Sesqui-Centennial History of Kentucky*, 640–42; Turner, "Patterns of Educational Initiative," 151–59.

17. Clark, *Kentucky*, 237; *KE*, 740; Tracy Campbell, *Short of the Glory: The Fall and Redemption of Edward F. Prichard, Jr.* (Lexington: Univ. Press of Kentucky, 1998), 22–23; Thelin, *A History of American Higher Education*, 218–19; Kenneth H. Williams, ed., "'I'm Sure There Were Some That Thought I Was Too Smart for My Own Good': The Ed Prichard Oral History Interviews," *Register of the Kentucky Historical Society* 104 (Summer–Autumn 2006): 395, 401–15, 419–39.

18. Thelin, *A History of American Higher Education*, 174–77.

19. Rudolph, *The American College and University*, 55.

20. Birdwhistell, *Kentucky Baptists*, 87–89; Snyder, *A History of Georgetown College*, 77; Fields, *A Sesquicentennial History of Georgetown College*, 9.

21. Fields, *A Sesquicentennial History of Georgetown College*, 9; Snyder, *A History of Georgetown College*, 81, 85, 87.

22. Fields, *A Sesquicentennial History of Georgetown College*, 9, 11–13; Ira J. Porter, "Georgetown College and Its Relation to Kentucky Baptists," 9, paper presented to the Ten Club, Louisville, October 25, 1960; Birdwhistell, *Kentucky Baptists*, 104–6, 110; Snyder, *A History of Georgetown College*, 87–96.

23. Thelin, *A History of American Higher Education*, 249–51; Rudolph, *The American College and University*, 463; Gutek, *A History of the Western Educational Experience*, 499–500; *KE*, 245, 157; James H. Taylor and Elizabeth Sue Wake, *"A Bright Shining City Set on a Hill": A Centennial History* (Williamsburg, KY: Cumberland College, 1988), 13, 48–112; Badgett, *History of Campbellsville University*, 68–107.

24. Ellis, *A History of Eastern Kentucky University*, 16–19; *KE*, 178.

25. *KE,* 178; Montgomery, "Rackyte Cax, Cowax, Cowax," 159, 250; Craig, *Centre College of Kentucky,* 89–90; Kitty Rogers Baird, "Women in Physical Education and Sports at Centre College, 1854–1978" (specialist in education thesis, Eastern Kentucky Univ., 1978), 1, 11, 38–39; Hardin and Hill, *Our Standard Sure,* 50–72.

26. Perkinson, *The Imperfect Panacea,* 136–37; Adams, "Central Kentucky Colleges," 119.

27. A Carnegie Foundation retiree, at least sixty-five years old with thirty years of service or more, received a pension based on one-half of the average of the person's salaries of the last five years of service. *KE,* 177–78; Adams, "Central Kentucky Colleges," 119–23, 127, 130–37, 200.

28. *KE,* 14, 896; Adams, "Central Kentucky Colleges," 46, 52, 54; Ward, *A Literary History of Kentucky,* 44; Wright, *Transylvania,* 243–46; Stevenson, *Lexington Theological Seminary,* 110–17.

29. *KE,* 515; Adams, "Central Kentucky Colleges," 77, 84–85, 208; Wright, *Transylvania,* 336–43; Stevenson, *Lexington Theological Seminary,* 165–204.

30. *KE,* 35, 516, 559, 859–60; Wallis and Tapp, *A Sesqui-Centennial History of Kentucky,* 632–36; Paul D. Ransdell, "Understanding Organizational Spirit in a Higher Education Context: A Case Study of Lindsey Wilson College" (Ed.D. diss., Peabody College of Vanderbilt Univ., 2000), 3–4, 30–33, 37, 79–80.

31. Dew and Weiss, *In Pursuit of the Dream,* 85, 91–99; Hamlett, *History of Education in Kentucky,* 298.

32. *KE:* 516, 569; Dew and Weiss, *In Pursuit of the Dream,* 99–149.

33. *KE,* 35–36; Joseph A. Thacker Jr., *Asbury College: Vision and Miracle* (Nappanee, IN: Evangel Press, 1990), 1–173; Michael Alexander Longinow, "Mysterious and Spontaneous Power: Shaping of an Evangelical Culture for Revivalist Higher Education in Henry Clay Morrison's *Pentecostal Herald*" (Ph.D. diss., Univ. of Kentucky, 1996), 362–65; Rogers, "A Study of Henry Clay Morrison," 118–20, 123–24, 126, 142, 160.

34. *KE,* 72, 359; Harrison and Klotter, *A New History of Kentucky,* 381–82; Klotter, *Kentucky,* 153–54; Adams, "Central Kentucky Colleges," 182–83, 188.

35. Wilson, *Berea College,* 75–101; Sandra Diane Hayslette, "'Not at the Top, but Climbing': Teaching and Learning about Appalachia and Identity at Berea College, 1920–1940" (Ph.D. diss., Univ. of North Carolina at Chapel Hill, 2002), 1–2.

36. Hayslette, "Not at the Top, but Climbing," 39–40; Wilson, *Berea College,* 103–4.

37. Hayslette, "Not at the Top, but Climbing," 43–52; Wilson, *Berea College,* 107–19.

38. *KE,* 13; Hilton, "The Leaders Are Here," iii, 8, 15, 17, 19–23, 77, 145, 213; Searles, *A College for Appalachia,* 60–93.

39. *EL,* 165, 841; *KE,* 122–23, 675, 791–92, 838, 880; Wallis and Tapp, *A Sesqui-Centennial History of Kentucky,* 709–10; *Lexington Herald-Leader,* May 29, 2007; Father Clyde Crews, personal communication; Crews, *An American Holy Land,* 213, 254–55.

40. *EL,* 902; Cox and Morison, *The University of Louisville,* 44–49; Sarah P. McNabb, "A History of Campus Planning at the University of Louisville" (master's thesis, Univ. of Louisville, 1999), 9, 10–11.

41. Cox and Morison, *The University of Louisville,* 57–74; Dean R. C. Ernest, *Progress in Engineering Education, 1925–1969* (Louisville: Speed Scientific School,

Univ. of Louisville, 1969), 2, 4, 6; McNabb, "Campus Planning at the University of Louisville," 14.

42. *KE*, 821, 822, 913; *EL*, 822–23; Cox and Morison, *The University of Louisville*, 88–96; Jackson, "Black Public Schooling in Louisville," 255–60; Wellyn F. Collins, "Louisville Municipal College: A Study of the College Founded for Negroes in Louisville, Kentucky" (master's thesis, Univ. of Louisville, 1971), 1–8; Wilson, "A Century of Negro Education in Louisville," 172; Lawrence H. Williams, *Black Higher Education in Kentucky, 1879–1930: The History of Simmons University* (Lewiston, NY: Edwin Mellen Press, 1987), 149–55; Oscar Fitzgerald Galloway, "Higher Education for Negroes in Kentucky" (Ph.D. diss., Univ. of Kentucky, 1931), 178–82; Hudson, "The History of Louisville Municipal College," 27–37.

43. *KE*, 514; Dwight Oliver Wendell Holmes, *The Evolution of the Negro College* (New York: AMS Press, 1970), 151, 153; John A. Hardin, *Fifty Years of Segregation: Black Higher Education in Kentucky, 1904–1954* (Lexington: Univ. Press of Kentucky, 1997), 31–35; Hardin, "Hope versus Reality," 183.

44. *KE*, 514; Gerald L. Smith, *A Black Educator in the Segregated South: Kentucky's Rufus B. Atwood* (Lexington: Univ. Press of Kentucky, 1994), 32–41; Hardin, *Fifty Years of Segregation*, 34–45; Terry Boston Foster, "A Historical Examination of the Changing Mission of Kentucky State University" (Ed.D. diss., Indiana Univ., 1992), 61–62; Hardin, *Onward and Upward*, 17–33.

45. Hardin, "Hope versus Reality," 64; Smith, *A Black Educator in the Segregated South*, 32–35, 41–47: Foster, "Changing Mission of Kentucky State University," 51–55, 91–92; Holmes, *The Evolution of the Negro College*, 151, 187, 199; *Lexington Herald-Leader*, February 25, 2007; Hardin, *Onward and Upward*, 35–41.

46. Klotter, *Kentucky*, 164–65; Talbert, *The University of Kentucky*, 31; Hamlett, *History of Education in Kentucky*, 281.

47. Adams, "Central Kentucky Colleges," 207; H. L. Donovan, "The Evolution of a University," *Filson Club History Quarterly* 21 (1947): 214–15; Wyatt, "Into the Promised Land," 14–15.

48. Hopkins, *The University of Kentucky*, 160–61, 182–83, 211–16; Birdwhistell, "Divided We Fall," 448, 451; Roark to Cherry, July 31, August 20, 1907, box 1, General Letters, Henry Hardin Cherry Papers, Western Kentucky Univ.; Ellis, *A History of Eastern Kentucky University*, 24–25; Wyatt, "Into the Promised Land," 23–24.

49. McVey, *The Gates Open Slowly*, 119; Hopkins, *The University of Kentucky*, 243–61; Cone, *The University of Kentucky*, 38.

50. *KE*, 713; Hopkins, *The University of Kentucky*, 262–70.

51. Kiesel, "Kentucky's Land-Grant Legacy," 11–12, 153–58, 202, 219–38; Hopkins, *The University of Kentucky*, 160–61, 276; Michael J. McCorkle, "Efficiency, Influence, and Leadership: The Transformation of State University, 1903–1940" (Ed.D. diss., Univ. of Kentucky, 2000), 5–6, 169–72.

52. Hopkins, *The University of Kentucky*, 268–79; Talbert, *The University of Kentucky*, 1–2.

53. Solomon, *In the Company of Educated Women*, 53–54; McCorkle, "Efficiency, Influence, and Leadership," 13–15, 41, 60–61, 168; Cone, *The University of Kentucky*, 51–67; Talbert, *The University of Kentucky*, 7–10, 24–34.

54. *KE*, 912; Cone, *The University of Kentucky*, 67–70; Talbert, *The University*

of Kentucky, 35–47; McCorkle, "Efficiency, Influence, and Leadership," 22, 45, 52, 64–67, 82, 97–98.

55. McVey, *The Gates Open Slowly*, 121–23; Cone, *The University of Kentucky*, 67–70; Talbert, *The University of Kentucky*, 35–49; *KE*, 911–12; McCorkle, "Efficiency, Influence, and Leadership," 98–102, 125–42.

56. *KE*, 181–82; Wyatt, "Into the Promised Land," 24–25, 78–82; Ellis, *A History of Eastern Kentucky University*, 21–43; Harrison, *Western Kentucky University*, 19–30; Carl P. Chelf, "A Selective View of the Politics of Higher Education in Kentucky and the Role of H. H. Cherry" (Ph.D. diss., Univ. of Nebraska, 1968), 24–26, 235–50.

57. Wyatt, "Into the Promised Land," 81–84; Harrison, *Western Kentucky University*, 31.

58. Ellis, *A History of Eastern Kentucky University*, 29–58; Wyatt, "Into the Promised Land," 78–86, 99–101; Junius Lathrop Merian, *Normal School Education and Efficiency in Teaching* (New York: Teachers College, Columbia, 1906), 112–13; Harrison, *Western Kentucky University*, 67–71.

59. Thelin, *A History of American Higher Education*, 199–204; Ellis, *A History of Eastern Kentucky University*, 39–41; Harrison, *Western Kentucky University*, 32, 37, 43; Snyder, *A History of Georgetown College*, 90–92; Dew and Weiss, *In Pursuit of the Dream*, 136–38; Talbert, *The University of Kentucky*, 50–51.

60. Rudolph, *The American College and University*, 487.

61. Talbert, *The University of Kentucky*, 51–61; *KE*, 196; McCorkle, "Efficiency, Influence, and Leadership," 170–74, 186; Taff, *History of State Revenue and Taxation in Kentucky*, 82–84.

62. McCorkle, "Efficiency, Influence, and Leadership," 168–71; Susan H. Gooden, "Tuning the Local Network to a National Channel: Educational Leadership and the College of Education at the University of Kentucky, 1917–27," *Register of the Kentucky Historical Society* 93 (Summer 1995): 307–20.

63. Talbert, *The University of Kentucky*, 68–70; McCorkle, "Efficiency, Influence, and Leadership," 185–88; Gooden, "Turning the Local Network to a National Channel," 320–32.

64. McCorkle, "Efficiency, Influence, and Leadership," 181–84, 199–201; McVey, *A University Is a Place*, 112–21; John Russell Groves Jr., "An Examination of Major Initiatives in Campus Planning at the University of Kentucky, 1919–1991" (Ph.D. diss., Univ. of Kentucky, 1992), 20–34; Talbert, *The University of Kentucky*, 76–80; Terry L. Birdwhistell, e-mail to the author, December 21, 2008.

65. Pangburn, *The Evolution of the American Teachers College*, 11–12, 93; Richard Hofstadter and C. Dewitt Hardy, *The Development and Scope of Higher Education in the United States* (New York: Columbia Univ. Press, 1952), 95–96; *KE*, 850; Harrison and Klotter, *A New History of Kentucky*, 396–97; Harrison, *Western Kentucky University*, 57, 59; Ellis, *A History of Eastern Kentucky University*, 43–45; Wyatt, "Into the Promised Land," 113–37, 142–46; Talbert, *The University of Kentucky*, 69–70; Herbst, *And Sadly Teach*, 151.

66. Klotter, *Kentucky*, 166–67; Wyatt, "Into the Promised Land," 118–33, 145; *KE*, 644, 649, 664, 873; Ralph H. Woods and members of the faculty, *Murray State University: Fifty Years of Progress, 1922–1972* (Murray, KY: Murray State Univ., 1973),

1–13; Flatt, *A Light to the Mountains*, 29–36; Harry Eugene Rose, "The Historical Development of a State College: Morehead Kentucky State College" (Ed.D. diss., Univ. of Cincinnati, 1965), 71–86, 128, 131–56.

67. *KE*, 23.

68. Ellis, "The Kentucky Evolution Controversy," 56–57; McVey, *A University Is a Place*, 17–25.

69. Dew and Weiss, *In Pursuit of the Dream*, 144–46; Snyder, *A History of Georgetown College*, 99; Longinow, "Mysterious and Spontaneous Power," 222–25; Rose, "The Historical Development of a State College," 187–88; Ellis, "The Kentucky Evolution Controversy," 95.

70. *KE*, 553, 584, 834; Ellis, "*A Man of Books and a Man of the People*," 105–23; Wright, *Transylvania*, 336–63; Rogers, "A Study of Henry Clay Morrison," 3, 160, 163, 165, 169–70, 178, 191.

71. *KE*, 113, 326; *EL*, 113–14; Thelin, *A History of American Higher Education*, 148–150, 152, 240–41; Cox and Morison, *The University of Louisville*, 53–56.

72. *EL*, 212; Cox and Morison, *The University of Louisville*, 75–76; Gooden, "Tuning the Local Network to a National Channel," 314.

73. *EL*, 212, 346; Doyle, Layson, and Thompson, *From the Fort to the Future*, 186–87; Cox and Morrison, *The University of Louisville*, 75–76.

74. *EL*, 212; Cox and Morison, *The University of Louisville*, 78–87; Doyle, Layson, and Thompson, *From the Fort to the Future*, 187.

75. *KE*, 79, 217–18; George W. Robinson, ed., *Bert Combs the Politician: An Oral History* (Lexington: Univ. Press of Kentucky, 1991), 2–3, 10–13; Albert B. Chandler, *Heroes, Plain Folks, and Skunks: The Life and Times of Happy Chandler* (Chicago: Bonus Books, 1989), 21.

76. Hilton, "The Leaders Are Here," 73–77.

77. Hayslette, "Not at the Top, but Climbing," 279–86, 332–33, 385–90.

78. Ellis, *A History of Eastern Kentucky University*, 56–57.

79. Baird, "Women in Physical Education," 39.

80. Birdwhistell, "An Educated Difference," 35, 38–40, 40–42, 60–66, 70–71, 162–63.

81. Carolyn Terry Bashaw, "'To Serve the People of the State of Kentucky': Sarah Gibson Blanding and the Development of Administrative Skill, 1923–1941," *Filson Club History Quarterly* 65 (April 1991): 281–301; Birdwhistell, "An Educated Difference," 121–25, 161–62; Ellis, *A History of Eastern Kentucky University*, 32, 36–37, 45–47, 56, 63–64.

82. Montgomery, "Rackyte Cax, Cowax Cowax," 107, 109, 111, 115, 121, 135, 143, 144, 150, 155, 178, 246; Morelock, *Taking the Town*, 2–11, 245–84; Hardin and Hill, *Our Standard Sure*, 169–70.

83. *KE*, 265–66, 787; Kindred, *Basketball*, 71–95, 115–24; Stanley, *Before Big Blue*, 128–33; Rose, "The Historical Development of a State College," 222; Ellis, *A History of Eastern Kentucky University*, 72–73, 82–83, 92, 95–97, 100.

84. *KE*, 178; John Y. Brown Sr., *Legend of the Praying Colonels* (Louisville: J. Marvin Gray, n.d.), 47–69; Chandler, *Heroes, Plain Folks, and Skunks*, 39–43.

85. *KE*, 218–19; Ellis, *A History of Eastern Kentucky University*, 52–53.

86. Thelin, *A History of American Higher Education*, 208–11; John R. Thelin,

Games Colleges Play: Scandal and Reform in Intercollegiate Athletics (Baltimore: Johns Hopkins Univ. Press, 1994), 13–67; *KE*, 793; Stanley, *Before Big Blue*, 151–54; Talbert, *The University of Kentucky*, 98–100, 113–14; Cone, *The University of Kentucky*, 105, 159–60; Ellis, *A History of Eastern Kentucky University*, 71, 81–82, 132.

87. Ellis, *A History of Eastern Kentucky University*, 73–75; Cone, *The University of Kentucky*, 99; Cox and Morison, *The University of Louisville*, 106–7; Harrison, *Western Kentucky University*, 93–96.

88. Ellis, *A History of Eastern Kentucky University*, 74–75; Hiram Brock Jr., interview by author, May 29, 1987.

89. Rose, "The Historical Development of a State College," 221, 226–28, 299–302; Flatt, *A Light to the Mountains*, 61–83.

90. Wright, *Transylvania*, 364–75; Dew and Weiss, *In Pursuit of the Dream*, 151–75.

91. Fields, *A Sesquicentennial History of Georgetown College*, 11–13, 15; Snyder, *A History of Georgetown College*, 98–99, 105–10.

92. Snyder, *A History of Georgetown College*, 106–7, 109; Porter, "Georgetown College and Its Relation to Kentucky Baptists," 9; Fields, *A Sesquicentennial History of Georgetown College*, 15.

93. Porter, "Georgetown College and Its Relation to Kentucky Baptists," 9; Fields, *A Sesquicentennial History of Georgetown College*, 15; Apple, Johnston, and Bevins, *Scott County*, 347; Snyder, *A History of Georgetown College*, 109–10, 116.

94. Blakey, *Hard Times and New Deal in Kentucky*, 74–77, 93–95, 199; Ellis, *A History of Eastern Kentucky University*, 78–81; Harrison, *Western Kentucky University*, 98–99; Cox and Morison, *The University of Louisville*, 102–3.

95. Thomas D. Clark, *My Century in History: Memoirs* (Lexington: Univ. Press of Kentucky, 2006), 184; "Gleanings from the Kentucky Kernel," *Kentucky Alumni* 78 (Spring 2007): 41; Talbert, *The University of Kentucky*, 92–129; David O. Levine, *The American Colleges and the Culture of Aspiration, 1915–1940* (Ithaca, NY: Cornell Univ. Press, 1986), 185–201; Malcolm M. Willey, *Depression, Recovery, and Higher Education: A Report by the Committee Y of the American Association of University Professors* (New York: McGraw-Hill, 1937), 454–504; *Statistical Abstract of the United States, 1942*, 142.

96. Erin Brisbay, "College Women in the 1930's: The Possibilities and the Realities," *Filson Club History Quarterly* 64 (January 1990): 32–59; Birdwhistell, "An Educated Difference," 166.

97. Ellis, *A History of Eastern Kentucky University*, 76–77, 86–87; Flatt, *A Light to the Mountains*, 68–69; Donovan to A. L. Crabb, January 23, 1932; Donovan to Joseph Rosier, March 12, 1934; "Summary of Facts regarding the Eastern Kentucky State Teachers College," all in box 91, Donovan Papers, Eastern Kentucky Univ. Archives.

98. Klotter, *Kentucky*, 309; Harrison, *Kentucky's Governors*, 171; Harrison, *Western Kentucky University*, 74–75, 90–91; Ellis, *A History of Eastern Kentucky University*, 77; Woods et al., *Murray State University*, 515.

99. *KE*, 851; Hackensmith, *Out of Time and Tide*, 216–17; Harrison and Klotter, *A New History of Kentucky*, 396; Klotter, *Kentucky*, 301; Adron Doran, "The Work of the Council on Public Higher Education in Kentucky" (Ed.D. diss., Univ. of

Kentucky, 1950), 53–59, 151–53, 163–66; Cathy Lynn Cole, "A Historical Perspective of the Kentucky Council on Higher Education" (Ph.D. diss., Southern Illinois Univ., 1983), 43–47, 60–61.

100. "Preliminary Statement of Conference between Governor Chandler and the Presidents of the State-Supported Colleges," March 24, 1936; Council on Public Higher Education in Kentucky Minutes, March 24, 1936, both in box 91, Eastern Kentucky Univ. Archives; Ellis, *A History of Eastern Kentucky University*, 86–88; Harrison, *Western Kentucky University*, 92–93; Talbert, *The University of Kentucky*, 111; Nathan Robert Myers, "Higher Education's Perfect System? State Planning for Colleges and Universities in Kentucky, 1930–1965" (Ph.D. diss., Univ. of Kentucky, 2005), 25–28.

101. Klotter, *Kentucky*, 308–9; Harrison and Klotter, *A New History of Kentucky*, 367–69; Donovan to Chandler, December 14, 1936, Donovan Papers, Eastern Kentucky Univ. Archives; Harrison, *Kentucky's Governors*, 171; Harrison, *Western Kentucky University*, 92–93.

102. Harrison, *Western Kentucky University*, 103–7; *KE*, 943.

103. Harrison, *Western Kentucky University*, 108–11; Klotter, "Promise, Pessimism, and Perseverance," 55.

104. Wyatt, "Into the Promised Land," 146–48; Harrison, *Kentucky's Governors*, 172–73; Harrison, *Western Kentucky University*, 135; Ellis, *A History of Eastern Kentucky University*, 86–88.

105. Clark, *My Century in History*, 129–30, 132, 163, 174, 177, 178–79, 216; Thomas D. Clark, "Part II: Commentary," *Register of the Kentucky Historical Society* 103 (Winter–Spring 2005): 377–78; Donovan, "The Evolution of a University," 217–18; McCorkle, "Efficiency, Influence, and Leadership," 227–28; Talbert, *The University of Kentucky*, 127–33; Myers, "Higher Education's Perfect System?" 34–37.

106. Talbert, *The University of Kentucky*, 133–36; Ellis, *A History of Eastern Kentucky University*, 89–90; McCorkle, "Efficiency, Influence, and Leadership," 228–33.

107. *KE*, 660; Harrison, *Kentucky's Governors*, 177–80; Ellis, *A History of Eastern Kentucky University*, 90; Mary F. Richards, interview by author, July 22, 1986; Martha K. Barksdale, interview by author, November 17, 1987; Chelf, "Politics of Higher Education in Kentucky," 246; McCorkle, "Efficiency, Influence, and Leadership," 233–35; Clark, "Part II, Commentary," 381–82.

108. Harrison and Klotter, *A New History of Kentucky*, 366; Calvin B. T. Lee, *The Campus Scene, 1900–1970* (New York: David McKay, 1970), 61–65; Cox and Morison, *The University of Louisville*, 104–5, 204–7.

109. Wright, *A History of Blacks in Kentucky*, 2:169–77; Chandler to Donovan, June 29, 1939; Donovan to McVey, June 12, 1939, Donovan Papers, Eastern Kentucky Univ. Archives; McVey, *The Gates Open Slowly*, 156–59; Hardin, *Fifty Years of Segregation*, 61–65; Michael Dennis, "The Illusion of Relevance: Southern Progressives and American Higher Education," *Journal of the Historical Society* 8 (June 2008): 229–71.

110. Klotter, *Kentucky*, 66–68, 241–44; Harrison and Klotter, *A New History of Kentucky*, 434; Wright, *A History of Blacks in Kentucky*, 2:89–90, 101–2; Ellis, Everman, and Sears, *Madison County*, 321–22; Tom McHone, interview by author, July 4, 1984.

111. Thelin, *A History of American Higher Education*, 78; Hopkins, *The University of Kentucky*, 59–64; Talbert, *The University of Kentucky*, 23, 51, 53–54, 140; Harrison, *Western Kentucky University*, 83; Woods et al., *Murray State University*, 130–31; Ellis, *A History of Eastern Kentucky University*, 88–89.

112. Ellis, *A History of Eastern Kentucky University*, 88–89; 91–92; Woods et al., *Fifty Years of Progress*, 129.

Chapter 7. Elementary and Secondary Education from World War II to the Threshold of Major Reform

1. Jeanne Boydston et al., *Making the Nation: The United States and Its People* (Upper Saddle River, NJ: Prentice Hall, 2002), 713–19.

2. Harrison and Klotter, *A New History of Kentucky*, 370–73.

3. Wendell P. Butler, *History of Education in Kentucky, 1939–1964* (Frankfort: Department of Education, 1963), 25–26; Harrison, *Kentucky's Governors*, 178; *KE*, 219; Schacter, *Kentucky on the March*, 118, 160–61; Frederick D. Ogden, ed., *The Public Papers of Governor Keen Johnson, 1939–1943* (Lexington: Univ. Press of Kentucky, 1982), 160; Doyle, Layson, and Thompson, *From the Fort to the Future*, 366.

4. McVey, *The Gates Open Slowly*, 251–53, Butler, *History of Education in Kentucky*, 27, 29, 31–45, 71; *Louisville Courier-Journal*, November 5, 6, 7, 1941; Ogden, *The Public Papers of Governor Johnson*, 128–29, 160.

5. McVey, *The Gates Open Slowly*, 251; Butler, *History of Education in Kentucky, 1939–1964*, 31–32, 39; Ogden, *The Public Papers of Governor Johnson*, 121, 129, 164–65, 232; Beauchamp, *The Kentucky School for the Deaf*, 25; *EL*, 478–79; *KE*, 511–12.

6. Butler, *History of Education in Kentucky*, 69–70; Howard W. Beers, *Kentucky: Designs for Her Future* (Lexington: Univ. of Kentucky Press, 1945), 243–44.

7. *EL*, 213–14; Schacter, *Kentucky on the March*, 60–61; Klotter, *Kentucky*, 337–39.

8. Harrison, *Kentucky's Governors*, 182–84; Klotter, *Kentucky*, 322–24; Doyle, Layson, and Thompson, *From the Fort to the Future*, 292; *Louisville Courier-Journal*, November 3, 4, 5, 6, 1943; Philip H. Losey, "The Election and Administration of Governor Simeon Willis, 1943–1947" (master's thesis, Eastern Kentucky Univ., 1978), 15–27.

9. Klotter, *Kentucky*, 337–38; Beers, *Kentucky*, v–vi, 223–52.

10. Doyle, Layson, and Thompson, *From the Fort to the Future*, 276–78.

11. Harrison, *Kentucky's Governors*, 183; Butler, *History of Education in Kentucky*, 53–75; Klotter, *Kentucky*, 324–27, 329; John Fred Williams, *Education on the March: A Progress Report* (Frankfort: Department of Education, 1947), 357–406; Losey, "The Election and Administration of Governor Simeon Willis," 30–85.

12. Klotter, *Kentucky*, 330–32; Harrison, *Kentucky's Governors*, 185–90; Butler, *History of Education in Kentucky*, 81–82; John Ed Pearce, *Divide and Dissent: Kentucky Politics, 1930–1963* (Lexington: Univ. Press of Kentucky, 1987), 50; *Louisville Courier-Journal*, November 5, 6, 1947.

13. Butler, *History of Education in Kentucky*, 82–83, 86, 91; Klotter, *Kentucky*, 331–33; Harrison, *Kentucky's Governors*, 186–89; Charlie Bush, ed. *A Citizen's Guide to the Kentucky Constitution*, Research Report no. 137 (Frankfort: Legislative Research Commission, 1989), 129; *Louisville Courier-Journal*, November 9, 10, 11, 1949.

14. Harrison, *Kentucky's Governors*, 188–89; Butler, *History of Education in Kentucky*, 83–85; Harrison and Klotter, *A New History of Kentucky*, 331–33; Doyle, Layson, and Thompson, *From the Fort to the Future*, 293–95; *Louisville Courier-Journal*, March 15, 1950.

15. Doyle, Layson, and Thompson, *From the Fort to the Future*, 279–81; Schacter, *Kentucky on the March*, 61–62; Butler, *History of Education in Kentucky*, 89, 96, 101, 108–9; *Louisville Courier-Journal*, March 11, 1950.

16. *KE*, 206; Harrison and Klotter, *A New History of Kentucky*, 401–2; Harrison, *Kentucky's Governors*, 192; Butler, *History of Education in Kentucky*, 85; John E. Kleber, ed., *The Public Papers of Governor Lawrence W. Wetherby, 1950–1955* (Lexington: Univ. Press of Kentucky, 1983), 2–3, 18–23, 26, 251–52; *Louisville Courier-Journal*, March 6, 7, 13, 15, 1951.

17. Butler, *History of Education in Kentucky*, 115; Harrison, *Kentucky's Governors*, 193–95; *Louisville Courier-Journal*, November 7, 1951; Kleber, *Papers of Wetherby*, 252–53.

18. Harrison, *Kentucky's Governors*, 193–95; Harrison and Klotter, *A New History of Kentucky*, 402; Kleber, *Papers of Wetherby*, 22, 260–62.

19. *KE*, 641; Hopkins, *KEA*, 48–51; Doyle, Layson, and Thompson, *From the Fort to the Future*, 291, 305–10; *Louisville Courier-Journal*, November 2, 4, 6, 1953; Kleber, *Papers of Wetherby*, 260–61.

20. *KE*, 641; Hopkins, *KEA*, 48–51; *The Constitution of the Commonwealth of Kentucky*, 192; Doyle, Layson, and Thompson, *From the Fort to the Future*, 306–11; Butler, *History of Education in Kentucky*, 118, 123–38; Kleber, *Papers of Wetherby*, 253, 267.

21. *KE*, 263; Butler, *History of Education in Kentucky*, 99; Gutek, *A History of the Western Education Experience*, 509–10; E. C. Bolmeier, *Landmark Supreme Court Decisions on Public School Issues* (Charlottesville, VA: Michie, 1973), 89–96.

22. Channing, *Kentucky*, 204; Pearce, *Divide and Dissent*, 54; John E. Kleber, "As Luck Would Have It: An Overview of Lawrence W. Wetherby as Governor, 1950–1955," *Register of the Kentucky Historical Society* 84 (Autumn 1986): 414–16; Kleber, *Papers of Wetherby*, 262–63, 264–65; Reese, *America's Public Schools*, 226–29.

23. Bush, *Guide to the Kentucky Constitution*, 128; Beauchamp, *The Kentucky School for the Deaf*, 66–67; Butler, *History of Education in Kentucky*, 127.

24. Wright, *A History of Blacks in Kentucky*, 2:197–99; *KE*, 263.

25. Azile Wofford, "Integrated Libraries," *Kentucky School Journal* 34 (December 1955): 16, 33; W. C. Lappin, "The Principal and Integration," *Kentucky School Journal* 34 (September 1955): 10–11, 33.

26. *KE*, 179, 612–13; Harrison and Klotter, *A New History of Kentucky*, 403; Harrison, *Kentucky's Governors*, 173–74; *Louisville Courier-Journal*, November 9, 1955; Malcolm E. Jewell and Everett W. Cunningham, *Kentucky Politics* (Lexington: Univ. of Kentucky Press, 1968), 136.

27. Harrison and Klotter, *A New History of Kentucky*, 388; Wright, *A History of Blacks in Kentucky*, 2:202; Doyle, Layson, and Thompson, *From the Fort to the Future*, 369; David L. Wolfford, "Kentucky after Brown," *Kentucky Humanities* 2 (2003): 16.

28. Butler, *History of Education in Kentucky*, 145–46; Harrison and Klotter, *A New History of Kentucky*, 403–6; Pearce, *Divide and Dissent*, 66–90; *Louisville Courier-Journal*, November 8, 9, 10, 1951; Bert T. Combs, interview, December

17, 1976; Jo M. Ferguson, interview, March 9, 1977; Edward F. Prichard Jr., Oral History Interview by Barry Peel, January 25, 1977; Wendell P. Butler, interview, February 3, 1977, all in Eastern Kentucky Univ. Archives.

29. William J. Reese, *History, Education, and the Schools* (New York: Palgrave Macmillan, 2007), 105–6; Perkinson, *The Imperfect Panacea*, 152–53, 214–16; *Advancing Education in Kentucky: Challenges-Processes-Outcomes, 1956–1957–1958–1959* (Frankfort: Kentucky Department of Education, n.d.), 942–43.

30. Butler, *A History of Education in Kentucky*, 146–74; Pearce, *Divide and Dissent*, 68; Harrison, *Kentucky's Governors*, 174; Harrison and Klotter, *A New History of Kentucky*, 405–6; Doyle, Layson, and Thompson, *From the Fort to the Future*, 310–11; *Advancing Education in Kentucky*, 885.

31. *KE:* 612–13; *Advancing Education in Kentucky*, 837, 865–67, 882–85, 900–903, 917, 973; R. E. Jaggers, "Rights and Realities," *Kentucky School Journal* 33 (March 1955): 7–8; *Louisville Courier-Journal*, September 20, 1956.

32. J. Marvin Dodson and Richard Van Hoose, interviews by Barry Peel, December 17, 1976, Eastern Kentucky Univ. Archives.

33. David L. Wolfford, "Resistance on the Border: School Desegregation in Western Kentucky, 1954–1964," *Ohio Valley History* 4 (Summer 2004): 41–42, 61; *Louisville Courier-Journal*, April 14, September 13, 14, 1955, September 9, October 21, 1956; *Hoops and Dreams: The Road to Equality in Sports*, a video by Angela Hardin about the Powell County Schools, 2006, copy in author's possession.

34. *Louisville Courier-Journal*, September 5–6, 8–9, 1956; Wolfford, "Kentucky after Brown," 16–17.

35. *Louisville Courier-Journal*, September 11–23, 25, 28–30, 1956; J. Harvie Wilkinson III, *From Brown to Bakke: The Supreme Court and School Integration, 1954–1978* (New York: Oxford Univ. Press, 1979), 63–64.

36. When asked how he wished to be remembered at the conclusion of the interview, Chandler said, with characteristic bravado, "I want you to say I was sober and I meant to do every damn thing I did." Albert B. Chandler, Oral History Interview, October 7, 1980, Eastern Kentucky Univ. Archives; Chandler, *Heroes, Plain Folks, and Skunks*, 173–242; *KE*, 179.

37. *Louisville Courier-Journal*, September 18, 19, 23, 1956; *KE*, 263; Harrison and Klotter, *A New History of Kentucky*, 388; *Lexington Herald-Leader*, May 17, 2004; Wright, *A History of Blacks in Kentucky*, 2:202–3; Wolfford, "Resistance on the Border," 41–62; Wolfford, "Kentucky after Brown," 15–16.

38. *EL*, 148–49, 160; *KE*, 164–65; Omer Carmichael and Weldon James, *The Louisville Story* (New York: Simon and Schuster, 1957), 70–72.

39. *KE*, 808; Carmichael and James, *The Louisville Story*, 14–15, 23–24, 30–35; Wright, *A History of Blacks in Kentucky*, 2:185, 196; Yater, *Two Hundred Years at the Falls of the Ohio*, 219–20.

40. Carmichael and James, *The Louisville Story*, 42–44; *Louisville Courier-Journal*, June 27, 1954; *EL*, 111; Yater, *Two Hundred Years at the Falls of the Ohio*, 225.

41. *EL*, 160; *KE*, 164–65; Wright, *A History of Blacks in Kentucky*, 2:203–4; Carmichael and James, *The Louisville Story*, 79–118; *Louisville Courier-Journal*, September 11, 12, 13, 18, 21, 1956; August 1, 2006; Yater, *Two Hundred Years at the Falls of the Ohio*, 225–26.

42. Harrison and Klotter, *A New History of Kentucky*, 388; Carmichael and James, *The Louisville Story*, 118–49; Wright, *A History of Blacks in Kentucky*, 2:204; *KE*, 262; *Louisville Courier-Journal*, September 13, 14, 1955.

43. *KE*, 507; Doyle, *Recalling the Record*, 356; *Lexington Herald-Leader*, February 13, 2008; Robinson, *The Bond-Washington Story*, 36–39, 95–105; *Louisville Courier-Journal*, April 14, 1955.

44. *Louisville Courier-Journal*, March 1–3, 1958; Butler, *History of Education in Kentucky*, 155–56; *Lexington Herald-Leader*, September 2, 2007; February 24, 2008; *Advancing Education in Kentucky*, 938–40.

45. Wright, *A History of Blacks in Kentucky*, 2:199, 201, 205; *EL*, 518; for the brief operation of a state-funded residential high school after the closure of Lincoln Institute, see Gayle Webb Ecton, "A History of the Lincoln School, Simpsonville, Kentucky, 1966–1970" (Ed.D. diss., Univ. of Kentucky, 1979).

46. *KE*, 58; *Lexington Herald-Leader*, March 23, 2008; David Wolfford, "Louis Stout," *Kentucky Monthly* (February 2007): 48–49, 51; Kindred, *Basketball*, 59–64; Wolfford, "Kentucky after Brown," 17–18; for information about pre-integration African American high school sports, see Louis Stout, *Shadows of the Past: A History of the Kentucky High School Athletic League* (Lexington: Host Communications, 2006).

47. Harrison, *Kentucky's Governors*, 198–99; Clark, "Kentucky Education," 195; Harrison and Klotter, *A New History of Kentucky*, 407–8; Robinson, *Bert Combs the Politician*, 100–101; Jewell and Cunningham, *Kentucky Politics*, 136–37.

48. Harrison, *Kentucky's Governors*, 198; Harrison and Klotter, *A New History of Kentucky*, 406–10; Pearce, *Divide and Dissent*, 110–45; Robinson, *Bert Combs the Politician*, 102–3, 106, 115, 119; *Louisville Courier-Journal*, February 19, 1960.

49. *KE*, 172–73; Doyle, Layson, and Thompson, *From the Fort to the Future*, 321–23; Pearce, *Divide and Dissent*, 126–28.

50. Doyle, Layson, and Thompson, *From the Fort to the Future*, 270, 323–26; *First Report of the Commission on Public Education* (Frankfort: Commonwealth of Kentucky, December 1961), 1–67.

51. *KE*, 146, 497–98; Butler, *History of Education in Kentucky*, 179–227: Ellis, *A History of Eastern Kentucky University*, 118; Prichard interview, January 25, 1977.

52. Butler, *History of Education in Kentucky*, 207–8; Reese, *History, Education, and the Schools*, 106.

53. *KE*, 172–73, 801, 904; Ronald Eller, *Uneven Ground: Appalachia since 1945* (Lexington; Univ. Press of Kentucky, 2008), 156–57; Caudill, *Night Comes to the Cumberlands*, 334–38; Pearce, *Divide and Dissent*, 50.

54. Harrison, *Kentucky's Governors*, 198–99; Pearce, *Divide and Dissent*, 129–33, 171; Clark, "Kentucky Education," 198–99; *Louisville Courier-Journal*, February 28, 1960.

55. *KE*, 519, 800–801; Doyle, Layson, and Thompson, *From the Fort to the Future*, 200–205; Elam, "That's Just The Way It Was," chap. 7; Paul D. Blanchard, "Conflict and Cohesion in Small Groups: A Comparative Study of Kentucky School Boards" (Ph.D. diss., Univ. of Kentucky, 1973), 2, 23, 32, 56–57, 68, 181; John W. Smith, interview by author, March 27, 2002; Forniss Park, private conversations, December 7, 2006; February 24, 2009; Sohn et al., *Education in Appalachia's Central Highlands*, 424–26.

56. Harrison and Klotter, *A New History of Kentucky*, 391–92.

57. Jackie Couture, e-mail to the author, October 23, 2007.

58. "Building a Program for the One-Teacher School," *Education Bulletin* (August 1947): 144–48; Elam, "That's Just the Way It Was," 119; *KE*, 696–97, 801; Jack E. Weller, *Yesterday's People: Life in Contemporary Appalachia* (Lexington: Univ. of Kentucky Press, 1965), 14, 22, 26, 107–13; John Fetterman, *Stinking Creek* (New York: E. P. Dutton, 1967), 101–10.

59. Adell English Martin, e-mail to the author, August 24, 2006.

60. Marshall Myers, e-mail to the author, November 28, 2005; Marshall Myers, "Mr. Grisso, Oolite School, and Eternity," *Back Home in Kentucky* (January–February 2003): 25, 32; Rennick, *Kentucky Place Names*, 221.

61. Rodney B. Piercey, e-mails to the author, November 25, 28, 2008; *Richmond Register*, September 28, 2008.

62. *KE*, 696, 801. For the most complete history of the one-room school, see Hartford, *The Little White Schoolhouse*.

63. Harrison and Klotter, *A New History of Kentucky*, 411–13; Harrison, *Kentucky's Governors*, 200–205; Doyle, Layson, and Thompson, *From the Fort to the Future*, 353; *Richmond Register*, October 15, 2003.

64. Harrison, *Kentucky's Governors*, 200–205; Harrison and Klotter, *A New History of Kentucky*, 411–13; *KE*, 498; *Louisville Courier-Journal*, March 2, 18, 20, 21, 1966.

65. Harrison and Klotter, *A New History of Kentucky*, 412; *Lexington Herald-Leader*, May 17, 2004; Wright, *A History of Blacks in Kentucky*, 2:204–5; *Annual Survey and Progress Report: Integration in the Public Schools of Kentucky* (Frankfort: State Department of Education, October 10, 1965), 2, 5–8, 10–22, 33–37; *Louisville Courier-Journal*, March 18, 1966.

66. Wright, *A History of Blacks in Kentucky*, 2:205–10; Doyle, *Recalling the Record*, 356, 376; Shackelford and Weinberg, *Our Appalachia*, 313; Jewell Gaton Lay, Oral History Interview by David R. Davis, October 8, 1980, Eastern Kentucky Univ. Archives and Special Collections; Doyle, Layson, and Thompson, *From the Fort to the Future*, 253; *KE*, 474–75; Wade Hall, *The Rest of the Dream: The Black Odyssey of Lyman Johnson* (Lexington: Univ. Press of Kentucky, 1988), 72–73; *Louisville Courier-Journal*, September 10, October 7, 1959.

67. Fairclough, *A Class of Their Own*, 400–405, 408–19; Wright, *A History of Blacks in Kentucky*, 2:209–10.

68. Linda Cornett, "The Desegregation of Teachers in Kentucky, 1954–1968," a paper presented in History 712, Univ. of Kentucky, December 11, 1991, 1–29; Kentucky Commission on Human Rights, *Kentucky Black Teacher Gap: An Analysis of Teacher Employment, 1954–1974* (Frankfort: Commonwealth of Kentucky, 1981), 1; *Kentucky Revised Statutes, July 1962* (Frankfort: Legislative Research Commission, 1962), 2:25.

69. Cornett, "The Desegregation of Teachers in Kentucky," 29–44.

70. *Louisville Courier-Journal*, March 2, 18, 25, 1966; Harrison, *Kentucky's Governors*, 203–4, 207–20; Harrison and Klotter, *A New History of Kentucky*, 413–15; Jewell and Cunningham, *Kentucky Politics*, 115–18; Klotter interview, February 28, 2008.

71. Harrison and Klotter, *A New History of Kentucky*, 414–15; Harrison, *Kentucky's Governors*, 207–8; David V. Hawpe, interview by author, November 27, 2006;

Robert F. Sexton and Lewis Bellardo Jr., eds., *The Public Papers of Governor Louis B. Nunn, 1967–1971* (Lexington: Univ. Press of Kentucky, 1975), 352–56.

72. *KE*, 498; Doyle, Layson, and Thompson, *From the Fort to the Future*, 292–301; *Louisville Courier-Journal*, February 25, 1960.

73. *KE*, 498, 685–66; Doyle, Layson, and Thompson, *From the Fort to the Future*, 292–301; *Louisville Courier-Journal*, February 25, 1960; Ornstein and Levine, *Foundations of Education*, 43–45; Sexton and Bellardo, *Public Papers of Nunn*, 573–78; Dana F. Beane, "A History of Efforts by the Kentucky Education Association toward Passage of a Professional Negotiations Law in the Kentucky General Assembly, 1968–1976" (Ed.D. diss., Univ. of Kentucky, 1978), 11–31.

74. Kentucky Education Association (KEA), *Beyond the Minimum, . . . A New Dimension for Kentucky's Foundation Program for Education: A Report by the KEA Committee for the Study of the Foundation Program* (Louisville: KEA, 1967), frontispiece, 4–6, 93–96; *EL*, 910.

75. Kentucky Education Association, *Beyond the Minimum*, 2, 12–17.

76. Ibid., 23–28, 30–31, 37–74, 77–81, 121–25; Harrison, *Kentucky's Governors*, 202–3; *Louisville Courier-Journal*, March 25, 1966; *KE*, 287; John R. Burch Jr., *Owsley County, Kentucky, and the Perpetuation of Poverty* (Jefferson, NC: McFarland, 2008), 40–41, 150.

77. Kentucky Education Association, *Beyond the Minimum*, 83–92, 126–31.

78. Harrison, *Kentucky's Governors*, 211–12; Robinson, *Bert Combs the Politician*, 187–91; Harrison and Klotter, *A New History of Kentucky*, 415; *Lexington Herald-Leader*, March 2, 1999; *Louisville Courier-Journal*, November 2, 1971.

79. *KE*, 24–25, 25–26, 716–77; Harrison and Klotter, *A New History of Kentucky*, 410; Eller, *Uneven Ground*, 31–32, 41–42, 52, 55, 75, 77, 80.

80. Eller, *Uneven Ground*, 26, 75, 100–101, 182–83, 187–88, 232–37; Elam, "That's Just the Way It Was," 178–80.

81. *KE*, 13, 425, 433, 724; Stoddart, *Challenge and Change in Appalachia*, 206–24; John W. Smith interview, March 27, 2002.

82. Woods et al., *Murray State University*, 385–407; Steven Connelly, "The Importance of Local Control in Educational Decisions: Fact or Folklore? A Study of the Merger of the Berea Independent School District with the Berea College Schools in 1966" (master's thesis, Eastern Kentucky Univ., 1996), 1–52.

83. Harrison, *Kentucky's Governors*, 211–18; Harrison and Klotter, *A New History of Kentucky*, 415; *Lexington Herald-Leader*, March 2, 1999; W. Landis Jones, ed., *The Public Papers of Wendell H. Ford, 1971–1974* (Lexington: Univ. Press of Kentucky, 1978), 213–16, 226; Beane, "Efforts by the Kentucky Education Association," 59–71.

84. Doyle, Layson, and Thompson, *From the Fort to the Future*, 216–17, 372; *KE*, 311–12, 716–17; Linda Jean Carpenter and R. Vivian Acosta, *Title IX* (Champaign, IL: Human Kinetics, 2005), 3–31; *Louisville Courier-Journal*, November 7, 1973; March 19, 1980.

85. Doyle, Layson, and Thompson, *From the Fort to the Future*, 326–30; Harrison, *Kentucky's Governors*, 218; Harrison and Klotter, *A New History of Kentucky*, 416; *Louisville Courier-Journal*, March 1, 7, 11, 17, 19, 20, 1978; Beane, "Efforts by the Kentucky Education Association," 93–135.

86. *KE*, 686; Daniel Tysen Smith, "Appalachia's Last One-Room School: A

Case Study" (Ed.D. diss., Univ. of Kentucky, 1988), 9, 94–100, 113–14, 121, 135, 153, 135–62; Sohn et al., *Education in Appalachia's Central Highlands*, 173–204; Alan DeYoung, interview by author, May 6, 2009.

87. Marie T. Doyle, "The Public School Merger Issue in Jefferson County, Kentucky" (Ed.D. diss., Univ. of Kentucky, 1974), 33, 46, 59–61, 67, 84.

88. Wright, *Lexington*, 193–200; David L. Wolfford, "The Fayette County School Integration Controversy, 1971–1972: Removing the Vestiges of Segregation," *Register of the Kentucky Historical Society* 101 (Summer 2003): 244–45, 247–49.

89. Wright, *Lexington*, 199–200; Wolfford, "The Fayette County Integration Controversy," 245–50; Wright, *A History of Blacks in Kentucky*, 2:205; Bolmeier, *Landmark Supreme Court Decisions on Public School Issues*, 179–88; Wilkinson, *From Brown to Bakke*, 126, 136–39; James T. Patterson, *Brown v. Board of Education: A Civil Rights Milestone and Its Troubled Legacy* (New York: Oxford Univ. Press, 2001), 155–59.

90. Wright, *Lexington*, 200; Wolfford, "The Fayette County School Integration Controversy," 250–74; Wolfford, "Kentucky after Brown," 19.

91. *EL*, 111, 916; Harrison and Klotter, *A New History of Kentucky*, 391; James W. Loewen, "Sundown Towns and Counties: Racial Exclusion in the South," *Southern Cultures* 15 (Spring 2009): 23, 26, 29, 31–32, 35. The term *Sundown* came from the warning to blacks that they must leave such a community before nightfall or face dire consequences.

92. Doyle, *Recalling the Record*, 690; *Louisville Courier-Journal*, April 12, 1974; Wright, *A History of Blacks in Kentucky*, 2:310–12; *KE*, 264; *EL*, 111; Harrison and Klotter, *A New History of Kentucky*, 391; Wolfford, "Kentucky after Brown," 19–20; J. David Woodard, "Busing Plans, Media Agendas, and Patterns of White Flight: Nashville, Tennessee, and Louisville, Kentucky" (Ph.D. diss., Vanderbilt Univ., 1978), 53; David V. Hawpe, personal conversation, November 25, 2009.

93. Wright, *A History of Blacks in Kentucky*, 2:211; Harrison and Klotter, *A New History of Kentucky*, 390–91; Harrison, *Kentucky's Governors*, 208.

94. Doyle, *Recalling the Record*, 565–66; *Louisville Courier-Journal*, September 24, 1972.

95. Judith Ann Birkhead, "Consolidation and Desegregation of Public Schools in Jefferson County, Kentucky" (Ed.D. diss., Univ. of Cincinnati, 1978), 173–75, 402–3; John Marshall Thompson, "School Desegregation in Jefferson County, Kentucky, 1954–1975" (Ed.D. diss., Univ. of Kentucky, 1976), 138, 149, 150, 161, 215, 241; *EL*, 148; *Louisville Courier-Journal*, April 2, 4, 1969; Doyle, "Merger Issue in Jefferson County," 118–26; Woodard, "Busing Plans, Media Agendas, and Patterns of White Flight," 139.

96. *Louisville Courier-Journal*, September 24, 1972; Reese, *America's Public Schools*, 246–48; Patterson, *Brown v. Board of Education*, 147–69; Thompson, "School Desegregation in Jefferson County," 172–73; Birkhead, "Consolidation and Desegregation," 181–82.

97. Robert A. Sedler, "The Louisville–Jefferson County School Desegregation Case: A Lawyer's Retrospective," *Register of the Kentucky Historical Society* 105 (Winter 2007): 3–7; *EL*, 148–49.

98. *EL*, 148–49; Wright, *A History of Blacks in Kentucky*, 2:210–11; Doyle,

"Merger Issue in Jefferson County," 97; Doyle, *Recalling the Record*, 589–91, 597–615; *KE*, 379; Thompson, "School Desegregation in Jefferson County," 226; Sedler, "The Louisville–Jefferson County School Desegregation Case," 6–15; Woodard, "Busing Plans, Media Agendas, and Patterns of White Flight," 54.

99. *EL*, 345; *Louisville Courier-Journal*, March 1, July 18, 31, 1975; September 21, 1980; September 4, 2005; Birkhead, "Consolidation and Desegregation," 441–42; Sedler, "The Louisville–Jefferson County School Desegregation Case," 25–27.

100. *Louisville Courier-Journal*, July 29, 30, 31, August 20, 21, 24, 27, 29, 30, October 3, 1975; January 25, 1976; *EL*, 148–49; Wright, *A History of Blacks in Kentucky*, 2:210–11.

101. *Louisville Courier-Journal*, September 3, 4, 5, 6, 7, 8, 1975; September 21, 1980; *EL*, 148–49; Birkhead, "Consolidation and Desegregation," 333–35; Woodard, "Busing Plans, Media Agendas, and Patterns of White Flight," 245.

102. *Louisville Courier-Journal*, October 3, 16, 20, 24, November 23, December 18, 1975; January 13, 1976; September 21, 1980; September 4, 2005; Wright, *A History of Blacks in Kentucky*, 2:210–11; Harrison, *Kentucky's Governors*, 218; *KE*, 379; Sedler, "The Louisville–Jefferson County Desegregation Case," 24–25.

103. Jeanne McCutcheon, e-mail to the author, February 11, 2009; Steve Vest, "Adolescence, Interrupted," *Kentucky Monthly* 7 (September 2005): 80; Steve Vest, e-mail to the author, March 16, 2009; Chris Atzinger, e-mail to the author, April 11, 2009; Linda Sherrell Perkey, "Effects of Sudden Involuntary Desegregation on Interracial Interaction and Attitudes in a Junior High School" (specialist in education thesis, Univ. of Louisville, 1976), iii, 2, 21–24, 42–48; Woodard, "Busing Plans, Media Agendas, and Patterns of White Flight," 181–85, 250.

104. *Louisville Courier-Journal*, September 4, 2005; *EL*, 149; David V. Hawpe, personal conversation, November 25, 2009.

105. *EL*, 165–66, 294–95, 781–82; Robert J. Samuelson, review of *Historical Statistics of the United States*, *Wilson Quarterly* 30 (Autumn 2006): 103; *Louisville Courier-Journal*, March 13, 1978; Father Clyde Crews, personal communication; Crews, *An American Holy Land*, 363–65.

106. Reese, *History, Education, and the Schools*, 113–38; information from the Web sites of Beth Haven Christian School and the Christian Academy of Louisville; *Louisville Courier-Journal*, October 26, 1975; January 19, 1976; September 26, 1977; March 10, 18, 24, June 15, October 5, 1978; October 10, 1979; March 25, 30, 1980; *Constitution of Kentucky*, Bill of Rights, 5, Right of Religious Freedom (Frankfort: Legislative Research Commission, 1952), 1.

107. *EL*, 475–76; *KE*, 638, 799; *Lexington Herald-Leader*, August 19, 2006; David V. Hawpe, personal conversation, November 25, 2009.

108. Sedler, reviews of *Silent Covenants: Brown v. Board of Education and the Unfilled Hopes for Racial Reform* (2004), by Derrick Bell, and *After Brown: The Rise and Retreat of School Desegregation* (2004), by Charles T. Clotfelter, *Register of the Kentucky Historical Society* 102 (Summer 2004): 444; Sedler, "The Louisville–Jefferson County School Desegregation Case," 3–4.

109. *KE*, 130; *Lexington Herald*, November 7, 1979; Harrison, *Kentucky's Governors*, 221–28; Doyle, Layson, and Thompson, *From the Fort to the Future*, appendix B.

110. Ornstein and Levine, *Foundations of Education*, 282–91; Jack Jones Early,

"Religious Practices in the Public Schools in Selected Communities in Kentucky" (Ed.D. diss., Univ. of Kentucky, 1956), 89, 173–76, 182, 197–207; Bolmeier, *Landmark Supreme Court Decisions on Public School Issues*, 111–29, 153–59; *Michie's Kentucky Revised Statutes* (Charlottesville, VA: Matthew Bender, 2006), 7:910–12; Frank R. Hatfield, interview by author, August 14, 2009.

111. Bolmeier, *Landmark Supreme Court Decisions on Public School Issues*, 153–59; *Louisville Courier-Journal*, January 13, 1976; William E. Ellis, "Recurring Crisis: The Evolution/Creation Controversy in Kentucky," *Journal of Kentucky Studies* 1 (1984): 132–35; *Michie's Revised Kentucky Statutes*, 7:912–13.

112. Ellis, "Recurring Crisis," 135–140; *Louisville Courier-Journal*, March 6, 11, 21, 25, 30, 1980.

113. William E. Ellis, "The Modern Evolution-Creation Controversy: The Historian as Observer, Participant, and Analyst," *History and Social Science Teacher* 24 (Summer 1989): 221–26; William E. Ellis, "Biology and Border State Beliefs," *Transaction: Social Science and Modern Society* 20 (January–February 1983): 26–30; *Louisville Courier-Journal*, January 10, 1982; William E. Ellis, "Creationism in Kentucky: The Response of High School Teachers in Kentucky," in *Science and Creation: Geological, Theological, and Educational Perspectives*, ed. Robert W. Hanson (New York: Macmillan, 1986), 72–91.

114. Ellis, "Recurring Crisis," 135–39; William E. Ellis, "The Odyssey of a Historian: Solving Mysteries, Murderous and Otherwise," *Register of the Kentucky Historical Society* 96 (Summer 1998): 299–301; *Lexington Herald*, August 17, 18, October 20, 1981; January 24, November 23, 1982; Leroy L. Sullivan, "The Arkansas Landmark Court Challenge of Creation Science," *College Board Review* 123 (Spring 1982): 12–17, 32.

115. Doyle, Layson, and Thompson, *From the Fort to the Future*, 373; Harrison, *Kentucky's Governors*, 223–28; Harrison and Klotter, *A New History of Kentucky*, 416–18; *Louisville Courier-Journal*, March 16, 26, 1980.

116. Rennick, *Kentucky Place Names*, 39; *KE*, 364–65; nine interviews conducted by Darrell Logan, "History of Buckeye School" Oral History Project, Eastern Kentucky Univ. Archives; DeYoung interview, May 6, 2009.

117. DeYoung and Barbara Kent Lawrence, "On Hoosiers, Yankees, and Mountaineers," *Phi Delta Kappan* 77 (October 1995): 6, 8 (from Academic Search Premier Database); DeYoung and Craig B. Howley, "The Rural Economy of Rural School Consolidation," *Peabody Journal of Education* 67 (Summer 1990): 63–89; Tom Boyd and DeYoung, "Experts vs. Amateurs: The Irony of School Consolidation in Jackson County, Kentucky," *Appalachian Journal* 13 (Spring 1986): 275–83; DeYoung interview, May 6, 2009.

118. DeYoung and Julia Damron Porter, "Multicultural Education in Appalachia: Origins, Prospects, and Problems," *Appalachian Journal* 7 (Autumn–Winter 1979–1980): 124–25, 132; DeYoung, Charles Vaught, and Julia D. Porter, "Evaluating Educational Performance in Appalachian Kentucky, *Appalachian Journal* 9 (Fall 1981): 57; DeYoung, "The Status of Formal Education in Central Appalachia," *Appalachian Journal* 10 (Summer 1983): 323–25, 331; DeYoung, *Struggling with Their Histories: Economic Decline and Educational Improvement in Four Rural Southeastern School Districts* (Norwood, NJ: Ablex, 1991), 177–243; *KE*, 801; Richard Ulack, ed.,

Atlas of Kentucky (Lexington: Univ. Press of Kentucky, 1998), 103–4; DeYoung interview, May 6, 2009.

119. *KE,* 741; Harrison and Klotter, *A New History of Kentucky,* 419; Campbell, *Short of the Glory,* 266–81; Robert F. Sexton, interview by author, April 13, 2009.

120. Reese, *America's Public Schools,* 215–16, 249–50, 289, 323–24; Reese, *History, Education, and the Schools,* 109, 113, chap. 8; Perkinson, *The Imperfect Panacea; A Nation at Risk: The Imperative for Educational Reform* (Washington, DC: U.S. Department of Education, National Commission on Excellence in Education, April 1983), 5, 11. For an exhaustive discussion of the issues of the time and the personalities involved in debating *A Nation at Risk,* see Beatrice Gross and Ronald Gross, eds., *The Great School Debate: Which Way for American Education?* (New York: Touchstone, 1985).

121. *KE,* 214–15; Harrison, *Kentucky's Governors,* 229–32; Doyle, Layson, and Thompson, *From the Fort to the Future,* appendix A, 351; *Louisville Courier-Journal,* March 8, November 9, 10, 1983.

122. Harrison, *Kentucky's Governors,* 231–33; Richard Elliott Day, "Each Child, Every Child: The Story of the Council for Better Education, Equity and Inadequacy in Kentucky's Schools" (Ed.D. diss., Univ. of Kentucky, 2003), 87–89.

123. Harrison, *Kentucky's Governors,* 231–33; Harrison and Klotter, *A New History of Kentucky,* 419; Campbell, *Short of the Glory,* 278–79; *Louisville Courier-Journal,* March 16, 1980; Sexton interview, April 13, 2009.

124. Elizabeth Duffy Fraas, ed., *The Public Papers of Governor Martha Layne Collins, 1983–1987* (Lexington: Univ. Press of Kentucky, 2006), 157–209; *Louisville Courier-Journal,* June 3, 1984.

125. Day, "Each Child, Every Child," 88–90, 94–101, 343; John W. Smith interview, March 27, 2002; Hatfield interview, August 14, 2009.

126. Sexton interview, April 13, 2009; Day, "Each Child, Every Child," 107–10, 343–34; Hatfield interview, August 14, 2009.

127. Day, "Each Child, Every Child," 108–111; Sexton interview, April 13, 2009; *Lexington Herald-Leader,* November 14, 15, 16, 1984; Fraas, *Public Papers of Collins,* 174–75; Hatfield interview, August 14, 2009.

128. Sexton interview, April 13, 2009; *KE,* 741.

129. *KE,* 741; *Lexington Herald-Leader,* January 20, February 25, 1985; Fraas, *Public Papers of Collins,* 189–207; Hawpe interview, November 27, 2006; Sexton interview, April 13, 2009.

130. Harrison and Klotter, *A New History of Kentucky,* 419–20; *Louisville Courier-Journal,* July 6, 8, 9, 10, 1985; Paul Blanchard, "Educational Reform and Executive-Legislative Relations in Kentucky," *Journal of Kentucky Studies* 10 (September 1993): 66–68.

131. *Louisville Courier-Journal,* July 9, 10, 11, 12, 13, 16, 21, 1985; *Lexington Herald-Leader,* July 19, 1985; Fraas, *Public Papers of Collins,* 210–20; Harrison, *Kentucky's Governors,* 233–34; Penny M. Miller, *Kentucky Politics and Government: Do We Stand United?* (Lincoln: Univ. of Nebraska Press, 1994), 251.

132. Day, "Each Child, Every Child," 112–14, 117–19, 124–26, 130–34, 139–48; *Louisville Courier-Journal,* November 22, 1985; Hatfield interview, August 14, 2009.

133. Day, "Each Child, Every Child," 160–61; Hawpe interview, November

27, 2006; *KE*, 287–88; Sexton interview, April 13, 2009; Blanchard, "Educational Reform and Executive-Legislative Relations," 68–73; Hatfield interview, August 14, 2009; Woody Barwick, "A Chronology of the Kentucky Case," *Journal of Education Finance* 15 (Fall 1989): 136–41.

Chapter 8. Higher Education

1. Ellis, *A History of Eastern Kentucky University*, 91–92; Terry L. Birdwhistell, e-mail to the author, December 21, 2008.

2. Harrison and Klotter, *A New History of Kentucky*, 372–75; Ellis, *A History of Eastern Kentucky University*, 92–93.

3. Flatt, *A Light to the Mountains*, 87; Ellis, *A History of Eastern Kentucky University*, 92–95; Cox and Morison, *The University of Louisville*, 110–11; Rose, "The Historical Development of a State College," 259.

4. Talbert, *The University of Kentucky*, 137–40; Herman Lee Donovan, *Keeping the University Free and Growing* (Lexington: Univ. of Kentucky Press, 1959), 56–59.

5. Thelin, *A History of American Higher Education*, 257–59; Thelin, *Games Colleges Play*, 66–67; Ellis, *A History of Eastern Kentucky University*, 93; Cox and Morison, *The University of Louisville*, 111–12; Wright, *Transylvania*, 396.

6. Smith, *A Black Educator in the Segregated South*, 98–99; Lee, *The Campus Scene*, 75–76; Talbert, *The University of Kentucky*, 140–42; Clark, *My Century in History*, 214–15; Birdwhistell, "An Educated Difference," 223.

7. Talbert, *The University of Kentucky*, 119, 156–59; Myers, "Higher Education's Perfect System?" 47–49; Cone, *The University of Kentucky*, 100–111; Donovan, *Keeping the University Free and Growing*, 73–76.

8. Flatt, *A Light to the Mountains*, 86–90; Harrison, *Western Kentucky University*, 122–26; Woods et al., *Murray State University*, 130–34.

9. Ellis, *A History of Eastern Kentucky University*, 93–96; Clark, *My Century in History*, 214.

10. Thacker, *Asbury College*, 183–85; Dew and Weiss, *In Pursuit of the Dream*, 184–87; Snyder, *A History of Georgetown College*, 119–21; Wilson, *Berea College*, 136–41; Ellis, Everman, and Sears, *Madison County*, 336; Wright, *Transylvania*, 386–89; Hardin and Hill, *Our Standard True*, 211–17.

11. Taylor and Wake, *"A Bright Shining City Set on a Hill,"* 153; Snyder, *A History of Georgetown College*, 116–22; Porter, *Georgetown College and Its Relations to Kentucky Baptists*, 11; Cox and Morison, *The University of Louisville*, 113–14.

12. Woods et al., *Murray State University*, 130–33; Flatt, *A Light to the Mountains*, 86–93; Ellis, *A History of Eastern Kentucky University*, 96–99; Harrison, *Western Kentucky University*, 126–27.

13. Foster, "Changing Mission of Kentucky State University," 76–77, 105–9, 116–17; Hardin, "Hope versus Reality," 183; Smith, *A Black Educator in the Segregated South*, 97–101; Hardin, *Fifty Years of Segregation*, 67–84; Hardin, *Onward and Upward*, 38–41.

14. Hardin, *Fifty Years of Segregation*, 59–75; Smith, *A Black Educator in the Segregated South*, 93–106; Hudson, "The History of Louisville Municipal College," 37–47.

15. Harrison, *Western Kentucky University*, 123; Wilson, *Berea College*, 140–41; Ellis, *A History of Eastern Kentucky University*, 94.

16. Cone, *The University of Kentucky*, 111–15; Talbert, *The University of Kentucky*, 133–51; Donovan, *Keeping the University Free and Growing*, 56–59.

17. Talbert, *The University of Kentucky*, 163, 186; Cone, *The University of Kentucky*, 116; Ellis, *A History of Eastern Kentucky University*, 96–98; Snyder, *A History of Georgetown College*, 122; Wilson, *Berea College*, 141; Woods et al., *Murray State University*, 134–35; Hardin and Hill, *Our Standard Sure*, 217; Cox and Morison, *The University of Louisville*, 111.

18. Michael J. Bennett, *When Dreams Came True: The GI Bill and the Making of Modern America* (Washington, DC: Brassey's, 1966); Lee, *The Campus Scene*, 76–87; Thelin, *A History of American Higher Education*, 262–68; Anthony J. Principi, "Veterans as Revolutionaries," *Wilson Quarterly* 25 (Summer 2001): 105; Ornstein and Levine, *Foundations of Education*, 181.

19. Thelin, *A History of American Higher Education*, 262–66; Norman Deeb, interview by author, October 1, 1987.

20. Wright, *Transylvania*, 388–89. Ellis, *A History of Eastern Kentucky University*, 98–99; Snyder, *A History of Georgetown College*, 121.

21. Harrison, *Western Kentucky University*, 128; Dew and Weiss, *In Pursuit of the Dream*, 196; Cox and Morison, *The University of Louisville*, 115; Cone, *The University of Kentucky*, 116–17; Talbert, *The University of Kentucky*, 160–61; Birdwhistell, "An Educated Difference," 216; Foster, "Changing Mission of Kentucky State University," 131.

22. Cone, *The University of Kentucky*, 116–17; Talbert, *The University of Kentucky*, 161–62; Snyder, *A History of Georgetown College*, 121; Dew and Weiss, *In Pursuit of the Dream*, 197–99; Harrison, *Western Kentucky University*, 128–29. Ellis, *A History of Eastern Kentucky University*, 98–99.

23. Thelin, *A History of American Higher Education*, 260–316; *KE*, 85–51, 220–21.

24. Doran, "The Council of Public Higher Education," 163–66; *KE*, 494–95; *Louisville Courier-Journal*, November 30, 1949; Klotter, *Kentucky*, 337–39; Schacter, *Kentucky on the March;* Cole, "The Kentucky Council on Higher Education," 62–63.

25. Thelin, *A History of American Higher Education*, 268–71, 284.

26. Myers, "Higher Education's Perfect System?" 16, 47–54; Talbert, *The University of Kentucky*, 172–74, 188–89; *KE*, 220–21; *ENK*, 676; Robert Anderson, "The Southern Regional Education Board," in *Emerging Patterns in American Higher Education*, ed. Logan Wilson (Washington, DC: American Council on Education, 1965), 191–95.

27. Harrison, *Kentucky's Governors*, 186–89; Talbert, *The University of Kentucky*, 152–55.

28. Harrison, *Kentucky's Governors*, 187–89; Williams, "I'm Sure There Were Some That Thought I Was too Smart for My Own Good," 519–24; Pearce, *Divide and Dissent*, 151–52; *Lexington Herald-Leader,* September 16, 2006.

29. *KE*, 945; Larry Douglas Stanley, "The Historical Development of the Two-Year Colleges in Kentucky, 1903–1964" (Ph.D. diss., Univ. of Kentucky, 1974), 40–41; Hardin, *Fifty Years of Segregation*, 57–66, 73–78; *EL*, 34–35; Smith, *A Black Educator in the Segregated South*, 130–34.

30. Hardin, *Fifty Years of Segregation*, 78–79; Smith, *A Black Educator in the Segregated South*, 132–37; Schacter, *Kentucky on the March*, 123–30.

31. *EL*, 450–51; Wright, *A History of Blacks in Kentucky*, 2:176–92; Hall, *The Rest of the Dream*, 154–57; Talbert, *The University of Kentucky*, 174–77.

32. Clark, *My Century in History*, 248–51; Donovan, *Keeping the University Free and Growing*, 95–99; Talbert, *The University of Kentucky*, 175–77.

33. Hall, *The Rest of the Dream*, 154–56; Cone, *The University of Kentucky*, 121–23.

34. Clark, "Part II: Commentary," 407–20; Clark, *My Century in History*, 248–51.

35. *KE*, 263; Butler, *History of Education in Kentucky*, 99; *Louisville Courier-Journal*, November 2, 1949; March 15, 17, 1950; Hudson, "The History of Louisville Municipal College," 108–12; Collins, "Louisville Municipal College," 31–37; Sharon Barrow Chiles, "The Integration of the First African-American Undergraduates at the University of Kentucky" (Ed.D. diss., Univ. of Kentucky, 2000), 55, 62–64, 78, 93–97, 102, 111, 119–27; Wright, *A History of Blacks in Kentucky*, 2:183–84.

36. Klotter, "Promise, Pessimism, and Perseverance," 52; Ellis, *A History of Eastern Kentucky University*, 113–14, 122–23; Harrison, *Western Kentucky University*, 146–47; Wolfford, "Resistance on the Border," 54; Glenn Murrell, "The Desegregation of Paducah Junior College," *Register of the Kentucky Historical Society* 43 (January 1969): 63–79; Jack Birdwhistell, e-mail to author, September 14, 2009.

37. Donovan, "The Evolution of a University," 222; Talbert, *The University of Kentucky*, 160–81; Cone, *The University of Kentucky*, 127–35; Kindred, *Basketball*, 71–113; Thelin, *Games Colleges Play*, 106–7, 117–27, 121; Donovan, *Keeping the University Free and Growing*, 102–16; Clark, *My Century in History*, 247.

38. McNabb, "Campus Planning at the University of Louisville," 28; Ernst, *Progress in Engineering Education*, 4, 6, 8, 18; Cox and Morison, *The University of Louisville*, 113–19.

39. Cox and Morison, *The University of Louisville*, 115–39; *EL*, 902–4; John W. Brown, e-mail to the author, August 9, 2009; *Louisville Courier-Journal*, March 18, 1964; November 13, 2008.

40. Cox and Morison, *The University of Louisville*, 126–30.

41. *Lexington Herald-Leader*, September 8, 9, 2008; *KE*, 57–59, 339, 504–5; Thelin, *Games Colleges Play*, 173–75, 193–94.

42. Snyder, *A History of Georgetown College*, 121–52; *EL*, 479; Apple, Johnston, and Bevins, *Scott County*, 393–94; *Louisville Courier-Journal*, February 25, 1960; William F. Taylor, "A Survey of the Development and Current Status of Junior and Community College Education in Kentucky" (Ed.D. diss., Univ. of Kentucky, 1965), 49; Birdwhistell, *Kentucky Baptists*, 117; *KE*, 74; James Duane Bolin, *Kentucky Baptists, 1925–2000: A Story of Cooperation* (Louisville: Kentucky Baptist Convention, 2000), 192–98; Porter, *Georgetown College and Its Relation to Kentucky Baptists*, 12–13; Badgett, *History of Campbellsville University*, 154–60.

43. Lindsey Apple, e-mail to the author, September 15, 2009; Brackney, *Congregation and Campus*, 120, 404.

44. *KE*, 157, 245; Taylor, *"A Bright Shining City Set on a Hill,"* 153–263, 335; Taylor, "Junior and Community College Education," 50, 51, 64, 76; Campbellsville University and University of the Cumberlands Internet Web sites; Badgett, *History of Campbellsville University*, 164–242.

45. Ron Murphy, e-mail to the author, June 19, 2009.

46. Ellis, *A History of Eastern Kentucky University*, 105–7.

47. *KE*, 632; Dew and Weiss, *In Pursuit of the Dream*, 189–95.

48. Dew and Weiss, *In Pursuit of the Dream*, 195–204; *KE*, 516.

49. *KE*, 516; Dew and Weiss, *In Pursuit of the Dream*, 205–42.

50. *KE*, 907; W. G. Marigold, ed., *Union College, 1879–1979* (Barbourville, KY: Union College, 1979), 117–19, 133, 142–43, 150–51, 214–15.

51. *KE*, 559, 859–60; "Sue Bennett College Closes," United Methodist News List (Web site); Ransdell, "Organizational Spirit in a Higher Educational Context," 45–48, 51–54, 72–82.

52. *KE*, 35–36, 631–62; Thacker, *Asbury College*, 174–237; Asbury College, Web site; *Lexington Herald-Leader*, August 16, 2009.

53. *KE*, 13; Hilton, "The Leaders Are Here," iii, 8, 77, 145, 213–20; Searles, *A College for Appalachia*, 76–162.

54. *KE*, 492, 636, 896; Wright, *Transylvania*, 383–434.

55. Wright, *Transylvania*, 391–92; Craig, *Centre College of Kentucky*, 111–13, 141; Norman L. Snider, "Centre College and the Presbyterians: Corporation and Partnership," *Register of the Kentucky Historical Society* 67 (April 1969): 117–18.

56. *KE*, 178; Craig, *Centre College of Kentucky*, 140–56; Hardin and Hill, *Our Standard Sure*, 222–42.

57. *KE*, 723; Alice Kinder, *Pikeville College Looks to the Hills: 1889–1989* (Pikeville, KY: Pikeville College, 1989), 1–80.

58. *Lexington Herald-Leader*, February 23, 2006; *KE*, 542, 723; Kinder, *Pikeville College Looks to the Hills*, 77–114.

59. *KE*, 68–69, 122–23, 791–92, 838, 880; *EL*, 84, 841–42; *ENK*, 876–77; Crews, *An American Holy Land*, 212–13, 287, 365–66; *Lexington Herald-Leader*, May 29, 2007; Wade Hall, *High upon A Hill: A History of Bellarmine College* (Louisville: Bellarmine College Press, 1999), 12–20, 30, 267, 270–82; Stanley, "The Two-Year Colleges in Kentucky," 47–49.

60. *KE*, 834; Gregory Lee Waltermire, "Academic Freedom in the Southern Baptist Seminaries: A Study in Epistemology and Response to Modernism" (Ph.D. diss., Univ. of Kentucky, 1996), 235–64.

61. *KE*, 441, 533, 584, 822; Stevenson, *Lexington Theological Seminary*, chap. 8, p. 258; Thacker, *Asbury College*, 242–44, 247, 258.

62. Donovan, *Keeping the University Free and Growing*, 46–47, 66; Talbert, *The University of Kentucky*, 172, 176, 189–91, 197; Kleber, *Papers of Wetherby*, 293.

63. Talbert, *The University of Kentucky*, 188–92; *Louisville Courier-Journal*, January 23, 27, 1948; Cox and Morison, *The University of Louisville*, 136–37.

64. Talbert, *The University of Kentucky*, 192–95; Cone, *The University of Kentucky*, 137; Harrison, *Kentucky's Governors*, 174–75; Chandler, *Heroes, Plain Folks, and Skunks*, 252–54.

65. Talbert, *The University of Kentucky*, 193–95; Cox and Morison, *The University of Louisville*, 137–38; *Louisville Courier-Journal*, June 16, 1957; Donovan, *Keeping the University Free and Growing*, 51–55.

66. *Lexington Herald-Leader*, August 8, 2009; Talbert, *The University of Kentucky*, 135, 183, 196–97; Cone, *The University of Kentucky*, 137–47; Clark, *My Century*

in History, 219; Thomas D. Clark, "Clark and the University of Kentucky," *Register of the Kentucky Historical Society* 103, Thomas D. Clark Memorial Issue (Winter–Spring 2005): 385.

67. *KE,* 269–70, 649–50; Flatt, *A Light to the Mountains,* 107–13, 166–91; Rose, "The Historical Development of a State College," 336–57, 466–70; Doran, "The Council on Public Higher Education," 152–53, 163–66; Gary S. Cox, interview by author, April 7, 2009.

68. *KE,* 943; Harrison, *Western Kentucky University,* 139–74.

69. Ellis, *A History of Eastern Kentucky University,* 117–19; Robinson, *Bert Combs the Politician,* 77–92; Robert F. Matthews, interview by author, November 30, 1976; Combs interview, December 17, 1976; Albert B. Chandler, interview by author, December 6, 1976.

70. Ellis, *A History of Eastern Kentucky University,* 117–21; Butler interview, February 3, 1977; Chandler interview, December 6, 1976; Combs interview, December 17, 1976.

71. Neil Cook Ward, "An Analysis of Issues, Findings, and Impact: Mandated Studies of Public Higher Education in Kentucky" (Ed.D. diss., Univ. of Kentucky, 1980), 6–14; James P. Chapman, interview by author, December 5, 2006; *KE,* 494–95.

72. *KE,* 279; Ellis, *A History of Eastern Kentucky University,* 117–52; Thomas D. Clark, interview by author, October 29, 2002; Cox and Morison, *The University of Louisville,* 176, 195; Butler interview, February 3, 1977; *Louisville Courier-Journal,* December 1, 1997; Prichard interview, January 25, 1977; Richard Wilson, interviews by author, April 18, 1977; March 9, 2000.

73. Wright, *A History of Blacks in Kentucky,* 2:179–83; Hardin, *Fifty Years of Segregation,* 110–21.

74. Wright, *A History of Blacks in Kentucky,* 2:215–16; Kramer, *Capital on the Kentucky,* 377–78; Smith, *A Black Educator in the Segregated South,* 145–65; Bacon, "White Town/Black Gown," 86.

75. Bacon, "White Town/Black Gown," 86–117, 153–61; Smith, *A Black Educator in the Segregated South,* 146–65; Foster, "Changing Mission of Kentucky State University," 189; Hardin, *Onward and Upward,* 50–51; M. M. Chambers, *Higher Education in the Fifty States* (Danville, IL: Interstate, 1970), 157–58; Cox interview, April 7, 2009; Gary S. Cox, e-mail to author, January 18, 2010.

76. Earlo Anderson, "Satisfaction and University Involvement among Black Undergraduate Students" (Ph.D. diss., Univ. of Kentucky, 1983), 76–77, 160–68.

77. *EL,* 845, 862–63; Thelin, *A History of American Higher Education,* 322, 332–35; Stanley, "The Two-Year Colleges in Kentucky," 103–18.

78. Stanley, "The Two-Year Colleges in Kentucky," 160–76; Ward, "Issues, Findings, and Impact," 5–9; Harrison, *Kentucky's Governors,* 196–99; Fitzpatrick to Martin, December 19, 1960, Robert R. Martin Papers, Eastern Kentucky Univ. Archives; Ellis F. Hartford, interview by author, December 14, 1976.

79. *KE,* 220–21, 497–98; Harrison, *Kentucky's Governors,* 196–99; Stanley, "The Two-Year Colleges in Kentucky," 160–86; *Lexington Herald,* November 3, 1961; *Lexington Leader,* November 3, 1961; Robinson, *Bert Combs the Politician,* 202–3; Adron Doran, interview by author, February 23, 1977; Arthur M. Cohen and Florence B. Brawer, *The American Community College* (San Francisco: Jossey-Bass, 1989), 13–14, 103.

80. *KE*, 220–21; *ENK*, 676; Taylor, "Junior and Community College Education," 76–84, 96, 103–4, 108–17; Stanley, "The Two-Year Colleges in Kentucky," 123–40, 187–206; Cohen and Brawer, *The American Community College*, 39, 307–11.

81. *Louisville Courier-Journal*, October 15, 1971; *Lexington Herald-Leader*, August 8, 2009; *EL*, 434; David Patrick Ecker, "A History of Jefferson Community College, 1960–1977: The Promise and the Complications of 'La Porta'" (Ph.D. diss., Univ. of Kentucky, 1991), 1–2, 81–84, 92–94, 100, 132–34, 147–48, 208–14.

82. Cone, *The University of Kentucky*, 147; *KE*, 220–21; Chapman interview, December 5, 2006; Cox interview, April 7, 2009.

83. *Lexington Herald-Leader*, August 8, 2009; Cone, *The University of Kentucky*, 144, 146; Talbert, *The University of Kentucky*, 195–97; Clark, *My Century in History*, 219–20; Clark, "Clark and the University of Kentucky," 385–86.

84. Cone, *The University of Kentucky*, 147–56; Frank G. Dickey, interview by author, January 5, 1977; Myers, "Higher Education's Perfect System?" 55–65; Thelin, *A History of American Higher Education*, 286–90; Perkinson, *The Imperfect Panacea*, 217–18.

85. Clark, *My Century in History*, 220–25; Clark, "Clark and John Oswald," *Register of the Kentucky Historical Society* 103, Thomas D. Clark Memorial Issue (Winter–Spring 2005): 421–44; Cone, *The University of Kentucky*, 149; *KE*, 196–97.

86. *Kentucky Kernel*, November 13, 1963; *Louisville Courier-Journal*, October 25, 1963; *KE*, 967; Doran to Martin, October 19, 1963; Woods to Martin, June 7, 1963; March 3, 1964, Robert R. Martin Papers, Eastern Kentucky Univ. Archives.

87. *Louisville Courier-Journal*, October 25, 1963; Ward, "Issues, Findings, and Impact," 7–8; Chambers, *Higher Education in the Fifty States*, 158–63; *KE*, 741, 851.

88. *Louisville Courier-Journal*, December 10, 1965; *Paducah Sun-Democrat*, June 9, 1963; Ellis, *A History of Eastern Kentucky University*, 133–37.

89. Robert E. Corlew, *Tennessee: A Short History* (Knoxville: Univ. of Tennessee Press, 1981), 532–36; *KE*, 850–51.

90. *Louisville Courier-Journal*, June 9, 1963; March 19, 1964; Ellis, *A History of Eastern Kentucky University*, 133–37; Harrison, *Western Kentucky University*, 161–67; Kenneth W. Kurzendoerfer, "A Perspective of the Kentucky Council on Higher Education" (master's thesis, Univ. of Louisville, 1990), 30–31.

91. Chambers, *Higher Education in the Fifty States*, 158–63; Myers, "Higher Education's Perfect System?" 20, chap. 7; E. Allan Dunham, *Colleges of the Forgotten Americans: A Profile of State Colleges and Regional Universities* (New York: McGraw-Hill, 1969), 27–45, 115–30, 155–66, 181; Charles Hamilton White, "The Kentucky Council on Public Higher Education: An Analysis of a Change in Structure" (Ph.D. diss., Ohio State Univ., 1967), 153–59, 214–21.

92. *KE*, 741, 851; Woods et al., *Murray State University*, 516–19; Ellis, *A History of Eastern Kentucky University*, 136; Harrison, *Kentucky's Governors*, 203; Chambers, *Higher Education in the Fifty States*, 161; Williams, "I'm Sure There Were Some That Thought I Was Too Smart for My Own Good," 601; Campbell, *Short of the Glory*, 233, 238, 248–49; Frank Steve Barkovich, "The Kentucky Council on Public Higher Education" (master's thesis, Univ. of Louisville, 1970), 27–38, 75; Kurzendoerfer, "Kentucky Council on Higher Education," 32–38; Cole, "The Kentucky Council on Higher Education," 90–92.

93. Harrison, *Kentucky's Governors,* 207–9; Ellis, *A History of Eastern Kentucky University,* 136.

94. Lee, *The Campus Scene,* 108–72; *EL,* 189–90; Harrison and Klotter, *A New History of Kentucky,* 413–14.

95. Cone, *The University of Kentucky,* 156–59; Ellis, *A History of Eastern Kentucky University,* 139–41; Harrison, *Western Kentucky University,* 164–67, 196–98.

96. Harrison, *Western Kentucky University,* 205–9; Chambers, *Higher Education in the Fifty States,* 161–63; *KE,* 664–65, 943–44; Cone, *The University of Kentucky,* 156–63; Smith, *A Black Educator in the Segregated South,* 176–77; Hardin, *Onward and Upward,* 53–81; Cox interview, April 7, 2009; Cox and Morison, *The University of Louisville,* 144; Harry M. Snyder, interview by author, December 11, 2009.

97. Harrison, *Kentucky's Governors,* 207; Louie B. Nunn, interview by author, February 16, 1977; *KE,* 538, 684–85; *ENK,* 676–79.

98. Myers, "Higher Education's Perfect System?" 64–65; *KE,* 823–24; Ward, "Issues, Findings, and Impact," 113; Otis Singletary, interview by Mark Wilburn, May 3, 1978, Eastern Kentucky Univ. Archives; Doran interview, February 23, 1977.

99. *EL,* 479, 903; Barkovich, "The Kentucky Council on Public Higher Education," 62–67; Cox and Morison, *The University of Louisville,* 143–44; Kris W. Kindelsperger, "A Study of Factors Leading to the Entrance of the University of Louisville into the State System of Higher Education in Kentucky" (master's thesis, Univ. of Louisville, 1976), 36, 49–53, 64.

100. Kindelsperger, "The Entrance of the University of Louisville into the State System of Higher Education," 33–34, 46–48, 53, 59; Cox and Morison, *The University of Louisville,* 144–45; Barkovich, "The Kentucky Council on Public Higher Education," 63–64; Nunn interview, February 16, 1977; Sexton interview, April 13, 2009.

101. Kindelsperger, "The Entrance of the University of Louisville into the State System of Higher Education," 60–82; Cox and Morison, *The University of Louisville,* 144–45; *EL,* 903; Klotter interview, February 28, 2008; Kurzendoerfer, "Kentucky Council on Higher Education," 40–42; Lyman A. Glenny, "State Systems and Plans for Higher Education," in Wilson, *Emerging Patterns in American Higher Education,* 91–103; *Louisville Courier-Journal,* April 1, 1969; White, "The Kentucky Council on Public Higher Education," 168–69; Richard Wilson, e-mail to author, December 3, 2009; Cole, "The Kentucky Council on Higher Education," 104–18.

102. *Lexington Herald-Leader,* November 18, 2007; August 8, 2009; Nunn interview, February 16, 1977; Groves, "Major Initiatives in Campus Planning at the University of Kentucky," 119.

103. Cone, *The University of Kentucky,* 163–67; Stephanie Lang, "1958–1983: The Heart of the Campus," *Ampersand: The Magazine of the College of Arts and Sciences* (Spring 2008): 28–29 (this is a UK publication); Horowitz, *Campus Life,* 244–46; Mitchell K. Hall, "'A Crack in Time': The Response of Students at the University of Kentucky to the Tragedy at Kent State, May 1970," *Register of the Kentucky Historical Society* 83 (Winter 1985): 36–63; *Lexington Herald,* May 6, 1970.

104. Hall, "A Crack in Time," 50–63; Sexton, *Public Papers of Nunn,* 352; Rita J. Pritchett, "The Battle between Promise and Privilege: The History of Women's Basketball at the University of Kentucky, 1972–2002 (Ed.D. diss., Univ. of Kentucky, 2007), 81.

105. Cox and Morison, *The University of Louisville*, 146–50; Cone, *The University of Kentucky*, 166–67; Ellis, *A History of Eastern Kentucky University*, 140–46, 154, 173, 177; Harrison, *Western Kentucky University*, 232–35, 247–57, 271; Prichard interview, January 25, 1977.

106. Cox interview, April 7, 2009; Klotter interview, February 28, 2008; Prichard interview, January 25, 1977; Gary S. Cox, e-mail to the author, January 18, 2010.

107. Kurzendoerfer, "Kentucky Council on High Education," 34–45; Prichard interview, January 25, 1977.

108. Harrison, *Kentucky's Governors*, 211–28; Kurzendoerfer, "Kentucky Council on Higher Education," 43–45.

109. Charles Paul Conn, *Julian Carroll of Kentucky* (Old Tappan, NJ: Revel, 1977), 117; Harrison, *Kentucky's Governors*, 218; Harrison and Klotter, *A New History of Kentucky*, 415–16; *KE*, 165.

110. Harrison, *Kentucky's Governors*, 218; Kurzendoerfer, "Kentucky Council on Higher Education," 46, 49–70; Thelin, *A History of American Higher Education*, 326–31.

111. *KE*, 967; Hawpe interview, November 27, 2006; Nunn interview, February 16, 1977; Flatt, *A Light to the Mountains*, 242–46; Ellis, *A History of Eastern Kentucky University*, 149.

112. *Louisville Courier-Journal*, November 7, 1973; Kurzendoerfer, "Kentucky Council on Higher Education," 46–49; Harrison, *Western Kentucky University*, 254; Snyder interview, December 11, 2009.

113. Harrison, *Kentucky's Governors*, 218; Kurzendoerfer, "Kentucky Council on Higher Education," 63–70; Cox interview, April 7, 2009; *KE*, 10; *ENK*, 676–79; *Lexington Herald-Leader*, April 11, 2009; Snyder interview, December 11, 2009.

114. *Louisville Courier-Journal*, September 27, 1977; March 10, 20, August 25, November 10, 1978; *Lexington Herald*, September 8, 1979; Ward, "Issues, Findings, and Impact," 39–40; Klotter interview, February 28, 2008; Harrison, *Western Kentucky University*, 254–57; Charles Douglas Whitlock, "An Analysis of Opinion about Public Higher Education in the Commonwealth of Kentucky" (Ed.D. diss., Univ. of Kentucky, 1981), 164–66.

115. Harrison, *Western Kentucky University*, 254–57; Kurzendoerfer, "Kentucky Council on Higher Education," 80; Ellis, *A History of Eastern Kentucky University*, 157; Campbell, *Short of the Glory*, 248–51, 260; *Louisville Courier-Journal*, October 16, 1975; June 5, October 23, 1977; Snyder interview, December 11, 2009; Cox interview, April 7, 2009.

116. *Louisville Courier-Journal*, June 22, 1978; March 26, 27, 1980.

117. Cox and Morison, *The University of Louisville*, 154–56.

118. Ellis, *A History of Eastern Kentucky University*, 148–49; Harrison, *Western Kentucky University*, 254–55; Snyder interview, December 11, 2009.

119. Kurzendoerfer, "Kentucky Council on Higher Education," 72–73; Ward, "Issue, Findings, and Impact," 39–42, 113–14, 164–75; *Louisville Courier-Journal*, August 4, 1971; October 3, 1975; February 28, 1976; November 10, 1978; Cole, "The Kentucky Council on Higher Education," 178–90; Snyder interview, December 11, 2009.

120. Cox interview, April 7, 2009; Kurzendoerfer, "Kentucky Council on Higher Education," 72–91; *Louisville Courier-Journal*, June 5, 1977; Snyder interview, December 11, 2009.

121. Cox and Morison, *The University of Louisville*, 154; Ward, "Issues, Findings, and Impact," 68; *Louisville Courier-Journal*, January 18, March 20, November 10, 1978.

122. *KE*, 494–95; Harrison, *Western Kentucky University*, 254–57; Ellis, *A History of Eastern Kentucky University*, 157; Snyder interview, December 11, 2009.

123. Miller, *Kentucky Politics and Government*, 238–40; Harrison, *Kentucky's Governors*, 221–27; *KE*, 741; Campbell, *Short of the Glory*, 266–81.

124. Kurzendoerfer, "Kentucky Council on Higher Education," 105–17; Cox interview, April 7, 2009; Ellis, *A History of Eastern Kentucky University*, 157–58; Harrison, *Western Kentucky University*, 255–57, 264–69; *Louisville Courier-Journal*, September 8, 1979; Snyder interview, December 11, 2009.

125. Cox interview, April 7, 2009; Sexton interview, April 13, 2009; *Louisville Courier-Journal*, November 7, 1979; Kurzendoerfer, "Kentucky Council on Higher Education," 110–17, appendixes 2, 4; *KE*, 851; Cole, "The Kentucky Council on Higher Education," 321–42; Snyder interview, December 11, 2009.

126. *KE*, 664–65, 943–44; Harrison, *Western Kentucky University*, 260–88; Fraas, *Public Papers of Collins*, 545–46; Ellis, *A History of Eastern Kentucky University*, 153–91.

127. *KE*, 650; Flatt, *A Light to the Mountains*, 251–62.

128. *KE*, 10, 650; Flatt, *A Light to the Mountains*, 262–76, 299–309; *Louisville Courier-Journal*, July 7, 1985; *Lexington Herald-Leader*, April 11, 14, 2009.

129. Cox and Morison, *The University of Louisville*, 159–61, 174–75; *KE*, 823–24, 912–13; Cone, *The University of Kentucky*, 230–31.

130. Ellis, *A History of Eastern Kentucky University*, 181; Harrison, *Western Kentucky University*, 255, 257, 267–71; Cox interview, April 7, 2009; Sexton interview, April 13, 2009; Snyder interview, December 11, 2009.

131. Sexton interview, April 13, 2009; *Louisville Courier-Journal*, July 16, 1985; Cox and Morison, *The University of Louisville*, 174–82; Cone, *The University of Kentucky*, 230; Harrison, *Western Kentucky University*, 266–69; Cox interview, April 7, 2009; *ENK*, 173–74; Snyder interview, December 11, 2009; Gary S. Cox, e-mail to the author, January 18, 2010.

132. Cox interview, April 7, 2009; *KE*, 515; David Wilson, "Going from Black to Black and White: A Case Study of the Desegregation of Kentucky State University" (Ed.D. diss., Harvard Univ., 1987), 79–85, 149–157, 176–78, 193; Hardin, *Onward and Upward*, 59–81; Snyder interview, December 11, 2009; Gary S. Cox, e-mail to the author, January 18, 2010.

133. Ward, "Issues, Findings, and Impact," 68; Cone, *The University of Kentucky*, 220, 222, italics in original.

134. *KE*, 851.

Epilogue

1. Harrison, *Kentucky's Governors*, 233–35.

2. Sexton interview, April 13, 2009; Hawpe interview, November 27, 2006; Blanchard, "Educational Reform and Executive-Legislative Relations in Kentucky," 68–73.

3. *KE*, 573, 956; Harrison and Klotter, *A New History of Kentucky*, 420; Harrison, *Kentucky's Governors*, 237–42

4. Robert F. Sexton, *Mobilizing Citizens for Better Schools* (New York: Teachers College Press, 2004), 51–56; Blanchard, "Education Reform and Executive-Legislative Relations in Kentucky," 67–70; Day, "Each Child, Every Child," 170–99, 212–18, 349, 351.

5. Holly Holland, *Making Change: Three Educators Join the Battle for Better Schools* (Portsmouth, NH: Heinemann, 1998), xix–xxvii; Hawpe interview, November 27, 2006; Sexton interview, April 13, 2009.

6. *KE*, 956; Harrison and Klotter, *A New History of Kentucky*, 420, 422; Blanchard, "Education Reform and Executive-Legislative Relations in Kentucky," 71–73; Hawpe interview, November 27, 2006; *Louisville Courier-Journal*, June 4, 2006.

7. Sexton, *Mobilizing Citizens for Better Schools*, 57–67; *ENK*, 770–71; Sexton interview, April 13, 2009; Hawpe interview, November 27, 2006; Miller, *Kentucky Politics and Government*, 251–54.

8. Sexton, *Mobilizing Citizens for Better Schools*, 57; *New York Times*, March 30, 1990; Hatfield interview, August 14, 2009; Sexton interview, April 13, 2009; Campbell, *Short of the Glory*, 283–84; John E. Kleber, ed., *Thomas D. Clark of Kentucky: An Uncommon Life in the Commonwealth* (Lexington: Univ. Press of Kentucky, 2003), 91–92; Thomas D. Clark, "We Still Have a Long Way to Go," *Kentucky Monthly* (January 2000): 56; *Lexington Herald-Leader*, June 21, 2002.

9. Holland, *Making Change*, 173–82; Sexton, *Mobilizing Citizens for Better Schools*, 80.

10. *KE*, 287–88, 861; *ENK*, 771; Sexton, *Mobilizing Citizens for Better Schools*, 79; Miller, *Kentucky Politics and Government*, 249–57; Hawpe interview, November 27, 2006.

11. Harrison, *Kentucky's Governors*, 248, 255, 258, 263, 267; Harrison and Klotter, *A New History of Kentucky*, 420–25; Miller, *Kentucky Politics and Government*, 245–46, 254–57.

12. *Richmond Register*, September 9, 2006; September 18, 2009; *Lexington Herald-Leader*, January 7, 1993; *Louisville Courier-Journal*, November 26, 2006.

13. Sedler, "The Louisville–Jefferson County School Desegregation Case," 3–4; *Richmond Register*, February 27, 2004; *Louisville Courier-Journal*, July 23, 2006.

14. *Louisville Courier-Journal*, June 8, 2006; February 25, 2007; *Richmond Register*, December 3, 2006; *Lexington Herald-Leader*, July 5, 2007.

15. *Lexington Herald-Leader*, July 4, 5, 28, 2007; *Louisville Courier-Journal*, June 29, July 31, 2007; May 10, 2008; *Washington Post*, June 29, 2007; *Meredith v. Jefferson County Board of Education*, Cornell School of Law, Web site; Sara Bullard, "Little Rock Betrayed," *Historically Speaking* 9 (September–October 2007): 31–32; Jefferson County Public Schools, Web site.

16. June Overton Hyndman, "A Study of Gender Patterns in the Kentucky Principalship" (Ph.D. diss., Univ. of Kentucky, 2008), abstract, 126–30; Marlene Helm, Oral History Interview, June 27, 2006, Eastern Kentucky Univ. Archives; Elaine Farris, interview by Richard E. Day and Jonah Brown, August 21, 2009; Dan Sharrard, e-mail to the author, April 28, 2008.

17. *Louisville Courier-Journal*, June 28, 1991; *Lexington Herald-Leader*, March 1, September 4, 1992; February 19, 1993; September 16, 2008; March 17, September 11, 2009; *Richmond Register*, April 28, 2009.

18. Reese, *America's Public Schools*, 328; *Lexington Herald-Leader*, December 13, 2005; June 6, 2006; *Louisville Courier-Journal*, June 15, 2006.

19. *Richmond Register*, December 12, 2006; November 27, February 27, May 5, 2009; *Lexington Herald-Leader*, April 19, 2009; Kentucky Center for School Safety, Web site; *Louisville Courier-Journal*, December 16, 2005.

20. *Lexington Herald-Leader*, November 30, 2005; September 22, 2006; March 16, 2009; Reese, *History, Education, and the Schools*, 156–57, 169; Reese, *America's Public Schools*, 1, 9, 322, 325, 329–30; *Daytona Beach News-Journal*, January 15, 2007; *Louisville Courier-Journal*, March 9, 2007.

21. *Lexington Herald-Leader*, April 17, 2006; August 13, September 5, 10, 2008; March 16, 2009; Thelin, *A History of American Higher Education*, 302–3; Reese, *America's Public Schools*, 238; *Richmond Register*, May 15, 2006.

22. *Lexington Herald-Leader*, February 14, 2007; March 23, September 16, November 9, 2008; February 23, 2009; *Louisville Courier-Journal*, August 14, 2005; September 5, 2008. The comments of Milburn were what I often heard from teachers taking my graduate courses at EKU from the beginning of KERA until my retirement in 1999.

23. *Lexington Herald-Leader*, March 3, 2006; July 30, August 3, November 9, 2008; *ENK*, 771; *Louisville Courier-Journal*, January 8, 2006; Hawpe interview, November 27, 2006.

24. *Lexington Herald-Leader*, March 5, 2008; February 10, 15, 23, March 12, 15, 18, 20, May 1, December 10, 2009; *Louisville Courier-Journal*, February 7, 20, March 20, 27, 2009; *Richmond Register*, March 15, 20, 2009; Hawpe interview, November 27, 2006.

25. *Lexington Herald-Leader*, October 7, 2006; February 13, 2007; Carl West editorial reprinted in the *Richmond Register*, June 2, 2007.

26. *Lexington Herald-Leader*, October 27, 2009; February 10, April 14, 18, 21, 22, 30, May 3, 5, 2010.

27. *Louisville Courier-Journal*, April 29, 2006; *Lexington Herald-Leader*, March 27, 2006; William E. Ellis, "Education, Education, Education," *Kentucky Monthly* (February 2007): 52; Alexis Seymore, e-mail to the author, February 8, 2007; Alexis Seymore, Oral History Interview, September 5, 2007, Eastern Kentucky Univ. Archives; David V. Hawpe, personal communication, November 25, 2009.

28. Cox interview, April 7, 2009; Margery Coulson-Clark, "From Process to Outcome: Performance Funding Policy in Kentucky Public Higher Education, 1994–1997" (Ph.D. diss., Univ. of Kentucky, 1999), 15–17.

29. Cox interview, April 7, 2009.

30. Harrison, *Kentucky's Governors*, 241–43; Cone, *The University of Kentucky*, 231–33; Cox and Morison, *The University of Louisville*, 178–79; Ellis, *A History of Eastern Kentucky University*, 177; Klotter, "Promise, Pessimism, and Perseverance," 55; Miller, *Kentucky Politics and Government*, 133; Harrison and Klotter, *A New History of Kentucky*, 420.

31. Harrison, *Kentucky's Governors*, 248–50; Miller, *Kentucky Politics and Government*, 133; Harrison and Klotter, *A New History of Kentucky*, 423–24; Cox and Morison, *The University of Louisville*, 179; Ellis, *A History of Eastern Kentucky University*, 177; Cox interview, April 7, 2009; Coulson-Clark, "From Process to Outcome," 15–19, 67–77.

32. Harrison, *Kentucky's Governors*, 251–63; Paul Blanchard, "Governor Paul Patton," *Register of the Kentucky Historical Society* 102 (Winter 2004): 74–80; Cox and Morison, *The University of Louisville*, 201–2; Ellis, *A History of Eastern Kentucky University*, 182–83; Snyder interview, December 11, 2009; Klotter interview, February 28, 2008.

33. Doug Cantrell, Thomas D. Matijasic, Richard E. Holl, Lorie Maltby, and Richard Smoot, *Kentucky through the Centuries: A Collection of Documents and Essays* (Dubuque, IA: Kendall/Hunt, 2005), 453–59; Sandra K. Mullins, "Kentucky Community and Technical College System from Inception to 2006" (Ed.D. diss., Univ. of Kentucky, 2007), 57–59, 88–89.

34. John R. Thelin, Oral History Interview, September 11, 2007, Eastern Kentucky Univ. Archives; Helm interview, June 27, 2006.

35. Ellis, *A History of Eastern Kentucky University*, 199; Robert W. Kustra, Oral History Interview, May 2, 2001, Eastern Kentucky Univ. Archives; *Lexington Herald-Leader*, March 15, April 15, August 8, September 2, 1999; February 23, March 3, 11, 15, 2000; *Louisville Courier-Journal*, February 23, June 18, 2000; *Eastern Progress*, December 9, 1999; April 20, 2000.

36. Ellis, *A History of Eastern Kentucky University*, 212–13; Helm interview, June 27, 2006; *Lexington Herald-Leader*, September 28, 2001; April 4, May 17, 26, June 3, 2002; April 3, May 13, August 7, 2003; *Louisville Courier-Journal*, May 5, 9, 10, 12, June 5, 2002; Al Smith, Oral History Interview, September 19, 2002, Eastern Kentucky Univ. Archives.

37. Harrison, *Kentucky's Governors*, 259–63; *Lexington Herald-Leader*, August 15, 2006; *Richmond Register*, August 15, 2006.

38. *Lexington Herald-Leader*, February 20, 2006; July 5, 2007; *Eastern Progress*, November 30, 2006; October 23, 2008; *Richmond Register*, September 22, 2008; December 4, 2009; *Louisville Courier-Journal*, October 8, 2006.

39. *Lexington Herald-Leader*, September 23, November 14, 2005; June 15, July 10, 2006; December 23, 27, 2007; November 17, 2008; October 17, 23, 2009; February 22, 2010; *Louisville Courier-Journal*, June 7, 15, 2006; *Kentucky Kernel*, July 13, 2006.

40. *Lexington Herald-Leader*, November 10, December 18, 2006; March 2, 2007; April 23, November 8, 2009; *Louisville Courier-Journal*, November 5, 2006; Sexton interview, April 13, 2009; Thelin interview, September 11, 2007; Hawpe interview, November 27, 2006.

41. Xiao-Bo Yuan, "Kentucky," *Chronicle of Higher Education* (August 25, 2006): 57; *Louisville Courier-Journal*, December 11, 2005; September 4, 2007; May 1, 2008; *Lexington Herald-Leader*, March 24, 25, April 1, August 15, 20, 2006; May 30, July 27, August 8, September 1, 13, 2007; April 15, 17, 27, 30, May 21, December 9, 2008; Hawpe interview, November 27, 2006; *Richmond Register*, April 30, December 10, 2008.

42. *Richmond Register*, September 15, 2006; July 17, August 8, 2007; *Lexington Herald-Leader*, June 20, September 15, November 29, 2006; *Louisville Courier-Journal*, December 17, 2006.

43. *Richmond Register*, December 4, 10, 2008; April 20, 2010; *Lexington Herald-Leader*, September 17, 2006; February 18, October 23, 2007; August 27, November 13, December 3, 10, 2008; May 25, 2009; April 24, 2010.

44. *Lexington Herald-Leader*, October 26, 2006; March 10, September 23, 2007;

February 28, 2009; Tenna Hammond Gomez, "Out-of-State Colleges Invading Kentucky," *Kentucky Monthly* (February 2007): 26, 28–29.

45. Harrison, *Kentucky's Governors*, 240–41; *Lexington Herald-Leader*, July 15, 2006; April 3, 2007; December 13, 2009; *Richmond Register*, July 30, 2006; April 12, 2009; Miller, *Kentucky Politics and Government*, 94, 142, 200.

46. "The Association of Independent Kentucky Colleges and Universities, 2007 Partners for the Commonwealth Annual Report," 1–25, Association of Independent Kentucky Colleges and Universities, Frankfort, KY; Cox interview, April 7, 2009; *Lexington Herald-Leader*, October 21, 2006; May 21, August 7, 17, 20, 2007; August 23, 2008; November 9, 19, 2009; *Louisville Courier-Journal*, April 10, 2006; Gary S. Cox, e-mail to the author, January 19, 2010.

47. *Lexington Herald-Leader*, October 19, 2006; September 17, 2008; June 1, 2009; "Through the Years: A Conversation with Professor Wayne Ward," *Baptists Today* (March 2009): 14; "A Conversation with Diana and David Garland," *Baptists Today* (July 2007): 4.

48. *Richmond Register*, August 31, 2007; *Louisville Courier-Journal*, May 20, 2008; *Lexington Herald-Leader*, July 5, 2006; September 10, 2008.

49. *Lexington Herald-Leader*, September 6, 2005; August 2, December 12, 2007; July 12, 2008, June 23, 24, 2010; *Louisville Courier-Journal*, July 18, September 12, 2008; July 10, 2009; *Richmond Register*, March 31, 2010; *LEO Weekly*, August 27, 2008, LEO Weekly Web site; Cone, *The University of Kentucky*, 233, 245; *Kentucky Kernel*, November 10, 2006; David Horowitz, *The Professors: The 101 Most Dangerous Academics in America* (Washington, DC: Regnery, 2006), 33–34.

50. *Kentucky Kernel*, October 13, 2009; Chapman interview, December 5, 2006; Thelin interview, September 11, 2007.

51. *Lexington Herald-Leader*, October 22, November 27, 2008; May 2, November 15, 2009; *Louisville Courier-Journal*, December 20, 2008; *Richmond Register*, March 6, 2010.

52. Klotter, "Promise, Pessimism, and Perseverance," 50; *Lexington Herald-Leader*, August 15, 2005.

53. Steve Vest, "Most Likely to Succeed," *Kentucky Monthly* (April 2010): 55–56; *Lexington Herald-Leader*, February 26, 2010; *Richmond Register*, March 30, 2010.

Index